EURIPIDES
BACCHAE

EDITED WITH

INTRODUCTION AND COMMENTARY

BY

E. R. DODDS

REGIUS PROFESSOR OF GREEK
IN THE UNIVERSITY OF OXFORD

SECOND EDITION

OXFORD
AT THE CLARENDON PRESS

Oxford University Press, Ely House, London W. 1

GLASGOW NEW YORK TORONTO MELBOURNE WELLINGTON
CAPE TOWN IBADAN NAIROBI DAR ES SALAAM LUSAKA ADDIS ABABA
DELHI BOMBAY CALCUTTA MADRAS KARACHI LAHORE DACCA
KUALA LUMPUR SINGAPORE HONG KONG TOKYO

ISBN 0 19 814120 3

First edition 1944
Reprinted 1953
Second edition 1960
Reprinted from sheets of the second edition
1963, 1966, 1970, 1974

Printed in Great Britain
at the University Press, Oxford
by Vivian Ridler
Printer to the University

PREFACE TO THE SECOND EDITION

I AM grateful to the Delegates of the Press for giving me the opportunity to revise this book in the light of work which has appeared since 1943. The intervening years have brought varied contributions. The two papyri cited in the first edition have been published, and a third, as yet unpublished, has been made available to me by the kindness of Mr. J. W. B. Barns and the Delegates (see Introduction, p. lix). The medieval manuscripts have been minutely studied by Professor Turyn (*The Byzantine Manuscript Tradition of the Tragedies of Euripides*, 1957). Professor Winnington-Ingram's admirable essay has appeared under the title *Euripides and Dionysus* (1948); the late Professor Norwood has presented his δεύτεραι φροντίδες on the *Bacchae* in *Essays on Euripidean Drama* (1954); and we have had interesting studies of the play from André Rivier (*Essai sur le tragique d'Euripide*, 1944, chap. v); F. Martinazzoli (*Euripide*, 1946, 387 ff.); J. Labarbe (*Miscellanea J. Gessler*, 1948, ii. 686 ff.); E. M. Blaiklock (*The Male Characters of Euripides*, 1952, chap. xi); F. M. Wassermann (*Studies presented to D. M. Robinson*, 1953, 559 ff.); H. Diller (*Abh. Mainz*, 1955, Nr. 5); and A.-J. Festugière (*Eranos*, lv, 1957, 127 ff.). There has been an edition with Italian commentary by P. Scazzoso (1957), and individual passages have been discussed by A. Y. Campbell, D. S. Colman, A.-J. Festugière, M. Gigante, J. C. Kamerbeek, R. Merkelbach, E. L. B. Meurig-Davies, K. O'Nolan, L. R. Palmer, D. S. Robertson, and others; especially valuable are the conjectures of the late John Jackson in his *Marginalia Scaenica* (1955). In addition, I must thank those scholars who have been good enough to send me unpublished criticisms and suggestions; they include Father Festugière, Professors Broadhead, Dover, Merkelbach, and W. R. Smyth, Mr. W. S. Barrett, Mr. Alan Ker, and Mr. W. B. Sedgwick.

I should probably have made fuller use of all this material

had I been able to approach it with a fresh mind. But it has at least enabled me to recognize, if not always to remedy, various weaknesses in my own treatment of the play. Users of the first edition will find here, besides the new papyrus evidence on lines 1154–9 and 1183–6, substantially modified views on lines 21–22, 135, 209, 506, 902–11, and 1220, fuller consideration of the problems presented by lines 406–8, 651–3, and 1066–7, correction of a good many minor inaccuracies, and a large number of small changes and additions which I hope will make the book more useful. I have also added two short indexes. Murray's text and *apparatus criticus* are retained—not for reasons of sentiment or modesty, as one reviewer suggested, but because resetting the Greek would make the book too expensive for the kind of reader for whom it is primarily designed.

E. R. D.

OXFORD
February 1959

PREFACE TO THE FIRST EDITION

No OTHER play of Euripides has been so much discussed as the *Bacchae*; very few have been the subject of such exact and careful study on the linguistic side. In the field of language and textual criticism a twentieth-century editor is unlikely to better very substantially the work of Elmsley and Hermann, Paley and Sandys and Wecklein, except where he is lucky enough to be armed with new evidence: the solid scholars of the last century stated all the major linguistic and textual problems of the play, and brought most of them as near to solution as they are likely to be brought in the absence of such evidence. Their successors may still occasionally find (or think they have found) new answers to old questions; but their best hope of reaching a closer understanding of a difficult work probably lies in asking new questions, arising out of that new approach to Greek tragedy of which Wilamowitz was the pioneer[1]—an approach which seriously concerns itself with the play not only as a piece of Greek but as a work of art and at the same time (like all works of art) a social document.

If the present commentary has any justification, it is, in the first place, that it asks a number of new questions, new at any rate in the sense that previous commentators have ignored them. That all or most of them are rightly answered is more than I dare hope; but if they are rightly framed I have done some service. In particular, I have aimed at bringing to bear on the interpretation both of individual passages and of the play as a whole that wider and deeper knowledge of Dionysiac religion which my generation owes

---

[1] In his great commentary on the *Heracles* (1889). He left no continuous commentary on the *Bacchae*, but I have learned much from his translation (1923), from the notes he contributed to Bruhn's edition (1891), and from his discussions of individual passages in *Griechische Verskunst* and elsewhere.

to the work of men like Rohde, Farnell, Wilamowitz, Kern, and Nilsson. If such matter bulks large in both Introduction and Commentary, the reason is that the last fifty years have achieved a greater and more fruitful advance in this field than in any other which has an equally important bearing on the play. I have also been enabled, thanks to the generosity of the Egypt Exploration Society, the Delegates of the Oxford University Press, and Mr. C. H. Roberts of St. John's College, Oxford, to add something to the positive evidence for the text by quoting the readings of two unpublished papyri (see Introduction, p. lvi).

In accordance with the plan of the series to which it belongs, the text (and *apparatus criticus*) of the present edition is, apart from correction of one or two misprints, that of Professor Murray (Euripides, Oxford Classical Texts, 2nd edition, 1913). In the Commentary, I have made it my first business to explain this text; but where I disagree with it I have said so, and have given my reasons. In the arrangement of my matter I have ventured to depart in two respects from the established custom of commentators. (i) Since I believe that linguistic, metrical, and literary interpretation are alike indispensable, and cannot be divorced without peril, I have incorporated in the Commentary both metrical analysis (presented, I hope, with a minimum of technicality) and discussion of the significance of the several scenes, instead of relegating the former to an unreadable appendix and the latter to an Introduction which may be left unread. (ii) Since this edition is intended for schoolboys as well as for scholars, I have enclosed certain matter in square brackets—matter which is for the most part controversial, and concerned mainly (though not exclusively) with textual criticism. I hope that those reading the play for the first time will in general ignore this bracketed stuff: it is addressed primarily to persons who are or wish to become professional scholars. If the love and knowledge of Greek literature ever die in this country, they will die of a suffocation arising from its exponents' industry. I do not wish to be accessory to the murder.

Like all editors, I have pillaged my predecessors, sometimes with acknowledgement, but often without. It is more important to acknowledge here what I owe to the learning and the unselfishness of my friends, and of two above all: Professor Eduard Fraenkel, who read the whole of my typescript and not only threw a completely fresh light on several passages but saved me from more errors than I care to count and introduced me to many new sources of knowledge; and Mr. J. D. Denniston, who generously sacrificed the scanty leisure of a temporary civil servant in war-time to do me a similar service. In addition, I have profited greatly by the expert advice of Dr. Paul Jacobsthal on archaeological matters and of Dr. Paul Maas on a number of metrical, linguistic, and textual points; Mr. R. P. Winnington-Ingram has permitted me to quote several acute observations from an unpublished essay on the play; Professor R. B. Onians has allowed me to consult the proofs of his forthcoming *Origins of European Thought*; and I have had valuable help of various kinds from Professor J. D. Beazley, Mr. E. L. B. Meurig-Davies, Dr. Rudolf Pfeiffer, Mr. Maurice Platnauer, and Mr. C. H. Roberts. Lastly, I must thank Professor Murray, to whose lectures on the *Bacchae* I, like so many others, owe my first real understanding of the play's greatness and of its religious background. All of this book is ultimately his: a part of it he made; the rest grew from seed he planted thirty years ago.

E. R. D.

OXFORD
November 1943

CONTENTS

NOTE

For the older fragments of the tragedians my references are to Nauck's *Tragicorum Graecorum Fragmenta*, second edition, except in the case of Sophocles where I have followed the new Liddell and Scott (L.S.⁹) in referring to Pearson's edition. For more recently discovered fragments I have where possible given references to Hunt, *Fragmenta Tragica Papyracea* (O.C.T., 1912), or Arnim, *Supplementum Euripideum* (Lietzmann's Kleine Texte, Bonn, 1913), or Page, *Greek Literary Papyri*, i (Loeb Library, 1942).

Kühner–Blass, Kühner–Gerth = R. Kühner, *Ausführliche Grammatik der griechischen Sprache*, Dritte Auflage, Teil i, besorgt von F. Blass; Teil ii, besorgt von B. Gerth.

Beazley, *A.R.V.* = J. D. Beazley, *Attic Red-Figure Vase-Painters* (Oxford, 1942).

INTRODUCTION

UNLIKE most Greek tragedies the *Bacchae* is a play about an historical event—the introduction into Hellas of a new religion.[1] When Euripides wrote, the event lay in the far past, and the memory of it survived only in mythical form; the new religion had long since been acclimatized and accepted as part of Greek life. But it still stood as the expression of a religious attitude, and the memorial of a religious experience, different from anything implied in the cult of the traditional Olympian gods; and the forces liberated and embodied by the original movement were active in other forms in the Athens of Euripides' day. If we are to understand this play, we must first know something about Dionysiac religion—the intention of certain of its rites, the meaning of certain of its myths, and the shapes it had assumed in Euripides' time. The disagreements of nineteenth-century critics should warn us that if we attempt to seize the poet's thought by a frontal attack, in disregard of the contemporary background, we shall be at the mercy of our own or other people's prejudices.

I. DIONYSUS

1. *The Nature of Dionysiac Religion*[2]

To the Greeks of the classical age Dionysus was not solely, or even mainly, the god of wine. Plutarch tells us

[1] The characteristics of Dionysiac worship are so different from those of most other Greek cults that we may justifiably speak of it in this way. But in its Greek form it was never a separate 'religion' in the sense of excluding other cults.

[2] The first modern writer who understood the Dionysiac psychology was Erwin Rohde; his *Psyche* (1st ed. 1891–4, Eng. trans. 1925) is still the fundamental book. See also Farnell, *Cults of the Greek States*, vol. v, chaps. 4–7, Wilamowitz, *Glaube der Hellenen*, ii. 60 ff., O. Kern, *Religion der Griechen*, i. 226 ff., W. K. C. Guthrie, *The Greeks and their Gods*,

as much, confirming it with a quotation from Pindar,[1] and the god's cult titles confirm it also: he is Δενδρίτης or Ἔνδενδρος, the Power in the tree; he is Ἄνθιος the blossom-bringer, Κάρπιος the fruit-bringer, Φλεύς or Φλέως, the abundance of life. His domain is, in Plutarch's words, the whole of the ὑγρὰ φύσις—not only the liquid fire in the grape, but the sap thrusting in a young tree, the blood pounding in the veins of a young animal, all the mysterious and uncontrollable tides that ebb and flow in the life of nature. Our oldest witness, Homer, nowhere explicitly refers to him as a wine god;[2] and it may well be that his association with certain wild plants, such as the fir and the ivy, and with certain wild animals, is in fact older than his association with the vine. It was the Alexandrines, and above all the Romans—with their tidy functionalism and their cheerful obtuseness in all matters of the spirit—who departmentalized Dionysus as 'jolly Bacchus' the wine-god with his riotous crew of nymphs and satyrs.[3] As such he was taken over from the Romans by Renaissance painters and poets; and it was they in turn who shaped the image in which the modern world pictures him. If we are to understand the *Bacchae*, our first step is to unthink all this: to forget the pictures of Titian and Rubens, to forget Keats and his 'god of breathless cups and chirping mirth', to remember that ὄργια are not orgies but acts of devotion (cf. 34 n.), and that βακχεύειν is not to 'revel' but to have a particular kind of religious experience—the experience of

chap. 6. Miss Harrison's *Prolegomena to the Study of Greek Religion* and W. F. Otto's *Dionysos* are interesting but should be used with caution. Some illuminating modern parallels are cited by H. Jeanmaire in his comprehensive but in parts decidedly speculative book, *Dionysos* (1951).

[1] *Is. et Os.* 35, 365 A, quoting Pindar, fr. 140 Bowra.

[2] This may of course be accidental; but it is odd, as Farnell says, that Maron, though a Thracian and a vine-rgower, is represented as a priest not of Dionysus but of Apollo.

[3] Horace is an exception: *Odes*, 2. 19 and 3. 25 show a deeper understanding of the god's true nature.

communion with God which transformed a human being
into a βάκχος or a βάκχη (cf. 115 n.).

To this experience the Greeks, like many other peoples,[1]
believed wine to be in certain circumstances an aid.
Drunkenness, as William James observed, 'expands, unites,
and says Yes: it brings its votary from the chill periphery
of things to the radiant core; it makes him for the moment
one with truth'.[2] Thus wine acquires religious value: he
who drinks it becomes ἔνθεος—he has drunk deity. But
wine was not the only or the most important means to
communion. The maenads in our play are not drunken:
Pentheus thought they were (260 ff.), but we are expressly
told that he was mistaken (686 f.); some of them preferred
to drink water, or even milk (704 ff.). In this Euripides is
probably correct from a ritual point of view: for the other
acts of his maenads belong to a *winter* ritual which seems
not to have been a wine festival, and would not naturally
be one.[3] The right time for holy drunkenness is in the spring,
when the new wine is ready to be opened; and it is then that
we find it, e.g. at the Athenian 'Feast of Cups' which formed
part of the Anthesteria.

But there were other ways of becoming ἔνθεος. The
strange ὀρειβασία or mountain dancing, which is described
in the πάροδος of the *Bacchae* and again in the first messenger-
speech, is no fancy of the poet but the reflection of a ritual
which was practised by women's societies at Delphi down
to Plutarch's time, and for which we have inscriptional
evidence from a number of other places in the Greek world.[4]
The rite took place in midwinter in alternate years (hence
the name τριετηρίς, *Ba.* 133). It must have involved considerable discomfort, and even risk: Pausanias says that

---

[1] Cf. Frazer, *Golden Bough*, iii. 248, and for an excellent modern
example Ruth Benedict, *Patterns of Culture*, 85.

[2] *The Varieties of Religious Experience*, 387.

[3] Farnell, *Cults*, v. 198 ff. Cf., however, *Ion*, 550–4.

[4] See my article 'Maenadism in the *Bacchae*', *Harvard Theological
Rev.* xxxiii (1940), 155 ff. (reprinted in part, with some additions and
corrections, as an appendix to *The Greeks and the Irrational*, 1951).

at Delphi the women went to the very summit of Parnassus (over 8,000 ft. high), and Plutarch describes an occasion, apparently in his own lifetime, when they were cut off by a snow-storm and a rescue party had to be sent out.[1]

What was the object of this practice? Many peoples dance out of doors to make their crops grow, by sympathetic magic. But such dances elsewhere are annual like the crops, not biennial like the ὀρειβασία; their season is spring, not midwinter; and their scene is the cornland, not the barren mountain-tops. Late Greek writers thought of the dances at Delphi as commemorative: 'they dance', says Diodorus (4. 3), 'in imitation of the maenads who are said to have been associated with the god in the old days'. Probably he is right, as regards his own time (or the time of his source); but ritual is usually older than the myth by which people explain it, and has deeper psychological roots. There must have been a time when the maenads or thyiads or βάκχαι really became for a few hours or days what their name implies—wild women whose human personality has been temporarily replaced by another. Whether this might still be so in Euripides' day we have no sure means of knowing: a Delphic tradition recorded by Plutarch[2] suggests that as late as the fourth century B.C. the rite sometimes produced a true disturbance of personality, but the evidence is slender.

There are, however, parallel phenomena in other cultures which may help us to understand the πάροδος of the *Bacchae* and the punishment of Agaue. In many societies, perhaps in all societies, there are people for whom 'ritual dances provide a religious experience that seems more satisfying and convincing than any other. . . . It is with their muscles that they most easily obtain knowledge of the divine.'[3] The best known examples are the Mohammedan dervishes, the American Shakers, the Jewish Hasidim, and the Siberian

---

[1] Paus. 10. 32. 5; Plut. *de primo frigido*, 18, 953 D.
[2] *mul. virt. 13.*
[3] Aldous Huxley, *Ends and Means*, 232, 235.

shamans. Often the dance induces a sense of being possessed by an alien personality. Such dancing is highly
infectious; it 'spreads like wildfire' (*Ba.* 778), and easily
becomes a compulsive obsession, taking possession even of
sceptics (like Agaue) without the consent of the conscious
mind. This happened in the extraordinary dancing madness
which periodically invaded Europe from the fourteenth to
the seventeenth century,[1] when people danced until they
dropped and lay unconscious (cf. *Ba.* 136 and n.): e.g. at
Liège in 1374 'many persons seemingly sound in mind and
body were suddenly possessed by the devils' and left house
and home to wander away with the dancers; Cadmus and
Teiresias had their counterparts in seventeenth-century
Italy, where 'even old men of ninety threw aside their crutches
at the sound of the tarantella, and as if some magic potion,
restorative of youth and vigour, flowed through their veins,
they joined the most extravagant dancers'. Many held that
the dancing madness could be imposed on people by cursing
them with it, as Dionysus cursed the daughters of Cadmus.
In some cases the obsession reappeared at regular intervals,

[1] See J. F. K. Hecker, *Die Tanzwuth* (1832; Eng. trans., Babington,
1888), A. Martin, 'Geschichte der Tanzkrankheit in Deutschland' in
Ztschr. d. Vereins f. Volkskunde, xxiv (1914). Such happenings are not
unknown even today. In 1921 there was an outbreak of dancing mania
in Thuringia, inspired by one Muck Lamberty. 'Policemen and public
servants were seen joining the dance and singing in open streets, and
there was a new kind of riot, against which the authorities seemed to be
helpless. . . . Dignity, profession, creed and political opinion lost their
meaning. . . . The new prophet became a power, esteemed even in high
quarters. Not only was it doubtful whether anybody could have been
found to call him to account, but this might even have resulted in a
general rising' (G. R. Halkett, *The Dear Monster*, 204 ff.). As Dionysus
was received at Delphi, so Muck preached in the Cathedral at Erfurt,
and succeeded for a time in establishing new forms of religious festival.
But Pentheus won in the end: Muck was discredited owing to moral
scandals. Similar outbreaks of mass hysteria occurred periodically in
Japan during the eighteenth and nineteenth centuries (see E. H.
Norman, *Far Eastern Survey*, xiv (1945), 65 ff.). Disturbed social
conditions seem to have been a predisposing cause both in Germany
and in Japan.

growing in intensity until St. John's or St. Vitus's day, when an outbreak occurred and was followed by a return to normality; hence there developed periodic 'cures' of afflicted patients by music and ecstatic dancing, which in some places crystallized into annual festivals.[1]

This last fact suggests the way in which in Greece the ritual ὀρειβασία at a fixed date may originally have developed out of spontaneous attacks of mass hysteria.[2] By canalizing such hysteria in an organized rite once in two years, the Dionysiac cult kept it within bounds and gave it a relatively harmless outlet. What the πάροδος of the *Bacchae* depicts is hysteria subdued to the service of religion; the deeds done on Cithaeron were manifestations of hysteria in the raw, the compulsive mania which attacks the unbeliever. Dionysus is at work in both: like St. John or St. Vitus, he is the cause of madness and the liberator from madness, Βάκχος and Λύσιος,[3] θεὸς δεινότατος, ἀνθρώποισι δ' ἠπιώτατος (*Ba.* 860). We must keep this ambivalence in mind if we are rightly to understand the play. To resist Dionysus is to repress the elemental in one's own nature; the punishment is the sudden complete collapse of the inward dykes when the elemental breaks through perforce and civilization vanishes.

The culminating act of the Dionysiac winter dance was the tearing to pieces, and eating raw, of an animal body, σπαραγμός and ὠμοφαγία. It is referred to in the regulations of the Dionysiac cult at Miletus (276 B.C.),[4] and attested

[1] Cf. the annual dancing procession at Esternach in the Rhineland, which is still believed to be a cure for psychopathic complaints (Martin, l.c., 129 ff.); also Jeanmaire, *Dionysos*, 167 ff.

[2] For other parallels which suggest that the 'maenad' is a real and not merely a mythological figure see notes on 748–64, and 'Maenadism in the *Bacchae*', 159 ff.

[3] Rohde, *Psyche*, chap. 9, n. 21, Farnell, *Cults*, v. 120. Cf. the story of the daughters of Proetus, who were driven mad by Dionysus and subsequently cured μετ' ἀλαλαγμοῦ καί τινος ἐνθέου χορείας [Apollod.] 2. 2. 2; and schol. Pindar, *Pyth.* 3. 139 καὶ τὸν Διόνυσον δὲ καθαρτικὸν μανίας φασί.

[4] *Milet* vi. 22 μὴ ἐξεῖναι ὠμοφάγιον ἐμβαλεῖν μηθενὶ πρότερον ἢ ἡ ἱέρεια ὑπὲρ τῆς πόλεως ἐμβάλῃ. ἐμβαλεῖν means, I think, 'throw to the crowd of

by Plutarch and others. In the *Bacchae* the σπαραγμός, first of the Theban cattle (734 ff.) and then of Pentheus (1125 ff.), is described with a gusto which the modern reader has difficulty in sharing. A detailed description of the ὠμοφαγία would perhaps have been too much for the stomachs even of an Athenian audience; Eur. speaks of it twice, *Ba.* 138 and *Cretans* fr. 472, but in each place he passes over it swiftly and discreetly. It is hard to guess at the psychological state that he describes in the two words ὠμοφάγον χάριν. But it is noteworthy that the days appointed for ὠμοφαγία were 'unlucky and black days';[1] and it appears that those who practise a comparable rite in our time experience in it a mixture of supreme exaltation and supreme repulsion: it is at once holy and horrible, fulfilment and uncleanness, a sacrament and a pollution—the same violent conflict of emotional attitudes that runs all through the *Bacchae* and lies at the root of all religion of the Dionysiac type.[2]

Late writers explained the ὠμοφαγία as they did the dancing: they supposed it to commemorate the day when the infant Dionysus was himself torn to pieces and devoured.[3] But (*a*) we can hardly dissociate the rite from the widespread belief in what Frazer called 'the homoeopathic effects of a flesh diet':[4] if you tear something to pieces and eat it warm and bleeding, you add its vital powers to your

celebrants' ('Maenadism in the *Bacchae*', 164); cf. the modern Arab ὠμοφαγία, where the priest on a terrace throws the victim to the mob of ecstatics below (R. Brunel, *Essai sur la confrérie religieuse des Aissâoûa au Maroc*, 177). For other evidence see Farnell, *Cults*, v. 302 f.

[1] Plut. *def. orac.* 14, 417 C, ἡμέρας ἀποφράδας καὶ σκυθρωπάς, ἐν αἷς ὠμοφαγίαι καὶ διασπασμοί.

[2] Cf. Benedict, *Patterns of Culture*, 179: 'the very repugnance which the Kwakiutl [Indians of Vancouver Island] felt towards the act of eating human flesh made it for them a fitting expression of the Dionysian virtue that lies in the terrible and the forbidden'.

[3] Schol. Clem. Alex. 92 P. (i. 318 Stählin), Firm. Mat. *err. prof. rel.* 6. 5, Photius, s.v. νεβρίζειν.

[4] See *Golden Bough*, v. ii, chap. 12.

own, for 'the blood is the life'; (b) it seems likely that the victim was felt to embody the vital powers of the god himself, which by the act of ὠμοφαγία were transferred to the worshippers. The most usual victim was a bull—that is why Aristophanes speaks of 'the Bacchic rites of bull-eating Cratinus'.[1] We hear also of ὠμοφαγίαι of wild goats or fawns, and the tearing of vipers;[2] while the women who rent Pentheus believed him to be a lion.[3] In several of these creatures we may recognize bestial incarnations of the god: cf. Ba. 1017–19, where the faithful cry to him to appear as bull, snake, or lion. For a cattle-herding people like those of Boeotia or Elis there is no more splendid symbol of nature's potency than the bull. It is in bull-shape, 'raging with bestial hoof', that Dionysus is invoked in the ancient hymn of the women of Elis,[4] as it is in bull-shape that he mocks his persecutor in the Bacchae (618); and the sculptors sometimes show him, as Pentheus saw him in a vision (Ba. 922), as a horned man.[5] In the Homeric hymn (7. 44) he manifests himself as a lion, and this may well be the oldest of his bestial shapes.[6]

We may regard the ὠμοφαγία, then, as a rite in which the god was in some sense present in his beast-vehicle and was in that shape torn and eaten by his people.[7] Did the cult once admit—as the Pentheus story suggests—a still more potent, because more dreadful, form of communion—the rending, even the rending and eating, of God in the shape

---

[1] Ran. 357 and schol. Cf. Ba. 743 ff., 1185; Oppian, Cyn. 4. 304 ff.

[2] Goat, Ba. 138, Arnobius, adv. nat. 5. 19; fawn, Phot., s.v. νεβρίζειν; viper, Galen, de antid. 1. 6. 14.

[3] Cf. Or. 1492, where the βάκχαι hunt a σκύμνος ὀρεία (i.e. a lion-cub?).

[4] Plut. Q.Gr. 36, 299 B, βοέῳ ποδὶ θύων, ἄξιε ταῦρε.

[5] Cf. his cult epithets δίκερως, ταυρωπός, ταυρομέτωπος, κερασφόρος. Occasionally his statues gave him a bull's body also (Athen. 476 A). Certain of his worshippers were called βουκόλοι, and at Argos he was worshipped as βουγενής (Plut. Is. et Os. 35, 364 F).

[6] There were no lions in Greece in historical times; but the lion survived in the god's earlier homes, in Asia Minor, Thrace, and Macedonia (Hdt. 7. 125, Xen. Cyn. 11, Paus. 6. 5. 4, Ar. Hist. An. 579ᵇ7). [7] Cf. Gruppe, Gr. Mythologie u. Religionsgeschichte, 732.

of man? We cannot be sure, and some scholars deny it. There are, however, scattered indications which point that way.[1] Theophrastus, *apud* Porph. *abst.* 2. 8, speaks of ἡ τῶν ἀνθρωποθυσιῶν βακχεία, and adds that the Bassares practise cannibalism as well. Pausanias (9. 8. 2) has heard that at Potniae, near Thebes, a boy was at one time sacrificed to Dionysus, until Delphi authorized a goat as a surrogate. He explains the rite as expiatory; but there is other evidence which may lead us to doubt this. Euelpis of Carystos (*ap.* Porph. *Abst.* 2. 55) knows that on two Aegean islands, Chios and Tenedos, σπαραγμός of a human victim was once practised in honour of Dionysus Omadios, the god of the ὠμοφαγία; and Clement (*Protr.* 3. 42) has culled from a Hellenistic history of Crete a similar tradition about Lesbos. It seems that on Tenedos, as at Potniae, an animal victim was later substituted, but the ritual retained curious and significant features: Aelian (*N.A.* 12. 34) tells us that they choose a cow in calf and treat her as if she were a human mother; when the calf is born, they put buskins on it and then sacrifice it to Dionysus Ἀνθρωπορραίστης, 'the Mansmasher'; 'but he who struck the calf with his axe is stoned by the people until he escapes to the sea-shore' (i.e. he is polluted, and must make as if to leave the country, like Agaue at the end of the *Bacchae*). To this evidence we may add the repeated occurrence of child-murder and human σπαραγμός in Dionysiac myths (see below); the fact that the human sacrifice alleged to have been performed before the battle of Salamis is said to have been offered to Dionysus Omestes;[2] and the allegation of ritual murder in connexion with the Italian Dionysiac movement which was suppressed in 186 B.C.[3]

[1] Collected by F. Schwenn, *Die Menschenopfer bei den Griechen u. Römern.* See also Farnell, *Cults,* v. 164 ff.

[2] Plut. *Them.* 13, on the authority of Aristotle's pupil Phanias. Even if the story be false, it shows what fourth-century Greeks thought of Dionysus Omestes.

[3] Livy, 39. 13, cf. Plaut. *Bacchides,* 371 f. Kern believed that the Λῆναι (Theocr. xxvi) was written to defend ritual child-murder (*Arch. f. Rel.* xxvi. 14 f.).

However this may be, the ὠμοφαγία and the bestial incarnations reveal Dionysus as something much more significant and much more dangerous than a wine-god. He is the principle of animal life, ταῦρος and ταυροφάγος,[1] the hunted and the hunter—the unrestrained potency which man envies in the beasts and seeks to assimilate. His cult was originally an attempt on the part of human beings to achieve communion with this potency. The psychological effect was to liberate the instinctive life in man from the bondage imposed on it by reason and social custom: the worshipper became conscious of a strange new vitality, which he attributed to the god's presence within him (cf. Ba. 187 ff., 194, 945-6, and notes). Euripides seems to hint likewise at a further effect, a merging of the individual consciousness in a group consciousness: the worshipper θιασεύεται ψυχάν (Ba. 75), he is at one not only with the Master of Life but with his fellow-worshippers; and he is at one also with the life of earth (Ba. 726-7, and note).

ii. Dionysiac Religion at Athens

The Greeks held, no doubt correctly, that these singular rites were not native to Hellas: Herodotus calls them νεωστὶ ἐσηγμένα (2. 49, where νεωστὶ seems to refer to the time of Melampus, before the Trojan War); and Euripides represents the Dionysiac cult as a sort of 'world religion', carried by missionaries (as no native Greek cult ever was) from one land to another. According to him, its original seat is the mountains of Lydia and Phrygia (Ba. 13, 55, 86, &c.), a view supported by the modern discovery that Βάκχος is the Lydian equivalent of Dionysus.[2] Elsewhere Dionysus is most often represented as a Thracian: Homer connects him with the Thracian Lycurgus (Il. 6. 130 ff., cf. Soph. Ant. 955), and in the fifth century Greek travellers knew of the

---

[1] Soph. fr. 668.
[2] Sardis, vi. i. 39, Lyd. Βακιϝαλις = Greek Διονυσικλῆς.

Dionysiac cult on Mounts Pangaeum and Rhodope.[1] This also we may accept: the highlands of Thrace and those of Asia Minor held peoples of kindred blood and culture (Hdt. 7. 73). The myths suggest that the new god may in fact have reached mainland Greece by two independent routes—overseas from the Asiatic coast by way of Cos, Naxos, Delos, and Euboea to Attica, and by land from Thrace to Macedonia, Boeotia, and Delphi.[2] His coming cannot be exactly dated, but must I think be a good deal earlier than was supposed, e.g., by Wilamowitz (who was prepared to put it as late as 700 B.C.): not only is Semele already a Theban princess for the author of the Διὸς ἀπάτη (*Il.* 14. 323 ff.), but the introduction myths are associated with very early conditions—the monarchy at Athens, the rule of the Minyae at Orchomenus and of the Proetids and Perseids at Argos, the Cadmean period at Thebes.[3]

In the course of the centuries which separate the first appearance of Dionysiac cult in Greece from the age of

[1] Cf. *Hec.* 1267, *Rhes.* 972, Hdt. 5. 7 and 7. 111. Hdt. also knows of orgiastic τριετηρίδες among the Scythian Geloni (4. 108). And the god's northern associations are recognized even in the *Bacchae* (lines 560–75).

[2] Cf. Kern, *Rel. der Griech.* i. 226 ff.; Nilsson, *Minoan-Mycenaean Religion*², 567 ff.

[3] Cf. Farnell, *Cults*, v. 109 ff., Foucart, *Culte de Dion. en Attique*, chap. 3, Deubner, *Arch. Jhb.* xlii (1927), 189. Since the above was written, the case for a very early dating of the introduction myths has been strengthened by Miss Lorimer, *Homer and the Monuments*, 471 f., and has received apparent confirmation from the decipherment on a fragmentary Pylos tablet, Xao6, of the name di-wo-nu-so-jo (Ventris and Chadwick, *Documents in Mycenaean Greek*, 127). Ventris and Chadwick point out that the name on the tablet is not necessarily that of a god; it seems, however, to presuppose knowledge of the divine name, and thus to date back Greek acquaintance with Dionysus to the thirteenth century B.C. at latest. If the decipherment is confirmed, it does not follow that the introduction myths are entirely without historical foundation; but the historical element will refer to a very remote period (the time of Herodotus' Melampus?), unless with Nilsson (*Minoan-Mycenaean Religion*², 575 ff.) we postulate a missionary movement in the Archaic Age which was in fact a reintroduction from abroad of ideas and rites that had been familiar to the Minoan world.

Euripides, it was brought under State control and lost much of its original character, at any rate in Attica. The Athenians of Euripides' time had no biennial winter rite, no mountain dancing, no ὠμοφαγία;[1] they were content to send a delegation of women to represent them at the Delphic τριετηρίς. So far as we know, their own Dionysiac festivals were very different: they were occasions for old-fashioned country gaiety and a little old-fashioned country magic, as at the rural Dionysia; or for pious and cheerful drunkenness, as at the Feast of Cups; or for a display of the civic and cultural greatness of Athens, as at the City Dionysia. Only the Lenaea may perhaps have kept something of the original fervour which its name betokens and which we may recognize on some of the so-called 'Lenaea-vases'.[2] The function of these genial Attic festivals was, in the words of Pericles,[3] to provide ἀνάπαυλαι τῶν πόνων: their value was more social than religious. This aspect of Dionysiac worship is not ignored in the *Bacchae*: Euripides has expressed it beautifully in the first stasimon, 370 ff. (see Commentary). But there was little or nothing in the *official* Athenian cult which could inspire the descriptions in the πάροδος and the messenger-speeches, or had any real relevance to the savage and primitive story of Pentheus' punishment.

Much of the play's primitive religious colouring is doubtless traditional, like the theme itself (see below). Its extraordinary vividness is possibly due in some measure to things that the poet saw or heard in Macedonia, where the play was written—for in Macedonia, if we are to believe Plutarch,

---

[1] It has been held that the 'orgiastic' rites never had a footing in Attica; but the name Lenaea—apparently from λῆναι, the wild women —suggests the contrary.

[2] Farnell, *Cults*, v. 208 f.; Frickenhaus, *Lenäenvasen*; Deubner, *Att. Feste*, 126 ff. The vases show a wine-offering made by women before a mask-idol of Dionysus, accompanied by a sacral dance with thyrsi and torches, to the music of flutes and castanets. This looks like a controlled and limited survival of the orgiastic female cult. But its connexion with the Lenaea is disputed (Nilsson, *Arch. Jahrb.* xxxi (1916), 331 f.).   [3] Thuc. 2. 38.

the Dionysiac cult was still in the fourth century sufficiently primitive to include such rites as snake-handling.[1] But I have suggested elsewhere[2] that Euripides' interest in the subject may also have been aroused by things that were happening nearer home. At Athens Dionysus had been tamed; but it does not follow that the Dionysiac temper had vanished, and there is in fact plenty of evidence that during the Peloponnesian War—probably as a result of the social stresses which it generated—religion of the orgiastic type began to emerge again under other names. Athens was invaded by a multitude of θεοὶ ξενικοί: it is at this time that Attic literature begins to be full of references to the eastern and northern mystery gods, Cybele and Bendis, Attis, Adonis, and Sabazius.[3] In relation to the *Bacchae* the last-named is of especial interest. He is an oriental counterpart of Dionysus—an unhellenized Dionysus whose cult retained the primitive appeal and much of the primitive ritual which the Attic Dionysus had long since lost. Sabazius still promised his initiates what Dionysus had once promised—identification with deity.[4] And to this end he offered them the old means—an ecstatic nocturnal rite performed to the music of flute and kettledrum.[5] Several of the old ritual elements mentioned in the πάροδος of the *Bacchae*—the καθαρμοί, the τύμπανα, the snake-handling, the fawnskins, the cult-title ἔξαρχος—are attested by Demosthenes for the Sabazius-cult as practised at Athens in the fourth century.[6]

[1] Plut. *Alex.* 2.

[2] 'Maenadism in the *Bacchae*', 171 ff.

[3] Cybele, Cratinus, fr. 82, Ar. *Av.* 876 f., Soph. *Phil.* 391 ff.; Bendis, Cratin. fr. 80, cf. *I.G.* i². 310. 208 (429/8 B.C.); Attis, Theopompus com. fr. 27; Adonis, Cratin. fr. 15, Ar. *Pax*, 420; Sabazius, Ar. *Vesp.* 9 f., *Av.* 875, *Lys.* 387–97. On the growth of superstition during the Peloponnesian War see Kern, *Rel. d. Griech.* ii. 287 ff., Nilsson, *Greek Popular Religion*, 130 ff.

[4] They became σάβοι, as the initiates of Bacchus became βάκχοι (Harpocrat. s.v. Σάβοι, schol. Ar. *Av.* 874, Plut. *Q. Conv.* 4. 6. 2).

[5] Ar. *Lys.* 388, fr. 566, Dem. *de cor.* 259, Iamb. *de myst.* 3. 9.

[6] *de cor.* 259 f., 284. We may add the ivy if the MS. reading κιττοφόρος is right in *de cor.* 260.

The past had in fact returned, or was trying to return. And it brought in its train a controversy of similar substance to the debate between Pentheus and Teiresias in the *Bacchae*. Echoes of that controversy survive in the fragments of Old Comedy, in the orators, and in Plato. Or rather, echoes from one side of it; for it happens that all our witnesses are hostile to the new religious movement. Aristophanes wrote a play, the *Horae*, in which 'Sabazius and certain other foreign gods' were put on trial and sentenced to banishment from Athens; the complaint seems to have been chiefly directed, like Pentheus' complaint against Dionysus, to the celebration of women's rites under cover of darkness, 'nocturnae pervigilationes'.[1] Nor was this an isolated attack on the new cults: the θεοὶ ξενικοί were satirized by Apollophanes in his *Cretans*, by Eupolis in his *Baptae*, by Plato comicus in his *Adonis*. In the fourth century, Demosthenes seeks to blacken his rival's character by repeated allusions to his association with the disreputable rites of Sabazius; Phryne is accused of introducing a 'new god' of Dionysiac type, Isodaites, and of forming unlicensed θίασοι;[2] while Plato takes so seriously the moral dangers of the movement that he would impose severe penalties on anyone who should be found 'practising private orgiastic rites'.[3]

Athenian public opinion is thus, so far as we happen to know it, on the side of law and order. What sort of emotional forces were engaged on the other side we may partly guess from the choruses of the *Bacchae*,[4] and the discourse of Teiresias may perhaps help us to reconstruct the intellectual case for the defence that was made in certain quarters. Conversely, we may understand better some parts of the

[1] Cic. *Leg.* 2. 37.

[2] Euthias, fr. 2 Baiter-Sauppe. Moral prejudice against foreign cults probably had something to do also with the condemnation of the two priestesses, Ninus and Theoris (cf. Foucart, *Associations*, 80 ff., 132 ff.).

[3] ὀργιάζων πλὴν τὰ δημόσια, *Leg.* 10, 910 BC.

[4] Partly also from certain vase-paintings: see below, p. xxxv f., and Webster, *Greek Art and Literature, 530–400 B.C.*, 174.

play if we relate them to this contemporary background. I do not suggest that the poet treated the coming of Dionysus to Thebes as an allegory of the coming to Athens of Sabazius and his like: even had he wished to do so, the outline of the story was too firmly fixed by tradition to lend itself to such treatment. But it seems probable that the contemporary situation helped to stimulate Euripides' interest in the mythical one; and that in writing certain passages of the *Bacchae*—notably the Pentheus–Teiresias scene[1]—he had in mind, and expected his audience to have in mind, the parallelism between the two.

II. TRADITIONAL ELEMENTS IN THE BACCHAE

i. *History and Ritual*

The story of Pentheus and Agaue is one of a series of cult-legends which describe the punishment of those rash mortals who refused to accept the religion of Dionysus. The first of them to appear in literature is the tale of Lycurgus the Thracian, of whom Homer relates (*Il.* 6. 130 ff.) that on the sacred mountain Nysa he hunted Dionysus and his 'nurses', drove them into the sea, and was blinded as a punishment. Later writers (and vase-paintings[2]) tell that he was punished with madness, and in his madness killed his own son ([Apollod.] 3. 5. 7, Hyg. *Fab.* 132). His end is variously described: he was entombed in a cave (Soph. *Ant.* 955 ff.), suffered σπαραγμός by horses ([Apollod.]) or panthers (Hyg.), or cut off his own legs (Serv. on *Aen.* 3. 14). A closely similar figure is the Thracian

---

[1] See introductory note on this scene, and 201–3 n., 222–3 n., 234 n., 274–85 n.

[2] The oldest evidence is a hydria painted about 440 (*C.V.A. Cracovie*, pl. 12; Beazley, *Greek Vases in Poland*, 44 ff.), which shows that this version is not a late borrowing from the Agaue story.

Boutes, who chased the maenads of Phthiotis into the sea, went mad, and drowned himself in a well (Diod. 5. 50). Another group of stories tells of *women* who were maddened by the god—the three daughters of Minyas at Orchomenos, who killed and devoured the child Hippasos (Plut. *Q. Gr.* 38); the three daughters of Proetus, who induced the women of Argos to kill their children and take to the mountains ([Apollod.] 2. 2. 2, from Hesiod, &c.); the daughters of Eleuther at Eleutherae, whose madness was a punishment for scorning a vision of the god (Suidas s.v. *Μέλαν*).

These legends are evidently related to the Theban myth of the madness of Cadmus' three daughters and the death of Pentheus at their hands. Many writers[1] find in them simply a reflection of historical events—a tradition of successive local conflicts between the fanatical adherents of the new religion and the representatives of law and order, the heads of the great families. That such conflicts occurred is probable in itself; that the infection of mountain-dancing should lay sudden hold of unbelievers is psychologically intelligible and has, as we have seen, its parallels in other cultures; that the god should make his first converts among the women is natural in view of the narrow and repressed lives which Greek women commonly led. But while we need not reject this view, it does not, I think, provide by itself a complete explanation of the myths. (*a*) It does not suit the Lycurgus story, which is located in the god's Thracian homeland. (*b*) It does not account for the odd fixity of outline displayed by the other group: always it is the king's daughters who go mad; always there are three of them (corresponding to the three θίασοι of maenads which existed at Thebes and elsewhere in historical times, cf. *Ba.* 680 n.); regularly they murder their children, or the child of one of them, as Lycurgus did his son, and as Procne murdered Itys at the τριετηρίς on Mount Rhodope (Ov. *Met.* 6. 587 ff.).

---

[1] e.g. Wilamowitz, *Glaube d. Hell.* 2. 66, Nilsson, *Hist. of Greek Religion*, 206 ff. Against this view, see now Guthrie, *The Greeks and their Gods*, 172 f., and Jeanmaire, *Dionysos*, 86 ff.

History no doubt repeats itself: but it is only ritual that repeats itself *exactly*. (c) The Minyad story is connected by Plutarch with a ritual pursuit of the 'maenads' by the priest of Dionysus which was still performed at Orchomenos in his own day—a pursuit which could end (and had on occasion ended) in a ritual murder. If we accept Plutarch's evidence, it is hard to avoid the conclusion that the pursuit of the Argive maenads by the priest Melampus, and that of the god's 'nurses' by Lycurgus and Boutes, reflect a similar ritual.[1]

These considerations suggest that Pentheus may be a figure compounded (like Guy Fawkes) of historical *and* ritual elements—at once the god's historical adversary and his ritual victim. Euripides has given him a character that suits the former role: he is the conservative Greek aristocrat, who despises the new religion as βάρβαρον, hates it for its obliteration of sex and class distinctions, and fears it as a threat to social order and public morals. But there are features in his story as the play presents it which look like traditional elements derived from ritual, and are not easily accounted for on any other hypothesis.[2] Such are Pentheus' perch on the sacred fir-tree (1058–75 n.), his pelting with fir and oak branches (1096–8 n.), and Agaue's delusion that she carries the severed head of one of the god's bestial incarnations, a bull-calf or a lion, on which she invites the Chorus to feast (1184–7 nn.). And if we accept these as reflecting a primitive sacrificial ritual, we may reasonably connect with the same ritual—and therefore recognize as in substance traditional—two major incidents of the story, the enchanting or bedevilling of Pentheus and his dressing

---

[1] Lycurgus' βουπλήξ (*Il.* 6. 135) looks like a ritual weapon. Does his imprisonment in the cave also reflect ritual? Cf. Livy, 39. 13. 13, in Italian Dionysiac cult 'raptos a diis homines dici, quos machinae illigatos ex conspectu in abditos specus abripiant': I am tempted to connect this with the cave-dwelling god or προφήτης of *Rhes.* 972 f. and Strabo, 7. 3. 5. (So now Festugière, *Mélanges d'Arch. et d'Hist.* 1954, 94 ff.)

[2] Cf. A. G. Bather, *J.H.S.* xiv (1894), 244 ff., Farnell, *Cults*, v. 171 f.

in ritual garb. If Pentheus is to be the god's victim, he must become the god's vehicle (that is the Dionysiac theory of sacrifice) : Dionysus must enter into him and madden him, not by drink or drugs or hypnotism, as modern rationalism too glibly suggests, but by a supernatural invasion of the man's personality (cf. introductory note to scene 3 c). Also, before the victim is torn, it must be consecrated by a rite of investiture: as the calf on Tenedos wore the god's buskin, so Pentheus must wear the god's μίτρα (831–3 n., 854–5 n.). We may say with some confidence that neither the bedevilling scene nor the 'toilet' scene is, in its main content, the poet's (or any poet's) invention as has been alleged, although from these traditional elements he has created something which is unique in its strangeness and compelling power. The same seems to be true of much of the content of the first messenger-speech (see Commentary).

ii. *Evidence from Earlier Dionysiac Plays*

The πάθη of Dionysus, the patron god of drama, may well be the oldest of all dramatic subjects. For us the *Bacchae* is a unique specimen of a Dionysiac passion-play; but for its first audience it was a rehandling of a theme already familiar to generations of Athenian play-goers. The ascription of a Πενθεύς to Thespis is probably a fiction; but in addition to the two Dionysiac tetralogies of Aeschylus we hear of a Lycurgus-tetralogy by Polyphrasmon, exhibited 467; a Βάκχαι by Xenocles, one of a set of plays which gained the first prize in 415; a Βάκχαι ἢ Πενθεύς by Sophocles' son Iophon; a Σεμέλη κεραυνουμένη by Spintharos (late fifth century); a Βάκχαι by Cleophon (period uncertain). No Dionysiac tragedies are attributed to Sophocles, unless his Ὑδροφόροι dealt, like the Σεμέλη ἢ Ὑδροφόροι of Aeschylus, with the birth of Dionysus (whom we know to have been mentioned in the play, fr. 674). The Διόνυσος of Chaeremon (in which Pentheus seems to have figured), the Σεμέλη of Carcinus, and the Σεμέλη of Diogenes probably belong to the fourth century; a longish extant passage from the last-named testifies to the continued interest of Athenian audiences in exotic orgiastic cults.

Of none of these do we know much beyond the title—the great popularity of the *Bacchae*[1] in later antiquity doubtless killed them. And even of Aeschylus' Dionysiac plays our knowledge is lamentably small.[2] His *Lycurgeia* consisted of the Ἠδωνοί, Βασσάραι (or Βασσαρίδες), Νεανίσκοι, and the satyr-play Λυκοῦργος (schol. Ar. *Thesm.* 134). As to the plays which made up his (presumed) Theban tetralogy there is much dispute. The Medicean catalogue offers us Βάκχαι, Ξάντριαι, Πενθεύς, Σεμέλη ἢ Ὑδροφόροι, Τροφοί (= Διονύσου Τροφοί, hyp. Eur. *Med.*). This is one too many: the likeliest guess is perhaps that the Βάκχαι is an alternative title for the Βασσάραι.[3] The Σεμέλη must have been the first play: it dealt with Semele's mysterious pregnancy and the beginning of the Dionysiac possession at Thebes (schol. Ap. Rh. 1. 636), and presumably ended with her death and the supposed death of her child;[4] the Chorus are women who have brought water for the ceremonial washing of the

---

[1] It was well known as a schoolbook (Call. *epigr.* 48 Wilam. = *Anth. Pal.* 6. 310); popular recitations were given from it (Lucian, *Ind.* 19); it was widely quoted and excerpted in the Roman period, as may be seen from the 'testimonia' cited in Kirchhoff's *apparatus*, and was imitated by Nonnus at a time when almost all memory of Greek tragedy was fading.

[2] To the fragments in Nauck's *T.G.F.* must be added *P. Oxy.* 2164, now conveniently accessible in Mr. Lloyd-Jones's appendix to the Loeb Aeschylus, and a few scraps collected by Mette in his *Fragmente der Tragödien des Aischylos* (Berlin, 1959). Discussion: Welcker, *Aisch. Trilogie*, 320 ff., Hermann, *Opusc.* v. 3 ff., Bruhn, Introd. to *Ba.*, Zielinski, *Tragodoumena*, 67 ff., Murray, *Aeschylus*, 153 ff., Deichgräber, *Gött. Nachr.* 1939, no. 8, Latte, *Philol.* xcvii (1948), 47 ff.

[3] Or for the Πενθεύς (as the Βάκχαι of Eur. and Iophon bore the alternative title Πενθεύς). In that case the Alexandrine scholar who made the catalogue has blundered surprisingly. On the view suggested in the text, the blunder may be that of a copyist, who wrote Βάκχαι Βασσάραι Γλαῦκος Πόντιος instead of Βάκχαι ἢ Βασσάραι Γλαῦκος Ποτνιεύς Γλαῦκος Πόντιος.

[4] Cf. fr. 221 Ζεὺς ὃς κατέκτα τοῦτον (i.e. Dionysus, cf. *Ba.* 244 f.?).

new-born infant.[1] Hera may have intervened to tempt Semele to her destruction (cf. *Ba.* 9), as she does in some later versions of the story. The Oxyrhynchus fragments, however, in which Hera figures, belong, if Asclepiades[2] can be trusted, not to this play but to the *Xantriae*. In the main fragment a chorus—presumably the 'wool-carding women' of the title—defend Semele's reputation against jealousy and slander concerning her union with Zeus (cf. *Ba.* 26 ff.).[3] To them enter Hera disguised as a begging priestess: her purpose is doubtless to stir up opposition against Semele's son (cf. *Ba.* 98, 294); I take her to be the person referred to elsewhere in the play as τῶνδε βούλευτις πόνων (fr. 172). (It is interesting that Euripides discards this supernatural intervention, making the opposition purely human and basing it on very human motives.) Dionysus' reply to Hera's plot is to send Lyssa to madden the unbelievers (fr. 169). (Observe, again, that whereas Aeschylus brought Lyssa in person on the stage, Euripides is content with a

---

[1] Others say, to put out the fire started by the lightning. But this unforeseen event seems to have occurred at or near the end of the play, and the entry of the Chorus could hardly be so long deferred. Descriptive titles elsewhere describe the *initial* situation, e.g. *Choephoroe*, *Ichneutae*, *Plyntriae*, *Hippolytus Stephanias*.

[2] *Apud* schol. Ar. *Frogs* 1344. Latte has argued forcibly that we should throw Asclepiades' testimony overboard and assign the fragments to the *Semele*, thus giving Hera the function which she has in some later versions of the story. His argument rests, however, on two assumptions: that the *Xantriae* dealt with the death of Pentheus, and that in the fragments Semele is implied to be still alive. Neither assumption seems to me secure. As to Pentheus' death see p. xxxi n. 1. Semele's life hangs on a supplement to an incomplete sentence, [Σ]εμέλας δ᾽ ε[ὑ]χόμεθ᾽ εἶναι διὰ πᾶν εὐθύπορον λα[, which Latte completes with λά[χος αἰοῦς, Lloyd-Jones with λά[χος ὄλβου. But other supplements are possible, e.g. λατρείαν (for the rhythm cf. *Agam.* 204): the sentence would then refer to the continuing cult at Semele's grave (cf. note on *Ba.* 6–12).

[3] They are therefore *not* the women who were punished with madness for their lack of faith. Hence Elmsley's view that Ξάντριαι = 'The Dismemberers' (of Pentheus) seems to be mistaken (it is also open to objection on the ground stated in n. 1 above).

passing allusion (977); he had used her in the *Heracles*, but here there is no room for such a purely symbolic figure.) In the Ξάντριαι I suspect that Dionysus did not appear in person but worked through his agent Lyssa; the god himself was reserved for the third piece. The Ξάντριαι may have ended where Euripides' *Bacchae* begins, with the retreat of the Theban women to Cithaeron, which we know was mentioned in it,[1] and Pentheus' threat to pursue them. The third piece, the Πενθεύς, will then have covered the same ground as Euripides' play, which agrees with the statement of Aristophanes of Byzantium in the ὑπόθεσις to the latter.[2] Enragingly, only one line of it survives, fr. 183 μηδ' αἵματος πέμφιγα πρὸς πέδῳ βάλῃς—an injunction which recalls *Ba.* 837 and was perhaps uttered in similar circumstances. Of the Διονύσου Τροφοί we know only that it dealt with, or mentioned, the rejuvenation of the Τροφοί and their husbands by Medea (fr. 50). This reward of the faithful would suit a satyr-play, having obvious humorous possibilities.

The fragments of Aeschylus' *Lycurgeia* offer some interesting parallels to the *Bacchae*. (*a*) In the 'Ἠδωνοί, as in our play, Dionysus was taken prisoner (schol. Ar. *Thesm.* 135), questioned about his birthplace, evidently in ignorance of his identity (fr. 61, cf. *Ba.* 460 ff.), and taunted with his effeminate appearance and costume (fr. 61 and probably 59, 60, 62, cf. *Ba.* 453–9 n., 831–3 n.). It looks as if the first scene between Pentheus and Dionysus in the *Bacchae*

---

[1] Schol. *Eum.* 26 νῦν φησιν ἐν Παρνασῷ εἶναι τὰ κατὰ Πενθέα, ἐν δὲ ταῖς Ξαντρίαις ἐν Κιθαιρῶνι. It is usually inferred from this that the death of Pentheus occurred in the Ξάντριαι, which was therefore the third play of the trilogy. But if so, (*a*) what was the second play about? (*b*) why does Aristophanes say that Aesch. treated the subject-matter of Eur.'s *Bacchae* ἐν Πενθεῖ? Cithaeron may well have figured both in the Ξάντριαι and in the Πενθεύς, and Pentheus' death may have been predicted in the former play.

[2] Πενθεύς here has sometimes been taken for the name of the whole trilogy. But Ar. parallels the *Phoenissae* with the *Septem*, not with the *Oedipodea*.

followed the older poet's model pretty closely. (*b*) Somewhere in the tetralogy there was an epiphany of the god in his true nature, whose effect on Lycurgus' palace was described in the line ἐνθουσιᾷ δὴ δῶμα· βακχεύει στέγη (fr. 58). We may probably infer that in the 'palace miracles' of the *Bacchae* Euripides was following tradition, although the words preserved need not imply an actual earthquake. Cf. Naevius, *Luc.* frs. 20, 23, quoted below, p. xxxiii, n. 1. (*c*) From two fragments of the *Βασσάραι* we may infer that Aeschylus—like Euripides—spoke of the god's dangerous bull-shape (fr. 23, cf. *Ba.* 618, 920, 1017) and represented him (if ἀστραπῆς is sound) as Master of the Lightning (Mette, *Suppl. Aesch.* fr. 31 = fr. 12 Weir-Smyth [Loeb] ἀστραπῆς πευκᾶεν σέλας on Mount Pangaeum, cf. *Ba.* 594–5 n., 1082–3 n.).

Three further conjectures may be added. (i) Some character in Aeschylus (?Lycurgus or Pentheus) applied the abusive term χαλιμίαι or χαλιμάδες to the bacchanal women (fr. 448), which suggests that the allegations of immorality put by Euripides into Pentheus' mouth are traditional charges. (ii) The imprisonment and miraculous escape of the bacchanals, briefly described in our play (443–8), figures in 'Apollodorus' ' summary of the Lycurgus story (*Bibl.* 3. 5. 1 Βάκχαι δὲ ἐγένοντο αἰχμάλωτοι . . . αὖθις δὲ αἱ Βάκχαι ἐλύθησαν ἐξαίφνης), and perhaps appeared also in the *Lucurgus* of Naevius (fr. 6, cf. Ribbeck, *Römische Tragödie*, 59 f.). 'Apollodorus' is not following Euripides, for he makes Lycurgus jail the satyrs too. We must suppose that he and Euripides (and Naevius?) are drawing here on a common source, in all likelihood the *Lycurgeia* of Aeschylus.[1] (iii) Naevius reproduces also the interrogation of the captive god (frs. 11–14) and the description of his effeminate dress,[2] which certainly go back to Aeschylus;

[1] Cf. Zielinski, *Tragodoumena*, 66.

[2] Naevius, fr. incerti nominis 4 'diabathra in pedibus habebat, erat amictus epicroco'. It seems fairly certain that Dionysus is the person described.

and the burning of the palace,[1] which probably does. Hence it may well be from the same source that he and Euripides derived the comparison of the maenads to birds and the account of their raid on the valley farms (frs. 7 and 3, quoted on *Ba.* 748–50). The impression left by the *Lucurgus* fragments as a whole is that Naevius did not borrow from the *Bacchae*, but used an original very similar to it both in general colouring and in the pattern of its plot. And the probabilities are that this original was the 'Ηδωνοί of Aeschylus.[2]

Of the Roman tragedies on the Pentheus story, the *Pentheus* of Pacuvius was based on Euripides, if we are to believe Servius on *Aen.* 4. 469; but some other source was apparently used as well, for Pentheus' prisoner was called Acoetes, as he is in Ovid. *Met.* 3. 574 ff. (where the narrative diverges widely from Euripides in other respects). The *Bacchae* of Accius appears from the fragments to have been a fairly close adaptation of Euripides' play.

iii. *Evidence from Vase Paintings*[3]

The death of Pentheus was, like other Dionysiac subjects, a great favourite with the vase painters; and from their treatment of it attempts have been made to draw inferences as to Aeschylus' handling of it and the innovations attributable to him or to Euripides.

1. The earliest extant representation of the scene appears on a psykter in Boston (and Freiburg), painted about 520 B.C. in the manner of Euphronios (*Arch. Jhb.* vii (1892), pl. 5, Philippart, pl. 12, No. 150, Beazley, *A.R.V.* p. 19. 5). The largest fragment shows Pentheus (identified by name)

---

[1] fr. 20 'ut uideam Volcani opera haec flammis flora fieri'; fr. 23 'late longeque transtros feruere'.

[2] Cf. Deichgräber, loc. cit., pp. 260 ff.

[3] Most fully collected and illustrated by H. Philippart, 'Iconographie des Bacchantes d'Eur.', *Rev. belge de phil. et d'hist.* ix (1930). Cf. also Sandys[4], Introd., pp. cvii ff., and L. Curtius, *Pentheus* (Berliner Winckelmannsprogramm 88, 1929).

being torn by two maenads, one of whom is named Galene;[1] the name of the other is missing. It has been inferred that in the oldest form of the myth the killers were not Agaue and her sisters but the followers of Dionysus; and that either Aeschylus or Euripides was the first to make Agaue the murderess.[2] This is not impossible, but the parallel myths of the Minyads and Proetids seem to me to tell against it; and the Villa Giulia cup (*infra*) is against making Euripides the innovator.

2. Other pre-Euripidean vases present nothing that conflicts with Euripides' account. That the ghastly play with the mangled limbs (*Ba.* 1133 ff.) is an invention neither of Euripides nor of Aeschylus appears from two early works: the Louvre cup G 69 (*Arch. Jhb.*, l.c., p. 162, Philippart, pl. 13 a, No. 151), which belongs to the last decade of the sixth century;[3] and the stamnos by the Berlin painter in Oxford (Beazley, *A.R.V.* 138. 112, *J.H.S.* xxxi (1911), 282, pl. 17), painted in the first decade of the fifth. The triumph-dance led by a maenad who carries Pentheus' head is shown on fragments of a cup in the Villa Giulia at Rome (*C.V.A. Villa Giulia*, fasc. 2, III. i. c, pl. 37) painted early in the last quarter of the fifth century B.C. Here the leading figure stands out from the others, and it is a reasonable guess to call her Agaue, though we cannot be absolutely certain.

3. About contemporary (at earliest) with Euripides' play is the Heidelberg pyxis (Curtius, Abb. 2–6, Philippart, No. 132, pl. VII b), which shows Pentheus setting out from his palace with net and hunting-spears, presumably to hunt the maenads (cf. the figurative hunting of the fawn, *Ba.* 868 ff.). Neither here nor elsewhere in Greek art is there

---

[1] A figure so named appears also in a Dionysiac θίασος on a red-fig. bell-krater, *c.* 430 B.C. (Reinach, *Répertoire des Vases*, ii. 6. 3, C. Fränkel, *Satyr- u. Bakchennamen auf Vasenbildern*, No. η). Elsewhere Galene is a Nereid or a local nymph.

[2] Aesch., P. Girard, *R.E.G.* xvii (1904), 190; Eur., Hartwig, *Arch. Jhb.* vii (1892), 157 ff., Wilamowitz, *Ba. übersetzt, Einleitung* 34.

[3] The dates assigned by Curtius ('*c.* 470') and Philippart ('early fifth century') are mistaken.

any indication that Pentheus is disguised. This may be
due merely to the difficulty of making a disguised Pentheus
easily recognizable (Huddilston, *Greek Tragedy in the Light
of Vase-paintings*, 16). And it is in any case rash to conclude,
as some do, that Euripides invented the disguising (cf.
supra, p. xxviii): more than one version of Pentheus' end
may well have been current before he wrote.

4. An Italiote kalpis (München 3267, Sandys, No. 1,
Curtius, Abb. 14, Philippart, No. 137, pl. VII a), roughly contemporary with the first performance of the *Bacchae*, shows
an *armed* Pentheus discovered in hiding between two trees;
and a series of other vases of similar date and origin[1] show
him in armed conflict with the maenads. This conception
has been thought to go back to Aeschylus,[2] on the strength
of *Eum.* 25 f. Βάκχαις ἐστρατήγησεν θεός, | λαγὼ δίκην Πενθεῖ
καταρράψας μόρον, which is understood as implying that
Dionysus led his women into pitched battle with Pentheus
and routed him (cf. *Ba.* 52, 798 f., which might carry a
reference to this version). The combination would be more
convincing if Aeschylus' words were more explicit and the
art tradition were traceable to a date nearer to Aeschylus'
time.

Speculations of this type are necessarily hazardous. What
does, however, emerge from a study of fifth-century paint-
ings of Dionysiac subjects is that some at least of the
painters had seen women in religious ecstasy (possibly at
the Lenaea).[3] And what they could see Euripides might
see also, without going to Macedonia for the purpose. But
the painters' conception of a maenad changed as the fifth
century advanced. Those by the great artists of the age
of the Persian wars[4] breathe the fiercest fire. In the last

---

[1] Philippart, Nos. 133, 134, 138, 139 = Sandys, Nos. 2, 6, 3, 4.

[2] G. Haupt, *Commentationes archaeol. in Aesch.* (Diss. phil. Hal.,
1897), 114 ff., Bruhn, *Einl.* 25 f.; *contra*, Séchan, *Études sur la Tragédie
grecque dans ses rapports avec la Céramique*, 102 ff., 308 ff.

[3] See above, p. xxii.

[4] e.g. the amphora by the Kleophrades painter, Pfuhl, figs. 379–80
(Beazley, *A.R.V.* 121. 5); white-ground cup by the Brygos painter

quarter of the fifth century noble maenads were still created, e.g. in the reliefs reflected by a Greek bronze krater[1] and by neo-Attic marble copies,[2] or on the Lenaea-stamnos in Naples.[3] These do not lack σεμνότης, but the animality and savage ecstasy of the older period is toned down—the ἀχάλινον and βάρος have given way to an ideal of tamed melodious beauty. It is the older pictures which best illustrate the spirit of Euripides' poem.

iv. *Formal Elements*

We have thus far considered only the content of the *Bacchae*. When we examine the form, we are at once struck by the archaic aspect which this very late play presents. In this it is not unique: a certain archaizing tendency shows itself here and there in all Euripides' later work.[4] But the *Bacchae* carries archaism further than any other of his plays; Murray even calls it 'the most formal Greek play known to us'.[5]

In a measure this is dictated by the plot. Here for once Euripides had a Chorus whose presence needed no apology and whose personal fortunes were intimately bound up with the action: they can thus συναγωνίζεσθαι in the manner approved by Aristotle (*Poet.* 1456[a]25), and to an extent which is unusual both in Euripides and in the surviving plays of Sophocles. Hence there was no need to curtail their part or to replace any of their songs by actor's solos

Furtwängler-Reichhold, pl. 49 (*A.R.V.* 247. 14); cup by Makron, Pfuhl, fig. 438 (*A.R.V.* 304. 37).

[1] W. Zuechner, *Der Berliner Mänadenkrater* (Berliner Winckelmannsprogramm 98).

[2] Gisela Richter, *A.J.A.* xl (1936), 11 ff.

[3] Pfuhl fig. 582 (*A.R.V.* 789. 2).

[4] Wilamowitz, *Eur. Herakles*, i[2], p. 145, cf. H. Burkhardt, *Die Archaismen des Eur.* (Diss. Erlangen, 1906), 95 ff., W. Kranz, *Stasimon*, 232. A striking example is Euripides' revival of the original metre of tragic dialogue, the trochaic tetrameter, which after a long interval of neglect reappears in the *Heracles* and is used in most of his subsequent plays.   [5] *Euripides and His Age*, 184.

(μονῳδίαι).[1] Further, the presentation of a miracle play, unless the producer commands the technical resources of Drury Lane, imposes an extensive use of narrative. The poet has put a psychological miracle at the centre of his stage action;[2] but the physical miracles have to be reported. And so the *Bacchae* reverts to the oldest dramatic model: not only are there two formal messenger-speeches, each over 100 lines long, but we have in addition the soldier's narrative (434–50) and that of the Stranger (616–37); all four describe miraculous events which could not be shown on the stage.

But it is significant that in diction and style also the play reverts to an older manner. A recent continental investigator finds more archaic forms in the *Bacchae* than in any other play of Euripides, and fewer colloquial or prose forms than in anything he had written since the *Troades*.[3] There is, it is true, an unusually high proportion of 'new' words, i.e. words not found in any earlier writer.[4] But few of these seem to be taken from contemporary speech: some of them belong to the language of Dionysiac religion, like θιασώτης or καταβακχιοῦσθαι: others are refinements of poetic diction, like χρυσορόης or σκιαρόκομος. There is a considerable Aeschylean element in the vocabulary,[5] and some unconscious echoes of Aeschylean phrases have been noticed[6] (probably we should find more if Aeschylus' Dionysiac plays were extant). The grave semi-liturgical style which

[1] It seems likely that the long solo, overdone in plays like the *Orestes* and no longer a novelty, had begun to bore audiences (cf. Ar. *Ran.* 849, 1329 ff.); for the contemporary *Oedipus Coloneus* shows a similar reversion to the older practice as compared with the *Philoctetes*.

[2] See note on Scene 3 (*c*), p. 172.

[3] J. Smereka, *Studia Euripidea* (Lwow, 1936), 117.

[4] Ibid. 241.

[5] Cf. Burkhardt, op. cit., 62 ff.

[6] O. Krausse, *de Euripide Aeschyli instauratore* (diss. Jena, 1905), 158–62. See esp. 850–3 n. and 1101–2 n. It is unsafe to attach much significance to stock tags like 764 οὐκ ἄνευ θεῶν τινος = *Pers.* 163, or 753 πάντ' ἄνω τε καὶ κάτω = *Eum.* 650, or to proverbial phrases like 795 πρὸς κέντρα λακτίζοιμι (cf. *Ag.* 1624).

predominates in the choral odes often recalls Aeschylus; there is little of the baroque preciosity and preoccupation with the decorative which characterizes most of Euripides' later lyrics. In keeping with this tone is the choice of rhythms associated with actual hymns of worship (Commentary, p. 183), and especially the extensive use of ionics (p. 72). So too is the introduction of refrains (876 ff., 991 ff.), which belong to the tradition of the cult hymn: it is noteworthy that Aeschylus uses them freely, Sophocles not at all, Euripides elsewhere only in Ion's hymn to Apollo and Electra's water-carrying song. The iambic trimeters give away the date of the play by the high proportion of resolved feet (one to every 2·3 trimeters, a frequency exceeded only in the *Orestes*); but the dialogue has nevertheless a certain archaic stiffness as compared, e.g., with the contemporary *Iphigeneia at Aulis*. One mark of this is the rarity in the spoken passages of ἀντιλαβή (division of a line between two speakers). In other late plays this is a favourite[1] device for conveying the swift cut-and-thrust of excited discussion, especially in the trochaic scenes; in the *Bacchae* iambic lines are divided in two places only (189, 966–70), trochaics never.

This severity of form seems to be deliberate: it goes beyond what the conditions of the theatre enforced. And in fact the play's tremendous power arises in part from the tension between the classical formality of its style and structure and the strange religious experiences which it depicts. As Coleridge said, the creative imagination shows itself most intensely in 'the balance or reconciliation of opposite or discordant qualities', and especially in combining 'a more than usual state of emotion with more than usual order'. Such a combination is achieved in the *Bacchae*.

---

[1] 52 spoken lines are so divided in the *Orestes*, 36 in the *IA.*, 53 in the *OC.*

III. THE PLACE OF THE *BACCHAE* IN EURIPIDES' WORK

After the production of the *Orestes* in the spring of 408 Euripides left Athens, never to return: he had accepted the invitation of Archelaus, the Hellenizing king of the semi-barbarous Macedonians, who was anxious to make his court a centre of Greek culture. The poet was over 70 and, as we have some reason to think, a disappointed man. If the prize-lists were any test, he had been relatively un-successful as a dramatist; he had become the butt of the comic poets; and in an Athens crazed by twenty years of increasingly disastrous war his outspoken criticisms of demagogy and of power-politics must have made him many enemies. There may well be truth in the tradition preserved in a fragment of Philodemus—φασὶν ἀχθόμενον αὐτὸν ἐπὶ τῷ σχεδὸν πάντας ἐπιχαίρειν πρὸς Ἀρχέλαον ἀπελθεῖν.[1] In Macedonia he continued to write, producing the *Archelaus*, a play about his host's eponymous ancestor, which may have been acted in the new theatre built by Archelaus at Dion. And when he died, in the winter of 407–406, three further pieces were found among his papers, the *Bacchae*, the *Alcmaeon at Corinth* (now lost), and the *Iphigeneia at Aulis*—the last-named probably unfinished. These were subsequently staged at Athens by the poet's son (or nephew), Euripides the younger,[2] and won the first prize.[3] The presumption thus created that the *Bacchae* was com-pleted, if not conceived, in Macedonia derives support from the complimentary references to Pieria (409–11 n.) and to the valley of the Ludias (568–75 n.)—both of them districts

---

[1] *De vitiis*, col. 13. 4. It is not certain that the words refer to Euripides, but it is highly probable. Cf. *vit. Eur.* l. 115 Nauck πλέον τι φρονήσας εἰκότως περιίστατο τῶν πολλῶν, οὐδεμίαν φιλοτιμίαν περὶ τὰ θέατρα ποιούμενος. . . . ἐπέκειντο δὲ καὶ οἱ κωμικοὶ φθόνῳ αὐτὸν διασύροντες. ὑπεριδὼν δὲ πάντα εἰς Μακεδονίαν ἀπῆρε.

[2] Schol. Ar. *Ran.* 67 (from the διδασκαλίαι); cf. *vit. Eur.*, l. 29.

[3] Suidas, s.v. Εὐριπίδης.

which Euripides is likely to have visited, since Dion was situated in the former and Aegae, the Macedonian capital, in the latter. I do not, however, think it probable that the play was designed primarily for a Macedonian audience: the allusions to contemporary theories and controversies at 201–3, 270–1, 274 ff., 890 ff., and elsewhere (see Commentary) are surely meant for Athenian ears;[1] and we have seen that at this period the social problem of orgiastic religion had at least as much topical interest at Athens as in Macedonia.

Why did Euripides, tireless innovator and experimenter as he had always been, leave as his final legacy to his fellow-countrymen this topical yet deeply traditional miracle-play, 'old-fashioned' in style and structure as in the incidents it depicted, yet charged with disturbing emotion? Had he some lesson which he wished to teach them? Most of his would-be interpreters have thought so, though they have failed to agree about the nature of the lesson. Since the play exhibits the power of Dionysus and the dreadful fate of those who resist him, the first explanation which occurred to scholars was that the poet had experienced (or thought it expedient to feign) a death-bed conversion: the *Bacchae* was a 'palinode', a recantation of the 'atheism' of which Aristophanes had accused its author (*Thesm.* 450 f.); it was written to defend Euripides against the charge of impiety which was soon to overwhelm his friend Socrates (Tyrwhitt, Schoene), or 'to put him right with the public on matters on which he had been misunderstood' (Sandys), or from a genuine conviction 'that religion should not be exposed to the subtleties of reasoning' (K. O. Müller) since 'he had found no satisfaction in his unbelief' (Paley). Oddly enough, good Christian editors seem to have been gratified by this notion of their poet's eleventh-hour conversion to pagan orthodoxy; and this or something like it remained the prevailing

[1] Cf. R. Nihard, *Le Problème des Bacchantes d'Euripide* (Publications du Musée Belge, No. 38, 1912), 33 ff., and 62, n. 2.

opinion till far on in the nineteenth century. At this period a generation arose which, having a different set of prejudices, admired Euripides for quite other reasons, and proceeded to make the *Bacchae* conform with its own views by radically reinterpreting it. Pointing out (correctly) that Cadmus and Teiresias are poor representatives of orthodoxy, and that Dionysus behaves with pitiless cruelty not only to his opponents Pentheus and Agaue but to his supporter Cadmus, they concluded that the real moral of the play was 'tantum religio potuit suadere malorum'. This interpretation, the germ of which appears already in Patin, was developed in the last decade of the century by Wilamowitz and Bruhn in Germany, Decharme and Weil in France; and later (with fantastic elaborations peculiar to themselves) by Norwood and Verrall in England. The devotional earnestness of the choral odes, to these critics an offence and a stumbling-block, was variously explained as a concession to a superstitious Macedonian audience (Weil) or as a successful characterization of fanaticism (Wilamowitz).

The more thoughtful among recent critics[1] have recognized the inadequacy both of the 'palinode' theory and of its rival. Each thesis fits some of the facts, but manifestly does not fit others: i.e. both are too crude.

(*a*) Closer study of the poet's work as a whole reveals no such abrupt *volte-face* as the 'palinode' thesis postulated.[2]

---

[1] Cf. Murray, 'The Bacchae of Euripides in relation to certain Currents of Thought in the Fifth Century', *Essays and Addresses*, 56 ff., Nihard, op. cit., F. M. Wassermann, 'Die Bakchantinnen des Eur.', *N. Jhb. f. Wiss. u. Jugendbildung*, v (1929), 272 ff., W. B. Sedgwick, *C.R.* xliv (1930), 6 ff., G. M. A. Grube, *Trans. Amer. Phil. Ass.* lxvi (1935), 37 ff., and *The Drama of Euripides*, 398 ff., H. D. F. Kitto, *Greek Tragedy*, 382 f. To these can now be added W. Schmid, *Geschichte der griech. Lit.* I. iii, 683 ff., A. Lesky, *Die griech. Tragödie*[2], 250 ff., F. Martinazzoli, *Euripide*, 387 ff., and E. M. Blaiklock, *The Male Characters of Euripides*, 209 ff.

[2] Hartung pointed this out a century ago: 'hi si magis quid carmina Euripidis docerent scrutari quam quid ipsi opinarentur effutire voluissent, eandem sententiam iuvenem atque senem profiteri intellexissent'.

On the one hand, his interest in, and sympathetic understanding of, orgiastic religion does not date from his Macedonian period: it appears already in the chant of the
initiates in the *Cretans* (fr. 472), the ode on the mysteries
of the Mountain Mother in the *Helena* (1301 ff.), and the
remains of an ode in the *Hypsipyle* (frs. 57, 58 Arnim = 31,
32 Hunt). The *Helena* was played in 412, the *Hypsipyle*
somewhat later; but the *Cretans* seems to be early work.[1]
The Choruses of the *Bacchae* are thus the last and fullest
utterance of feelings which had haunted[2] Euripides for
at least six years before his death, and probably for much
longer. So too the attacks on 'cleverness', and praise of
the instinctive wisdom of simple people, which have surprised critics of the *Bacchae*, are in reality nothing new:
see notes on 399–401, 430–3, 890–2, 910–11. On the other hand,
the discrepancy between the moral standards implied in
the myths and those of civilized humanity, to which many
of Euripides' characters call attention, is not ignored in
the *Bacchae*. The vengeance of Dionysus is as cruel and
undiscriminating as the vengeance of Aphrodite in the
Hippolytus. In each play one of the god's humble worshippers pleads against this unmorality, and pleads in vain
(*Ba.* 1348–9 n.). And each play ends with the sympathies
of the audience concentrated solely upon the god's victims.
It is not thus that Euripides, or anyone else, would have
composed a palinode.[3]

For further evidence see my paper 'Euripides the Irrationalist', *C.R.*
xliii (1929), 97 ff.

[1] Wilamowitz, *Berl. Kl. Texte*, v. 2, p. 79, Zielinski, *Tragodoumena*,
226 (no resolutions in the 40 surviving trimeters).

[2] Significant in this connexion is his especial fondness for the *metaphorical* use of βάκχη, βακχεύειν, and related terms. I have counted over
20 examples, against 2 in Aeschylus and 1 in Sophocles.

[3] One may add that the supposed 'conversion' to 'orthodoxy' must
have been followed by an immediate backsliding. For one of the
implications of the *I A.*—presumably the poet's last work, since he seems
to have left it unfinished—is certainly 'tantum religio . . .' (cf. the
judgement of the Chorus-leader, 1403 τὸ τῆς θεοῦ νοσεῖ).

(b) But we must not leap to the conclusion that Euripides regarded Aphrodite and Dionysus either as fiends or as fictions. To such an interpretation of the *Bacchae* one fatal obstacle is the characterization of Pentheus. If Dionysiac worship is an immoral superstition and nothing more, it follows that Pentheus is one of the martyrs of enlightenment. But it is much easier to blacken Dionysus than to whitewash Pentheus. Some rationalist critics have essayed the latter task; but it takes a resolutely blinkered vision to discover in him 'the defender of conjugal faith', 'a consistently lovable character'.[1] Euripides could conceivably have represented him thus; he could certainly have made him a second Hippolytus, fanatical, but with a touching and heroic fanaticism. He has not chosen to do so. Instead, he has invested him with the traits of a typical tragedy-tyrant:[2] absence of self-control (214, 343 ff., 620 f., 670 f.); willingness to believe the worst on hearsay evidence (221 ff.), or on none (255 ff.); brutality towards the helpless (231, 241, 511 ff., 796 f.); and a stupid reliance on physical force as a means of settling spiritual problems (781–6 n.). In addition, he has given him the foolish racial pride of a Hermione (483–4 n.), and the sexual curiosity of a Peeping Tom (222–3 n., 957–60 n.).[3] It is not thus that martyrs of enlightenment are represented.[4] Nor do such martyrs at the moment of death recant their faith as Pentheus does (1120 f.).

---

[1] Masqueray, *Euripide et ses idées*, 147; Pohlenz, *Die griech. Tragödie*[2], i. 455.

[2] Cf. Murray's translation, note on 215–62, M. Croiset, *Journal des Savants*, 1909, 250, and now especially H. Diller, *Abh. Mainz* 1955, Nr. 5, 458–63.

[3] Pentheus' 'libidinosa spectandorum secretorum cupido' was already noticed by Hartung. It is this curiosity which delivers him into his enemy's hands (see Commentary on the temptation scene). As Zielinski has well said (*N. Jhb.*, 1902, 646), primitive things rise against him not only in Thebes but in his own breast.

[4] Nihard, op. cit. 103 f., instructively contrasts the character of Zopire in Voltaire's *Mahomet*. (We must, of course, avoid the opposite error of seeing in Pentheus a mere stage villain: if he were that, the poet could not invite our pity for him as he plainly does in the later

What of the divine Stranger? He displays throughout qualities antithetic to those of his human antagonist: therein lies the peculiar effectiveness of the conflict scenes. Pentheus is flurried, irascible, full of an unhealthy excitement; the Stranger preserves from first to last an unruffled smiling calm (ἡσυχία, 621–2 n.)—a calm which we find at first touching, then vaguely disquieting, in the end indescribably sinister (439 n., 1020–23 n.). Pentheus relies on a parade of military force; the Stranger's only weapon is the invisible power which dwells within him. And to the σοφία of the King, the 'cleverness' or 'realism' which would measure everything by the vulgar yardstick of average experience, he opposes another kind of σοφία, the wisdom which, being itself a part of the order of things, knows that order and man's place in it. In all these ways the Stranger is characterized as a supernatural personage, in contrast with his all-too-human adversary: ἡσυχία, σεμνότης, and wisdom are the qualities which above all others the Greek artists of the classical age sought to embody in the divine figures of their imagination. The Stranger behaves οἷα δὴ θεός, as a Greek god should behave: he is the counterpart of the serene and dignified being whom we see on certain red-figure vases, or in sculptured works of Attic inspiration.

But the Stranger is not simply an idealized being from outside man's world; he is Dionysus, the embodiment of those tragic contradictions—joy and horror, insight and madness, innocent gaiety and dark cruelty—which, as we have seen, are implicit in all religion of the Dionysiac type. From the standpoint, therefore, of human morality he is and must be an ambiguous figure. Viewing him from that standpoint, Cadmus at the end of the play explicitly condemns

scenes. As lines 45–46 show, he is a man of conventional conservative piety, not a *contemptor deum* like Virgil's Mezentius, and he believes himself to be acting in the interest of the State. But neither in Greek tragedy nor in real life do good intentions save men from the consequences of false judgement.)

his heartlessness. But the condemnation is as futile as is the similar condemnation of Aphrodite in the *Hippolytus*. For, like Aphrodite, Dionysus is a 'person', or moral agent, only by stage necessity. What Aphrodite really is, the poet has told us plainly: φοιτᾷ δ' ἀν' αἰθέρ', ἔστι δ' ἐν θαλασσίῳ | κλύδωνι Κύπρις, πάντα δ' ἐκ ταύτης ἔφυ· | ἥδ' ἐστὶν ἡ σπείρουσα καὶ διδοῦσ' ἔρον, | οὗ πάντες ἐσμὲν οἱ κατὰ χθόν' ἔγγονοι (*Hipp.* 447 ff.). To ask whether Euripides 'believed in' *this* Aphrodite is as meaningless as to ask whether he 'believed in' sex. It is not otherwise with Dionysus. As the 'moral' of the *Hippolytus* is that sex is a thing about which you cannot afford to make mistakes,[1] so the 'moral' of the *Bacchae* is that we ignore at our peril the demand of the human spirit for Dionysiac experience. For those who do not close their minds against it such experience can be a deep source of spiritual power and εὐδαιμονία. But those who repress the demand in themselves or refuse its satisfaction to others transform it by their act into a power of disintegration and destruction, a blind natural force that sweeps away the innocent with the guilty. When that has happened, it is too late to reason or to plead: in man's justice there is room for pity, but there is none in the justice of Nature; to our 'Ought' its sufficient reply is the simple 'Must'; we have no choice but to accept that reply and to endure as we may.

If this or something like it is the thought underlying the play, it follows that the flat-footed question posed by nineteenth-century critics—was Euripides 'for' Dionysus or 'against' him?—admits of no answer in those terms. In himself, Dionysus is beyond good and evil; for us, as Teiresias says (314–18), he is what we make of him. The nineteenth-century question rested in fact on the assumption, common to the rationalist school and their opponents,[2]

---

[1] R. G. Collingwood, *An Essay on Metaphysics*, 210.

[2] As Grube expresses it (*Drama of Eur.* 399), 'both schools are guilty of the same fundamental error: they put the poet himself in front of his play instead of behind it'. Cf. Zielinski, *N. Jhb.*, 1902, 649, 'War er

and still too often made, that Euripides was, like some of his
critics, more interested in propaganda than in the dramatist's proper business. This assumption I believe to be false.
What is true is that in many of his plays he sought to inject
new life into traditional myths by filling them with a new
contemporary content—recognizing in the heroes of old
stories the counterparts of fifth-century types, and restating
mythical situations in terms of fifth-century conflicts. As
we have seen, something of the kind may have been
intended in the *Bacchae*. But in his best plays Euripides
used these conflicts not to make propaganda but as a
dramatist should,[1] to make tragedy out of their tension.
There was never a writer who more conspicuously lacked
the propagandist's faith in easy and complete solutions.
His favourite method is to take a one-sided point of view,
a noble half-truth, to exhibit its nobility, and then to
exhibit the disaster to which it leads its blind adherents—
because it is after all only part of the truth.[2] It is thus that
he shows us in the *Hippolytus* the beauty and the narrow
insufficiency of the ascetic ideal, in the *Heracles* the
splendour of bodily strength and courage and its toppling
over into megalomania and ruin; it is thus that in his
revenge plays—*Medea, Hecuba, Electra*—the spectator's
sympathy is first enlisted for the avenger and then made to
extend to the avenger's victims. The *Bacchae* is constructed
on the same principle: the poet has neither belittled the

Pentheus, war er Dionysus, Teiresias? Alles das, und noch vieles dazu'.
Blaiklock quotes the judgement of André Gide (*Journal*, 21 August
1940): 'Euripides takes sides no more than does Ibsen, it seems to me.
He is content to illuminate and develop the conflict between natural
forces and the soul that claims to escape their domination.'

[1] Cf. Virginia Woolf on the *Antigone*: 'When the curtain falls we
sympathise even with Creon himself. This result, to the propagandist
undesirable . . . suggests that if we use art to propagate political
opinions, we must force the artist to clip and cabin his gift to do us a
cheap and passing service. Literature will suffer the same mutilation
that the mule has suffered; and there will be no more horses' (*Three
Guineas*, 302).

[2] Cf. Murray, *Euripides and His Age*, 187.

joyful release of vitality which Dionysiac experience brings
nor softened the animal horror of 'black' maenadism;
deliberately he leads his audience through the whole gamut
of emotions, from sympathy with the persecuted god,
through the excitement of the palace miracles and the
gruesome tragi-comedy of the toilet scene, to share in the
end the revulsion of Cadmus against that inhuman justice.
It is a mistake to ask what he is trying to 'prove': his concern in this as in all his major plays is not to prove anything
but to enlarge our sensibility—which is, as Dr. Johnson
said, the proper concern of a poet.

What makes the *Bacchae* different from the rest of
Euripides' work is not anything new in its technique or in
its author's intellectual attitude. It is rather what James
Adam felt when he said that the play expressed 'an added
dimension of emotion', and that it was 'pervaded by
the kind of joyous exaltation which accompanies a new
discovery or illumination'.[1] It is as if the renewed contact
with nature in the wild country of Macedonia, and his re-
imagining there of the old miracle story, had released some
spring in the aged poet's mind, re-establishing a contact
with hidden sources of power which he had lost in the self-
conscious, over-intellectualized environment of late-fifth-
century Athens, and enabling him to find an outlet for
feelings which for years had been pressing on his consciousness without attaining to complete . expression. We may
guess that Euripides said to himself in Macedonia very

---

[1] *The Religious Teachers of Greece*, 316 f. Cf. André Rivier, *Essai sur
le tragique d'Euripide*, 96: 'La révélation d'un au delà libéré de nos
catégories morales et de notre raison, tel est le fait religieux fonda-
mental sur quoi repose la tragédie des *Bacchantes*.' The depth and sin-
cerity of the religious feelings expressed in the choral odes has recently
been emphasized by Festugière, *Eranos*, lv (1957), 127 ff. This seems to
me right, so long as we are talking of feelings and not of convictions.
But it remains perfectly possible that, as Jaeger puts it, 'Euripides
learnt how to praise the joy of humble faith in one of the religious
truths which pass all understanding, simply because he himself had no
such happy faith' (*Paideia*, i. 352, Eng. trans.).

much what Rilke said to himself at the beginning of his last period:

> 'Werk des Gesichts ist gethan:
> tue nun Herzwerk
> an den Bildern in dir, jenen gefangenen. Denn du
> überwältigtest sie; aber nun kennst du sie nicht.'

The 'added dimension of emotion' proceeds from no intellectual conversion, but from the work of the heart—from vision directed inward upon images long imprisoned in the mind.

Note. In the above discussion I have not dealt, save by implication, with the ingenious fancies of Verrall and (in his youth) Norwood,[1] which had a vogue in this country[2] fifty years ago but lie outside the main current of thought about the play. So far as scholars are concerned, it might be sufficient to say that time has dealt with them;[3] but since Verrall at least is still, I believe, read in English schools, it may be useful to state briefly here some of the grounds which make it impossible to accept their two main theses,[4] viz. that the miracles in which the play abounds are meant to be understood by the audience as bogus miracles, and that Pentheus'

---

[1] Gilbert Norwood, *The Riddle of the Bacchae* (1908); A. W. Verrall *The Bacchants of Euripides and Other Essays* (1910). Verrall had already interpreted other plays of Euripides on similar lines.

[2] It is interesting that no continental scholar of standing has ever (so far as I know) taken Verrall's interpretation of Euripides really seriously.

[3] Since this was written, the late Professor Norwood has dealt with them himself, in a characteristically honest and forthright manner. In his *Essays on Euripidean Drama* (1954) he recanted both the theses I have criticized, and gave his reasons. He still held that the destruction of the palace can only be an illusion in the mind of the Chorus, but he had come to believe that the illusion, and also the many physical miracles reported in the play, are to be accepted as divinely occasioned, and that the Stranger is none other than the god.

[4] Some of their interpretations of individual passages are considered in the Commentary. Most of them I am unable to accept, but it is only fair to say that both writers have helped me in places to a better understanding.

prisoner is not the god Dionysus but a human priest or adept.

(a) These contentions ignore the conditions of the Greek theatre[1] (and of all theatres), under which an audience must inevitably accept stage personages and stage happenings as being—for the purposes of the play—what they profess to be, unless someone on the stage knows better and says so. Nothing would have been easier than to have Pentheus expose the false miracles—denying the reality of the earthquake,[2] impugning the good sense or the good faith of the Herdsman—had the poet so chosen. But the King, so quick to scent licence and venality, is allowed on these points no single word of doubt. Again, the prologue, whose speaker is at pains to make it clear to the meanest intelligence that he is a god preparing to masquerade as a man, becomes either on Norwood's early view or on Verrall's a gratuitous mystification. According to the former, he is in fact a man masquerading as a god masquerading as a man. Verrall, perceiving that this monstrous formula was too complicated for any audience to grasp (even were it explained to them, as it is not), and that Dionysus prologizes in virtue of the same convention as other gods in other plays, admitted the Dionysus of prologue and epilogue as a 'theatrical deity', distinct from the 'adept' who represents him in the body of the play. But how should the cleverest audience distinguish the man on the stage, who continually hints that he is a god, and is seen by them to exercise divine power, from the god-made-flesh who has been promised them? That promise is on Verrall's theory a plain lie, whose only discernible effect is to befog the spectator. Was Euripides really such a bungler?

[1] Verrall was in fact driven to maintain that Euripides' plays were, like the poetic dramas of his own time, written with an eye to the study rather than the theatre: 'to the ultimate purpose the stage-exhibition at the Dionysia was indifferent' (Introduction to the *Ion*, p. xlv). Yet Aristotle a century later still thought exclusively in terms of the stage-exhibition.

[2] On the supposed difficulties of the earthquake scene see pp. 147 ff.

(b) The supposition that Euripides thought it worth while to write a play about the sham miracles of a sham god, having already represented similar sham miracles in a whole series of other plays, is intelligible only if we assume that fifth-century Athens shared the burning interest in the historicity of mythical miracles characteristic of late-Victorian England. Such an assumption is highly improbable: myths were myths, not scripture, and no man was required to profess belief in them—e.g. the devout Pindar could write ὑπὲρ τὸν ἀλαθῆ λόγον | δεδαιδαλμένοι ψεύδεσι ποικίλοις ἐξαπατῶντι μῦθοι.[1] Verrall's theories are in fact a classic instance of that insularity in time which, blinding men to the uniqueness both of their own and of past ages, drives them to impose upon the past the fleeting image of their own preoccupations.

(c) The final condemnation of these bleak ingenuities is, for me at least, that they transform one of the greatest of all tragedies into a species of esoteric and donnish witticism (a witticism so ill contrived that it was twenty-three centuries before anyone saw the point).[2] Did Earth, for example, acknowledge her Master by yielding at the touch of his holy wand 'milk and wine and nectar of the bee' (704 ff.)? Doubtless, replied Norwood; but the clever spectator will realize that they came there in the picnic basket and were 'planted', as the police say, to give the messenger a little surprise.[3] The οἰκεία ἡδονή of tragedy can be enjoyed in more forms than Aristotle knew; but (as Grube observes) it cannot be enjoyed by those who are continuously occupied in sniggering up their sleeve.

---

[1] *Ol.* 1. 29. Cf. J. Burnet, 'The Religious and Moral Ideas of Euripides', reprinted in his *Essays and Addresses*, 46 ff.

[2] Verrall claimed (*Euripides the Rationalist*, 106, 212) that his general view of Euripidean gods was anticipated by Aristophanes (*Thesm.* 450 f.) and by Lucian (*Iup. Tr.* 41). But the claim rests on a wilful mistranslation of the former passage and a wilful misunderstanding of the latter.

[3] Op. cit. 73, n. 1.

IV. SOURCES OF THE TEXT

i. *The Transmission*[1]

We possess two distinct groups of plays by Euripides, which derive from two different ancient sources. One group, the plays to which ancient commentaries (scholia) are attached, appears to be descended from a school edition of select plays of Euripides with notes, produced under the Roman Empire.[2] It resembled the school editions from which the extant plays of Aeschylus and Sophocles descend, and was perhaps made by the same man. The majority of our MSS., including the oldest and best (M A V B and the Jerusalem palimpsest H), contain only plays of this group. The other group, which has no scholia, evidently represents a fragment of a comprehensive library edition of Euripides in which the plays were arranged in alphabetic order; for all the plays of this group have titles beginning with *E, H, I,* or *K*. From this comprehensive edition two nests (τεύχη) of papyrus rolls[3] survived by some accident longer than the rest, and came into the hands of an unknown scholar of early[4] Byzantine times, who copied the select plays (without their scholia) and the additional plays from his new find into a single codex, thus producing a combined edition of the nineteen plays which we possess to-day. This combined edition is represented for us by two rather late MSS., L and P.

[1] For a general account of the transmission of the text of Euripides see Mr. W. S. Barrett's introduction to his forthcoming edition of the *Hippolytus*, which corrects and replaces Wilamowitz's description in *Einleitung in die griech. Tragödie*, Kap. iii.

[2] The edition cannot be dated with any certainty, but such slender indications as we have suggest the second century A.D.

[3] See B. Snell, *Hermes*, lxx (1935), 119 f. His ingenious theory is not, however, free from difficulties.

[4] We may infer this from the considerable divergence between M A V B and L P in the tradition of the select plays which are common to both. And I learn from Dr. Maas that Eustathius (1850. 35 ff.) speaks of the *Cyclops* as extant in the twelfth century.

The position of the *Bacchae* is peculiar. Like the 'alphabetic' plays, it survives only in the MSS. of the combined
edition—in P, and down to l. 755 in L. But it cannot be
part of the unknown Byzantine scholar's papyrus find.
For (a) a roll with title-initial *B* (or *Π* if the alternative
title *Pentheus* was used) would not be found in the same
nest with rolls having title-initials *E* to *K*, unless it had
strayed into the wrong pigeon-hole. (b) Like most of the
'select' plays, but unlike any of the 'alphabetic' plays, it
has two ὑποθέσεις, one of which is attributed by name (like
the second hypotheses of *Med., Phoen., Or.*, which are 'select'
plays) to Aristophanes of Byzantium. (c) It was known to
the author of the *Christus Patiens* (see below), who otherwise
shows acquaintance only with 'select' plays. (d) Although
it has been transmitted to us, like the 'alphabetic' plays,
without scholia,[1] it is quoted by the Euripidean scholiasts
far oftener than any 'non-select' play.

We must conclude that it formed part of the Roman
edition of select plays.[2] If we accept the numerals attached
to the plays in L as representing the original order, it was
the last play in the select edition.[3] And if so, we can better
understand its absence from M A V B, its incomplete pre-
servation in L, and the mutilated state of its ending in P:
bored copyists are tempted to omit the last piece in their

---

[1] Apart from three glosses in L (on 151, 451, 611) and a few metrical
notes in the same MS.

[2] This conclusion is now (1959) confirmed by the second Antinoë
papyrus (see below, p. lix), which shows that as early as the sixth
century the *Bacchae* was being copied along with annotated 'select'
plays.

[3] As L lacks the *Troades*, the *Bacchae* is numbered 9 (θ'). These
marginal numerals in L have generally been attributed to the scribe,
but according to P. G. Mason (*C.Q.* xlviii (1954), 56) and Turyn (*The
Byzantine Manuscript Tradition of the Tragedies of Euripides*, 240)
they are in the hand of *l*. We need not, however, assume with Turyn
(242) that they represent merely *l*'s private fancy; he may have
found them in an independent source, or even in the margins of L's
exemplar—to which, according to Turyn himself (246), he must have
had access.

exemplar,[1] especially if it be defective or blurred; and the last pages of a book are especially liable to injury.

ii. *The Medieval Sources*

Laurentianus xxxii. 2 (Murray's L, also known as C) is a MS. of the early fourteenth century which was brought to Italy by its owner, Simon Atumanus, Bishop of Gerace in Calabria, in or before 1348; subsequently it passed into the Laurentian collection at Florence, where it now is. It contains all the extant plays of Euripides except the *Troades* and the latter part of the *Bacchae*, together with 6 of Sophocles, 3 of Aeschylus, and Hesiod's *Works and Days*. Of the *Bacchae* it never contained more than ll. 1–755, which are followed by some pages left blank.[2] The whole of the work was checked with the exemplar by a contemporary διορθωτής, or, as Turyn thinks, by the scribe himself; he corrected occasional errors and omissions in the copy and added here and there variants or glosses (probably from the margins of the exemplar): e.g. it seems to have been he who added γε in 401, the gloss ἐμοῦ on 451, and the note ἡμιχ(όριον) at 590. Unfortunately correction did not rest there: another hand, identified by Turyn as that of the well-known Byzantine scholar Demetrius Triclinius, has introduced numerous conjectural emendations, in some cases obliterating all trace of the original text. His readings (marked *l* in Murray's *apparatus*) have no more authority than the conjectures of modern scholars, whereas those of the διορθωτής (L[2] in Murray) represent the tradition; but unluckily

[1] Most of these copyists omitted more: B lacks *Rhes.* and *Tro.*; A lacks *Alc.*, *Rhes.*, *Tro.*; M lacks *Med.*, *Alc.*, *Rhes.*, *Tro.* V contains all the plays which have scholia, and may once have contained *Bacch.*, since it is mutilated at the end.

[2] Wilamowitz thought the *Bacchae* was written in a different hand from the rest, and concluded that it was copied from a different exemplar (*Analecta Euripidea,* 4 f.). But it is now generally agreed that although the ink is different the hand is the same which wrote most of the other plays (Spranger, *Studi Italiani,* x (1932), 315 ff.; Mason, loc. cit.; Turyn, op. cit. 235 f.).

there is often difficulty in deciding to which hand a particular correction is due. In the *Bacchae l* has been successful
in removing a number of small corruptions, e.g. in mending
lame syntax at 55 and lame trimeters at 227 and 503, and
in correcting the meaningless κλύειν at 653. He knew that
strophe and antistrophe should correspond,[1] and tried to
restore responsion at 392–3 and 421—and I strongly suspect
at 115 also, though there Murray thinks ὅστις may be a
genuine old reading preserved by L². An example of *l*'s
recklessness in emendation, and the harm caused by it,
may be seen at 102, where his feeble and unnecessary conjecture θυρσοφόροι survives even in some twentieth-century
texts because it is 'a manuscript reading'.

The Palatinus (P) was written at some time in the
fourteenth century; by about 1420 it was split into two
parts, one of which is preserved in the Vatican as Palatinus
287, the other at Florence as Laurentianus Conv. Suppr.
172.[2] It contains all the extant plays of Euripides together
with 3 of Aeschylus, 6 of Sophocles, and 2 homilies of John
Chrysostom. Like L, it was checked by a contemporary
διορθωτής (P²). The Palatine part, which includes the
Bacchae and 12 other plays of Euripides, came into the
possession of Marcus Musurus (*c.* 1470–1517), who used it,
together with a copy of L, as the basis of the Aldine edition
(1503, the first printed edition which contains the *Bacchae*).
It may have been Musurus who introduced some or all of
the numerous later corrections (*p*) which appear in the
Palatine part. *p* was a rather better scholar than *l*, and
found the right correction for a good many small slips in
the *Bacchae*, e.g. at 737 πόριν for πόλιν, 929 καθήρμοσα for
καθώρμισα, 1277 τίνος for τί μου. There are other places
where he is less happy, e.g. 477, 747, 1227. At 314 he quotes
a (false) variant from Stobaeus, whose readings he has

---

[1] On *l* as a metrician see Denniston's introduction to the *Electra*,
pp. xli f.
[2] That these are parts of the same MS. was first recognized by
C. Robert, *Hermes*, xiii (1878), 133.

introduced in other plays also; but apart from this instance there is no evidence that he had MS. authority for any of his readings in the *Bacchae* (he seems in this play not even to have used L or a copy of L).

The relationship of P to L—which was long completely obscured, and is still to some extent obscured, by the ravages of *p* and *l*—appears to be different in different plays. (*a*) In the 9 'alphabetic' plays it now seems pretty certain that P is a derivative of L, whose only value lies in preserving readings of L which *l* erased.[1] (*b*) In some at least of the 'select' plays P is at least partially independent of L, since it not infrequently agrees with M A V against L. (*c*) In the *Troades*, and in *Bacch.* 756–1392, both of which L lacks, P is an independent witness. His source, which I will call [Q], is probably the same for both;[2] and to judge by P's wide divergence from V in *Tro.*, [Q] is more likely to have been a MS. of the combined edition than a MS. of the select plays. In *Bacch.* 1–755 P may depend in part on L: in one place (568) his text looks like the result of misreading L's handwriting. But he must have drawn also on [Q], since he preserves l. 14 and the word παρεῖται in 635, both of which L omits.

Had the scribe of P taken his text of the *Bacchae* from a MS. of the select plays, we should be much better off: we should have a valuable dual tradition for ll. 1–755, and probably also a more complete text of the last 100 lines. We know from the adaptations in the *Christus Patiens* that a more complete text existed in the twelfth century;[3] and

---

[1] See esp. Wecklein, *Sitz.-Ber. Bayer. Akad.*, 1899, ii. 297 ff., and 1922, Abh. 5. 61; P. Maas, *Gnomon*, 1926, 156 f. Turyn, who maintains that P is throughout a twin of L, derived from the same exemplar (op. cit. 264 ff.), does not seem to me to have disposed of their very strong arguments for the dependence of P on L in the alphabetic plays: cf. H. Lloyd-Jones, *Gnomon*, xxx (1958), 505 ff.

[2] It can be plausibly argued from the distribution of lacunas that both descend in P from an archetype which had on each page two columns of 35 to 38 verses: see 755–7 n.

[3] See Murray's note at end of text, and my Appendix. On the date of the *Chr. Pat.*, see Brambs's preface to the Teubner edition, 18 ff.

we can be fairly certain that the MS. from which its author[1] quarried the material for his curious mosaic contained select plays only, since he shows knowledge of no others. It provided him with a text of the *Bacchae* which was not only fuller but in some places at least more accurate than P's: cf. 694, 1161, 1213, and especially 1084 and 1087, where the text deducible from *Chr. Pat.* is now confirmed by a papyrus.[2] The indirect evidence furnished by the *Chr. Pat.* for several hundred lines of our play must, however, be used with great caution; for the author altered his originals freely, not only adapting them to a new purpose but often modernizing them in language and metre.

iii. *Papyri*

The text of the *Bacchae* thus rests on a more slender foundation than the text of any other 'select' play of Euripides. And apart from the *Chr. Pat.* and a few ancient citations we have hitherto had no means of testing the strength of this foundation. Line 1, it is true, occurs in a schoolboy's exercise book, P. Teb. iii. 901; line 642 in a grammatical fragment, P. Lit. Lond. 183; and the tail-piece (1388–92) in P. Hibeh i. 25. But none of these tells us anything. Thanks, however, to the kindness of the Egypt Exploration Society, the Delegates of the Oxford University Press, and Mr. C. H. Roberts, I have been allowed to make use of two unpublished papyri.[3] The more interesting of their readings are quoted and discussed individually in the

---

[1] Possibly Constantine Manasses (K. Horna, *Hermes*, lxiv (1929)' 429); anyhow not Gregory of Nazianzus.

[2] As it is also at *Rhes*. 52. The opinion of Kirchhoff, that the author of *Chr. Pat.* used a MS. similar to L P and no better, was refuted by Doering, *Philol.* xxiii. 517 ff., xxv. 221 ff. In the plays with a dual tradition the *Chr. Pat.* supports now the one, now the other group of MSS., but is usually free from errors peculiar to one group: i.e. it seems to represent a stage in the tradition prior to the bifurcation.

[3] Since published as P. Oxy. 2223 and P. Ant. 24 respectively. To these two I am now (1959) able to add another fragment from Antinoë: see below, p. lix.

commentary; but a word may be said here about the general bearing of the new evidence on the reliability of the text.

(a) An Oxyrhynchos fragment, written in a handsome professional book-hand assigned by Mr. Roberts to the second century A.D., contains ll. 1070–1136, but with beginnings of lines missing in the first column (1070–1104) and ends of lines in the second (1105–36). It looks like a careless copy made from an excellent text—a much better text than P. Its faults are numerous but superficial: with one possible exception (1131) its visibly false readings are such as could be corrected at a glance even without the help of P. Nowhere (apart from spellings like ἱέρεια) does it agree with P in a manifestly false reading; in the three places where it supports a text that has been seriously doubted (1098, 1103, 1125) the grounds for doubt are, I think, inconclusive. On the other hand, it confirms no fewer than thirteen modern corrections, most of them old[1] and extremely obvious. What is disturbing, however, is that besides omitting (I suspect rightly) a line which has never been doubted (1092), and adding a new line (after 1104) whose absence has never been felt, it presents defensible new readings in seven other places where the tradition of P has not been questioned. One of these (κάρα 1087) happens to be confirmed by the *Chr. Pat.*; two others seem to me definite improvements (βρόμον 1085, δ' ἄρ' 1113); the remainder (τ(ε)ιμωρεῖτ' ἐμοί 1081, σεμνόν 1083, ὁ [σός] 1118, πλευροῖσιν 1126) are more or less indifferent variants, such as we encounter fairly often in the medieval tradition of Euripides.

The general effect is not to strengthen one's belief either in the reliability of P or in the possibility of correcting it outside rather narrow limits. It looks on this evidence as if the text of the *Bacchae* had suffered considerable alteration since Roman times, including the introduction not only of

---

[1] The most recent critic of whose labours it takes any account is Paley—a distressing illustration of the law of diminishing returns to which conjectural emendation is subject.

many superficial errors which the critics have been able
to put right but probably of a good many others which
remain unsuspected. This appearance conflicts with the
conclusion usually, and rightly, drawn from the study of
papyri in general and of Euripidean papyri in particular.[1]
The difference is probably due to the exceptional manner
in which the *Bacchae* has been transmitted; if we could
read it as it stood in the edition with scholia, the relation
between the medieval and the Roman tradition might well
appear in a different light.

In the same hand as the Oxyrhynchos fragment are four
beginnings of unrecognized lines on a detached piece of
papyrus, which will be found in the Appendix; they may or
may not be lost lines of the *Bacchae*.

(*b*) Mr. Roberts's other contribution consists of three
scraps from a papyrus codex found at Antinoë and assigned
by him to the fifth century A.D. The largest scrap has on
the verso fragments of ll. 459–71, on the recto fragments of
ll. 496–508. The other two have on both sides fragments
of unrecognized lines; these are printed in the Appendix,
where I have given reasons for attributing the two longer
of them to the *Bacchae* and situating them in the lacuna
after 1329. The fragments of extant lines are too meagre
to justify any confident generalization about the character
of the text they represent. So far as they go, however,
they tend to support the conclusion that the L P tradition
of the *Bacchae* is decidedly inferior to that current in
Roman times. This papyrus, like the other, nowhere agrees
with the medieval tradition in manifest error. The scribe
has made one slip (omission of δέ in 465); on the other hand,
he avoids four blunders common to L and P, confirming in
one case (503) an ancient citation, in the other three the
conjectures of early editors. In the two remaining places

---

[1] e.g. Schubart, *Einführung i. d. Papyruskunde*, 88, says that 'in
general, papyri of the Roman period have the text which we read today'; D. L. Page, Introd. to *Medea*, xl, that Euripidean papyri of post-
Alexandrian date 'differ very little from our own manuscripts'.

where the papyrus differs from L P, either text is possible, with the balance of probability perhaps slightly in favour of the new reading (Διόνυσος αὐτός μ' 466, οὐδ' εἰσορᾷς 502). At 469, where L and P differ from each other, the papyrus confirms L.

(c) In the present (second) edition I have been enabled by the kindness of Mr. J. W. B. Barns and the Delegates of the Press to cite the readings of a further papyrus scrap, as yet unpublished. It comes from Antinoë, but not from the same text as P. Ant. 24, described above. Mr. Barns tells me that it is in the same fifth- or sixth-century hand as P. Ant. 23 (*Medea*, with scholia), and almost certainly from the same codex (or set of codices).[1] It contains only fragments of (recto) lines 1154–9 and (verso) lines 1183–6. But scanty as it is, it confirms two modern corrections, Ἄιδα for Ἄιδαν at 1157, and τλᾶμον for τλάμων at 1184. Its evidence thus points in the same direction as that of the other *Bacchae* papyri.

---

[1] The surviving scrap of the *Bacchae* includes no scholia; but what looks like an interlinear letter 'μ' added (perhaps by a second hand) above ὁ μόσχος at 1185 is possibly a reference numeral applying to a scholion which has not been preserved.

ΒΑΚΧΑΙ

ΥΠΟΘΕΣΙΣ ΒΑΚΧΩΝ

Διόνυσον οἱ προσήκοντες οὐκ ἔφασαν εἶναι θεόν· ὃ δὲ αὐτοῖς τιμωρίαν
ἐπέστησε τὴν πρέπουσαν. ἐμμανεῖς γὰρ ἐποίησε τὰς τῶν Θηβαίων
γυναῖκας, ὧν αἱ τοῦ Κάδμου θυγατέρες ἀφηγούμεναι τοὺς θιάσους ἐξῆγον
ἐπὶ τὸν Κιθαιρῶνα. Πενθεὺς δέ, ὁ τῆς Ἀγαύης παῖς, παραλαβὼν τὴν
βασιλείαν ἐδυσφόρει τοῖς γινομένοις καί τινας μὲν τῶν Βακχῶν 5
συλλαβὼν ἔδησεν, ἐπ᾽ αὐτὸν δὲ τὸν θεὸν ἄλλως ἀπέστειλεν. οἳ δὲ
ἑκόντος αὐτοῦ κυριεύσαντες ἦγον πρὸς τὸν Πενθέα, κἀκεῖνος ἐκέλευσεν
δήσαντας αὐτὸν ἔνδον φυλάττειν, οὐ λέγων μόνον ὅτι θεὸς οὐκ ἔστι
Διόνυσος, ἀλλὰ καὶ πράττειν πάντα ὡς κατ᾽ ἀνθρώπου τολμῶν. ὃ δὲ
σεισμὸν ποιήσας κατέστρεψε τὰ βασίλεια, ἀγαγὼν δὲ εἰς Κιθαιρῶνα 10
ἔπεισε τὸν Πενθέα κατόπτην γενέσθαι τῶν γυναικῶν λαμβάνοντα
γυναικὸς ἐσθῆτα· αἱ δ᾽ αὐτὸν διέσπασαν, τῆς μητρὸς Ἀγαύης καταρ-
ξαμένης. Κάδμος δὲ τὸ γεγονὸς καταισθόμενος τὰ διασπασθέντα
μέλη συναγαγὼν τελευταῖον τὸ πρόσωπον ἐν ταῖς τῆς τεκούσης ἐφώρασε
χερσίν. Διόνυσος δὲ ἐπιφανεὶς τὰ μὲν πᾶσι παρήγγειλεν, ἑκάστῳ δὲ 15
ἃ συμβήσεται διεσάφησεν †ἔργοις, ἵνα μὴ λόγοις† ὑπό τινος τῶν
ἐκτὸς ὡς ἄνθρωπος καταφρονηθῇ.

ΑΡΙΣΤΟΦΑΝΟΥΣ ΓΡΑΜΜΑΤΙΚΟΥ ΥΠΟΘΕΣΙΣ

Διόνυσος ἀποθεωθεὶς μὴ βουλομένου Πενθέως τὰ ὄργια αὐτοῦ
ἀναλαμβάνειν εἰς μανίαν ἀγαγὼν τὰς τῆς μητρὸς ἀδελφὰς ἠνάγκασε 20
Πενθέα διασπάσαι. ἡ μυθοποιία κεῖται παρ᾽ Αἰσχύλῳ ἐν Πενθεῖ.

Argumenta habet P: om. L   3 θιάσους Elmsley: θράσους P
ἐξῆγον Kirchhoff: εἰσῆγον P   4 Ἀγαύης p: spatium vacuum reli-
querat is qui argumentum scripsit in P, ut etiam Agavae nomen in
personarum indice ignorabatur   παραλαβὼν Elmsley: παραβὼν P
6 ἄλλως] ἀγγέλους Elmsley: δμῶας Wecklein   9 ἀνθρώπου Hermann: ἄνθρωπον P   12 κατα*ξαμ (asterisco supra μ posito) P: corr. p
15 τὰ μὲν Elmsley: μὲν P   16 ἵνα μὴ ἔργοις ἢ λόγοις Elmsley:
fortasse λόγοις, ἵνα μὴ ἔργοις   21 διασπάσαι Musurus: διασπα-
σθῆναι P

ΤΑ ΤΟΥ ΔΡΑΜΑΤΟΣ ΠΡΟΣΩΠΑ

ΔΙΟΝΥΣΟΣ	*ΘΕΡΑΠΩΝ*
ΧΟΡΟΣ	*ΑΓΓΕΛΟΣ*
ΤΕΙΡΕΣΙΑΣ	*ΕΤΕΡΟΣ ΑΓΓΕΛΟΣ*
ΚΑΔΜΟΣ	*ΑΓΑΥΗ*
ΠΕΝΘΕΥΣ	

Διόνυσος ὁ προλογίζων

Personarum indicem in ordinem reduxit Elmsley : sic habent L P
διόνυσος. πενθεύς. χορός (χορὸς βακχῶν P). θεράπων. τειρεσίας. ἄγγελος.
κάδμος. ἕτερος ἄγγελος. γυνή (καὶ γυνή P): apparet haec e codice
descripta esse in quo nomina sic disposita erant

Διόνυσος.	*θεράπων.*
χορός.	*ἄγγελος.*
Τειρεσίας.	*ἕτερος ἄγγελος.*
Κάδμος.	*Ἀγαύη.*
Πενθεύς.	

Cf. ad Person. indicem Phoenissarum. Eodem fere ritu expli-
candi sunt ordines dati a B V⋅in Medea (sed παῖδες omissi erant in archetypo), a P in Alcestide (omissi παῖς et χορός in archetypo), alii
   Pro *θεράπων. ἄγγελος. ἕτερος ἄγγελος* mavult *θεράπων. βουκόλος.*
ἕτερος θεράπων Wecklein   verba *Διόνυσος ὁ προλογίζων* om. P

   Acta paullo post annum A.C. 406 mortuo poeta (Schol.
Ar. Ran. 67). Codices L P : L post v. 755 deficit. Scholia
paucissima.

ΒΑΚΧΑΙ

ΔΙΟΝΥΣΟΣ

Ἥκω Διὸς παῖς τήνδε Θηβαίων χθόνα
Διόνυσος, ὃν τίκτει ποθ᾿ ἡ Κάδμου κόρη
Σεμέλη λοχευθεῖσ᾿ ἀστραπηφόρῳ πυρί·
μορφὴν δ᾿ ἀμείψας ἐκ θεοῦ βροτησίαν
πάρειμι Δίρκης νάματ᾿ Ἰσμηνοῦ θ᾿ ὕδωρ.   5
ὁρῶ δὲ μητρὸς μνῆμα τῆς κεραυνίας
τόδ᾿ ἐγγὺς οἴκων καὶ δόμων ἐρείπια
τυφόμενα Δίου πυρὸς ἔτι ζῶσαν φλόγα,
ἀθάνατον Ἥρας μητέρ᾿ εἰς ἐμὴν ὕβριν.
αἰνῶ δὲ Κάδμον, ἄβατον ὃς πέδον τόδε   10
τίθησι, θυγατρὸς σηκόν· ἀμπέλου δέ νιν
πέριξ ἐγὼ ᾿κάλυψα βοτρυώδει χλόῃ.
λιπὼν δὲ Λυδῶν τοὺς πολυχρύσους γύας
Φρυγῶν τε, Περσῶν θ᾿ ἡλιοβλήτους πλάκας
Βάκτριά τε τείχη τήν τε δύσχιμον χθόνα   15
Μήδων ἐπελθὼν Ἀραβίαν τ᾿ εὐδαίμονα
Ἀσίαν τε πᾶσαν, ἣ παρ᾿ ἁλμυρὰν ἅλα
κεῖται μιγάσιν Ἕλλησι βαρβάροις θ᾿ ὁμοῦ
πλήρεις ἔχουσα καλλιπυργώτους πόλεις,

Εὐριπίδου Βάκχαι suprascr. in P: consentiunt didascalia Strabo
Plutarchus Athenaeus alii: cf. Schol. Ar. Ran. 67: Εὐριπίδου Πενθεύς
L: consentiunt codd. Stobaei bis, fl. 36. 9 et 74. 8: cf. Hippolyti
init.   1 Θηβαίων L P et Σ Tro. 1: Θηβαίαν gramm. Ambros. in
Keil. Anal. Gr. p. 10, 22. Anecd. Chisiana de re metr. (Mangelsdorf
p. 26), Schol. Hephaest. p. 183: Θηβαίαν κάτα Priscian ii. p. 151
8 Δίου Barnes: δίου τε L P: τυφομένην ἁδροῦ Plut. Solon 1: δίου τ᾿
ἔτι πυρὸς Porson   13 τοὺς Elmsley: τὰς L P   γύας L et Strab. i.
p. 27, xv. p. 687: γυίας *l* P   14 om. L   θ᾿ om. Bothe et, ut videtur, Chr. Pat. 1588   15 δύσχιμον Elmsley: δύσχειμον L P Strab.
Chr. Pat. 1589   16 ἐπελθὼν L P cum Strab. p. 27: ἐπῆλθον Strab.
p. 687: παρελθὼν Chr. Pat. 1590

ἐς τήνδε πρῶτον ἦλθον Ἑλλήνων πόλιν,   20
τἀκεῖ χορεύσας καὶ καταστήσας ἐμὰς
τελετάς, ἵν᾽ εἴην ἐμφανὴς δαίμων βροτοῖς.
  πρώτας δὲ Θήβας τῆσδε γῆς Ἑλληνίδος
ἀνωλόλυξα, νεβρίδ᾽ ἐξάψας χροὸς
θύρσον τε δοὺς ἐς χεῖρα, κίσσινον βέλος·   25
ἐπεί μ᾽ ἀδελφαὶ μητρός, ἃς ἥκιστα χρῆν,
Διόνυσον οὐκ ἔφασκον ἐκφῦναι Διός,
Σεμέλην δὲ νυμφευθεῖσαν ἐκ θνητοῦ τινος
ἐς Ζῆν᾽ ἀναφέρειν τὴν ἁμαρτίαν λέχους,
Κάδμου σοφίσμαθ᾽, ὧν νιν οὕνεκα κτανεῖν   30
Ζῆν᾽ ἐξεκαυχῶνθ᾽, ὅτι γάμους ἐψεύσατο.
τοιγάρ νιν αὐτὰς ἐκ δόμων ᾤστρησ᾽ ἐγὼ
μανίαις, ὄρος δ᾽ οἰκοῦσι παράκοποι φρενῶν·
σκευήν τ᾽ ἔχειν ἠνάγκασ᾽ ὀργίων ἐμῶν,
καὶ πᾶν τὸ θῆλυ σπέρμα Καδμείων, ὅσαι   35
γυναῖκες ἦσαν, ἐξέμηνα δωμάτων·
ὁμοῦ δὲ Κάδμου παισὶν ἀναμεμειγμέναι
χλωραῖς ὑπ᾽ ἐλάταις ἀνορόφοις ἧνται πέτραις.
δεῖ γὰρ πόλιν τήνδ᾽ ἐκμαθεῖν, κεἰ μὴ θέλει,
ἀτέλεστον οὖσαν τῶν ἐμῶν βακχευμάτων,   40
Σεμέλης τε μητρὸς ἀπολογήσασθαί μ᾽ ὕπερ
φανέντα θνητοῖς δαίμον᾽ ὃν τίκτει Διί.
  Κάδμος μὲν οὖν γέρας τε καὶ τυραννίδα
Πενθεῖ δίδωσι θυγατρὸς ἐκπεφυκότι,
ὃς θεομαχεῖ τὰ κατ᾽ ἐμὲ καὶ σπονδῶν ἄπο   45
ὠθεῖ μ᾽, ἐν εὐχαῖς τ᾽ οὐδαμοῦ μνείαν ἔχει.

---

20 πόλιν] χθόνα Chr. Pat. 1595: fortasse ἐς τήνδε δήποτ᾽ ἦλθον Ἑλ
λήνων χθόνα   21 τἀκεῖ Wilamowitz: κἀκεῖ L P: quo servato v. 20
post 22 trai. Pierson: codicum ordinem tuetur Chr. Pat. 1594 sq.
22 εἴη P   23 δὲ L P: γε l   malim πρώτην δὲ Θήβην τήνδε
25 βέλος Stephanus: μέλος L P   26 ἥκιστ᾽ ἐχρῆν L P   31 ἐξε
καυχώμεθ᾽ L P: corr. Elmsley   32 οἴστρησ᾽ L P: corr. Elmsley
38 ἀνορόφους ἧνται πέτρας Elmsley   46 οὐδαμοῦ P et Chr. Pat.
1571: οὐδαμῶς L

ὧν οὕνεκ' αὐτῷ θεὸς γεγὼς ἐνδείξομαι
πᾶσίν τε Θηβαίοισιν. ἐς δ' ἄλλην χθόνα,
τἀνθένδε θέμενος εὖ, μεταστήσω πόδα,
δεικνὺς ἐμαυτόν· ἢν δὲ Θηβαίων πόλις   50
ὀργῇ σὺν ὅπλοις ἐξ ὄρους βάκχας ἄγειν
ζητῇ, ξυνάψω μαινάσι στρατηλατῶν.
ὧν οὕνεκ' εἶδος θνητὸν ἀλλάξας ἔχω
μορφήν τ' ἐμὴν μετέβαλον εἰς ἀνδρὸς φύσιν.

ἀλλ', ὦ λιποῦσαι Τμῶλον ἔρυμα Λυδίας,   55
θίασος ἐμός, γυναῖκες, ἃς ἐκ βαρβάρων
ἐκόμισα παρέδρους καὶ ξυνεμπόρους ἐμοί,
αἴρεσθε τἀπιχώρι' ἐν πόλει Φρυγῶν
τύμπανα, Ῥέας τε μητρὸς ἐμά θ' εὑρήματα,
βασίλειά τ' ἀμφὶ δώματ' ἐλθοῦσαι τάδε   60
κτυπεῖτε Πενθέως, ὡς ὁρᾷ Κάδμου πόλις.
ἐγὼ δὲ βάκχαις, ἐς Κιθαιρῶνος πτυχὰς
ἐλθὼν ἵν' εἰσί, συμμετασχήσω χορῶν.

ΧΟΡΟΣ

—   Ἀσίας ἀπὸ γᾶς
       ἱερὸν Τμῶλον ἀμείψασα θοάζω   65
       Βρομίῳ πόνον ἡδὺν
       κάματόν τ' εὐκάματον, Βάκ-
       χιον εὐαζομένα.
—   τίς ὁδῷ τίς ὁδῷ; τίς;
       μελάθροις ἔκτοπος ἔστω, στόμα τ' εὔφη-
       μον ἅπας ἐξοσιούσθω·   70

52 συνάψω P   53 sq. del. Bernhardy   55 λιποῦσαι l cum
Chr. Pat. 1602 et Strab. x. p. 469: λιποῦσα L P   57 συνεμπόρους L
59 τύπανα Nauck   62 πτύχας L P   64–71 nullam esse re-
sponsionem vidit Wilamowitz: cf. Med. 130–7, Aesch. Sept. 78 sqq.
67 post εὐαζομένα add. θεόν, metri gr. ut putabat, l   68 τὶς (ter)
Bruhn: cf. Soph. Trach. 865, Pind. Pyth. x. 4   post τίς non post
μελάθροις distinxit Elmsley: cf. I. T. 1210   70 ἐξοσιούσθω L P:
ἐξ erasit l

τὰ νομισθέντα γὰρ αἰεὶ
Διόνυσον ὑμνήσω.

—   ὦ   [στρ.
μάκαρ, ὅστις εὐδαίμων
τελετὰς θεῶν εἰδὼς
βιοτὰν ἁγιστεύει καὶ
θιασεύεται ψυχὰν   75
ἐν ὄρεσσι βακχεύων
ὁσίοις καθαρμοῖσιν,
τά τε ματρὸς μεγάλας ὄρ-
για Κυβέλας θεμιτεύων,
ἀνὰ θύρσον τε τινάσσων,   80
κισσῷ τε στεφανωθεὶς
Διόνυσον θεραπεύει.

—   ἴτε βάκχαι, ἴτε βάκχαι,
Βρόμιον παῖδα θεὸν θεοῦ
Διόνυσον κατάγουσαι   85
Φρυγίων ἐξ ὀρέων Ἑλ-
λάδος εἰς εὐρυχόρους ἀ-
γυιάς, τὸν Βρόμιον·

—   ὅν   [ἀντ.
ποτ᾽ ἔχουσ᾽ ἐν ὠδίνων
λοχίαις ἀνάγκαισι
πταμένας Διὸς βροντᾶς νη-   90
δύος ἔκβολον μάτηρ
ἔτεκεν, λιποῦσ᾽ αἰῶ-
να κεραυνίῳ πληγᾷ·
λοχίοις δ᾽ αὐτίκα νιν δέ-

71 διόνυσσον L   ὑμνήσω] metrum sanum : cf. sequentia   75 θιασ-
σεύεται P   76 ὄρεσι L P   77 ὁσίοις L : ὁσίοισι L² P   καθαρμοῖσι P :
καθαρμοῖς in ras. *l* vel L²   79 θεμιτεύων Musgrave : θεμιστεύων L P
81 κατὰ κισσῷ στεφανωθεὶς Hermann   82 διόνυσσον L   83 sic L
nunc : ὦ ἴτε βάκχαι ἴτε βάκχαι P et ante rasuram L   87 εὐρυχόρους
fortasse primitus P : εὐρυχώρους L P   92 ἔτεκε L P   93 κεραυνίῳ
L : κεραυνία P   πλαγᾶ *l*

ξατο θαλάμαις Κρονίδας Ζεύς,   95
κατὰ μηρῷ δὲ καλύψας
χρυσέαισιν συνερείδει
περόναις κρυπτὸν ἀφ' Ἥρας.

—   ἔτεκεν δ', ἀνίκα Μοῖραι
τέλεσαν, ταυρόκερων θεὸν   100
στεφάνωσέν τε δρακόντων
στεφάνοις, ἔνθεν ἄγραν θηροτρόφον μαινάδες ἀμφι-
βάλλονται πλοκάμοις.

—   ὦ Σεμέλας τροφοὶ Θῆ-   [στρ.
βαι, στεφανοῦσθε κισσῷ·   106
βρύετε βρύετε χλοήρει
μίλακι καλλικάρπῳ
καὶ καταβακχιοῦσθε δρυὸς
ἢ ἐλάτας κλάδοισι,   110
στικτῶν τ' ἐνδυτὰ νεβρίδων
στέφετε λευκοτρίχων πλοκάμων
μαλλοῖς· ἀμφὶ δὲ νάρθηκας ὑβριστὰς
ὁσιοῦσθ'· αὐτίκα γᾶ πᾶσα χορεύσει—
Βρόμιος ὅστις ἄγῃ θιάσους—   115
εἰς ὄρος εἰς ὄρος, ἔνθα μένει
θηλυγενὴς ὄχλος
ἀφ' ἱστῶν παρὰ κερκίδων τ'
οἰστρηθεὶς Διονύσῳ.   119

—   ὦ θαλάμευμα Κουρή-   [ἀντ.

95 θαλάμαις Wecklein : θαλάμοις L P   97 χρυσέαισιν *l* : χρυσέαις L P
102 θηροτρόφον post Musgravium Wecklein : θηροτρόφοι P et, ut
vid., ante ras. L : θυρσοφόροι *l*   107 χλοήρει Hermann : χλοηρεῖ
L P : α super εῖ scr. *l*   108 σμίλακι *l* : cf. 703   καλικάρπῳ L
109 καταβακχιοῦσθε L : corr. *l*   110 ἢ 'ν ἐλάτας Blomfield : sed
cf. Phoen. 1515: ἢ ἐλάτας ἐν κλάδοις *l*   111 ἐνδυκτὰ P   115 ὅστις
L² vel *l*: ὅτ' L P : εὖτ' ἂν Elmsley : sed sensus videtur esse 'Bacchus
fit quicumque ducit thiasos' : cf. 141   ἄγει L² vel *l*   118 ἀμφ'
ἱστῶν P et μ erasa L   119 διονύσσῳ P

τῶν ζάθεοί τε Κρήτας
Διογενέτορες ἔναυλοι,
ἔνθα τρικόρυθες ἄντροις
βυρσότονον κύκλωμα τόδε
μοι Κορύβαντες ηὗρον·   125
βακχείᾳ δ' ἀνὰ συντόνῳ
κέρασαν ἀδυβόᾳ Φρυγίων
αὐλῶν πνεύματι ματρός τε 'Ρέας ἐς
χέρα θῆκαν, κτύπον εὐάσμασι Βακχᾶν·
παρὰ δὲ μαινόμενοι Σάτυροι   130
ματέρος ἐξανύσαντο θεᾶς,
ἐς δὲ χορεύματα
συνῆψαν τριετηρίδων,
αἷς χαίρει Διόνυσος.

—   ἡδὺς ἐν ὄρεσιν, ὅταν ἐκ θιάσων δρομαί-   [ἐπῳδ.
       ων πέσῃ πεδόσε, νε-   136
βρίδος ἔχων ἱερὸν ἐνδυτόν, ἀγρεύων
αἷμα τραγοκτόνον, ὠμοφάγον χάριν, ἱέμε-
νος ἐς ὄρεα Φρύγια, Λύδι', ὁ δ' ἔξαρχος Βρόμιος,   140
εὐοῖ.
ῥεῖ δὲ γάλακτι πέδον, ῥεῖ δ' οἴνῳ, ῥεῖ δὲ μελισσᾶν
νέκταρι.
Συρίας δ' ὡς λιβάνου κα-

121 κρήτας L P: κρῆτες ut vid. l: utrumque in codd. Strabonis
p. 469   123 ἄντροις Musgrave: ἐν ἄντροις L P: ἀνθοῖς Strabo
125 ηὗρον L P: εὗρον l   126 ἀνὰ δὲ βακχείᾳ (βακχείῳ Strabo) L P
Strabo: trai. Dobree : ἀνὰ δὲ βάκχια apogr. Par.   127 ἡδυβόα
L P: ἀδυβοᾶν fortasse Strabo, qui κέρας ἀνὰ δύο βοᾶν habet   128 τε
paene erasum in L   129 εὐάσμασι Canter: ἐν ἄσμασι L P: καλ-
λίκτυπον εὔασμα Strabo   131 θεᾶς L P: 'Ρέας Strabo   133 προσ-
ῆψαν Strabo   134 οἷς Strabo   135 ἡδύ γ' Dobree: ἀδὺ δ'
Wecklein: intellego 'Dulcis est ille'; cf. 225-238   ὃς ἂν R. Gompf:
sed unus tantum vir   136 πέσῃ L: πεύσῃ P   πεδόσσε P
138 ἀγ*ρεύων L: ἀγορεύων P   140 verba ὁ δ'... εὐοῖ ante ἡδὺς v. 135
collocat Wilamowitz   143 νέκταρ συρείας P   144 sq. καπνὸν...
ἀνέχων Wilamowitz: καπνός.... δ' ἔχων L P (δ' ἔχων πῦρ primitus P)

πνὸν ὁ Βακχεὺς ἀνέχων   145
πυρσώδη φλόγα πεύκας
ἐκ νάρθηκος ἀίσσει
δρόμῳ καὶ χοροῖσιν
πλανάτας ἐρεθίζων
ἰαχαῖς τ' ἀναπάλλων,
τρυφερόν ⟨τε⟩ πλόκαμον εἰς αἰθέρα ῥίπτων.   150
ἅμα δ' εὐάσμασι τοιάδ' ἐπιβρέμει·
   ῍Ω ἴτε βάκχαι,
   [ὦ] ἴτε βάκχαι,
Τμώλου χρυσορόου χλιδᾷ
μέλπετε τὸν Διόνυσον   155
βαρυβρόμων ὑπὸ τυμπάνων,
εὔια τὸν εὔιον ἀγαλλόμεναι θεὸν
ἐν Φρυγίαισι βοαῖς ἐνοπαῖσί τε,
λωτὸς ὅταν εὐκέλαδος   160
ἱερὸς ἱερὰ παίγματα βρέμῃ, σύνοχα
φοιτάσιν εἰς ὄρος εἰς ὄρος· ἡδομέ-   165
να δ' ἄρα, πῶλος ὅπως ἅμα ματέρι
φορβάδι, κῶλον ἄγει ταχύπουν σκιρτήμασι βάκχα.

ΤΕΙΡΕΣΙΑΣ

τίς ἐν πύλαισι; Κάδμον ἐκκάλει δόμων,   170
Ἀγήνορος παῖδ', ὃς πόλιν Σιδωνίαν
λιπὼν ἐπύργωσ' ἄστυ Θηβαίων τόδε.

146–147 inverso ordine habuit L, sed numeris appositis correxit
147 χοροῖς L P   148 ἐρεθίζων πλανάτας L : ἐρεθίζων πλάνας P : trai.
Wilamowitz   149 ἂν ἀπ' ἄλλων L   150 τε add. Wilamowitz
151 δ' ἐπ' εὐάσμασιν ἐπιβρέμει τοιάδ' L P : ἐπ' del. Elmsley : traieci ob
metrum   post ἐπιβρέμει in L adscript. ἐπι λίγει (ἐπιλέγει Wilamowitz)
ἠχεῖ glossemata   153 ὦ erasum in L   154 Τμώλου] Πακτωλοῦ
Wecklein   155 διόννσσον L   156 ante 155 trai. Wilamowitz
159 βολαῖς primitus P   164 βρέμει suprascr. η P   165 ἀδομένα
Dindorf   169 βάκχα Musgrave : βάκχου L P   170 Τε. praescr. L P :
sed cum eadem nota ante 173 stet in L, Θερ(άπων) hic praescr. l
ἐκκάλει Bergler : ἐκκαλεῖ nullo post πύλαισι puncto L P

ἴτω τις, εἰσάγγελλε Τειρεσίας ὅτι
ζητεῖ νιν· οἶδε δ' αὐτὸς ὧν ἥκω πέρι
ἅ τε ξυνεθέμην πρέσβυς ὢν γεραιτέρῳ,   175
θύρσους ἀνάπτειν καὶ νεβρῶν δορὰς ἔχειν
στεφανοῦν τε κρᾶτα κισσίνοις βλαστήμασιν.

ΚΑΔΜΟΣ

ὦ φίλταθ', ὡς σὴν γῆρυν ᾐσθόμην κλύων
σοφὴν σοφοῦ παρ' ἀνδρός, ἐν δόμοισιν ὤν·
ἥκω δ' ἕτοιμος τήνδ' ἔχων σκευὴν θεοῦ·   180
δεῖ γάρ νιν ὄντα παῖδα θυγατρὸς ἐξ ἐμῆς
[Διόνυσον ὃς πέφηνεν ἀνθρώποις θεὸς]
ὅσον καθ' ἡμᾶς δυνατὸν αὔξεσθαι μέγαν.
ποῖ δεῖ χορεύειν, ποῖ καθιστάναι πόδα
καὶ κρᾶτα σεῖσαι πολιόν; ἐξηγοῦ σύ μοι   185
γέρων γέροντι, Τειρεσία· σὺ γὰρ σοφός.
ὡς οὐ κάμοιμ' ἂν οὔτε νύκτ' οὔθ' ἡμέραν
θύρσῳ κροτῶν γῆν· ἐπιλελήσμεθ' ἡδέως
γέροντες ὄντες.

Τε.   ταῦτ' ἐμοὶ πάσχεις ἄρα·
κἀγὼ γὰρ ἡβῶ κἀπιχειρήσω χοροῖς.   190

Κα.   οὐκοῦν ὄχοισιν εἰς ὄρος περάσομεν;

Τε.   ἀλλ' οὐχ ὁμοίως ἂν ὁ θεὸς τιμὴν ἔχοι.

Κα.   γέρων γέροντα παιδαγωγήσω σ' ἐγώ.

Τε.   ὁ θεὸς ἀμοχθὶ κεῖσε νῷν ἡγήσεται.

Κα.   μόνοι δὲ πόλεως Βακχίῳ χορεύσομεν;   195

Τε.   μόνοι γὰρ εὖ φρονοῦμεν, οἱ δ' ἄλλοι κακῶς.

Κα.   μακρὸν τὸ μέλλειν· ἀλλ' ἐμῆς ἔχου χερός.

Τε.   ἰδού, ξύναπτε καὶ ξυνωρίζου χέρα.

182 del. Dobree: om. (quod sane nihili est) Chr. Pat. 1152: cf. 860
πέφην' L P   184 δεῖ Musurus: δὴ L P   ποῖ alterum] ποῦ Wecklein
188 ἡδέως Milton: ἡδέων L P   189 ταυτά μοι L P   190 nota Cadmi
hic praescripta personas usque ad v. 200 permutat P   192 ὁ θεὸς ἂν
Porson: ἂν θεὸς Wecklein   ἔχει suprascr. οι P   194 ἀμοχθεὶ L P : corr.
Elmsley   νῷιν L P   195 βακχείω L P : corr. l p   198 ξυνάπτω Wecklein

Κα. οὐ καταφρονῶ 'γὼ τῶν θεῶν θνητὸς γεγώς.

Τε. οὐδὲν σοφιζόμεσθα τοῖσι δαίμοσιν.　　　　　　　200
πατρίους παραδοχάς, ἅς θ' ὁμήλικας χρόνῳ
κεκτήμεθ', οὐδεὶς αὐτὰ καταβαλεῖ λόγος,
οὐδ' εἰ δι' ἄκρων τὸ σοφὸν ηὕρηται φρενῶν.
ἐρεῖ τις ὡς τὸ γῆρας οὐκ αἰσχύνομαι,
μέλλων χορεύειν κρᾶτα κισσώσας ἐμόν;　　　　　　205
οὐ γὰρ διήρηχ' ὁ θεός, οὔτε τὸν νέον
εἰ χρὴ χορεύειν οὔτε τὸν γεραίτερον,
ἀλλ' ἐξ ἁπάντων βούλεται τιμὰς ἔχειν
κοινάς, διαριθμῶν δ' οὐδέν' αὔξεσθαι θέλει.

Κα. ἐπεὶ σὺ φέγγος, Τειρεσία, τόδ' οὐχ ὁρᾷς,　　　　210
ἐγὼ προφήτης σοι λόγων γενήσομαι.
Πενθεὺς πρὸς οἴκους ὅδε διὰ σπουδῆς περᾷ,
Ἐχίονος παῖς, ᾧ κράτος δίδωμι γῆς.
ὡς ἐπτόηται· τί ποτ' ἐρεῖ νεώτερον;

ΠΕΝΘΕΥΣ

ἔκδημος ὢν μὲν τῆσδ' ἐτύγχανον χθονός,　　　　　215
κλύω δὲ νεοχμὰ τήνδ' ἀνὰ πτόλιν κακά,
γυναῖκας ἡμῖν δώματ' ἐκλελοιπέναι
πλασταῖσι βακχείαισιν, ἐν δὲ δασκίοις
ὄρεσι θοάζειν, τὸν νεωστὶ δαίμονα
Διόνυσον, ὅστις ἔστι, τιμώσας χοροῖς·　　　　　　220
πλήρεις δὲ θιάσοις ἐν μέσοισιν ἑστάναι
κρατῆρας, ἄλλην δ' ἄλλοσ' εἰς ἐρημίαν
πτώσσουσαν εὐναῖς ἀρσένων ὑπηρετεῖν,

200 οὐδ' ἐνσοφιζόμεσθα Musgrave, sed cf. Hclit. fr. 78, 79, 83 Diels
201 πατρίους, cl. Plut. Mor. 756 B, Valckenaer: πρς L: πατρὸς P
202 αὐτά] δῆτα Dalmeyda　　　καταβαλεῖ Scaliger: καταβάλλει L:
καταβάλλῃ P　　　203 ἄκρας ... φρενός Plut. l. c.　　　εὕρηται L P
204 ἀρεῖ, ut videtur, primitus P　　　205 χωρεύειν primitus P
206 sq. οὔτε ... οὔτε Matthiae: εἴτε ... εἴτε L P: quo servato χρῄζει
pro εἰ χρὴ Wecklein　　　207 χηρεύειν P　　　209 delet Bernhardy:
δι' ἀριθμῶν δ' οὐδὲν L P: corr. Heath　　　210 Τε. L: om. P　　　215 τήνδ'
primitus P　　　217 δώματ' L: σώματ' P　　　220 διόνυσος P

πρόφασιν μὲν ὡς δὴ μαινάδας θυοσκόους,
τὴν δ᾽ Ἀφροδίτην πρόσθ᾽ ἄγειν τοῦ Βακχίου.   225
ὅσας μὲν οὖν εἴληφα, δεσμίους χέρας
σώζουσι πανδήμοισι πρόσπολοι στέγαις·
ὅσαι δ᾽ ἄπεισιν, ἐξ ὄρους θηράσομαι,
[Ἰνώ τ᾽ Ἀγαύην θ᾽, ἥ μ᾽ ἔτικτ᾽ Ἐχίονι,
Ἀκταίονός τε μητέρ᾽, Αὐτονόην λέγω.]   230
καὶ σφᾶς σιδηραῖς ἁρμόσας ἐν ἄρκυσιν
παύσω κακούργου τῆσδε βακχείας τάχα.

λέγουσι δ᾽ ὥς τις εἰσελήλυθε ξένος,
γόης ἐπῳδὸς Λυδίας ἀπὸ χθονός,
ξανθοῖσι βοστρύχοισιν εὐοσμῶν κόμην,   235
οἰνῶπας ὅσσοις χάριτας Ἀφροδίτης ἔχων,
ὃς ἡμέρας τε κεὐφρόνας συγγίγνεται
τελετὰς προτείνων εὐίους νεάνισιν.
εἰ δ᾽ αὐτὸν εἴσω τῆσδε λήψομαι στέγης,
παύσω κτυποῦντα θύρσον ἀνασείοντά τε   240
κόμας, τράχηλον σώματος χωρὶς τεμών.
ἐκεῖνος εἶναί φησι Διόνυσον θεόν,
ἐκεῖνος ἐν μηρῷ ποτ᾽ ἐρράφθαι Διός,
ὃς ἐκπυροῦται λαμπάσιν κεραυνίαις
σὺν μητρί, Δίους ὅτι γάμους ἐψεύσατο.   245
ταῦτ᾽ οὐχὶ δεινῆς ἀγχόνης ἔστ᾽ ἄξια,
ὕβρεις ὑβρίζειν, ὅστις ἔστιν ὁ ξένος;

ἀτὰρ τόδ᾽ ἄλλο θαῦμα, τὸν τερασκόπον
ἐν ποικίλαισι νεβρίσι Τειρεσίαν ὁρῶ
πατέρα τε μητρὸς τῆς ἐμῆς—πολὺν γέλων—   250

227 πανδήμοις L P : corr. l   στέγαις L : δόμοις P   229 οἰνώ
primitus L   ἀγαυήν oxytone ut solent L P : non notatur amplius
229–230 del. Collmann : cf. 337   233 ὥς τις Musurus : ὅστις L P
235 εὐοσμῶν Tyrrell : εὔοσμον L P   236 οἰνῶπας Scaliger : οἰνωπά
τ᾽ L : οἰνωπάς τ᾽ P : οἰνωπός, Barnes   ὅσοις P (τε γ᾽ ὅσσοις p)
243 ἐρράφθαι Reiske : ἐρράφη L P   246 δεινὰ κἀγχόνης Mau   ἐπάξια
Elmsley   247 suspectus Wilamowitzio   248 ἄλλον P

νάρθηκι βακχεύοντ'· ἀναίνομαι, πάτερ,
τὸ γῆρας ὑμῶν εἰσορῶν νοῦν οὐκ ἔχον.
οὐκ ἀποτινάξεις κισσόν; οὐκ ἐλευθέραν
θύρσου μεθήσεις χεῖρ', ἐμῆς μητρὸς πάτερ;
σὺ ταῦτ' ἔπεισας, Τειρεσία· τόνδ' αὖ θέλεις   255
τὸν δαίμον' ἀνθρώποισιν ἐσφέρων νέον
σκοπεῖν πτερωτοὺς κἀμπύρων μισθοὺς φέρειν.
εἰ μή σε γῆρας πολιὸν ἐξερρύετο,
καθῆσ' ἂν ἐν βάκχαισι δέσμιος μέσαις,
τελετὰς πονηρὰς εἰσάγων· γυναιξὶ γὰρ   260
ὅπου βότρυος ἐν δαιτὶ γίγνεται γάνος,
οὐχ ὑγιὲς οὐδὲν ἔτι λέγω τῶν ὀργίων.

Χο.   τῆς δυσσεβείας. ὦ ξέν', οὐκ αἰδῇ θεοὺς
Κάδμον τε τὸν σπείραντα γηγενῆ στάχυν,
Ἐχίονος δ' ὢν παῖς καταισχύνεις γένος;   265

Τε.   ὅταν λάβῃ τις τῶν λόγων ἀνὴρ σοφὸς
καλὰς ἀφορμάς, οὐ μέγ' ἔργον εὖ λέγειν·
σὺ δ' εὔτροχον μὲν γλῶσσαν ὡς φρονῶν ἔχεις,
ἐν τοῖς λόγοισι δ' οὐκ ἔνεισί σοι φρένες.
θράσει δὲ δυνατὸς καὶ λέγειν οἷός τ' ἀνὴρ   270
κακὸς πολίτης γίγνεται νοῦν οὐκ ἔχων.
οὗτος δ' ὁ δαίμων ὁ νέος, ὃν σὺ διαγελᾷς,
οὐκ ἂν δυναίμην μέγεθος ἐξειπεῖν ὅσος
καθ' Ἑλλάδ' ἔσται. δύο γάρ, ὦ νεανία,
τὰ πρῶτ' ἐν ἀνθρώποισι· Δημήτηρ θεά—   275
γῆ δ' ἐστίν, ὄνομα δ' ὁπότερον βούλῃ κάλει·
αὕτη μὲν ἐν ξηροῖσιν ἐκτρέφει βροτούς·
ὃς δ' ἦλθ' ἔπειτ', ἀντίπαλον ὁ Σεμέλης γόνος

251 βακχεύοντας l   252 ἔχων primitus L   257 φέρειν l :
φέρων L P   261 γάνος L : γάμος P   263 δυσσεβείας Reiske :
εὐσεβείας L P : ἀσεβείας Chr. Pat. 191   265 ante 264 trai. Musgrave
270 θράσει Madvig : θρασὺς L P   δὲ L : τε P   270 sq. del. Dindorf :
habet Stob. fl. 45. 2   276 ὄνομα] ὁπόμα (ab ὁπότερον sequenti) P
278 ὃς δ' Fix : ὅδ' L P   ἦλθ' ἔπειτ' ἀντίπαλον Housman (ἀντίπαλος
malit Marchant) : ἦλθεν (ἦλθ' P) ἐπὶ τἀντίπαλον L P

βότρυος ὑγρὸν πῶμ' ηὗρε κεἰσηνέγκατο
θνητοῖς, ὃ παύει τοὺς ταλαιπώρους βροτοὺς   280
λύπης, ὅταν πλησθῶσιν ἀμπέλου ῥοῆς,
ὕπνον τε λήθην τῶν καθ' ἡμέραν κακῶν
δίδωσιν, οὐδ' ἔστ' ἄλλο φάρμακον πόνων.
οὗτος θεοῖσι σπένδεται θεὸς γεγώς,
ὥστε διὰ τοῦτον τἀγάθ' ἀνθρώπους ἔχειν.   285
    καὶ καταγελᾷς νιν, ὡς ἐνερράφη Διὸς
μηρῷ; διδάξω σ' ὡς καλῶς ἔχει τόδε.
ἐπεί νιν ἥρπασ' ἐκ πυρὸς κεραυνίου
Ζεύς, ἐς δ' Ὄλυμπον βρέφος ἀνήγαγεν θεόν,
Ἥρα νιν ἤθελ' ἐκβαλεῖν ἀπ' οὐρανοῦ·   290
Ζεὺς δ' ἀντεμηχανήσαθ' οἷα δὴ θεός.
ῥήξας μέρος τι τοῦ χθόν' ἐγκυκλουμένου
αἰθέρος, ἔθηκε τόνδ' ὅμηρον ἐκδιδούς,

    •   •   •   •   •   •   •   •   •

Διόνυσον Ἥρας νεικέων· χρόνῳ δέ νιν
βροτοὶ ῥαφῆναί φασιν ἐν μηρῷ Διός,   295
ὄνομα μεταστήσαντες, ὅτι θεᾷ θεὸς
Ἥρᾳ ποθ' ὡμήρευσε, συνθέντες λόγον.
    μάντις δ' ὁ δαίμων ὅδε· τὸ γὰρ βακχεύσιμον
καὶ τὸ μανιῶδες μαντικὴν πολλὴν ἔχει·
ὅταν γὰρ ὁ θεὸς ἐς τὸ σῶμ' ἔλθῃ πολύς,   300
λέγειν τὸ μέλλον τοὺς μεμηνότας ποιεῖ.
Ἄρεώς τε μοῖραν μεταλαβὼν ἔχει τινά·
στρατὸν γὰρ ἐν ὅπλοις ὄντα κἀπὶ τάξεσιν
φόβος διεπτόησε πρὶν λόγχης θιγεῖν.
μανία δὲ καὶ τοῦτ' ἐστὶ Διονύσου πάρα.   305

---

279 πῶμ' Elmsley: πόμ' L P   281 πληθῶσιν P: corr. p
286–297 suspecti Boeckhio   289 θεόν] νέον Musurus: θεῶν Mekler
post 293 lacunam indicavi: ex. gr. αὐτὸν δὲ δοὺς ἔσωσε Νυσαίαις κόραις
vel αὐτὸν δ' ὀρείαις δοὺς θεαῖς ἐρρύσατο: cf. Apollod. iii. 4. 3: mavult
Wilamowitz ἔσωσε pro ἔθηκε, nulla lacuna   295 ῥαφῆναι Pierson :
τραφῆναι L P   ἐκ μῆρς διός P   304 θίγειν L P

ἔτ' αὐτὸν ὄψῃ κἀπὶ Δελφίσιν πέτραις
πηδῶντα σὺν πεύκαισι δικόρυφον πλάκα,
πάλλοντα καὶ σείοντα βακχεῖον κλάδον,
μέγαν τ' ἀν' Ἑλλάδα. ἀλλ' ἐμοί, Πενθεῦ, πιθοῦ·
μὴ τὸ κράτος αὔχει δύναμιν ἀνθρώποις ἔχειν,   310
μηδ', ἣν δοκῇς μέν, ἡ δὲ δόξα σου νοσῇ,
φρονεῖν δόκει τι· τὸν θεὸν δ' ἐς γῆν δέχου
καὶ σπένδε καὶ βάκχευε καὶ στέφου κάρα.

οὐχ ὁ Διόνυσος σωφρονεῖν ἀναγκάσει
γυναῖκας ἐς τὴν Κύπριν, ἀλλ' ἐν τῇ φύσει   315
[τὸ σωφρονεῖν ἔνεστιν εἰς τὰ πάντ' ἀεί]
τοῦτο σκοπεῖν χρή· καὶ γὰρ ἐν βακχεύμασιν
οὖσ' ἥ γε σώφρων οὐ διαφθαρήσεται.

ὁρᾷς, σὺ χαίρεις, ὅταν ἐφεστῶσιν πύλαις
πολλοί, τὸ Πενθέως δ' ὄνομα μεγαλύνῃ πόλις·   320
κἀκεῖνος, οἶμαι, τέρπεται τιμώμενος.
ἐγὼ μὲν οὖν καὶ Κάδμος, ὃν σὺ διαγελᾷς,
κισσῷ τ' ἐρεψόμεσθα καὶ χορεύσομεν,
πολιὰ ξυνωρίς, ἀλλ' ὅμως χορευτέον,
κοὐ θεομαχήσω σῶν λόγων πεισθεὶς ὕπο.   325
μαίνῃ γὰρ ὡς ἄλγιστα, κοὔτε φαρμάκοις
ἄκη λάβοις ἂν οὔτ' ἄνευ τούτων νοσεῖς.

Χο. ὦ πρέσβυ, Φοῖβόν τ' οὐ καταισχύνεις λόγοις,
τιμῶν τε Βρόμιον σωφρονεῖς, μέγαν θεόν.

Κα. ὦ παῖ, καλῶς σοι Τειρεσίας παρήνεσεν.   330
οἴκει μεθ' ἡμῶν, μὴ θύραζε τῶν νόμων.

306 ἐν δελφοῖς ante ἔτ' habet L, nimirum scholii vestigia   δελφίσι L :
δελφοῖσιν P   πέτραις in L erasit praeter π et ν scripsit, tum πέτραις
in marg. rescripsit antiqua manus alias non obvia : primo, ut videtur,
textum corrigere voluit, tum se errare vidit   307 πεύκοισι P
308 πάλλοντα Matthiae : βάλλοντα L P   309 Ἑλλάδ' L P
311 νοσεῖ L P   314 σωφρονεῖν L P cum Chr. Pat. 261 : μὴ σωφρονεῖν
p cum Stob. fl. 5. 15 et 74. 8 : μὴ φρονεῖν Musgrave : ἀφρονεῖν Salmasius
315 εἰς τὴν φύσιν Stob. fl. 74. 8   316 = Hip. 79 : omisit hic Stob.
fl. 74. 8 : habet 5. 15 : et fortasse habuit Chr. Pat. 264 : delevit Kirchhoff
320 οὔνομα L P   327 νοσεῖς] νόσου Dobree

νῦν γὰρ πέτῃ τε καὶ φρονῶν οὐδὲν φρονεῖς.
κεἰ μὴ γὰρ ἔστιν ὁ θεὸς οὗτος, ὡς σὺ φῄς,
παρὰ σοὶ λεγέσθω· καὶ καταψεύδου καλῶς
ὡς ἔστι, Σεμέλη θ' ἵνα δοκῇ θεὸν τεκεῖν,   335
ἡμῖν τε τιμὴ παντὶ τῷ γένει προσῇ.

ὁρᾷς τὸν Ἀκτέωνος ἄθλιον μόρον,
ὃν ὠμόσιτοι σκύλακες ἃς ἐθρέψατο
διεσπάσαντο, κρεῖσσον' ἐν κυναγίαις
Ἀρτέμιδος εἶναι κομπάσαντ', ἐν ὀργάσιν.   340
ὃ μὴ πάθῃς σύ· δεῦρό σου στέψω κάρα
κισσῷ· μεθ' ἡμῶν τῷ θεῷ τιμὴν δίδου.

Πε.   οὐ μὴ προσοίσεις χεῖρα, βακχεύσεις δ' ἰών,
μηδ' ἐξομόρξῃ μωρίαν τὴν σὴν ἐμοί;
τῆς σῆς ⟨δ'⟩ ἀνοίας τόνδε τὸν διδάσκαλον   345
δίκην μέτειμι. στειχέτω τις ὡς τάχος,
ἐλθὼν δὲ θάκους τοῦδ' ἵν' οἰωνοσκοπεῖ
μοχλοῖς τριαίνου κἀνάτρεψον ἔμπαλιν,
ἄνω κάτω τὰ πάντα συγχέας ὁμοῦ,
καὶ στέμματ' ἀνέμοις καὶ θυέλλαισιν μέθες.   350
μάλιστα γάρ νιν δήξομαι δράσας τάδε.

οἳ δ' ἀνὰ πόλιν στείχοντες ἐξιχνεύσατε
τὸν θηλύμορφον ξένον, ὃς ἐσφέρει νόσον
καινὴν γυναιξὶ καὶ λέχη λυμαίνεται.
κἄνπερ λάβητε, δέσμιον πορεύσατε   355
δεῦρ' αὐτόν, ὡς ἂν λευσίμου δίκης τυχὼν
θάνῃ, πικρὰν βάκχευσιν ἐν Θήβαις ἰδών.

Τε.   ὦ σχέτλι', ὡς οὐκ οἶσθα ποῦ ποτ' εἶ λόγων.
μέμηνας ἤδη· καὶ πρὶν ἐξέστης φρενῶν.
στείχωμεν ἡμεῖς, Κάδμε, κἀξαιτώμεθα   360

335 Σεμέλη θ' Tyrwhitt: σεμέλης L P   336 ἡμῶν Scaliger
337 Ἀκτέωνος L² vel l: Ἀκταίωνος L P: cf. Dittenb. Syll. Inscr. 9. 10
338 ὃν l: τὸν L P   339 κυνηγίαις L P: corr. Matthiae   343 χεῖρα
P: χεῖρα καὶ L   345 δ' add. Matthiae   346 δίκην Elmsley:
δίκη L P   347 τοῦδ' Musgrave: τοὐσδ' L P   οἰωνοσκοπῇ P
348 τριαίνου L: τριαίνης P

ὑπέρ τε τούτου καίπερ ὄντος ἀγρίου
ὑπέρ τε πόλεως τὸν θεὸν μηδὲν νέον
δρᾶν. ἀλλ᾽ ἕπου μοι κισσίνου βάκτρου μέτα,
πειρῶ δ᾽ ἀνορθοῦν σῶμ᾽ ἐμόν, κἀγὼ τὸ σόν·
γέροντε δ᾽ αἰσχρὸν δύο πεσεῖν· ἴτω δ᾽ ὅμως,   365
τῷ Βακχίῳ γὰρ τῷ Διὸς δουλευτέον.
Πενθεὺς δ᾽ ὅπως μὴ πένθος εἰσοίσει δόμοις
τοῖς σοῖσι, Κάδμε· μαντικῇ μὲν οὐ λέγω,
τοῖς πράγμασιν δέ· μῶρα γὰρ μῶρος λέγει.   369

Χο. —   Ὁσία πότνα θεῶν,   [στρ.
              Ὁσία δ᾽ ἃ κατὰ γᾶν
              χρυσέαν πτέρυγα φέρεις,
              τάδε Πενθέως ἀίεις;
              ἀίεις οὐχ ὁσίαν
              ὕβριν ἐς τὸν Βρόμιον, τὸν   375
              Σεμέλας, τὸν παρὰ καλλι-
              στεφάνοις εὐφροσύναις δαί-
              μονα πρῶτον μακάρων; ὃς τάδ᾽ ἔχει,
              θιασεύειν τε χοροῖς
              μετά τ᾽ αὐλοῦ γελάσαι   380
              ἀποπαῦσαί τε μερίμνας,
              ὁπόταν βότρυος ἔλθῃ
              γάνος ἐν δαιτὶ θεῶν, κισ-
              σοφόροις δ᾽ ἐν θαλίαις ἀν-
              δράσι κρατὴρ ὕπνον ἀμ-   385
              φιβάλλῃ.

     —   ἀχαλίνων στομάτων   [ἀντ.
              ἀνόμου τ᾽ ἀφροσύνας
              τὸ τέλος δυστυχία·

365 γέροντες δ᾽ P   372 χρυσέαν Brunck : χρύσεα L : χρυσέα P
373 τὰ δὲ L P   375 ἐς P : εἰς L   379 θιεύσειν P   385 ἀμφι-
βάλη L : ἀμφὶ βάλη P : corr. Barnes

ὁ δὲ τᾶς ἡσυχίας
βίοτος καὶ τὸ φρονεῖν   390
ἀσάλευτόν τε μένει καὶ
συνέχει δώματα· πόρσω
γὰρ ὅμως αἰθέρα ναίον-
τες ὁρῶσιν τὰ βροτῶν οὐρανίδαι.
τὸ σοφὸν δ' οὐ σοφία   395
τό τε μὴ θνητὰ φρονεῖν.
βραχὺς αἰών· ἐπὶ τούτῳ
δέ τις ἂν μεγάλα διώκων
τὰ παρόντ' οὐχὶ φέροι. μαι-
νομένων οἵδε τρόποι καὶ   400
κακοβούλων παρ' ἔμοι-
γε φωτῶν.

—   ἱκοίμαν ποτὶ Κύπρον,   [στρ
νᾶσον τᾶς Ἀφροδίτας,
ἵν' οἱ θελξίφρονες νέμον-
ται θνατοῖσιν Ἔρωτες,
Πάφον θ' ἃν ἑκατόστομοι   405
βαρβάρου ποταμοῦ ῥοαὶ
καρπίζουσιν ἄνομβροι.
οὗ δ' ἁ καλλιστενομένα
Πιερία μούσειος ἕδρα,
σεμνὰ κλιτὺς Ὀλύμπου,   410

392 δώματα P : δῶμα in ras. l   πόρσω γὰρ Elmsley : πόρρω γὰρ
Stob. fl. 58. 3 : πρόσω γὰρ ἀλλ' L P   394 ὁρῶσιν L sed σιν in ras. l :
ὁρῶσι P   396 θνατὰ Elmsley   398 μεγάλα L : τὰ μεγάλα P :
μακρὰ Heimsoeth   399 φέρει L P   400 μαινομένων δ' Stob.
fl. 22. 17   401 ἔμοιγε L² P : ἐμοὶ L   402 Κύπρον Elmsley : τὰν
κύπρον L P   403 τᾶς] τὰν Petersen   404 ἵν' οἱ Heath : ἵνα
L P : ἐν ᾇ Nauck   406 sq. lectio suspecta : sed cf. Hel. 151 : Βωκάρου
ποταμοῦ Meursius : cf. Pauly–Wissowa s.v. et Tac. Hist. ii. 3, Plin.
N. H. ii. 210   409 οὗ Schoene : ὅπου L P : ποῦ Nauck   δ' ἁ L P :
del. l   410 πιερεία P   411 κλειτὺς L P

ἐκεῖσ᾽ ἄγε με, Βρόμιε Βρόμιε,
πρόβακχ᾽ εὔιε δαῖμον.
  ἐκεῖ Χάριτες,
ἐκεῖ δὲ Πόθος· ἐκεῖ δὲ βάκ-   415
χαις θέμις ὀργιάζειν.

—   ὁ δαίμων ὁ Διὸς παῖς   [ἀντ.
χαίρει μὲν θαλίαισιν,
φιλεῖ δ᾽ ὀλβοδότειραν Εἰ-
ρήναν, κουροτρόφον θεάν.   420
ἴσαν δ᾽ ἔς τε τὸν ὄλβιον
τόν τε χείρονα δῶκ᾽ ἔχειν
οἴνου τέρψιν ἄλυπον·
μισεῖ δ᾽ ᾧ μὴ ταῦτα μέλει,
κατὰ φάος νύκτας τε φίλας   425
εὐαίωνα διαζῆν,
σοφὰν δ᾽ ἀπέχειν πραπίδα φρένα τε
περισσῶν παρὰ φωτῶν·
      τὸ πλῆθος ὅ τι   430
τὸ φαυλότερον ἐνόμισε χρῆ-
ταί τε, τόδ᾽ ἂν δεχοίμαν.

ΘΕΡΑΠΩΝ

Πενθεῦ, πάρεσμεν τήνδ᾽ ἄγραν ἠγρευκότες
ἐφ᾽ ἣν ἔπεμψας, οὐδ᾽ ἄκρανθ᾽ ὡρμήσαμεν.   435
ὁ θὴρ δ᾽ ὅδ᾽ ἡμῖν πρᾶος οὐδ᾽ ὑπέσπασεν
φυγῇ πόδ᾽, ἀλλ᾽ ἔδωκεν οὐκ ἄκων χέρας
οὐδ᾽ ὠχρός, οὐδ᾽ ἤλλαξεν οἰνωπὸν γένυν,

412 μ᾽ ὦ Hartung : sed cf. 545   413 πρόβακχ᾽ εὔιε Hermann :
προβακχήιε L P   δαίμων l   415 βάκχαισι P : βάκχαισιν L
419 εἰρήνην P   421 ἴσαν l : ἴσα L P   427 ἄπεχε Hermann,
cf. 412   πραπίδα L : παρ᾽ ἀσπίδα P   430 ὅ τι τὸ Brunck : ὅτι
τε (τε in ras.) l : ὅτι περ P et fortasse L   431 τε, τόδ᾽ ἂν δεχοίμαν
Kirchhoff : τε τόδε τοι λέγοιμ᾽ ἂν L : τ᾽ ἐν τῷδε λεγοίμην ἄν P : totius
v. lectio dubia   438 οὐκ ὠχρός Kirchhoff

γελῶν δὲ καὶ δεῖν κἀπάγειν ἐφίετο
ἔμενέ τε, τοὐμὸν εὐτρεπὲς ποιούμενος.   440
κἀγὼ δι' αἰδοῦς εἶπον· *Ω ξέν', οὐχ ἑκὼν
ἄγω σε, Πενθέως δ' ὅς μ' ἔπεμψ' ἐπιστολαῖς.

ἃς δ' αὖ σὺ βάκχας εἶρξας, ἃς συνήρπασας
κἄδησας ἐν δεσμοῖσι πανδήμου στέγης,
φροῦδαί γ' ἐκεῖναι λελυμέναι πρὸς ὀργάδας   445
σκιρτῶσι Βρόμιον ἀνακαλούμεναι θεόν·
αὐτόματα δ' αὐταῖς δεσμὰ διελύθη ποδῶν
κλῇδές τ' ἀνῆκαν θύρετρ' ἄνευ θνητῆς χερός.
πολλῶν δ' ὅδ' ἀνὴρ θαυμάτων ἥκει πλέως
ἐς τάσδε Θήβας. σοὶ δὲ τἄλλα χρὴ μέλειν.   450

Πε. μέθεσθε χειρῶν τοῦδ'· ἐν ἄρκυσιν γὰρ ὢν
οὐκ ἔστιν οὕτως ὠκὺς ὥστε μ' ἐκφυγεῖν.

ἀτὰρ τὸ μὲν σῶμ' οὐκ ἄμορφος εἶ, ξένε,
ὡς ἐς γυναῖκας, ἐφ' ὅπερ ἐς Θήβας πάρει·
πλόκαμός τε γάρ σου ταναός, οὐ πάλης ὕπο,   455
γένυν παρ' αὐτὴν κεχυμένος, πόθου πλέως·
λευκὴν δὲ χροιὰν ἐκ παρασκευῆς ἔχεις,
οὐχ ἡλίου βολαῖσιν, ἀλλ' ὑπὸ σκιᾶς,
τὴν Ἀφροδίτην καλλονῇ θηρώμενος.
πρῶτον μὲν οὖν μοι λέξον ὅστις εἶ γένος.   460

Δι. οὐ κόμπος οὐδείς· ῥᾴδιον δ' εἰπεῖν τόδε.
τὸν ἀνθεμώδη Τμῶλον οἶσθά που κλύων.

Πε. οἶδ', ὃς τὸ Σάρδεων ἄστυ περιβάλλει κύκλῳ.

Δι. ἐντεῦθέν εἰμι, Λυδία δέ μοι πατρίς.

Πε. πόθεν δὲ τελετὰς τάσδ' ἄγεις ἐς Ἑλλάδα;   465

Δι. Διόνυσος ἡμᾶς εἰσέβησ', ὁ τοῦ Διός.

Πε. Ζεὺς δ' ἔστ' ἐκεῖ τις, ὃς νέους τίκτει θεούς;

440 εὐπρεπὲς L P : corr. Canter : εὐπετὲς Nauck   442 ἐγώ σε et
ἔπεμψεν P   443 βάχκας L   448 κληῖδ' ἐστ' L   449 ἀνὴρ L P
451 μέθεσθε Burges : μαίνεσθε L P : punctum post μαίνεσθε fortasse voluit
L, non post τοῦδ' : γρ. λάζυσθε suprascr. p   τοῦδ'] suprascr. ἐμοῦ L²,
ut videtur   457 λ**κὴν P : corr. p   ἐκ παρασκευῆς Hermann :
εἰς παρασκευὴν L P   466 εἰσέβησ' Abresch : εὐσέβησ' L P

Δι. οὔκ, ἀλλ' ὁ Σεμέλην ἐνθάδε ζεύξας γάμοις.

Πε. πότερα δὲ νύκτωρ σ' ἢ κατ' ὄμμ' ἠνάγκασεν;

Δι. ὁρῶν ὁρῶντα, καὶ δίδωσιν ὄργια. 470

Πε. τὰ δ' ὄργι' ἐστὶ τίν' ἰδέαν ἔχοντά σοι;

Δι. ἄρρητ' ἀβακχεύτοισιν εἰδέναι βροτῶν.

Πε. ἔχει δ' ὄνησιν τοῖσι θύουσιν τίνα;

Δι. οὐ θέμις ἀκοῦσαί σ', ἔστι δ' ἄξι' εἰδέναι.

Πε. εὖ τοῦτ' ἐκιβδήλευσας, ἵν' ἀκοῦσαι θέλω. 475

Δι. ἀσέβειαν ἀσκοῦντ' ὄργι' ἐχθαίρει θεοῦ.

Πε. τὸν θεὸν ὁρᾶν γὰρ φῂς σαφῶς, ποῖός τις ἦν;

Δι. ὁποῖος ἤθελ'· οὐκ ἐγὼ 'τασσον τόδε.

Πε. τοῦτ' αὖ παρωχέτευσας εὖ κοὐδὲν λέγων.

Δι. δόξει τις ἀμαθεῖ σοφὰ λέγων οὐκ εὖ φρονεῖν. 480

Πε. ἦλθες δὲ πρῶτα δεῦρ' ἄγων τὸν δαίμονα;

Δι. πᾶς ἀναχορεύει βαρβάρων τάδ' ὄργια.

Πε. φρονοῦσι γὰρ κάκιον Ἑλλήνων πολύ.

Δι. τάδ' εὖ γε μᾶλλον· οἱ νόμοι δὲ διάφοροι.

Πε. τὰ δ' ἱερὰ νύκτωρ ἢ μεθ' ἡμέραν τελεῖς; 485

Δι. νύκτωρ τὰ πολλά· σεμνότητ' ἔχει σκότος.

Πε. τοῦτ' ἐς γυναῖκας δόλιόν ἐστι καὶ σαθρόν.

Δι. κἀν ἡμέρᾳ τό γ' αἰσχρὸν ἐξεύροι τις ἄν.

Πε. δίκην σε δοῦναι δεῖ σοφισμάτων κακῶν.

Δι. σὲ δ' ἀμαθίας γε κἀσεβοῦντ' ἐς τὸν θεόν. 490

Πε. ὡς θρασὺς ὁ βάκχος κοὐκ ἀγύμναστος λόγων.

Δι. εἴφ' ὅ τι παθεῖν δεῖ· τί με τὸ δεινὸν ἐργάσῃ;

Πε. πρῶτον μὲν ἁβρὸν βόστρυχον τεμῶ σέθεν.

Δι. ἱερὸς ὁ πλόκαμος· τῷ θεῷ δ' αὐτὸν τρέφω.

468 οὔκ, ἀλλ' ὁ (ὃς P) σεμέλης ἐνθάδ' ἔξευξεν γάμοις L P: corr.
Stephanus, Musgrave: ἀλλ' ὁ Σεμέλης ἐνθάδε ζευχθεὶς γάμοις Kirchhoff
469 σ' P: om. L   κατ' ἦμαρ ἤγνισεν Elmsley   ὄμμ' L: ὄμματ' P
475 θέλω l: θέλων L P, 'recte cum aposiopesi' Verrall   476 ἀ-
σκοῦνθ' ὄργι' L P   477 ὁρᾶν γὰρ Musgrave: γὰρ ὁρᾶν L P:
post ὁρᾶν suprascr. σὺ p   ἦν Musgrave: ἢ P: om. L: ὢν l
480 φρονεῖν] λέγειν Stob. fl. 4. 18   484 δὲ L: om. P   490 ἀμαθίας
γε κἀσεβοῦντ' L: ἀμαθίας ἀσεβοῦντ' P: ἀμαθίας γ', οὐκ εὐσεβοῦντ' Pierson

Πε. ἔπειτα θύρσον τόνδε παράδος ἐκ χεροῖν. 495

Δι. αὐτός μ' ἀφαιροῦ· τόνδε Διονύσου φορῶ.

Πε. εἰρκταῖσί τ' ἔνδον σῶμα σὸν φυλάξομεν.

Δι. λύσει μ' ὁ δαίμων αὐτός, ὅταν ἐγὼ θέλω.

Πε. ὅταν γε καλέσῃς αὐτὸν ἐν βάκχαις σταθείς.

Δι. καὶ νῦν ἃ πάσχω πλησίον παρὼν ὁρᾷ. 500

Πε. καὶ ποῦ 'στιν; οὐ γὰρ φανερὸς ὄμμασίν γ' ἐμοῖς.

Δι. παρ' ἐμοί· σὺ δ' ἀσεβὴς αὐτὸς ὢν οὐκ εἰσορᾷς.

Πε. λάζυσθε· καταφρονεῖ με καὶ Θήβας ὅδε.

Δι. αὐδῶ με μὴ δεῖν σωφρονῶν οὐ σώφροσιν.

Πε. ἐγὼ δὲ δεῖν γε, κυριώτερος σέθεν. 505

Δι. οὐκ οἶσθ' ὅ τι ζῇς, οὐδ' ὃ δρᾷς, οὐδ' ὅστις εἶ.

Πε. Πενθεύς, Ἀγαύης παῖς, πατρὸς δ' Ἐχίονος.

Δι. ἐνδυστυχῆσαι τοὔνομ' ἐπιτήδειος εἶ.

Πε. χώρει· καθείρξατ' αὐτὸν ἱππικαῖς πέλας
φάτναισιν, ὡς ἂν σκότιον εἰσορᾷ κνέφας. 510
ἐκεῖ χόρευε· τάσδε δ' ἃς ἄγων πάρει
κακῶν συνεργοὺς ἢ διεμπολήσομεν
ἢ χεῖρα δούπου τοῦδε καὶ βύρσης κτύπου
παύσας, ἐφ' ἱστοῖς δμωίδας κεκτήσομαι.

Δι. στείχοιμ' ἄν· ὅ τι γὰρ μὴ χρεών, οὔτοι χρεὼν 515
παθεῖν. ἀτάρ τοι τῶνδ' ἄποιν' ὑβρισμάτων
μέτεισι Διόνυσός σ', ὃν οὐκ εἶναι λέγεις·
ἡμᾶς γὰρ ἀδικῶν κεῖνον εἰς δεσμοὺς ἄγεις.

Χο. — . . . .
        Ἀχελῴου θύγατερ,   [στρ.
        πότνι' εὐπάρθενε Δίρκα,   520

502 αὐτὸν Elmsley   503 με καὶ Θήβας *l* et Schol. Ar. Ran. 103:
μου καὶ θήβης L P : fortasse κερτομεῖ pro καταφρονεῖ   506 ὅ τι ζῇς
('quid sit tua vita'): ὃ χρήζεις Wilamowitz   ὃ δρᾷς οὐδ' Reiske :
ὁρᾷς οὔθ' L P   510–518 singulis versibus notae personarum minio
olim praescriptae tum erasae in L : Δι. notam in ras. scr. *l*   513 κτύπους P   514 παύσας P : πάσας L   515 οὔτοι Porson : οὔτι L :
οὔτε P   aut ante 519 versus excidit (ὦ καλλίστα κρανᾶν suppl. Barnes)
aut 537 spurius est

σὺ γὰρ ἐν σαῖς ποτε παγαῖς
τὸ Διὸς βρέφος ἔλαβες,
ὅτε μηρῷ πυρὸς ἐξ ἀ-
θανάτου Ζεὺς ὁ τεκὼν ἥρ-
πασέ νιν, τάδ' ἀναβοάσας·   525
Ἴθι, Διθύραμβ', ἐμὰν ἄρ-
σενα τάνδε βᾶθι νηδύν·
ἀναφαίνω σε τόδ', ὦ Βάκ-
χιε, Θήβαις ὀνομάζειν.
      σὺ δέ μ', ὦ μάκαιρα Δίρκα,   530
στεφανηφόρους ἀπωθῇ
θιάσους ἔχουσαν ἐν σοί.
τί μ' ἀναίνῃ; τί με φεύγεις;
ἔτι ναὶ τὰν βοτρυώδη
Διονύσου χάριν οἴνας,   535
ἔτι σοι τοῦ Βρομίου μελήσει.

—   οἵαν οἵαν ὀργὰν   [ἀντ.
      ἀναφαίνει χθόνιον
γένος ἐκφύς τε δράκοντός
ποτε Πενθεύς, ὃν Ἐχίων   540
ἐφύτευσε χθόνιος,
ἀγριωπὸν τέρας, οὐ φῶ-
τα βρότειον, φόνιον δ' ὥστε γίγαντ' ἀντίπαλον θεοῖς·
ὃς ἔμ' ἐν βρόχοισι τὰν τοῦ   545
Βρομίου τάχα ξυνάψει,
τὸν ἐμὸν δ' ἐντὸς ἔχει δώ-

523 μηρῷ P   524 ἥρπασε] ἥρμοσε Kayser   525 τάδ' ἀναβοάσας
revera P: om. L: τάδ' ἀναβοήσας l: τᾷδ' ἀναβώσας Nauck, τάδ' ἀμβοάσας
Dindorf, frustra   526 ἴθι Hermann: ἴθ' ὦ L P   528 ἀναφαίνω
Hermann: ἀναφανῶ L P   530 Δίρκα] Θήβα Middendorf   534 ναὶ
L P: νὴ p   537 vid. ad 519   544 θεοῖς P et sine dubio L,
θεοῖσιν l   545 ἔμ' ἐν Dobree: με L P: ἐμὲ Hartung fortasse recte.
cf. 412   546 συνάψει L P   547 δ' erasum in L

ματος ἤδη θιασώταν
σκοτίαις κρυπτὸν ἐν εἰρκταῖς.

ἐσορᾷς τάδ', ὦ Διὸς παῖ   550
Διόνυσε, σοὺς προφήτας
ἐν ἁμίλλαισιν ἀνάγκας;
μόλε, χρυσῶπα τινάσσων,
ἄνα, θύρσον κατ' Ὄλυμπον,
φονίου δ' ἀνδρὸς ὕβριν κατάσχες.   555

— 	πόθι Νύσας ἄρα τᾶς θη-
ροτρόφου θυρσοφορεῖς
θιάσους, ὦ Διόνυσ', ἢ
κορυφαῖς Κωρυκίαις;
τάχα δ' ἐν ταῖς πολυδένδρεσ-   560
σιν Ὀλύμπου θαλάμαις, ἔν-
θα ποτ' Ὀρφεὺς κιθαρίζων
σύναγεν δένδρεα μούσαις,
σύναγεν θῆρας ἀγρώτας.

μάκαρ ὦ Πιερία,   565
σέβεταί σ' Εὔιος, ἥξει
τε χορεύσων ἅμα βακχεύ-
μασι, τόν τ' ὠκυρόαν
διαβὰς Ἀξιὸν εἱλισ-
σομένας Μαινάδας ἄξει,   570

---

549 σκοτίαισι κρυπτὸν εἰρκταῖς Bothe, cf. 530   551 σοὺς L : σὰς P
552 omissum postmodo add. L vel *l*   553 χρυσωπέ Usener   554 ἄνα,
Hermann : ἀνὰ L : ἀνα P   Ὀλύμπου Kirchhoff   556 Νύσης L P
ἄρα τᾶς θηροτρόφου P et, puto, L : ἄρα θηροτρόφου *l*   θυρσοφορεῖς P :
θυρσοφοραῖς scr. ει super αι L : θυρσοφοραῖσιν *l*   558 διόννσε ἢ L P
560 ταῖσι P et primitus L   πολυδένδρεσιν L : πολυδένδραισιν P :
corr. *l*   561 θαλάμαις Barnes : θαλάμοις L P   563 σύναγε
L P : συνάγει hic et v. sequenti Dobree   564 θῆρας L P
565 μάκαρ Hermann : μάκαιρ' L P   567 χορεύσων] σων in rasura
in L   βακχεύμασιν P et primitus L   568 ὠκυρόαν L : ὦ
κύρῖαν P   569 Ἀξιὸν L : ἄξιον P   570 τε μαινάδας L P : τε
del. Heath

Λυδίαν πατέρα τε, τὸν
τᾶς εὐδαιμονίας βροτοῖς
ὀλβοδόταν, τὸν ἔκλυον
εὔιππον χώραν ὕδασιν
    καλλίστοισι λιπαίνειν.   575

Δι.   ἰώ,
    κλύετ' ἐμᾶς κλύετ' αὐδᾶς,
    ἰὼ βάκχαι, ἰὼ βάκχαι.

Χο. — τίς ὅδε, τίς ⟨ὅδε⟩ πόθεν ὁ κέλαδος
    ἀνά μ' ἐκάλεσεν Εὐίου;

Δι.   ἰὼ ἰώ, πάλιν αὐδῶ,   580
    ὁ Σεμέλας, ὁ Διὸς παῖς.

Χο. — ἰὼ ἰὼ δέσποτα δέσποτα,
    μόλε νυν ἡμέτερον ἐς
    θίασον, ὦ Βρόμιε Βρόμιε.

Δι.   ⟨σεῖε⟩ πέδον χθονὸς Ἔννοσι πότνια.   585

Χο. — ἆ ἆ,
    τάχα τὰ Πενθέως μέλαθρα διατι-
    νάξεται πεσήμασιν.
  — ὁ Διόνυσος ἀνὰ μέλαθρα·
    σεβετέ νιν. — σέβομεν ὤ.   590
  — εἴδετε λάινα κίοσιν ἔμβολα

571–573 Λυδίαν τε τὸν hic, πατέρα τε τὸν infra ante ἔκλυον habent
L P : trai. Wilamowitz   572 τᾶς L : τὰς P   573 ὀλβοδόταν
πατέρα, τὸν Bothe   574 ὕδασι L P   576 ἁμᾶς Wecklein :
sed cf. 580, 581   578 ὅδε alterum add. post Hermannum Wecklein
583 νῦν L P   ἀμέτερον Dindorf   585–603 nullas personarum
notas exhibent L P, nisi 590 ἡμιχ. σέβομεν L P (minio scr. L² P² ut
vid.) : 590 Διον. σέβετε l, 592 Χο. βρόμιος L, 596 ἡμιχ. ἆ ἆ l : 'certum
est haec a singulis chori personis cantari' Kirchhoff : notas et paragraphos post Tyrwhittum Bruhnium alios praescripsimus   585 σεῖε
add. Wilamowitz   πέδον an πέδου habeant L P incertum   Ἔννοσι
scripsi : ἔνοσι L P   588 διατινάζεται P   591 εἴδετε Dobree :
ἴδετε L : ἴδετε τὰ P, fortasse recte   κίοσιν om. P

διάδρομα τάδε; Βρόμιος ⟨ὅδ'⟩ ἀλαλάζεται στέγας ἔσω.

Δι. ἅπτε κεραύνιον αἴθοπα λαμπάδα·
σύμφλεγε σύμφλεγε δώματα Πενθέος.   595

Χο. ἆ ἆ,
πῦρ οὐ λεύσσεις, οὐδ' αὐγάζῃ,
Σεμέλας ἱερὸν ἀμφὶ τάφον, ἅν
ποτε κεραυνόβολος ἔλιπε φλόγα
Δίου βροντᾶς;
δίκετε πεδόσε τρομερὰ σώματα   600
δίκετε, Μαινάδες· ὁ γὰρ ἄναξ
ἄνω κάτω τιθεὶς ἔπεισι
μέλαθρα τάδε Διὸς γόνος.

Δι. βάρβαροι γυναῖκες, οὕτως ἐκπεπληγμέναι φόβῳ
πρὸς πέδῳ πεπτώκατ'; ᾔσθησθ', ὡς ἔοικε, Βακχίου   605
διατινάξαντος †δῶμα Πενθέως· ἀλλ' ἐξανίστατε†
σῶμα καὶ θαρσεῖτε σαρκὸς ἐξαμείψασαι τρόμον.

Χο. ὦ φάος μέγιστον ἡμῖν εὐίου βακχεύματος,
ὡς ἐσεῖδον ἀσμένη σε, μονάδ' ἔχουσ' ἐρημίαν.

Δι. εἰς ἀθυμίαν ἀφίκεσθ', ἡνίκ' εἰσεπεμπόμην,   610
Πενθέως ὡς ἐς σκοτεινὰς ὁρκάνας πεσούμενος;

Χο. πῶς γὰρ οὔ; τίς μοι φύλαξ ἦν, εἰ σὺ συμφορᾶς τύχοις;
ἀλλὰ πῶς ἠλευθερώθης ἀνδρὸς ἀνοσίου τυχών;

Δι. αὐτὸς ἐξέσωσ' ἐμαυτὸν ῥᾳδίως ἄνευ πόνου.

592 ὅδ' add. Bruhn   ἀλαλάζεται P: ἀλαλάξεται L: ἠλάλαξε τᾶς
Tyrwhitt   595 Πενθέος L: πενθέως P   596 αὐγάζῃ sanum,
passive: cf. Hec. 637   597 τόνδε Σεμέλας Wilamowitz metri paeonici
causa   598 κεραυνοβόλος L P: tum Διὸς βροντά Hervagiana secunda
599 βροντῆς L   600 πεδόσσε primitus L   σώματα Schol. Phoen.
641 (δίκετε τρομερὰ σώματα) et Etym. M. 279. 20 (δίκετε παῖδα δίκετε
τρομερὰ σώματα μαινάδες ordine verborum fortasse meliore): δώματα
L P   602 τίθει P   603 γόνος διόννσος L   605 πεπτώκαθ' L P
ἤσθη∗θ' L nunc: ᾔσθεσθ' Canter   606 τὰ Πενθέως δώματ' ἐκ δ' ἀνίστατε
post Musgravium Wilamowitz   607 σαρκὸς Reiske: σάρκας L P
612 μοι P et suprascr. L: μου L   τύχας P   613 ἐλευθερώθης P
τυχών] fortasse μυχῶν

Χο. οὐδέ σου συνῆψε χεῖρε δεσμίοισιν ἐν βρόχοις;   615
Δι. ταῦτα καὶ καθύβρισ' αὐτόν, ὅτι με δεσμεύειν δοκῶν
οὔτ' ἔθιγεν οὔθ' ἥψαθ' ἡμῶν, ἐλπίσιν δ' ἐβόσκετο.
πρὸς φάτναις δὲ ταῦρον εὑρών, οὗ καθεῖρξ' ἡμᾶς ἄγων,
τῷδε περὶ βρόχους ἔβαλλε γόνασι καὶ χηλαῖς ποδῶν,
θυμὸν ἐκπνέων, ἱδρῶτα σώματος στάζων ἄπο,   620
χείλεσιν διδοὺς ὀδόντας· πλησίον δ' ἐγὼ παρὼν
ἥσυχος θάσσων ἔλευσσον. ἐν δὲ τῷδε τῷ χρόνῳ
ἀνετίναξ' ἐλθὼν ὁ Βάκχος δῶμα καὶ μητρὸς τάφῳ
πῦρ ἀνῆψ'· ὁ δ' ὡς ἐσεῖδε, δώματ' αἴθεσθαι δοκῶν,
ᾖσσ' ἐκεῖσε κᾆτ' ἐκεῖσε, δμωσὶν Ἀχελῷον φέρειν   625
ἐννέπων, ἅπας δ' ἐν ἔργῳ δοῦλος ἦν, μάτην πονῶν.
διαμεθεὶς δὲ τόνδε μόχθον, ὡς ἐμοῦ πεφευγότος,
ἵεται ξίφος κελαινὸν ἁρπάσας δόμων ἔσω.
κᾆθ' ὁ Βρόμιος, ὡς ἔμοιγε φαίνεται, δόξαν λέγω,
φάσμ' ἐποίησεν κατ' αὐλήν· ὁ δ' ἐπὶ τοῦθ' ὡρμημένος 630
ᾖσσε κἀκέντει φαεννὸν ⟨αἰθέρ'⟩, ὡς σφάζων ἐμέ.
πρὸς δὲ τοῖσδ' αὐτῷ τάδ' ἄλλα Βάκχιος λυμαίνεται·
δώματ' ἔρρηξεν χαμᾶζε· συντεθράνωται δ' ἅπαν
πικροτάτους ἰδόντι δεσμοὺς τοὺς ἐμούς· κόπου δ' ὕπο
διαμεθεὶς ξίφος παρεῖται· πρὸς θεὸν γὰρ ὢν ἀνὴρ   635
ἐς μάχην ἐλθεῖν ἐτόλμησε. ἥσυχος δ' ἐκβὰς ἐγὼ
δωμάτων ἥκω πρὸς ὑμᾶς, Πενθέως οὐ φροντίσας.
ὡς δέ μοι δοκεῖ—ψοφεῖ γοῦν ἀρβύλη δόμων ἔσω—
ἐς προνώπι' αὐτίχ' ἥξει. τί ποτ' ἄρ' ἐκ τούτων ἐρεῖ;
ῥᾳδίως γὰρ αὐτὸν οἴσω, κἂν πνέων ἔλθῃ μέγα.   640
πρὸς σοφοῦ γὰρ ἀνδρὸς ἀσκεῖν σώφρον' εὐοργησίαν.

---

615 χεῖρε Nauck: χεῖρα L P   618 καθεῖργ' Wecklein   619 ἔβαλε P
621 δ' P: γ' L   622 θάσσων P: θᾶσσον L   625 ᾗσσ' L: ᾗσο' P
629 βρώμιος L   630 φάσμ' Jacobs: φῶς L P ('recte: leg. κελαινῶν
628' Verrall)   ἐποίησε P   631 κἀκέντα P   αἰθέρ' add. Canter:
cf. Hel. 584, supra 293   632 τάδ' P: τὰ δ' L   635 παρεῖται P:
om. L   636 ἐτόλμησε L   ἐκβὰς ἐγὼ Heinisch: ἐκ βάκχας ἄγων
L P: ἐκ βακχάδων Hermann   639 ἄρ' L P   641 ἀσκεῖν L:
ἀρκεῖ P   εὐοργησία L

28   ΕΥΡΙΠΙΔΟΥ

Πε. πέπονθα δεινά· διαπέφευγέ μ' ὁ ξένος,
     ὃς ἄρτι δεσμοῖς ἦν κατηναγκασμένος.
     ἔα ἔα·
     ὅδ' ἐστὶν ἀνήρ· τί τάδε; πῶς προνώπιος   645
     φαίνῃ πρὸς οἴκοις τοῖς ἐμοῖς, ἔξω βεβώς;
Δι. στῆσον πόδ', ὀργῇ δ' ὑπόθες ἥσυχον πόδα.
Πε. πόθεν σὺ δεσμὰ διαφυγὼν ἔξω περᾷς;
Δι. οὐκ εἶπον—ἢ οὐκ ἤκουσας—ὅτι λύσει μέ τις;
Πε. τίς; τοὺς λόγους γὰρ ἐσφέρεις καινοὺς ἀεί.   650
Δι. ὃς τὴν πολύβοτρυν ἄμπελον φύει βροτοῖς.
Πε. .   .   .   .
Δι. ὠνείδισας δὴ τοῦτο Διονύσῳ καλόν.
Πε. κλῄειν κελεύω πάντα πύργον ἐν κύκλῳ.
Δι. τί δ'; οὐχ ὑπερβαίνουσι καὶ τείχη θεοί;
Πε. σοφὸς σοφὸς σύ, πλὴν ἃ δεῖ σ' εἶναι σοφόν.   655
Δι. ἃ δεῖ μάλιστα, ταῦτ' ἔγωγ' ἔφυν σοφός.
     κείνου δ' ἀκούσας πρῶτα τοὺς λόγους μάθε,
     ὃς ἐξ ὄρους πάρεστιν ἀγγελῶν τί σοι·
     ἡμεῖς δέ σοι μενοῦμεν, οὐ φευξούμεθα.

ΑΓΓΕΛΟΣ
     Πενθεῦ κρατύνων τῆσδε Θηβαίας χθονός,   660
     ἥκω Κιθαιρῶν' ἐκλιπών, ἵν' οὔποτε
     λευκῆς χιόνος ἀνεῖσαν εὐαγεῖς βολαί.
Πε. ἥκεις δὲ ποίαν προστιθεὶς σπουδὴν λόγου;
Αγ. βάκχας ποτνιάδας εἰσιδών, αἳ τῆσδε γῆς

645 ἀνήρ L P   647 πόδα] cf. Soph. in Berl. Kl. Text. v. 2, p. 65, v. 13
649 ἢ om. P   post 651 lacunam indicavit Reiske (ex. gr. κακόν
γε δῶρον, παραφρονεῖν ὠνωμένος): post 652, quem Pentheo tribuit,
Hermann   notam ante 653 om. L: 653–656 notas inversas
habet P, tum 657 Baccho tribuit   653 κλείειν l : κλύειν L P
655 σύ ex Chr. Pat. 1529 Porson: εἰ P : γ' εἰ L   658 ἀγγελῶν
P   659 φευξόμεθα L: corr. l   660 ΑΓΓΕΛΟΣ] ΒΟΥΚΟΛΟΣ malit
Wecklein   662 ἀνεῖσαν χιόνος Ludv. Dindorf   ἐξαυγεῖς Elmsley,
cf. Rhes. 304   v. fictum ad aposiopesin tegendam censet Verrall: cf.
I. T. 253   663 δὲ ποίαν Porson: δ' ὁποίαν L P

οἴστροισι λευκὸν κῶλον ἐξηκόντισαν, 665
ἥκω φράσαι σοὶ καὶ πόλει χρῄζων, ἄναξ,
ὡς δεινὰ δρῶσι θαυμάτων τε κρείσσονα.
θέλω δ' ἀκοῦσαι, πότερά σοι παρρησίᾳ
φράσω τὰ κεῖθεν ἢ λόγον στειλώμεθα·
τὸ γὰρ τάχος σου τῶν φρενῶν δέδοικ', ἄναξ, 670
καὶ τοὐξύθυμον καὶ τὸ βασιλικὸν λίαν.

Πε. λέγ', ὡς ἀθῷος ἐξ ἐμοῦ πάντως ἔσῃ.
τοῖς γὰρ δικαίοις οὐχὶ θυμοῦσθαι χρεών.
ὅσῳ δ' ἂν εἴπῃς δεινότερα βακχῶν πέρι,
τοσῷδε μᾶλλον τὸν ὑποθέντα τὰς τέχνας 675
γυναιξὶ τόνδε τῇ δίκῃ προσθήσομεν.

Αγ. ἀγελαῖα μὲν βοσκήματ' ἄρτι πρὸς λέπας
μόσχων ὑπεξήκριζον, ἡνίχ' ἥλιος
ἀκτῖνας ἐξίησι θερμαίνων χθόνα.
ὁρῶ δὲ θιάσους τρεῖς γυναικείων χορῶν, 680
ὧν ἦρχ' ἑνὸς μὲν Αὐτονόη, τοῦ δευτέρου
μήτηρ Ἀγαύη σή, τρίτου δ' Ἰνὼ χοροῦ.
ηὗδον δὲ πᾶσαι σώμασιν παρειμέναι,
αἱ μὲν πρὸς ἐλάτης νῶτ' ἐρείσασαι φόβην,
αἱ δ' ἐν δρυὸς φύλλοισι πρὸς πέδῳ κάρα 685
εἰκῇ βαλοῦσαι σωφρόνως, οὐχ ὡς σὺ φῂς
ᾠνωμένας κρατῆρι καὶ λωτοῦ ψόφῳ
θηρᾶν καθ' ὕλην Κύπριν ἠρημωμένας.

ἡ σὴ δὲ μήτηρ ὠλόλυξεν ἐν μέσαις
σταθεῖσα βάκχαις, ἐξ ὕπνου κινεῖν δέμας, 690
μυκήμαθ' ὡς ἤκουσε κεροφόρων βοῶν.
αἱ δ' ἀποβαλοῦσαι θαλερὸν ὀμμάτων ὕπνον

---

667 cf. 716: θαυμάτων τ' ἐπάξια habet Chr. Pat. 2213   669 τά-
κεῖθεν L P   673 del. Nauck, cl. fr. 287. 1   675 τὰς L: om. P
678 βόσκων Sandys   680 γυναικίων P   681 τοῦ Scaliger: τοῦ
δὲ L P   682 τρίτου Musurus, et teste Wilamowitzio primitus
L: τρίτη L P: τρίτη δ' Ἰνὼ τρίτου Hermann   683 εὖδον L P
684 νῶτον primitus L   687 οἰνωμένας L P: corr. Elmsley   ψήφῳ P:
corr. p   688 ἠρεμωμένας P: ἠρημωμένην Wecklein

ἀνῇξαν ὀρθαί, θαῦμ' ἰδεῖν εὐκοσμίας,
νέαι παλαιαὶ παρθένοι τ' ἔτ' ἄζυγες.

καὶ πρῶτα μὲν καθεῖσαν εἰς ὤμους κόμας 695
νεβρίδας τ' ἀνεστείλανθ' ὅσαισιν ἀμμάτων
σύνδεσμ' ἐλέλυτο, καὶ καταστίκτους δορὰς
ὄφεσι κατεζώσαντο λιχμῶσιν γένυν.
αἳ δ' ἀγκάλαισι δορκάδ' ἢ σκύμνους λύκων
ἀγρίους ἔχουσαι λευκὸν ἐδίδοσαν γάλα, 700
ὅσαις νεοτόκοις μαστὸς ἦν σπαργῶν ἔτι
βρέφη λιπούσαις· ἐπὶ δ' ἔθεντο κισσίνους
στεφάνους δρυός τε μίλακός τ' ἀνθεσφόρου.
θύρσον δέ τις λαβοῦσ' ἔπαισεν ἐς πέτραν,
ὅθεν δροσώδης ὕδατος ἐκπηδᾷ νοτίς· 705
ἄλλη δὲ νάρθηκ' ἐς πέδον καθῆκε γῆς,
καὶ τῇδε κρήνην ἐξανῆκ' οἴνου θεός·
ὅσαις δὲ λευκοῦ πώματος πόθος παρῆν,
ἄκροισι δακτύλοισι διαμῶσαι χθόνα
γάλακτος ἐσμοὺς εἶχον· ἐκ δὲ κισσίνων 710
θύρσων γλυκεῖαι μέλιτος ἔσταζον ῥοαί.
ὥστ', εἰ παρῆσθα, τὸν θεὸν τὸν νῦν ψέγεις
εὐχαῖσιν ἂν μετῆλθες εἰσιδὼν τάδε.

ξυνήλθομεν δὲ βουκόλοι καὶ ποιμένες,
κοινῶν λόγων δώσοντες ἀλλήλοις ἔριν 715
ὡς δεινὰ δρῶσι θαυμάτων τ' ἐπάξια·
καί τις πλάνης κατ' ἄστυ καὶ τρίβων λόγων
ἔλεξεν εἰς ἅπαντας· Ὦ σεμνὰς πλάκας
ναίοντες ὀρέων, θέλετε θηρασώμεθα
Πενθέως Ἀγαύην μητέρ' ἐκ βακχευμάτων 720
χάριν τ' ἄνακτι θώμεθα; εὖ δ' ἡμῖν λέγειν

694 τ' ἔτ' ἄζυγες ex Chr. Pat. 1834 Musgrave: τε κἄζυγες L P
696 ὀμμάτων P   698 λιχμῶσιν Heath: λιχμῶσαν L P   γέναν P
701 μαζὸς L P: corr. Brunck   σπαρτῶν P   703 ἀνθεσφόρου
Hervagiana prima: ἀνθεσφόρους L P   704 λαβοῦσα L   709 διαμῶσαι L P: λικμῶσαι suprascr. l   710 ἐσμοὺς L P   715 vix
sanus   716 del. Dobree: cf. 667   721 θώμεθ' Elmsley: θῶμεν L P

ἔδοξε, θάμνων δ᾽ ἐλλοχίζομεν φόβαις
κρύψαντες αὑτούς· αἳ δὲ τὴν τεταγμένην
ὥραν ἐκίνουν θύρσον ἐς βακχεύματα,
Ἴακχον ἀθρόῳ στόματι τὸν Διὸς γόνον   725
Βρόμιον καλοῦσαι· πᾶν δὲ συνεβάκχευ᾽ ὄρος
καὶ θῆρες, οὐδὲν δ᾽ ἦν ἀκίνητον δρόμῳ.
    κυρεῖ δ᾽ Ἀγαύη πλησίον θρῴσκουσά μου·
κἀγὼ ᾽ξεπήδησ᾽ ὡς συναρπάσαι θέλων,
λόχμην κενώσας ἔνθ᾽ ἐκρυπτόμην δέμας.   730
ἣ δ᾽ ἀνεβόησεν· Ὦ δρομάδες ἐμαὶ κύνες,
θηρώμεθ᾽ ἀνδρῶν τῶνδ᾽ ὕπ᾽· ἀλλ᾽ ἕπεσθέ μοι,
ἕπεσθε θύρσοις διὰ χερῶν ὡπλισμέναι.
    ἡμεῖς μὲν οὖν φεύγοντες ἐξηλύξαμεν
βακχῶν σπαραγμόν, αἳ δὲ νεμομέναις χλόην   735
μόσχοις ἐπῆλθον χειρὸς ἀσιδήρου μέτα.
καὶ τὴν μὲν ἂν προσεῖδες εὔθηλον πόριν
μυκωμένην ἔχουσαν ἐν χεροῖν δίχα,
ἄλλαι δὲ δαμάλας διεφόρουν σπαράγμασιν.
εἶδες δ᾽ ἂν ἢ πλεύρ᾽ ἢ δίχηλον ἔμβασιν   740
ῥιπτόμεν᾽ ἄνω τε καὶ κάτω· κρεμαστὰ δὲ
ἔσταζ᾽ ὑπ᾽ ἐλάταις ἀναπεφυρμέν᾽ αἵματι.
ταῦροι δ᾽ ὑβρισταὶ κἀς κέρας θυμούμενοι
τὸ πρόσθεν ἐσφάλλοντο πρὸς γαῖαν δέμας,
μυριάσι χειρῶν ἀγόμενοι νεανίδων.   745
θᾶσσον δὲ διεφοροῦντο σαρκὸς ἐνδυτὰ
ἢ σὲ ξυνάψαι βλέφαρα βασιλείοις κόραις.
χωροῦσι δ᾽ ὥστ᾽ ὄρνιθες ἀρθεῖσαι δρόμῳ

722 ἐλοχίζομεν P   723 αὑτοὺς L p : αὐτοὺς P   726 συνεβάκχευ᾽
Porson, cl. de Sublimitate xv. 6 (ubi codd. συνεβάκχευεν) : συνεβάκχευσ᾽ L P
728 κύρει L P : corr. p   730 ἔνθ᾽ L : ἔνδ᾽ P   ἐκρύπτομεν L P
732 ὕπ᾽ l p : ὑπ᾽ L P   734 φυγόντες Elmsley   735 σπαραγμῶν L
νεμόμεναι P   737 πόλιν P : corr. p   738 δίχα Reiske (et
ἕλκουσαν) : δίκα L P : δίκῃ Elmsley : ἀκμαῖς Nauck   740 πλεύρ᾽
Barnes : πλευρὰν L P   743 κεῖς L P   746 ἔνδυτα L P   747 σὲ
L : σὺ P (tum ξυνάψαις p)

πεδίων ὑποτάσεις, αἱ παρ' Ἀσωποῦ ῥοαῖς
εὔκαρπον ἐκβάλλουσι Θηβαίων στάχυν·   750
Ὑσιάς τ' Ἐρυθράς θ', αἱ Κιθαιρῶνος λέπας
νέρθεν κατῳκήκασιν, ὥστε πολέμιοι,
ἐπεσπεσοῦσαι πάντ' ἄνω τε καὶ κάτω
διέφερον· ἥρπαζον μὲν ἐκ δόμων τέκνα·
ὁπόσα δ' ἐπ' ὤμοις ἔθεσαν, οὐ δεσμῶν ὕπο   755
προσείχετ' οὐδ' ἔπιπτεν ἐς μέλαν πέδον,
οὐ χαλκός, οὐ σίδηρος· ἐπὶ δὲ βοστρύχοις
πῦρ ἔφερον, οὐδ' ἔκαιεν. οἳ δ' ὀργῆς ὕπο
ἐς ὅπλ' ἐχώρουν φερόμενοι βακχῶν ὕπο·
οὗπερ τὸ δεινὸν ἦν θέαμ' ἰδεῖν, ἄναξ.   760
τοῖς μὲν γὰρ οὐχ ἥμασσε λογχωτὸν βέλος,
κεῖναι δὲ θύρσους ἐξανιεῖσαι χερῶν
ἐτραυμάτιζον κἀπενώτιζον φυγῇ
γυναῖκες ἄνδρας, οὐκ ἄνευ θεῶν τινος.
πάλιν δ' ἐχώρουν ὅθεν ἐκίνησαν πόδα,   765
κρήνας ἐπ' αὐτὰς ἃς ἀνῆκ' αὐταῖς θεός.
νίψαντο δ' αἷμα, σταγόνα δ' ἐκ παρηίδων
γλώσσῃ δράκοντες ἐξεφαίδρυνον χροός.

τὸν δαίμον' οὖν τόνδ' ὅστις ἔστ', ὦ δέσποτα,
δέχου πόλει τῇδ'· ὡς τά τ' ἄλλ' ἐστὶν μέγας,   770
κἀκεῖνό φασιν αὐτόν, ὡς ἐγὼ κλύω,
τὴν παυσίλυπον ἄμπελον δοῦναι βροτοῖς.
οἴνου δὲ μηκέτ' ὄντος οὐκ ἔστιν Κύπρις
οὐδ' ἄλλο τερπνὸν οὐδὲν ἀνθρώποις ἔτι.

---

749 αἰσωποῦ P   750 Θηβαίων L: θηβαῖον P: Θηβαίοις Brunck
751 ὑσίας L P   τ'] δ' Brunck   ἐρυθρὰς P: ἐρυθρᾶς L p   θ' om. P
754 τέκνα] τύχη Madvig: locus difficilis: hiatum post 754 Har-
tungus, alterum post 756 Middendorfius ponit: τέκνα habuit Nonnus,
xlv. 294   755 post ὕπο explicit L: λείπει adscr. l   758 ἔκαιεν
Elmsley: ἐκαίεθ' P   οἵ p: ἤ P   761 τοῖς Stephanus: τᾶς P: τὰς
Brodeau   764 γυναῖκες Musurus: γυναῖκας P   766 ἔπ', αὐτὸς
Bruhn   768 δράκοντες Reiske: δράκοντος P   ἐξεφέδρυνον P:
corr. p   773 οἴνου] fortasse τούτου

Χο. ταρβῶ μὲν εἰπεῖν τοὺς λόγους ἐλευθέρους   775
     πρὸς τὸν τύραννον, ἀλλ' ὅμως εἰρήσεται·
     Διόνυσος ἥσσων οὐδενὸς θεῶν ἔφυ.

Πε. ἤδη τόδ' ἐγγὺς ὥστε πῦρ ὑφάπτεται
     ὕβρισμα βακχῶν, ψόγος ἐς Ἕλληνας μέγας.
     ἀλλ' οὐκ ὀκνεῖν δεῖ· στεῖχ' ἐπ' Ἠλέκτρας ἰὼν   780
     πύλας· κέλευε πάντας ἀσπιδηφόρους
     ἵππων τ' ἀπαντᾶν ταχυπόδων ἐπεμβάτας
     πέλτας θ' ὅσοι πάλλουσι καὶ τόξων χερὶ
     ψάλλουσι νευράς, ὡς ἐπιστρατεύσομεν
     βάκχαισιν· οὐ γὰρ ἀλλ' ὑπερβάλλει τάδε,   785
     εἰ πρὸς γυναικῶν πεισόμεσθ' ἃ πάσχομεν.

Δι. πείθῃ μὲν οὐδέν, τῶν ἐμῶν λόγων κλύων,
     Πενθεῦ· κακῶς δὲ πρὸς σέθεν πάσχων ὅμως
     οὔ φημι χρῆναί σ' ὅπλ' ἐπαίρεσθαι θεῷ,
     ἀλλ' ἡσυχάζειν· Βρόμιος οὐκ ἀνέξεται   790
     κινοῦντα βάκχας ⟨σ'⟩ εὐίων ὀρῶν ἄπο.

Πε. οὐ μὴ φρενώσεις μ', ἀλλὰ δέσμιος φυγὼν
     σώσῃ τόδ'; ἢ σοὶ πάλιν ἀναστρέψω δίκην;

Δι. θύοιμ' ἂν αὐτῷ μᾶλλον ἢ θυμούμενος
     πρὸς κέντρα λακτίζοιμι θνητὸς ὢν θεῷ.   795

Πε. θύσω, φόνον γε θῆλυν, ὥσπερ ἄξιαι,
     πολὺν ταράξας ἐν Κιθαιρῶνος πτυχαῖς.

Δι. φεύξεσθε πάντες· καὶ τόδ' αἰσχρόν, ἀσπίδας
     θύρσοισι βακχῶν ἐκτρέπειν χαλκηλάτους.

Πε. ἀπόρῳ γε τῷδε συμπεπλέγμεθα ξένῳ,   800

776 πρὸς e Chr. Pat. 2222 et 2244 Wecklein: εἰς P   778 ὑφάπτεται
Chr. Pat. 2227: ἐφάπτεται P   784 ἐπιστρατεύσωμεν P: corr. p
786 πεισόμεθ' P: corr. p   787–842 quae Dionysi sunt Nuntio
tribuit P: corr. Tyrwhitt: cf. ad 798   787 κλύειν λόγων Chr.
Pat. 2277   791 κινοῦντα Canter: κινοῦντι P quo servato v. ante
790 trai. Verrall: κινοῦν τι Schoene   σ' add. Lenting   ὀρῶν P
793 δίκην] χέρας Wecklein   796 ἄξιος Wilamowitz   797 πτύχαις P
798 sq. Pentheo continuat, 800–2 Nuntio trib. P: corr. Tyrwhitt: cf.
ad 787–842   798 φεύξεσθε Elmsley: φευξεῖσθε P   799 ἐντρέπειν
Nauck

ὃς οὔτε πάσχων οὔτε δρῶν σιγήσεται.
Δι. ὦ τᾶν, ἔτ' ἔστιν εὖ καταστῆσαι τάδε.
Πε. τί δρῶντα; δουλεύοντα δουλείαις ἐμαῖς;
Δι. ἐγὼ γυναῖκας δεῦρ' ὅπλων ἄξω δίχα.
Πε. οἴμοι· τόδ' ἤδη δόλιον ἔς με μηχανᾷ.   805
Δι. ποῖόν τι, σῶσαί σ' εἰ θέλω τέχναις ἐμαῖς;
Πε. ξυνέθεσθε κοινῇ τάδ', ἵνα βακχεύητ' ἀεί.
Δι. καὶ μὴν ξυνεθέμην—τοῦτό γ' ἔστι—τῷ θεῷ.
Πε. ἐκφέρετέ μοι δεῦρ' ὅπλα, σὺ δὲ παῦσαι λέγων.
Δι. ἆ.   810
      βούλῃ σφ' ἐν ὄρεσι συγκαθημένας ἰδεῖν;
Πε. μάλιστα, μυρίον γε δοὺς χρυσοῦ σταθμόν.
Δι. τί δ' εἰς ἔρωτα τοῦδε πέπτωκας μέγαν;
Πε. λυπρῶς νιν εἰσίδοιμ' ἂν ἐξῳνωμένας.
Δι. ὅμως δ' ἴδοις ἂν ἡδέως ἅ σοι πικρά;   815
Πε. σάφ' ἴσθι, σιγῇ γ' ὑπ' ἐλάταις καθήμενος.
Δι. ἀλλ' ἐξιχνεύσουσίν σε, κἂν ἔλθῃς λάθρᾳ.
Πε. ἀλλ' ἐμφανῶς· καλῶς γὰρ ἐξεῖπας τάδε.
Δι. ἄγωμεν οὖν σε κἀπιχειρήσεις ὁδῷ;
Πε. ἄγ' ὡς τάχιστα, τοῦ χρόνου δέ σοι φθονῶ.   820
Δι. στεῖλαί νυν ἀμφὶ χρωτὶ βυσσίνους πέπλους.
Πε. τί δὴ τόδ'; ἐς γυναῖκας ἐξ ἀνδρὸς τελῶ;
Δι. μή σε κτάνωσιν, ἢν ἀνὴρ ὀφθῇς ἐκεῖ.
Πε. εὖ γ' εἶπας αὖ τόδ'· ὥς τις εἶ πάλαι σοφός.
Δι. Διόνυσος ἡμᾶς ἐξεμούσωσεν τάδε.   825
Πε. πῶς οὖν γένοιτ' ἂν ἃ σύ με νουθετεῖς καλῶς;
Δι. ἐγὼ στελῶ σε δωμάτων ἔσω μολών.

801 ὃς Musgrave: ὡς P   802 ὦ τᾶν Scaliger: ὅταν P   803 δου-
λίαις P: corr. p   805 δούλιον primitus P   808 μὴν p: μὴ P
ἔστι P: intellego 'Pactum habetis tu et mulieres.' 'Immo ego et deus:
hoc quidem verum': ἴσθι Musgrave: ξυνεθέμην τοῦτό γ' ἔς τι Tyrwhitt
814 νιν] μὲν Bruhn   ἐξοινωμένας P   816 γ' Musurus: δ' P
817 ἐξιχνεύουσι κἂν P: supplevit Musgrave   ἔλθῃς Pierson: θέλῃς P
818 τόδε Hermann   820 δέ σοι Nauck: δέ σ' οὐ P   821 νυν
Canter: νιν P   824 αὖ τόδ' ὡς Wecklein: αὐτὸ καὶ P

Πε. τίνα στολήν; ἢ θῆλυν; ἀλλ' αἰδώς μ' ἔχει.

Δι. οὐκέτι θεατὴς μαινάδων πρόθυμος εἶ.

Πε. στολὴν δὲ τίνα φῂς ἀμφὶ χρῶτ' ἐμὸν βαλεῖν;   830

Δι. κόμην μὲν ἐπὶ σῷ κρατὶ ταναὸν ἐκτενῶ.

Πε. τὸ δεύτερον δὲ σχῆμα τοῦ κόσμου τί μοι;

Δι. πέπλοι ποδήρεις· ἐπὶ κάρᾳ δ' ἔσται μίτρα.

Πε. ἢ καί τι πρὸς τοῖσδ' ἄλλο προσθήσεις ἐμοί;

Δι. θύρσον γε χειρὶ καὶ νεβροῦ στικτὸν δέρας.   835

Πε. οὐκ ἂν δυναίμην θῆλυν ἐνδῦναι στολήν.

Δι. ἀλλ' αἷμα θήσεις συμβαλὼν βάκχαις μάχην.

Πε. ὀρθῶς· μολεῖν χρὴ πρῶτον εἰς κατασκοπήν.

Δι. σοφώτερον γοῦν ἢ κακοῖς θηρᾶν κακά.)

Πε. καὶ πῶς δι' ἄστεως εἶμι Καδμείους λαθών;   840

Δι. ὁδοὺς ἐρήμους ἵμεν· ἐγὼ δ' ἡγήσομαι.

Πε. πᾶν κρεῖσσον ὥστε μὴ 'γγελᾶν βάκχας ἐμοί.
  ἐλθόντ' ἐς οἴκους . . . ἂν δοκῇ βουλεύσομαι.

Δι. ἔξεστι· πάντῃ τό γ' ἐμὸν εὐτρεπὲς πάρα.

Πε. στείχοιμ' ἄν· ἢ γὰρ ὅπλ' ἔχων πορεύσομαι   845
  ἢ τοῖσι σοῖσι πείσομαι βουλεύμασιν.

Δι. γυναῖκες, ἀνὴρ ἐς βόλον καθίσταται,   848
  ἥξει δὲ βάκχας, οὗ θανὼν δώσει δίκην.   847

  Διόνυσε, νῦν σὸν ἔργον· οὐ γὰρ εἶ πρόσω·
  τεισώμεθ' αὐτόν. πρῶτα δ' ἔκστησον φρενῶν,   850
  ἐνεὶς ἐλαφρὰν λύσσαν· ὡς φρονῶν μὲν εὖ
  οὐ μὴ θελήσῃ θῆλυν ἐνδῦναι στολήν,
  ἔξω δ' ἐλαύνων τοῦ φρονεῖν ἐνδύσεται.
  χρῄζω δέ νιν γέλωτα Θηβαίοις ὀφλεῖν

829 μενάδων P   833 κάρα P   835 γε Hermann : τε P   838 ἐς
hic P   840 καδμίους P : corr. p   842 'γγελᾶν Pierson Reiske :
γελᾶν P   843 et 844 paragraphos, 845 ἀγγ. praescr. P : corr. Heath
843 ἐλθών γ' Nauck   ἂν] ἀν P   844 εὐτρεπὲς Canter : εὐπρεπὲς P
846 τοῖς σοῖσι πείθομαι P : corr. Musurus   847 post 848 trai.
Musgrave : delet Middendorf : si recte positus, fortasse ἥξεις . . . δώσεις
848 ἀνὴρ P   847 βάκχαις Lenting   851 λίσσαν P : corr. p
852 θελήσει P   854 ὄφλειν P

γυναικόμορφον ἀγόμενον δι' ἄστεως　　　　　855
ἐκ τῶν ἀπειλῶν τῶν πρίν, αἷσι δεινὸς ἦν.
ἀλλ' εἶμι κόσμον ὅνπερ εἰς Ἅιδου λαβὼν
ἄπεισι μητρὸς ἐκ χεροῖν κατασφαγείς,
Πενθεῖ προσάψων· γνώσεται δὲ τὸν Διὸς
Διόνυσον, ὃς πέφυκεν ἐν τέλει θεός,　　　　　860
δεινότατος, ἀνθρώποισι δ' ἠπιώτατος.

Χο. 　— 　　ἆρ' ἐν παννυχίοις χοροῖς　　　　　[στρ.
θήσω ποτὲ λευκὸν
πόδ' ἀναβακχεύουσα, δέραν
εἰς αἰθέρα δροσερὸν ῥίπτουσ',　　　　　865
ὡς νεβρὸς χλοεραῖς ἐμπαί-
ζουσα λείμακος ἡδοναῖς,
ἡνίκ' ἂν φοβερὰν φύγῃ
θήραν ἔξω φυλακᾶς
εὐπλέκτων ὑπὲρ ἀρκύων,　　　　　870
θωΰσσων δὲ κυναγέτας
συντείνῃ δράμημα κυνῶν·
μόχθοις τ' ὠκυδρόμοις τ' ἀέλλαις θρῴσκει πεδίον
παραποτάμιον, ἡδομένα
βροτῶν ἐρημίαις σκιαρο-　　　　　875
κόμοιό τ' ἔρνεσιν ὕλας.

— 　　τί τὸ σοφόν; ἢ τί τὸ κάλλιον
παρὰ θεῶν γέρας ἐν βροτοῖς
ἢ χεῖρ' ὑπὲρ κορυφᾶς

855 ἄστεος P　　　　856 ante 855 trai. Wecklein　　　　857 ἄδου P
860 ἐν τέλει θεός = τελείως θεός　　　862 παννυχίοισι P : corr. Musurus
864 δέρην P　　　865 αἰθέρ' ἐς Musgrave　　　867 ἐμπέζουσα P : corr. p
ἀδοναῖς Elmsley　　　868 sq. φοβερὰν . . . θήραν Nauck : φοβερὰν . . .
θήραμ' P : φοβερὸν . . . θήραμ' Musurus　　　872 δρόμημα P　　　873 μόχθοις
primitus P　　　μόχθοις δ' ὠκυδρόμοις ἀελλὰς Hermann　　　874 παρὰ
ποτάμιον P　　　ἀδομένα Dindorf　　　875 σκιαροκόμοιό τ' ἔρνεσιν Nauck :
σκιαροκόμου θ' ἔρνεσιν P : σκιαροκόμου τ' ἐν ἔρνεσιν Musurus

τῶν ἐχθρῶν κρείσσω κατέχειν;　　880
ὅ τι καλὸν φίλον ἀεί.

— ὁρμᾶται μόλις, ἀλλ' ὅμως　　　[ἀντ.
πιστόν ⟨τι⟩ τὸ θεῖον
σθένος· ἀπευθύνει δὲ βροτῶν
τούς τ' ἀγνωμοσύναν τιμῶν-　　885
τας καὶ μὴ τὰ θεῶν αὔξον-
τας σὺν μαινομένᾳ δόξᾳ.
κρυπτεύουσι δὲ ποικίλως
δαρὸν χρόνου πόδα καὶ
θηρῶσιν τὸν ἄσεπτον. οὐ　　890
γὰρ κρεῖσσόν ποτε τῶν νόμων
γιγνώσκειν χρὴ καὶ μελετᾶν.
κούφα γὰρ δαπάνα νομί-
ζειν ἰσχὺν τόδ' ἔχειν,
ὅ τι ποτ' ἄρα τὸ δαιμόνιον,
τό τ' ἐν χρόνῳ μακρῷ νόμιμον　　895
ἀεὶ φύσει τε πεφυκός.

— τί τὸ σοφόν; ἢ τί τὸ κάλλιον
παρὰ θεῶν γέρας ἐν βροτοῖς
ἢ χεῖρ' ὑπὲρ κορυφᾶς
τῶν ἐχθρῶν κρείσσω κατέχειν;　　900
ὅ τι καλὸν φίλον ἀεί.

— εὐδαίμων μὲν ὃς ἐκ θαλάσσας
ἔφυγε χεῖμα, λιμένα δ' ἔκιχεν·
εὐδαίμων δ' ὃς ὕπερθε μόχθων
ἐγένεθ'· ἑτέρᾳ δ' ἕτερος ἕτερον　　905

880 κρέσω P　　　　883 τι add. Nauck: τό γε θεῖον Musurus
886 ἄζοντας Wecklein, cl. Soph. O. C. 134　　　887 συμμαινομένα ex
σημαινομένα factum in P　　δόξᾳ] δοκᾷ Hermann: δοκοῖ Musgrave,·
cl. El. 747　　890 θηρῶσι P　　892 καὶ καὶ P　　893 γὰρ P, sed
ἀρ in ras.　　894 τόδ' Heath: τ' P　　902 θαλάσσης P　　905 ἑτέρα
(i.e. ἑτέρᾳ) P: ἕτερα Elmsley

ὄλβῳ καὶ δυνάμει παρῆλθεν.
μυρίαι δ' ἔτι μυρίοις
εἰσὶν ἐλπίδες· αἱ μὲν
τελευτῶσιν ἐν ὄλβῳ
βροτοῖς, αἱ δ' ἀπέβησαν·
τὸ δὲ κατ' ἦμαρ ὅτῳ βίοτος   910
εὐδαίμων, μακαρίζω.

Δι.   σὲ τὸν πρόθυμον ὄνθ' ἃ μὴ χρεὼν ὁρᾶν
σπεύδοντά τ' ἀσπούδαστα, Πενθέα λέγω,
ἔξιθι πάροιθε δωμάτων, ὄφθητί μοι,
σκευὴν γυναικὸς μαινάδος βάκχης ἔχων,   915
μητρός τε τῆς σῆς καὶ λόχου κατάσκοπος·
πρέπεις δὲ Κάδμου θυγατέρων μορφὴν μιᾷ.

Πε.   καὶ μὴν ὁρᾶν μοι δύο μὲν ἡλίους δοκῶ,
δισσὰς δὲ Θήβας καὶ πόλισμ' ἑπτάστομον·
καὶ ταῦρος ἡμῖν πρόσθεν ἡγεῖσθαι δοκεῖς   920
καὶ σῷ κέρατα κρατὶ προσπεφυκέναι.
ἀλλ' ἦ ποτ' ἦσθα θήρ; τεταύρωσαι γὰρ οὖν.

Δι.   ὁ θεὸς ὁμαρτεῖ, πρόσθεν ὢν οὐκ εὐμενής,
ἔνσπονδος ἡμῖν· νῦν δ' ὁρᾷς ἃ χρή σ' ὁρᾶν.

Πε.   τί φαίνομαι δῆτ'; οὐχὶ τὴν Ἰνοῦς στάσιν   925
ἢ τὴν Ἀγαύης ἑστάναι, μητρός γ' ἐμῆς;

Δι.   αὐτὰς ἐκείνας εἰσορᾶν δοκῶ σ' ὁρῶν.
ἀλλ' ἐξ ἕδρας σοι πλόκαμος ἐξέστηχ' ὅδε,
οὐχ ὡς ἐγώ νιν ὑπὸ μίτρᾳ καθήρμοσα.

Πε.   ἔνδον προσείων αὐτὸν ἀνασείων τ' ἐγὼ   930
καὶ βακχιάζων ἐξ ἕδρας μεθώρμισα.

Δι.   ἀλλ' αὐτὸν ἡμεῖς, οἷς σε θεραπεύειν μέλει,

907 δ' ἔτι μυρίοις Hartung : μυρίοισιν ἔτ' P   909 αἱ δ' ἐμάτησαν
Stadtmueller   913 σπεύδοντά Musurus : σπένδοντά P   917 μορφὴν
Musgrave : μορφῇ P : μορφῇ δὲ ... πρέπεις μιᾷ Brunck   920 ἡγεῖσθαι
supra suppletum in P   923 notam Dionysi omisit, 924 praescr. P :
corr. Tyrwhitt   923 ὢν p : ὂν P   926 μητρός γ' p : μητρὸς P
929 καθήρμοσα p : καθώρμισα P, fortasse recte, cf. 931   930, 931 in
marg. postmodo additos habet P   932 μέλει p : μέλη P

πάλιν καταστελοῦμεν· ἀλλ' ὄρθου κάρα.

Πε. ἰδού, σὺ κόσμει· σοὶ γὰρ ἀνακείμεσθα δή.

Δι. ζῶναί τέ σοι χαλῶσι κοὐχ ἑξῆς πέπλων   935
στολίδες ὑπὸ σφυροῖσι τείνουσιν σέθεν.

Πε. κἀμοὶ δοκοῦσι παρά γε δεξιὸν πόδα·
τἀνθένδε δ' ὀρθῶς παρὰ τένοντ' ἔχει πέπλος.

Δι. ἦ πού με τῶν σῶν πρῶτον ἡγήσῃ φίλων,
ὅταν παρὰ λόγον σώφρονας βάκχας ἴδῃς.   940

Πε. πότερα δὲ θύρσον δεξιᾷ λαβὼν χερὶ
ἢ τῇδε, βάκχῃ μᾶλλον εἰκασθήσομαι;

Δι. ἐν δεξιᾷ χρὴ χἄμα δεξιῷ ποδὶ
αἴρειν νιν· αἰνῶ δ' ὅτι μεθέστηκας φρενῶν.

Πε. ἀρ' ἂν δυναίμην τὰς Κιθαιρῶνος πτυχὰς   945
αὐταῖσι βάκχαις τοῖς ἐμοῖς ὤμοις φέρειν;

Δι. δύναι' ἄν, εἰ βούλοιο· τὰς δὲ πρὶν φρένας
οὐκ εἶχες ὑγιεῖς, νῦν δ' ἔχεις οἵας σε δεῖ.

Πε. μοχλοὺς φέρωμεν; ἢ χεροῖν ἀνασπάσω
κορυφαῖς ὑποβαλὼν ὦμον ἢ βραχίονα;   950

Δι. μὴ σύ γε τὰ Νυμφῶν διολέσῃς ἱδρύματα
καὶ Πανὸς ἕδρας ἔνθ' ἔχει συρίγματα.

Πε. καλῶς ἔλεξας· οὐ σθένει νικητέον
γυναῖκας· ἐλάταισιν δ' ἐμὸν κρύψω δέμας.

Δι. κρύψῃ σὺ κρύψιν ἥν σε κρυφθῆναι χρεών,   955
ἐλθόντα δόλιον μαινάδων κατάσκοπον.

Πε. καὶ μὴν δοκῶ σφᾶς ἐν λόχμαις ὄρνιθας ὡς
λέκτρων ἔχεσθαι φιλτάτοις ἐν ἕρκεσιν.

Δι. οὐκοῦν ἐπ' αὐτὸ τοῦτ' ἀποστέλλῃ φύλαξ·
λήψῃ δ' ἴσως σφᾶς, ἢν σὺ μὴ ληφθῇς πάρος.   960

---

936 ὑπὸ] ἐπὶ Blass   940 παραλόγον P: παράλογον Porson
941 δεξιᾷ p: δεξιὸν ut vid. P   944 αἴρειν Musurus: αἴρει P
946 αὐτῆσιν ἐλάταις, quod e Bacchis citat Σ Phoen. 3, hic eum legisse
censebat Valckenaer   951 τὰ Stephanus: τᾶν P   952 Πανὸς
Brodeau: καπνὸς P   953 καλῶν primitus P   954 ἐλάταισι
δ' P: fortasse ἐλάταις δ' ἀμὸν ἐγκρύψω   955 κρυφῆναι P: corr.
Musurus

Πε.   κόμιζε διὰ μέσης με Θηβαίας χθονός·
      μόνος γὰρ αὐτῶν εἰμ' ἀνὴρ τολμῶν τόδε.
Δι.   μόνος σὺ πόλεως τῆσδ' ὑπερκάμνεις, μόνος·
      τοιγάρ σ' ἀγῶνες ἀναμένουσιν οὓς ἐχρῆν.
      ἔπου δέ· πομπὸς [δ'] εἰμ' ἐγὼ σωτήριος,   965
      κεῖθεν δ' ἀπάξει σ' ἄλλος.   Πε. ἡ τεκοῦσά γε.
Δι.   ἐπίσημον ὄντα πᾶσιν.   Πε. ἐπὶ τόδ' ἔρχομαι.
Δι.   φερόμενος ἥξεις . . .   Πε. ἁβρότητ' ἐμὴν λέγεις.
Δι.   ἐν χερσὶ μητρός.   Πε. καὶ τρυφᾶν μ' ἀναγκάσεις.
Δι.   τρυφάς γε τοιάσδε.   Πε. ἀξίων μὲν ἅπτομαι.   970

Δι.   δεινὸς σὺ δεινὸς κἀπὶ δείν' ἔρχῃ πάθη,
      ὥστ' οὐρανῷ στηρίζον εὑρήσεις κλέος.
      ἔκτειν', Ἀγαύη, χεῖρας αἵ θ' ὁμόσποροι
      Κάδμου θυγατέρες· τὸν νεανίαν ἄγω
      τόνδ' εἰς ἀγῶνα μέγαν, ὁ νικήσων δ' ἐγὼ   975
      καὶ Βρόμιος ἔσται. τἄλλα δ' αὐτὸ σημανεῖ.

Χο.   —   ἴτε θοαὶ Λύσσας κύνες ἴτ' εἰς ὄρος,   [στρ.
               θίασον ἔνθ' ἔχουσι Κάδμου κόραι,
               ἀνοιστρήσατέ νιν
               ἐπὶ τὸν ἐν γυναικομίμῳ στολᾷ   980
               λυσσώδη κατάσκοπον μαινάδων.
               μάτηρ πρῶτά νιν λευρᾶς ἀπὸ πέτρας
               ἢ σκόλοπος ὄψεται
               δοκεύοντα, μαινάσιν δ' ἀπύσει·
               Τίς ὅδ' ὀρειδρόμων   985
               μαστὴρ Καδμείων ἐς ὄρος ἐς ὄρος ἔμολ'
               ἔμολεν, ὦ βάκχαι; τίς ἄρα νιν ἔτεκεν;

961 χθονός] πόλεως Nauck   962 γὰρ εἰμ' αὐτῶν P : corr. Elmsley
964 οὓς σε χρή Fix   965 δ' seclusi   εἰμ' Musurus   σωτήριος
omissum et postmodo additum in P   977 λύσσης P   981 μαινάδων
κατάσκοπον λυσσώδη P : trai. Bothe   982 νιν πρῶτα Headlam
985 sq. Καδμείων μαστὴρ ὀριοδρόμων P : corr. Nauck   986 εἰς ut
solet P (bis)   ἔμολεν ἔμολεν ὦ P : corr. Elmsley : cf. 1007

οὐ γὰρ ἐξ αἵματος
γυναικῶν ἔφυ, λεαίνας δέ τινος
ὅδ' ἢ Γοργόνων Λιβυσσᾶν γένος.   990

— ἴτω δίκα φανερός, ἴτω ξιφηφόρος
φονεύουσα λαιμῶν διαμπὰξ
τὸν ἄθεον ἄνομον ἄδικον Ἐχίονος   995
γόνον γηγενῆ.

— ὃς ἀδίκῳ γνώμᾳ παρανόμῳ τ' ὀργᾷ   [ἀντ·
περὶ ⟨σά⟩, Βάκχι', ὄργια ματρός τε σᾶς
μανείσᾳ πραπίδι
παρακόπῳ τε λήματι στέλλεται,   1000
τἀνίκατον ὡς κρατήσων βίᾳ,
γνωμᾶν σωφρόνα θάνατος ἀπροφάσιστος ἐς τὰ θεῶν ἔφυ·
βροτείως τ' ἔχειν ἄλυπος βίος.

τὸ σοφὸν οὐ φθονῶ·   1005
χαίρω θηρεύουσα· τὰ δ' ἕτερα μεγάλα
φανερά τ'· ὤ, νάει⟨ν⟩ ἐπὶ τὰ καλὰ βίον,
ἦμαρ ἐς νύκτα τ' εὐ-
αγοῦντ' εὐσεβεῖν, τὰ δ' ἔξω νόμιμα
δίκας ἐκβαλόντα τιμᾶν θεούς.   1010

---

989 sq. ὅδ' ante ἔφυ habet P : ante ἢ trai. Hermann   993 λαιμῶν
Tyrwhitt : δαίμων P   996 γόνον: cf. 1016: idem utrobique
legendum monuit Elmsley   998 σά suppl. Scaliger   ὄργια]
ἱρὰ Mekler: metro satisfaceret περὶ σά, Βάκχε, σᾶς τ' ὄργια ματέρος
999 μανεῖσα P   1001 τἀνίκατον Wilamowitz : τὰν ἀνίκατον P :
cf. 981   1002 γνώμαν σώφρονα P   1002–4 locus paene con-
clamatus: fortasse hoc dicit: 'qui iniuste &c. (v. 997), ei senten-
tiarum castigatrix in rebus divinis indeprecabilis Mors est': de sub-
stantivo σωφρόνη vid. Stephanum s.v.   1003 εἰς P: fortasse περὶ:
cf. stropham   1004 βροτείως] βροτείῳ P   1005 φθόνῳ P
1007 φανερά τ'· ὤ, νάειν ('ah, vitam fluere vel εὔροιαν habere precor,'
cf. H 179) scripsi: φανερὰ τῶν ἀεὶ P : φανέρ' ἄγοντ' ἀεὶ Fix : tum ποτὶ
pro ἐπὶ Sandys   1008 εὖ ἄγουντ' P : corr. Hermann

— ἴτω δίκα φανερός, ἴτω ξιφηφόρος
   φονεύουσα λαιμῶν διαμπὰξ
   τὸν ἄθεον ἄνομον ἄδικον Ἐχίονος   1015
   τόκον γηγενῆ.

— φάνηθι ταῦρος ἢ πολύκρανος ἰδεῖν   [ἐπῳδ.
   δράκων ἢ πυριφλέγων ὁρᾶσθαι λέων.
      ἴθ᾽, ὦ Βάκχε, θηραγρευτᾷ βακχᾶν   1020
   γελῶντι προσώπῳ περίβαλε βρόχον
   θανάσιμον ὑπ᾽ ἀγέλαν πεσόντι τὰν μαινάδων.

ΑΓΓΕΛΟΣ Β

      ὦ δῶμ᾽ ὃ πρίν ποτ᾽ εὐτύχεις ἀν᾽ Ἑλλάδα,
   Σιδωνίου γέροντος, ὃς τὸ γηγενὲς   1025
   δράκοντος ἔσπειρ᾽ Ὄφεος ἐν γαίᾳ θέρος,
   ὥς σε στενάζω, δοῦλος ὢν μέν, ἀλλ᾽ ὅμως
   [χρηστοῖσι δούλοις συμφορὰ τὰ δεσποτῶν].

Χο. τί δ᾽ ἔστιν; ἐκ βακχῶν τι μηνύεις νέον;

Αγ. Πενθεὺς ὄλωλεν, παῖς Ἐχίονος πατρός.   1030

Χο. ὦναξ Βρόμιε, θεὸς φαίνῃ μέγας.

Αγ. πῶς φῄς; τί τοῦτ᾽ ἔλεξας; ἦ ᾽πὶ τοῖς ἐμοῖς
   χαίρεις κακῶς πράσσουσι δεσπόταις, γύναι;

Χο.   εὐάζω ξένα μέλεσι βαρβάροις·

1014 δαίμων P, cf. 993   1019 fortasse δράκων πυριφλέγων θ᾽
1020 θηραγρευτᾷ Dindorf: θηραγρότα P, sed o in ras. (fuerat, ut videtur, ω): θὴρ θηραγρέτᾳ Tyrrell   1021 metro melius conveniret
προσώπῳ γελῶντι   1022 sq. θανάσιμον ὑπ᾽ Bruhn: ἐπὶ θανάσιμον P
πεσόντι Scaliger: πεσόντα P   1024 ΑΓΓΕΛΟΣ] ΘΕΡΑΠΩΝ malit
Wecklein   εὐτυχεῖς P   ἀν᾽ ex ἐν factum in P   1025 ὃς p:
ὥς P   1026 ὄφεος P cum Greg. Cor. 402, Choerob. Cann. i. 194,
Theodos. in Bekk. Anecd. 981. 13: nomen proprium esse vidit
Wilamowitz   1028 del. Dobree: cf. Med. 54   τὰ Medeae
codd.: τῶν P   1029 τί δ᾽ ex τό δ᾽ factum in P   τί μηνύεις P
1031 claudicat metrum: σὺ φαίνῃ Kirchhoff, cl. Chr. Pat. 2100, 2542
(Ἄναξ ἄναξ ἄφθιτε, σὺ θεὸς μέγας): θεὸς θεὸς Hermann: sed suspectum
φαίνῃ   1032 ἦ P

οὐκέτι γὰρ δεσμῶν ὑπὸ φόβῳ πτήσσω. 1035

Αγ. Θήβας δ' ἀνάνδρους ὧδ' ἄγεις . . .

. . . . ;

Χο. ὁ Διόνυσος ὁ Διόνυσος, οὐ Θῆβαι
κράτος ἔχουσ' ἐμόν.

Αγ. συγγνωστὰ μέν σοι, πλὴν ἐπ' ἐξειργασμένοις
κακοῖσι χαίρειν, ὦ γυναῖκες, οὐ καλόν. 1040

Χο. ἔννεπέ μοι, φράσον, τίνι μόρῳ θνῄσκει
ἄδικος ἄδικά τ' ἐκπορίζων ἀνήρ;

Αγ. ἐπεὶ θεράπνας τῆσδε Θηβαίας χθονὸς
λιπόντες ἐξέβημεν Ἀσωποῦ ῥοάς,
λέπας Κιθαιρώνειον εἰσεβάλλομεν 1045
Πενθεύς τε κἀγώ—δεσπότῃ γὰρ εἱπόμην—
ξένος θ' ὃς ἡμῖν πομπὸς ἦν θεωρίας.
πρῶτον μὲν οὖν ποιηρὸν ἵζομεν νάπος,
τά τ' ἐκ ποδῶν σιγηλὰ καὶ γλώσσης ἄπο
σῴζοντες, ὡς ὁρῷμεν οὐχ ὁρώμενοι. 1050
ἦν δ' ἄγκος ἀμφίκρημνον, ὕδασι διάβροχον,
πεύκαισι συσκιάζον, ἔνθα μαινάδες
καθῆντ' ἔχουσαι χεῖρας ἐν τερπνοῖς πόνοις.
αἱ μὲν γὰρ αὐτῶν θύρσον ἐκλελοιπότα
κισσῷ κομήτην αὖθις ἐξανέστεφον, 1055
αἱ δ', ἐκλιποῦσαι ποικίλ' ὡς πῶλοι ζυγά,
βακχεῖον ἀντέκλαζον ἀλλήλαις μέλος.
Πενθεὺς δ' ὁ τλήμων θῆλυν οὐχ ὁρῶν ὄχλον
ἔλεξε τοιάδ'· Ὦ ξέν', οὗ μὲν ἕσταμεν,

1036 hiatum indicaverunt Brunck Seidler   1037 fortasse ὁ
Διόνυσος ὁ διόγονος   1039 notam om., 1040 ἀγγ. praescr. P : corr.
Musurus   1041 τίνι Chr. Pat. 653 : τίνει P   1044 ῥοᾶς P : corr.
Musurus   1048 ποιηρὸν Musurus : πικρὸν P : χλοηρὸν Chr. Pat. 676
1050 ὁρῶμεν P   1051 ἀμφίκρημνον P : ὑψίκρημνον Schol. B. Hephaest.
p. 183 Gaisf. (ἦν δ' ἄγκος ὑψίκρημνον, ὄρεσι περίδρομον) et idem voluit
Anecd. Metr. Chis. p. 26 (ὑψίκομον scriptum)   1053 κάθηντ' P
1055 αὖτις P

οὐκ ἐξικνοῦμαι μαινάδων ὅσσοις νόθων· 1060
ὄχθων δ' ἔπ', ἀμβὰς ἐς ἐλάτην ὑψαύχενα,
ἴδοιμ' ἂν ὀρθῶς μαινάδων αἰσχρουργίαν.

τοὐντεῦθεν ἤδη τοῦ ξένου ⟨τὸ⟩ θαῦμ' ὁρῶ·
λαβὼν γὰρ ἐλάτης οὐράνιον ἄκρον κλάδον
κατῆγεν, ἦγεν, ἦγεν ἐς μέλαν πέδον· 1065
κυκλοῦτο δ' ὥστε τόξον ἢ κυρτὸς τροχὸς
τόρνῳ γραφόμενος περιφορὰν ἕλκει δρόμον·
ὡς κλῶν' ὄρειον ὁ ξένος χεροῖν ἄγων
ἔκαμπτεν ἐς γῆν, ἔργματ' οὐχὶ θνητὰ δρῶν.
Πενθέα δ' ἱδρύσας ἐλατίνων ὄζων ἔπι, 1070
ὀρθὸν μεθίει διὰ χερῶν βλάστημ' ἄνω
ἀτρέμα, φυλάσσων μὴ ἀναχαιτίσειέ νιν,
ὀρθὴ δ' ἐς ὀρθὸν αἰθέρ' ἐστηρίζετο,
ἔχουσα νώτοις δεσπότην ἐφήμενον·
ὤφθη δὲ μᾶλλον ἢ κατεῖδε μαινάδας. 1075
ὅσον γὰρ οὔπω δῆλος ἦν θάσσων ἄνω,
καὶ τὸν ξένον μὲν οὐκέτ' εἰσορᾶν παρῆν,
ἐκ δ' αἰθέρος φωνή τις, ὡς μὲν εἰκάσαι
Διόνυσος, ἀνεβόησεν· Ὦ νεάνιδες,
ἄγω τὸν ὑμᾶς κἀμὲ τἀμά τ' ὄργια 1080
γέλων τιθέμενον· ἀλλὰ τιμωρεῖσθέ νιν.
καὶ ταῦθ' ἅμ' ἠγόρευε καὶ πρὸς οὐρανὸν
καὶ γαῖαν ἐστήριξε φῶς σεμνοῦ πυρός.

σίγησε δ' αἰθήρ, σῖγα δ' ὕλιμος νάπη
φύλλ' εἶχε, θηρῶν δ' οὐκ ἂν ἤκουσας βοήν. 1085
αἱ δ' ὠσὶν ἠχὴν οὐ σαφῶς δεδεγμέναι

1060 ὅσσοις Canter: ὅσοι P   νόθων cf. 224: ὅποι μόθων Musgrave
1061 ὄχθων δ' ἐπ' ἐμβὰς εἰς ἐλάτην P: corr. Bruhn: ὄχθον δ' ἐπεμβὰς ἢ
'λάτην Tyrwhitt   1062 αἰχουργίαν primitus P   1063 τὸ supplevi:
cf. 760, I. T. 320: τι add. p: θαῦμ' εἰσορῶ Dalmeyda   1064 οὐρανίον
an οὐρανίου P incertum   1066 κυκλοῦτο Musurus: κυκλοῦται P
1067 περιφορᾶν P   ἕλκει (mut. in ἕλκη) δρόμον P: ἑλικόδρομον Reiske:
ἑλκεδρόμον Scaliger   1078 φωνήν Reiske   1083 ἐστήριξε Chr.
Pat. 2259: ἐστήριξε P   1084 ὕλιμος Chr. Pat. 2260: εὔλειμος P

ἔστησαν ὀρθαὶ καὶ διήνεγκαν κόρας.
ὁ δ' αὖθις ἐπεκέλευσεν· ὡς δ' ἐγνώρισαν
σαφῆ κελευσμὸν Βακχίου Κάδμου κόραι,
ᾖξαν πελείας ὠκύτητ' οὐχ ἥσσονες   1090
ποδῶν τρέχουσαι συντόνοις δραμήμασι,
μήτηρ Ἀγαύη σύγγονοί θ' ὁμόσποροι
πᾶσαί τε βάκχαι· διὰ δὲ χειμάρρου νάπης
ἀγμῶν τ' ἐπήδων θεοῦ πνοαῖσιν ἐμμανεῖς.
ὡς δ' εἶδον ἐλάτῃ δεσπότην ἐφήμενον,   1095
πρῶτον μὲν αὐτοῦ χερμάδας κραταιβόλους
ἔρριπτον, ἀντίπυργον ἐπιβᾶσαι πέτραν,
ὄζοισί τ' ἐλατίνοισιν ἠκοντίζετο.
ἄλλαι δὲ θύρσους ἵεσαν δι' αἰθέρος
Πενθέως, στόχον δύστηνον· ἀλλ' οὐκ ἤνυτον.   1100
κρεῖσσον γὰρ ὕψος τῆς προθυμίας ἔχων
καθῆσθ' ὁ τλήμων, ἀπορίᾳ λελημμένος.
τέλος δὲ δρυΐνους συγκεραυνοῦσαι κλάδους
ῥίζας ἀνεσπάρασσον ἀσιδήροις μοχλοῖς.
ἐπεὶ δὲ μόχθων τέρματ' οὐκ ἐξήνυτον,   1105
ἔλεξ' Ἀγαύη· Φέρε, περιστᾶσαι κύκλῳ
πτόρθου λάβεσθε, μαινάδες, τὸν ἀμβάτην
θῆρ' ὡς ἕλωμεν, μηδ' ἀπαγγείλῃ θεοῦ
χοροὺς κρυφαίους. αἱ δὲ μυρίαν χέρα
προσέθεσαν ἐλάτῃ κἀξανέσπασαν χθονός·   1110
ὑψοῦ δὲ θάσσων ὑψόθεν χαμαιριφὴς
πίπτει πρὸς οὖδας μυρίοις οἰμώγμασιν

1090 sq. ἥσσονα ποδῶν ἔχουσαι Heath   1091 τρέχουσαι Hartung
ex Chr. Pat. 2015 ποδῶν δράμωσι συντόνοις ὁρμήμασιν (v. l. δρομήμασιν):
ἔχουσαι P   δρομήμασι P   1096 κραταιβόλους Chr. Pat. 667:
κραταβόλους P   1098 τ' Hermann: δ' P   1099 ἄλλαι Brodeau:
ἄλλοι P   1100 στόχον Reiske: τ' ὄχον P   1102 καθῆστο τλῆμον
P: corr. Brunck Musurus   λελημμένος Musgrave: λελησμένος P
1103 δρυΐνοις συντριαινοῦσαι κλάδοις Hartung: lectio dubia   1104 ἀνε-
σπάρασον P   1111 χαμαιριφὴς vel χαμαὶ ῥιφεὶς Chr. Pat. 1430:
χαμαιπετὴς P

Πενθεύς· κακοῦ γὰρ ἐγγὺς ὢν ἐμάνθανεν.

πρώτη δὲ μήτηρ ἦρξεν ἱερέα φόνου
καὶ προσπίτνει νιν· ὃ δὲ μίτραν κόμης ἄπο   1115
ἔρριψεν, ὥς νιν γνωρίσασα μὴ κτάνοι
τλήμων Ἀγαύη, καὶ λέγει, παρηίδος
ψαύων· Ἐγώ τοι, μῆτερ, εἰμί, παῖς σέθεν
Πενθεύς, ὃν ἔτεκες ἐν δόμοις Ἐχίονος·
οἴκτιρε δ᾽ ὦ μῆτέρ με, μηδὲ ταῖς ἐμαῖς   1120
ἁμαρτίαισι παῖδα σὸν κατακτάνῃς.

ἡ δ᾽ ἀφρὸν ἐξιεῖσα καὶ διαστρόφους
κόρας ἑλίσσουσ᾽, οὐ φρονοῦσ᾽ ἃ χρὴ φρονεῖν,
ἐκ Βακχίου κατείχετ᾽, οὐδ᾽ ἔπειθέ νιν.
λαβοῦσα δ᾽ ὠλένης ἀριστερὰν χέρα,   1125
πλευραῖσιν ἀντιβᾶσα τοῦ δυσδαίμονος
ἀπεσπάραξεν ὦμον, οὐχ ὑπὸ σθένους,
ἀλλ᾽ ὁ θεὸς εὐμάρειαν ἐπεδίδου χεροῖν·
Ἰνὼ δὲ τἀπὶ θάτερ᾽ ἐξειργάζετο,
ῥηγνῦσα σάρκας, Αὐτονόη τ᾽ ὄχλος τε πᾶς   1130
ἐπεῖχε βακχῶν· ἦν δὲ πᾶσ᾽ ὁμοῦ βοή,
ὃ μὲν στενάζων ὅσον ἐτύγχαν᾽ ἐμπνέων,
αἳ δ᾽ ἠλάλαζον. ἔφερε δ᾽ ἣ μὲν ὠλένην,
ἣ δ᾽ ἴχνος αὐταῖς ἀρβύλαις· γυμνοῦντο δὲ
πλευραὶ σπαραγμοῖς· πᾶσα δ᾽ ἡματωμένη   1135
χεῖρας διεσφαίριζε σάρκα Πενθέως.

κεῖται δὲ χωρὶς σῶμα, τὸ μὲν ὑπὸ στύφλοις
πέτραις, τὸ δ᾽ ὕλης ἐν βαθυξύλῳ φόβῃ,
οὐ ῥᾴδιον ζήτημα· κρᾶτα δ᾽ ἄθλιον,
ὅπερ λαβοῦσα τυγχάνει μήτηρ χεροῖν,   1140

1114 ἱερέα cf. Or. 261 : ἱερεία P   1115 προσπιτνεῖ P   1116 κτάνῃ P
1124 βακχείου P   1125 ὠλένης Kirchhoff : ὠλέναις P   fortasse
λαβοῦσα χεῖρα δ᾽ ὠλένης ἀριστερὰν vel ἀλλ᾽ ὠλένης λαβοῦσα χεῖρ᾽ ἀριστερὰν   1132 στενάζων Musurus : στυγνάζων P   ἐτύγχανε πλέων
P (πνέων p): corr. Reiske   1133 ἔφερε Duport : ἀνέφερε P
ὠλένην Musurus : ἐλένην P   1136 διεσφέριζε P   1137 στυφλοῖς
(sic) Barnes: τυφλοῖς P   1138 φόβῃ p : φόβους ut vid. P

πήξασ' ἐπ' ἄκρον θύρσον ὡς ὀρεστέρου
φέρει λέοντος διὰ Κιθαιρῶνος μέσου,
λιποῦσ' ἀδελφὰς ἐν χοροῖσι μαινάδων.
χωρεῖ δὲ θήρᾳ δυσπότμῳ γαυρουμένη
τειχέων ἔσω τῶνδ', ἀνακαλοῦσα Βάκχιον   1145
τὸν ξυγκύναγον, τὸν ξυνεργάτην ἄγρας,
τὸν καλλίνικον, ᾧ δάκρυα νικηφορεῖ.
ἐγὼ μὲν οὖν ⟨τῇδ'⟩ ἐκποδὼν τῇ ξυμφορᾷ
ἄπειμ', Ἀγαύην πρὶν μολεῖν πρὸς δώματα.
τὸ σωφρονεῖν δὲ καὶ σέβειν τὰ τῶν θεῶν   1150
κάλλιστον· οἶμαι δ' αὐτὸ καὶ σοφώτατον
θνητοῖσιν εἶναι κτῆμα τοῖσι χρωμένοις.

Χο. — ἀναχορεύσωμεν Βάκχιον,
ἀναβοάσωμεν ξυμφορὰν
τὰν τοῦ δράκοντος Πενθέος ἐκγενέτα·   1155
ὃς τὰν θηλυγενῆ στολὰν
νάρθηκά τε, πιστὸν Ἅιδαν,
ἔλαβεν εὔθυρσον,
ταῦρον προηγητῆρα συμφορᾶς ἔχων.
βάκχαι Καδμεῖαι,   1160
τὸν καλλίνικον κλεινὸν ἐξεπράξατε
ἐς στόνον, ἐς δάκρυα.
καλὸς ἀγών, χέρ' αἵματι στάζουσαν
περιβαλεῖν τέκνου.

1141 πήξασ' Stephanus: πτήξασ' P   1147 ᾧ Reiske: ῇ P: nihil
ad rem Chr. Pat. 1300: ῇ Heath   1148 τῇδ' suppl. Reiske
1151 δ' Chr. Pat. 1146 et Orion Anth. iv. p. 55: γ' P   1152 κτῆμα
Orion: χρῆμα P et Chr. Pat.   1153 Βάκχιον Hermann: βακχείων P
1155 Πενθέος ἐκγενέτα Wilamowitz: ἐκγενέτα πενθέως P   1157 πιστὸν
Ἅιδαν varie tentatus: ἐπιστολάδαν Headlam: ὁπλισμὸν Ἅιδα Wilamowitz   1161 ἐξεπράξατε Scaliger (et Chr. Pat. 1051): ἐξεπράξατο P
1162 ἐς στόνον scripsi, cf. Chr. Pat. 1051 εἰς θρῆνον: εἰς γόνον P: ἐς γόον
Canter   1163 χέρ' αἵματι στάζουσαν Wilamowitz: ἐν αἵματι στάζουσαν
χέρα P (et ἐν αἵμασι Chr. Pat. 1051)   1164 τέκνῳ Kirchhoff

— ἀλλ', εἰσορῶ γὰρ ἐς δόμους ὁρμωμένην   1165
Πενθέως Ἀγαύην μητέρ' ἐν διαστρόφοις
ὄσσοις, δέχεσθε κῶμον εὐίου θεοῦ.

ΑΓΑΥΗ

[στρ.

    Ἀσιάδες βάκχαι—   Χο. τί μ' ὀροθύνεις, ὤ;

Αγ.   φέρομεν ἐξ ὀρέων

    ἕλικα νεότομον ἐπὶ μέλαθρα,   1170

    μακάριον θήραν.

Χο.   ὁρῶ καί σε δέξομαι σύγκωμον.

Αγ.   ἔμαρψα τόνδ' ἄνευ βρόχων

    ⟨λέοντος ἀγροτέρου⟩ νέον ἶνιν·

    ὡς ὁρᾶν πάρα.   1175

Χο.   πόθεν ἐρημίας;

Αγ.   Κιθαιρὼν . . .   Χο. Κιθαιρών;

Αγ.   κατεφόνευσέ νιν.

Χο.   τίς ἁ βαλοῦσα;   Αγ. πρῶτον ἐμὸν τὸ γέρας.

    μάκαιρ' Ἀγαύη κληζόμεθ' ἐν θιάσοις.   1180

Χο.   τίς ἄλλα;   Αγ. τὰ Κάδμου . . .

Χο.   τί Κάδμου;   Αγ. γένεθλα

    μετ' ἐμὲ μετ' ἐμὲ τοῦδ'

    ἔθιγε θηρός· εὐτυχής γ' ἅδ' ἄγρα.

1165 εἰς P: πρὸς Wecklein   δόμους Stephanus: δρόμους P
1167 ὄσσοις P   1168 sqq. *ΑΓΑΥΗ* Musurus: γυνὴ P sed inde a 1251
Agavae nota etiam in P   1168 μ' ὀροθύνεις, ὤ Hermann: με ὀρθεῖς
ὤ P: με θροεῖς τάδ', ὤ vel με θροεῖς, ἰώ Fix   1169 ὀρέων P: ὄρεος
Plut. Crass. 33, Polyaen. vii. 41   1171 μακάριον θήραν Polyaenus:
μακαρίαν θήραν Plut. l. c.: μακάριον θήραμα P et Plut. Mor. 501 C
1174 νέον νιν P: lacunam indicavit Canter: suppl. ex. gr. post
Macnaghten Wecklein: νέον λίν Stephanus   1177 τί Κιθαιρών P:
τί delevi: cf. 1193, item 1181 sq., 1197 sq.   1178 fortasse κατα-
φονεύει   1179 Αγ. πρῶτον Hartung: πρῶτα; Γυν. P (vid. ad 1168),
πρώτα; Αγ. Hermann, cf. 1195 sqq.   ἐμὸν Plut. Crass. 33: ἐμὸν ἐμὸν P
1180 Χο. μάκαιρ' ἀγαύη. Γυν. κληζόμεθ' P (vid. ad 1168): corr. Seidler
Hermann: cf. 1196   1181 verba τίς ἄλλα τὰ κάδμου Agavae continuat P: corr. Heath   γένεθλα γένεθλα P: corr. Heath   1183 Χο.
εὐτυχεῖς τάδ' ἄγρα (τᾆδ' ἄγρᾳ Musurus): corr. Nauck

Χο.   .   .   .   .   .

       .   .   .   .   .

Αγ. μέτεχέ νυν θοίνας.   Χο. τί; μετέχω, τλᾶμον;   [ἀντ.

Αγ.   νέος ὁ μόσχος ἄρ-   1185
     τι γένυν ὑπὸ κόρυθ' ἁπαλότριχα
     κατάκομον θάλλει.

Χο.   πρέπει γ' ὥστε θὴρ ἄγραυλος φόβῃ.

Αγ.   ὁ Βάκχιος κυναγέτας
     σοφὸς σοφῶς ἀνέπηλ' ἐπὶ θῆρα   1190
     τόνδε μαινάδας.

Χο.   ὁ γὰρ ἄναξ ἀγρεύς.

Αγ.   ἐπαινεῖς;   Χο. ἐπαινῶ.

Αγ.   τάχα δὲ Καδμεῖοι . . .   1194

Χο.   καὶ παῖς γε Πενθεὺς . . .   Αγ. ματέρ' ἐπαινέσεται,
     λαβοῦσαν ἄγραν τάνδε λεοντοφυῆ.

Χο.   περισσάν.   Αγ. περισσῶς.

Χο.   ἀγάλλῃ;   Αγ. γέγηθα,
     μεγάλα μεγάλα καὶ
     φανερὰ τᾷδ' ἄγρᾳ κατειργασμένα.

Χο.   δεῖξόν νυν, ὦ τάλαινα, σὴν νικηφόρον   1200
     ἀστοῖσιν ἄγραν ἣν φέρουσ' ἐλήλυθας.

Αγ.   ὦ καλλίπυργον ἄστυ Θηβαίας χθονὸς

post 1183 duos excidisse trimetros censet Wilamowitz   1184 μέτ-
εχε νῦν P   τί μετέχω τλάμων; P: corr. Hartung Wilamowitz
1187 θάλλει Musgrave: βάλλει P   1188 Agavae (sc. Γυναικί) continuat P: corr. Tyrwhitt   πρέπει γὰρ ὥστε θηρὸς ἀγραύλου φόβῳ P:
corr. Kirchhoff (φόβῃ iam Brodeau)   1189 Βακχεῖος P: corr.
Musurus   1190 sq. σοφῶς Brunck: σοφὸς P   ἀνέπηλεν P
θῆρα τόνδε Brodeau: θήρα τόνδε P: θήρᾳ τοῦδε Hermann   1193 τί
δ' ἐπαινῶ; Musurus: cf. 1177   1194 δὲ Καδμεῖοι Musurus: δὲ καὶ
καδμεῖοι P   1195 sqq. Χο. καὶ παῖς . . . Γυ. ἀγάλλῃ. Χο. γέγηθα . . .
κατειργασμένα P: personas secundum strophae rationem disposuerunt
Hermann alii   1195 ματέρα ἐπαινεύσεται P   1196 λεοντοφυᾶ
Dindorf   1197 περισσάν Brodeau: περισσὰς P   1199 τᾷδ'
ἄγρᾳ Nauck: τάδ' ἔργα P: τᾷδε γᾷ Ludv. Dindorf   1200 νῦν P

ναίοντες, ἔλθεθ' ὡς ἴδητε τήνδ' ἄγραν,
Κάδμου θυγατέρες θηρὸς ἣν ἠγρεύσαμεν,
οὐκ ἀγκυλητοῖς Θεσσαλῶν στοχάσμασιν,   1205
οὐ δικτύοισιν, ἀλλὰ λευκοπήχεσι
χειρῶν ἀκμαῖσιν. κᾆτα κομπάζειν χρεὼν
καὶ λογχοποιῶν ὄργανα κτᾶσθαι μάτην;
ἡμεῖς δέ γ' αὐτῇ χειρὶ τόνδε θ' εἵλομεν,
χωρίς τε θηρὸς ἄρθρα διεφορήσαμεν.   1210
   ποῦ μοι πατὴρ ὁ πρέσβυς; ἐλθέτω πέλας.
Πενθεύς τ' ἐμὸς παῖς ποῦ 'στιν; αἰρέσθω λαβὼν
πηκτῶν πρὸς οἴκους κλιμάκων προσαμβάσεις,
ὡς πασσαλεύσῃ κρᾶτα τριγλύφοις τόδε
λέοντος ὃν πάρειμι θηράσασ' ἐγώ.   1215

Κα.   ἕπεσθέ μοι φέροντες ἄθλιον βάρος
Πενθέως, ἕπεσθε, πρόσπολοι, δόμων πάρος,
οὗ σῶμα μοχθῶν μυρίοις ζητήμασιν
φέρω τόδ', εὑρὼν ἐν Κιθαιρῶνος πτυχαῖς
διασπαρακτόν, κοὐδὲν ἐν ταὐτῷ πέδῳ   1220
λαβών, ἐν ὕλῃ κείμενον δυσευρέτῳ.
   ἤκουσα γάρ του θυγατέρων τολμήματα,
ἤδη κατ' ἄστυ τειχέων ἔσω βεβὼς
σὺν τῷ γέροντι Τειρεσίᾳ Βακχῶν πάρα·
πάλιν δὲ κάμψας εἰς ὄρος κομίζομαι   1225
τὸν κατθανόντα παῖδα Μαινάδων ὕπο.
καὶ τὴν μὲν Ἀκτέων' Ἀρισταίῳ ποτὲ
τεκοῦσαν εἶδον Αὐτονόην Ἰνώ θ' ἅμα

1203 ὡς ἴδετε P: corr. Musurus   1205 ἀγκυλητοῖς Nauck:
ἀγκυλώτοις P et Schol. Hec. 1156 (qui etiam στοχίσμασιν praebet)
1209 γ' αὐτῇ Kirchhoff: ταύτῃ P   τόνδε Musurus: τόδε P
1210 χωρὶς σιδήρου τ' Pierson   1212 αἰρέσθω P: ἀράσθω Scaliger
1213 πηκτῶν Barnes: cf. Chr. Pat. 1263 πηκτὰς κλίμακος πρὸς ἐμβάσεις:
πλεκτῶν P   1218 μόχθων Wecklein   1219 Κιθερῶνος P
1223 ἔσω hic P   1224 πάρα Musgrave: πέρι P   1227 ἀκταίων·
ἀριστέω P: cf. 337 (ἀριστέα p)

ἔτ᾽ ἀμφὶ δρυμοὺς οἰστροπλῆγας ἀθλίας,
τὴν δ᾽ εἶπέ τίς μοι δεῦρο βακχείῳ ποδὶ 1230
στείχειν Ἀγαύην, οὐδ᾽ ἄκραντ᾽ ἠκούσαμεν·
λεύσσω γὰρ αὐτήν, ὄψιν οὐκ εὐδαίμονα.

Αγ. πάτερ, μέγιστον κομπάσαι πάρεστί σοι,
πάντων ἀρίστας θυγατέρας σπεῖραι μακρῷ
θνητῶν· ἁπάσας εἶπον, ἐξόχως δ᾽ ἐμέ, 1235
ἣ τὰς παρ᾽ ἱστοῖς ἐκλιποῦσα κερκίδας
ἐς μεῖζον᾽ ἥκω, θῆρας ἀγρεύειν χεροῖν.
φέρω δ᾽ ἐν ὠλέναισιν, ὡς ὁρᾷς, τάδε
λαβοῦσα τἀριστεῖα, σοῖσι πρὸς δόμοις
ὡς ἀγκρεμασθῇ· σὺ δέ, πάτερ, δέξαι χεροῖν· 1240
γαυρούμενος δὲ τοῖς ἐμοῖς ἀγρεύμασιν
κάλει φίλους ἐς δαῖτα· μακάριος γὰρ εἶ,
μακάριος, ἡμῶν τοιάδ᾽ ἐξειργασμένων.

Κα. ὦ πένθος οὐ μετρητὸν οὐδ᾽ οἷόν τ᾽ ἰδεῖν,
φόνον ταλαίναις χερσὶν ἐξειργασμένων. 1245
καλὸν τὸ θῦμα καταβαλοῦσα δαίμοσιν
ἐπὶ δαῖτα Θήβας τάσδε κἀμὲ παρακαλεῖς.
οἴμοι κακῶν μὲν πρῶτα σῶν, ἔπειτ᾽ ἐμῶν·
ὡς ὁ θεὸς ἡμᾶς ἐνδίκως μέν, ἀλλ᾽ ἄγαν,
Βρόμιος ἄναξ ἀπώλεσ᾽ οἰκεῖος γεγώς. 1250

Αγ. ὡς δύσκολον τὸ γῆρας ἀνθρώποις ἔφυ
ἔν τ᾽ ὄμμασι σκυθρωπόν. εἴθε παῖς ἐμὸς
εὔθηρος εἴη, μητρὸς εἰκασθεὶς τρόποις,
ὅτ᾽ ἐν νεανίαισι Θηβαίοις ἅμα
θηρῶν ὀριγνῷτ᾽· ἀλλὰ θεομαχεῖν μόνον 1255
οἷός τ᾽ ἐκεῖνος. νουθετητέος, πάτερ,

1229 δρυμοὺς Bruhn: δρυμοῖς P   1230 τήνδ᾽ P   1232 αὐτήν
Scaliger: αὐτῆς P   1237 μεῖζον Chr. Pat. 163   θῆρας in ras. scr. p
1240 ἀγκρεμασθῇ Hermann: ἂν κρεμασθῇ P   1241 ἐκγαυριῶν coni.
Wecklein: vid. sub fine fabulae frag. 2   ἐμοῖς Musurus: ἐμῆς P
1245 ἐξειργασμένον p   1252 σκυθρωπόν Musurus: σκυθρωπός P
1254 ὅτ᾽ ἐν] ὅπως Wecklein: malim ἄγρᾳ pro ἅμα

σοῦστίν. τίς αὐτὸν δεῦρ' ἂν ὄψιν εἰς ἐμὴν
καλέσειεν, ὡς ἴδη με τὴν εὐδαίμονα;

Κα. φεῦ φεῦ· φρονήσασαι μὲν οἷ' ἐδράσατε
ἀλγήσετ' ἄλγος δεινόν· εἰ δὲ διὰ τέλους   1260
ἐν τῷδ' ἀεὶ μενεῖτ' ἐν ᾧ καθέστατε,
οὐκ εὐτυχοῦσαι δόξετ' οὐχὶ δυστυχεῖν.

Αγ. τί δ' οὐ καλῶς τῶνδ' ἢ τί λυπηρῶς ἔχει;

Κα. πρῶτον μὲν ἐς τόνδ'·αἰθέρ' ὄμμα σὸν μέθες.

Αγ. ἰδού· τί μοι τόνδ' ἐξυπεῖπας εἰσορᾶν;   1265

Κα. ἔθ' αὐτὸς ἤ σοι μεταβολὰς ἔχειν δοκεῖ;

Αγ. λαμπρότερος ἢ πρὶν καὶ·διειπετέστερος.

Κα. τὸ δὲ πτοηθὲν τόδ' ἔτι σῇ ψυχῇ πάρα;

Αγ. οὐκ οἶδα τοὔπος τοῦτο. γίγνομαι δέ πως
ἔννους, μετασταθεῖσα τῶν πάρος φρενῶν.   1270

Κα. κλύοις ἂν οὖν τι κἀποκρίναι' ἂν σαφῶς;

Αγ. ὡς ἐκλέλησμαί γ' ἃ πάρος εἴπομεν, πάτερ.

Κα. ἐς ποῖον ἦλθες οἶκον ὑμεναίων μέτα;

Αγ. Σπαρτῷ μ' ἔδωκας, ὡς λέγουσ', Ἐχίονι.

Κα. τίς οὖν ἐν οἴκοις παῖς ἐγένετο σῷ πόσει;   1275

Αγ. Πενθεύς, ἐμῇ τε καὶ πατρὸς κοινωνίᾳ.

Κα. τίνος πρόσωπον δῆτ' ἐν ἀγκάλαις ἔχεις;

Αγ. λέοντος, ὥς γ' ἔφασκον αἱ θηρώμεναι.

Κα. σκέψαι νυν ὀρθῶς· βραχὺς ὁ μόχθος εἰσιδεῖν.

Αγ. ἔα, τί λεύσσω; τί φέρομαι τόδ' ἐν χεροῖν;   1280

Κα. ἄθρησον αὐτὸ καὶ σαφέστερον μάθε.

Αγ. ὁρῶ μέγιστον ἄλγος ἡ τάλαιν' ἐγώ.

1257 σοῦστίν Kirchhoff: σοί τ' ἐστιν P: σοί τ' ἐστὶ κἀμοὶ μὴ σοφοῖς
χαίρειν κακοῖς. | ποῦ 'στιν; Musurus, ipse, ut vid., interpolator
1267 διιπετέστερος P: corr. Elmsley   1268 τόδέ τι P   1271 σαφῶς
Reiske: σοφῶς P   1272 ἐκλέλησμαι Musurus: ἐλέλησμαι P
1274 ὡς λέγουσ'] ἐς δόμους F. Gu. Schmidt   1276 ἐμῇ Musurus:
ἐμοί P   1277 τίνος p ut videtur: τί μου P   1279 sq. notam
Agavae ante βραχὺς posuit, ante v. 1280 om. P: corr. Musurus
1280 φέρομεν Elmsley   1281 αὐτό] αὖθις (αὖτις solet scr. P)
Reiske

Κα. μῶν σοι λέοντι φαίνεται προσεικέναι;

Αγ. οὔκ, ἀλλὰ Πενθέως ἡ τάλαιν' ἔχω κάρα.

Κα. ὠμωγμένον γε πρόσθεν ἢ σὲ γνωρίσαι.　　　　　1285

Αγ. τίς ἔκτανέν νιν;—πῶς ἐμὰς ἦλθεν χέρας;

Κα. δύστην' ἀλήθει', ὡς ἐν οὐ καιρῷ πάρει.

Αγ. λέγ', ὡς τὸ μέλλον καρδία πήδημ' ἔχει.

Κα. σύ νιν κατέκτας καὶ κασίγνηται σέθεν.

Αγ. ποῦ δ' ὤλετ'; ἦ κατ' οἶκον; ἢ ποίοις τόποις;　　　1290

Κα. οὗπερ πρὶν Ἀκτέωνα διέλαχον κύνες.

Αγ. τί δ' ἐς Κιθαιρῶν' ἦλθε δυσδαίμων ὅδε;

Κα. ἐκερτόμει θεὸν σάς τε βακχείας μολών.

Αγ. ἡμεῖς δ' ἐκεῖσε τίνι τρόπῳ κατήραμεν;

Κα. ἐμάνητε, πᾶσά τ' ἐξεβακχεύθη πόλις.　　　　　1295

Αγ. Διόνυσος ἡμᾶς ὤλεσ', ἄρτι μανθάνω.

Κα. ὕβριν ⟨γ'⟩ ὑβρισθείς· θεὸν γὰρ οὐχ ἡγεῖσθέ νιν.

Αγ. τὸ φίλτατον δὲ σῶμα ποῦ παιδός, πάτερ;

Κα. ἐγὼ μόλις τόδ' ἐξερευνήσας φέρω.

Αγ. ἦ πᾶν ἐν ἄρθροις συγκεκλημένον καλῶς;　　　　1300

. . . .

Αγ. Πενθεῖ δὲ τί μέρος ἀφροσύνης προσῆκ' ἐμῆς;

Κα. ὑμῖν ἐγένεθ' ὅμοιος, οὐ σέβων θεόν.

τοιγὰρ συνῆψε πάντας ἐς μίαν βλάβην,

ὑμᾶς τε τόνδε θ', ὥστε διολέσαι δόμους

κἄμ', ὅστις ἄτεκνος ἀρσένων παίδων γεγὼς　　　　1305

τῆς σῆς τόδ' ἔρνος, ὦ τάλαινα, νηδύος

1283 προσεοικέναι P : corr. Brunck　　　1285 ὠμωγμένον lex. Messan. ed. H. Rabe, N. Mus. Rhen. 47. p. 413: οἰμωγμένον P : ἠμαγμένον Musgrave　　　1286 ἔκτανέ P　　　ἦλθεν Elmsley: ἦλθες P: ἦλθ' ἐς Musurus　　　1289 κασίγνητοι P : corr. Musgrave　　　1290 ἦ κατ' P 1291 ἀκταίωνα P: vid. ad 337　　　1295 ἐμάνη τὲ P　　　1297 γ' suppl. Heath　　　1300 ἦ et συγκεκλημένον P (συγκεκλειμένον p) post 1300 versum Cadmi deesse indicavit Victorius, sed nescio an melius hic sileat Cadmus　　vv. 1298–300 hinc alieni ex iis quae post 1329 perierunt superesse videntur Wilamowitzio : mavult Robert magnam post 1300 lacunam ponere in qua fuerint compositio membrorum Penthei et Agavae in se ipsam accusatio : vide sub fine fabulae

αἴσχιστα καὶ κάκιστα κατθανόνθ' ὁρῶ,
ᾧ δῶμ' ἀνέβλεφ'—ὃς συνεῖχες, ὦ τέκνον,
τοὐμὸν μέλαθρον, παιδὸς ἐξ ἐμῆς γεγώς,
πόλει τε τάρβος ἦσθα· τὸν γέροντα δὲ   1310
οὐδεὶς ὑβρίζειν ἤθελ' εἰσορῶν τὸ σὸν
κάρα· δίκην γὰρ ἀξίαν ἐλάμβανες.
νῦν δ' ἐκ δόμων ἄτιμος ἐκβεβλήσομαι
ὁ Κάδμος ὁ μέγας, ὃς τὸ Θηβαίων γένος
ἔσπειρα κἀξήμησα κάλλιστον θέρος.   1315
ὦ φίλτατ' ἀνδρῶν—καὶ γὰρ οὐκέτ' ὢν ὅμως
τῶν φιλτάτων ἔμοιγ' ἀριθμήσῃ, τέκνον—
οὐκέτι γενείου τοῦδε θιγγάνων χερί,
τὸν μητρὸς αὐδῶν πατέρα προσπτύξῃ, τέκνον,
λέγων· Τίς ἀδικεῖ, τίς σ' ἀτιμάζει, γέρον;   1320
τίς σὴν ταράσσει καρδίαν λυπηρὸς ὤν;
λέγ', ὡς κολάζω τὸν ἀδικοῦντά σ', ὦ πάτερ.
    νῦν δ' ἄθλιος μέν εἰμ' ἐγώ, τλήμων δὲ σύ,
οἰκτρὰ δὲ μήτηρ, τλήμονες δὲ σύγγονοι.
εἰ δ' ἔστιν ὅστις δαιμόνων ὑπερφρονεῖ,   1325
ἐς τοῦδ' ἀθρήσας θάνατον ἡγείσθω θεούς.
Χο. τὸ μὲν σὸν ἀλγῶ, Κάδμε· σὸς δ' ἔχει δίκην
παῖς παιδὸς ἀξίαν μέν, ἀλγεινὴν δὲ σοί.
Αγ. ὦ πάτερ, ὁρᾷς γὰρ τἄμ' ὅσῳ μετεστράφη

·   ·   ·   ·   ·   ·   ·

ΔΙΟΝΥΣΟΣ

·   ·   ·   ·   ·   ·

δράκων γενήσῃ μεταβαλών, δάμαρ τε σὴ   1330

1308 ᾧ P: ὃν suprascr. p   ἀνέβλεπεν P: corr. Elmsley   1312 ἐλάμβανες Hermann: ἐλάμβανεν P: cf. Hdt. i. 115, vii. 39   1317 τέκνον
Reiske: τέκνων P   1318 θιγγάνων Brodeau: θιγγάνω P   1319 προσ-
πτέξῃ primitus P   1320 τίς ἀδικεῖ Barnes: τίς σ' ἀδικεῖ P
1329 Post h. v. lacunam magnam statuit Tyrwhitt: vide sub fin.
fabulae   1330 om. P: suppl. Bredow e Schol. Dion. Per. 391, qui
h. v. cum duobus sequentibus citat

ἐκθηριωθεῖσ' ὄφεος ἀλλάξει τύπον,
ἣν Ἄρεος ἔσχες Ἁρμονίαν θνητὸς γεγώς.
ὄχον δὲ μόσχων, χρησμὸς ὡς λέγει Διός,
ἐλᾷς μετ' ἀλόχου, βαρβάρων ἡγούμενος.
πολλὰς δὲ πέρσεις ἀναρίθμῳ στρατεύματι   1335
πόλεις· ὅταν δὲ Λοξίου χρηστήριον
διαρπάσωσι, νόστον ἄθλιον πάλιν
σχήσουσι· σὲ δ' Ἄρης Ἁρμονίαν τε ῥύσεται
μακάρων τ' ἐς αἶαν σὸν καθιδρύσει βίον.

    ταῦτ' οὐχὶ θνητοῦ πατρὸς ἐκγεγὼς λέγω   1340
Διόνυσος, ἀλλὰ Ζηνός· εἰ δὲ σωφρονεῖν
ἔγνωθ', ὅτ' οὐκ ἠθέλετε, τὸν Διὸς γόνον
εὐδαιμονεῖτ' ἂν σύμμαχον κεκτημένοι.

Κα. Διόνυσε, λισσόμεσθά σ', ἠδικήκαμεν.

Δι. ὄψ' ἐμάθεθ' ἡμᾶς, ὅτε δὲ χρῆν, οὐκ ᾖδετε.   1345

Κα. ἐγνώκαμεν ταῦτ'· ἀλλ' ἐπεξέρχῃ λίαν.

Δι. καὶ γὰρ πρὸς ὑμῶν θεὸς γεγὼς ὑβριζόμην.

Κα. ὀργὰς πρέπει θεοὺς οὐχ ὁμοιοῦσθαι βροτοῖς.

Δι. πάλαι τάδε Ζεὺς οὑμὸς ἐπένευσεν πατήρ.

Αγ. αἰαῖ, δέδοκται, πρέσβυ, τλήμονες φυγαί.   1350

Δι. τί δῆτα μέλλεθ' ἅπερ ἀναγκαίως ἔχει;

Κα. ὦ τέκνον, ὡς ἐς δεινὸν ἤλθομεν κακὸν
⟨πάντες,⟩ σύ θ' ἡ τάλαινα σύγγονοί τε σαί,
ἐγώ θ' ὁ τλήμων· βαρβάρους ἀφίξομαι

1332 ἁρμονίας P : corr. Musurus   1333 ὄχον Musurus : ὄχων P
1334 ἐλᾷς P   1341 σοφρονεῖν P : corr. p   1342 ἔγνωθ' p :
ἄγνωθ' P   1343 εὐδαιμονοῖτ' P : post Musgravium correxi
1344, 1346, 1348 Cadmo tribuit P : Agavae edd. post Elmsleium
1344 λισσόμεθα P   1345 ἐμάθεθ' . . . ᾖδετε Musurus : ἐμέθετ' . . .
εἴδετε P : adfert Elmsleius Bekk. Anecd. p. 98 ᾖδεται (ᾔδετε leg.)·
Εὐριπίδης Βάκχαις   δ' ἐχρῆν P   1347 ὑμῶν Victorius : ἡμῶν P
1349 τάδε Musurus : τάγε P   ἐπένευσεν p : ἐπαίνεσε P   1350 τήλ-
μονες P   1353 πάντες om. P : suppl. Kirchhoff ex Chr. Pat. 1701
(ὦ φίλος, ὡς εἰς δεινὰ φῂς ἐλθεῖν κακὰ πάντας, κἄμ' αὐτὸν συγγόνους τ'
ἄρδην ἐμούς): σύ, θ⟨ύγατερ,⟩ ἡ τάλαινα suppl. Marchant : παῖς τε post
τάλαινα Hermann

γέρων μέτοικος· ἔτι δέ μοι τὸ θέσφατον   1355
ἐς Ἑλλάδ' ἀγαγεῖν μιγάδα βάρβαρον στρατόν.
καὶ τὴν Ἄρεως παῖδ' Ἁρμονίαν, δάμαρτ' ἐμήν,
δράκων δρακαίνης ⟨φύσιν⟩ ἔχουσαν ἀγρίαν
ἄξω 'πὶ βωμοὺς καὶ τάφους Ἑλληνικούς,
ἡγούμενος λόγχαισιν· οὐδὲ παύσομαι   1360
κακῶν ὁ τλήμων, οὐδὲ τὸν καταιβάτην
Ἀχέροντα πλεύσας ἥσυχος γενήσομαι.

Αγ. ὦ πάτερ, ἐγὼ δὲ σοῦ στερεῖσα φεύξομαι.
Κα. τί μ' ἀμφιβάλλεις χερσίν, ὦ τάλαινα παῖ,
    ὄρνις ὅπως κηφῆνα πολιόχρων κύκνος;   1365
Αγ. ποῖ γὰρ τράπωμαι πατρίδος ἐκβεβλημένη;
Κα. οὐκ οἶδα, τέκνον· μικρὸς ἐπίκουρος πατήρ.

Αγ.   χαῖρ', ὦ μέλαθρον, χαῖρ', ὦ πατρία
         πόλις· ἐκλείπω σ' ἐπὶ δυστυχίᾳ
         φυγὰς ἐκ θαλάμων.   1370
Κα.   στεῖχέ νυν, ὦ παῖ, τὸν Ἀρισταίου

      ·   ·   ·   ·

Αγ.   στένομαί σε, πάτερ.   Κα. κἀγὼ ⟨σέ⟩, τέκνον,
         καὶ σὰς ἐδάκρυσα κασιγνήτας.
Αγ.   δεινῶς γὰρ τάνδ' αἰκείαν
         Διόνυσος ἄναξ τοὺς σοὺς ϵἰς   1375
         οἴκους ἔφερεν.
Δι.   καὶ γὰρ ἔπασχον δεινὰ πρὸς ὑμῶν,

1355 ἔτι δέ μοὐστὶ M. Haupt : ἔστι γὰρ τὸ Chr. Pat. 1670   1358 φύσιν
suppl. Musurus : om. P : σχῆμ' suppl. Nauck, cl. Ion. 992, et in fine
ἀγρίας   1363 στερεῖσα Barnes : στερηθεῖσα P   1365 πολιόχρων
Musgrave : πολιόχρως P   κύκνον Heath   1368, 1371, 1374 notas
om. P : add. Musurus   1368 πατρία Elmsley : πατρῴα P
post 1371 lacunam statuit Hermann   1372–92 spurios iudicat
Nauck   1372 στένομαι Elmsley : στέρομαι P   σέ suppl. Barnes
1373 κασιγνήτους P : corr. Barnes   1374 γὰρ] γάρ τοι Hermann :
δεινῶς Brunck (Musuro duce)   αἰκίαν L P : vide Kühner–Blass Gr.
Gr. I. p. 215 : accentum Ionicum dubiṭanter servavi   1376 ἔφερε P
1377 Κα. καὶ γὰρ ἔπασχεν post Bothium Hermann

ἀγέραστον ἔχων ὄνομ' ἐν Θήβαις.

Αγ.   χαῖρε, πάτερ, μοι.   Κα. χαῖρ', ὦ μελέα
θύγατερ. χαλεπῶς ⟨δ'⟩ ἐς τόδ' ἂν ἥκοις.   1380

Αγ.   ἄγετ', ὦ πομποί, με κασιγνήτας
ἵνα συμφυγάδας ληψόμεθ' οἰκτράς.

ἔλθοιμι δ' ὅπου
μήτε Κιθαιρὼν ⟨ἔμ' ἴδοι⟩ μιαρὸς
μήτε Κιθαιρῶν' ὄσσοισιν ἐγώ,   1385
μήθ' ὅθι θύρσου μνῆμ' ἀνάκειται·
Βάκχαις δ' ἄλλαισι μέλοιεν.

Χο.   πολλαὶ μορφαὶ τῶν δαιμονίων,
πολλὰ δ' ἀέλπτως κραίνουσι θεοί·
καὶ τὰ δοκηθέντ' οὐκ ἐτελέσθη,   1390
τῶν δ' ἀδοκήτων πόρον ηὗρε θεός.
τοιόνδ' ἀπέβη τόδε πρᾶγμα.

1378 ἀγέρατον ὄνομ' ἔχων P : corr. Musurus Barnes   1379 πάτερ
Musurus : ὦ πέρ P   1380 δ' add. Reiske   1382 ληψώμεθ' P
1384 ἔμ' ἴδοι suppl. Schoenii monitu Kirchhoff   1387 βάκχαισι P
1388–92 cf. fines Alc. Med. Andr. Hel.   1391 πόρων εὗρε P
Subscr. τέλος εὐριπίδου βακχῶν P

Quod ad lacunam post v. 1329 explendam attinet, cf. Apsinem in
Rhet. Gr. ed. Walz ix. p. 587 παρὰ τῷ Εὐριπίδη τοῦ Πενθέως ἡ μήτηρ
Ἀγαύη, ἀπαλλαγεῖσα τῆς μανίας καὶ γνωρίσασα τὸν παῖδα τὸν ἑαυτῆς
διεσπασμένον, κατηγορεῖ μὲν ἑαυτῆς ἔλεον δὲ κινεῖ: ib. p. 590 τοῦτον
τὸν τρόπον κεκίνηκεν Εὐριπίδης οἶκτον ἐπὶ τῷ Πενθεῖ κινῆσαι βουλόμενος.
ἕκαστον γὰρ αὐτοῦ τῶν μελῶν ἡ μήτηρ ἐν ταῖς χερσὶ κρατοῦσα καθ' ἕκαστον
αὐτῶν οἰκτίζεται. Fragmenta ex Bacchis citata quae hoc loco sedem
habere potuisse videntur haec sunt:

1.   εἰ μὴ γὰρ ἴδιον ἔλαβον ἐς χέρας μύσος
Ex Eur. Bacchis citat Schol. Ar. Plut. 907.

2. Antiatticista in Bekk. Anecd. p. 87 γαυριᾶν· καὶ τοῦτο μέμφονται.
Δημοσθένης περὶ τοῦ Στεφάνου. Εὐριπίδης Βάκχαις: cf. tamen v. 1144,
1241.

3. Id. ib. p. 105 λελάβημαι· ἀντὶ τοῦ εἴλημμαι . . . Εὐριπίδης Βάκχαις:
cf. v. 1102.

Cf. Lucian. Piscator 2 καθάπερ τινὰ Πενθέα ἢ 'Ορφέα
λακιστὸν ἐν πέτραισιν εὑρέσθαι μόρον.

v. huc rettulit Musgrave, parum probabiliter.

Praeterea integro codice Baccharum videntur usi esse et argumenti primi scriptor, cf. vv. 16–18, et quod maioris momenti est Pseudo-Gregorius, *Christi Patientis* scriptor: cuius vv. 1312 sq. Porson, 1466–8 Burges, alios alii et in primis Kirchhoff ex hoc loco repetiverunt: cf. Kirchhoff in Philol. viii. pp. 78 sqq., Hartung, *Eur. Restit.* ii. 556, Bruhn, pp. 127 sq.: habes infra vv. qui maiore cum probabilitate hinc fluxisse videri possunt: uncis inclusi quae certe non Euripidea sunt.

Ex Agavae oratione:

Chr. Pat. 1311 sqq.

> τίς ἐστιν οὗτος ὃν νέκυν χεροῖν ἔχω;
> πῶς καί νιν ἡ δύστηνος εὐλαβουμένη
> πρὸς στέρνα θῶμαι; τίνα ⟨δὲ⟩ θρηνήσω τρόπον
> 1315 καὶ πᾶν (κατασπάσαι με) σὸν μέλος, τέκνον

ib. 1256 sq.

> ὅπως (κατασπάσαιμι) καὶ σύμπαν μέλος,
> κυνοῦσα σάρκας ἅσπερ ἐξεθρεψάμην.

ib. 1466 sqq.

> φέρ', ὦ γεραιέ, κρᾶτα τοῦ (τρισολβίου)
> ὀρθῶς προσαρμόσωμεν, εὔτονον δὲ πᾶν
> σῶμ' ἐξακριβώσωμεν εἰς ὅσον πάρα.
> ὦ φίλτατον πρόσωπον, ὦ νέα γένυς,
> ἰδοὺ καλύπτρα τῇδε σὴν κρύπτω (κάραν·)
> τὰ δ' αἱμόφυρτα καὶ κατηλοκισμένα
> μέλη . . .

ib. 1122 sqq.

> (e.g. ποίοις δὲ πέπλοις κατακαλύψω σοι μέλη;
> τίνες δὲ κηδεύσουσιν, ὦ τέκνον, χέρες;)

Euripides fortasse τρισαθλίου, et σὸν κρύπτω κάρα. Cf. etiam 1504, 1825–9.

Hos vv. ut videtur Agavae, sequentes Dionysi suppeditavit oratio (cf. arg. primum ad finem ἑκάστῳ ἃ συμβήσεται διεσάφησεν) de Pentheo sic locuti:

ib. 1664 ἐς δεσμά τ' ἦλθε καὶ (λόγους ἐμπαιγμάτων)
1663 τοίγαρ τέθνηκεν ὧν ἐχρῆν ἥκισθ' ὕπο.
1667 καὶ ταῦτα μὲν πέπονθεν οὗτος (οὐκ ἄκων)

Cf. etiam 1438, 1440.

(Euripides fortasse λόγων ὑβρίσματα et ἐνδίκως.)

de Thebanis (cf. Hdt. v. 61 ἐξανιστέαται Καδμεῖοι ὑπ' Ἀργείων καὶ τρέπονται ἐς τοὺς Ἐγχελέας)

1668 ἃ δ' αὖ παθεῖν δεῖ λαὸν οὐ κρύψω κακά.
1669 λίπῃ πόλισμα, βαρβάροις εἴκων, (ἄκων)

1678   πόλεις δὲ πολλὰς εἰσαφίκωνται, ζυγὸν
       δούλειον (ἀνέλκοντες) οἱ δυσδαίμονες.
1672   αἰχμαῖς ἀλωτούς, πόλλ' ἀνατλάντας κακά.
  Cf. etiam 1713–16, 1665 sq.

de Agave et sororibus:

1674 sqq. λιπεῖν πόλιν τήνδ', ἀνοσίου μιάσματος
       δίκην τίν(οντας) τῷδ' ὃν ἔκτειναν (φθόνῳ),
       καὶ μηκέτ' (ἰδεῖν) πατρίδ'· οὐ γὰρ εὐσεβὲς
       μένειν φονευτὰς (ἐν τάφοις νεκρουμένων.)
(fortasse τινούσας et ἐσιδεῖν).

de Cadmo:

1689   οὗτος δ' ἃ μέλλει πήματ' ἐκπλήσειν φράσω·
  (fortasse αὐτὸς δ' ἃ μέλλεις) quem versum Bac. 1330 brevi intervallo
excepisse credibile est.

  Cf. etiam 1639–40 fortasse a vv. de Dionyso ipso dictis derivatos

      σαφῶς γὰρ αὐτὸν τοῖσιν ἐξειργασμένοις
      θεὸν νομίζω.

COMMENTARY

Hypotheses

These are prefatory notes, originally prefixed to two different ancient editions of the play. The first is a ὑπόθεσις in the original sense, i.e. a synopsis of the subject-matter, and is presumably the work of some μυθογράφος of Alexandrine or Roman date. Its only interest for us lies in the last sentence (unfortunately corrupt), which summarizes the closing scene of the play; the writer evidently had an unmutilated text of this scene (see 1329 n.). The second hypothesis is an extract from the preface to the *Bacchae* composed by the great Alexandrine scholar Aristophanes of Byzantium (*c.* 257–180 B.C.) for his edition of the plays. On the content of Aristophanes' prefaces, which were all built on the same formal plan, see Page's *Medea*, pp. liii ff. Here Aristophanes disposes of the plot in a sentence, as he commonly does, and then notes that the subject was treated by Aeschylus in his *Pentheus* (cf. Introd., p. xxxi), after which the extract breaks off.

[l. 6. ἄλλως, if right, = 'rashly': the mission was not 'in vain'. But ἀπέστειλεν lacks an object, and οἱ δέ lacks a reference. Neither Elmsley's ἀγγέλους nor Wecklein's δμῶας is convincing: the former does not suit persons charged to make an arrest, the latter is a purely poetic word. Perhaps simply ἄλλους (cf. οἱ δέ, v. 352), in contrast with the agents implied in συλλαβὼν ἔδησεν.]

[l. 16. I suspect that some words have dropped out, an accident to which these hypotheses are for some reason peculiarly liable. Pohlenz proposes ἔργοις ⟨δ' ἔφη τοὺς ἐν γένει νουθετῆσαι⟩, ἵνα μὴ λόγοις, κτλ.: τῶν ἐκτός then = 'people outside the family'. But it may perhaps be used in the Hellenistic sense of 'people outside the religious community'.]

Scene

Outside the Royal Castle on the Cadmeia or acropolis of Thebes. On the stage is a tomb from whose neighbourhood smoke rises (6); over the fence surrounding it vine-shoots may trail (11 f.). The façade of the castle, which forms the back-scene, is in the Doric style, with columns supporting an entablature (591, 1214).

Prologue (1–63)

Like the majority of Eur.'s plays, the *Bacchae* opens with a soliloquy (whereas Sophocles prefers dialogue). Here as elsewhere one purpose of the soliloquy is to situate the action in its context of legendary tradition, by giving its time and place, a summary of the events leading up to it, and the relationships of the principal characters. This technique is not peculiar to Eur.; the opening speeches of the *Trachiniae* and the *Philoctetes* have a similar function. But in Eur.'s hands it had hardened into something like a stage convention (cf. *Frogs* 946), in which dramatic relevance is deliberately subordinated to the need for rapid and lucid exposition of τὰ ἔξω τοῦ δράματος before the action begins.

Both in tone and in substance this prologue resembles Aphrodite's in the *Hippolytus*: each opens with an emphatic assertion of the speaker's divinity (ἥκω Διὸς παῖς ∼ *Hipp.* 1 πολλὴ . . . θεὰ κέκλημαι), shows how that divinity is slighted, and announces a design for obtaining vengeance. But Dion. differs from Aphrodite and the other prologizing gods familiar to Eur.'s audiences in that he will not vanish from the action when his sinister message has been delivered, but will mingle unrecognized, *in human form*, with the actors in the human drama. This point must be 'put across' to every member of the audience: hence it is made not once but three times (4, 53, 54).

1. Ἥκω: a favourite word with supernatural visitants: so *Hec.* 1 (the ghost), *Tro.* 1 (Poseidon), *Ion* 5 (Hermes), *PV.* 284 (Oceanus). Διὸς παῖς . . . Διόνυσος: 'the imperious affirmation of the divine personality rings out like a challenge and a threat' (Méridier). Cf. 27 Διόνυσον . . . Διός, 466 Διόνυσος . . . ὁ τοῦ Διός, 550 f. ὦ Διὸς παῖ Διόνυσε, 859 f. τὸν Διὸς Διόνυσον. Eur. seems to connect the two names etymologically, perhaps taking Διόνυσος to mean 'son of Zeus', as do many moderns. [Several grammarians quote the line with Θηβαίαν, and this is the form which Eur. uses everywhere else: cf. 660, 961, 1043, 1202, *Phoen.* 287, &c. But he may have preferred the gen. here as stressing Dion.'s mission to the *people* of Thebes.]

3. 'With the lightning flame for midwife.'   ἀστραπηφόρῳ (a ἅπαξ λεγόμενον) may be either passive in sense, 'lightning-borne' (from ἀστραπήφορος), or active, 'lightning-carrying' (from ἀστραπηφόρος). For the latter, cf. πανοῦχον φλόγα, 'the torch-holding flame', i.e. the torch-flame, Fr. trag. adesp. 160.

5. πάρειμι (*adsum*) implies previous motion: hence it is regularly used even in prose with εἰς, and occasionally by Eur. with a simple accus. of the goal of motion (*Cycl.* 95, 106, *El.* 1278). Dirce and Ismenus are the rivers of Thebes, the διπόταμος πόλις (Eur. *Supp.* 621, cf. *Her.* 572 f., *Phoen.* 825 ff.).

6–12. Any place (or person) struck by lightning was felt in antiquity to be uncanny, a point where the natural world had been touched by the supernatural. Just as Capaneus became a ἱερὸς νεκρός when the lightning slew him, and must be buried in a place apart (Eur. *Supp.* 934 ff., quoted by Wilamowitz), so the spot of earth which the lightning has marked as its own becomes in Greece an ἐνηλύσιον, in Italy a *bidental*, and is kept taboo, ἄβατον (line 10).[1] Such places were dedicated to Ζεὺς καταιβάτης (*Etym. Magn.* s.v. ἐνηλύσια), and sacrifice was offered at them (Artemidorus 2. 9).[2] Such an ἄβατον existed at Thebes in Eur.'s day and for long after. [It is referred to in a recently discovered Delphic inscription of the third century B.C. (*Delph.* iii. 1, p. 195), where it is called, as here, Semele's σηκός or 'precinct' (properly the precinct of a heru-tomb, Usener, *Rh. Mus.* xxix. 49); and it was still preserved as an ἄβατον and shown to tourists as a holy place in the second century A.D., when Pausanias (9. 12. 3) and Aristides (*Or.* 25. 2, p. 72 Keil) visited Thebes. Both these call it Semele's θάλαμος; from Pausanias' account it was apparently part of 'the old house of Cadmus', of which some ruins survived on the acropolis (Eur.'s δόμων ἐρείπια). The Σεμέλης μνῆμα Paus. found elsewhere, in the Lower Town near the Proetid Gate (9. 16. 7), whereas Eur. puts it close to the new palace of Pentheus, and apparently within the σηκός—the fire is among the ἐρείπια (7 f.) and 'about the tomb of Semele' (596 f.). This may be for dramatic convenience; or the μνῆμα in the Lower Town may be an invention of later guides. In any case Eur. clearly has some knowledge of the Theban cult and cult-places. (On his familiarity with Thebes see J. Mesk, *Wien. Stud.* lv [1937], 54.)]

Semele figures as the Theban bride of Zeus and mother of Dion. in the later stratum of epic tradition, *Il.* 14. 323 ff., Hes. *Theog.* 940 ff. Hesiod says that she bore Dion. ἀθάνατον θνητή· νῦν δ' ἀμφότεροι θεοί εἰσιν. This reverses the historical development. It is probable that she was originally an Anatolian earth goddess (Kretschmer, *Aus der Anomia*, 17 ff., derived her name from the root *ghem*, meaning 'earth', which appears in χαμαί, *humus*, Nova Zembla).[3] When the legends of Dion. were grafted upon Theban tradition she became a mortal princess; but traces of her original exalted status survived both in saga and in cult, and the learned guessed that she was Mother Earth (F. Gr. H. 244 F 131 Jacoby, Diodorus 3. 62). It is as earth goddess that she became the Bride of the Thunderbolt: in southern Europe the thunderstorm is beneficent as well as terrible—the lightning blasts, but the rain quickens the seed in the earth, so that Semele perishes and Dion. is born. But

---

[1] Cf. the parasite who was nicknamed Κεραυνός because he made dinner-parties unapproachable (ἀβάτους) by descending on them (Anaxippus, fr. 3 Kock).

[2] For a full statement and discussion of the evidence see A. B. Cook, *Zeus*, ii. 13 ff.

[3] But her alleged appearance alongside Zeus in a Phrygian inscription is apparently an error: see Calder, *Monumenta Asiae Minoris Antiqua*, vii, p. xxix.

Semele does not stay dead. As Pindar puts it (*Ol.* 2. 25), ζώει
ἀποθανοῖσα: in legend, Dion. brings her back from Hades ([Apollod.]
3. 5. 3, &c.); in ritual, she has at Delphi and elsewhere a periodic
ἄνοδος or ἀναγωγή like that of Kore.[1] In the *Bacchae*, though she is
mortal, she has a place in her son's cult: see 997–1001 n.

7–8. 'And the ruins of her home that smoulder with the yet living flame
of the fire of Zeus.' Murray, I think rightly, follows Hermann in
taking φλόγα as internal accus. with the intransitive middle participle
τυφόμενα. There is no exact parallel, but such bold extensions of
the 'cognate' usage are characteristic of Eur.'s later style: e.g. *Ion*
1238 τίνα φυγὰν πτερόεσσαν . . . πορευθῶ; *Phoen.* 334 στενάζων ἀράς:
ib. 1431 τετρωμένους . . . καιρίους σφαγάς: *Or.* 479 δράκων στίλβει
νοσώδεις ἀστραπάς. [Others follow Paley in putting a comma after
τυφόμενα and taking φλόγα in 'partial' apposition to ἐρείπια τυφόμενα,
but the effect is awkward, as another appositional phrase of a different type follows. The unmetrical[2] τε which the MSS. have after δίου
seems to have been inserted by a scribe to simplify the construction
(as at Aesch. *Supp.* 42, and often). Porson's δίου τ' ἔτι πυρός is open
to the objection that if the fire is actually visible at this point the
effect of its apparition at 596 is spoilt. The same applies to Elmsley's
τυφόμεν' ἁδροῦ τε: moreover ἁδρός is non-tragic (though Soph. has
ἁδρύνειν, fr. 979), and Δίου is supported by 599 Δίου βροντᾶς, *Alc.* 5
Δίου πυρός, and the antithesis with Ἥρας in the next line. Plutarch's
citation of the line, from which ἁδροῦ comes, has evidently been
adapted to its context either by a copyist or by Plutarch himself.]

9. ἀθάνατον . . . ὕβριν: 'the undying outrage', i.e. an undying token of
the outrage. Cf. Eur. *El.* 1261, where μῆνιν similarly stands in
apposition to the sentence in the sense 'an act of wrath'. The sense
of ἀθάνατον is fixed by ἔτι ζῶσαν above and 523 πυρὸς ἐξ ἀθανάτου.
When Semele's chthonic character was forgotten, her blasting by
the lightning was explained by the story that Hera tempted her
to require Zeus to appear to her in his true form ([Apollod.] 3.
4. 3).

11. θυγατρὸς σηκόν: family feeling is characteristic of Cadmus (cf. 181,
334 n.). The vine marks the spot as a Dionysiac holy place; in
another version of the story it is not a vine but a miraculously rapid
growth of ivy (sch. *Phoen.* 651, τῶν Καδμείων βασιλείων κεραυνωθέν-
των κισσὸς περὶ τοὺς κίονας φυεὶς ἐκάλυψεν αὐτόν [sc. Διόνυσον], from
the Alexandrine geographer Mnaseas).

13. λιπών regularly introduces the *starting-point* of a journey (cf. 661),

---

[1] Cf. now Jeanmaire, *Dionysos*, 343 f.

[2] Prato's attempt (*Maia*, ix, 1957) to show that Euripides admitted
anapaests elsewhere than in the first foot of the trimeter does not carry
conviction.

and Dion.'s starting-point was Phrygia and Lydia (55, 86, 234, 462 ff., cf. Introd., p. xx), so we must construe only γύας with λιπών and take the other accusatives with ἐπελθών: θ' in 14 then links πλάκας with τείχη, &c. [*Christus Patiens* 1588 (not 1583) reproduces the line without this θ', and its omission would, as Paley says, 'make the sense plainer to readers of Greek who are not Greeks'; it appears, however, in Strabo's two quotations of the passage.] πολυχρύσους refers to the proverbial wealth of Lydia, and especially to the gold-dust found in the sands of the Pactolus, cf. 154 n., *IA*. 786 αἱ πολύχρυσοι Λυδαί, Archilochus fr. 25 οὔ μοι τὰ Γύγεω τοῦ πολυχρύσου μέλει. [Elmsley's τούς for τάς is universally accepted. But it is a little odd that the same mistake occurs *Hel.* 89, and odder that Strabo twice quotes the present line with τάς, as does Lydus also (*Mag.* 3. 58). Eur. has a liking for unusual forms: did he here use the by-form γύη, attested by Hesychius and *Etym. Magn.* s.v.?]

14. πλάκας: here *upland* plains, plateaux (cf. 307, 718 f., and *Ion* 1267 Παρνασοῦ πλάκες); Persia is high country, as fifth-century Greeks must have known.

15. τείχη: walled towns.   δύσχιμον: either 'bleak', in reference to the climate, which Strabo says is cold (11. 13. 7); or, more generally, 'grim', 'sinister'.

16. Ἀραβίαν εὐδαίμονα: 'rich Arabia', presumably from its wealth of spices (Hdt. 3. 107). The epithet, like the others, is decorative, not distinguishing: there is no contrast with the Arabian desert such as is implied in the later term Arabia Felix. Herodotus saw the Greek Dionysus in the Arabian god Orotalt (3. 8).

17. Ἀσίαν, in the restricted sense of western Asia Minor, as the context shows. Eur. represents it as already colonized by Greeks in the days of Cadmus; tragedy is generally indifferent to this sort of anachronism.

19. καλλιπυργώτους: neologism for καλλιπύργους (*infra* 1202). It is in form a passive verbal adjective, though there is no verb καλλιπυργόω: cf. χρυσοκόλλητος beside χρυσόκολλος, εὐκύκλωτος beside εὔκυκλος, and other examples quoted by Wilamowitz on *Her.* 290.

20-22. With this text we must, I think, translate 'I came to this city of Greeks *first when* (i.e. only when) I had set Asia dancing (χορεύσας causative, as at *Her.* 871) and established there my mysteries, that I might be manifest to mankind as god'. (So Verrall, *Bacchants of Eur.* 32, n. 1, except that he somewhat awkwardly keeps κἀκεῖ [MSS.] as 'even in Asia'.) Dion. explains why he comes so late to his native Thebes: his mission is to all mankind, and he began it among the βάρβαροι, passing then to the mixed populations of the Asiatic coast (18), and last of all to Greece. The common rendering of 20, 'I came to this city first in Greece', (a) leaves the following participles as a weak tail dangling from the sentence, (b) makes 23 a repetition of 20; we might also expect πρώτην (Cobet), though the distinction between adj. and adv. is not invariably maintained. [But even on the view suggested above the balance of the sentence is poor (Kitto, *C.R.* lx [1946], 65), and there is good reason to doubt whether Wilamowitz's τἀκεῖ is the right way out of the difficulty. Keeping κἀκεῖ, one might with Paley suppose a line lost after 22, containing a statement of the god's design for Greece; but I now incline to prefer (with Campbell, *C.Q.* xlix [1956], 56) Pierson's remedy of putting 20 after 22. Paley objected that this brought two tautologous lines together; but the tautology vanishes if at the end of 20 we read χθόνα (*Chr. Pat.*) in place of πόλιν (L P), which could easily have come in by assimilation to the end of 19.[1] The sequence of thought is then natural: 'I converted the eastern lands before coming to Greek soil (τήνδε . . . Ἑλλήνων χθόνα). And on Greek soil my first convert was Thebes.' If this is right, the corruption is an old one; for the author of the *Christus Patiens* would seem to have found the lines in the same order in which they stand in L P.]

23. [τῆσδε should perhaps be τάσδε (Pierson), 'Thebes here'. Murray suggests altering to πρώτην δὲ Θήβην τήνδε (Thebe being the eponymous nymph of Thebes), presumably to provide a personal object for ἀνωλόλυξα: but cf. Eur. *El.* 691 ὀλολύξεται πᾶν δῶμα, *Her.* 1085 ἀν' αὖ βακχεύσει Καδμείων πόλιν. With χροός and χεῖρα the reader naturally, after ἀνωλόλυξα, supplies τῶν γυναικῶν.]

24. ἀνωλόλυξα: 'I stirred to women's cries', roused Thebes to the joy-cry 'ololu' (for the causative force of ἀνα- cf. ἀναβακχεύειν, *Her.* 1085, *Or.* 338). The ὀλολυγή is the *women's* ritual cry of triumph or thanksgiving. [φωνὴ γυναικῶν ἣν ποιοῦνται ἐν τοῖς ἱεροῖς εὐχόμεναι, *Etym. Magn.* s.v., cf. Pollux 1. 28, Eust. on *Od.* 4. 767. ὀλολυγή is first mentioned in connexion with the worship of Athena, *Il.* 6. 301. For its use in orgiastic cults, cf. Menander fr. 326 Kock; in cult of Cybele, Lucian, *Tragodopod.* 30 ff., *Anth. Pal.* 6. 173; of Dionysus, Lucian, *Dion.* 4 αἱ μαινάδες σὺν ὀλολυγῇ ἐνεπήδησαν αὐτοῖς, and the *ululatus* of the Italian bacchanals, Livy 39. 10.]   νεβρίδα: see 111 n.

25. On the thyrsus see 113 n., on the ritual use of ivy 81 n.   κίσσινον βέλος, 'my ivied javelin' (Murray). This is no mere metaphor: the thyrsus is actually used as a missile (762, 1099). Cf. *Ion* 217 where Dion. slays a giant ἀπολέμοισι κισσίνοισι βάκτροις. The thyrsus was formed by inserting a bunch of ivy leaves in the hollow tip of a fennel-rod (176 n., 1054–5 n.). [MSS. have μέλος, but β and μ are notoriously similar in many minuscule hands.]

26. [I should keep ἥκιστ' ἐχρῆν (L P), since it seems pretty clear that

---

[1] One must admit, however, that χθόνα could no less easily be the result of adaptation to the context in the *Chr. Pat.* (V. Longo, *Antiquitas*, i [1946], 43).

Eur. used ἐχρῆν as well as χρῆν. Cf. Platnauer, *C.R.* lvi (1942), 4 f., Harrison, ibid. 6 f., and *infra*, line 964.]

28. νυμφευθεῖσαν: 'made a woman', a euphemism for 'seduced', cf. *Ion* 1371.

29. 'Fathered on Zeus her maidenhood's mischance' (Sandys). For the (unusual) word-order cf. Eur. *El.* 368 αἱ φύσεις βροτῶν, *I A.* 72 ὁ μῦθος Ἀργείων, and Denniston–Page on Aesch. *Ag.* 637.

30. Κάδμου σοφίσμαθ': accus. in apposition to the sentence Σεμέλην ... ἀναφέρειν: Semele's sisters uncharitably thought that the story of her mating with Zeus was invented by Cadmus to screen her lapse from virtue. [The words have sometimes actually been taken as in apposition to ἔφασκον, as if Cadmus were the author of the idea that Semele was seduced by a mortal (so, most surprisingly, Wilamowitz in his translation, followed by Deichgräber, *Hermes* lxx. 327, and apparently by Kitto, *Greek Tragedy*, 375). This is manifestly wrong, as appears from line 10, and still more from 333–6.]

31. ἐξεκαυχῶνθ': 'they published gloatingly' (ἅπ. λεγ.): the term expresses the malicious triumph of the sisters. καυχάομαι and its cognates occur in comedy, but are elsewhere avoided by the tragedians.

32–33. νιν αὐτάς: 'those same sisters': their allegation that Semele was punished brought punishment on themselves.   **ὅρος:** Cithaeron (62), which lies about 8 miles from Thebes. It is still thickly wooded with silver firs (the ἐλάται of 38), whence its modern name Ἐλατί. The summit is rocky.

34. σκευήν ... ὀργίων ἐμῶν: 'the livery of my service'. ὄργια, from same root as ἔργον, are properly 'things done' in a religious sense (cf. ἔρδειν, to sacrifice), the actions of a religious ritual: *H. Dem.* 473 ff. ἡ δέ ... δεῖξε ... δρησμοσύνην θ' ἱερῶν καὶ ἐπέφραδεν ὄργια πᾶσι. Custom restricted the application of the word mainly to the private rites of the mystery cults (see L.S.⁹ s.v.), more especially those of Dion. (ὄργια τὰ μυστήρια, κυρίως δὲ τὰ Διονυσιακά, *Etym. Magn.* 629). The modern sense of 'orgies' derives from the Hellenistic and Roman conception of the nature of Dionysiac religion: it must not be imported into the *Bacchae*.

35–36. With this punctuation ὅσαι γυναῖκες ἦσαν is purely tautologous after πᾶν τὸ θῆλυ σπέρμα, like γυναιξὶ θηλείαις *Or.* 1205. It cannot limit the meaning of τὸ θῆλυ σπέρμα by excluding the unmarried, for παρθένοι are included, 694; nor by excluding children (Musgrave, &c.), for γυνή does not mean a grown woman in contrast with a girl. Tautology can be avoided by putting the comma after σπέρμα (H. von Arnim, Bruhn): Καδμείων ὅσαι γυναῖκες ἦσαν then limits the meaning by excluding slaves. But the repetition may be designed to emphasize the exclusion of men: this is a point of importance in the drama—cf. Pentheus' unjust suspicions, 223, 354, and their refutation, 686. Eur.'s usage, however, favours Arnim: he dislikes a strong pause before the last iambus (Wilamowitz on *Her.* 280).

37. 'With the daughters of Cadmus amongst them': in the Dionysiac worship gentle and simple mix without distinction. Wilamowitz took ἀναμεμειγμέναι to mean 'in disorder', comparing Soph. *El.* 715 ὁμοῦ δὲ πάντες ἀναμεμειγμένοι, which describes drivers 'bunched together' at the start of a chariot race. But 693 θαῦμ' ἰδεῖν εὐκοσμίας is against this, and the Sophocles passage strongly suggests that ὁμοῦ coheres with ἀναμεμειγμέναι (cf. 18 μιγάσιν ὁμοῦ), instead of governing παισίν as on Wilamowitz's view it must do.

38. ἀνορόφοις πέτραις : in contrast with overhanging rocks or caves (Philoctetes' cave is called a πέτρα, Soph. *Phil.* 16, 272: cf. also *Il.* 4. 107). For the local dat. cf. Eur. *El.* 315 θρόνῳ κάθηται: it is quite needless to alter to accusatives (Elmsley, Bruhn).

40. ἀτέλεστον οὖσαν : best taken as equivalent to an object clause after ἐκμαθεῖν, 'this town must learn its lesson to the end (ἐκ-), that it has still to gain the blessing of my worship'. Elmsley and Bruhn, objecting that Thebes knows this already, would take the participle as causal and understand τὰ ἐμὰ βακχεύματα as obj. of ἐκμαθεῖν: but this is less natural. The god implies that the Thebans must learn to the full, *suo cum malo*, what it means to neglect something profound and holy.

43–44. Κάδμος μέν prepares us for a Πενθεὺς δέ, which is, however, replaced by ὅς (45).   οὖν, resumptive, bringing us back to the past after lines 39–42 which hint at the future.   δίδωσι: 'has given', cf. 213 n.

45. θεομαχεῖ τὰ κατ' ἐμέ : 'opens war on deity in my person'. The rather rare verb θεομαχεῖν is twice again used (325, 1255) of Pentheus' hopeless struggle against Dion. It has the same implication of a hopeless resistance to overwhelming power at *I A.* 1408 τὸ θεομαχεῖν γὰρ ἀπολιποῦσ', ὅ σου κρατεῖ, | ἐξελογίσω τὰ χρηστὰ τἀναγκαῖά τε, and Menander fr. 187 Kock, while at Xen. *Oec.* 16. 3 it is used of a futile struggle against nature. The author of *Acts* may have had echoes of the *Bacchae* in his head when he wrote εἰ δὲ ἐκ Θεοῦ ἐστιν, οὐ δυνήσεσθε καταλῦσαι αὐτούς· μήποτε καὶ θεομάχοι εὑρεθῆτε (5. 39): he had probably read the play (see on 443–8 and 795).[1]

49. τἀνθένδε, used by a sort of attraction for τὰ ἐνθάδε, under the influence of the associated idea of motion which is already implied in ἐς ἄλλην χθόνα. The idiom is common even in prose, e.g. Plato, *Apol.* 40 C μεταβολὴ καὶ μετοίκησις τοῦ τόπου τοῦ ἐνθένδε εἰς ἄλλον τόπον (Kühner–Gerth i, § 448, n. 1).—According to 'Apollodorus'

---

[1] The history of the word and the idea has been traced by J. C. Kamerbeek, 'On the conception of θεομάχος in relation to Greek Tragedy', *Mnemos.* 1948, 271 ff.

(3. 5. 2), Dion. went on from Thebes to Argos, where he was again opposed and again cursed the women with madness.

52. ξυνάψω, sc. μάχην (as Hdt. 4. 80, Ar. *Ach.* 686), 'I shall engage them'. μαινάσι with στρατηλατῶν (cf. Eur. *El.* 321, 917): like ἡγεῖσθαι and other verbs of leadership, στρατηλατεῖν is used either with the gen. (stressing the office) or with the dat. (stressing the physical act of leading).— Pentheus does not in fact attempt to recover the women by force, though he is on the point of doing so (784, 809, 845); so that the god's threat is never carried out. Bruhn saw evidence here that Eur. left the play unrevised at his death, arguing that when he wrote the prologue he intended to follow a version which involved a fight, but later changed his mind. Such a version appears in fourth-century vase-paintings, and may be older (see Introd., p. xxxv). But Bruhn's inference is unjustified. It is an old trick of Eur. to reserve a surprise for his audience by using a little judicious *suggestio falsi* in the prologue (Dalmeyda, *R.E.G.* xxviii [1915], 43 ff.; Zielinski, *Tragodoumena* Lib. I). [Thus *Ion* 71 f. suggests a course of events which is quite different from the course they take in the play but may correspond to the version followed in the *Creusa* of Sophocles. A similar device appears to be used in the prologues of the *Hipp.* (where I believe line 42 to be sound) and the *Medea* (where again line 42 is, I think, genuine in substance, though the passage seems to have been garbled by actors). So too in the prologue to the *Suppliants* (25 f.) Eur. carefully keeps open the question whether the settlement with the Argives will be achieved by persuasion, as in the *Eleusinians* of Aeschylus, or by force of arms. The point is interesting, since it shows that the element of surprise had more importance in Greek stage-craft than modern critics usually allow.]

53–54. Hermann found the tautology 'putida'. Sandys offers the triple defence that μετέβαλον εἰς clears up the ambiguity of ἀλλάξας (which can mean 'change to' or 'change from', like Lat. *muto*); that ἀνδρός makes more precise the vague θνητόν; and that this 'parallelism of sense' at the end of the monologue has the same rhetorical effectiveness as the 'parallelism of sound' at the end of Shakespeare's speeches, which often close with a rhyming couplet. But there is also a good practical reason for the repetition, in the necessity of making it quite clear to the audience that the speaker, whom they accept as a god, will be accepted as a man by the people on the stage. [This motive might of course have led an actor to interpolate the lines, as Bernhardy thought; and the rather clumsy repetition of ὧν οὕνεκ' from 47, where it is more clearly appropriate, lends some colour to his suspicion, though it is hardly decisive. Hermann tried to palliate the tautology by reading ἐγώ for ἔχω and omitting τ', Bothe by reading θεῖον for θνητόν: but these half-measures do not convince. θνητόν is supported by *Chr. Pat.* 1512 ὧν οὕνεκ' εἶδος προσλαβὼν θνητὸν φέρεις.] **ἀλλάξας ἔχω:** the so-called 'schema Sophocleum', common also in Eur., originally developed from phrases like λαβὼν ἔχω 'I have taken and keep', but in Herodotus and tragedy often practically equivalent to an English perfect (Goodwin, *M. and T.*, § 47).

55–61. The god addresses himself to the Chorus. They give no sign of having heard his words, and probably they are not meant to hear them, for ἐμά (59) comes too near giving away his identity; but they may nevertheless, as if in response to his will, begin at this point to file into the orchestra through one of the side passages (πάροδοι). The device of making the prologist introduce the Chorus to the audience is characteristic Euripidean technique: cf. *Cycl.* 36 ff., *Hipp.* 54 ff., *Supp.* 8 ff., *IT.* 63 f., *Or.* 132. Eur. usually takes this or some other opportunity to motive his Chorus's presence: e.g. in his *Philoctetes* he made the Chorus of Lemnians begin with an apology for not having called on Philoctetes sooner, whereas in Aeschylus' play on the same subject no explanations were offered (Dio Chrys. 52. 7).

55. Τμῶλον: Mount Tmolus (mod. Musa Dagh), the great ridge which forms the backbone of Lydia and dominates Sardis (463) and the basins of the Hermus and the Cayster. It is a holy mountain (65, Aesch. *Pers.* 49), i.e. the Lydian bacchants practised their ὀρειβασία on its heights, as do the bacchants in Nonnus (40. 273); it is in this sense that *H. Orph.* 49. 6 calls it καλὸν Λυδοῖσι θόασμα. Its lower slopes were famous for their vineyards (Virg. *Georg.* 2. 98, Ov. *Met.* 6. 15).

56–57. θίασος ἐμός, γυναῖκες: 'my sisterhood of worshippers'. θίασος is a word of quite uncertain etymology, perhaps pre-Greek. It could be applied to any religious confraternity which existed for the purpose of private as distinct from civic worship (e.g. there were θιασῶται of Aphrodite at the Peiraeus); but it describes especially the characteristic unit of organization of Dionysiac religion, cf. 680 n. **παρέδρους καὶ ξυνεμπόρους:** 'comrades in rest and march' (Sandys).

58. πόλει, here not in the literal but in the social sense, and so = 'country'; Eur. applies the term to Euboea (*Ion* 294) and even to the Peloponnese (fr. 730).

59. τύμπανα: 'tambourines' or 'kettledrums'. The τύμπανον consisted of a wooden hoop covered on one side with hide (124 βυρσότονον κύκλωμα); sometimes it had pairs of small cymbals fastened round the rim, like the 'jingles' on a modern tambourine. It is, with the flute, the characteristic instrument of the orgiastic cults (on the reason for this see A. E. Crawley, *Dress, Drink and Drums*, 248 ff.); hence it is 'the invention of Dionysus and Rhea (= Cybele)': cf. 120–34 n. [Similarly in fr. 586 Eur. speaks of Dion. ὃς ἀν' Ἴδαν |

τέρπεται σὺν ματρὶ φίλᾳ | τυμπάνων ἐπ' ἰαχαῖς. For its use in the cult of the 'Great Mother' cf. Pindar fr. 61 σεμνᾷ μὲν κατάρχει | ματέρι πὰρ μεγάλᾳ ῥόμβοι τυπάνων, Diog. Ath. Trag. fr. 1, Catull. 63. 10; in the related Thracian cult of Cotyto, Aesch. fr. 57, where its music is compared to the rumbling of an earthquake; in the cult of Sabazius at Athens, Dem. *de cor.* 284; in various orgiastic women's rites at Athens, Ar. *Lys.* 1-3, 388. The tympanum seems to have had no place in the official Athenian worship of Dion., which was not orgiastic. In Attic vase-paintings of maenads it becomes common only with the vogue of oriental cults at Athens late in the fifth century, and it is always associated with the wilder sort of dances (Frickenhaus, *Lenäenvasen,* 16; L. B. Lawler in *Memoirs Amer. Acad. Rome,* vi [1927], 107 f.).]

[Where the metre requires it, a short final syllable is lengthened in tragedy before initial ῥ (which was originally a double sound), e.g. Aesch. *PV.* 1023 μέγα ῥάκος; and it is quite possible that here Eur. wrote not τύμπᾰνᾰ ῥ- but τύπᾰνᾱ ῥ- (cf. *Hel.* 1347 and Housman in *P. Oxy.* vol. xiii, p. 43). There are, however, instances in tragedy of a vowel remaining short before initial ῥ-, e.g. *PV.* 713 and 992, *Ba.* 128 (lyr.) and 1338 (where see note).]

61. ὡς ὁρᾷ: final subjunctive, 'that the people of Cadmus may come and see'.

Parodos (64-169)

This falls into three parts. (1) 64-71 are a prelude (προοίμιον), which announces the following hymn and links it to the prologue but is not itself part of the hymn: hence it is quite properly astrophic (cf. *Med.* 131 ff., *Hel.* 164 ff.), and strophic correspondence should not be forced upon it by altering the text. It is sung as the Chorus enter the orchestra, and thus constitutes the πάροδος in the narrower sense of the term. Murray divides it between two solo voices, but there is no proof of this. (2) 72-134, two pairs of strophes, forming the body of the hymn. (3) 135-69, a long epode, so long that it may almost be considered a second hymn without strophic correspondence. As Kranz notes (*Stasimon,* 240), such lengthy epodes are characteristic of Eur.'s last period (cf. e.g. *IA.* 277 ff., 773 ff.).

Both in form and in content the ode seems to be fairly closely modelled on an actual cult hymn (K. Deichgräber, *Hermes,* lxx. 323 ff.). This is a return to the oldest dramatic practice: cf. the statement attributed to Aristotle (Them. *Or.* 16. 316 D) that τὸ μὲν πρῶτον ὁ χορὸς εἰσιὼν ᾖδεν εἰς τοὺς θεούς, and Prof. E. Fraenkel in *Philologus,* lxxxvi. 3 ff. The Chorus themselves emphasize the point: they use a formula which must be designed to give the illusion of a religious procession (68-70), and announce that they are about to sing 'the traditional things in honour of Dionysus' (71). The hymn

is written mainly in a traditional cult metre (see below); it opens
with a traditional 'beatitude' (72–75 n.); it introduces ritual cries like
ἴτε βάκχαι, ἴτε βάκχαι (83, 152) and εἰς ὄρος, εἰς ὄρος (116, 165); and
there is a marked tendency to end on a *nomen sacrum*—71 Διόνυσον
ὑμνήσω, 82 Διόνυσον θεραπεύει, 87 τὸν Βρόμιον, 119 Διονύσῳ, 134
Διόνυσος. In content, it presents, as Zielinski has said (*Neue Jahrb.*
1902, p. 646), the three essential elements of all religions—dogma
(στρ. α΄), myth (ἀντ. α΄, ἀντ. β΄), and ritual (στρ. β΄, epode). In keeping
with the eastern origin of the singers, the song has a vividly oriental
colouring. Asiatic associations are repeatedly stressed (64 f., 86,
127, 140, 144, 154, 159); the cult of Dion. is linked with those of Cybele
(78–79 n.) and the Cretan Zeus (120–34 n.); the myths are primitive
and barbarous; the ritual described is not Athenian, perhaps in
some of its details not Greek (Introd., p. xxii); and the singers
accompany their words with the wild eastern music of the kettledrum (58, 124). There is no reference to the Eleusinian Mysteries,
as Sandys and others have imagined.

Metre

προοίμιον and **στρ.+ἀντ. α΄**: ionics *a minore*. This is the characteristic
metre of the *Bacchae*. Its use was doubtless traditional for Dionysiac
plays, since it is proper to Dionysiac cult-hymns: it appears in the
refrain of Philodamos' Delphic hymn to Dion., and in the Iacchos-
hymn of the *Frogs* (324 ff.). The standard line consists of two μέτρα
(65 and 69 have three), either

(a) 'straight' form, ∪∪ − − | ∪∪ − − (Hor. *Odes* 3. 12 is composed
    entirely in this form),

or (b) 'anaclastic' or broken form (anacreontics), ∪∪ − ∪ | − ∪ − − .

(b) yields a swifter and more emotional rhythm than (a). Both
forms are illustrated by Kipling's line:
∪   ∪ ∠   −   ∪   ∪ ∠   −   ∪   ∪ − ∪ − ∪ − ⨉
And the sunshine | and the palmtrees | and the tinkly | temple bells .
    Variations include (1) 'catalexis', suppressing the last syllable of
the second μέτρον and occasionally of the first (64 = ∪∪ − ⨉ |
∪∪ − ⨉); (2) 'syncopation', suppressing a short syllable within the
μέτρον (71 = ∪∪ − ∪ | − · − −); (3) 'resolution' of either long into
two shorts (79 = ∪∪∪∪ − | ∪∪ − −); (4) the reverse substitution
of a long for two shorts (81 = − − − | ∪∪ − −).
[It is by no means certain that the opening lines of στρ.+ἀντ. α΄ *are*
pure ionics. To make them scan as such Murray has to treat the
opening syllable ὧ (= ὅν) as *extra metrum*, and the final syllable of 74
(= 90) does not fit into the scheme. Schroeder and Wilamowitz
arrange 72–77 = 88–93 like 105–10, as choriambus+∪ − − or ∪ − − −

A. M. Dale (*The Lyric Metres of Greek Drama*, 121 f.) analyses them, I think more naturally, as a mixture of ionic and aeolic lines.

στρ. + ἀντ. β′. In 105–10 = 120–5 the first element is a choriambus – ◡ ◡ – (resolved in 107 = 122 into ◡◡ ◡ ◡ ◡◡); the second is either an iambic μέτρον (109 = 124, with the last long resolved) or a bacchius ◡ – – (perhaps equivalent to a syncopated iambic μέτρον ◡ – · –). In the remainder, ionics (113–14) are mixed with glyconics (see on stasimon 1, 402 ff., which for the beginner forms a better introduction to this metre) and dactyls. The last-named describe the rush of the dancers to the mountains (116–17); and in general the excited and swiftly changing rhythms seem to reflect, as Deich-gräber observes, the Dionysiac unrest.

Scheme:

105, 120	– ◡ ◡ – ◡ – –	chor. + ba.
	– ◡ ◡ – ◡ – –	chor. + ba.
	◡◡ ◡ ◡ ◡◡ ◡ – –	chor. + ba.
	– ◡ ◡ ◡◡ ◡ – –	chor. + ba.
	– ◡ ◡ – ◡ – ◡ ◡◡	chor. + iamb.
110, 125	– ◡ ◡ – ◡ – –	chor. + ba.
	– – – ◡ ◡ – ◡ –	glyc.
	◡◡ ◡ – ◡ ◡ – ◡ ◡ –	? glyc. with trisyllabic close.
	– – – ◡ ◡ – – ◡ ◡ – –	3 ion.
	◡ ◡ – – ◡ ◡ – – ◡ ◡ – –	3 ion.
115, 130	◡◡ ◡ – ◡ ◡ – ◡ ◡ –	? glyc. with trisyllabic close.
	– ◡ ◡ – ◡ ◡ – ◡ ◡ – ⋏	4 dact.
	– ◡ ◡ – ◡ ◡	2 dact.
	◡ – – ◡ ◡ – ◡ –	glyc.
	– – – ◡ ◡ – –	pher.

ἐπῳδή. Metrically difficult. The rhythm of the opening lines is so uncertain (see separate notes) that the beginner had better not trouble with it. 144–53 are arranged by Murray as straight ionics (catalēxis 145, 151; syncopation 148–9; ὦ *extra metrum*, 152). Then glyconic rhythms (154–6) lead over to the final breathless gallop of paeons (– ◡ ◡ ◡) and dactyls in which the rush of the maenads is described.

Scheme:

135	– ◡ ◡ ◡◡ ◡ ◡◡ – ◡ ◡ – ◡ –	? 2 dochm.
	– ◡ – ◡◡ ◡ –	? 2 cretics.
	◡ ◡◡ – ◡ ◡◡ – ◡ ◡ – – –	? 2 dochm.
	– ◡ ◡ ◡ – ◡ ◡ – ◡ ◡ – ◡ ◡	5 dact.

140 ⏕⏑⏑ ⏕⏑⏑ –⏑⏑ –– –⏑⏑ – ⋌   ? 6 dact.
     ––   ? exclam. *extra metrum*

–⏑⏑ –⏑⏑ –– ⏓⏓ –⏑⏑ ––   6 dact.
           –⏑⏔   ? cretic (anceps).
            ⏑⏑–– ⏑⏑––   2 ion.

145   ⏑⏑–– ⏑⏑– ⋌   2 ion.
        ––– ⏑⏑––   2 ion.
        ––– ⏑⏑––   2 ion.
        ·⏑–– ·⏑––   2 ion.
        ·⏑–– ⏑⏑––   2 ion.
        ·⏑–– ⏑⏑––   2 ion.

150   ⏑⏑–⏕ ⏑⏑–– ⏑⏑––   3 ion.
    ⏑⏑–– ⏑⏑–⏕ ⏑⏑– ⋌   3 ion.
        – ⏑⏑––   adoneus.
         ⏑⏑––   ion.
       –– –⏑⏑– ⏑–   glyc.

155   –⏑⏑– ⏑⏑––   chor.+ion. (or pher.)

       ⏕⏑ –⏑⏑– ⏑–   glyc.
   –⏑⏑⏑ –⏑⏑⏑ –⏑⏑ –⏑⏑   2 pae.+2 dact.
   –⏑⏑ –⏑⏑ –⏑⏑ –⏑⏑   4 dact.

160   –⏑⏑⏑ –⏑⏑⏑   2 pae.
   ⏕⏑⏕⏑ –⏑⏑⏑ –⏑⏑⏑   tr.+2 pae.

165 –⏑⏑ –⏑⏑ –⏑⏑ –⏑⏑   4 dact.
   –⏑⏑ –⏑⏑ –⏑⏑ –⏑⏑   4 dact.
–⏑⏑ –⏑⏑ –⏑⏑ –– –⏑⏑ ––   6 dact.

65–67. 'I am swift in my sweet labours for the Roaring God, work that is love's work, crying "euhoi" to the Lord of Bacchanals.' **πόνον** internal accus. with θοάζω. That the humblest or most toilsome work, when performed in God's service, is transfigured by the blessing which rests upon it, is a standing paradox of the religious consciousness: so Ion sweeping the temple steps sings κλεινὸς δ' ὁ πόνος μοι | θεοῖσι δούλαν χέρ' ἔχειν | οὐ θνατοῖς, ἀλλ' ἀθανάτοις· | εὐφάμους δὲ πόνους | μοχθεῖν οὐκ ἀποκάμνω (*Ion* 131 ff.), and cf. the phrase of the English Prayer-book, 'whose service is perfect freedom' (Silenus, of course, feels otherwise, *Cycl.* 1.) But perhaps there is in addition a hint here of the easy power which is the especial gift of Dion. (cf. 194 n.). **Βρόμιος**, from √βρέμω, a very common title of Dion. in poetry. Diod. (4. 5. 1) explains it ἀπὸ τοῦ κατὰ τὴν γένεσιν αὐτοῦ γενομένου βρόμου (thunder). But Dion. is himself a 'Roarer', as bull-god, lion-god, earthquake-god (hence he is ἐρίβρομος *H. Hymn* 7. 56, etc., ἐριβόας Pind. fr. 63. 10); and his kettledrums roar too (156, *Anth. Pal.* 6. 165. 5). **Βάκχιος**, adj.

of Βάκχος, and commoner in our play than Βάκχος as a title of the god.

68-70. Those who are in the street (ὁδῷ) are to make way for the procession (ἔκτοπος ἔστω); *all*, including those indoors (μελάθροις), are to 'hush their tongues to reverence', lit. 'let every man make himself completely (ἐξ-) holy in respect of a mouth that speaks no unlucky word (εὔφημον predicative)'. This is the customary prelude to a ritual act (religious procession, Eur. fr. 773. 66 ff., Aesch. *Eum.* 1035; offering of χοαί, Eur. *IT.* 123; sacrifice, Ar. *Ach.* 239 ff.; Dionysiac dance, Semos *ap.* Athen. 622 B–C); Aristophanes parodies it, *Frogs* 354 ff., εὐφημεῖν χρὴ κἀξίστασθαι τοῖς ἡμετέροισι χοροῖσιν, κτλ. [Elmsley suggested punctuating τίς ὁδῷ τίς ὁδῷ; τίς; μελάθροις ἔκτοπος ἔστω ('let him be withdrawn in his house'), and several edd. adopt this. It no doubt makes the sequence of question and injunction more logical. But (*a*) the third τίς standing by itself seems to me unlikely after the reduplicated ritual cry; (*b*) the citizens are not prohibited from *watching*, as this reading would suggest—they are meant to watch (61).[1]—The proposal to write τὶς is not, I think, justified by the passages quoted in Murray's critical note (cf. Jebb on *Trach.* 865, Gildersleeve on *Pyth.* 10. 4).]

71. αἰεί with νομισθέντα: cf. 201. [Διόνυσον ὑμνήσω (two ionic μέτρα with anaclasis and syncopation) presents no metrical difficulty except on the mistaken theory that it must correspond to 67 -χιον εὐαζομένα.]

72-75. 'O blessed is he who, by happy favour knowing the sacraments of the gods, leads the life of holy service and is inwardly a member of God's company.' Such formulas of beatitude are traditional in Greek poetry (cf. B. Snell, *Hermes*, lxvi [1931], 75), e.g. Alcman, *Maidensong*, 2 ὁ δ' ὄλβιος ὅστις εὔφρων | ἁμέραν διαπλέκει | ἄκλαυτος. But they have a deeper meaning in the language of the mystery cults: thus the *Hymn to Demeter* says of the Eleusinian Mysteries ὄλβιος ὃς τάδ' ὄπωπεν ἐπιχθονίων ἀνθρώπων (480); Pindar (fr. 121 Bowra) ὄλβιος ὅστις ἰδὼν κεῖν' εἶσ' ὑπὸ χθόν'· | οἶδε μὲν βίου τελευτάν, | οἶδεν δὲ διόσδοτον ἀρχάν: Sophocles (fr. 837 Pearson) ὡς τρισόλβιοι | κεῖνοι βροτῶν οἳ ταῦτα δερχθέντες τέλη | μόλωσ' ἐς Ἅιδου· τοῖσδε γὰρ μόνοις ἐκεῖ | ζῆν ἔστι. The present passage, like these, bases the promise of happiness on a religious experience, but its promise, unlike theirs, is for this world, not for the next—the happiness which Dion. gives is here and now.   **μάκαρ** describes this happiness from the point of view of an observer; **εὐδαίμων** (one of the keywords of the play) gives it from the experient's point of view, and suggests the reason for it ('having a good δαίμων'): cf. 910 f. ὅτῳ βίοτος | εὐδαίμων, μακαρίζω.   **τελετάς,** a word originally applicable to many sorts of ritual (e.g. Pindar calls the Olympic games

---

[1] Cf. now Festugière, *Mus. Helv.* ix (1952), 244.

a τελετή), but from the later fifth century onwards used chiefly of
the rites practised in the mystery cults. It does not always mean
'initiations': initiation can happen only once, but the δεισιδαίμων
of Theophrastus goes to the Ὀρφεοτελεσταί every month τελεσθησό-
μενος. Cf. Kern, *Religion d. Griechen*, ii. 187 f., Nock, *Conversion*, 29,
and C. Zijderveld's Τελετή.   **εἰδώς:** the mystery cults offered their
adepts a supposedly potent kind of *knowledge*, from which the
profane were excluded; cf. 472–4, *Rhes.* 973 σεμνὸς τοῖσιν εἰδόσιν θεός,
Bowra, *Class. Phil.* xxxii (1937), 109 f.   **βιοτὰν ἁγιστεύει** refers to
outward ritual observance (cf. τὰς ὁσίους ἁγιστείας of the Eleusinian
initiates, ps.-Plat. *Axiochus* 371 D); **θιασεύεται ψυχάν** to the inward
feeling of unity with the θίασος and through it with the god (Verrall's
'congregationalises his soul' is the nearest English equivalent):
such merging of individual consciousness in group consciousness
is the attraction and the danger of all religion of the Dionysiac
type.[1]

76. ὄρεσσι: this Homeric dative ending (required here by the metre) is
admitted by Eur. at least five times in lyrics and perhaps once in
dialogue (*Alc.* 756).

77. καθαρμοῖσιν: ritual (not moral) 'purifications'. This side of Dionysiac religion was especially exploited by Orphism, but we need not
see a reference to Orphism here (or anywhere in the play): Plato
associated Dionysiac dances with καθαρμούς τε καὶ τελετάς τινας
(*Laws* 815 c); Varro says that 'Liberi patris sacra ad purgationem
animae pertinebant' (Servius on Virg. *Georg.* 1. 166).

78–79. It is surprising to find the ὄργια of Dion. so intimately associated, if not identified, with those of the Asiatic Cybele, whose cult
was first introduced to Greece in the fifth century. [The explanation
seems to be that from very early times a Divine Mother and a Divine
Son were worshipped with dances and ὀρειβασία under different
names on different Asiatic and Cretan mountains: the Mother was
in Asia Minor Kubele or Dindymene or Zemelo, in Crete Rhea (cf.
Farnell, *Cults*, iii, chap. vi); the son was Sabazios or Bakkos or
Diounsis or the Cretan 'Zeus'. The Greeks early adopted the Cretan
Rhea (whom in cult they usually called ἡ Μήτηρ τῶν θεῶν, or simply
ἡ Μήτηρ), and also the Phrygian Dionysus; but these two, being
of different local origin, were not regarded as a mother-and-son pair,
and their cults and myths remained unconnected. But in the fifth
century Asiatic immigrants brought the divine pair afresh to Greece
under the names of Cybele and Sabazius, and embraced them in
a common cult (cf. Strabo 10. 3. 18 ταῦτα γάρ ἐστι σαβάζια καὶ μητρῷα,
of the rites described in the *de corona*). Rhea's essential identity

[1] On the whole passage see now Festugière's detailed study, *Eranos*,
54 (1956), 72 ff.

with the Asiatic Mother was then perceived (see on 120–34); and
Dionysus, if not identified until later with Sabazius, was yet felt
to be 'in a sense the Son of the Mother', as Strabo says of Sabazius
(10. 3. 15), and as the similarity of his ritual showed. It is as the Son
of the Mother that Eur. speaks of him in fr. 586, Διονύσου . . . ὃς ἀν'
Ἴδαν | τέρπεται σὺν ματρὶ φίλα | τυμπάνων ἐπ' ἰαχαῖς, and that old
relationship underlies the linking of his cult with hers both here and
at *Hel.* 1364 f. The cult of the Thracian Dionysus seems to have been
similarly linked with that of the Thracian goddess Cotyto in the
Edoni of Aesch. (fr. 57). But Greek myth, in making Semele a
Theban princess, had given him a human mother; and Greek mytho-
graphers made shift to clear up the resulting confusion either by
distinguishing Dionysus son of Semele from Dionysus Sabazius
(Diod. 4. 4, Cic. *N.D.* 3. 23) or, as Eur. does here, 130 ff., by making
the Theban Dionysus *borrow* his rites and his music from Rhea–
Cybele ([Apollod.] *Bibl.* 3. 5. 1, Sch. Ven. on *Il.* 6. 132).]

80. Tmesis for ἀνατινάσσων, purposely paralleled by a similar tmesis
at the same point in the antistrophe. The thyrsus was swung high
in the dance: cf. 553, fr. trag. adesp. 406 θύρσον ἀνασείει θεῶν, and the
epithet θυρσοτινάκτης.

81. Cf. 177. Ivy-crowned maenads may be seen on many vases. The
ivy was used not merely, as Plutarch (*Q. Conv.* 3. 2) and Sandys suppose, as a handy winter substitute for vine leaves or to cool the
fevered brow of the drinker, but because in its evergreen vitality
it typifies the victory of vegetation over its enemy the winter, as
do also the μῖλαξ (108) and the fir (110). That is why Chaeremon
(fr. 5) called it ἐνιαυτοῦ παῖς. That it was thought of as a vehicle
of the god himself seems to be implied by the worship of Dion. as
'Ivy-lord' (Κισσός) at Acharnae (Paus. 1. 31. 6) and by the rending
and chewing (σπαραγμός and ὠμοφαγία) of the ivy still practised
in Plutarch's day (*Q. Rom.* 112, 291 A); cf. Soph. *Trach.* 218 ἀνα-
ταράσσει εὐοῖ μ' ὁ κισσός. In any case its place in Dionysiac ritual is
primitive, perhaps older than the place of the vine: Pliny notes the
persistence of its use among the primitive Thracian tribes—'hedera
. . . Liberi patris, cuius dei et nunc adornat thyrsos (cf. 25) galeasque
ac scuta in Thraciae populis in sollemnibus sacris' (*NH* 16. 144)
[The line is metrically sound: κισσῷ τε = 97 as read by *l* χρῡσέαισιν.
Hermann's κατὰ κισσῷ derives only weak support from the omission
of τε in a citation by Strabo (10. 3. 13).]

84. θεὸν θεοῦ: for the emphatic collocation, 'son God of God', cf. Soph.
OT. 660 τὸν πάντων θεῶν θεὸν πρόμον.

85. κατάγουσαι: 'bringing home'. [The expression is perhaps connected
with the ritual of the Καταγώγια, a Dionysiac festival celebrated in
Ionia and, in later times at least, at Athens, which is thought to
have taken its name from the 'bringing back' of Dionysus as the

god of annual vegetation. Cf. Wiegand, *Milet*, vi. 23, No. 262, line 21
τοῖς δὲ Καταγωγίοις κατάγειν τὸν Διόνυσον τοὺς ἱερεῖς καὶ τὰς ἱερείας
τοῦ Διονύσου: *Inschr. Priene* 174, τοῖς Καταγωγίοις καθηγήσεται (sc.
ὁ ἱερεύς) τῶν συγκαταγόντων τὸν Διόνυσον: Nilsson in Pauly–Wissowa
s.v. Καταγώγια.]

87. εὐρυχόρους ἀγυιάς: 'spacious streets'. The phrase is traditional
(Pind. *Pyth.* 8. 55, oracle in Dem. *Meid.* 52), and Hellas is tradition-
ally εὐρύχορος (*Il.* 9. 478). The application of the word to countries
seems to show that even if it meant originally 'wide enough for
dancing' it was early connected with χῶρος, not χορός. The association of Dion. with ἀγυιαί appears both in the oracle mentioned above
and in Soph. *Ant.* 1135 Θηβαίας ἐπισκοποῦντ' ἀγυιάς.

88–98. Myth of the Double Birth. On the thunder-birth from Semele
see 6–12 n. The second birth from the thigh of Zeus is mentioned
by Hdt. (2. 146. 2), and occasionally depicted on vases and in other
works of art (Philippart, *Iconographie des Ba.* Nos. 21–22, 24–27, 30;
Heydemann, *Berl. Winckelmannsprogamm* 10, pp. 12 ff.; A. B. Cook,
Zeus, iii, 80 ff.). Arrian localizes it in Bithynia (*F.H.G.* 3. 592);
Theocritus (26. 33) on Drakanon (in Cos?), which had an old cult of
Dionysus (cf. *H. Hymn* 1. 1) doubtless derived from the Asiatic mainland. Its origin and significance are an unsolved puzzle. [There is a
parallel Indian myth about Soma, a Vedic god who is the animating
principle of the fermented drink of the same name: one of the oldest
upanishads, the Taittirîya, states that the gods took Soma and
put him (or it) into the right thigh of the supreme sky-god Indra
(A. Kuhn, *Zeitschr. f. Vergl. Sprachforschung*, 1851, cf. Gladys M. N.
Davies, *The Asiatic Dionysos*, 167). It looks from this as if the tale
in any case belonged to the common stock of Indo-European myths:
if so, it is illegitimate to found on it, as Miss Harrison and others
have done, inferences about early Greek society. It has in fact
a fairly close parallel as far afield as Southern Nigeria, where the
natives tell of magicians who cause a child to be brayed in a mor-
tar and made into soup, and subsequently produce him alive from
the right thigh of the man who has swallowed the soup (Amaury
Talbot, *Life in Southern Nigeria*, 72). Other stories of miraculous
births—not, however, rebirths—from thigh or knee are quoted by
Cook, l.c. They may rest, as Prof. Onians suggests (*Origins of
European Thought*, 182 f.) on the belief that the marrow in the thigh-
bones or the fluid in the knee-cap was the stuff of life.]

88–92. 'Whilst his mother was carrying him, the lightning of Zeus
took wing, and in forced pangs of labour she dropped him from her
womb untimely.' ἔχουσα, 'pregnant', as Hdt. 5. 41. ἐν ... ἀνάγκαισι
not (as Sandys) with ἔχουσα, but, as λοχίαις shows, with ἔτεκεν.
πταμένας ... βροντᾶς is better taken as genitive absolute than as
dependent on ἀνάγκαισι, which already has a dependent genitive in

ὠδίνων.   ἔκβολον in the sense of the prose word ἐκβόλιμος: cf.
L.S.⁹ s.vv. ἐκβάλλω VI, ἐκβολή IV.

94–95. λοχίοις . . . θαλάμαις: 'in secret recesses of birth', explained by
μηρῷ. [MSS. θαλάμοις 'chambers', which might express the same
thing metaphorically, whereas θαλάμαι is a technical term for cavities
in physiology. The rendering 'in Semele's bedroom' is not only
unpoetic but false to the tradition: for the child was first washed
in the waters of Dirce (521 f.), then, as the vase-paintings show
(Philippart, Nos. 14–18), brought to Zeus by Athena or Hermes.—If
θαλάμαις is right, λοχίοις here is hardly consistent with λοχίαις 89.
The adj. has three terminations elsewhere in Eur. (*Supp.* 958,
Ion 452, *IT.* 1097).]

98. κρυπτὸν ἀφ' Ἥρας, cf. *H. Hymn* 1. 7 κρύπτων λευκώλενον Ἥρην. The
motive sounds like a Greek attempt to make sense of the old myth.

99. For the *Μοῖραι* as Birth-goddesses cf. *IT.* 206 f., Pind. *Ol.* 6. 41 ff.,
Nem. 7. 1; for *Μοῖραι τέλεσαν,* Pind. *Isthm.* 6. 46 μοιρίδιον τελέσαι.
The supernatural pregnancy completes its term, in contrast (marked
by the repetition of ἔτεκεν) with the premature birth from Semele.

100. ταυρόκερων: so Dion. is called βούκερως by Sophocles (fr. 959
Pearson) and ταυρωπός by Ion of Chios (fr. 9 Bergk). Hellenistic
and Roman art often depicts him in this way, as a young man with
bull's horns; but this tradition seems not to go back to the fifth century (E. Thraemer in Roscher, *Lex Myth.* i. 1149 ff., cf. Sandys⁴, pp.
cxl ff.). On the significance of Dion.'s bull-nature see Introd., p. xviii.

101–4. A miniature example of an 'aetiological myth', or story of how
a custom began. In such cases the custom is commonly the source
of the story, and not vice versa. Snake-handling was once really
practised in certain forms of Dionysiac cult (Dem. *de cor.* 259,
Plut. *Alex.* 2), as it is today in the American 'Holiness Church'
(see my *Greeks and the Irrational,* 275 f., and Guthrie, *The Greeks and
their Gods,* 148, n. 2); and the 'snaky snood' survived as a conventional attribute of the maenads of fiction (Hor. *Odes* 2. 19. 19 'nodo
coerces viperino Bistonidum sine fraude crines'). It is nicely seen in
the beautiful vase-painting by Brygos at Munich, No. 2645 (Beazley,
A.R.V., p. 247. 14, Furtwängler–Reichhold, Taf. 49). Cf. also 695–
8 n., and Naevius, *Lucurgus* fr. 2 'iubatos angues inlaesae gerunt'.
ἔνθεν, 'from which cause', like 465 πόθεν 'from what cause'. To take
it as equivalent to a partitive gen. (Wecklein) is to miss the aetiological point.   **ἄγραν θηροτρόφον:** 'their beast-brood spoil', i.e.
the snakes they have caught: the adj. is hardly more than a poetic
variant for θηριώδη. [θηροτρόφοι, the reading of P, which probably
stood originally in L also, would apply quite well to the maenads as
'beast-keepers'; but ἄγραν needs an adj. much more than μαινάδες.
θυρσοφόροι, which some modern edd. have revived, is the worthless
guess of Triclinius.]

107. βρύετε, βρύετε: 'abound, abound', a word belonging to the language of poetry and religion; for its use here cf. Ar. *Frogs* 328 ff. πολύκαρπον μὲν τινάσσων | περὶ κρατὶ σῷ βρύοντα | στέφανον μύρτων, of the garland worn by the μύσται: Eubulus fr. 56 κισσῷ κάρα βρύουσαν, of a wine-cup: Bacchyl. 6. 8 f. Repetition of words is especially characteristic of Eur.'s later lyric style (cf. Aristophanes' parody, *Frogs* 1352 ff., and Breitenbach, *Untersuchungen zur Sprache der E. Lyrik*, 214 ff.); but most of the instances in the *Bacchae* (68, 83, 107, 116, 152, 165, 370, 412, 537(?), 577 f., 582, 584, 595, 986, 1183, 1198) seem to be either ritual cries or the natural expression of religious exaltation.

108. μίλακι: Sandys showed that this is the *smilax aspera*, an evergreen (χλοήρει) creeper with clusters of white flowers (cf. 703 μίλακός τ' ἀνθεσφόρου) and bright scarlet berries (καλλικάρπῳ); he suggested 'bryony' (which gets its name from βρύειν) as the nearest English equivalent. Pliny, *NH* 16. 155, disapproves its ritual use as a substitute for ivy.

109–10. 'And consecrate yourselves with twigs of oak or fir.' Sandys took the κλάδοι to be branches carried in the hand (? identical with the thyrsus), and is followed in this by Prof. Murray and Mr. Lucas. His view gets some support from the scholiast on Ar. *Knights* 408, who speaks of τοὺς κλάδους οὓς οἱ μύσται φέρουσι and says that these κλάδοι were called βάκχοι (which would give special point to καταβακχιοῦσθε). But the scholiast goes on to say that certain garlands were also called βάκχοι, quoting a line of Nicander in illustration; and on the whole it seems more likely that the reference here is still to garlands: cf. 703 στεφάνους δρυός, and for wreaths made of κλάδοι Alc. 759 στέφει δὲ κρᾶτα μυρσίνης κλάδοις, Delphic Hymn to Apollo 24 f. ἀμφὶ πλόκ[αμον . . .] δάφνας κλάδον πλεξάμενος. [The hiatus in 110 is often mended by writing ἢ 'ν ἐλάτας: but the same words with the same hiatus occur *Phoen.* 1515, where the cure is not so easy; Murray there compares *H. Ven.* 264 ἢ ἐλάται ἠὲ δρύες. The phrase seems to be a fossilized epicism: in epic and Pindar a vowel after ἤ ('or') is apparently not felt as a hiatus (P. Maas, *Griech. Metrik*, § 141, cf. Wilamowitz, *Sitzb. Berl. Ak.*, Phil.-hist. Kl. 1903, p. 598, n. 1).—For Dion. as Lord of Trees cf. his cult titles Ἔνδενδρος (in Boeotia, Hesych. s.v.), Δενδρεύς (Studemund, *Anecd. Varia*, i. 268), Δενδρίτης (Plut. *Q. Conv.* 5. 3. 1, 675 F), and Jeanmaire, *Dionysos*, 12 ff. There were in Hellenistic times δενδροφορίαι in his honour (Strabo 10. 3. 10, Artemidorus, p. 141. 13 Hercher), though these may be due in part to the influence of the Attis-cult. Oak and fir are the typical trees of Cithaeron (Sandys), as of many Greek forests; but there may be ritual reasons for their frequent appearance in the *Bacchae* (oak 685, 703, 1103; fir 684, 1061, 1098). A θίασος of Dionysus Δρυοφόρος existed at Philippi close to Mt. Pangaeum, one of the original homes of the cult (*Bull. Corr. Hell.* 1900, pp. 322 f.); on a fifth-century coin of Abdera we see the god carrying a fir-tree in his hand (Münzer-Strack, *Münzen von Thrakien*, I. i, pl. 2, No. 4); and the fir-tree on which Pentheus sat was a holy tree (1058 n.).]

111. The fawnskin, the traditional cloak of the maenad both in poetry and on vases, served no doubt as a necessary protection against the cold of the winter ὀρειβασία; but it is also a ἱερὸν ἐνδυτόν (137), originally worn because it communicated to the wearer the Dionysiac virtue of the fawn (cf. 866), as the lion-skin gives Heracles the virtue of the lion. Cf. *Hel.* 1358 μέγα τοι δύναται νεβρῶν | παμποίκιλοι στολίδες. It was apparently retained until fairly recently by the Viza mummers (Dawkins, *J.H.S.* xxvi [1906], 194). The skin of the ὠμοφάγιον has a like magical value among Arabs who practise the rite today (Brunel, *Aïssâoûa*, 179).

112. στέφετε is usually translated here 'fringe' or 'trim'. But no satisfactory parallel or explanation has been adduced: Tac. *Germ.* 17, which edd. quote, refers to the furrier's device of stitching together furs of contrasting colours, and is not really relevant; the object of the practice enjoined here cannot have been mere embellishment— we are dealing with a series of ritual prescriptions. Dr. P. Jacobsthal has suggested to me that στέφετε means 'deck with στέμματα (strands of wool)', and that these strands were wreathed round the girdle which supported the νεβρίς, in the same way as round the suppliant's θάλλος (cf. Aesch. *Eum.* 43 ff. κλάδον | λήνει μεγίστῳ σωφρόνως ἐστεμμένον, | ἀργῆτι μαλλῷ). He points out that a vase figured by Frickenhaus, *Lenäenvasen*, 72, pl. 2, 14 (= Beazley, *A.R.V.*, p. 327. 15) shows the fawnskin girt by a belt which has the appearance of being decorated by a series of tufts. If this view is right, as I believe it is, λευκοτρίχων πλοκάμων μαλλοῖς will be a descriptive periphrasis for στέμμασι, as ἀργῆτι μαλλῷ is in *Eum.* 45. The word τρίχες is applicable to wool (Hes. *Op.* 517), and though πλόκαμος is normally a tress of human hair, the golden lamb is called by Eur. καλλιπλόκαμος, *El.* 705.[1] With λευκοτρίχων πλοκάμων, in which the second part of the compound adj. simply repeats the idea of the noun, cf. 169 κῶλον ταχύπουν: this is a favourite stylistic trick, especially with Eur. (Pearson on *Hel.* 154). [Musgrave, and subsequently Housman, proposed πλοκάμοις μαλλῶν, 'braids of white wool'; but in a late Euripidean lyric the more artificial phrase is the more

---

[1] *El.* 705 is, however, metrically faulty as it stands in the MSS., and it may be that καλλίποκον (Heath) should be read there *metri gratia*. Mr. W. S. Barrett suggests to me that we might similarly read πόκων at *Ba.* 112 and Φρυγῶν in the corresponding line 127, which would yield a normal glyconic. But the recurrence of the identical rhythm at 115 = 130 makes me hesitate to accept a double correction here.

probable.] The function of the στέμματα, as of the garlands, is to consecrate the worshipper to the service of her god (cf. G. Hock, *Griech. Weihegebräuche*, 111 ff.). Trans. 'Gird for a consecration your cloaks of dappled fawnskin with white curls of braided wool'.

113. Again a strange phrase. It seems to mean 'Be reverent in your handling of the violent wands' (like ὅσιοι περὶ ξένους, 'scrupulous in their dealings with guests', *Cycl.* 125; ἀμφὶ Δίκτυνναν ἀνίερος, 'failing in your religious duty towards Dictynna', *Hipp.* 145 f.). Such versions as Mr. Lucas's 'Be purified by joining the haughty bearers of the fennel wand' give an impossible sense to ἀμφί. The startling conjunction of ὁσιότης with ὕβρις expresses the dual aspect of Dionysiac ritual as an act of *controlled violence* in which dangerous natural forces are subdued to a religious purpose (Introd., p. xvi). The thyrsus is the vehicle of these forces; its touch can work beneficent miracles (704 ff.), but it can also inflict injury (762), and, as the adj. θυρσοπλήξ shows, it can cause madness: hence Dion. is θύρσῳ δεινός (*Anth. Pal.* 16. 185) and 'gravi metuende thyrso' (Hor. *Odes* 2. 19).
[In its original form, as we see it on sixth-century Attic vases, it was literally a βακχεῖον κλάδον (308), a branch of the god's holy tree (θύρσος = Lat. *fustis*?): to carry it was to carry deity. In fifth-century pictures this begins to be replaced by the νάρθηξ or fennel rod, which is in itself a profane object (used e.g. for caning boys, schol. *Or.* 1492) but becomes a θύρσος by the addition of the magical (81 n.) bunch of ivy leaves fastened to its tip. The νάρθηξ is thus strictly a *part* of the thyrsus, but in the *Bacchae* the two words seem to be often synonymous (251 νάρθηκι = 254 θύρσου, 704 θύρσον = 706 νάρθηκα). In later art the bunch of leaves is more and more stylized and simplified until it eventually looks like, and is mistaken for, a pine-cone (θύρσου κωνοφόρου *Anth. Pal.* 6. 165). See F.-G. v. Papen, *Der Thyrsos i. d. gr. u. röm. Literatur u. Kunst*, Diss. Bonn, 1905; A. Reinach in *Rev. de l'Hist. des Religions*, lxvi (1912), 1 ff.; Lorenz in *P.-W.* s.v. 'thyrsos'. A descendant of the primitive Thracian θύρσος is perhaps to be recognized in the 'saplings some 10 or 12 feet long' carried by certain of the Viza mummers (Dawkins, *J.H.S.* xxvi [1906], 197). A curious indication of its original potency survives in the Rules of the Iobacchi, a Dionysiac association at Athens in the second century A.D.: if any member misbehaves, a steward is to bring τὸν θύρσον τοῦ θεοῦ and set it beside the offender, whereupon the latter must leave the banqueting hall.]

114. γᾶ πᾶσα: 'all (the people of) this land', in contrast with the θηλυγενὴς ὄχλος. Cf. the Delphic Hymn to Dion. 19 f. πᾶσα δ᾽ ὑμνοβρύης χόρευ|ε[ν Δελφῶ]ν ἱερὰ μάκαιρα χώρα.

115. 'Whosoever leads the worshipping companies is Bromius', i.e. the leader of the ὀρειβασία is in the sacrament identified with the god: cf. 141 ὁ δ᾽ ἔξαρχος Βρόμιος. We know very little of the organization of actual ὀρειβασίαι, but such evidence as we have is consistent with the view that it was originally a women's rite with a single male celebrant (cf. Nilsson, *Studi e mat. di storia delle religioni*, x [1934], 3; Dodds, *Harv. Theol. Rev.* xxxiii [1940], 170).[1] If the celebrant was identified with the god, we can see why the god as well as the worshipper is called ταυροφάγος (Soph. fr. 668); why Diodorus (4. 3) speaks of an 'epiphany' of Dion. at the τριετηρίς; and why in descriptions of the latter the god himself is represented as carrying the torch (*Ion* 714 ff., fr. 752, Ar. *Clouds* 603 ff., &c.). Some degree of identification with the god seems to be implied in calling human participants in Dionysiac rites βάκχαι and βάκχοι (Pentheus calls the Stranger ὁ βάκχος, 491): cf. the proverb πολλοὶ μὲν ναρθηκοφόροι, παῦροι δέ τε βάκχοι, which appears to mean that many perform the ritual but few experience identification. It is *possible* (though there is no direct evidence of it outside this passage) that the supreme degree of such identification, open only to the ἔξαρχος, was expressed by giving him the holy name Bromius (or if not, that Eur. thought so). Conversely, the god sometimes received in cult the title Καθηγεμών (*I.G.* ii. 3067, 3068, &c.). The organization would be like that of a witches' coven, where the single male leader was known to his congregation as 'the devil'. [While adopting this provisionally as the most natural explanation of the MS. text of 135-41, I prefer Elmsley's generally accepted εὗτ' ἄν here. (*a*) If ὅστις was introduced into the Laurentian by the διορθωτής (L²) it *may* be an old reading; but the superfluous correction ἄγει which accompanies it does not strengthen its claims, and if it is due, as Wecklein thought, to the later corrector (*l*) it is (like all his readings) a mere guess, *metri gratia*, and wholly devoid of authority. (*b*) As a guess, εὗτ' ἄν is clearly better: the parenthetic statement is very abrupt, and the rare εὗτε, which is glossed ὅτε in Hesych., would be more exposed to corruption than the common ὅστις. Prof. Murray told me in 1940 that he no longer thought ὅστις right.]

120-34. Myth of the origin of the τύμπανον (the βυρσότονον κύκλωμα of 124, cf. *Hel.* 1347 τύπανα βυρσοτενῆ): (*a*) it was invented in a Cretan cave by the Curetes or Corybantes (to drown the cries of the infant 'Zeus', lest his father Kronos should find and devour him, cf. Lucr. 2. 629 ff.); they then presented it, along with the Phrygian flute, to Rhea (mother of the Zeus-child), to be used in her orgiastic rites; (*b*) from her the Satyrs obtained it and introduced it into the Dionysiac rite of the τριετηρίς. This is 'aetiology' again: (*a*) explains why the kettledrum was used in the Cretan cult of the Mother and Son, (*b*) explains why it also appears in that of Dionysus. (*a*) may be old; (*b*) looks like a fifth-century invention to account for the

---

[1] But see below, p. 86 n. 2.

observed similarity (for the true explanation cf. 78–79 n.). [(b) is related in a form so brief as to be for us obscure. 'Apollodorus' (*Bibl.* 3. 5. 1) tells a much fuller story: Διόνυσος . . . Ἥρας μανίαν αὐτῷ ἐμβαλούσης περιπλανᾶται Αἴγυπτόν τε καὶ Συρίαν. . . . αὖθις δὲ εἰς Κύβελα τῆς Φρυγίας ἀφικνεῖται, κἀκεῖ καθαρθεὶς ὑπὸ Ῥέας καὶ τὰς τελετὰς ἐκμαθὼν καὶ λαβὼν παρ' ἐκείνης τὴν στολήν, ἐπὶ Ἰνδοὺς διὰ τῆς Θράκης ἠπείγετο. Here the Indians at least are post-Euripidean; but the madness sent by Hera (perhaps invented to explain the Homeric epithet μαινόμενος, *Il.* 6. 132, cf. schol. Ven. A *ad loc.*) was known to Eur. (*Cycl.* 3) and presumably furnished the occasion on which the satyrs, 'mad' like their master, borrowed the kettledrum which was used in the corybantic rite for the cure of madness (cf. Ar. *Wasps* 119 f. and schol. *ad loc.*). Eur., like the author of the *Bibliotheca* and later antiquity generally, seems to identify Rhea with Cybele (who is already for Pindar the Mother of the Gods, fr. 77 Bowra), just as he appears to identify the Curetes, mythical ministers of Rhea, with the Corybantes, mythical ministers of Cybele; such 'syncretism' is characteristic of the late fifth century, when people began trying to reduce to order the chaos of old and new cults and myths. On the Cretan 'Zeus', who is a vegetation-god with orgiastic cult, more akin to Dionysus than to the Hellenic Zeus, see Farnell, *Cults*, i, pp. 36–38; Guthrie, *The Greeks and their Gods*, 40 ff., 154 ff.]

120. 'After the birth-place of the god's mother they address the birth-place of his father; and the moral is perhaps that Thebes should not be less eager to celebrate the son than Crete the father' (Winnington-Ingram). **θαλάμευμα:** 'secret chamber', a poetic variation for θαλάμη, which was a *vox propria* for a sacred cave (schol. Nicander, *Alexipharm.* 8 Λοβρίνης θαλάμαι· τόποι ἱεροί, ὑπόγειοι, ἀνακείμενοι τῇ Ῥέᾳ: cf. Hesych. θαλάμη· τρώγλη, and Eur. *Ion* 394 where the oracle-cave of Trophonius is his θαλάμαι). Such sacred caves were the earliest cult centres in Crete and Anatolia; they had a place also in the Greek cult of Dion. (Delphic Hymn, 139; Macrob. *Saturn.* 1. 18. 3; Paus. 2. 23. 1; Cumont, *A.J.A.* 1933, 250 f., &c.). In *H. Hymn* 26, line 6, Dion. like the Cretan 'Zeus' is brought up in a cave.

123. τρικόρυθες, 'with triple helmet'. It is not clear what is meant. The scholiast on *Or.* 1480 τρικόρυθος Αἴας compares τρίπτυχος ('composed of three layers of material'?), applied by Homer to Hector's helmet, *Il.* 11. 353; and offers the alternative guess that the word means τρίλοφος 'three-crested'. The three-*crested* helmet is worn, e.g., by Athena in fifth-century sculpture; but the epithet should suggest something alien and remote, not something perfectly familiar. On the other hand, archaeological evidence does not support Wilamowitz's assertion that Eur. is describing 'the old Cretan helmet, resembling the papal tiara, which must have survived in ritual'. Perhaps he had nothing specific in mind, but merely introduced a grand epical-sounding word which he had found in older poetry. [Instead of dropping ἐν before ἄντροις we should perhaps read τρικόρυθες ἔνθ' ἐν ἄντροις (Dobree), thus avoiding the interlinear hiatus which in this song occurs nowhere else within the strophic unit (save for 152–3 which is a special case). The words may have been transposed into prose order, as often.]

126–9. 'And in the tense ecstatic dance they mingled it (the kettle-drum) with the sweetly calling breath of Phrygian flutes, and put it into the hand of Mother Rhea to beat time for the joy-cries of her worshipping women.' ἀνά ... κέρασαν, tmesis. συντόνῳ can be taken with πνεύματι in the sense of 'shrill' or 'excited', but with our reading it is preferable to take it with βακχείᾳ as πνεύματι already has an adj. βακχείᾳ and Βακχᾶν have troubled editors, since the worship described is that of Rhea, not of Dion.; but the same transference appears in fr. 472. 13 ff., μητρί τ' ὀρείῳ δᾷδας ἀνασχὼν | καὶ Κουρήτων | βάκχος ἐκλήθην ὁσιωθείς. It is justified by the similarity, and in ultimate origin identity, of the two cults (78–79 n.). For Φρυγίων αὐλῶν in the cult of the Mother cf. Catull. 63. 22, Lucr. 2. 620. The flute is ὀργιαστικόν (Arist. *Pol.* 1341ᵃ21); Menander's Theophoroumene, who is possessed by the Mother, or by the Cory-bantes, dances to its music (*Theoph.* 27 f., p. 101 f. Koerte³).

[Dobree's transposition, adopted in the text, is not indispensable. It makes the metrical correspondence with 111 exact; but Eur. does not insist on strict correspondence in the glyconic base (cf. 404–5 n.). Nor can decisive weight be given to Hermann's objection that βάκχια is nowhere else used for 'Bacchic rites' (βακχεῖα, which the metre excludes): the adjs. βάκχιος and βακχεῖος are hardly distinguishable in meaning; and if Eur. could call the Dionysiac dance βάκχιον χόρευμα (*Phoen.* 655, where MSS. have βακχεῖον as here), why should he not use for it the vaguer term βάκχια? If we write ἀνὰ δὲ βάκχια, βάκχια is not governed by ἀνεκέρασαν—for the βάκχια cannot be described as a κτύπος—but by ἀνά (with extended local sense, like ἅμ φόνον *Il.* 10. 298). ἀνακεράννυμι is not used elsewhere of musical composition (whereas κεράννυμι is), nor does it occur in tragedy at all, an objection which has led Campbell to propose βακχείᾳ δ' ἅμα (*C.Q.* xlix (1956), 56).]

133. τριετηρίδων: 'the feast of the second year' ('third' by the Greek method of inclusive reckoning). This is the biennial orgiastic festival: see Introd., pp. xiii f.

135. ἡδύς: probably 'welcome' (if ὅταν is sound), expressing the worshippers' joy in the god's epiphany; the word is several times so used by Sophocles of someone newly arrived, *OT*. 82 (cf. Jebb ad loc.), *El.* 929, *Phil.* 530. As the text stands, the person referred to can only be Dion. Hermann objected that the god would then be contrasted with himself (by the δέ in 141, ὁ δ' ἔξαρχος Βρόμιος).[1] To avoid that conclusion, many edd. alter ὅταν to ὅς ἄν: they then either emend ἡδύς as well (ἥδος Musgrave, which is non-Attic, ἡδύ γ' Dobree) or take it to mean 'joyful'—a rendering which is hardly sufficiently supported by *Hipp.* 289 ἡδίων γενοῦ (= 'cheer up!') and similar colloquial uses in prose, apparently always of the comparative. But it may be the god *in the person of his* ἔξαρχος or celebrant priest who takes part in the ὀρειβασία and ὠμοφαγία: see 115 n., 136 n. The words ὁ δ' ἔξαρχος Βρόμιος are then explanatory of what precedes; δέ has often in tragedy something of the force of γάρ (Denniston, *Particles*, 169). On this hypothesis there is no need either to alter the sense of 135 or to adopt Wilamowitz's bold remedy of transferring ὁ δ' ἔξαρχος Βρόμιος, εὐοί to the beginning of the epode. But I feel no certainty about the passage.[2]

[The metre is also obscure. The lines can be read in several ways, but as the text stands no analysis is very convincing. With Murray's colometry 135 and 137 must, I think, be taken as dochmiac; but dochmii are somewhat surprising in this metrical context. Paeons seem far more likely (cf. 160-2): by writing ὄρεσσιν (Schoene, cf. 76) we get a paeonic opening, and as Denniston pointed out to me νεβρίδος . . . ἀγρεύων makes a paeonic tetrameter catalectic. As to the intervening words, ἐκ θιάσων δρομαίων echoes the rhythms of the preceding stanza (105 ff. = 120 ff.); but the isolated iambic metron πέση πεδόσε is a little unexpected. At a guess, Eur. may have written

ἡδὺς ἐν ὄρεσσιν, ὅταν	2 paeons
ἐκ θιάσων δρομαίων	chor. + ba.
– ∪ ∪ – πέσῃ πεδόσε,	chor. + iamb. } cf. 108-9
νεβρίδος ἔχων ἱερὸν ἐνδυτόν, ἀγρεύων	4 paeons (catal.)

[1] Kamerbeek, *Mnemos.* 1953, 192, has proposed to remove the difficulty by the elementary expedient of writing ὅδ' ἔξαρχος Βρόμιος, but the deictic pronoun is hardly intelligible in this context.

[2] Since the above was written, Prof. K. J. Dover has suggested to me that ἡδύς can be applied to the worshipper as 'well pleasing' to the god: cf. Soph. fr. 959 P. Νῦσαν, ἣν ὁ βουκέρως | Ἴακχος αὑτῷ μαῖαν ἡδίστην νέμει, and Xen. *Hiero* 4. 1 ποῖος θεράπων ἡδὺς ἀπιστούμενος; I am now inclined to take it so, and to read ὅς ἄν. Murray's objection to that reading, 'unus tantum vir', is true of the situation on Cithaeron at the moment; but if it is intended generally, it does not fit the assumptions of the play: γᾶ πᾶσα χορεύσει (114) must include the men (the women are dancing already); and Teiresias says (206 ff.) explicitly that *all* must join in the worship. At Delphi the παννυχίς appears to have been attended by women only, but that elsewhere men were admitted to the ὄργια, at least in the fifth century, is implied by Hdt. 4. 79, and by the inscription from Cumae referring to τὸν βεβαχχευμένον (*Not. degli scavi* 1906, 378).

The missing choriambus (?) might be e.g. ⟨ἔνθεος ὤν⟩. But no approach to certainty is attainable. πέσῃ . . . ἀγρεύων can also be read as 2 iamb.+glyc. (scanning νέβρ- and ἀγρ-).]

136. πέσῃ πεδόσε: 'falls to the ground' (not 'to the plain', cf. 600 and Soph. *Trach.* 786 ἐσπᾶτο γὰρ πέδονδε). Why does he fall? Paley says 'through fatigue', comparing 683; but gods are not fatigued, nor are Dion.'s votaries while the god is within them (cf. 187). Possibly to tear the dying goat (Murray in lectures); but it seems to happen during the hunt, not at the moment of the kill (ἀγρεύων, not ἀγρεύ-σας). I suspect that the words describe a moment when the celebrant falls unconscious and the god enters into him. This happens in other orgiastic dances, e.g. with the Siberian shamans. In the dancing mania of A.D. 1374 'those affected fell to the ground sense-less, panting and labouring for breath. They foamed at the mouth, and suddenly springing up began their dance amidst strange con-tortions' (J. F. K. Hecker, *Die Tanzwuth*, trans. Babington, p. 107). In the Ghost Dance of the North American Indians 'the dancers, one after the other, fell rigid, prostrate on the ground. During their seizure they had visions . . . and meanwhile the dance continued and others fell' (R. Benedict, *Patterns of Culture*, 92). Cf. also T. K. Oesterreich, *Possession*, 241, 251, 362, 371 (Eng. trans.). The falling maenad is occasionally recognizable in vase-paintings, e.g. Berlin 2471 (Beazley, *A.R.V.* 724. 1; Pfuhl, fig. 560).

138. 'Blood of the goat that is slain, joy of the living flesh devoured.' For the first phrase cf. *Or.* 833 ματροκτόνον αἷμα, Aesch. fr. 327 αἵματος χοιροκτόνου; for the second, *Her.* 384 χαρμοναῖσιν ἀνδροβρῶσι, fr. 537 ἀνδροβρῶτας ἡδονάς. This is the supreme rite of the τριετηρίς: for evidence about it, and a discussion of its meaning, cf. Introd., pp. xvi ff.

141. ἔξαρχος: a cult title in the kindred worship of Sabazius (Dem. *de cor.* 260), and probably in that of Dion. also, though it has not yet turned up in an inscription. If the view taken above is right, the Chorus here speak more truth than they know ('tragic irony'): their Leader is in fact Bromius in the literal and not merely in the religious sense. [The whole passage ἱέμενος . . . νέκταρι is again metrically odd, particularly the resolved dactyls (∪∪∪∪) in 140 and the isolated νέκτᾰρῑ (should εὐοῖ be transposed to follow νέκταρι?).]

142-3. 'A beautiful dreamlike effect after the horror of the ὠμοφαγία' (Murray). Cf. 704-11 n. The same Dionysiac miracles were described in similar terms by the Chorus of Eur.'s *Hypsipyle*, as appears from the mutilated papyrus scraps Διόνυσος . . . ῥεῖ δὲ γά . . . στάζε . . . νέκταρ . . . λιβάνου . . . μύρνας καπν . . . (frs. 57, 58 Arnim).

144-50. 'The Bacchic One (i.e. the god temporarily incarnate in the celebrant), lifting high the blazing flame of the pine torch, sweet as

the smoke of Syrian frankincense, lets it stream from his wand
(i.e. the flame trails behind him as he runs), with racing and with
dances spurring the stragglers and rousing them with his call, his
long curls rippling in the wind.' I take ἀνέχων and ἀίσσει as governing
φλόγα, ἐρεθίζων and ἀναπάλλων as governing πλανάτας. For ἀίσσειν
transitive cf. Or. 1427 ff. αὔραν . . . πρὸ παρηίδος ἀίσσων, 'making the
breeze stream across my cheek'. If it is taken intrans. here, ἐκ
νάρθηκος has to go with ἀνέχων—a less natural word-order and a less
natural use of ἐκ. For the sense of ἐρεθίζων cf. Ar. Clouds, 312
εὐκελάδων τε χορῶν ἐρεθίσματα (of Dionysiac dances); for that of
ἀναπάλλων cf. 1190. On the long hair see 455–6 n., and on πλόκαμον
ῥίπτων 862–5 n.; cf. also Lucian's picture of a sham ecstatic σείων τὴν
κόμην ἄνετον ὥσπερ οἱ . . . ἐνθεαζόμενοι (Alex. 13). The νάρθηξ seems
to be used here not as a component part of the θύρσος but as a torch-
holder; the maenads in vase-paintings often carry both thyrsus
and torch, though the latter is usually a simple bundle of pine-twigs
(πεύκη), not attached to a νάρθηξ.

145. [The MS. reading can hardly be right: the second ionic μέτρον is
a syllable short, and Συρίας δ' ὡς λιβάνου καπνός is not a sentence—
to make it one we have to supply not 'is', which would be easy, but
(since καπνός has no article) 'there is', which is difficult. The correction in the text (Wilamowitz's) is convincing: if the first N was
accidentally omitted from ἀνέχων, A would be read as Δ, and
καπνόν, having then no construction, would be altered to καπνός.
Cf. Eur. Ion 716 Βάκχιος ἀμφιπύρους ἀνέχων πεύκας, in a description
of the same rite.]

148. [δρόμῳ καὶ χοροῖς (MSS.) is unsatisfactory metrically (a dochmius
is not in place here). By writing χοροῖσιν and adopting Wilamowitz's
transposition in the next line (to lengthen the last syllable of
χοροῖσιν) Murray obtains ionics.]

150. [To make the ionics right we must either insert τε as in text or
(with Earle) alter πλόκαμον to βόστρυχον, which is glossed πλόκαμον
schol. Phoen. 787.]

151. 'Among the maenad cries his voice rings deep.' [Murray's transposition in conjunction with Elmsley's deletion of ἐπ' (on which L
has the interlinear note περισσόν, 'superfluous'), makes this line for
the first time plausible metrically: the ionics continue (-ᾰδ' ἐπ- = a
resolved long syllable). Hiatus before and after exclamations, as
here before and after ὦ, is not unusual.] It is not clear how much of
what follows is spoken by the Βακχεύς. Wilamowitz, arguing (I do
not know why) that the god could not refer to himself in the third
person (155 τὸν Διόνυσον), attributes to him only the ritual cry ὦ
ἴτε βάκχαι, which is then taken up by the Chorus; and so apparently
Murray in his translation. But would a ritual cry be introduced
by τοιάδε? I believe (with Bruhn and Mr. Lucas) that it introduces

all the imperatives, and that the Βακχεύς ends, as he began, with
a repeated ritual formula (165 εἰς ὄρος, εἰς ὄρος), after which the
Chorus describes the maenads' response.

152-69. ' "On, my Dancers! On, my Dancers! With the glitter of
Tmolus that runs with gold sing praise of Dionysus to the beat
of the rumbling drums, in joy glorifying the Lord of Joy with
Phrygian crying and calling, when the sweet and holy music of the
pipe peals its holy gaiety, climbing with you as you climb—to the
Mountain, to the Mountain!" Oh happily then as a filly beside its
dam in the pasture, with limbs drawn and swift feet the Dancer
leaps!'

152-4. Τμώλου χρυσοροόου, because the river Pactolus, as Hdt. says
(5. 101), ψῆγμα χρυσοῦ καταφορέει ἐκ τοῦ Τμώλου. For the gold mines
of Tmolus cf. Strabo 13. 1. 23. [Wecklein's Πακτωλοῦ for Τμώλου is
pedantic and metrically unconvincing.] I do not see how χλιδᾷ can
refer to gold *ornaments* (Wecklein, Dalmeyda): it must be instrumental with μέλπετε. The instruments referred to can hardly be
gilded τύμπανα (Bruhn): you cannot 'play on the kettledrum to the
beat of (ὑπό) the kettledrum'. (This difficulty might be evaded by
taking βαρυβρόμων ὑπὸ τυμπάνων with ἀγαλλόμεναι, but see next note.)
Possibly they are gilded κρόταλα (castanets): the use of these in
Dionysiac dances is attested by *Cycl.* 205 (where they are associated
with τύμπανα), *Hel.* 1308, and the vase-paintings; but they are not
mentioned in the *Bacchae*. [It seems on the whole safer to return,
with Wilamowitz, to χλιδά (Victorius, and most edd. before Wecklein)—'O pride of Tmolus' (abstract for concrete). The word suggests the showy trappings of the oriental woman: cf. Aesch. *Supp.*
234 ff., where the Danaids are called ὅμιλον τόνδ' ἀνελληνόστολον |
πέπλοισι βαρβάροισι κἀμπυκώμασι | χλίοντα.]

155-6. [Wilamowitz's transposition of these two lines might well have
been adopted: it greatly improves the rhythm (by getting the
two glyconic lines together), and also results in a more natural and
effective word-order.]

157-9. εὔια: internal accus. with ἀγαλλόμεναι, equivalent to an adv.
ἐν βοαῖς: cf. Soph. *Phil.* 1393 ἐν λόγοις πείσειν, *Ant.* 961, Aesch. *Sept.*
280. In such phrases ἐν seems to mark the sphere in which an
activity takes place (Wilamowitz on *Her.* 932); but we may see in
them the starting-point of the development towards the Hellenistic
use with an instrumental dat. (cf. 277, 1165-7 n.). ἐνοπαί are always
loud or excited cries (cf. Denniston on Eur. *El.* 1302). [One rather
expects two purely dactylic lines here, balancing 165-7. This could
be obtained by altering εὔια τὸν εὔιον to εὔιον εὔι' (suggested to me
by Dr. P. Maas).]

Scene i (170-369): Teiresias, Cadmus, then Pentheus.
     There are violent differences of opinion about the meaning of

this scene. Its function in the structure of the play is or should be clear enough: before we see Dionysus and Pentheus in collision we must be introduced to each of them separately, so that we may understand the strength and obstinacy of the colliding forces. That is the careful, logical technique of the ancient dramatist: we find it in other conflict plays, e.g. *Antigone* and *Hippolytus*. And the two old men provide, as Winnington-Ingram says, 'a prosaic background to the lyrical exaltation' of the Chorus. But there is no agreement about the emotional tone of the scene or about its character-drawing.

Murray and Nihard (*Problème des Bacchantes*, 44 f.) think that the point of the opening dialogue between the two old men is to exhibit a Dionysiac miracle of rejuvenation: by the magic of the god they are filled for a time with 'a mysterious strength and exaltation' (Murray's stage direction at 187). Certainly both claim to have forgotten their age; and it is probably not accidental that there is no mention of the attendant who in other plays leads the blind Teiresias on to the stage (*Phoen.* 834, Soph. *Ant.* 989, *OT.* 297). Nihard cites as a parallel the rejuvenation of Iolaos in the *Heraclidae*, 796, 851 ff. (this is, however, οὐδὲν πρὸς τὸν Διόνυσον, and the messenger who reports it is in any case made to present it expressly as a second-hand story). One might quote also Medea's rejuvenation of 'the nurses of Dionysus', which Aeschylus is said to have related in his Διονύσου τροφοί (fr. 50). But the most relevant parallels are the Iacchos dance in the *Frogs*, in which γόνυ πάλλεται γερόντων | ἀποσείονται δὲ λύπας | χρονίους τ᾽ ἐτῶν παλαιῶν ἐνιαυτοὺς | ἱερᾶς ὑπὸ τιμᾶς (345 ff.); and Plato, *Laws* 666 B ἐπίκουρον τῆς τοῦ γήρως αὐστηρότητος ἐδωρήσατο (sc. ὁ Διόνυσος) τὸν οἶνον φάρμακον, ὥστε ἀνηβᾶν ἡμᾶς. In the light of these passages we may take it that ll. 187-90 describe a traditional Dionysiac effect (cf. Introd. p. xv). Yet Eur. seems to treat this 'miracle' with a certain irony. If the old men are filled with power, it should be because they are filled with faith. But Cadmus at least is not filled with faith, only with a timid worldliness. His real creed is, as Dalmeyda puts it, 'the solidarity of the family': Dion. is after all his daughter's son (181), and must be accepted for family reasons, 'that Semele may be thought to have given birth to a god, and the whole family may share in the credit' (335 f.). As for his mysterious strength, he shows little confidence in it: he suggests taking a cab to Cithaeron (191), and is nervous of finding himself in a minority (195). Altogether, not the right kind of old man to be the subject of a miracle.

That the slight portrait of Cadmus is touched with humour seems to me evident. But many interpreters, from Walter Pater (*Greek Studies*, 62) down to Prof. Grube (*Trans. Amer. Phil. Ass.* lxvi. 39 f.), go much farther than this. Taking literally the bitter remark

of Pentheus that the old gentleman in his fancy dress is 'a great joke'
(πολὺν γέλων, 250), they hold that the scene should be played frankly
to get laughs. I doubt if this interpretation is justified by the text,
and I do not think it stands up to the test of production—at any
rate when the scene was produced on these lines at Cambridge in 1930
it appeared to me to jar, and to injure the effect of what followed.

What is hardest to assess is the significance of Teiresias. One
thing is clear: he stands for a different notion of Dionysiac religion
from that presented in the preceding choral ode. For him Dion. is
not the mystical beast-god, the spirit of the ὠμοφαγία, but an abs-
traction—a personification of wine as Demeter is of bread (274–85).
And he explains away the central mystery of the Double Birth
by an etymological fantasy about a 'hostage' (285–97), which the
Chorus subsequently ignore (523 ff.). He appears to be a man of the
fifth century, an intellectual of sorts who has read his Protagoras
and his Prodicus (see on 201–3 and 274–85); and it is probable that
to understand his part fully we should have to know much more
than we do of fifth-century controversies about religion—his
speeches are, as Nihard says, 'des documents pour l'histoire de la
mentalité religieuse de l'époque'. We need not take his opinions to
be those of the poet, as do Nestle and others. Euripides had been
poking fun at soothsayers all his life (Decharme, *Eur. et l'esprit
de son théâtre*, 96 ff.; Radermacher, *Rh. Mus.* liii. 501 ff.), and he
was about to have a last whack at them in the *IA*. (520 f., 956 ff.):
it seems unlikely that he should here have chosen such a man as
his mouthpiece. What Teiresias does perhaps represent is the
ecclesiastical politics of Delphi (with which Eur. elsewhere shows
little sympathy): he predicts the acceptance of Dion. by Delphi
(306 ff.), and the Chorus-leader congratulates him on becoming
Dionysiac without ceasing to be Apolline (328 f.). That is to say,
his is the type of mind which would harness to the cause of doc-
trinal conservatism the spontaneous emotional forces generated by
a religious revival: he would not reject the new foreign cults which
were disturbing Athens in Eur.'s day (Introd., pp. xxiii ff.), but he
would Hellenize and rationalize them, as Delphi once Hellenized
and rationalized the foreigner Dion. 'A regulated ecstasy has lost
its germ of danger' (Nilsson, *History of Greek Religion*, 208). Tyrrell
was not, I think, far from the mark when he compared Teiresias to
a Broad Church dean.

On the character of Pentheus see 214 n., and Introd., p. xliii.

170. Like *Phoen.* 1067 f. ὠή, τίς ἐν πύλαισι δωμάτων κυρεῖ; | ἀνοίγετε.
'The cue is "Bacchanal"—foal-like and nimble; the entry is that of
a figure, wearing Bacchic costume indeed, but male and old and blind'
(Winnington-Ingram).

171–2. In accordance with the usual practice of the Greek stage (cf.

Wilamowitz, *Analecta Eur.* 199 ff.), Cadmus is formally introduced—presumably for the benefit of the less literate members of the audience. Eur. had described him in almost the same words in the opening lines of an earlier play, the *Phrixus* (fr. 819).

176. ἀνάπτειν: lit. 'to tie', i.e. *make* a thyrsus by tying a bunch of ivy leaves to a narthex (cf. 113 n., 1054–5 n.). Vase-paintings often show the ivy leaves lashed on to the tip of the narthex. [The rendering 'kindle' will not do, unless we read πυρσούς (Housman): the torch is called νάρθηξ (147, Nonn. *Dion.* 7. 340), but never θύρσος. And the parallel passage 248–54 confirms θύρσους. Wecklein explained ἀνάπτειν as 'attach to yourself', i.e. carry ceremoniously, quoting fr. 752 Διόνυσος . . . θύρσοισι καὶ νεβρῶν δοραῖς | καθαπτός: but there θύρσοισι can be taken with καθαπτός only by a zeugma.] On the fawnskins see 111 n., on the ivy wreaths 81 n.   ἔχειν: 'to wear'.

178. 'Dear friend—for I heard and recognized your voice.' ὡς is causal: 'rationem reddit cur carissimum appellaverit Tiresiam, priusquam viderit. Dicit enim haec, dum aperiuntur fores' (Hermann). [Cobet approved Portus's ἡδόμην (with ὡς exclamatory), but ᾐσθόμην is confirmed by the closely parallel passage *Hec.* 1114 f., ὦ φίλτατ᾽· ᾐσθόμην γάρ, Ἀγάμεμνον, σέθεν | φωνῆς ἀκούσας, as well as by *Chr. Pat.* 1148.]

179. σοφὴν σοφοῦ: σοφία, true or false, is a recurrent motif in the play, and especially in this scene (186, 200, 203, 266 ff., 311 f., 332).

182. This line is often rejected on the grounds of its resemblance to 860 and its superfluity here. [Certainly the unconscious humour of the sentence emerges more obviously if it be omitted. And lines were sometimes interpolated in order to bring in proper names, for the sake of greater clearness, e.g. 1092, *Phoen.* 428, Soph. *Tr.* 362–4 (cf. G. Jachmann, *Nachr. Gött. Ges.*, Phil.-hist. Kl., 1936, 194 ff.). But the objections are hardly conclusive. It is natural that Cadmus, having hinted at the real reason for his devotion (ὄντα παῖδα θυγατρὸς ἐξ ἐμῆς), should enlarge on the official one—there has been a revelation (for πέφηνεν cf. 22, 42, 1031). And we may say with P. W. Harsh (*Hermes*, lxxii [1937], 443) that here and at 860 Eur. 'is deliberately varying a formula'.]

183. αὔξεσθαι μέγαν: 'be magnified to greatness' (not 'grow up' as L.S. surprisingly translates). αὔξειν often of honouring a god: for the passive in this sense cf. 209. 'To increase the power of a deity by appropriate ritual seems to be the aim and object of ancient sacrifice in its earliest form, before it was thought of as a present to win his favour', Skutsch and Rose, *C.Q.* xxxii (1938), 223 (who interpret 'macte esto' in this way).

184. ποῖ δεῖ χορεύειν: not 'Whither must I dance?' (as 191 shows, he does not propose to *dance* from Thebes to Cithaeron), but 'where must I (go and) dance?' The use of ποῖ for ποῦ in both questions is due to

an *implied* verb of motion, as in *Alc.* 863 ποῖ στῶ; *Her.* 74 ποῖ πατὴρ
ἄπεστι γῆς; Ar. *Eccl.* 837 ὅποι δειπνήσετε.

185. κρᾶτα σεῖσαι: see on 862-5.   **ἐξηγοῦ:** 'expound'. The word is
probably meant, as Verrall suggested, to recall the ἐξηγηταὶ Πυθό-
χρηστοι appointed by the Delphic Oracle to act as consultants on
questions of religious law and custom: cf. Aesch. *Eum.* 609. Teiresias
is conceived as the prototype of such personages, and it is in this
sense that Cadmus here calls him σοφός, 'expert'.

188-9. ἀντιλαβή (division of a line between speakers) is very sparingly
used in this play. It usually suggests excitement—here perhaps
Teiresias' excited pleasure in comparing symptoms.   **γέροντες
ὄντες:** Eur. not infrequently admits such jangling assonances, to
which Greek ears may have been less sensitive than ours (cf. Denniston on *El.* 606). [The correction ἡδέως for ἡδέων was first made by
the poet Milton, who noted it with other conjectures in the margin
of his copy of Euripides, now in the Bodleian Library at Oxford.
These emendations were not published in full until 1814, when they
were printed in the *Museum Criticum.*]

192. [This line violates in its third foot (-ως ἂν ὁ) the rule which
prohibits 'trochaic caesura of a dactyl', i.e. the distribution between
two independent words of the two short syllables (which should
cohere closely because they represent the resolution of a single long
syllable). There is no such cohesion between ἂν and ὁ as there is
between preposition and noun in 816 σι|γῇ γ' ὑπ' ἐ|λάταις or between
article and noun in 206 διῄ|ρηχ' ὁ θε|ός. It is easy to 'correct' the
rhythm here by writing ὁ θεὸς ἄν, but it is not logical to do so unless
we are prepared also to emend lines like 285 ὥστε δι|ά, 807 κοιν|ῇ
τάδ', ἵ|να, *Or.* 2 οὐδὲ πά|θος, *Or.* 632 σὸν πόδ' ἐ|πί. Descroix, *Le
trimètre iambique*, 187 ff., carrying further the work of Hermann
and C. F. Mueller, has traced the progressive relaxation of the
rigour of the rule; he shows that unqualified violations of it appear
in the latest plays of Eur. (*Or., Ba., IA., Hypsipyle*), but not elsewhere in tragedy. For the penthemimeral caesura separating ἄν
from ὁμοίως cf. *Heraclid.* 743 τοιοῦτος· οἵαν ‖ ἂν τροπὴν Εὐρυσθέως.]

193. As Dobree, and more recently Earle and Zielinski, have pointed
out, this ought to be printed as a question, to which 194 is the answer.
It seems to be, like 195, an expression of doubt: 'shall one old man
be nursemaid to another?' Cf. the servant's doubts about old Iolaus,
Heraclid. 729 ἦ παιδαγωγεῖν γὰρ τὸν ὁπλίτην χρεών; According to
Gellius (*N.A.* 13. 19. 3 = Soph. fr. 695 P.) the present line occurred
also in the *Phthiotides* of Soph.

194. ἀμοχθεί: the Dionysiac effortlessness of which we had a hint at 66;
we shall meet it again later. Cf. Ar. *Frogs* 402, where the μύσται
pray to Iacchos δεῖξον ὡς ἄνευ πόνου | πολλὴν ὁδὸν περαίνεις. This
is something different from the commonplace that all things are

easy to a god (Aesch. *Supp.* 100, &c.): it is a power communicated by this god to his worshippers. [The spelling ἀμοχθεί (L P) may be right: cf. ἀσυλεί from ἄσυλος, *I.G.* i². 58. 14 (5th cent.).]

198. The blind man stretches out his hand: 'There, take it in yours and make a pair of them.'

200. δαίμοσιν used to be explained either as a dat. of hostile direction, 'we (Cadmus and I) do not argue against the gods', or as a dat. of relation, 'we do not rationalize with respect to the gods'. But σοφίζεσθαι is not a verb of hostile intention, and the so-called dat. of relation seems always to be used of *things* and to have a local or instrumental sense (see 683 n.). If the text is right it appears necessary to take δαίμοσιν, with Wilamowitz and Murray, as dat. of the person judging, 'we (men) have no cleverness in the eyes of the gods', the thought being then like Heraclitus' ἀνὴρ νήπιος ἤκουσε πρὸς δαίμονος. [This sense, however, seems to me less relevant in the present context. Moreover σοφίζεσθαι, except in the perfect, is in classical Greek to *use* cleverness rather than to be clever. I should prefer to write οὐδ' ἐνσοφιζόμεθα with Musgrave, &c.: 'nor do we use cleverness on the gods'. In Teiresias' mouth, however, the connective is hardly in place at this point, where he breaks off the stichomythia and turns to the audience. Unless we change Musgrave's οὐδ' into οὐκ (suggested to me by Prof. Fraenkel), I think we must on this view give the line to Cadmus (D. S. Robertson, *Proc. Camb. Philol. Soc.* no. 178 [1945], 29); for the shift from singular to plural cf. 669 n. The verb ἐνσοφίζεσθαι does not occur elsewhere, but cf. ἐγγυμνάζεσθαί τινι to practise on a person, ἐγκιλικίζειν τινι to play the Cilician on a person (i.e. cheat him), and Denniston, *C.R.* l (1936), 117, on the taste for ἐν- compounds. An alternative possibility is that after 200 a line or more has fallen out (Kirchhoff) containing a verb to which δαίμοσιν belonged and a verb which governed παραδοχάς (see note on αὐτά, 202).]

201-3. 'The traditions which we have received from our fathers, old as time itself, no argument shall overthrow them, whatever subtleties have been invented by deep wits.' The opening phrase was correctly understood by Plutarch (*Erot.* 756 B) as meaning ἡ πατρία καὶ παλαιὰ πίστις: a prose writer would have said ἃς κεκτήμεθα παραδοχάς, πατρίους οὔσας ὁμήλικάς τε χρόνῳ. **ὁμήλικας χρόνῳ:** not coeval *in* time (with us), but coeval *with* time. A dateless antiquity is their sanction, as it is the sanction of the ἄγραπτα θεῶν νόμιμα to which Antigone appeals: οὐ γάρ τι νῦν γε κἀχθὲς ἀλλ' ἀεί ποτε | ζῇ ταῦτα, κοὐδεὶς οἶδεν ἐξ ὅτου 'φάνη (*Ant.* 456 f.). So the Chorus of the *OT.* speak of νόμοι . . . ὧν "Ολυμπος | πατὴρ μόνος, οὐδέ νιν | θνατὰ φύσις ἀνέρων | ἔτικτεν (865 ff.), and Lysias of unwritten laws οὓς οὐδείς πω κύριος ἐγένετο καθελεῖν οὐδὲ ἐτόλμησεν ἀντειπεῖν, οὐδὲ αὐτὸν τὸν θέντα ἴσασιν (*Andoc.* 10). But this language is surprising here: for in the

play Dion. is a *new* god (219, 272, 467), and it is Pentheus, not
Dion., who is entitled to appeal to tradition. Verrall held that
the λόγος was the Dionysiac doctrine of the Chorus and the παραδοχαί the Apolline religion of Delphi; but the context makes it
perfectly evident that Teiresias' sneer is directed against the sceptics, not against the enthusiasts. And it is hardly sufficient to say
that his appeal is to the tradition of respect for deity as such:
Dionysus' opponents are no atheists (as lines 45-46 show); they
merely refuse to recognise the newcomer's claim to godhead. The
explanation seems to be that Eur. has made Teiresias speak as a
man of the fifth century, I think deliberately : the glaring anachronism is a warning to the audience that the debate which follows will
represent a fifth-century controversy transposed into the mythical
past (cf. Nihard, *Problème des Bacchantes*, 46 ff., P. Corssen, *Rh.
Mus.* lxviii [1913], 306).   καταβαλεῖ: Hdt. (8. 77) uses this word
in the same way, of 'upsetting' the belief in oracles (cf. Ar. *Clouds*
1229 τὸν ἀκατάβλητον λόγον, and Democritus B 125 Diels). It is a
metaphor from wrestling, like *I A.* 1013 ἀλλ' οἱ λόγοι γε καταπαλαίουσιν
λόγους. Protagoras wrote a work entitled Καταβάλλοντες (sc. Λόγοι),
'Destructive Essays', which began with his famous Essay on Truth
and may also have contained (E. Meyer, *Gesch. d. Altertums*, iv.
265) the Essay on the Gods, of which the opening words were περὶ
μὲν θεῶν οὐκ ἔχω εἰδέναι, οὔθ' ὡς εἰσὶν οὔθ' ὡς οὐκ εἰσὶν οὔθ' ὁποῖοί
τινες ἰδέαν (B 4 Diels). It is possible (as Bernays, *Rh. Mus.* vii
[1850], 464 ff., was the first to suggest), though it is hardly certain,
that the choice of the word καταβαλεῖ was meant to remind an
Athenian audience of this book : cf. another possible allusion to it,
Her. 757 ff., τίς ὁ θεοὺς ἀνομίᾳ χραίνων, θνητὸς ὤν, | ἄφρονα λόγον |
οὐρανίων μακάρων κατέβαλ', ὡς ἄρ' οὐ | σθένουσιν θεοί; However this
may be, 203 certainly seems to carry a reference to fifth-century
agnosticism of the Protagorean type (cf. 890-2 n.).   αὐτά: such
redundant pronouns are common in the colloquial style of Hdt. and
Plato ; and cf. the redundant νιν at Soph. *OT*. 248, *Tr.* 287. For the
neuter plural Sandys quotes Thuc. 6. 10. 2 σπονδαὶ ἔσονται· οὕτω
γὰρ . . . ἔπραξαν αὐτά (sc. τὰ περὶ τὰς σπονδάς). [But the text is open
to question : the redundant pronoun comes surprisingly soon after
the noun which it resumes. Proposed corrections for αὐτά are τάσδε,
Herwerden (transcriptionally very improbable), and δῆτα, Dalmeyda
(unidiomatic). I should prefer to suppose with Kirchhoff that the
beginning of the sentence is lost. M. Croiset (*Journ. des Savants*,
1909, p. 250) proposed to insert before 201 θεοὶ δ' ὅσ' ἔδοσαν, εἴτε
καινὰς εἴτε καί, claiming that thus 'le sens est rétabli et la grammaire
est satisfaite' (but Porson's law is not, nor is Eur.'s usage in the
matter of *enjambement*).   ηὕρηται might be middle (with the
personal subject implied in λόγος) ; but this form is usually passive.

Hermann preferred to keep εὕρηται and take it as a subjunctive, 'ut in re incerta'; but fifth-century agnosticism is a 'res certa'. καταβάλλει (L: καταβάλλῃ P) is perhaps defensible on the same ground.]

205. [Wecklein wrote χορεύσειν, on the ground that where μέλλω implies intention the tragedians use the future infinitive if metre allows. But cf. *Alc.* 513 θάπτειν τιν' ἐν τῇδ' ἡμέρᾳ μέλλω νεκρόν.]

206–7. γάρ: 'Not so: for . . .'. Similarly Aeschylus says of Dionysiac dancing κοὐδεὶς παλαιῶν οὐδὲ τῶν νεωτέρων ἑκὼν ἄπεστι τῶνδε διστοί-χω[ν χορῶν], fr. 276 Lloyd-Jones (= *P. Oxy.* 2162), lines 73 f. [With εἴτε . . . εἴτε (MSS.), the εἰ is redundant. Of a number of possible corrections the best is perhaps χρείη for εἰ χρή (W. Wolff, H. A. J. Munro), despite the irregular tense sequence. 'The corruption would arise from χρή being written for χρείη and then εἰ added in the margin or above. This opt. is common enough, and yet it is constantly corrupted' (Munro).]

209. διαριθμῶν δ' οὐδέν: separating no one in his count, 'putting none in a class apart'. Cf. the Delphic oracle quoted by Demosthenes, *Meid.* 52, ordering the Athenians to give thanks to Dion. ἄμμιγα πάντας. [The MS. tradition can equally represent δι' ἀριθμῶν δ' οὐδέν (adopted in the first edition of Murray's text) or διαριθμῶν δ' οὐδέν': the word-division in our Byzantine MSS. has no ancient authority. For διαριθμῶν cf. Plato, *Gorg.* 501 A οὐδὲν διαριθμησαμένη, 'classifying nothing'; also Aeschines, *Ctes.* 207 διηριθμημένους, 'sorted out'; Ar. *Av.* 1622, where διαριθμῶν ἀργυρίδιον is probably 'sorting small money' and not merely 'counting change'; and *IT.* 965 f., where the διά in διηρίθμησε seems to refer to the sorting of the votes into two heaps. But δι' ἀριθμῶν is also, I believe, defensible—and preferable, as giving a more pointed antithesis to ἐξ ἁπάντων . . . κοινάς. Wilamowitz (*Berl. Sitzb.* 1909, 831, n. 2) argued from an obscure phrase of Pindar, πρεσβυτέραν ἀριθμοῦ πρᾶξιν (fr. 112 Bowra, 127 Snell), that ἀριθμός could be used in the technical sense of 'age-group'. But Festugière, *Cl. Phil.* xlviii (1953), 237, has persuaded me that interpretation should start from the well-attested usage of ἀριθμός (L.S.⁹ s.v. I. 4) as 'item' or 'unit', a member of a collection considered in isolation from the rest. Euripides was fond of this usage: he has ὁ δεύτερος ἀριθμός, 'the second item' (*Ion* 1014); ἀριθμοὺς ναυαγίων, 'separate pieces of wreckage' (*Hel.* 410); οὐκ ἀριθμὸν ἀλλ' ἐτητύμως ἄνδρα (*Heraclid.* 997, cf. *Tro.* 476). It would be no great extension of this to use ἀριθμῶν, 'isolated units', here to denote individuals in contrast with the collection (ἁπάντων) to which they belong. Dionysiac worship was essentially collective: see note on 75 θιασεύεται ψυχάν. In any case I see no need to alter the text to διαιρῶν δ' οὐδέν (Brady) or διαγράφων δ' οὐδέν' (Denniston), or to delete the line with Bernhardy.]

211. προφήτης σοι λόγων is certainly not 'a prophet to you of the coming conversation with Pentheus', as some of the older edd. took it: προφήτης is not normally 'prophet' (cf. Wackernagel, *Vorl. üb. Syntax*, ii. 239 f.). Paley, &c., make it 'a speaker for you of words you would have spoken had you not been blind'—because 'it would have been in accordance with the usage of Eur. to make Teiresias end his speech by announcing the approach of Pentheus' (Tyrrell). But probably the phrase means merely 'an interpreter in words to you (of what is happening)'. Cadmus perhaps jests on the point that he, not Teiresias, is the 'seer' on this occasion.

213. δίδωμι, 'I have given': the present is used because the effect of the action persists. So 44 δίδωσι, 11 τίθησι, 42 τίκτει.

214. ὡς ἐπτόηται: 'how excited he is!'—a hint to the producer. Pentheus is characterized throughout by lack of self-control, in contrast with the supernatural ἡσυχία of Dion. His behaviour in this scene is, as Murray says, that of a typical tragedy-tyrant: those who are tempted to whitewash him, as Norwood does, should compare it closely with the behaviour of Creon in the *Antigone*—both show the same suspiciousness, the same prickly egotism, the same blind faith in physical force as a means of settling spiritual problems.   **νεώτερον,** 'fresh', perhaps with the implication 'untoward', like νέον in 362.

215-47. Greek stage convention allows Pentheus to ignore the presence of the old gentlemen for over thirty lines, after which he observes them with a start of horror (the break is marked by ἀτάρ, as often, cf. Denniston, *Particles*, 52). His monologue serves an expository purpose: it is a sort of second prologue (Schadewaldt, *Monolog u. Selbstgespräch*, 241), a counter-manifesto to the first—having heard the god's programme of action, we now listen to the man's. Similar expository monologues, *Hel.* 386 ff., *Or.* 356 ff.; in the latter passage Menelaus, like Pentheus here, fails to notice the persons on the stage.

219. θοάζειν: 'gad about'. So Cassandra is called a μαινὰς θοάζουσα, *Troad.* 349.   **τὸν νεωστί:** more contemptuous than τὸν νέον, almost 'this parvenu god': cf. *Med.* 366, 514.

222-3. 'They slink off one by one to lonely places to serve the lust of males.' Similar accusations were apparently levelled at the new mystery-cults at Athens in Eur.'s day: Aristophanes in his *Horae* attacked 'novos deos et in his colendis nocturnas pervigilationes', and cf. Lucian, *adv. indoct.* 27 on the *Baptae* of Eupolis. This may be one reason why Pentheus is made to harp on the charge (237 f., 260 f., 353 f., 487) and return to it (957 f.) even after it has been disproved by the evidence of an eyewitness (686 f.). But this insistence on the theme of sex is also significant, as Wilamowitz and Zielinski have seen, for Pentheus' psychology. His attitude to the Bacchanal women is not one of simple repulsion: unlike Hippolytus, he is the dark puritan whose passion is compounded of horror and unconscious desire, and it is this which leads him to his ruin (cf. introductory note to Scene 3 (c)).[1]

225. ἄγειν: 'rank'. Strict logic would demand ἀγούσας: but anger is not logical, and the final jeer gains in force by being thrown into the same construction as ἑστάναι and ὑπηρετεῖν.

226. χέρας, accus. of relation with δεσμίους, lit. 'bound as to their hands'.

227. πανδήμοισι ... στέγαις: 'in the common gaol'—a stylized version of the prose euphemism by which the prison is called τὸ δημόσιον (Thuc. 5. 18) and the executioner ὁ δήμιος. [P's uneuphonious δόμοις may have been introduced into the text by an unconscious echoing of the middle syllables of πανδήμοισι. But such synonymous variants are common in the tradition of Eur., and are often very old (Wecklein, *Sitzb. Akad. München*, 1896, pp. 471 ff.): cf. 1118 n.]

229–30. A possible but not, I think, certain instance of the interpolation of proper names (182 n.). [Collmann rejected the lines on the pedantic ground that ὅσαι ἄπεισιν includes other women besides the daughters of Cadmus. A stronger objection is the form Ἀκταίονος: elsewhere in the play (337, 1227, 1291) the oblique cases have ω as they have in Aesch. (fr. 241) and in Nonnus. But Callimachus has Ἀκταίονα (*Lav. Pall.* 109) and Ovid 'Actaeŏn' (*Metam.* 3. 243, &c.). Choeroboscus (*Grammatici Gr.* iv. i. 273) quotes 230, and says the o form is used *metri gratia*: cf. Ἠλεκτρύονος, which should probably be read at *Alc.* 839, and Ἠλεκτρύωνα (*Her.* 17).[2] Though unpleasing to a modern taste, the lines are appropriate enough dramatically: Pentheus feeds his rage on the thought that the women of his own family are among the culprits (cf. Grube, *Drama of Eur.* p. 403 n. 1). And the mention of Actaeon as his cousin prepares for the parallel which Cadmus draws (337 ff.) between Pentheus' impiety and his. Moreover, Cadmus' family is an artificial creation (presumably of some Theban poet, Wilamowitz, *Pindaros*, 46), and the family relationships might well be unfamiliar to some members of Eur.'s audience. Ino, Actaeon, Aristaeus (1371) seem to be old gods or δαίμονες who have been worked into the genealogy.]

234. γόης ἐπῳδός: 'a wizard conjuror'. So Theseus taunts Hippolytus with being ἐπῳδὸς καὶ γόης (*Hipp.* 1038). This was doubtless, as

---

[1] Some scholars, like Pohlenz and Diller, have found this psychological interpretation too subtle, or too 'modern'. But it is not easy to account on any other view for such lines as 812 and 957–8. Euripides, as the ancients knew, was an acute observer of μανίαι τε καὶ ἔρωτες: it is hardly an exaggeration to say with Jaeger (*Paideia* i. 350, Eng. trans.) that 'he created the pathology of the mind'.

[2] See now G. Björck, *Das Alpha Impurum*, 111, who is prepared to accept Ἀκταίονος.

Prof. Tierney has observed, a current charge against propagators of mystery-cults at Athens: cf. Plato, *Rep.* 364 B, C.

235. On the long hair and feminine beauty of Dion. see 453–9 nn.; for his golden curls cf. *Cycl.* 74 f. ὦ φίλε Βακχεῖε . . . ποῖ ξανθὰν χαίταν σείεις; To scent the hair was a fashion of Lydian origin (Xenophanes, fr. 3, where it is condemned as a ἁβροσύνη ἀνωφελής). [εὐοσμῶν (Tyrrell) for εὔοσμον (MSS.) is recommended by the frequency of the confusion between ω and o (cf. 233, 279, 622, 802). But with this text the dat. βοστρύχοισιν is somewhat awkward; and εὐοσμεῖν occurs only in Theophrastus. I should prefer to write εὔοσμον (internal accus.) κομῶν (ptcp.): cf. fr. 203 κομῶντα κισσῷ, Pherecrates fr. 189 K. ὦ ξανθοτάτοις βοτρύχοισι κομῶν. Badham proposed εὐόσμοις κομῶν: but this rather spoils the balance of the line, and it is hard to see why it should be corrupted to εὔοσμον κόμην.]

236. 'With the charm of Aphrodite winedark in his eyes.' [But the reading is, I think, false. The physiognomists described an οἰνωπὸς ὀφθαλμός as like a goat's and indicative of lunacy ([Arist.] *Phgn.* 812^b6). 438 οἰνωπὸν γένυν strongly suggests that the reference here is to the Stranger's flushed cheeks (cf. also Nonn. *Dion.* 18. 343 οἰνωπῇσι παρηίσι, *Anth. Pal.* 11. 36. 1 παρειαῖς οἰνωπαῖς, and Page, *G.L.P.*, i. 11. 14 f., from Eur. *Cretans*, where Wilamowitz rightly took οἰνωπόν with γένυν): and there is no authority for understanding ὄσσοις as 'face'. Also the second-declension form οἰνωπός occurs half a dozen times in Eur., οἰνώψ never (though Soph. has οἰνῶπα Βάκχον, *OT.* 211). I prefer Barnes's οἰνωπός, as do almost all modern edd.]

237–8. 'Who day and night keeps company with young girls, dangling before them his mysteries of joy'.   συγγίγνεται is purposely suggestive, as when the jealous Aphrodite describes Hippolytus παρθένῳ ξυνὼν ἀεί (*Hipp.* 17).

239. [στέγης is a little odd: Pentheus objects to the Stranger's activities not merely in the Castle but in the country at large, and orders his men to arrest him ἀνὰ πόλιν (352); on the other hand, the words can hardly mean 'If I catch and bring him to my house', or 'to yonder prison'. Norwood's ληψόμεσθα γῆς (*C.R.* xix, 1905) is attractive: the shift from plural to sing., though not in fact uncommon (cf. 669 n.), might lead to corruption.]

240. κτυποῦντα θύρσον: 'making his thyrsus ring' against the ground. This was apparently a movement of the Dionysiac dance, cf. 188 θύρσῳ κροτῶν γῆν: Stat. *Ach.* 2. 155 'Thyrsos pariterque levant pariterque reponunt.' [βύρσαν (R. B. Cross, *C.R.* xvi [1902]) is at first sight tempting, in view of 513 f. χεῖρα . . . βύρσης κτύπου παύσας. But it is the women who carry kettledrums; the Stranger carries a thyrsus (495).]

241. τράχηλον: 'his head'. On this use of τράχηλος, αὐχήν, δέρη for 'head' see J. E. Powell, *C.R.* liii (1939), 58. To the examples he quotes

may be added Aesch. *Cho.* 883 f. ἔοικε νῦν αὐτῆς ... αὐχὴν πεσεῖσθαι,
and in Latin Suet. *Caligula* 33 'cervix demetur'. The phrase is
brutal: a 'sympathetic' character would not be made to speak thus
(cf. Murray, *Rise of the Gk. Epic*[4], 128); decapitation was felt to be
ὠμὸν καὶ οὐχ Ἑλληνικόν (schol. B on *Iliad* 13. 203). In the end it is
Pentheus who suffers the mutilation he would have inflicted on the
Stranger.

242–3. The repeated ἐκεῖνος is very emphatic—*this* is the disreputable
charlatan on whose word the story of Dion.'s divinity depends.
ἐρράφθαι, sc. Διόνυσον. Under the influence of ἐκεῖνος the word was
transcribed ἐρράφη by someone who forgot that for Pentheus the
Stranger and the god are two, not one. [Other views of this passage:
(1) Verrall suggested that ἐκεῖνος ... ἐρράφη could stand, 'this is the
man who was (metaphorically) "sewn into the thigh of Zeus" ',
i.e. this is the man who claims to have shared in a mystical sense the
experience of his god. But, apart from other objections, ὅς could
not then refer to Dion., as it must do. (2) Failing to see the point
of the emphatic reference to the Stranger's character, some would
remove it by making the pronouns refer to Dion.: Elmsley wrote
ἐκεῖνον εἶναι ... ἐκεῖνος ... ἐρράφη (understanding with 243 ὡς
φησὶν ὁ ξένος); Robert (*Hermes*, xlix [1914]) proposed ἐκεῖνον εἶναι ...
ἐκεῖνον ... ἐρράφθαι. This line of attack was adequately answered
by Hermann. (3) The second ἐκεῖνος has been thought an accidental
repetition of the first: P. Corssen (*Rh. Mus.* lxviii [1913]) proposed
ἐπείπερ ἐν μηρῷ ποτ' ἐρράφη. But cf. *Or.* 595 f. ἐκεῖνον ἡγεῖσθ' ἀνόσιον
καὶ κτείνετε· | ἐκεῖνος ἥμαρτ', οὐκ ἐγώ. (4) Dindorf struck out 243,
Wecklein and Tyrrell the whole passage 242–7. But 242–5 make
a point essential to Pentheus' case, and the removal of 243 involves
removing also Teiresias' answer to it, 286–97. On 246–7 see below.
(5) A more plausible proposal is to transpose 239–41 to follow
247 (Kirchhoff). This clarifies the train of thought by making
the scornful ἐκεῖνος follow immediately on the description of the
Stranger; but angry men are sometimes less than perfectly lucid,
and 239–41 can be regarded as a parenthetic outburst (Bruhn).]

244. ὃς ἐκπυροῦται: '(Dionysus) who was (in fact) destroyed by fire.'
[Tyrrell's objection to 'the wrong use of ἐκπυροῦται' rests on a confusion.]

245. 'Because she lied that she was loved by Zeus.' An echo, probably
intended by Eur., of 31: Pentheus makes it clear that he accepts
his mother's naturalistic explanation of Semele's baby; and the
audience guesses that he will be punished for it no less than she.

246–7. 'Does not this call for the hideous noose, to commit such acts
of insolence, be the Stranger who he may?' Since ἀγχόνη is almost
always used with reference to suicide, several scholars take ἀγχόνης
ἄξια to mean 'enough to make one hang oneself', comparing *OT*.

1374 ἔργα . . . κρείσσον' ἀγχόνης, *Heraclid.* 246 τάδ' ἀγχόνης πέλας,
Ar. *Ach.* 125 ταῦτα δῆτ' οὐκ ἀγχόνη; That ἄξια can mean 'sufficient
to cause' is shown by *Alc.* 229 ἄξια σφαγᾶς τάδε. But though this
rendering is possible, it seems to suit Pentheus' character and
situation less well than the threat of hanging. That the latter is
inconsistent with 241 matters little: 356 is inconsistent with both,
but Pentheus is in a temper. Eur. uses βραχίονος ἀγχόναι of Heracles
strangling the Nemean lion (*Her.* 154). [247 was at one time condemned by Wilamowitz; both lines were rejected by Wecklein and
Tyrrell. In 246 Tyrrell objected to δεινῆς, as 'ludicrously feeble', and
to the violation of Porson's law (ἔστ'||ἄξια). The point of the former
may perhaps be that hanging is a particularly dirty death (cf.
Hel. 299 f., *Odyssey* 22. 462 ff., Servius ad *Aen.* 12. 603); but Mau's
δεινὰ κἀγχόνης is very plausible (*K* misread as *IC*, and the resulting
δειναις emended to δεινῆς). The latter is if anything evidence of
authenticity: the use of a long monosyllable, or elided trochaic
word, at the beginning of the fifth foot is characteristic of Eur.,
and especially of his latest style (Descroix, *Trimètre iambique,*
328 f.): cf. 252 νοῦν οὐκ ἔχον, 271 νοῦν οὐκ ἔχων, *IT.* 501 δός τῇ τύχῃ,
Or. 1035 δεῖ δ' ἢ βρόχους, *IA.* 507 σοῦ τ' ἀξίως, 975 σοῦ τ' ἄξια, 1026
χρή μ' ἀθλίαν, &c.; and for this particular word, *Or.* 615 ἐστ' ἀξία,
Bellerophon fr. 299 ἐστ' ἀσθενῆ. 247 looks a little weak: but ὕβρεις
ὑβρίζειν is an especially Euripidean phrase (*Her.* 741, cf. *Her.* 708,
Hel. 785, *IA.* 961, and *infra* 1297); and Pentheus' doubt about the
identity of the Stranger nicely balances his doubt about the identity
of Dion. (220). The forgery, if such it be, is as painstaking as it is
motiveless.]

251. βακχεύοντ' may be dual, but is I think more probably singular.
ἐν ποικίλαισι νεβρίσι will then apply to Teiresias only, as its position
suggests it should (for the plural cf. Nonn. 45. 86 χρύσεα πέπλα φέρων,
οὐ νεβρίδας), and it will be balanced by νάρθηκι βακχεύοντ' applying
to Cadmus. This is supported by 322, which seems to show that
Teiresias understands πολὺν γέλων as referring only to Cadmus.
ἀναίνομαι: best taken closely with εἰσορῶν, 'I shrink from seeing', like
IA. 1503 θανοῦσα δ' οὐκ ἀναίνομαι, 'I do not shrink from dying'. P. is
shocked because τῷ γήρᾳ φιλεῖ | ὁ νοῦς ὁμαρτεῖν (Soph. fr. 260): cf. the
similar reproach at Soph. *OC.* 930, and Cornford, *C.Q.* vi (1912), 203 f.
πάτερ: 'sir' (denoting respect, not relationship): cf. 1322. Pentheus is
fond of his grandfather (1318 ff.), and lays the blame for his conduct
on the priest. [Tyrrell through some misunderstanding asserted that
πάτερ was not in the MSS.; he also, like earlier edd., attributed to
the first hand in C (= L) the worthless conjecture βακχεύοντας.
Murray's text is that of the MSS., and there are no valid reasons for
doubting it.]

255–7. 'By introducing one more (τόνδ' αὖ) god as a novelty to mankind, you hope to have fresh occasion to watch the birds and take more pay for reading the signs in the burnt offering.' The sentence is perhaps better written as a question, with Dindorf, &c.: Pentheus turns to Teiresias, the younger man and the stronger character, and says: 'This is your doing—what was your motive?' Venality is a traditional charge against seers from the *Odyssey* (2. 186) onwards: both Creon and Oedipus throw it at Teiresias (*Ant.* 1050, *OT.* 388).

258–60. This again is like Oedipus' εἰ δὲ μὴ 'δόκεις γέρων | εἶναι, παθὼν ἔγνως ἂν οἷά περ φρονεῖς (*OT.* 402 f.). **εἰσάγων** is casual.

261. γάνος: 'the liquid gleam'. The root meaning of the word seems to be 'brightness' (τὸ λαμπρόν, schol. Ar. *Plut.* 166, cf. γανάω); it is used especially to describe the sheen or sparkle of liquids. [The genuineness of the line has sometimes been groundlessly suspected: see 384–5 n.]

262. 'I say that then there is nothing wholesome in their mysteries.' Pentheus' speech ends as it began, on the theme of impropriety. οὐδὲν ὑγιές is one of the colloquialisms introduced into tragic diction by Eur. (Soph. has it once in a late play, *Phil.* 1006). Cf. Ar. *Thesm.* 393 f. τὰς οἰνοπότιδας . . . τὰς οὐδὲν ὑγιές, and for the construction with dependent gen. Eur. *Hel.* 746 οὐδ' ἦν ἄρ' ὑγιὲς οὐδὲν ἐμπύρου φλογός.

263. τῆς δυσσεβείας is taken as exclamatory gen., like Ar. *Ach.* 87 τῶν ἀλαζονευμάτων. Elsewhere in tragedy such genitives are always preceded by an interjection (e.g. Soph. *El.* 920 φεῦ, τῆς ἀνοίας) or invocation (*I A.* 327 ὦ θεοί, σῆς ἀναισχύντου φρενός, *Or.* 1666 ὦ Λοξία μαντεῖε, σῶν θεσπισμάτων), or else by ἀλλά (when an exclamatory infinitive follows, as *Alc.* 832 ἀλλὰ σοῦ τὸ μὴ φράσαι). The naked genitive is a colloquialism possible in the mouth of Dicaeopolis, or of the lower-middle-class housewives in Theocr. 15, but alien so far as we can tell to any dignified or formal speech, and certainly ill suited to the highly stylized utterance of a Chorus-leader. [I therefore agree with Hermann that δυσσεβείας is a false emendation (despite the similar corruption at *Hel.* 1021). Still less, of course, can τῆς εὐσεβείας (MSS.) be defended as an ironical exclamatory gen. (Chorus-leaders do not indulge in irony); nor can it depend on αἰδῆ or on θεούς ('the gods of piety' would be a phrase without parallel in Greek). But the corrupt words may be θεούς, for which Musgrave proposed σθένος, Camper σέβας, Hartung κράτος. The most plausible of these is σθένος (cf. 883 τὸ θεῖον σθένος). I doubt, however, if σθένος is a possible object of αἰδώς, which is the feeling of respect for a *moral* claim. I suggest in preference τῆς Εὐσεβείας . . . θρόνους, 'the majesty of Religion': cf. Aesch. *Sept.* 409 f. τὸν Αἰσχύνης θρόνον τιμῶντα. Εὐσέβεια is similarly half personified by Empedocles, fr. 4. 5, πέμπε παρ' Εὐσεβίης ἐλάουσ' εὐήνιον ἅρμα: by Critias 2. 21 f. Bergk πρὸς τὴν τερπνοτάτην τε θεῶν θνητοῖς Ὑγίειαν | καὶ τὴν Εὐσεβίης

γείτονα Σωφροσύνην: and *H. Orph. prooem.* 14 f. (in a list of divinities)
καὶ τὸ Δικαιοσύνης τε καὶ Εὐσεβίης μέγ' ὄνειαρ | κικλήσκω: cf. the
goddess 'Οσία (370) and my note there. An alternative possibility
is that something has fallen out. It may be significant that in the
Chr. Pat. this line is represented by two (191–2): τῆς ἀσεβείας·
ὦ τάλ', οὐ φοβῇ Θεόν; | οὐ θεσμὸν αἰδῇ τῶν βροτῶν τῆς οὐσίας | Ἀδάμ
τε τὸν σπείραντα κτλ. Eur. may possibly have written something
like

τῆς Εὐσεβείας, ὦ ξέν', ⟨οὐ φοβῇ κράτος
θεσμόν τε τὸν παλαιόν;⟩ οὐκ αἰδῇ θεοὺς

(cf. 201 and fr. 360 l. 45 προγόνων παλαιὰ θέσμια).]

264–5. On P.'s ancestry see 537–41 n. [Musgrave's transposition of
these two lines gives rather more point to τὸν σπείραντα γηγενῆ
στάχυν by making it explanatory of γένος, but the argument is
hardly decisive.]

266–71. Teiresias' speech has a more formal structure than the angry
tirade of Pentheus. In accordance with Greek oratorical practice it
includes a προοίμιον (266–71), a series of πίστεις or pleas, and an
ἐπίλογος or peroration (319–27). The προοίμιον is of a type much
favoured by the orators—a denunciation of the opposing speaker's
abuse of professional skill. But it is not, I think, purely conventional:
reflections on the harm done by the art of suggestion (πειθώ), when
it is exercised by men without principle, appear repeatedly in Eur.,
and seem to represent a lesson which he wished to bring home to
his audience—cf. *Med.* 580 ff., *Hipp.* 486 ff., *Hec.* 1187 ff., *Phoen.*
526 f., *Or.* 907 ff., *Antiope* fr. 189. This was in fact the greatest
danger of ancient as of modern democracies. That Eur. had it in
mind here is suggested by the γνώμη about the κακὸς πολίτης
(270 f.), which is barely appropriate in the mouth of a subject
addressing a king (and seems designed, as Sandys pointed out, for
Athenian rather than Macedonian ears).

266–9. τῶν λόγων...καλὰς ἀφορμάς: 'an honest case to argue'. ἀφορμή
(-αί), 'what one starts from', developed a number of technical
senses: in military language it is the base of operations, in commercial
language capital, in the language of the courts the lawyer's 'case'
or 'brief'. Eur. is fond of using it in the last of these senses: *Hec.*
1238 f. τὰ χρηστὰ πράγματα | χρηστῶν ἀφορμὰς ἐνδίδωσ' ἀεὶ λόγων,
Her. 236 ἀφορμὰς τοῖς λόγοισιν (cf. Wilamowitz ad loc.), *Phoen.* 199
ἀφορμὰς τῶν λόγων. In all these passages ἀφορμαί refers to the
factual basis, λόγοι to the verbal presentation. It is one of those
prose words by means of which Eur. tried to give actuality to the
speech of tragedy.   **μέγ' ἔργον**, 'a big undertaking', is again a
colloquial expression (Plato, *Symp.* 187 E μέγα ἔργον ταῖς ... ἐπιθυμίαις
καλῶς χρῆσθαι, Ar. *Frogs* 1100 χαλεπὸν οὖν ἔργον διαιρεῖν).   **φρένες**

here denotes an abstract quality, 'good sense'; all connexion with its original meaning as the name of a bodily organ has vanished, so that it can be 'in' a man's words. [Cf. B. Meissner, *Mythisches und Rationales in der Psychologie der euripideischen Tragödie*, 96.] Teiresias says in effect 'It is easy to make a good speech, given two things—dexterity (σοφία) and a sound case. You have the nimble tongue of the σοφός, but the *content* of your pleas is foolish.'

270-1. 'The ready speaker who owes his influence (only) to his self-assurance (θράσει, the emphatic word) proves a bad citizen; for he lacks good sense.' Not '*becomes* a bad citizen *if* he lacks good sense', which, as Sandys says, would require μή. νοῦν οὐκ ἔχων is virtually a *tu quoque* to Pentheus' taunt, 252: that is why Teiresias puts it categorically. [The MS. reading in 270 is barely defensible as equivalent to θρασὺς δὲ ἀνήρ, δυνατὸς ὢν κα ἰοιός τε ὢν λέγειν. δυνατός may be a gloss on οἷός τε (cf. Hesych. οἷόν τε· δυνατὸν λέγουσιν), which has supplanted some other word (θρασὺς δὲ ⟨γλώσσῃ⟩ Wecklein, θρασύς τ' ⟨ἐν ἀστοῖς⟩ Badham). Madvig's correction is, however, supported by *Or.* 903 ἀνήρ τις ἀθυρόγλωσσος, ἰσχύων θράσει. These two lines should not in my judgement be rejected: see note on 266-71.]

274-85. What underlies this passage is (1) the traditional opposition of the Dry and the Wet (τὸ ξηρόν and τὸ ὑγρόν) as elements of the world's body and of man's body, which goes back to Ionian thought; and (2) the fifth-century identification of Demeter and Dion. with the most valuable forms of the Dry and the Wet, bread and wine respectively. For the latter cf. the opinion of the sophist Prodicus that πάντα τὰ ὠφελοῦντα τὸν βίον ἡμῶν οἱ παλαιοὶ θεοὺς ἐνόμισαν διὰ τὴν ἀπ' αὐτῶν ὠφέλειαν . . . καὶ διὰ τοῦτο τὸν μὲν ἄρτον Δήμητραν νομισθῆναι, τὸν δὲ οἶνον Διόνυσον (Sext. Emp. *adv. math.* 9. 18 = Diels *Vors.* 84 (77) B 5). Though Eur. was probably a good many years senior to Prodicus, the biographical tradition made him P.'s pupil (Gell. 15. 20. 4, *Vit. Eur.* 2, Suidas s.v. Εὐρ.), and he would certainly in any case be acquainted with P.'s views (we have no warrant for assuming, with Bruhn and Nestle, that he shared them). [It has been thought surprising that he should put words which recall this 'atheistic' doctrine into the mouth of the pious Teiresias, especially after the priest's profession οὐκ ἐνσοφίζεσθαι τοῖς δαίμοσιν— and it would be, were the doctrine really atheistic. But though Prodicus sometimes figures in ancient lists of ἄθεοι, it was possible to claim that he had 'put piety on a sound foundation' (Themistius 30, 349 B = Diels *Vors.* 84 (77) B 5). His was apparently the ambiguous position of the 'modernist' (cf. H. Gomperz, *Sophistik u. Rhetorik*, 113-17)—that is why he is quoted by the modernist Teiresias. (At a later date the Stoics similarly materialized and depersonalized the gods without ceasing to regard them as proper objects of worship. And the Irishman who being asked 'How can bread be God?'

replied 'What else would it be?' was not a man devoid of religious feeling.) Nor is the theory, thus understood, entirely anachronistic. Demeter and Dion. had not always been anthropomorphic personages. Whether Δη-μήτηρ means the Earth Mother, as some Greeks believed (Diod. 1. 12. 4, Sext. Emp. *adv. math.* 9. 189, Cic. *ND* 2. 67) or, as seems more probable, the Corn Mother (Mannhardt, cf. Cretan δηαί, 'barley'), Teiresias is right about her essential nature. And although Dion. is more than the Giver of Wine, the feeling that wine is his substance is as primitive as the complete identification in Indian thought of the god Soma with the drink Soma (284–5 n.). For the association of Demeter and Dion. cf. Pindar, *Isthm.* 7. 4 πάρεδρον Δαμάτερος . . . Διόνυσον: Moschion, fr. 6. 23 ff. (*T.G.F.* p. 814) τόθ' ηὑρέθη μὲν καρπὸς ἡμέρου τροφῆς | Δήμητρος ἁγνῆς, ηὑρέθη δὲ Βακχίου | γλυκεῖα πηγή: schol. Aratus, *Diosem.* 1068 οἱ παλαιοὶ τὸν Διόνυσον τῇ Δημήτρᾳ συγκαθιέρωσαν, αἰνιττόμενοι τὸ γόνιμον τῆς ὑγρότητος: and the inscriptional evidence cited by Vollgraff, *Mém. Acad. Inscr.* xiv (1951), 344 ff.]

276. γῆ δ' ἐστίν: the same identification in the *Phoenissae*, 685 ff. Δαμάτηρ θεά, | πάντων ἄνασσα, πάντων δὲ γᾶ τροφός. In cult Demeter and Ge were always distinct, though in many respects parallel. For the indifference as to names cf. Aesch. *PV*. 209 f. Θέμις | καὶ Γαῖα, πολλῶν ὀνομάτων μορφὴ μία.

277. ἐν ξηροῖσιν, where prose would use a simple instrumental dat.: cf. 157–9 n.

278. ἀντίπαλον, adj. with πῶμα, 'the liquor of the grape to match Demeter's bread'. [It is possible to retain what is practically the reading of L, ὁ δ' ἦλθεν ἐπὶ τἀντίπαλον, ὁ Σεμέλης γόνος· translating either 'But the other came to render the complementary service' (cf. 967 ἐπὶ τόδ' ἔρχομαι) or 'But the other entered into rivalry with her'. The resulting asyndeton is, however, a little harsh; and if we avoid it by writing ὃς δ' we should also accept Housman's neat correction of the following words, which is very close to the reading of P and yields much more natural Greek.]

282–3. Wine was the usual sleeping-draught of antiquity: cf. 385, *Cycl.* 574 εἰς ὕπνον βαλεῖ, Ar. *Wasps* 9 ὕπνος μ' ἔχει τις ἐκ Σαβαζίου, Hor. *Odes* 3. 21. 4. [P was formerly supposed to have ὕπνου, and this reading was adopted by some of the older edd. (as a subjective gen.); but later collations showed that both MSS. had ὕπνον.] **ἄλλο:** most naturally understood as 'other than wine'. Cf. fr. 1079, where someone attacks this use of wine as a λύπης φάρμακον, and 421–3 n.

284–5. 'He, being god, is poured out in offering to the gods, so that to him men owe all their blessings' (because the libation of wine was a part of prayer).   **σπένδεται** is quite certainly passive (not middle as L.S.⁸), nor is there any play on the middle sense (as

Paley, &c., fancied)—the statement that Dionysus 'makes a truce with the gods' would have no meaning in the context. The thought is curious, recalling Paul's mystical ἐγὼ γὰρ ἤδη σπένδομαι (2 *Tim.* 4. 6), 'I am poured out as an offering'. A closer parallel is the Indian belief in the identity of the god Soma with the soma-libation (an intoxicating drink made from a wild plant and offered to the gods): 'some of the finest and most spiritual of the Vedic hymns are addressed to Soma, and yet it is hard to say whether they are addressed to a person or a beverage' (Sir Charles Eliot, *Hinduism and Buddhism*, i. 58). It is tempting to see here not merely the rediscovery but the survival of an ancient religious idea (cf. Farnell, *Cults*, v. 97, 121, on the Thracian cult of Διόνυσος Βότρυς, 'Dionysus the Vine-cluster'). In any case I see no reason for regarding the thought either as a sophism put into Teiresias' mouth in order to discredit him (Bruhn) or as 'the last word of scientific rationalism' (Norwood). The elementary jokes cracked by the Cyclops about a god choosing to live in a bottle (*Cycl.* 525–7) tell us that the god-wine equation was current in some sense at Athens; they do not tell us what the sense was, still less what Eur. thought about it. [On the trochaic caesura ὥστε || δι-, which Porson wished to avoid by writing διὰ τοῦτον ὥστε, see 192 n.]

286–97. [Dindorf, Tyrrell, and Wecklein, following a suggestion of Boeckh's, dismissed this passage as spurious (though they failed to discover any plausible motive for its interpolation); and even Sandys thought its genuineness 'open to serious doubt'. But more recent scholars have rightly retained the lines. The main grounds of objection were (1) the absurdity of the explanation (μηρός a mistake for ὅμηρος); (2) the feebleness and obscurity of the ὅμηρος story; (3) the inconsistency of that story with the Chorus's acceptance of the doctrine of the Double Birth (94 ff.) and subsequent reiteration of it (523 ff.); (4) the inappropriateness of this 'sophistry' in the mouth of Teiresias. These objections lose a good deal of their force upon closer consideration. (1) Teiresias is not alone in attempting to explain the origin of a rejected myth (an early example is Pindar, *Ol.* 1. 46 ff.), or in basing his explanation on a supposed confusion of words—Nihard well compares Hdt. 1. 122, where the myth that Cyrus was suckled by a bitch is explained by the story that his foster-mother's name was Spako, σπάξ being the Median word for a dog. (2) It is probable on other grounds that our text has been injured (see 292–4 n.), and the injury may well be responsible for the obscurity of the narrative. Paley, a good judge of such questions, found nothing un-Euripidean in the style. (3) The difference of opinion between Teiresias and the Chorus has a close parallel in the *Helena*, where Helen as an educated woman cannot commit herself to the belief that she came out of an egg

(17 ff., 257 ff.), whereas her friends the washerwomen continue in the simple faith that she did (214 ff., 1144 ff.). As Sandys mildly expresses it, 'it is not necessary to have a perfect consistency of opinion between all the characters of the play'. (4) The passage is not out of character: Teiresias is trying to bring a barbarous myth, whose meaning had long been lost, into harmony with modern 'science'—for, as Winnington-Ingram says, 'ether, then as now, was a word to conjure with'. The thigh-birth lent itself too easily to ribald humour, as Lucian saw (*Dial. Deor.* 9), and as the Old Comedy poet Polyzelus, author of a *Διονύσου Γοναί*, doubtless saw before him.]

286. καταγελᾷς: not elsewhere with the accus., but Aeschylus uses the passive (*Ag.* 1271), and the tendency to make similar compounds transitive is strong in the later fifth century (cf. καταφρονεῖν 503 and Thuc. 6. 34, κατασκῆψαι Med. 94, καταπνεῦσαι Med. 839, καταβοᾶν Ar. *Ach.* 711, κατακράζειν Ar. *Eq.* 287).

289. θεόν, with predicative force—'as a god'. [Emendation is not, I think, necessary: for the thought cf. Theognis 1347 f. ἁρπάξας δ' ἐς *Ὄλυμπον ἀνήγαγε, καί μιν ἔθηκεν | δαίμονα*: as regards the repetition θεόν . . . θεός see 647 n.]

291. οἷα δὴ θεός: 'in a manner worthy of a god', cf. Plato, *Critias* 113 E τὴν νῆσον οἷα δὴ θεὸς εὐμαρῶς διεκόσμησεν.

292–4. 'He broke off a portion of the ether which surrounds the earth, and handing this over (to Hera) made it a hostage (for his future good behaviour); (but the real child he gave to the nymphs to rear, and thus saved) Dionysus from the jealousy of Hera.' **τόνδε** is attracted (from τόδε) to the gender of the secondary predicate ὅμηρον in accordance with an established Greek idiom.—Ether is not the air but the stuff of which the sky is made (οὐρανοῦ καὶ ἄστρων οὐσίαν αἰθέρα καλοῦμεν, [Arist.] *de mundo* 392ᵃ5). For its use as a raw material in the manufacture of dummies cf. the false Helen, who was made of οὐρανός (*Hel.* 34) or αἰθήρ (ibid. 584). [The view of Corssen and Pohlenz, that what Zeus surrendered to Hera was not an εἴδωλον of Dion. but (*a*) a portion of his realm and (*b*) the real Dion. (τόνδε) as security for her undisturbed possession of it, must I think be rejected: it gives a strange meaning to ῥήξας, and makes 291 pointless—there would be nothing clever about such a policy of appeasement.] We are not told what Hera did with the dummy Dion., but presumably she threw it out of Heaven: I have a suspicion that it may be identical with the mysterious 'log' which fell from Heaven into Semele's θάλαμος at the time of her death and was preserved at Thebes under the name Dionysus Cadmeius (Paus. 9. 12. 4, cf. *Fouilles de Delphes*, III. i. 195, 198)—where else should the bastard go but back to his mother? If a piece of Theban aetiology underlies the story, Eur. had a good reason for putting it into the mouth of the Theban seer. As for the true Dion., Zeus sent him away to be brought up by the nymphs of Nysa (*H. Hymn* 26. 3 ff., [Apollodorus] 3. 4. 3): hence Murray's supplement. It may well be that more than one line is missing, and that the function and fate of the μέρος αἰθέρος were made clearer than they are in our text. [Attempts to construe the text without the assumption of a lacuna shipwreck on the impossibility of finding a construction for νεικέων: neither ἐκδιδοὺς νεικέων, 'putting Dion. out of the way of Hera's jealousy', nor ὅμηρον νεικέων, 'a hostage to Hera's jealousy', has any parallel in Greek. We might read νείκεσιν (Usener), and translate either 'he made this into a Dion., surrendering it as a hostage to Hera's jealousy', or 'he made this a hostage to Hera's jealousy, putting Dion. out to nurse'; but on the former view the word-order is hopelessly contorted, and on the latter ἐκδιδούς is an oddly ambiguous verb to describe what Zeus did with the true Dion. The best attempts to mend the construction on the assumption that nothing is missing are Wilamowitz's ἔσωσε for ἔθηκε (governing Διόνυσον), and Dalmeyda's διάλυσιν for Διόνυσον, but neither is quite convincing: the former postulates a rather improbable corruption, and the latter leaves the following νιν rather obscure.]

295. [Most edd. retain τραφῆναι, which in itself is certainly defensible (cf. Aesch. *Eum.* 665 ἐν σκότοισι νηδύος τεθραμμένη). But ῥαφῆναι is perhaps to be preferred as answering more exactly to ὡς ἐνερράφη in 286 and to Pentheus' ἐρράφθαι (243).]

296–7. 'By the change of a word they made the story, because he was once a hostage to Hera, god to goddess.' **ὡμήρευσε:** this verb means either 'to be a hostage' or (*Rhes.* 434) 'to make into a hostage'. If we give it the latter sense, θεός = Zeus, and we must supply νιν as object from 294. But θεός in emphatic conjunction with θεᾷ looks like an assertion of *Dion.*'s divinity (cf. 84, 289). On either view the language is a little odd: Dion. and the dummy seem to be identified. But if I am right in suspecting that the dummy was identical with the revered fetish called Dionysus Cadmeius, it is easier to understand its being styled θεός.

298–301. In Thrace Dion. was a god of trance-mediumship: Herodotus (7. 111) describes his oracle on a mountain-top in the country of the Thracian Satrae, where he spoke through the lips of a priestess κατά περ ἐν Δελφοῖσι (i.e. she went into trance); hence Eur. elsewhere calls him ὁ Θρηξὶ μάντις (*Hec.* 1267: cf. Paus. 9. 30. 9, and the mysterious Βάκχου προφήτης in a cave on Mount Pangaeum, *Rhes.* 972). When Dion. came to Greece he found there an established mantic god, Apollo, with whom it was difficult to compete; yet at least one Dionysiac oracle on Greek soil lasted down to Roman times, that of Amphikleia in Phocis, where the god prophesied through an entranced priest (πρόμαντις δὲ ὁ ἱερεύς ἐστι, χρᾷ δὲ ἐκ τοῦ θεοῦ κάτοχος, Paus. 10. 33. 11). Teiresias' claim is thus based on more than the etymological connexion between μανία and μαντική which is hinted at in 299 and asserted in Plato's *Phaedrus* (244 C, where the τ is said to have been introduced into μαντική 'by a vulgar error', ἀπειροκάλως). On the dramatic significance of his claim see next note.—I do not think that l. 300 means merely 'when a man has drunk a great deal of wine' (Welcker, Bruhn), though Plutarch perhaps understood it so (*def. orac.* 40. 432 E οἶνος ἀναθυμιαθεὶς ἕτερα πολλὰ κινήματα καὶ λόγους ἀποκειμένους καὶ λανθάνοντας ἀποκαλύπτει· τὸ γὰρ βακχεύσιμον καὶ τὸ μανιῶδες μαντευτικὴν πολλὴν ἔχει κατ' Εὐριπίδην). Teiresias has disposed earlier of Dion.'s function as a wine-god (278–85); here he is presented as the cause of two unaccountable modes of behaviour, second-sight and panic, two μανίαι (305) whose common characteristic is that in both of them human will and reason are submerged by a mysterious impulse coming from outside the individual consciousness, and therefore, in the belief of antiquity, from a higher power. All such psychological states, which could be neither explained nor controlled, were attributed to an external psychic interference : cf. the language which Eur. uses to describe the uncontrollable impulse of desire breaking down the agent's will, *Hipp.* 443 Κύπρις γὰρ οὐ φορητός, ἦν πολλὴ ῥυῇ.

302–4. The assertion that Dion. 'shares in a certain portion of Ares' province' is explained by the two following lines—he is capable of injecting panic into armed and disciplined troops. There is not much to support the view that he was primitively a war-god. [In the first of the two passages quoted by Sandys in this connexion, βρόμιε, δορατοφόρ', ἐνυάλιε, πολεμοκέλαδε, some at least of the epithets belong not to Dion. but to Ares: it continues with πάτερ Ἄρη (Fragm. Mel. Chor. Adesp. 22 Diehl). The second, Macrobius, *Sat.* I. 19. 1, is a dubious piece of very late syncretism which proves, at most, that Dion. was somewhere called ἐνυάλιος (as he is ἄρειος in an inscription from S. Russia, *IPE.* iv. 199, fourth century B.C., and ἀρήιος in *H. Orph.* 30. 4). Except in representations of the Battle of the Gods and Giants he seldom or never appears in sculpture or painting as an armed god, at any rate before Hellenistic times, when he was imagined as a divine prototype of Alexander the Great.] But Teiresias does not claim that he is a war-god. Nor is it implied that the infection of terror which turns an army into a mob is *always* the work of Dion. Such terror was commonly attributed to Pan, as our name for it testifies. [I see no reason to suppose with Wilamowitz (*Glaube d. Hellenen*, i. 248, n. 2) that Pan merely borrowed a power which belonged primitively to Dion. : cf. Deichgräber, *Hermes*, lxx. 335.] What is meant is a special kind of panic— the moral and physical collapse of those who attempt to resist by normal means the fury of the possessed worshippers. These lines **are**

a preparation for the description of such an incident in 761–4 (where see note), just as 298–301 may be taken as a preparation for Dion.'s concluding prophecy. The lines are also in character for Teiresias: he perceives, as Winnington-Ingram says, 'that he can relate Dionysus' functions to those of Phoebus and of Ares, and so build yet another bridge for the new god peaceably to enter the Hellenic pantheon'. Phoebus is Teiresias' patron; the reason for the slightly artificial introduction of Ares is perhaps the special position which he held in Theban legend (cf. Aesch. *Sept.* 104 προδώσεις, παλαίχθων Ἄρης, τὰν τεάν; and 135 f., Eur. *Phoen.* 1006 ff.).

306–9. Teiresias predicts the acceptance of Dion. 'one day' (ἔτι) at Delphi, which shall make him μέγαν ἀν' Ἑλλάδα. And it is probable that this was in historical fact the decisive step which led to the final Hellenization of the dangerous Thracian god who had already established his orgiastic ritual at Orchomenos and Thebes (cf. Farnell, *Cults*, v. 112 f., Nilsson, *History of Greek Religion*, 208 f.). The curious division of powers which existed in classical times at Delphi looks like the result of a deliberate compromise between two rival cults; the divine brothers played Box and Cox, Apollo being undisputed master for nine months of the year, while Dion. had a free field for his ὄργια during the three winter months when Apollo was 'absent' and the oracle closed. Provided the Apolline priesthood retained complete control of the oracle and of the political power which the oracle wielded, they were willing not only to make room for the younger god but actively to propagate his cult elsewhere, as they did at Athens, Corinth, Sicyon, Methymna, Magnesia, and other places (cf. Parke and Wormell, *The Delphic Oracle* i. 330 ff.), and as the Apolline priest Teiresias does here.   πηδῶντα . . . πλάκα: for this accus. of space traversed cf. Soph. *Aj.* 30 πηδῶντα πεδία, and *infra* 749, 873. The 'upland between the two peaks' is probably the plateau of Livadi, the stretch of wild but fairly level country which lies behind the two summits of the Phaedriades, immediately above Delphi. For the pine-torch carried by the priest, the god's representative, cf. 144 ff. The reference is surely to the actual nocturnal mountain dancing in which the god himself was believed to take part (115 n.), not to optical illusions produced by 'cloud-effects at sunset' (Sandys).   πάλλοντα, 'brandishing': cf. 553, and Soph. *Ichn.* 220 θύρσο[ο]ν εὐπαλῆ. [βάλλοντα (MSS.) is perhaps defensible: cf. 762 and 1099 where the thyrsus is used as a missile, and 25 where it is called a βέλος. We should expect, however, σείοντα καὶ βάλλοντα.[1]]

310–12. 'Be not over-sure that force is what dominates human affairs;

---

[1] Hermann made βάλλοντα govern πλάκα, 'striking the upland (with light)', cf. *Supp.* 650 f. ἀκτὶς ἡλίου . . . ἔβαλλε γαῖαν. But this seems impossible without a word meaning 'light'.

nor, if you have a thought and your thought is sick, mistake that thought for wisdom.' For the danger of stubborn reliance upon an unproved δόξα cf. Soph. *Ant.* 323 ἦ δεινόν, ᾧ δοκῇ γε, καὶ ψευδῆ δοκεῖν (which shows that φρονεῖν need not be supplied with δοκῇς). For φρονεῖν τι 'to be clever' (τι in ironical deprecation, like the American use of 'some') cf. Thuc. 5. 7. 3, where we are told that Cleon ἐπίστευσέ τι φρονεῖν, thought himself 'some' general. [The older English edd. retain νοσεῖ, explaining that ἡ δέ . . . νοσεῖ is parenthetical and not part of the condition, despite the μέν and δέ. But the sense thus obtained is as poor as the syntax is odd, and the confusion of ει and ηι is frequent.]

314–18. The answer to 221–5: 'It is not Dionysus' part to force chastity on women: you must look for that (the moral factor) in human character; for even in the ecstatic rite the pure will not lose her purity.' Dion. is not immoral; he is non-moral—morality is ir-relevant to religion of the Dionysiac type (cf. Farnell, *Cults*, v. 238 f.). For the thought that it is φύσις, not νόμος—as we should say, character and not circumstance—that determines conduct, cf. fr. 810 μέγιστον ἄρ' ἦν ἡ φύσις, *Hipp.* 79 f. (quoted below), and other passages which I have discussed, *C.R.* xliii (1929), 99. Here once more Teiresias speaks the language of the fifth century and thinks in terms popularized by the Sophistic movement. [314 has suffered from the attentions of persons who did not perceive that the lines present a perfectly good, and typically Euripidean, answer to Pentheus. In the MSS. of Stobaeus, or (less probably) in those used by him, μή was inserted (unmetrically) before σωφρονεῖν: and the same 'correc-tion' was introduced into P by a late hand, almost certainly from Stobaeus, whose readings the same hand has introduced elsewhere, e.g. *Supp.* 238, 324, 486. Later pedants have read ἀφρονεῖν or μὴ φρονεῖν: but the former verb does not occur in Attic Greek; and apart from the awkwardness of φρονεῖν (312) followed two lines later by μὴ φρονεῖν in a different sense, μὴ φρονεῖν ἐς τὴν Κύπριν is a very odd way of describing unchastity. On the other hand, the sentence beginning ἀλλ' ἐν τῇ φύσει presents a genuine difficulty. Stobaeus quotes the passage twice—presumably from two different earlier anthologies, whose editors used different recensions of the Eur. text, since in one place (3. 5. 1 Hense = 5. 15 Meineke) he calls the play Βάκχαι, in the other (4. 23. H. = 74. 8 M.) Πενθεύς. His Βάκχαι text agrees in 315–16 with LP; his Πενθεύς text has εἰς τὴν φύσιν and omits 316. The main question is whether 316 is genuine. (*a*) If it is, we must either put a stop at ἀεί and make ἔνεστιν mean 'depends on' (unexampled, though Thuc. uses γίγνεσθαι ἐν in this sense, 1. 74. 1); or else read εἰ τῇ φύσει, with comma at ἀεί (Porson). The latter proposal is supported by Menander, fr. 89 Kock, ἀλλ' εἰ πλείονα | τὰ συμφέροντ' ἔνεστι, τοῦτο χρὴ σκοπεῖν, which might be an unconscious echo of the present passage. Prof. Murray told me in 1940 that he was now inclined to accept it. It makes excellent sense, and also accounts neatly for the variants: if εἰ was miswritten εἰς by assimilation to εἰς τὴν Κύπριν, εἰς τῇ φύσει would inevitably become either ἐν τῇ φύσει or εἰς τὴν φύσιν, and those who adopted the latter reading would have to drop 316 as meaningless. (b) Alternatively— but I think less probably—we may say that, not seeing the construction of ἐν τῇ φύσει, one ancient editor emended the words to make them parallel with εἰς τὴν Κύπριν, while another 'postulated a lacuna' and filled it up with a line which he concocted out of a vague recollection of Hipp. 79 ff. ὅσοις διδακτὸν μηδέν, ἀλλ' ἐν τῇ φύσει | τὸ σωφρονεῖν εἴληχεν ἐς τὰ πάνθ' ὁμῶς (or πάντ' ἀεί), | τούτοις δρέπεσθαι, τοῖς κακοῖσι δ' οὐ θέμις. Cf. G. Jachmann in Nachr. Ges. Wiss. Gött., Phil.-hist. Kl. 1936, p. 210. The construction ἐν τῇ φύσει τοῦτο σκοπεῖν χρή is in fact difficult: I have found no example in tragedy of σκοπεῖν τι ἔν τινι. Therefore, if we cut out 316, it is, I think, preferable to punctuate, with Kirchhoff and Wecklein, ἀλλ' ἐν τῇ φύσει τοῦτο· σκοπεῖν χρή· 'But that depends on character: look at the facts—even in the ecstatic rite . . .' Cf. El. 388 ff. οὐδὲ γὰρ δόρυ | μᾶλλον βραχίων σθεναρὸς ἀσθενοῦς μένει· |ἐν τῇ φύσει δὲ τοῦτο: and for σκοπεῖν χρή, Tro. 729 f. ἔχεις γὰρ ἀλκὴν οὐδαμῇ. σκοπεῖν δὲ χρή· | πόλις τ' ὄλωλε καὶ πόσις.—Various late authors relate an anecdote about Plato and the hedonist Aristippus in which the latter is made to quote καὶ γάρ—διαφθαρήσεται. In one version of the anecdote (Suidas, s.v. Ἀρίστιππος) 318 appears in the form ὁ νοῦς ὁ σώφρων οὐ διαφθαρήσεται, which Boeckh and Nestle were inclined to introduce into our text of the Bacchae: but the line has clearly been adapted to suit the position of a male philosopher.]

319–21. Gods, like kings, demand to be treated with respect: cf. Aphrodite in the Hippolytus (7 f.), ἔνεστι γὰρ δὴ κἀν θεῶν γένει τόδε· | τιμώμενοι χαίρουσιν ἀνθρώπων ὕπο: and Death in the Alcestis (53), τιμαῖς κἀμὲ τέρπεσθαι δόκει. The argument is one which Pentheus, himself a stickler for τιμή (1310 ff.), may be expected to appreciate.

326–7. 'For you are mad, cruelly mad: no drug can cure your sickness, but some drug has caused it.' τούτων must refer to φαρμάκοις, not to ἄκη: for οὔτε φαρμάκοις and οὔτ' ἄνευ τούτων are clearly antithetic. As the snake feeds his rage on evil drugs (βεβρωκὼς κακὰ φάρμακ'· ἔδυ δέ τέ μιν χόλος αἰνός Il. 22. 94), so homicidal rage or other folly in men is conventionally ascribed to a like cause: cf. Aesch. Ag. 1407 ff. τί κακόν . . . ἐδανὸν ἢ ποτὸν πασαμένα . . . τόδ' ἐπέθου θύος; Ar. Th. 534 ἢ πεφάρμαχθ' ἢ κακόν τι μέγα πεπόνθατ' ἄλλο, Eur. Hipp. 318 μῶν ἐξ ἐπακτοῦ πημονῆς ἐχθρῶν τινος; with scholion μή τίς σε οὖν τῶν ἐχθρῶν ἐφάρμαξε; Banquo speaks in the same convention when he asks, after the meeting with the witches, 'Have we eaten on the insane root that takes the reason prisoner? (Macbeth, 1. 3. 83). [The text has been much suspected, but Prof. Fraenkel has convinced me that it is probably sound. Of the suggested corrections, the most plausible are Dobree's νόσου (dep. ἄκη) for νοσεῖς and Headlam's νῦν τε for the second οὔτε. The former makes a sentence of the same type as Ar. *Lys.* 1038 f. ἐστίν . . . οὐ κακῶς εἰρημένον | οὔτε σὺν πανω-λέθροισιν οὔτ' ἄνευ πανωλέθρων, and others quoted by Wilamowitz on *Her.* 1106. But νόσου is a weakish supplement to a sense already complete.]

332. 'For now you are all in the air, and your wit is without wisdom', Winnington-Ingram. For πέτῃ cf. Theogn. 1053 τῶν γὰρ μαινομένων πέτεται θυμός τε νόος τε, Ar. *Av.* 169 ἄνθρωπος ὄρνις ἀστάθμητος πετόμενος, and the English word 'flighty'. The νόμοι in question are the prescriptions of religious tradition, the πάτριοι παραδοχαί of 201.

324. καταψεύδου καλῶς: 'lie for credit's sake'. A καλὸν ψεῦδος is not a 'noble lie', but one which makes a good impression (cf. Thuc. 6. 12. 1 τὸ ψεύσασθαι καλῶς χρήσιμον). Cadmus is partly the timid old man anxious to keep on the right side of τὸ θεῖον (341, cf. 199), partly the shrewd 'Hauspolitiker'. Winnington-Ingram calls attention to the repeated μεθ' ἡμῶν (331, 342): the family must hang together. Ion suspects Creusa of taking a similar line about his parentage, *Ion* 1523 ff.

335. [I doubt if Tyrwhitt's widely accepted emendation is any improvement on the MS. reading ὡς ἔστι Σεμέλης, ἵνα . . . . The νόμοι require Pentheus to profess that 'this god', Dionysus, exists (παρὰ σοὶ λεγέσθω, sc. εἶναι); family honour requires him to profess that the god is Semele's baby (ὡς ἔστι Σεμέλης), and not simply the latest importation from the orient (cf. 467–8). These are two distinct pleas—Pentheus might accept the first while rejecting the second—whereas with Tyrwhitt's text καταψεύδου ὡς ἔστι merely repeats the sense of παρὰ σοὶ λεγέσθω.]

336. παντὶ τῷ γένει: in apposition to ἡμῖν and defining its meaning: cf. 619.

337–40. The old man, who lives for his family, recalls the fate of his other grandson, Pentheus' cousin Actaeon, who was torn to pieces by his own dogs on Cithaeron (1291) because like Pentheus he had scorned a deity. The parallel is closer than Cadmus knows: Pentheus too will suffer σπαραγμός in the same place. That seems to be the reason why Actaeon crops up so often in the *Bacchae* (230, 1227, 1291). [Varying accounts of his offence are given. Our oldest authorities (Stesichorus fr. 68, Acusilaos fr. 33 Jacoby) make him compete with Zeus for the hand of Semele: this version probably derives from a Hesiodic *Eoe* (L. Malten, *Kyrene*, 18 ff.). When Semele became Actaeon's aunt this was no longer suitable, and he transferred his attentions to Artemis (Diod. 4. 81. 4), or was turned into a punished boaster like Eurytus (*Od.* 8. 224 ff.) or Agamemnon in Sophocles' *El.* (564 ff.): Eur. is the oldest authority for this. The story which finally established itself, that he surprised Artemis bathing, appears first in Callimachus (*Lav. Pall.* 110 ff.). For modern theories (all highly speculative) about the original nature of Actaeon and the meaning of his story see Malten, op. cit., 85 ff.]

337. ὁρᾷς : introducing the warning example, cf. *Or.* 588, Soph. *Ant.* 712, Antiphanes fr. 231. 3 Kock, Plato, *Gorg.* 470 D : we say 'You have seen', 'You have before you'.

338. [*l*'s ὅν for τόν is probably right : see 712 n.]

340. ὀργάσιν : apparently something like 'mountain glades' (rather than 'meadow-lands', L.S.⁹). Harpocration tells us that ὀργὰς καλεῖται τὰ λοχμώδη καὶ ὀρεινὰ χωρία καὶ οὐκ ἐπεργαζόμενα, and this agrees with Eur.'s usage of the word: cf. *El.* 1163 ὀργάδων δρύοχα, *Rhes.* 282 Ἴδης ὀργάδας, and *infra*, 445. [See further E. Norden, *Aus altrömischen Priesterbüchern*, 22 ff. N. equates ὀργάς with Lat. *tescum*, and shows that like *tescum* it was used especially of *loca religiosa*, places filled with a supernatural presence, cf. L.S.⁹ s.v. 2. Such an implication would give additional point here and at 445: Actaeon was a trespasser on holy ground ;[1] it was to holy ground that the liberated maenads fled.]

341. μὴ πάθῃς : jussive. Many edd. make it a final clause depending on στέψω. But it is a stock formula, as Prof. Fraenkel points out to me, to round off a warning ('don't let that happen to *you*') ; cf. Soph. *OC.* 1538 ὁ μὴ σύ, τέκνον Αἰγέως, βούλου παθεῖν: Dem. *Lept.* 50 ὁ μὴ πάθητε νῦν ὑμεῖς. **στέψω :** aor. subj., 'come here and let me crown you' : cf. Theopompus comicus fr. 32, δεῦρο δὴ γεμίσω σ' ἐγώ.

343-4. οὐ belongs to all three verbs : it is a stronger way of saying μὴ πρόσφερε, ἀλλὰ βάκχευε μηδὲ ἐξομόργνυσο: 'Hands off! Take yourself to your mummeries, and do not smear your folly upon me!' On the origin of the construction see Goodwin, *Moods and Tenses*, Appendix II, Pearson on *Hel.* 437 (appendix). For the contemptuous ἰών cf. Soph. *Ant.* 768 φρονείτω μεῖζον ἢ κατ' ἄνδρ' ἰών.—Pentheus speaks of Bacchism as if it were a physical infection transmissible by contact (as all forms of pollution were long held to be). His violent horror of such contact is a fine psychological stroke : something in him knows already the fascination and the mortal peril which the new rites hold for him. [The καί before βακχεύσεις in L arose, I think, through βα being read as κα (β and κ are barely distinguishable in some minuscule hands) ; having written κα the copyist recognized his mistake but did not erase the letters.]

345-6. δίκην internal, διδάσκαλον external accus. with μέτειμι ; cf. 516 f.

---

[1] The word order favours taking ἐν ὀργάσιν with κομπάσαντ' rather than (as Murray's punctuation requires) with διεσπάσαντο.

and Aesch. *Eum.* 230 f. δίκας μέτειμι τόνδε φῶτα. [MSS. δίκη: either δίκην or δίκῃ is possible; for the latter cf. 712 f. τὸν θεόν ... εὐχαῖσιν ἂν μετῆλθες and Thuc. 4. 62. 3 τιμωρίαις μετιόντες τοὺς ἀδικοῦντας.] **στειχέτω τις**: the attendants in Greek tragedy cannot be addressed by name, as they would be on the modern stage, for convention requires that they shall be anonymous.

347. Teiresias' Seat, like Semele's Bedchamber, was one of the 'sights' shown to tourists at Thebes (Paus. 9. 16. 1). Hence perhaps the mention of it here and Soph. *Ant.* 999—unless it was these passages which stimulated the Theban guides to 'discover' it. The blind seer could read omens in the birds' cries (*Ant.* 1001 ff.), and would have their movements described to him by an acolyte (cf. ibid. 1012). [MSS. τούσδε: but Paley's defence of this as deictic will hardly do—the language of 346-7 clearly implies that the οἰωνοσκοπεῖον was (as we should expect) in some fairly remote spot, not visible from the Cadmeia.]

350. στέμματα: *infulae*, 'holy ribbands'. The hanging up of these woollen bands consecrated the seat as a place of divination (G. Hock, *Griech. Weihegebräuche*, 25): cf. the στέμματα hung on the ὀμφαλός at Delphi (Eur. *Ion* 224), and Philostr. *Imag.* 2. 33. 1 στέμματα δ' ἀνῆπται τῆς δρυός (at Dodona), ἐπειδή ... χρησμοὺς ἐκφέρει. P.'s order is thus a command formally to desecrate the place.

352. πόλιν: probably 'state' (cf. 58 n.). The stranger is most likely to be found on Cithaeron (217 ff., 237).

356. Cf. Eurystheus' threat, *Heraclid.* 60, οὗ σε λεύσιμος μένει δίκη. Stoning was an exceptional mode of execution, which seems to have had the character of a ritual atonement, since it was used especially in cases of (*a*) ἐγγενὴς φόνος (*Or.* 50, Heliod. 1. 13. 4), (*b*) as here, sacrilege (Kinkel, *Ep. Fragm.* i, p. 49, offence against Cassandra; Eur. *Ion* 1237, against Apollo's servant; Hdt. 9. 120, against a heroshrine; Paus. 8. 5. 12, against a priestess). See R. Hirzel, *Die Strafe der Steinigung*, Abh. Sächs. Ges. der Wiss., Phil.-hist. Kl. xxvii (1909), 225 ff., and Fraenkel on *Agam.* 1616. On ὡς ἄν see 1240 n.

357. πικράν predicative : 'having seen a bitter end to his rites in Thebes'. So 634 and *Med.* 1388 πικρὰς τελευτὰς τῶν ἐμῶν γάμων ἰδών.

359. 'Your earlier folly has turned to a settled madness now.' Teiresias clearly means that Pentheus' state of mind as revealed by his last speech is worse than before. The contrast between ἐξέστης φρενῶν and μέμηνας is not, I think, between two degrees of folly (for even before Pentheus' last speech T. has said μαίνῃ ὡς ἄλγιστα), but between the temporary loss of control described by μαίνῃ ('you are behaving madly') or ἐξέστης φρενῶν ('you lost your head') and the permanent state of derangement expressed by the perfect μέμηνας. Cf. the climax in Men. *Epit.* 494 (558 Koerte[3]) ὑπομαίνεθ' οὗτος, νὴ τὸν Ἀπόλλω, μαίνεται, | μεμάνητ' ἀληθῶς. [Text and punctuation are thus sound: we should not write μέμηνας· ἤδη καὶ πρίν (Musgrave, &c.), or ἐξεστώς for ἐξέστης (Badham), since either of these would blur the contrast; while ἐκστῆναι (Weil) would imply the sort of foreknowledge which Teir. disclaims at 368.]

360–3. Wilamowitz, who disliked priests, found it 'hypocritical' that the priest should propose to pray for Pentheus and in the next breath (367) threaten him with his approaching doom. This seems perverse: Teiresias' intention to pray and his fear for Pentheus—based not on μαντική but on the conviction that 'God is not mocked' —are surely alike genuine. The situation is like that at the end of the first scene in the *Hippolytus*, where the old servant prays to Aphrodite on his master's behalf. In both cases, having heard the prologue, the audience knows that the prayer will not be answered; in both there is the same effect of pathos—the old and humble praying for the young and arrogant to unpitying gods, or rather, to unpitying natural forces. **μηδὲν νέον:** 'nothing strange', i.e. nothing sinister, a common euphemism: cf. Aesch. *Supp.* 1016 θεοῖς γὰρ εἴ τι μὴ βεβούλευται νέον.

363–5. This sort of thing is part of the conventional stage characterization of old men (cf. *Ion* 738 ff., Wilamowitz, *Herakles*[2], p. 237.) But it has also a particular psychological significance here: the old men are deeply discouraged, and in their discouragement the Dionysiac illusion of youth (187 ff.) has abandoned them. **ἕπου μοι:** 'come with me' (not 'follow me'). **πειρῶ:** second person imperative middle. **ἴτω δ' ὅμως:** 'still, let come what may' (sc. 'even though we fall'), dismissing a disagreeable thought, as Medea responds with ἴτω to the suggestion that the murder of her children will ruin her life (*Med.* 819, cf. ibid. 798, *Heraclid.* 455): ἴτω is the Greek for a shrug of the shoulders.

367. 'O Pentheus, named of sorrow! Shall he claim From all thy house fulfilment of his name?' (Murray). εἰσοίσει is perhaps an ironic echo of Pentheus' ἐσφέρει (353). The same play on the significant name Pentheus, Chaeremon fr. 4 (Nauck, *T.G.F.* p. 783) Πενθεὺς ἐσομένης συμφορᾶς ἐπώνυμος. The king's name may have been unconsciously altered to match his fate (cf. Wilamowitz on *Her.* 56), if Photius is right in saying that Hecataeus (fr. 31 Jac.) knew him as Tentheus.

Examples of such tragic 'punning' (ἐτυμολογεῖν) are many, especially in Aesch. and Eur. (cf. Kranz, *Stasimon* 287 ff., Platnauer on *IT.* 32). Elmsley, who collected and discussed them (on *Bacch.* 508), found the practice ψυχρόν. The Greeks did not, because they kept something of the primitive feeling that the connexion between a person and his name is significant, not accidental, φύσει not νόμῳ— names are for them, in Norden's words, 'visible pictures of invisible realities'. To us a pun is trivial and comic because it calls attention to the irrelevant; but the Greek felt that it pointed to something deeply relevant.

369. τοῖς πράγμασιν: 'by the facts' (cf. Eur. *Supp.* 747 φίλοις μὲν οὐ πείθεσθε, τοῖς δὲ πράγμασιν). The art of μαντική is treated with little respect in Eur.'s plays (see introductory note to this scene); but Teiresias is more than a soothsaying charlatan—he is a man who knows that, in the words of the next chorus, ἀχαλίνων στομάτων τὸ τέλος δυστυχία. Cf. *Hel.* 757 γνώμη δ' ἀρίστη μάντις ἥ τ' εὐβουλία, and fr. 973 μάντις δ' ἄριστος ὅστις εἰκάζει καλῶς.

Stasimon 1 (370–433)

A lyrical comment on the preceding scene, in two pairs of strophic stanzas. The strophes are directly related to the dramatic situation: στρ. α' denounces the ὕβρις which Pentheus has just shown, and appeals from it to the spirit of Reverence ('Οσία); στρ. β' expresses the Chorus's longing to escape to lands where their rite is not proscribed as it is in Thebes. The antistrophes look away from the immediate situation to state the underlying conflict in wider terms, by means of a series of γνῶμαι: the struggle between Pentheus and the new god becomes a type of all struggles between the arrogant 'cleverness' of the godless intellectuals and the instinctive religious feeling of the people. The same structure—strophe dramatic, antistrophe 'universalizing'—appears in the third stasimon, 862 ff., and in the fourth, 977 ff., though in other Euripidean lyrics the movement of thought is more often from universal to particular, e.g. *Alc.* 962 ff., *Med.* 410 ff., 627 ff. (C. Moeller, *vom Chorlied bei Eur.* 78). The leading ideas of the Cadmus–Teiresias scene are taken up in this song and given emotional expression. Taking their cue from the ῥῆσις of Teiresias and forgetting their character as orientals, the Chorus celebrate this time not the mysterious god of ecstasy but the Dion. whom the Athenian δῆμος knew, the genial wine-god of the Attic festivals (see Introd., p. xxii, and Jeanmaire, *Dionysos*, 27 ff.): lines 376–85 express lyrically what Teiresias in lines 272–85 has already expressed theologically, and the concluding stanza returns to this theme, presenting the religious life as the life of piety, gaiety, and humility. As Deichgräber has observed, the keyword is εὐφροσύνη (377), the gladness which is also good sense (cf. εὖ φρονοῦμεν 196); it is contrasted with the ἀφροσύνη of men like Pentheus (387), and the thought is resumed in εὐαίωνα (426). Opposed to this 'eudaemonist' attitude is that of the μαινόμενοι καὶ κακόβουλοι φῶτες (399 ff.), who are denounced in much the same terms which the old men had applied to Pentheus: he had a εὔτροχος γλῶσσα (268), they have ἀχάλινα στόματα (386); he was θύραζε τῶν νόμων (331), they are ἄνομοι (387); he was filled with false wisdom (311, 332), and so are they (394). It is tempting to try to go deeper, and detect in certain phrases of this lyric the personal voice of Eur. himself: see on 389–90, 402–16, 424–6, 430–3. But while there are themes here which seem to have had a special significance for the poet in his later years, there is little or nothing which by its dramatic irrelevance *compels* us to regard it as his personal utterance. And it should be remembered that, in Burnet's words (*Essays and Addresses*, 55), Euripidean choruses usually 'express a mood rather than a conviction'.

Metre

This is in the main an easy song metrically. The first pair of stanzas are written in 'straight' ionics (∪∪ – – | ∪∪ – –, see metrical note on πάροδος). The second μέτρον is often catalectic (∪∪ – ⏑). In the middle and at the end are lines of 3 μέτρα (378, 385). Otherwise the only variations are the resolution of a long syllable in 372 (∪∪ – ⏑⏑ | ∪∪ – ⏑) and 398, and the last line (*clausula*) which has the peculiar abbreviation form ∪∪ – – | ∪∪ – ⏑̄ | · ∪ – – or (more probably) ∪∪ – – | ∪∪ – ∪ | – · – ⏑̄ (anaclastic): cf. 536. Interlinear hiatus is admitted twice, after 380 and 388.

The second pair of stanzas are glyconic throughout, except lines 412 and 414 (= 428 and 430), which are iambic with resolutions. The glyconic and its variations are the commonest type of lyric metre in Soph. and Eur., and are not difficult for the beginner to master. The glyconic line is normally built round a central choriambus (– ∪ ∪ –) which is preceded by a disyllabic (occasionally, by resolution, trisyllabic) 'base' of indeterminate quantity (⏒ ⏒), and followed by ∪ – (rarely – –). This is the '(second) glyconic'. When the ending is shortened to –, as in 402, 403, 405, &c., the line is called a pherecratean. Sometimes the choriambus is transferred to the beginning of the line (415, 'first pherecratean') or to the end (409, 410, 'third glyconic': in 410 the base has become trisyllabic by resolution). These 'first' and 'third' glyconics are now often called 'choriambic dimeters', though they have only one choriambus.

Scheme of στρ. + ἀντ. β:

	∪ – – ∪ ∪ – –	pher.[2]
	– – – ∪ ∪ – –	pher.[2]
	∪ – – ∪ ∪ – ∪ –	glyc.[2]
405, 420	– – – ∪ ∪ – –	pher.[2]
	∪ – – ∪ ∪ – ∪ –	glyc.[2]
	– ∪ – ∪ ∪ – ∪ –	glyc.[2]
	– – – ∪ ∪ – –	pher.[2]
	– – – – – ∪ ∪ –	glyc.[3]
410, 425	⏒ ⏒ – – – ∪ ∪ –	glyc.[3]
	– – – ∪ ∪ – –	pher.[2]
	∪ – ∪ ⏑⏑ ∪ ⏑⏑ ∪ ⏑⏑	2 iamb. (427 is corrupt)

∪– –∪∪– –   pher.²
∪– ∪ ∪ω   iamb.
∪– ∪ω ∪ω ∪–   2 iamb.
–∪∪– ∪– –   pher.¹

370–2. 'Holiness, queen in Heaven! Holiness, passing on golden wing across the face of Earth!' πότνα θεῶν is an archaic religious formula borrowed from the language of epic: πότνα seems to be in origin a voc. form corresponding to the nom. πότνια (W. Schulze, *Kleine Schriften*, 325 ff.): the gen. is probably partitive both here and in *H. Dem.* 118, where Demeter is called πότνα θεάων (cf. *Alc.* 460 ὦ φίλα γυναικῶν, and the common Homeric δῖα θεάων). The peculiar use of δέ with the repeated voc. perhaps marks a certain contrast between the two aspects of 'Οσία (Hermann), as a Power accepted in the world of the gods and watchful also in man's world: cf., however, Soph. *Phil.* 827 Ὕπν᾽ ὀδύνας ἀδαής, Ὕπνε δ᾽ ἀλγέων, where there is no sharp antithesis. **κατὰ γᾶν:** probably 'across the earth' rather than 'earthward' (despite occasional uses like *Batrachom.* 267 ἔβαν . . . κατὰ λίμνην, 'down into the pool'). **χρυσέαν πτέρυγα φέρεις:** lit. 'thou carryest thy golden wing', an artificial variation on the more natural phrase χρυσέᾳ πτέρυγι φέρει (which W. H. Thompson unnecessarily proposed to restore here).—ὁσία or ὁσιότης may be defined as the quality of scrupulousness, especially in religious matters (Plato, *Gorg.* 507 B), which makes a man keep within the limits of what is permitted (ὅσιον): in this sense it is opposed to the οὐχ ὁσία ὕβρις of 375. But the word and its cognates seem to have been often in the mouths of the devotees of mystery cults, and to have acquired in this context a deeper and more positive significance: cf. 70, 77, 114, Ar. *Frogs* 327 ὁσίους θιασώτας, 336 ὁσίοις μύσταις, *H. Orph.* 84. 3 ὁσίους μύστας, Plato, *Rep.* 363 C συμπόσιον τῶν ὁσίων, and espec. Eur. fr. 472. 15 Βάκχος ἐκλήθην ὁσιωθείς—where the participle appears to mean something like 'consecrated', as it certainly does in a later passage referring to mystery cults, Lucian, *Lexiph.* 10. I suspect that this has something to do with the introduction here of 'Οσία as a quasi-personal Power or 'goddess': elsewhere she appears explicitly as such only in an anonymous tragic line (fr. trag. adesp. 501), 'Οσίᾳ δ᾽ Ἀνάγκη πολεμιωτάτη θεός. [Greek poets from Homer downwards have this way of personalizing and objectifying abstractions, but Eur. has an especial fondness for it: cf. Πόθος in this song, the sword-bearing Δίκη of 991, and (?) Εὐσέβεια in 263. as well as the 'goddesses' Εὐλάβεια (*Phoen.* 782), Λήθη (*Or.* 213), Λύπη (ibid. 399)—that is one reason why Aristophanes makes him pray to a 'private goddess' Ξύνεσις (*Frogs* 893). 'Gods' of this kind were not in any formal sense objects of worship; yet the ascription of divinity to them was more than a mere *façon de parler* or 'figure of speech'—a word like 'Οσία or Δίκη stood not only for a human quality but for a force controlling man's life, something which man has not made but finds given and must therefore bow to. This sort of feeling about ὁσία comes out very clearly in a sentence of Demosthenes, *Meid.* 126 ὁ θεός (sc. Διόνυσος) ᾧ χορηγὸς ἐγὼ καθειστήκειν, καὶ τὸ τῆς ὁσίας ὁτιδήποτ' ἐστίν, τὸ σεμνὸν καὶ τὸ δαιμόνιον, συνηδίκηται. Such forces move swiftly and invisibly about their purposes: that is why 'Οσία has wings here, as Love and Death and Victory are winged beings. Cf. Farnell, *Cults,* v. 443 ff.; A. C. Pearson, *Verbal Scholarship and the Growth of Some Abstract Terms,* 23 ff.; Wilamowitz on *Her.* 557, and on Hesiod, *Op. et Di.* 218–24. Johanna C. Bolkestein, "Οσιος *en* Εὐσεβής (Amsterdam, 1936), offers a valuable collection of material, but does not seem to me to make good her contention that ὁσία is primarily a moral and not a religious idea.[1]]

373. Πενθέως is disyllabic (synizesis).

378–81. 'This is his kingdom: to make men one in the dance; to be gay with the music of the pipes; to set an end to cares.' For the implications of θιασεύειν cf. on 75 θιασεύεται ψυχάν. It seems best to take it as transitive here (as *Ion* 552, ὅς με Δελφίσιν κόραις | ἐθιάσευσε), and to understand Dion. as the subject of all three infinitives. For Dion. as the smiling god cf. 439 γελῶν, 1021 γελῶντι προσώπῳ: for Dion. as the liberator from care, 280 ff. and Plut. *de adul. amic.* 27, 68 D, (Διονύσῳ) λύοντι τὸ τῶν δυσφόρων σχοινίον μεριμνῶν, κατὰ Πίνδαρον.

383. γάνος: see 261 n.   δαιτὶ θεῶν: an epic phrase (*Od.* 3. 336, &c.) for the sacrificial meal which men share with the gods. It seems possible that its use here was meant to remind a Greek audience of something specifically Dionysiac—the Theodaisia, a festival which many Greek towns observed in honour of Dion.

384–5. ἀνδράσι: primarily in contrast with θεῶν: but in addition the Chorus have their answer by implication Pentheus' charge that the *women's* rites were accompanied by drunkenness. The echo of 261, βότρυος ἐν δαιτὶ γάνος, is thus intentional, and should not be made a ground for suspecting the authenticity of that line.

389–92. ὁ τᾶς ἡσυχίας βίοτος: Dion. is repeatedly represented as ἥσυχος (435 ff., 622, 636) in contrast with Pentheus, the excitable man of action (214, 647, 670 f., 789 f.). But although ἡσυχία is proper to a god as such (Introd., p. xliv), orgiastic religion is not, to our thinking, particularly ἥσυχον, and one is tempted to discover here a secondary reference to the contemporary war-time controversy about quietism or the 'ivory tower' attitude, ἡσυχία or ἀπραγμοσύνη, which has been discussed by Nestle, *Philologus,* lxxxi (1925), 129 ff., and more

---

[1] Cf. the criticisms of M. H. van der Valk, *Mnemos.* 1942, 113 ff.; also Jeanmaire, 'Le substantif Hosia', *Rev. Ét. Gr.* 1945, 66 ff.

briefly by Prof. Wade-Gery, *J.H.S.* lii (1932), 224 f.[1] Eur. seems to make veiled allusions to this controversy as early as the *Medea* (217, 296, 807 f.), and we know that it was elaborately debated in a later play of his, the *Antiope* (cf. also *Ion* 598 ff.). That in the present passage he is moving, consciously or unconsciously, in the same circle of ideas, or in one closely related to it, is suggested not only by the reference to Εἰρήνη (419) but by comparison with the lines in Aristophanes' *Birds*, 1320 ff., which enumerate the presiding Powers of Cloud-Cuckoo-Land—Σοφία Πόθος Ἀμβροσία Χάριτες | τό τε τῆς ἀγανόφρονος Ἡσυχίας | εὐήμερον πρόσωπον. These are the gods of the war-weary 'escapist', and it is hardly accidental that four out of the five recur in the present lyric. But I do not suggest that this is more than a secondary theme or context of feeling.   συνέχει δώματα: the Chorus are presumably thinking of the rift between Pentheus and his family produced by the young man's lack of φρόνησις.

392–4. Cf. Aesch. *Eum.* 287 and Eur. fr. 255, from the contemporary *Archelaus*, δοκεῖς . . . τὴν Δίκην που μάκρ' ἀπῳκίσθαι βροτῶν· ἢ δ' ἐγγύς ἐστιν, οὐχ ὁρωμένη δ' ὁρᾷ.

395. τὸ σοφὸν οὐ σοφία: 'cleverness is not wisdom', 'the world's Wise are not wise' (Murray). Here again the Chorus take up a thought expressed in the preceding scene: τὸ σοφόν has the same implication as in 203; it is the false wisdom of men like Pentheus, who φρονῶν οὐδὲν φρονεῖ (332, cf. 266 ff., 311 f.), in contrast with the true wisdom of devout acceptance (179, 186). [These parallels, and the whole trend of the lyric are surely quite decisive against the view of Verrall (*Bacchants* 151) and Deichgräber (*Hermes* lxx [1935], 340) that the Chorus are here criticizing *Teiresias*.] For the 'wisdom' of Dion. cf. Diphilus fr. 86 Kock ὦ πᾶσι τοῖς φρονοῦσι προσφιλέστατε | Διόνυσε καὶ σοφώτατε: for the paradoxical form, *I.A.* 1139 ὁ νοῦς ὅδ' αὐτὸς νοῦν ἔχων οὐ τυγχάνει, *Or.* 819 τὸ καλὸν οὐ καλόν. Such paradoxes are the characteristic product of an age when traditional valuations are rapidly shifting in the way described in the famous passage of Thucydides on the transvaluation of values, 3. 82. They should be distinguished from purely verbal witticisms of the type illustrated by Denniston on *El.* 1230 and parodied by Aristophanes, *Ach.* 397 οὐκ ἔνδον ἔνδον ἐστίν, εἰ γνώμην ἔχεις.

397–9. 'Life is short: he that on such a tenure pursues great things will miss what lies at hand.'   ἐπὶ τούτῳ = ἐπὶ τῷ βραχὺν εἶναι τὸν αἰῶνα, marking the limitation to which the pursuit of ambitious ends is subject—the same use of ἐπί as in ἐπὶ ῥητοῖς, 'on stated terms'. For the thought cf. fr. 1076 τῶν ἀμηχάνων δ' ἔρως | πολλοὺς ἔθηκε τοῦ

[1] See now V. Ehrenberg, 'Polypragmosyne', *J.H.S.* lxvii (1947), 46 ff., and in particular pp. 53 f. on Euripides.

παρόντος ἀμπλακεῖν, Democritus fr. 191 Diels ἐπὶ τοῖς δυνατοῖς οὖν δεῖ ἔχειν τὴν γνώμην καὶ τοῖς παρεοῦσιν ἀρκέεσθαι, and Browning, *Grammarian's Funeral*, 'This high man, aiming at a million, misses a unit' (quoted by Sandys); but the accent here is religious as in *Psalm* 131. 1 'Lord, my heart is not haughty, nor mine eyes lofty: neither do I exercise myself in great matters, or in things too high for me.' [Many edd. follow the Aldine in reading τό τε μὴ θνητὰ φρονεῖν βραχὺς αἰών (sc. ἐστί), 'to have thoughts too proud for mortality is (i.e. spells, results in) shortness of life'. This is linguistically bold, but may be defended as an extension of the normal usage seen in 1004 βροτείως τ' ἔχειν ἄλυπος βίος or *IT.* 1121 f. τὸ δὲ μετ' εὐτυχίας κακοῦ|σθαι θνατοῖς βαρὺς αἰών. It is hardly bolder than Pindar's ποτὶ κέντρον δέ τοι | λακτίζεμεν τελέθει | ὀλισθηρὸς οἶμος (*Pyth.* 2. 94 ff.). With this punctuation ἐπὶ τούτῳ = ἐπὶ τῷ βραχὺν εἶναι αἰῶνα τὸ μὴ θνητὰ φρονεῖν. The argument in its favour is that in place of a generality which applies no more to Pentheus' case than to any other man's we get a further allusion to the preceding scene— a reinforcement of Teiresias' final warning (367 ff.) that Pentheus' ὕβρις will bring him to a bad end. Cf. Homer's words about another opponent of Dion., οὐδὲ γὰρ οὐδὲ Δρύαντος υἱὸς κρατερὸς Λυκόοργος | δὴν ἦν, ὅς ῥα θεοῖσιν ἐπουρανίοισιν ἔριζεν (*Il.* 6. 130 f.).—There is no need to alter μεγάλα to μακρά. For the pejorative sense of μέγας cf. μέγα φρονεῖν, μέγα λέγειν, μέγα ἔργον (Pind. *Nem.* 10. 64); for two short syllables answering to one long cf. 372 πτέρυγ- = 388 δυστ-.] **φέροι**, in the sense of φέρεσθαι, as Soph. *OT.* 1189 τίς ἀνὴρ πλέον | τᾶς εὐδαιμονίας φέρει | ἢ τοσοῦτον ὅσον δοκεῖν; [But it seems better to write with Tyrwhitt and Headlam (*J. Phil.* xxvi. 234) τίς . . . φέροι; 'who would pursue ambitious aims and not put up with things as they are?' This is the natural meaning of φέρειν τὰ παρόντα, for which Headlam compared Lucian, *Cyn.* 17 τὰ μὲν παρόντα φέρειν οὐκ ἐθέλετε, τῶν δὲ ἀπόντων ἐφίεσθε. And the word-order suggests a question rather than an indefinite clause (in which one would expect ἄν τις).]

399–401. The Chorus still have Pentheus in mind: μαινομένων picks up 326 μαίνῃ, 359 μέμηνας. But the words are of course capable of a wider application: cf. the very similar phrase—κακοφρόνων ἀνδρῶν παράνοια, *Or.* 824—which Eur. used a few years earlier to describe the philosophy of violence, the 'realism' whose motto is εὖ κακουργεῖν. **παρ' ἔμοιγε:** 'in my verdict', as *Med.* 762 f. γενναῖος ἀνήρ, | Αἰγεῦ, παρ' ἐμοὶ δεδόκησαι and often even in prose, the person being regarded as a court of judgement (cf. Hdt. 3. 160. 1 παρὰ Δαρείῳ κριτῇ = iudice Dario).

402–16. The 'escape-prayer' is frequent in Euripidean lyrics (e.g. *Hipp.* 732–51, *Hel.* 1478–86)—partly, perhaps, because they are war-time lyrics. Sometimes such prayers have little dramatic relevance and read like personal utterances of the poet (Wilamowitz, *Hippo-lytos*, p. 217 f.); and the present one has been taken to mean that Eur. himself hoped to find 'the peace of Dionysus in the cool shadow of a princely court, Evagoras' (in Cyprus or Archelaos' (in Mace-donia)' (Zielinski, *N. Jahrb.* 1902, 647 f.). That is quite possible, but we are not compelled to assume it: it is perfectly natural that the Chorus should long to flee from the persecutor to a peaceful place where βάκχαις θέμις ὀργιάζειν. And their choice of Pieria is equally natural (see on 409–11). But why Cyprus? Verrall asked this question, and finding no answer, was led to frame fantastic hypotheses. We need not follow these; nor need we imagine, with Norwood, that Eur. has deliberately made the Chorus give away the sensual character of their cult by dragging in Cyprus and Aphrodite. (*a*) Cyprus represents the eastern limit of the Greek world, as Olympus the northern limit: since Dion. is a god of the East and the North, it is natural that his worshippers should look eastward and northward for a place of refuge. Perhaps there is also a vague reminiscence of the Homeric Hymn, 7. 28, where the pirates propose to carry Dion. to Egypt, Cyprus, or the Hyperboreans. (*b*) In an 'escapist' poem there is nothing incongruous in giving Aphrodite a place beside Πόθος and the Χάριτες, Ἡσυχία and Εἰρήνη: cf. Ar. *Ach.* 989 ὦ Κύπριδι τῇ καλῇ καὶ Χάρισι ταῖς φίλαις ξύντροφε Διαλλαγή (= Εἰρήνη): *Peace* 455, where in celebration of the peace Trygaeus prays Ἑρμῇ Χάρισιν Ὥραισιν Ἀφροδίτῃ Πόθῳ. In the present context she is a symbol not of sensuality but of the happiness and liberation which comes from the gay and reverent acceptance of natural impulse. Her association with Dion., the other great Nature-power, is rooted both in popular thought and in the imagination of poets and artists. [For the former, cf. *infra*, 773, and the tradition by which the first round of drinks was dedicated to Dion., the Χάριτες, and the Ὧραι, the second to Dion. and Aphrodite (Panyasis fr. 13 Kinkel). For the latter, Anacreon fr. 2 Diehl, addressing Dion. as ὦναξ, ᾧ δαμάλης Ἔρως | καὶ Νύμφαι κυανώπιδες | πορφυρέη τ' Ἀφροδίτη | συμπαίζουσιν: *Cycl.* 69 ff. ἴακχον ἴακχον ᾠδὰν | μέλπω πρὸς τὰν Ἀφροδίταν | ἂν θηρεύων πετόμαν | βάκχαις σὺν λευκόποσιν: and the vase-paintings which show Aphrodite among the Maenads, e.g. the B.M. hydria F 20 (*Cat.* iv, pl. 2) or the Louvre lecythos L 59 (Pfuhl, *Malerei*, iii, fig. 592). The association is in some measure reflected even in cult: the two deities shared a temple at Argos (Paus. 2. 23. 8), and at Bura in Achaea (Paus. 7. 25. 9); and Aphrodite figures in the *lex Iobacchorum*, apparently as a character in a Dionysiac masque or mystery-play.]

403. [Petersen's νᾶσον τὰν Ἀφροδίτας may well be right. The un-metrical τάν before Κύπρον in our MSS. looks like a remnant of this reading:[1] τάν survived as a marginal variant and was eventually inserted in the wrong place.]

404–5. 'Where the Loves haunt, enchanters of the mortal heart.' θνατοῖσιν, with θελξίφρονες.   οἱ, which was inserted *metri gratia* by Heath, is understood by Paley as the article, by Bruhn as the pronoun (= Ἀφροδίτᾳ, ethic dat.): the former view is preferable, as two datives would make the sentence a little clumsy, and Eur. elsewhere avoids the demonstrative οἱ. [It is doubtful if the insertion is really necessary (Wilamowitz, *Griech. Verskunst*, 258 f.): Eur. does not always attempt strict correspondence in the glyconic base, e.g. *Hipp.* 737–9 = 747–9; and if the MSS. are right the same correspondence of ∪ ∪ to ∪ – occurs just below in 406 = 421.]

406–8. 'And Paphos which the waters of the alien river, with its hundred mouths, make fruitful without rain.' This passage is a standing puzzle. That 'the alien river' must be the Nile would seem indisputable if it had not been disputed: the combination of the many mouths (ἑκατόν is the language of poetry, not of arithmetic), the fertilizing waters, the adj. βαρβάρου (proper to Egypt, but hardly to Cyprus under the rule of Athens' friend Evagoras), and the adj. ἄνομβροι, is surely decisive: for the last, cf. Hdt. 2. 22. 3 ἄνομβρος ἡ χώρη, of the country about the sources of the Nile; 2. 25. 5 ὁ Νεῖλος ἐὼν ἄνομβρος: Eur. *Hel.* 1 ff. Νείλου . . . ῥοαί, | ὃς ἀντὶ δίας ψακάδος Αἰγύπτου πέδον | λευκῆς τακείσης χιόνος ὑγραίνει γύας: fr. 228 (from the *Archelaos*, contemporary with the *Bacchae*) Νείλου . . . ὃς ἐκ μελαμβρότοιο πληροῦται ῥοὰς | Αἰθιοπίδος γῆς, ἡνίκ' ἂν τακῇ χιών. But Paphos is a town on the SW. coast of Cyprus, 3,600 stades from Alexandria according to Strabo (14. 6. 3): in what sense can the Nile 'make it fruitful'? (*a*) Hermann's idea that the reference is to the profits of the Cypriot trade with Egypt clearly will not do: even if καρπίζειν could bear this meaning, ἄνομβροι is left quite pointless. (*b*) Much more plausible is Paley's suggestion that Eur. supposed the Nile current to be strong enough to 'fertilize' Paphos by depositing the rich Nile mud on its shores; it does in fact make the sea turbid for a considerable distance from the Egyptian coast, as later antiquity knew (Stat. *Theb.* 8. 361 f.). In support of this Murray adduces *Hel.* 151, where Teucer, anxious for a favourable wind to take him from Egypt to Cyprus, is reassured by Helen with the words πλοῦς, ὦ ξέν', αὐτὸς σημανεῖ, 'the voyage of itself will set your course'—which *may* refer to the Nile current.[2] But would the silting

---

[1] Dr. Maas suggests, as did Matthiae earlier, the possibility of retaining τὰν in 402 and writing in 417 πάϊς (epic and lyric, but not elsewhere in tragedy).

[2] For a later period we have (as John Jackson pointed out) more explicit testimony in Manilius' line (*Astr.* 4. 635) 'Aegyptique Cypros

up of a coast be called 'rainless fertilization'? Cf. Hesych. καρπί-
ζουσι· ποτίζουσιν, εὔκαρπα ποιοῦσι. (c) Alternatively, I am tempted
to guess that Eur. is alluding to the belief, held today by Cypriot
peasants and reported as far back as 1816 by the Turkish traveller
Ali Bey, that the island's numerous, rather brackish springs are
fed not by local rainfall but by water which has passed under the
sea (Unger-Kotschy, *Cypern*, 70; Hill, *Hist. of Cyprus*, i. 6). If
antiquity believed it to be *Nile* water—as for instance it believed
the river Inopus in Delos to be fed by Nile water (Call. *Dian*. 171,
Lycophr. 576 and schol., Paus. 2. 5. 3)—the puzzle would be explained
and the adjs. βαρβάρου ('foreign') and ἄνομβροι would have special
point. But direct ancient evidence is lacking. [Three types of
emendation have been attempted. (1) Eliminate Paphos. Φάρον
Reiske. But he did not explain why the Chorus should wish to visit
this small island 7 stades from Alexandria. Proteus, it is true, lived
there (*Hel*. 4 f.), and later tradition made Proteus welcome Dionysus
when he visited Egypt ([Apollod.] 3. 5. 1, cf. K. O'Nolan, *C.R.* lxxii
[1958], 204); but the connection is a slender one. Ἐ|πάφου (mythical
king of Egypt) Petersen, making 405 and 420 glyconics (θεάν disyll.).
But the mythological allusion is frigid and the rhythm impossible.
Πάφον a gloss on 404-5, which has ousted χθόνα (Meineke) or the like?
Possible but not very probable. (2) Eliminate the Nile. Βωκάρου for
βαρβάρου Meursius. This is alleged to be the name of a river in
Cyprus. The evidence for the allegation is very weak: see M. R.
James, *J.H.S.* ix (1888), 182 f., and Hill, l.c. And that the Bocarus
was ἑκατόστομος there is no evidence whatever: 'the rivers in Cyprus
are little more than mountain torrents' (Storrs and O'Brien, *Hand-
book of Cyprus*, 4); we are driven to explain the 'hundred mouths'
(feebly) as artificial irrigation runlets, or to read ἐρατόστομοι with
Musgrave. The further difficulty of ἄνομβροι is not met by reading ἄν-
ομβρον and referring to the superstition about the open-air altar of
Aphrodite at Paphos on which the rain always avoided falling (Tac.
Hist. 2. 3, Plin. *NH*. 2 .210): that it never rains at all in Paphos no
one thought or could think (the place has an average rainfall of
18 inches). (3) Separate Paphos from the Nile. Πάφον θ' ἄν ⟨θ'⟩
Schoene, sc. γᾶν (cf. *Troad*. 825). Simple, but leaves Paphos bare
of the expected adjectival compliment, and makes an odd, illogical
enumeration, 'Cyprus . . . and Paphos and Egypt'. At first sight
it is tempting to read Πάφον, ἄν θ' (apparently first proposed

pulsatur fluctibus amnis', on which Housman remarked 'idem Euripides si non dixit at dixisse videri potest in obscurissimis versibus.'
Manilius' authority, or his source's authority, may in fact be our
passage; if so, his text was the same as ours, and he understood it as
Paley did.

by Shilleto). *Πάφον* then becomes object of *νέμονται* (which is transitive, so far as I know, everywhere else in tragedy); and we get exact metrical correspondence with 421 as read in L P. Cf. Nonn. 13. 456 καὶ Πάφον, ἀβροκόμων στεφανηφόρον ὅρμον Ἐρώτων. The longing of the Chorus to be in Egypt could be explained by the theory that Dionysus is Osiris and Egypt is an earlier home of his cult (Hdt. 2. 42. 2, 49. 2): *H. Hymn* 1. 9 already associates him with that country. But even with this reading *Πάφον* is bare and abrupt; and to put the pause after *Πάφον* upsets the rhythm and balance of the composition (cf. antistrophe).]

409–11. Pieria, the exquisite hill-country on the northern side of the *massif* of Olympus, is the traditional birth-place of the Muses (Hes. *Theog.* 53, *Op. et Di.* 1). It was at Dion in this region that according to Diodorus (17. 16. 3) Archelaos, Euripides' host in Macedonia, established dramatic competitions dedicated to Zeus and the Muses. Hence, on the assumption that the *Bacchae* was written for production at this festival, these lovely lines have generally been taken as a graceful compliment from the great Athenian poet to his last audience (see, however, Introd., p. xl). But be that as it may, Pieria was in fact Dionysiac country: the Delphic paean (54 f.) records the god's visit to it; and it was there, according to 'several authors', that Orpheus was torn to pieces by the Maenads for refusing recognition to Dion. (Hygin. *Astron.* 2. 7, Kern, *Orph. Fragm.* test. 117, cf. test. 114, 115, 125, 129, 144). The association of Dion. with the Muses appears also in the *Antigone* (965), and is attested by the curious ritual of the Boeotian Agrionia, where the women search for Dion. and, failing to find him, declare that 'he has taken refuge with the Muses' (Plut. *Q. Conv.* 8 prooem., 717 A, cf. the tradition preserved by Eustathius, on *Od.* 17. 205, that 'the nurses of Dionysus' are the Muses). Aeschylus seems to have called him ὁ μουσόμαντις (fr. 60).

413. 'Spirit who leadest my worship, master of my joy.' [προβακχήιε MSS., with Ionic ending as in ἀνθρωπήιος. This seems not adequately supported by the use in tragedy of a few words like γάϊος, δάϊος, νάϊος, normally if not always with Doric spelling. Perhaps πρόβακχ' ἤιε, though ἤιος occurs elsewhere only as an epithet of Apollo. Neither προβακχήιος nor πρόβακχος is found elsewhere.]

414. For *Πόθος* and the *Χάριτες* cf. Ar. *Birds* 1320 (quoted on 389–92) and *Peace* 455 (quoted on 402–16). *Πόθος* appears also Aesch. *Supp.* 1039, where he is the child of Aphrodite. Vase-paintings show him in Dionysiac scenes: e.g. on the Pothos painter's bell-krater in Providence (*C.V.A. Providence*, i, pl. 23; Beazley, *A.R.V.* 801. 1), painted in the early years of the last quarter of the fifth century B.C., a boyish winged Pothos accompanies with the flute the dance of satyrs and maenads. On a pelike after the Meidias painter (Beazley, l.c. 835. 9), painted in the very last years of the century, Pothos has a tympanon. The Χάριτες, before they became the 'Graces' familiar to us from Latin poetry and Botticelli's picture, were ancient Minyan goddesses (Pind. *Ol.* 14. 4 Χάριτες Ἐρχομενοῦ, παλαιγόνων Μινυᾶν ἐπίσκοποι), and their cult was early associated with that of Dion.: in the very old prayer of the women of Elis (Plut. *Q. Graec.* 36. 299 B) he is besought to come in his bull-shape σὺν Χαρίτεσσιν, and at Olympia he and they shared a common altar (Paus. 5. 14. 10, schol. Pind. *Ol.* 5. 10); Servius on *Aen.* 1. 720 makes them his daughters.

415. 'And there thy Chosen have licence to serve thee.'

419–20. ὀλβοδότειραν Εἰρήναν, κουροτρόφον θεάν. Neither epithet needs explanation in our time. The second is as old as Hesiod (*Op. et Di.* 228); for the first cf. Bacchyl. fr. 4.61 Snell[7] τίκτει δέ τε θνατοῖσιν εἰρήνα μεγαλάνορα πλοῦτον, and for both, Eur. *Supp.* 490 f. τέρπεται δ' εὐπαιδίᾳ (sc. Εἰρήνη), | χαίρει δὲ πλούτῳ. A well-known statue at Munich, after Cephisodotus, shows Eirene with the child Ploutos in her arms. The longing for peace often finds expression in Eur.'s plays, e.g. *Cresphontes* fr. 453 Εἰρήνα βαθύπλουτε καὶ | καλλίστα μακάρων θεῶν, | ζῆλός μοι σέθεν, ὡς χρονίζεις, κτλ., and *Or.* 1682 f. τὴν καλλίστην | θεῶν Εἰρήνην. But the introduction of Εἰρήνη is not irrelevant here: Dion. too gives increase and enrichment of life, and for that reason the vase-paintings sometimes show her as a member of his thiasos (C. Fraenkel, *Satyr- u. Bakchennamen*, 53); war is Βρομίου παρά-μουσος ἑορταῖς (*Phoen.* 785).

421–3. 'In equal measure to rich and humble he gives the griefless joy of wine.' ὄλβιος and χείρων in the social sense, as often. διδόναι εἰς, instead of the dat., occurs also *Hel.* 1425, *Phoen.* 1757; but in all three places its use seems to be due to the presence of another word to which εἰς is more closely attached—ἴσαν here, εὔνοιαν in *Hel.* 1425 ἣν σὴν εἰς ἔμ' εὔνοιαν διδῷς, ἀχάριτον in *Phoen.* 1757 χάριν ἀχάριτον ἐς θεοὺς διδοῦσα.   ἄλυπον: either 'assuaging grief' or more probably 'causing no grief', 'innocent'. [It seems to have the former sense in Soph. fr. 172 P., where wine is called ἄλυπον ἄνθος (?ἄλθος) ἀνίας, on which Phrynich. *Soph.* p. 153. 23 observes εἰ θέλοις εἰπεῖν ἐπί τινος πράγματος ὅ λύπης ἀπαλλάττει, οὕτως ἂν χρήσαιο. Cf. 280 f., 381, 772 τὴν παυσίλυπον ἄμπελον, and Astydamas fr. 6 (*T.G.F.* p. 780) τὴν ἀκεσφόρον λύπης . . . ἄμπελον. But the latter is the usual and natural meaning (cf. M. N. Tod, *B.S.A.* xlvi [1951], 187), and is supported by fr. 897 where Eur. speaks of Eros as ἄλυπον τέρψιν τιν' ἔχων and the passages quoted in next note. When the comic poet Hermippus calls Chian wine ἄλυπος he presumably means that 'there isn't a headache in a hogshead' (fr. 82. 5 Kock).] Dion. is a demo-cratic god: he is accessible to all, not like Pythian Apollo through priestly intermediaries, but directly in his gift of wine and through membership of his θίασος. His worship probably made its original appeal mainly to people who had no citizen rights in the aristocratic 'gentile state' and were excluded from the older cults associated with the great families (Gernet-Boulanger, *Le génie grec dans la religion*, 124 f.). And in the classical age it seems to have retained a good deal of this popular character (cf. *Frogs* 405 ff., Plut. *cupid. div.* 8. 527 D, ἡ πάτριος τῶν Διονυσίων ἑορτὴ τὸ παλαιὸν ἐπέμπετο δημοτικῶς καὶ ἱλαρῶς). [At the Πιθοίγια (part of the Anthesteria) the Πιθοίγια (part of the Anthesteria) οὔτε οἰκέτην οὔτε μισθωτὸν εἴργειν τῆς ἀπολαύσεως τοῦ οἴνου θεμιτὸν ἦν, ἀλλὰ θύσαντας πᾶσι μεταδιδόναι τοῦ δώρου τοῦ Διονύσου (schol. Hes. *Op. et Di.* 368, from Plutarch): the same idea perhaps underlies the cult-title Ἰσοδαίτης. For later periods we have inscriptional evidence that even slaves might be admitted to membership of Dionysiac θίασοι (*C.I.L.* iii. 704, dedication by a *servus actor*, member of a *thiasus Liberi patris Tasibasteni* in Macedonia; iii. 7437, slaves admitted to a βακχεῖον alongside freedmen in the age of the Severi). —ἴσα L P, which should perhaps be retained even if Πάφον θ' is read in 406: see on 404-5.]

424–6. 'But he abhors the man whose thought is not this—by day and happy darkness to live to the end the life of blessedness.' **φίλας,** because the Dionysiac ἱερά take place νύκτωρ τὰ πολλά (486). **εὐαίωνα**: cf. εὐαίωνι σὺν ὄλβῳ in the refrain of the Delphic hymn to Dion. It is a strong word, implying *permanent* happiness such as man attributes to the gods: Eur. *Ion* 126 f. εὐαίων εἴης, ὦ Λατοῦς παῖ, Aesch. *Pers.* 711 βίοτον εὐαίωνα Πέρσαις ὡς θεὸς διήγαγες. The 'hedonism'—it would be more exact to call it religious eudaemonism —of this and other passages in the *Bacchae* (cf. 910–11 n. and 1004) has surprised some critics. But (*a*) it is dramatically appropriate: Dion. is the dispenser of natural joys, Pentheus the joy-hating Puritan. The same spirit breathes in the prayer to Dion. written by Ion of Chios (Athen. 10. 447 D = fr. 26 Blumenthal) χαῖρε· δίδου δ' αἰῶνα, καλῶν ἐπιήρανε ἔργων, | πίνειν καὶ παίζειν καὶ τὰ δίκαια φρονεῖν. A Ruvo amphora shows Εὐδαιμονία as a member of his thiasos (Beazley, *A.R.V.*, pp. 803–4; Furtwängler–Reichhold, ii, Abb. 107, p. 329). (*b*) The longing for security and an anodyne, natural to a war-weary world, is often expressed by Eur. Cf. especially *Her.* 503 ff. μικρὰ μὲν τὰ τοῦ βίου, | τοῦτον δ' ὅπως ἥδιστα διαπεράσετε, | ἐξ ἡμέρας ἐς νύκτα μὴ λυπούμενοι: *Antiope* fr. 196 τί δῆτ' ἐν ὄλβῳ μὴ σαφεῖ βεβηκότες | οὐ ζῶμεν ὡς ἥδιστα μὴ λυπούμενοι; *Telephus* fr. 714 σμίκρ' ἂν θέλοιμι καὶ καθ' ἡμέραν ἔχων | ἄλυπος οἰκεῖν: *Hipp.* 1111 ff.: *Supp.* 953 f. 'The contemplation of that mindless ease may have brought him an enhanced sense of his own agonies and his deprivation of modes of escape that were open to others but not to him' (Winnington-Ingram). When Eur.'s contemporary Antiphon invented and advertised a τέχνη ἀλυπίας (87 A 6 Diels), he was supplying a felt want.

427–9. 'And to withhold the mind and understanding in true wisdom (σοφάν predicative) from men who reject the common rule.' The περισσοὶ φῶτες are those 'superior persons' who, like Pentheus, refuse to recognize the limitations imposed by θνητὰ φρονεῖν: cf. the Nurse's warning to Phaedra that Cypris punishes ὃν ἂν περισσὸν καὶ φρονοῦνθ' εὕρῃ μέγα (*Hipp.* 445), and Theseus' taunt against Hippolytus as claiming to be περισσὸς ἀνήρ, one exempt from the common frailty of humanity (*Hipp.* 948).   παρά is a little odd: after ἀπέχειν we expect ἀπό (which Reiske wished to restore) or the simple gen. But the variation may be deliberately sought, as in 118 ἀφ' ἱστῶν παρὰ κερκίδων τ'. The difficulty is at any rate less than that of the other view (Hermann, Blass), which makes the words mean 'keep at arm's length the clever wit and subtlety *that proceed from* men who reject the common rule': as Tyrrell pointed out, πραπίς and φρήν, both originally names of physical organs, signify not the product of thought, which can 'proceed from' the thinker, but the seat of thought; and we should anyhow expect τὰν παρά. [The words σοφὰν δ' ἀπέχειν seem to be metrically faulty: the intrusion of an anapaest here, thought not quite unparalleled (Denniston, 'Lyric Iambics', in *Greek Poetry and Life*, 138), is improbable, especially as 412 has no anapaest (for we must scan μὲ not μὲ, cf. 545–6 n.). See Blass, *Rh. Mus.* lxii. 265. σοφὰν δ' ἀπεχε (Hermann) makes exact metrical correspondence; but the second sing. imperative addressed to the world at large is unusual in a chorus (Paley), and certainly rather abrupt here. σοφὸν ἀπέχειν, 'it is wise to withhold', Wilamowitz. Perhaps the easiest correction is σοφὰ δ' ἀπέχειν, which Dindorf once proposed: the idiomatic neuter plural (like δίκαια γὰρ τόνδ' εὐτυχεῖν, Soph. *Aj.* 1126) would be peculiarly exposed to corruption.]

430–3. 'Whatever the simple many have taken as their rule and usage, that would I accept.' The φαῦλοι are the 'simple' people both in the social and in the intellectual sense: Eur. frequently contrasts them with the σοφοί (e.g. *Andr.* 379 φαῦλός εἰμι κοὐ σοφός, and 481 f.; *Phoen.* 495 f.; fr. 635), and not always to their disadvantage: cf. *Ion* 834 f. φαῦλον χρηστὸν ἂν λαβεῖν φίλον | θέλοιμι μᾶλλον ἢ κακὸν σοφώτερον: fr. 473 φαῦλον ἄκομψον, τὰ μέγιστ' ἀγαθόν, | πᾶσαν ἐν ἔργῳ περιτεμνόμενον | σοφίαν, λέσχης ἀτρίβωνα: fr. 289 τῆς δ' ἀληθείας ὁδὸς | φαύλη τίς ἐστι. In the light of these passages it seems a mistake to suppose with Bruhn (*Einl.* 22) and Lindskog (*Stud. z. antiken Drama*, 30) that φαυλότερον is a 'depreciatory' epithet which gives away the Chorus's case. The antithesis in the present passage is substantially the same which Teiresias drew between τὸ σοφόν and the πάτριοι παραδοχαί (201–3). To those critics who are surprised to find a pupil of the sophists writing in this vein we may reply (a) that it is dramatically appropriate, since Dion. is peculiarly a god of the φαυλότερον πλῆθος (see 421–3 n.): cf. the 'olim iussa deo simplicitas facilis' which is praised on the gravestone of a Thracian worshipper of Dion., Heuzey, *Mission arch. de Macédoine*, 128; (b) that like many poets Eur. may well have felt at times a deeper kinship with the intuitive wisdom of the people than with the arid cleverness of the intellectuals: this feeling seems to be expressed in some of the passages quoted above, and especially in the *Electra*, where the Αὐτουργός is a type of the φαῦλος ἄκομψος. 'Faith in the "simple man" is characteristic of most idealists and most reformers. It implies the doctrine of Equality—a doctrine essentially religious and mystical, continually disproved in every fresh sense in which it can be formulated, and yet remaining one of the living faiths of men' (Murray, *Essays and Addresses*, 84). [The text is uncertain, though the general sense is not in doubt. Originally *both* MSS. had λεγοίμην ἄν (λέγοιμ' ἄν L² or *l*). For this, Musgrave's δεχοίμαν is convincing (Λ for Δ). But it *may* be an optative of wish: τε τόδε τοι δεχοίμαν Bernhardy, τε τόδ' ἀεὶ δεχοίμαν Adrian, Wilamowitz, *Analecta*, 49 (keeping βάκχαισι in 415). These readings are closer than Kirchhoff's to L as it now stands; they yield, however, a much less probable rhythm (iambic), and L has traces of two erased letters (? ἐν) between τε and τόδε, while τοι is added above the line—suggesting that it had originally ἐν τῷδε, like P. χρῇ|ταί τ' ἐν τῷδε, δεχοίμαν is good sense—ἐν τῷδε, 'in this matter', limiting their faith in the common man to the field of religion—and not impossible metrically: as a second glyconic may answer to a third glyconic or 'choriambic dimeter' (e.g. Eur. *Supp.* 1000 πρός σ' ἔβαν δρομὰς ἐξ ἐμῶν = 1023 σὲ τὸν θανόντ' οὔποτ' ἐμᾷ), so a second pherecratean (⌣ ⌣ – ⌣ ⌣ – –) is an admissible substitute for a first pherecratean or 'choriambic dimeter catalectic' (– ⌣ ⌣ – ⌣ – –), e.g. Eur. *El.* 192 -πηνᾶ φάρεα δῦναι = 168 σὰν ἀγρότει|ραν αὐλάν.]

Scene 2 (434–518): a soldier, Pentheus, the Stranger.

The soldier and one or more companions (κωφὰ πρόσωπα) enter from the audience's right (as coming ἐκ πόλεως, 352, cf. Pollux 4. 126); with them the Stranger, held by his arms. Pentheus may perhaps have remained on the stage throughout the preceding song, as e.g. Medea seems to do at *Med.* 410–45 and 627–62.

This is the first of the three scenes between man and god, Pentheus and the Stranger. They form a sort of triptych, beautifully built with the balanced antithetical symmetry in which classical art delights. At this short first meeting the strong plays at being the weak, while the weak mistakes himself for the strong: it ends in the seemingly complete victory of the man over the supernatural being. The long, carefully constructed central scene (642–861) exhibits the process by which the relation is slowly reversed. The third scene (912-76), again short, shows the reversal completed. This conflict in its three stages is the dramatic kernel of the play: everything else leads up to it or flows from it.—In the calm and patient courage which the Stranger here exhibits in face of Pentheus' jeers and threats Horace perceived a symbol of the superiority of moral to physical strength: he put an adaptation of certain of the Stranger's lines (492, 498) into the mouth of a Stoic sage, 'vir bonus et sapiens' (*Ep.* 1. 16. 73 ff.). Two centuries later we find Clement of Alexandria putting others of his lines (470, 472, 474, 476) into Christ's mouth. We may conclude that the sympathies of ancient, as of modern, audiences were in this scene with the prisoner. As for the soldier, he is a specimen of the πλῆθος φαυλότερον in whose intuitive good sense the Chorus have just expressed their confidence. His account of the Stranger's arrest shows that he possesses the αἰδώς or moral sensitiveness (441) which his master lacks (263).

436. ὁ θὴρ δ' ὅδ' ἡμῖν πρᾶος: 'but we found this wild beast tame.' Sc. ἦν: a relatively rare ellipse, but not unexampled (e.g. Plato, *Rep.* 503 B). ἡμῖν ethic dat. as in 217. In calling the Stranger a θήρ the soldier merely continues the metaphor of 434; but there is tragic irony in his words. Before the end Pentheus will perceive the beast-nature of his adversary visibly manifested (922). After that Pentheus himself will be hunted and caught like a wild animal (1107 f.), so that when the action is over the two opponents will be seen to have exchanged places, as the two women change places in the course of the *Andromache*, or the two men in Thomas Hardy's *Mayor of Casterbridge*.

438. Murray's punctuation seems to imply that he takes ὠχρός as parallel to ἄκων, 'not unwilling or pale'. But the adverbial use of ὠχρός is not so natural as that of ἄκων, and it appears preferable to supply ἦν again, putting a comma at the end of 437. The Stranger showed his tameness (1) by not running away but surrendering, (2) by not *even* turning pale. [οὐκ ὠχρός is possible but hardly necessary.]

439. γελῶν: the actor who played the Stranger no doubt wore a smiling mask throughout. Cf. 380, and *H. Hymn.* 7. 14 ὁ δὲ μειδιάων ἐκάθητο (of Dion. captured by the pirates). It is an ambiguous smile—here the smile of the martyr, afterwards the smile of the destroyer (1021). It appeared again in the *Bacchae* of Accius, fr. 11 (18) 'praesens praesto irridens (irridetis codd.) . . . nobis stupe⟨factis sese⟩ ultro ostentum obtulit.'

440. τοὐμὸν εὐτρεπὲς ποιούμενος: lit. 'making my (task) ready,' i.e. help-ing me in my duty of tying his hands and arresting him. The use of the middle, which has troubled some edd., seems merely to stress the Stranger's personal participation in the action, as in πόλεμον ποιεῖσθαι and similar periphrases (Kühner–Gerth, i. § 374. 5): cf.

Hdt. I. 119. 3 εὔτυκα ποιησάμενος (τὰ κρέα), '(Astyages) having made the meat ready (for Harpagus)'. [MSS. εὐπρεπές, 'turning for himself my task to seemliness' (Tyrrell²). But this hardly accounts so well for the αἰδώς felt by the soldier (441); and εὐτρεπές is strongly supported by 844, where τό γ' ἐμὸν εὐτρεπές is a quite certain correction for τό γ' ἐμὸν εὐπρεπές. L has the same confusion at *Her.* 497 and *Hec.* 565. Nauck's εὐπετές has less transcriptional probability. εὐτρεπές (or -ῇ) ποιεῖσθαι occurs also *El.* 689, *IT.* 245.]

442. ἐπιστολαῖς: 'by the commission' of P.—the oldest meaning of the word.

443–8. δ' αὖ marks the transition to a different arrest (L.S.⁹ s.v. αὖ II. 2). The liberation of the imprisoned women (those referred to at 226 f.) serves no obvious purpose in the economy of the play beyond giving Pentheus the unheeded warning that the supernatural cannot be controlled by lock and key. It is introduced primarily because it is a traditional Dionysiac miracle: see Introd., p. xxxii. Dion. has power to bind and to loose: he binds with the magic vine (Lucian, *Dial. Deor.* 18, Nonnus 21. 30 ff.); he looses already in *H. Hymn.* 7. 13 f. τὸν δ' οὐκ ἴσχανε δεσμά, λύγοι δ' ἀπὸ τηλόσ' ἔπιπτον | χειρῶν ἠδὲ ποδῶν, and cf. 498 n. Memories of the present passage may have helped to shape the story of the miraculous freeing of Peter in *Acts* 12: with 447–8 cf. *Acts* 12. 7 ἐξέπεσον αὐτοῦ αἱ ἁλύσεις ἐκ τῶν χειρῶν, and 10 (ἡ πύλη) αὐτομάτη ἠνοίχθη αὐτοῖς, also 16. 26. See 45 n., 795 n., and O. Weinreich, 'Gebet und Wunder', in *Genethliakon W. Schmid* (Tübinger Beitr. z. Alt. v), 284 ff., 326 ff.—Observe the effective use of resolved feet in 445–8 (six in four lines): the verses which describe the liberation are themselves liberated and swift. The harsh lack of euphony in 443, where the syllable ας occurs six times, is perhaps also a deliberate or instinctive adaptation of sound to sense. On ὀργάδας see 340 n.   [ποδῶν (447) is sometimes altered to πεδῶν (Meineke) because Pentheus at 226 mentions the chaining of the women's hands, not of their feet; but the objection is a little pedantic.]

449–50. The soldier half confesses his faith in the Stranger, then breaks off in fear of offending his master—'but what shall happen next is your concern, not mine'.

451–2. 'Let go his hands: now that he is in my net, he is not so nimble that he shall get away from me.' Cf. the similar though differently motived command, *IT.* 468 μέθετε τῶν ξένων χέρας, and for the middle, *Hec.* 400 τῆσδ' ἑκοῦσα παιδὸς οὐ μεθήσομαι. **ἐν ἄρκυσιν** takes up the metaphor of 434–6. [The corruption of μέθεσθε to μαίνεσθε would be helped by the common confusion of ε and αι, which were pronounced alike from Hellenistic times onward. Other views: (1) the reading of L P is defended by Tyrrell and Dalmeyda, who punctuate μαίνεσθε· χειρῶν τοῦδ' ἐν ἄρκυσιν γὰρ ὤν, take χειρῶν

ἄρκυσιν together (like *Alc.* 984 ἐν ἀφύκτοισι χερῶν . . . δεσμοῖς), and
suppose τοῦδε to be Pentheus (it is glossed ἐμοῦ in L). But (*a*) the
postponement of γάρ goes much beyond normal tragic practice
(cf. Denniston, *Particles*, 96): the only comparable example is Soph.
Phil. 1451 καιρὸς καὶ πλοῦς ὅδ᾽ ἐπείγει γάρ (where I should be tempted
to read with Burges ὅδ᾽ ἐπείγει γὰρ καιρὸς καὶ πλοῦς). (*b*) As Sandys
says, we should expect χειρῶν τῶνδε, and also μαίνῃ (whereas the
plur. μέθεσθε is natural since the Stranger is presumably held by
two men). (*c*) An order to unhand the captive is required here in
view of the order to seize him at 503. (2) The last two objections
apply also to Bothe's μαίνεσθε χεῖρον τοῦδ᾽ (revived by G. Rudberg,
Symb. Oslo. iv [1926], 29). Moreover, this would not mean 'You are
madder than the Stranger' (which is a possible exaggeration for an
angry man), but 'You are mad in a more sinister manner' (which
is merely absurd). (3) λάζυσθε, whether due to *p* or (Wilamowitz)
to P², is not more than a bad guess, inconsistent with 437 and 503.
(4) φθείρεσθε χειρῶν τοῦδ᾽ (J. U. Powell), 'Let go his hands, damn
you!', is not impossible (cf. *Androm.* 715), but seems an unnecessarily
violent form of command. (5) μαίνεσθε ⟨. . . . . . | μέθεσθε⟩ χειρῶν
τοῦδ᾽, Verrall, *Bacchants*, 61, on the ground that 'to drop μαίνεσθε
makes P. pass in silence the escape of the bacchanals and the man's
miraculous explanation'. This is plausible; but having laid hands
on the principal, P. may perhaps be allowed to neglect the sub-
ordinates.]

453-9. P. turns from the soldiers to study the prisoner (ἀτάρ, 'Well!',
marking the change of attention, cf. 248). These lines give one of
those relatively detailed descriptions of stage personages which are
characteristic of late-fifth-century tragedy (Webster, *Greek Art and
Literature, 530-400 B.C.*, 187); they belong to a time when mask
and costume were being made more individual and realistic, and
may be partly designed as stage directions. Winnington-Ingram
observes acutely that 'the sensual appearance of the Stranger
is precisely the form in which Dionysus should and could reveal
himself to the suppressed sensuality of Pentheus'. The girlishness
of Dion. (θηλύμορφον 353) is not, however, Eur.'s own invention.
Aristophanes quotes from the *Edoni* of Aesch. (Ar. *Thesm.* 134 ff. =
Aesch. fr. 61) the question ποδαπὸς ὁ γύννις; addressed to the captive
Dion. (cf. *infra*, 460). [In comedy he wears the feminine κροκωτός
(Ar. *Frogs* 46, cf. Cratinus fr. 38), and is mocked for his effeminacy.
Cf. also Hesych. Διονῦς· ὁ γυναικίας καὶ παράθηλυς. In painting and
sculpture the dignified bearded god of archaic and early classical
art begins to be replaced in the late fifth century by a graceful
beardless youth whose features and contours already show something of the feminine character which is so marked in Hellenistic
representations (see Farnell, *Cults*, v, chap. 7, E. Thraemer in Roscher

s.v. 'Dionysos'). The ephebic type is as old in literature as the Homeric hymn, where Dion. appears νεηνίη ἀνδρὶ ἐοικὼς | πρωθήβῃ· καλαὶ δὲ περισσείοντο ἔθειραι (7. 3 f.). But there he has στιβαροὶ ὦμοι: the effemination seems to begin in the fifth century. The change in the art type results in part from a general change in the representation of gods and heroes; but the conception of the womanish god may have deeper roots in eastern and northern religious ideas. Cf. the use of women's guise in Dionysiac ritual (854-5 n.); the effemination of the priests of Cybele, of Scythian μάντιες (Hdt. 4. 67. 2), and of Siberian shamans; and for possible explanations, Frazer, *Golden Bough*, IV. ii. 253 ff., van Gennep, *Rites de passage*, 246, R. H. Lowie, *Primitive Religion*, 243 ff.]

454. ὡς ἐς γυναῖκας: 'to a woman's taste, at least' ('considering that it is with a view to women': ὡς limitative, cf. L.S. s.v. Ab. II 2).

455. οὐ πάλης ὕπο: 'proving you no wrestler', lit. 'by not wrestling'. οὐ negatives the single word πάλης, like our 'non-' in compound nouns: so 458, 1287, *Hipp.* 195 f. δι' ἀπειροσύνην ἄλλου βιότου | κοὐκ ἀπόδειξιν ('non-revelation') τῶν ὑπὸ γαίας, and often in Thuc., e.g. 3. 95. 2 τὴν οὐ περιτείχισιν. This turn of speech is an invention of the late fifth century, and was afterwards found convenient by the philosophers, e.g. Plato, *Theaet.* 201 E μὴ οὐσία 'non-being', Lucr. 2. 930 'ex non sensibus' (Wackernagel, *Vorl. üb. Syntax*, ii. 263 ff.).—Close-cropped hair was affected by athletes, no doubt for convenience, and perhaps also as a mark of manliness (Lucian, *Dial. Mer.* 5. 3 ἐν χρῷ . . . καθάπερ οἱ σφόδρα ἀνδρώδεις τῶν ἀθλητῶν ἀποκεκαρμένη, of an Eton-cropped girl): cf. Eur. *El.* 528, which seems to refer to the bristliness induced in the wrestler's hair by frequent cutting. The long side-curls, 'rippling right down the cheek', are seen in many representations of Dion., e.g. the Wemyss head (Farnell, *Cults*, v. 271, pl. li) or the Capitoline head (Sandys, p. 26).

457. λευκήν describes a fair, not a pale, complexion (cf. 438). On δέ answering to τε see Denniston, *Particles*, 513. The shift to the adversative mode of expression is probably to be explained here by the intrusion in the second clause of the idea of purpose (ἐκ παρασκευῆς) which is not applicable to the first (Wecklein).   ἐκ παρασκευῆς : 'by deliberate contrivance' (explained in the next line). Cf. Antiphon 6. 19 μὴ ἐκ προνοίας μηδ' ἐκ παρασκευῆς γενέσθαι τὸν θάνατον, 'not premeditated or planned', Lys. 13. 22 ἐκ παρασκευῆς ἐμηνύετο. [εἰς παρασκευήν (MSS.) could hardly mean 'to the extent of using cosmetics' (Paley, Tyrrell): this would be inconsistent with the next line, and would require a verb like θηρεύεις instead of ἔχεις. It might just possibly mean 'with a view to preparation' for seducing women, explained by 459. But confusion of EK and EIC is easy and frequent.]

458. This seems to be like 455: οὐχ in effect negatives βολαῖσιν, despite the following ἀλλά—'by avoiding the sun's rays and by (keeping in) the shade'. To be ἐσκιατροφηκώς was a mark of effeminacy (Plato, *Rep.* 556 D, cf. *Phdr.* 239 C, Ar. *Vesp.* 1413); to be sunburnt, a mark of manliness (*Rep.* 474 E). And σκιατροφεῖσθαι was thought to be especially characteristic of Lydians (Clearchus fr. 43a Wehrli, *apud* Athen. 515 E).

461. οὐ κόμπος οὐδείς: these words are not an answer to the question τίς εἶ γένος; the implied antithesis to ῥᾴδιον εἰπεῖν is a false one; and the construction is not very clear. It is not quite easy to supply ἐστί μοι (on the analogy of stock phrases like οὐδεὶς φθόνος, Aesch. *PV.* 628, Plato *Tim.* 23 D, &c.), still less to supply εἰρήσεται (Elmsley). If we put a comma at οὐδείς and construe τόδε (the answer to your question) οὐκ ἔστι κόμπος οὐδείς, ῥᾴδιον δ᾽ εἰπεῖν, we get a construction at the cost of stressing the false antithesis. Cf. Thuc. 2. 41. 2 οὐ λόγων ἐν τῷ παρόντι κόμπος τάδε. But Thuc. continues with the natural antithesis μᾶλλον ἢ ἔργων ἐστὶν ἀλήθεια. [The text has been suspected by earlier scholars, from Musgrave onwards. The papyrus fragment from Antinoë (Introd., p. lviii), which begins at 459, unfortunately preserves only the letters]σουδ[. By writing κομπός (cf. *Phoen.* 600 and schol. ad loc.) and understanding εἰμί, we should remove the syntactical difficulty; but could one be a braggart by birth? κάματος, suggested to me by Mr. C. H. Roberts, is not impossible (cf. fr. trag. adesp. 350 οὐδεὶς κάματος εὐσεβεῖν θεούς), but seems rather too strong a word. I believe the true reading is Wakefield's οὐκ ὄκνος, revived by Mr. E. L. B. Meurig-Davies, *C.R.* lvii (1943), 69, who quotes a convincing parallel from the *Peirithous* (Arnim, *Suppl. Eur.* p. 41, line 5 = Page, *Literary Papyri*, i, no. 15, line 20), where to a question about his identity and intentions Heracles replies οὐδεὶς ὄκνος πάντ᾽ ἐκκαλύψασθαι λόγον. | ἐμοὶ πατρὶς μὲν Ἄργος . . . .]

462–3. On Tmolus as a centre of Dionysiac religion see 55 n. It seems to have been really ἀνθεμώδης: saffron was made from its crocuses (Virg. *Georg.* 1. 56). And it 'had Sardis in its arms' in the sense that the city was overlooked on the south by the main range, on the west by one of its spurs.   οἶσθα . . . οἶδα: this way of opening a stichomythia is a stock convention in Eur. (E. Fraenkel, *de media et nova comoedia quaestt. sel.* 55 f.): cf. *Supp.* 116, *Ion* 936, 987, *IT.* 517, 812, *Or.* 1183. Fraenkel points out that Sophocles imitated it in the *Trachiniae* (1191, 1219) and that comedy later took it over (Anaxandrides 9 Kock, and often in Terence, e.g. *Phormio* 62).

465. πόθεν: not 'whence' but 'how comes it that', as the answer shows: cf. 648, Aesch. *Cho.* 515.

466. εἰσέβησ᾽: it is not clear whether we should supply εἰς Ἑλλάδα or εἰς τὰς τελετάς. The first would make the sentence a more direct

answer to Pentheus' question. But the second is perhaps linguistic-
ally the more probable: cf. ἐμβατεύειν 'to be initiated' (inscript. in
Jahresh. Öst. Arch. xv. 46, *Ep. Col.* 2. 18), and εἴσβασις used of an
initial magical operation (*P. Mag. Par.* 1. 397). [P. Ant. has]νυσο-
σαυτοσμϵι]. This confirms the emendation εἰσέβησα' (adopted by
almost all edd. since Hermann), but offers a new reading αὐτός μ'
for ἡμᾶς. This may well be right: αὐτός adds something—the
Stranger's mission was given by no human priest, but by the god
in person—and it helps to motive Pentheus' question at 469. If
αὐτός fell out through homoeoteleuton it would be natural to fill the
metrical gap by substituting ἡμᾶς for μϵ on the model of 825.]

467–8. For Pentheus' ironical suggestion that the new god's father is
not Zeus (since the age of miracles is past in Greece) but some more
vigorous eastern namesake cf. *Hel.* 489 ff. With the corrections
adopted in the next line by Murray, the retort is 'No, we have the
same Zeus who wedded Semele here in Thebes'. [P. Ant., however,
has]αλλασεμελην ενθ[, which confirms Canter's less violent correction,
οὐκ, ἀλλὰ Σεμέλην ἐνθάδ' ἐζευξεν γάμοις. Elmsley accepted this as
'certissima'; most subsequent edd. have been misled into rejecting
it by the over-subtle criticisms of Hermann. L may once have had
ἀλλά, not ἀλλ' ὅ: ὅ is in an erasure.]

469–70. P. 'And was it in a dream or in your waking sight that he
laid compulsion on you?' D. 'It was face to face, and he gave me
rites (or symbols).' The divine call visits some men in sleep, as it
did Lucius in the *Metamorphoses* of Apuleius; others, like St. Paul,
in a waking vision. The latter mode is naturally the more authorita-
tive.   **ἠνάγκασεν:** God's will is a compulsion (cf. 34, *Phoen.* 1000,
I.A. 760 f. θεοῦ μαντόσυνοι . . . ἀνάγκαι, and A. D. Nock, *Conversion*,
154). But in Pentheus' mouth the word is ironic: he believes that
the Stranger has come to Thebes not in obedience to a religious 'call'
but to gratify his lusts (454). I see no reason for doubting the text.
[P. Ant. supports L against P in omitting σ', which is not indispensable.] **δίδωσιν ὄργια:** this belongs to the technical language of
the cult: the Delphic Oracle, issuing instructions for the institution
of a cult of Dion. at Magnesia by 'maenads' imported from Thebes,
says αἳ δ' ὑμῖν δώσουσι καὶ ὄργια καὶ νόμιμ' ἐσθλά (Kern, *Inschr. v.
Magnesia*, no. 215 = 338 Parke-Wormell). Are the ὄργια verbal
prescriptions for the conduct of the rites (as in *H. Cer.* 273 ὄργια δ'
αὐτὴ ἐγὼν ὑποθήσομαι ὡς ἂν ἔπειτα . . . ἱλάσκοισθε), or (Paley, Murray)
secret cult objects, the contents of a 'cista mystica' (on Dionysiac
κιστοφόροι see Cumont, *A.J.A.* 1933, 246 f.)? The latter sense of the
word is not recognized by L.S.; but it seems to be applied to things,
not actions, at Theocr. 26. 13 σὺν δ' ἐτάραξε ποσὶν μανιώδεος ὄργια
Βάκχου, where the ὄργια are apparently ἱερὰ ἐκ κίστας ποπανεύματα
laid on improvised altars; the singular, ὄργιον, is certainly so used

by Clem. Alex. *Protrept*. 2. 22 (p. 17. 7 Stählin); an inscription (*Berl. Sitzb*. 1905, 547) speaks of a priestess of Dionysus who ὄργια πάντα καὶ ἱρὰ ἤνεικεν, and when Latin poets speak of 'orgia ferre' (Prop. 3. 1. 4, Stat. *Ach*. 1. 812, Sen. *H.O.* 594) it is natural to give the word the concrete sense. If we could assume that sense here, the line would gain in point, since the bestowal of physical objects would be proof of the god's physical presence. On the other hand, the instances I have quoted are Hellenistic or Roman, and at 482, as elsewhere in the play, ὄργια is certainly 'rites' (471 and 476 are indecisive). The question must, I think, remain open.

471. τίν' ἰδέαν ἔχοντα: 'of what kind', if the ὄργια are rites; 'of what appearance', if they are physical objects. Fifth-century writers use ἰδέα in both senses (cf. Wilamowitz, *Platon*, ii. 248 ff.). With ἔχειν the second might seem the more natural; but cf. Plato, *Euthyph.* 5 D (πᾶν τὸ ἀνόσιον) ἔχον μίαν τινὰ ἰδέαν. It is mainly a prose word, found in tragedy here only; its synonym εἶδος is used freely by the tragedians, but always, so far as I know, of physical appearance. Notice the word-order: P. picks up D.'s word ὄργια, which is consequently put in the emphatic position at the expense of postponing the interrogative. Cf. 661–3 ἥκω . . . ἥκεις δὲ ποίαν . . .; 828–30 στολήν . . . στολὴν δὲ τίνα . . .; and the many exx. quoted by G. Thomson, *C.Q.* xxxiii (1939), 148. In 473 ἔχει ὄνησιν is put first because this is the fresh point, the next step in the interrogation: cf. 832 and Thomson, ibid., p. 149. In the following lines the Stranger skilfully excites, without satisfying it, Pentheus' curiosity about the rites (as P. himself observes, 475). This prepares the ground for the temptation scene.

475. 'You faked that answer cleverly, to make me want to hear' (bad money is κίβδηλος, from κίβδος 'dross'). [This line violates in its fourth foot the rule which prohibits a break between the second and the third syllable of a tribrach. We may perhaps say that ἵνα is treated as a proclitic, like τίνα in 471, *Or*. 266, *Ion* 931; and that the elision helps to bind it to the succeeding word (Descroix, *Trimètre iambique*, 166 f.). Such relative laxity is typical of late tragedy (cf. 192 n., 826 n.).—θέλω (*l*) for θέλων (L P) is a necessary correction, and technically easy since ν at the end of a line was often represented merely by a horizontal stroke. Verrall's overworked notion of aposiopesis is particularly unconvincing here.]

477. γάρ: 'since', introducing the reason for the question which follows. For its postponed position cf. Denniston, *Particles*, 96; the MSS. have the prose order, *contra metrum*.

479. 'Skilfully side-tracked again—with an empty phrase!' παροχετεύειν, properly to divert a watercourse—an operation often necessary in Greek farming—metaph. to 'turn off' a verbal or physical assault (so Eur. *Supp*. 1111 παρεκτρέποντες ὀχετόν). Plato plays on the two meanings, *Laws* 844 A. In κοὐδὲν λέγων Wecklein took the καί as copulative, 'cleverly and emptily' (cf. 490 n.); but it may be concessive, 'though there is nothing in what you say' (like e.g. καὶ ἐσσύμενον *Il.* 13. 787). Not 'telling me nothing': for οὐδὲν λέγων is the antithesis of σοφὰ λέγων in the next line. This idiom, common in Aristophanes and Plato, does not appear in this form elsewhere in tragedy; but cf. *Her.* 279 ἦν τί σοι δοκῶ λέγειν, 'if you think there is anything in what I say'; Soph. *OT.* 1475 λέγω τι; 'am I right?'

480. For the thought cf. *Med.* 298 f. The Stranger ἀμαθεῖ σοφὰ ἔλεγεν in saying that Dion. appeared ὁποῖος ἤθελε: it was a hint of the god's penchant for disguise, whose significance Pentheus missed. [Stobaeus' λέγειν for φρονεῖν is accounted for by assimilation: the reverse corruption would be hard to explain.]

482. πᾶς ... βαρβάρων, 'every one of the foreigners', is more emphatic than πάντες βάρβαροι: cf. Soph. *O.C.* 597 πᾶς τοῦτό γ' Ἑλλήνων θροεῖ. ὄργια: internal accusative; the sacral dance *is* the ὄργια.

483-4. P. 'Because foreigners are much sillier than Greeks.' D. 'Wise, rather, in this case, though their customs are different.' μᾶλλον may be *magis*, sc. τῶν Ἑλλήνων: but since we should then expect ἄμεινον it is perhaps better to take it as *potius* (Bruhn), correcting Pentheus' statement. P. is here the typical arrogant Greek. We must not take him as being the mouthpiece of his author: cf. *Andr.* 243 f., where the Greek princess's arrogant claim, οὐ βαρβάρων νόμοισιν οἰκοῦμεν πόλιν, is answered by the Trojan slave with the quiet retort κἀκεῖ τά γ' αἰσχρὰ κἀνθάδ' αἰσχύνην ἔχει. The recognition that different cultures have different codes of behaviour (*IA.* 558 f. διάφοροι δὲ φύσεις βροτῶν, διάφοροι δὲ τρόποι), and that the Greek code is not necessarily in all points the best, is one of the advances in thought due to the sophistic movement: cf. Hdt.'s view that we ought not to laugh at the religious customs of any people, however repugnant to our own notions (3. 38).

485-6. μεθ' ἡμέραν: 'by day', cf. μετὰ νύκτας (Pind. *Nem.* 6. 6), μεθημερινός. νύκτωρ τὰ πολλά: cf. 425, 862, *Frogs* 342 νυκτέρου τελετῆς φωσφόρος ἀστήρ, Ov. *Met.* 6. 588 ff., and the god's cult title νυκτέλιος (Paus. 1. 40. 6, Plut. *de EI ap. Delph.* 9, 389 A, Ov. *Met.* 4. 15).

487-9. Pentheus excitedly smells immorality again, and when the Stranger explains that morals don't depend on the time of day, he loses his temper—observe the explosive δ- δ- δ- in 489 (so Jason in his rage cries δώμασιν δώσει δίκην, *Med.* 1298). Hippolytus has a like objection to nocturnal rites, *Hipp.* 106 οὐδείς μ' ἀρέσκει νυκτὶ θαυμαστὸς θεῶν. Their moral dangers seem to have been a topic of controversy in Eur.'s day: cf. 222-3 n., also Eur. fr. 524, *Ion* 550 ff. (and the many stories in New Comedy of girls seduced at a παννυχίς).

490. The causal ptcp. ἀσεβοῦντα is parallel to the causal gen. ἀμαθίας, and linked with it by καί: 'for your blindness and as a blasphemer.'

491. ὁ βάκχος: the bacchant (not the god), 'this mystery-priest' (Murray): see 115 n.

492. τί... τὸ δεινόν because 489 implies an intention to do *something* δεινόν. Cf. 758-60 n. The phrase belongs to the language of everyday life: at Ar. *Lys.* 366 the old men respond to the women's implied threat by asking τί μ' ἐργάσει τὸ δεινόν;

493-7. Stage business with the Stranger's side curls and with his thyrsus. Murray thinks that Pentheus carries out his threats there and then—a symbolic act of ὕβρις, like the carpet-walking in the *Agamemnon*. But if this were the poet's intention we should expect more explicit indications in the text. As it is, it looks rather as if the mortal recoiled at 497 from the challenge of his divine adversary, and fell back on threatening future action.   **ἁβρὸν βόστρυχον**: 'your love-locks', implying a taunt of effeminacy (cf. 966-70 n.); βόστρυχος and πλόκαμος probably in the collective sense, as *Hipp.* 202, Aesch. fr. 313.   **τῷ θεῷ δ' αὐτὸν τρέφω**: there is of course irony here, as also in 496, 500, 502—irony which is lost if with Verrall we refuse to identify the Stranger and the god. Throughout the latter part of this scene 'le dieu se laisse entrevoir partout et ne se découvre jamais' (M. Croiset). [For the custom of growing one's hair to be cut off and dedicated cf. Aesch. *Cho.* 6 and Tucker ad loc.: Diphilus fr. 66. 5 ff., describing a runaway slave who grows his hair long to hide the brand on his forehead, κόμην τρέφων ... ἱερὰν τοῦ θεοῦ, | ὥς φησιν: Virg. *Aen.* 7. 391 'sacrum tibi (sc. Dionyso) pascere crinem': W. H. D. Rouse, *Greek Votive Offerings*, 240 ff. The hair was felt as a detachable, and therefore conveniently dedicable, extension of its owner's personality.]   **Διονύσου**: possessive gen., with predicative force—'this wand I carry is the god's' (and therefore not mine to give). The Rules of the Iobacchi speak similarly of τὸν θύρσον τοῦ θεοῦ (see 113 n., ad fin.).

498. A Greek audience would be reminded of Dionysus Λύσιος, a cult title which was explained in the Theban temple-legend as referring to an occasion when the god liberated (ἔλυσεν) certain prisoners (Paus. 9. 16. 6, cf. Heraclides Ponticus, fr. 101 Voss = 155 Wehrli). See O. Weinreich in *Genethliakon W. Schmid*, 285 f.

499. 'Sensus horum verborum est *Nunquam*', Elmsley. It seems to be implied that the god cannot be summoned save by the *collective* ritual—of which indeed he is in one aspect the 'projection'.

501. καὶ ποῦ 'στιν; 'And where *is* he, eh?' Cf. Soph. *El.* 928 καὶ ποῦ 'στιν οὗτος; and on καί in contemptuous questions generally Denniston, *Particles*, 309 ff.

502. παρ' ἐμοί: 'Where I am' (Murray). The irony vanishes if we translate 'Beside me' (πλησίον in 500 is πλησίον σου). [οὐδ' εἰσορᾷς

P. Ant., perhaps rightly—'You cannot even see him' (much less understand him). Elmsley's αὐτόν for αὐτός (the pronoun trajected as in *Ion* 293 ξένος σ' ὤν ἔσχεν) is a needless change. Vision demands not only an objective condition—the god's presence—but a subjective one—the percipient must *himself* be in a state of grace. Cf. Callimachus, *H. Ap.* 9 'Ὠπόλλων οὐ παντὶ φαείνεται, ἀλλ' ὅτις ἐσθλός : Plotinus 6. 5. 12. 28 Bréhier οἱ θεοὶ πόλλων παρόντων ἑνὶ φαίνονται πολλάκις, ὅτι ὁ εἷς ἐκεῖνος μόνος δύναται βλέπειν : *Ev. Luc.* 24. 16 οἱ δὲ ὀφθαλμοὶ αὐτῶν ἐκρατοῦντο τοῦ μὴ ἐπιγνῶναι αὐτόν.]

503. See 286 n. Thuc. has καταφρονεῖν twice with the accus. (6. 34, 8. 82). Schol. Ar. *Frogs* 103 calls such substitution of transitive for intransitive construction 'Attic', and quotes the present line as an illustration, thus confirming *l*'s doubtless conjectural emendation of the Byzantine text. It is rash to tamper further with the line. [P. Ant. also has με καὶ Θήβας, though the verb is not preserved. The genitives in L P must be due to a Byzantine copyist who knew a little grammar but no metric.]

506. 'You know not what your life is (?), nor the thing you do, nor what you are.' If ὅ τι ζῇς is sound, the sense must, I think, be, as Prof. Fraenkel suggests to me, 'You do not realize your status as a mere mortal'. ὅ τι is taken as an internal accus. with ζῇς. The closest parallel is Persius' 'quidnam victuri gignimur' (3. 67); but Dem. often has a neut. pl. relative as internal accus. with ζῆν or βιῶναι (*Meid.* 196 φθόνον ἐξ ὧν [= τούτων ἅ] ζῇς, 'unpopularity arising from your manner of life', cf. ibid. 134, *de cor.* 130). By ὅστις εἶ Dion. means 'what your position is (in relation to me)': the man mistakes himself for the god's master. Cf. M. Ant. 8. 52 οὐκ οἶδεν ὅστις ἐστίν ('what sort of being he is'): Men. *Samia* 175 f. ἐν τῇ πόλει | ὄψει σεαυτὴν νῦν ἀκριβῶς ἥτις εἶ : and Plato, *Gorg.* 447 D, where Chaerephon is momentarily puzzled by the question ὅστις ἐστὶν ὁ Γοργίας until Socrates explains that it means 'what is G.'s profession?' Pentheus too is puzzled, and answers as if the Stranger had accused him of forgetting his own name. Kitto compares the literalness of the Chorus-leader at Aesch. *Ag.* 1088 : in each case the prosaic response symbolizes the lack of contact between the normal mind and a mind gifted with supernormal insight. I doubt if Pentheus speaks 507 in mockery (Murray): I think with Denniston that he is bewildered, and a little frightened. [The text has been much disputed. One question is settled by P. Ant., which has] θοδρασουθοστ[, confirming Reiske's ὁ δρᾷς for ὁρᾷς. As to the negatives, οὐκ . . . οὐδ' . . . οὔθ' (MSS.) is impossible. We expect οὐκ . . . οὐδ' . . . οὐδ': but (οὐκ) . . . οὔθ' . . . οὔθ' (P. Ant.) is possibly defensible (Denniston, *Particles*, 509): cf. Soph. *Tr.* 1058 ff., Eur. *Med.* 1354 ff., Bacchyl. fr. 21 Snell. There remains considerable doubt about the first clause, which is unfortunately not preserved in the papyrus. Though defensible in point of syntax (see above), the words are decidedly obscure. And could an actor distinguish by his intonation ὅ τι ζῇς from the much commoner, but here non-sensical, ὅτι ζῇς? Many corrections have been proposed. Perhaps P. does not know what he wants (Wilamowitz compared Hippocrates, ep. 17 οὔτε ὅ τι θέλει οἶδε οὔτε ὅ τι ἔρδει): ὅ τι χρῇς Madvig, but the lengthened final syllable before χρ- is hardly possible; ὁ χρῄζεις Wilamowitz, with little transcriptional probability. Or what he is saying: ὁ βάζεις Cobet, improbably. Or with whom he is dealing: ὅτου ψῇς A. Y. Campbell olim, cf. Soph. Ant. 960 ff. (but can ψάω = ψαύω?); ὅτου φῇς L. Solomon (sc. κυριώτερος εἶναι, but the ellipse is too harsh). Less bad, I think, than any of these is ὁ τείσεις (ὁ τίσεις Schoene), giving an effect of climax—'you do not know the penalty or the offence or even the agent'. Written οτιϲειϲ in a Hellenistic copy, this might be corrupted through false word division.[1]]

508. 'You bear a name apt for calamity', lit. 'You are suitable as to your name to be unfortunate in (under) it'. This use of epexegetic infinitives compounded with ἐν is a late-fifth-century mannerism. Developing from phrases in which ἐν- has a simple local sense, e.g. Hdt. 9. 7. 2 ἐπιτηδεότατόν ἐστι ἐμμαχέσασθαι τὸ πεδίον, the usage is extended to expressions like Hipp. 1096 ὡς ἐγκαθηβᾶν πόλλ' ἔχεις εὐδαίμονα and Thuc. 2. 44. 1 ἐνευδαιμονῆσαί τε ὁ βίος ὁμοίως καὶ ἐντελευτῆσαι ξυνεμετρήθη. For ἐνδυστυχῆσαι so used cf. Phoen. 727, and for further examples, Cope on Arist. Rhet. 2. 4. 12, Wackernagel, Vorl. über Syntax, ii. 177 f., Denniston, C.R. l (1936), 117. On the significant name see 367 n.: the priest's warning is now reinforced by the god's—a deliberate cumulative effect.

509-10. Pentheus can stand it no longer, and is impatient to be rid of the Stranger's presence.   ἱππικαῖς πέλας φάτναισιν: not 'near to the stables' (too vague a direction), but 'in the neighbouring stables' (cf. 618). Stables as improvised prison also Or. 1449.

513. δούπου τοῦδε is explained by βύρσης κτύπου: for καί connecting words in apposition cf. 919 (Denniston, Particles, 291). [P's κτύπους yields a grammatically possible but much less tidy construction.] Pentheus here notices the Chorus for the first time: have they called attention to themselves by thumping their kettledrums (as τοῦδε suggests) to emphasize the Stranger's warning at 508? The proposal to enslave them is drastic, and could hardly be put in the mouth of

[1] I once thought of ⟨ἔθ'⟩ ὅ τι φῇς, which Campbell has since commended (C.Q. xlix, 1956), and I am now inclined to revert to it. It matches the simplicity of δρᾷς and εἶ, makes the obvious comment on Pentheus' claim to be κυριώτερος σέθεν, and is fairly plausible transcriptionally: if Ε Θ fell out after Cθ, ζῇς would be a natural makeshift metri gratia.

a character intended to be sympathetic: cf. *IT.* 1431 ff. Stage necessity of course prevents its execution: the Chorus must remain in the orchestra.

515–16. 'I am ready to go: for what is not to be I have not to suffer'— the negative counterpart of *Her.* 311 ὃ χρὴ γὰρ οὐδεὶς μὴ χρεὼν θήσει ποτέ. The next words are spoken as he is led out by his guards; they are unheard by Pentheus, who has probably already left the stage.   **ἀτάρ τοι:** 'Be sure, however', changing the subject as at 248. For the construction of **ἄποινα** cf. 345–6 n.

518. Irony again: the words are literally true, but for the people on the stage they express the same religious truth as 'Inasmuch as ye have done it unto one of the least of these my brethren, ye have done it unto me'.

Stasimon 2 (519–75)

A song in time of tribulation, comparable in tone and temper to some of the Psalms. The Chorus make a last appeal to Thebes; they reaffirm their faith in the mystery of the Twice-born, and denounce the persecutor; the song culminates in a solemn ὕμνος κλητικός, an appeal to their god to save them and a picture of his coming as the heavenly dancer, the Prince of Joy. It thus reinforces, like Stasimon 1, the emotional effect of the preceding scene; it also leads up to the following one, in which their prayer receives instant and surprising answer. The Chorus here συναγωνίζονται in the full sense: they are personally affected by the action of the play, and what they do in turn affects the action.

Metre. A single pair of strophes followed by a long epode, the whole written in ionics a minore (often anaclastic) save for the end of the epode (571–5) which is here reconstructed as glyconic. Catalexis, 519, 522, &c.; resolutions, 522, 525, 571; – for ∪ ∪, 537, but see note; 536 (clausula) like 385, see metrical note on stasimon 1.

Scheme of the glyconics:

```
571   – ∪  – ∪ ∪ ∪  –          pher.²
      – –  – ∪ ∪ –  ∪ –         glyc.²
      – ∪ ∪ –  ∪ –  ∪ ∪         glyc.¹
      – –  – –  – ∪ ∪ –         glyc.³
      – –  – ∪ ∪ –  –           pher.²
```

519–20. Either the opening line of the strophe is lost or the words οἵαν οἵαν ὀργάν at the beginning of the antistrophe are spurious: see on 537–41. The Achelous (mod. Aspropotamo) is Dirce's 'father' because he is in Mure's words 'the patriarch and eponyme hero of the whole fresh-water creation of Hellas': schol. T Hom. *Il.* 21. 195 ὁ Ἀχελῷος πηγὴ τῶν ἄλλων πάντων. According to Wilamowitz (*Glaube d. Hellenen*, i. 93, 219) he is the old water-god of the mainland who was ousted by Oceanus and sank to the status of a river. Cf.

625-6 n. **εὐπάρθενε**: 'Blessed maiden.' We might expect the word to mean 'blessed with maidens' on the analogy of εὔανδρος &c. But cf. εὔπαις 'blessed child' *Her.* 689, *IT.* 1234 (elsewhere 'blessed with children'), καλλίπαις 'fair child' *Or.* 964 (elsewhere 'having fair children'), μονόπαις 'only child' *Alc.* 906; and for this type of compound in general, Jebb on *OT.* 846, Wilamowitz on *Her.* 689.

521-2. The γάρ sentence explains why they invoke Dirce, and introduces a digression which leaves the vocatives 'hanging', to be picked up at 530. Cf. Pind. *Ol.* 4. 1 ff., and the many examples quoted by Fraenkel, commentary on *Agam.*, p. 698. For the washing of the infant Dion. by the nymphs cf. *Anth. Pal.* 9. 331, and Plut. *Lys.* 28. 7, who associates it with the spring Kissoussa near Haliartus. Eur. is the sole authority for Dirce's connexion with the story.

523-5. μηρῷ ... ἥρπασε: 'snatched ... (and hid) in his thigh.' [Kayser's ἥρμοσε is no improvement without the further (and very improbable) change of ὁ τεκών to ἀνελών: otherwise ἥρμοσε is at least as difficult with ἐκ πυρός as ἥρπασε with the local dative μηρῷ. 525 is metrically sound: for the correspondence of τᾶδ' ἄν to 544 ἄντ cf. 372 = 388, 522 = 541.]

526. διθύραμβος is the name of (1) a Dionysiac choral performance; (2) a member of the Dionysiac thiasos, who is perhaps a 'projection' of the choral song, as Linus of the Linus-song (the name appears on vases); (3) Dionysus himself (first here, also in the Delphic hymn and Athen. 30 B, 465 A: cf. θριαμβοδιθύραμβε [read Θρίαμβε Διθύραμβε?] Pratinas, fr. lyr. 1). Ancient scholars explained it as ὁ δὶς θύραζε βεβηκώς, 'he who came twice to the gates of birth' (*Et. Magn.* s.v., &c.); and doubtless in using the title here and here only Eur. had this derivation in mind, as had Plato when he spoke of Διονύσου γένεσις, οἶμαι, διθύραμβος λεγόμενος (*Laws* 700 B). [It will not in fact do: Δῑ- cannot represent δίς. Many moderns incline to interpret the word as 'divine-three-step', comparing θρίαμβος, triumphus, perhaps ἴαμβος. On this view, (1) is the original meaning, out of which first (2) and then (3) developed, the last with the help of false etymology. Calder, however, regards it as an old Asiatic cult title meaning 'Lord of the tomb' (Phryg. dithrera, 'tomb'). See on the whole subject Pickard-Cambridge, *Dithyramb, Tragedy, and Comedy*, 14 ff.]

528-9. 'I reveal thee to Thebes, O Bacchic One that she call thee (ὀνομάζειν epexegetic) by this name.' For ἀναφαινειν used of religious revelation cf. *IG.* iii. 713 ὃς τελετὰς ἀνέφηνε. The content of the revelation is the *nomen sacrum*, Διθύραμβος. [Hermann's ἀναφαίνω for ἀναφᾶνῶ is required for the sake of the metre.]

532. ἐν σοί: 'on thy banks' (Dalmeyda): cf. L.S.⁹ s.v. ἐν A. I. 4. We need not resort to the explanation that Dirce, a river in 521, has here become a symbol of Thebes; still less emend Δίρκα in 530 to Θήβα.

537–41. 'What rage, what rage he shows, the earth-child, the old dragon's breed, Pentheus whose father was earthborn Echion!' Echion ('Snake-man') was one of the Σπαρτοί ('sown men') who sprang from the dragon's teeth which Cadmus sowed. References to P.'s curious ancestry are strikingly frequent in the play (cf. 265, 507, 995 f., 1025 f., 1155, 1274 ff.). Winnington-Ingram thinks that we are meant to see in it a symbol of the Dionysiac element in this man, which makes him, like the snake, a potential vehicle of the god. The Chorus, however, draw here and at 995 the simpler conclusion that like the earthborn giants who fought against the gods he comes of a monstrous, inhuman stock and is therefore the natural enemy of what is divine. Cf. Nonnus 44. 211, where he is called ὀψίγονον τιτῆνα, and ibid. 46. 74 ff. The giants are traditional types of ὕβρις (Bacchyl. 15 [14]. 59 ff., &c.). [The words οἵαν οἵαν ὀργάν, which correspond to nothing in the strophe, were struck out by Bothe and Hermann as an addition made by someone who wrongly thought that the sense required them (*l* had already written, above the first οἵαν, περισσόν, 'superfluous'). Their omission leaves in fact a good idiomatic sentence—'P. reveals his earthborn origin, that he is descended from the dragon' (τε epexegetic). For ἀναφαίνει γένος cf. Soph. *OT.* 1059 φανῶ τοὐμὸν γένος: for the participial construction, Plato, *Crit.* 108 c τοὺς πολίτας ἀγαθοὺς ὄντας ἀναφαίνειν, Soph. *El.* 1359 ξυνών μ' ἔληθες οὐδ' ἔφαινες. The two 'revelations'— of Dionysus' birth and of Pentheus'—are then contrasted, as the recurrence of the same verb ἀναφαίνειν suggests they should be. One may add that the repeated οἵαν occurs in another passage which is suspect of being interpolated, *Hec.* 175; while there is no indication that anything is lacking at the beginning of the strophe.[1] It is perhaps a little strange (Winnington-Ingram) that an interpolator who was indifferent to strophic correspondence should yet know enough about metre to produce these metrically correct but not very obvious molossi (– – – for – ⏑ ⏑ –, cf. 81). Nevertheless, my feeling is that Bothe's solution is probably the right one.]

542–4. τέρας &c., are in apposition to ὄν: they might have been nominatives, but by throwing them into the relative clause the Chorus imply that these characteristics are in Pentheus' heredity. ὥστε = ὥσπερ. θεοῖς, monosyllable.

545–6. [For συνάπτειν ἐν βρόχοις cf. 615. The more obvious correction of με βρόχοισι (which is a syllable short) to ἐμὲ βρόχοισι is open to question. Lengthening of a final vowel before mute and liquid certainly occurs in the lyrics of Sophocles and Euripides, e.g. Soph. *Ant.* 612 τὸ πρίν, Eur. *Alc.* 101 ἐπὶ προθύροις, *Tro.* 833 σὰ δροσόεντα

---

[1] The slightly loose structure of the strophe belongs to this type of poetry (Norden, *Agnostos Theos* 157) and is surely natural.

λουτρά. Usually, however, the words are closely linked in sense, as in the above examples. Cf. Fraenkel, *Agam.*, Appendix E.]

549. [Here and here only in the play a 'straight' Ionic dimeter corresponds to an 'anaclastic' (530). The irregularity can be corrected by reading σκοτίαισι κρυπτὸν εἱρκταῖς (prepositions are sometimes interpolated for clarity). But the intention may be to link 549 in metre, as in sense, with what precedes, whereas 530 is linked by both metre and sense to what follows. The same irregularity occurs at Ar. *Frogs* 327∼44 and 336∼52, in a hieratic passage.]

550-2. ἐσορᾷς, like *Hec.* 1115 εἰσορᾷς ἃ πάσχομεν; (Sandys's ἐφορᾷς is thus needless). σοὺς προφήτας: 'thy preachers' (not 'prophets'). ἐν ἁμίλλαισιν ἀνάγκας: I think 'at grips with oppression' (cf. 643), rather than 'torn between two compulsions'.

553-5. 'Come, Lord, down from (?) Olympus, shaking thy golden staff of magic: restrain the violence of this man of blood.' ἄνα may be (1) an old voc. of ἄναξ which survived in formulas of prayer (Hom., Pind., and Soph. *OC.* 1485: elsewhere in tragedy the voc. is ἄναξ); or (2) an exclamation, 'Up!' (but its position is decidedly against this); or (3) in 'anastrophic tmesis' with τινάσσων (seeming examples of such tmesis, the preposition *following* the verb, are Aesch. *Pers.* 871, Soph. *Phil.* 343, Eur. *Hec.* 504). The first is, I think, likeliest: an old sacral form is in place in this context; for Dion. as ἄναξ cf. 601, 1192. χρυσῶπα = χρυσοῦν, as κοιλωπός (*IT.* 263) = κοῖλος: Eur. has a liking for such formations. [Most edd. repeat Hermann's weak explanation that the word refers to the inconspicuous yellowish flowers of the ivy with which the wand is tipped (surely rather, if to ivy at all, to the yellow *berries* of the variety called χρυσόκαρπος, Diosc. *Mat. Med.* 2. 210, Pliny, *NH.* 16. 147). But this botanical fancy seems far less likely than Sandys's view that the wand is 'golden' because it is the sceptre of Διόνυσος ἄναξ. Cf. *Eleg. in Maecenatem*, i. 63 (Vollmer, *Poet. Lat. min.* i. 148) 'et tibi thyrsus erat gemmis ornatus et auro', addressed to Dion.; and the wand wielded by a figure usually taken for Dion. on a Yale bell-krater discussed by Beazley, who calls it 'a narthex scepterised for greater splendour by twining a gold band round it' (*A.J.A.* xliii [1939], 629). Dion. is similarly χρυσομίτρας, Soph. *OT.* 209. Dr. Jacobsthal writes: 'That gods have everything of gold is common from Homer onwards. Golden or gilded accessories in statuary, not only in chryselephantine technique, are the rule. An example from vase-painting is the gold sceptre of Hera on the Munich cup, Furtwängler–Reichhold, pl. 65. 1 (Beazley, *A.R.V.*, p. 556. 14), about 460 B.C.' Cf. H. L. Lorimer in *Greek Poetry and Life*, 24 f. Usener's χρυσωπέ is no improvement: Dion. is οἰνωπός, 236, 438.] κατ' Ὄλυμπον as 'down from O.' is not adequately defended by Homer's exceptional use of καταβαίνω with an accusative

expressing the place whence (*Od.* 18. 206, 23. 85), nor by Aristarchus' reading κατ' οὐρανόν at *Il.* 6. 128. But 'down from O.' is
surely the sense required. We must write κατ' 'Ολύμπου (Kirchhoff).

556–9. 'O where then on Nysa, nursing mother of beasts, or on Corycian
heights, does thy wand wave over the worship?' **Νύσας,** partitive
gen. **ἄρα** implies 'if only one knew' (Denniston, *Particles*, 39).
θιάσους, obj. of the transitive action implied though not expressed
in θυρσοφορεῖς, as equivalent to 'lead with the thyrsus'. Cf. δορυ-
φορεῖν τινα, to 'spear-carry' a person, i.e. guard him, and χειροτονεῖν
τινα, 'to hand-stretch' a person, i.e. elect him by show of hands
(Kühner–Gerth, i, p. 301 f.).—The list of places where the god may
be found is traditional in Greek prayers: cf. e.g. *Il.* 16. 514 f., Aesch.
Eum. 292 ff., Ar. *Clouds* 269 ff., Theocr. 1. 123 ff., and L. Weniger,
Arch. f. Rel. xxii (1923/4), 16 ff. Dion., the god of the ὀρειβασία,
is naturally to be found on mountains—Nysa, Parnassus, Olympus.
[For Olympus as a Dionysiac mountain see 409–11 n. The κορυφαὶ
Κωρύκιαι are surely the heights near the Corycian cave in the massif
of Parnassus, not its Cilician namesake: cf. Soph. *Ant.* 1126 ff.,
where the Κωρύκιαι Νύμφαι of Parnassus are associated with Dion.,
and Aesch. *Eum.* 22 ff. That the god's acceptance by Delphi is still
in the future according to Teiresias (306 ff.) matters little. Nysa is
less easy to locate. The *Iliad* (6. 133) seems to place it in Thrace;
H. Hymn. 1. 9 puts it 'near the streams of Nile'; and others elsewhere—Hesychius calls it 'a mountain not confined to any one
place', and proceeds to enumerate fifteen local Nysas. But it is
always the mountain of Dion. It looks as if it were, in Leaf's words,
'a mystic, not a geographical name'—as if any mountain where
ὀρειβασία was practised might receive the cult-title Nysa, a title
which is perhaps linked with the second element in the god's name.
But Eur. seems to think of it as an individual place—possibly the
Thracian Pangaeum, a famous Dionysiac mountain which might be
expected to figure in the play.]

560–4. τάχα, 'perhaps', sc. θυρσοφορεῖς. **θαλάμαις,** 'coverts' (Hesych.
θαλάμη· τρώγλη, κατάδυσις). For **πολυδένδρεσσιν** cf. Virg. *Georg.*
1. 282 'frondosum Olympum'; for the magical music (**μούσαις**) of
Orpheus, *IA.* 1211 ff., Aesch. *Ag.* 1629 ff., Simonides fr. 27 Diehl,
Hor. *Od.* 1. 12. 6 ff., 3. 11. 13 ff. He is a figure closely related to
Dion., though the original character of their relationship is not
clear; here it seems to be thought of as a friendly one.

565. [**μάκαρ,** rare as a feminine adj., is required by metre here; in
the MSS. it has been corrupted to the common μάκαιρα. Cf. 991–
5 n.]

567. χορεύσων, perhaps transitive (Wilamowitz), 'to set thee dancing':
cf. 21.

568-75. The Axios (Vardar) and Ludias (Mavronero) are Macedonian rivers which the god must cross on his way (apparently from Thrace) to Pieria. The latter stream flowed beneath the walls of Aegae, Archelaos' capital; it may be in compliment to his Macedonian hosts that Eur. transfers to it the praise which in an earlier play he had given to a Thessalian river—*Hec.* 451 ff. καλλίστων ὑδάτων πατέρα | φασὶν Ἀπιδανὸν πεδία λιπαίνειν. Similarly the choice of the epithet εὔιππον may possibly have been guided by a recollection of Archelaus' special interest in the Macedonian cavalry (Thuc. 2. 100. 2); a horse is figured on his coinage.   βροτοῖς, governed by the verbal force in ὀλβοδόταν, like Aesch. *PV.* 612 πυρὸς βροτοῖς δοτῆρα: the whole phrase = τὸν διδόντα βροτοῖς τὸν ὄλβον τῆς εὐδαιμονίας. The τόν before ἔκλυον is a relative. [In 571-3 text and metre are uncertain. L P have Λυδίαν τε τὸν τᾶς (τὰς P) εὐδαιμονίας βροτοῖς ὀλβοδόταν πατέρα τε τὸν ἔκλυον κτλ. But (a) this is unmetrical, (b) it seems to introduce a third river which is (improbably) left nameless. It is easy to eliminate the third river by removing the second τε (Bothe); and if in addition we strike out τᾶς (Hermann) we get a choriambic rhythm (scanning ἔκλυον, like *Her.* 150 ἐκλήθης, *Or.* 12 ἐπέκλωσεν) –∪ –∪∪ – –∪∪ – | ∪ – –∪∪ – | ∪∪∪ – – ∪∪. The more elaborate correction in the text (Wilamowitz's) yields glyconics like 574-5: it is based on the assumption that πατέρα was accidentally omitted and replaced in front of the wrong τε τόν. But the abnormal position thus given to τε in 571 (instead of Λυδίαν τε πατέρα) may make us hesitate, though parallels exist (Denniston, *Particles*, 517).]

Scene 3 (576-861).

   This long ἐπεισόδιον falls into three parts: (a) the palace miracles, 576-656; (b) the first messenger-scene, 657-786; (c) the tempting of Pentheus, 787-861. The first of these subdivides in turn into (i) the earthquake scene, 576-603 (lyrical dialogue); (ii) the Stranger's narrative, 604-41 (trochaic tetrameters); (iii) Pentheus' second meeting with the Stranger, 642-56 (iambic trimeters).
   Scene 3 (a). *The earthquake scene.* This comes as an answer to the Chorus's prayer. At 576 a voice is heard 'off': it is Dion. crying out to his προφῆται, not in his assumed person as the Stranger, but in his true person as the god. Once more the Chorus invoke his presence (582 ff.), and now the voice is heard calling upon Ἔννοσις, the destructive potency in Nature. Thereupon a chorister predicts that the palace will be shaken, and in a moment another points to the physical results of the shock (591 f.). The voice speaks again, calling now upon the lightning: the Chorus claim to see the flames leap up 'about the holy tomb of Semele', and in fear and awe they fling themselves upon their faces. Their god has manifested himself—

but as the master of dangerous magic, the Son of the Lightning.
[585 and 594–5 certainly belong (*pace* Grube) to the divine voice: to
command the earthquake and the lightning is not for the Chorus
but for their Master. It is clear that 591 and 596 are addressed by
a part of the Chorus to the rest; also 590, unless σέβετέ νυν is spoken
by the Voice. The MSS. attribute 590 σέβομεν ὤ to ἠμιχ(όριον), but
in this scene of confusion and excitement a formal distribution
between semi-choruses seems out of place. Murray's horizontal
lines (παράγραφοι) indicate his conjectural distribution among a
number of solo voices. The change from the plural in 591 to sing.
in 596 perhaps means that 591–3 are sung by a solo voice (cory-
phaeus?) and 596–9 by the rest of the Chorus.]

The stage, meanwhile, is empty of mortal presences. What
happens on it? According to some rationalizing critics (Norwood,
Verrall, Rose) nothing at all happens: the Chorus are victims of
mass suggestion, as the intelligent spectator will at once perceive.
'By a master stroke of his art', says Norwood, 'Euripides has shown
us the thing *not happening*.' There is, however, one way, and one
way only, to show a thing not-happening on the stage—you must
introduce a character to point out that it has not happened. This
could easily have been done: Pentheus was at hand to do it. But
Pentheus denies nothing. And in the absence of such a denial the
audience is bound to accept what it is told: cf. *PV.* 1080 ff., *Her.*
904 ff., *Tro.* 1295 ff., *Hec.* 823, in all of which the Chorus or an actor
describes what is happening, and the audience imagines it happening,
with or without a little help from the stage manager.

The difficulties which have been invoked against the common
view of the scene are largely imaginary (cf. Wilamowitz, *Gr. V.* 581 f.).
(*a*) We do not know exactly how an earthquake was represented on
the Greek stage; but we know that it could be represented, or
adequately symbolized, for there are earthquakes in the *PV.* and
the *Heracles.* The modern producer will take 591 f. and 596 ff. as
stage directions, as in the Cambridge performance of 1930, when the
miracle was indicated by the partial collapse of an architrave of
the castle and a burst of flame from the smouldering fire (cf. 8)
within Semele's precinct. Whether the ancient producer could
achieve this modest degree of realism is uncertain (see on 591–3),
but unimportant: he could at any rate show the occurrence of the
earthquake by noises 'off' (cf. Haigh, *Attic Theatre³*, 218). (*b*) It is
true that Pentheus does not comment on the damage, and that the
messengers from Cithaeron do not interrupt their business to remark
'Dear me, there has been an earthquake here'. Theseus in the
Heracles shows the same lack of interest in the material damage.
This is 'unnatural', by the standards of modern realism. But people
in Greek plays do not waste time in saying what is natural unless it

THE EARTHQUAKE SCENE 149

is dramatically relevant; and after the scene is over comments and
explanations would be irrelevant dramatically, so they are simply
dropped (cf. Kitto, *Greek Tragedy*, 379 f.). Probably there was little
or nothing on the stage to provoke comment: the façade of the
castle is still standing (639, 645), as it must be since it forms the
backscene; the δώματα which have collapsed (633) must be somewhere at the back, and need not be identical with the 'house of
Pentheus', which was merely 'shaken' (606, 623)—a Greek palace
consisted of a number of buildings grouped round a central courtyard (αὐλή, 630).

It may be added that the earthquake is probably not Eur.'s
invention, but a traditional feature of Dionysiac plays (see Introd.,
p. xxxii); and that Horace at least did not take it for a conjuring
trick (*Od.* 2. 19. 14 'tectaque Penthei | disiecta non leni ruina').

Metre. 576, 580, 581 are best read (Wilamowitz, *Gr. V.* 580) as
pherecrateans with resolved base (∪∪ ∪), echoing the final rhythm
of the preceding stasimon (ἰὼ ἰώ in 580 and 582 seems to be ∪ ∪ ∪ –,
the first ω shortened before hiatus, cf. Aesch. *Ag.* 1136, Soph.
Phil. 759). 577 is perhaps two syncopated dochmii. 585 as restored
in the text is dactylic like the remaining utterance of the Voice,
594–5. The Chorus sing in lyric trochees (leading up to the regular
trochaic tetrameters of 604 ff.), with much resolution (∪∪ ∪ for – ∪)
and syncopation (∟ for – ∪), interspersed with dactylic κῶλα (582,
591). 596 should probably be read not as 4 spondees but as a trochaic tetrameter (8 syncopated trochees, cf. Aesch. *Eum.* 925): the
rhythm seems to express the Chorus's stupefaction at the miracle.
At the beginning of 597 we should, I think, insert τόνδε (Wilamowitz), giving a run of 'paeons' (– ∪ ∪ ∪), i.e. trochaic μέτρα in which
the first trochee is syncopated and the second resolved. In 600–1
the MSS. (and Murray) present an impossible jumble of trochees
and dactyls: the word-order preserved by a citation in the *Ety-
mologicum Magnum* must be the true one [to the references in
Murray's *app. crit.* add *Etym. gen.* B (Miller, *Mélanges*, 33) s.v.
ἀνδίκτης· δίκετε τρομερὰ σώματα Εὐριπίδης]. In the scheme below
I follow Hermann's arrangement of 600–3,

> δίκετε πεδόσε δίκετε τρομερὰ
> σώματα, Μαινάδες·
> ὁ γὰρ ἄναξ ἄνω κάτω τιθεὶς ἔπεισι
> μέλαθρα τάδε Διὸς γόνος.

∪ –	exclam. extra metrum
576 ∪∪∪ –∪∪– –	pher.[2]
∪ – – – ∪ – – –	? 2 dochm.
∪∪∪ ∪∪∪ ∪∪∪ ∪∪∪	} 4 tr.
∪∪∪ ∪∪∪ –∪ – ∪̆	

4003.9　　　　　　O

150 COMMENTARY

580
⏑⏑⏑ —⏑⏑— — pher.²
⏑⏑⏑ —⏑⏑— — pher.²
⏑⏑⏑ L —⏑⏑ —⏑⏑ tr.+2 dact.
⏑⏑⏑ L ⏑⏑⏑ L } 4 tr.
⏑⏑⏑ L ⏑⏑⏑ ⏑⏑⏑
585 —⏑⏑ —⏑⏑ —⏑⏑ —⏑⏑ 4 dact.
·— — exclam. extra metrum
⏑⏑⏑ —— ⏑⏑⏑ ⏑⏑⏑ } 4 tr.
—⏑ —⏑ —⏑ —⏑̆
⏑⏑⏑ —⏑ ⏑⏑⏑ —⏑ } 4 tr.
590 ⏑⏑⏑ L ⏑⏑⏑ —⏑̆
—⏑⏑ —⏑⏑ —⏑⏑ —⏑⏑ 4 dact.
⏑⏑⏑ ⏑⏑⏑ ⏑⏑⏑ ⏑⏑⏑ } 4 tr.
—⏑ —⏑ —⏑ — ⏑̆
—⏑⏑ —⏑⏑ —⏑⏑ —⏑⏑ 4 dact.
595 —⏑⏑ —⏑⏑ —⏑⏑ —⏑⏑ 4 dact.
— — exclam. extra metrum
L L L L L L L L 4 tr.
⟨L ⏑⟩⏑⏑ L⏑⏑⏑ L⏑⏑⏑ L } 6 tr.
⏑⏑⏑ L ⏑⏑⏑ ⏑⏑⏑ ⏑⏑̆
L L L L 2 tr.
600 ⏑⏑⏑ ⏑⏑⏑ ⏑⏑⏑ ⏑⏑⏑ 2 tr.
—⏑⏑ —⏑⏑ 2 dact.
⏑⏑⏑ —⏑ —⏑ —⏑ —⏑ 3 tr.
⏑⏑⏑ ⏑⏑⏑ —⏑ —⏑̆ 2 tr.

585. 'Shake the floor of the world, sovereign Spirit of Earthquake!' [Wilamowitz's supplement σεῖε restores sense and metre for the first time. Cf. in the parallel *Heracles* scene *Her.* 905 θύελλα σείει δῶμα. Earlier scholars explained πέδον, unconvincingly, either as an exclamation or as governed by the verbal force in ἔνοσι: others read πέδου, with a weak sense. Ἔνοσι πότνια is metrically possible, as a resolved trochaic μέτρον: but trochees seem to belong to the Chorus, not to the Voice. Ἔννοσι πότνια makes a dactylic line: for the spelling cf. Ἐννοσίγαιος and Hesych. ἔννοσις· κίνησις.]

587-8. διατινάξεται: probably passive in meaning, like many 'future middle' forms. πεσήμασιν, modal dat., though in English we say 'shall be shaken *to* its fall'. Πενθέως, dissyll.

591-3. 'You saw how yonder stone lintels upon the columns gaped apart? It is the Lord of Thunder who lifts the cry within those walls.' The ἔμβολα are the long cross-pieces which rest upon the columns of the façade and compose the architrave (ἐπιστύλιον). The earthquake shock has loosened them and cracks have suddenly appeared between them. (We need not suppose that the cracks are visible to the audience, still less that any part of the backscene falls down at this point—it is doubtful if built-up sets were in use even at the end of the fifth century.) κίοσιν is construed with ἔμβολα as the equivalent of ἐμβεβλημένα. ἀλαλάζεται, in reference to the ritual cry ἰὼ βάκχαι (577): ἡ γὰρ ἀλαλαγή . . . λέγεται καὶ ἐπὶ τῶν ἐκβακχευμάτων, schol. Pind. Ol. 7. 68. For the middle cf. Soph. fr. 534 P. [The text is uncertain in some details. ἴδετε (L) is unmetrical; and ἴδετε τά (P) is very doubtfully defensible as a resolved dactyl (cf. E. Fraenkel in Rh. Mus. lxxii [1918], 178). ὅδ' is inserted to make up the metre.]

594–5. For Dion. as Master of the Lightning cf. Introd., p. xxxii; also Pindar fr. 61. 12 (70 b. 15 Snell) ἐν δ' ὁ παγκρατὴς κεραυνὸς ἀμπνέων | πῦρ κεκίνηται, describing the god's thiasos; and the cry of the worshippers in Oppian, ἰὼ μάκαρ ὦ Διόνυσε | ἅπτε σέλας φλογερὸν πατρώιον, ἂν δ' ἐλέλιξον | γαῖαν (Cyn. 4. 301 ff.).

596–9. οὐδ' αὐγάζῃ may seem tautologous after οὐ λεύσσεις, and the middle, though used by Homer, does not occur elsewhere in tragedy (αὐγάζεις Nauck). Murray and L.S.⁹ take as passive, 'and are you not shone upon (i.e. dazzled)?' But this sense is hardly guaranteed by Hec. 637 τὰν . . . Ἅλιος αὐγάζει, which may mean merely 'whom the sun sees'. I think the second question is more precise than the first: 'Do you not see fire? do you not perceive, about the holy tomb of Semele, the flame of the bolt of Zeus which she left behind long ago when she was thunder-stricken?'

601–3. 'For, making high things low, our Lord assails this house, the son of Zeus.' For the stanza ending on a *nomen sacrum* cf. above, p. 72. Pat on the word the son of Zeus walks on to the stage, though the Chorus do not know it.

The Stranger's Narrative (604–41). After the Chorus has been reassured, we learn from the disguised god himself what happened behind the castle wall during the scene we have just witnessed. The physical occurrences described are those which the Chorus observed—the shaking of the castle and the blazing up of the fire on Semele's tomb, 623—followed by the collapse of a building (δώματα 633), apparently the stable in which the Stranger was imprisoned: this last was invisible to Chorus and audience, but the crash was perhaps heard at line 600 when the Chorus were moved to declare that their god was 'bringing things down'. Dionysus has proved his power over material things. He has also played tricks with Pentheus' mind, setting him to bind the Dionysiac principle not in its human but in its bestial shape (618–21 n.), and sending him in pursuit of a hallucination (629–31). Dion. is here the whimsical magician, the master of fantasies—a traditional role which he already exercises in *H. Hymn*. 7. 34 ff. (cf. G. Méautis, *L'Âme hellénique d'après les vases grecs*, 101 ff.). The tone of the narrative is correspondingly light, almost humorous (a fact which Verrall noticed but misinterpreted). 'To the god all this is child's play, and his calm and contemptuous amusement makes us realise his power far more than any anger could' (Grube, *T.A.P.A.* lxvi [1935], 46). Too grave a tone would, in fact, have injured the balance of the dramatic composition: this scene is only preparation for the clash of wills which lies ahead—the audience must not take it for a climax. The lightness of tone is matched by the use of the light and lively trochaic tetrameter, the oldest tragic metre, revived by Eur. in his later plays after some forty years' neglect. He employs it most often as a vehicle for swift repartee, usually in the familiar style (conversations with servants, *Hel.* 1627 ff., *Ion* 1250 ff., *Or.* 1506 ff., *IA.* 855 ff.; comedy, *Ion* 510 ff., *IT.* 1203 ff.); formally, its use here resembles that in *Her.* 855 ff., where it is employed as here for a ῥῆσις descriptive of swift and violent action, introduced by a brief dialogue. Cf. W. Krieg, *Philol.* xci (1936), 42 ff.

604. βάρβαροι γυναῖκες, 'Women of Asia'. The word does not imply contempt as Norwood imagines: Aeschylus' Persians regularly speak of themselves as βάρβαροι (*Pers.* 255, 337, &c.), and so do the Chorus in our play (1034) and in the *Phoenissae* (1301). But its use here is doubtless suggested by the fact that prostration is an oriental posture (cf. *Or.* 1507 and Plut. *Superstit.* 3. 166 A, where ῥίψεις ἐπὶ πρόσωπον are listed among the βάρβαρα κακά due to δεισιδαιμονία).

606. Corrupt, as the metre shows, though the sense is not in doubt. [The Musgrave–Wilamowitz correction (see app. crit.) assumes a complex corruption which is not easy to account for; and the substitution of δέ for the hortative ἀλλά is not an improvement. I am inclined to suspect, with Wecklein, that δῶμα Πενθέως is an intrusive gloss. Perhaps τὰ Πενθέως· ἀλλ' ⟨ἄγ'⟩ ἐξανίστατε (τά Elmsley, ἄγ' Reiske): τὰ Πενθέως = 'P.'s place' seems to be colloquial (Ar. *Wasps* 1432, Dem. 43. 62, Theocr. 2. 76, &c.), but need not on that account be excluded from a passage like this. Or τύραννα δώματ'· ἀλλ' [ἐξ]ανίστατε: cf. *Andr.* 303 where τυράννων δόμων ἕδραν is glossed οἰκήσεις τοῦ Νεοπτολέμου, and *Med.* 58 where in L P and the papyrus δεσποίνης has been supplanted by Μηδείας. The intrusion of ἐξ- may be due to the scribe's eye catching ἐξαμείψασαι in the next line.]

607. [σάρκας (MSS.) appears defensible either on the analogy of the double accusative after verbs like ἀφαιρεῖσθαι, or as object of the transitive action implied in the complex ἐξαμείψασαι-τρόπον, equivalent to 'obfirmantes' (Hermann): cf. 1288 n.]

608. 'O light supreme for us in the joyful worship.' For φάος (φῶς) applied metaphorically to a person cf. *Il.* 18. 102, *Hec.* 841 ὦ δέσποτ', ὦ μέγιστον ῞Ελλησιν φάος, *Ion* 1439, *Her.* 531 with Wilamowitz ad loc. It is used especially for the 'light' of deliverance, as in the first and last of these passages and at Aesch. *Cho.* 809, &c.

611. ὁρκάνας: either literal, 'dungeons' (ὁρκάνη· εἰρκτή, δεσμωτήριον Hesych.) or metaphorical, 'snares' (κυρίως ἡ ἀγρευτικὴ λίνος, scholion here in L; so also schol. Aesch. *Sept.* 346). The former sense suits σκοτεινάς better. Etymologically the word = 'means of shutting off', standing to εἴργω as χοάνη, 'means of pouring', i.e. 'funnel', to χέω: cf. schol. Theocr. 4. 61 τὴν τῶν προβάτων ὁρκάνην.

612. This is simply the past form of a general supposition in present time, τίς μοι φύλαξ ἐστὶν, ἐὰν σὺ συμφορᾶς τύχῃς; 'What protector have I if at any time you meet with trouble?' This is now reported as a past thought. Cf. Hdt. 9. 13. 3 ἐξήλαυνε δὲ τῶνδε εἴνεκεν, ὅτι . . . εἰ νικῷτο συμβαλών, ἀπάλλαξις οὐκ ἦν, where the thought reported is ἐὰν νικῶμαι, ἀπάλλαξις οὐκ ἔστιν.

613. Editors construe ἀνδρός with τυχών: 'But how were you liberated after chancing upon a man of sin?' Cf. *Alc.* 10 ὁσίου γὰρ ἀνδρὸς ὅσιος ὢν ἐτύγχανον, | παιδὸς Φέρητος. But the effect here is oddish and weakish: we expect 'after falling into the power of a man of sin'. J. Rappold has proposed to take ἀνδρός with ἠλευθερώθης (cf. Hdt. 5. 62. 1 τυράννων ἐλευθερώθησαν), and understand ἠλευθερώθης τυχών as = ἔτυχες ἐλευθερωθείς—'how did you succeed in getting free from the man of sin?' This is tempting; but although ἦλθες λαθών is as good Greek as ἔλαθες ἐλθών, and Goodwin and Kühner-Gerth recognize a similar construction with τυχών, I can find no real example of the latter (at *I A.* 958 τυχών is conditional, 'if he is lucky'; at *IT.* 252 the emendation κἀντυχόντες for καὶ τυχόντες has been confirmed by the Hibeh papyrus. [τυχών may have been introduced by assimilation to τύχοις at the end of 612. μυχῶν *ci.* Murray (but μυχοὶ ἀνδρός are not μυχοὶ δόμων); βρόχων Wecklein (does not suit 615); τεχνῶν Sybel (does not suit the facts); χερῶν F. W. Schmidt; perhaps φυγών.]

614. The literal fulfilment of the prediction at 498.   ἄνευ πόνου, cf. 194 n.

615. [The MSS. have χεῖρα, which looks like a mistake for χεῖρε. But for some reason tragedy appears to avoid the nom. and accus. dual of χείρ and πούς. According to E. Hasse, *Der Dualis im Attischen*, 47, there are no tragic examples of πόδε and only one of χεῖρε (*Andr.* 115 περὶ χεῖρε βαλοῦσα in a hexameter, like *Od.* 11. 211 περὶ χεῖρε βαλόντε—but at *Ag.* 1559 MSS. have περὶ χεῖρα βαλοῦσα).]

616–17. ταῦτα (internal accus. = ταύτην τὴν ὕβριν), is explained by the ὅτι clause: 'That was just (καί) the laugh I had against him, that . . .'. οὔτ' ἔθιγεν οὔθ' ἥψαθ': not quite synonymous, 'he did not touch or grasp'. For ἐλπίσι βόσκεσθαι cf. *Phoen.* 396, fr. 826, Soph. *Ant.* 1246, fr. 948 P.

618–21. The bull is a Dionysiac beast, a potential vehicle of the god (Introd., p. xviii). Winnington-Ingram sees here a piece of symbolism: 'in binding the bull with effort and strain Pentheus is performing the futile task of constraining the animal Dionysus within himself'; but this is, as I now think, over-subtle. In a late hexameter poem on the Lycurgus story (Page, *Literary Papyri* i, no. 129), the god imposes a converse error upon his adversary: Lycurgus mistakes human beings for snakes (Dionysiac creatures again).   περὶ . . . ἔβαλλε: tmesis, to avoid the form περιέβαλλε which seems to be non-tragic. [The only tragic examples I find of augmented tenses of περί compounds are περιέστησεν in a corrupt line of Critias (fr. 1. 37) and the disputable forms with apocope, Aesch. *Ag.* 1147 περεβάλοντο, *Eum.* 634 περεσκήνωσεν. περιέτρεψεν occurs in adesp. 547. 4, but this may be from a comedy (Hense, Stobaeus, vol. v, p. 942). In augmented tenses Eur. replaces περιβάλλω by ἀμφιβάλλω, *Andr.* 799, *Her.* 465.]   γόνασι καὶ χηλαῖς defines τῷδε more closely ('whole and part apposition', σχῆμα 'Ιωνικόν), as in ἅπτεσθαί τινος χερός, βαλεῖν τινα τὸν ὦμον, σοὶ τέρψιν ἐμβαλῶ φρενί (*Tro.* 635); cf. Wilamowitz on *Her.* 162.   θυμὸν ἐκπνέων, 'panting his rage', rather more vivid than *Rhes.* 786 θυμὸν πνέουσαι, *Phoen.* 454 θυμοῦ πνοάς, Aesch. *Sept.* 52 θυμὸς ἔπνει. The model is the Homeric μένεα πνείοντες (*Iliad* 3. 8, &c.). On such phrases, which originate in the belief that the air in the lungs is the material vehicle of the emotion, see Prof. Onians' *Origins of European Thought*, 50 ff.   χείλεσιν διδοὺς ὀδόντας, 'biting his lips'. As Wilamowitz pointed out, Eur. often uses διδόναι where we expect a more precise verb, e.g. *Tro.* 1175 f. βόστρυχον φιλήμασιν ἔδωκεν, 'she kissed your hair'; *Her.* 1402 δίδου δέρῃ σὴν χεῖρα, 'put your arm about my neck'; *IA.* 1221 γόνασι σοῖσι σῶμα δοὺς ἐμόν, 'sitting on your knee'; and *infra* 715. Here he might as well or better have said ὀδοῦσι διδοὺς χείλη (cf. *Hel.* 1383 λουτροῖς χρόα ἔδωκα with *Or.* 42 οὐ λούτρ' ἔδωκε χρωτί).

621–2. πλησίον δ' ἐγὼ παρών: the Stranger uses about himself the language he used earlier (500) about the god—a plain hint of their identity.   ἥσυχος, cf. 636, 640: amid the physical turmoil of the earthquake and the moral turmoil of the baffled Pentheus, the Stranger's calm marks him as something supernatural; it is like the sinister calm at the heart of a typhoon.

625–6. Ἀχελῷον, simply 'water', as in *Andr.* 167, *Hypsipyle* fr. 753, Ar. *Lys.* 381 and fr. 351. This 'metonymy' may go back to a time when Achelous was the supreme water-god (cf. 519–20 n.): Ephorus ap. Macrob. *Sat.* 5. 18 (F. Gr. Hist. 70 F 20 Jacoby) says that the expression belongs to the language of ritual, being used in oaths, prayers, and formulae of sacrifice. But here the magniloquent phrase carries if anything a suggestion of ridicule, while in Virgil's *pocula Acheloia* (*Georg.* 1. 9) it has become a stylistic trick: Sandys compared Shakespeare's 'A cup of hot wine with not a drop of allaying Tiber in 't' (*Coriolanus* ii. 1. 53), and its echo in Lovelace,

'When flowing cups run swiftly round With no allaying Thames'.
μάτην πονῶν, since the house was *not* on fire.

628. The epithet κελαινὸν is also applied by Soph. to a sword (*Aj.*
231), and to a spear (*Trach.* 856); Eur. has μέλαν ξίφος *Hel.* 1656,
Or. 1472. The primary reference is presumably to the colour of the
metal (μέλας σίδηρος, Hes. *Op. et Di.* 151), but both words have also
the sinister associations of Lat. 'ater', Eng. 'dark', which may have
been felt in all these passages (cf. Wilamowitz on *Her.* 780 κελαινὸν
ἅρμα). [Verrall's κελαινῶν is not an improvement, and does not
justify retaining φῶς in 630.—It is not very clear why P. rushes
indoors to look for his escaped prisoner. Does he suppose the
Stranger to be hiding in another part of the castle? Wilamowitz
provided him with a different but still not wholly satisfactory
motive by reading ἁρπάσαι (infinitive of purpose?).]

629-31. 'And then the Lord of Thunder made, or so I think—I give
you guesswork here—a phantom in the courtyard. And the King
rushed at it in passion and tried to stab bright vapour, thinking
that he spilled my blood.'   δόξαν in contrast with ἐπιστήμην (cf.
IT. 1164 τί τοὐκδιδάξαν τοῦτό σ'; ἢ δόξαν λέγεις;): the Stranger
pretends, as he must, that he knows the god's act only by inference
from Pentheus' behaviour.   αὐλήν is, I think, used in its proper
sense (as *Ion* 185) rather than in the vaguer sense of 'dwelling' (as
Hipp. 68): Pentheus was in the courtyard when the δώματα collapsed, which accounts for his escaping injury. [In 630 φῶς (MSS.)
seems too vague (despite 1083): why should the King mistake 'a light'
for his prisoner? But if the μ of φάσμα were accidentally omitted,
φαεννόν in the next line might easily suggest φῶς to a puzzled copyist.
φῶτ' (Tyrrell) will not do: it would mean a real man, not a phan-
tasm.—In 631 the noun to which φαεννόν belongs has dropped out.
⟨αἰθέρ'⟩ is perhaps the most probable supplement, this being the
customary stuff of such ghostly duplicates (cf. 292-4 n.); with Verrall's ⟨οὐδέν⟩ the natural meaning would be 'nothing bright' rather
than 'the bright nothing'.[1]]

633-4. 'All is shattered: he has seen a bitter end to my imprisonment.'
This is the god's retort to Pentheus' boast at 357.   συντεθράνωται
(ἅπ. λεγ.) is glossed συμπέπτωκε by Hesychius, evidently with
reference to this passage. συν- implies that the building has 'fallen
together', i.e. collapsed upon itself. The word is probably connected
not with θρᾶνος but with θραύω: cf. θραΰσσειν, 'to smash', Lycophr.
664. [So Sütterlin, *Z. Gesch. d. Verba denominativa*, 107, and Solmsen,
Unters. z. griech. Laut- u. Verslehre, 88. Some explain 'the beam-ends

---

[1] M. Gigante, *Dioniso*, xviii (1955), 174, would keep φῶς in 630 and
supply ⟨εἶδος⟩ here, comparing Sappho fr. 34 Lobel-Page, where φαεννὸν
εἶδος is used of the stars.

have been brought together (by buckling)'. But θρᾶνοι are beams, not beam-ends (L.S.[8] was wrong in citing Pollux 10. 49 as evidence for the latter meaning). Verrall's rendering of the line, 'Bacchus dashed the buildings to the ground, though (now, by magic) its beams have all been put together (again)', hardly needs formal refutation: the *Bacchae* is not a Christmas pantomime.]

635. παρεῖται, pf. mid. of παρίημι, 'he is exhausted'.

636. [ἐκ βάκχας ἄγων (MSS.) makes neither metre nor sense (there were no bacchants in the palace). ἐκβὰς ἐγώ is the accepted correction, and may be right: if for βάς a copyist absently wrote the familiar βάκχας, the further corruption might follow in an attempt to make sense. But Hermann's ἐκ βακχάδων, 'from that god-infested house', is attractive, enhancing by the antithesis the force of ἥσυχος, and may well represent the original sense: cf. *infra* 726, *IT*. 1243 βακχεύουσαν Διονύσῳ Παρνάσιον κορυφάν, and esp. Aesch. fr. 58 ἐνθουσιᾷ δὴ δῶμα· βακχεύει στέγη. The form βακχάδων is, however, nowhere attested, and if it existed would hardly be glossed (as Hermann postulated) by the rare verb βακχασάντων. It would be better to write ἐκ βακχίων, with the same meaning: in a MS. without accents or division of words this might be read as ἐκβακχιῶν (cf. 109 καταβακχιοῦσθε), which an unintelligent reader might gloss βάκχας ἄγων. For βάκχιος (-ειος) = βακχεύων cf. 1230 βακχείῳ ποδί. Tyrrell's εὖχος ἐς βάκχας δ' ἄγων, though technically neat, involves taking δωμάτων with φροντίσας, which is both awkward and feeble; moreover ἥσυχος is important for the characterization (621–2 n.).]

638–9. ψοφεῖ γοῦν ἀρβύλη: 'there is certainly a tramp of feet.' γοῦν introduces the certain fact on which the uncertain inference ἥξει is based (Denniston, *Particles*, 451); ὥς μοι δοκεῖ qualifies the latter. So Ar. *Pax* 232 f. ἐξιέναι γνώμην ἐμὴν | μέλλει· θορυβεῖ γοῦν ἔνδον. For the noisiness of the ἀρβύλη cf. *Or*. 140 f. σῖγα, σῖγα, λεπτὸν ἴχνος ἀρβύλης | τίθετε, μὴ κτυπεῖτε and Theocr. 7. 26 πᾶσα λίθος πταίοισα ποτ' ἀρ-βυλίδεσσιν ἀείδει.   **προνώπια:** τὰ ἔμπροσθεν τῶν πυλῶν (Hesych.). The indication of place is repeated in προνώπιος, 645, as if Eur. wished to stress that the antagonists are now to emerge from the fantasy-haunted castle and meet again in the daylight on the plane of normal experience.   **ἐκ τούτων**, 'after this'. The Stranger affects a mild curiosity about the King's reactions.

640. '(No matter), for I shall take him placidly, though he come with tempest in his lungs.'   **ῥᾳδίως . . . οἴσω**, like *Andr*. 744 τοὺς σοὺς δὲ μύθους ῥᾳδίως ἐγὼ φέρω. On **πνέων μέγα** cf. 618–21 n. So πνέοντες μεγάλα, *Andr*. 189, and τοσόνδ' ἔπνευσας, ibid. 327.

Pentheus' second meeting with the Stranger (642–56). This short passage of dialogue makes the transition from the Palace Scene to the Messenger Scene, being linked to the former by its subject, to the latter by its metre. It does not directly advance the action: its function (as 639 suggests) is to show the dawning of a new relationship between the antagonists, brought about by the strange happenings behind the scenes. Pentheus' bluster cannot wholly conceal his bewilderment and inner dread: in face of the uncanny he is beginning to lose his nerve. And the Stranger for his part speaks now for the first time with a hint of supernatural authority (647). The consequences of this changed relationship are to be developed later.

644. ἔα, a gasp of astonishment, perhaps representing the sound of a sharp intake of breath: being a noise, not a word, it is often doubled and placed *extra versum*, as here, and is naturally confined to excited dialogue or monologue; Eur. uses it very freely (cf. 1280), Ar. and Aesch. fairly freely, Soph. once; Plato gives it, with comic effect, to the shocked janitor at *Prot.* 314 D, St. Luke to the startled demoniac, 4. 34. Cf. Page on *Med.* 1004, Denniston on *El.* 341.

646. πρὸς οἴκοις τοῖς ἐμοῖς: an escaped prisoner strolling outside his prison adds insult to injury.

647. 'Halt there! and halt your anger to quietness!' To 'put a quiet foot under one's anger' is to 'go easy' with it. [To avoid the repetition it has been proposed to substitute βάσιν or τρόπον or φρένα for the second πόδα. But (a) the Greek ear, and Eur.'s ear in particular, was less sensitive to such things than ours: cf. 1060–2, Tucker on *Cho.* 51, Jebb on *OC.* 554, Pearson on *Hel.* 674, A. B. Cook, *C.R.* xvi (1902), 263 ff.; and for recurrence of a word in the same line, Eur. *El.* 1005 ἐκβεβλημένη | δόμων πατρῴων δυστυχεῖς οἰκῶ δόμους, *Ion* 2 θεῶν παλαιὸν οἶκον ἐκτρίβων, θεῶν | μιᾶς ἔφυσε Μαῖαν, *Hel.* 775 πρὸς τοῖσιν ἐν Τροίᾳ δέκα | ἔτεσι διῆλθον ἑπτὰ περιδρομὰς ἐτῶν. (b) The repetition is made tolerable by an implied antithesis: the first πόδα is literal, the second metaphorical. (c) ἥσυχον πόδα is confirmed by the new line referred to in the app. crit., τί μέλλετ'; οὐ χρῆν ἥσυχον κεῖσθαι π[ό]δα (Hunt, *Fr. trag. pap.* iii, l. 13), which is now known to come not from Sophocles but from the *Telephus* of Euripides:[1] cf. also *Med.* 217 οἱ δ' ἀφ' ἡσύχου ποδός (metaphorical, 'easy-going folk'), *Or.* 136 f. ἡσύχῳ ποδὶ | χωρεῖτε (literal). Despite the criticisms of Campbell, *C.Q.* xlix (1956), 57, I still see nothing amiss with this line.]

648-50. πόθεν, 'how comes it that ...' (cf. 465 n.). ἢ οὐκ, scanned as one syllable (synizesis). For the parenthetic alternative cf. *Tro.* 299 πιμπρᾶσιν—ἢ τί δρῶσι—Τρῳάδες μυχούς; *Cycl.* 121, *Rhes.* 565 f. The reference is to 498. τοὺς λόγους κτλ.: 'This is queer talk that you keep introducing' (καινούς predicative). [Cf. *Ion* 1340 τί φῇς; ὁ μῦθος εἰσενήνεκται νέος, which disposes of Wecklein's doubts about ἐσφέρεις.]

651-3. Both the formal continuity of the stichomythia and the logical

---

[1] See Handley and Rea, 'The *Telephus* of Euripides', *Bull. Inst. Class. Stud.* (London), Supplement 5, 1957.

continuity of the debate are interrupted here. The double breach makes it pretty certain that one or more lines have fallen out. If 652 is given to the Stranger, as in text, it must have been preceded by a line in which Pentheus said something rude about the effects of wine: to this the Stranger replies 'The thing you make a reproach to Dionysus is in fact his glory' ('In thy scorn his glory lies', Murray); καλόν is predicative. Cf. *I.A.* 304 f., where the old servant is told that he is too loyal to his master, and replies καλόν γέ μοι τοὔνειδος ἐξωνείδισας, also *Phoen.* 821. [But this arrangement is open to doubt on more than one ground. (*a*) The word-order in 652 suggests, as does the δή, that the emphasis should fall on ὠνείδισας rather than on καλόν (Kitto, *C.R.* lx [1946], 65). This could be met by reading τοῦθ' ὅ for τοῦτο (Campbell, *C.Q.* xlix [1956], 58). (*b*) Pentheus' words in 653 are left unmotived. 654 shows that the order to 'lock the towers' (i.e. the gates in the city wall, surmounted by towers as in medieval cities) must be an attempt to prevent *the god* (who in Pentheus' eyes is but a human accomplice) from leaving Thebes. How does P. know that the god is in Thebes? He might infer it from the fact that he has so recently liberated the Stranger; but we should expect the inference to be explicitly drawn and the purpose of the order indicated. Greek dialogue is seldom as elliptical as this. I incline on the whole to Hermann's view that 652 is spoken by P. and is followed, not preceded, by a lacuna. καλόν is then ironical, as in *Med.* 514 καλόν γ' ὄνειδος τῷ νεωστὶ νυμφίῳ, and the line means 'Your words are a *reproach* to your god,[1] a pretty reproach' (P. associates the behaviour of the Theban women with their use of wine, 221 f., 260 ff.). The missing link between this and 653 may be (*a*) a single line in which the Stranger indicates that the god is in Thebes, e.g. καλῶν μὲν οὖν τήνδ' ἦλθε τὴν πόλιν πλέως (Wecklein); or (*b*) more probably a longer passage of stichomythia, in which P. asks where Dion. is now (cf. 501) and announces his intention to lay hands on him (Robert, *Hermes*, xiii [1878], 137); or (*c*) P. may have continued with something like

⟨κλαίων δ' ἄρ' οἴνῳ τὰς γυναῖκας ἐκμανεῖ
ἥνπερ νιν ἐντὸς περιβολῶν λάβω πόλεως·⟩
κλῄειν κτλ.,

making, as Paley suggested, a 4-line speech to balance 656–9.]
654–5. τί δέ; 'and what of that?' (Denniston, *Particles*, 175 f.). P.'s reply is like the impatient retort of Hermione when she is worsted in argument by Andromache, σοφὴ σοφὴ σύ· κατθανεῖν δ' ὅμως σε δεῖ (*Andr.* 245). Cf. 179 n.

---

[1] Strictly speaking, Pentheus believes that 'Dionysus', Semele's child, is dead (242 ff., 517); but he may perhaps be allowed to use here the language of his adversary.

Scene 3 (b). This first Messenger Scene is essential to the psychological dynamics of the play, since its effect is to divert Pentheus'
rage from the god and his priest on to his own subjects. It also depicts
for the audience what could not be shown on the stage, the strange
working of the Dionysiac madness upon the Theban women, as it
appeared in all its beauty and horror to a simple-minded observer.
It should be remembered that what is described here is not the
organized and controlled maenadism of Dionysiac cult, as sketched
e.g. in the πάροδος, but a 'black maenadism' which has been sent as
a punishment upon the too respectable and has swept them away
against their will: critics of the play have too often ignored this
distinction. Yet even these 'black' maenads do no harm to man or
beast until they are attacked. The description is probably in its
main lines traditional (see on 699-702, 704-11, 734-47, 748-64). And
there is some ground for guessing that the group of herdsmen who
at first pursue the maenads but are eventually converted is itself
a traditional feature. [Cf. the Thracian 'Boutes' and his men who
attacked the maenads of Phthiotis (Diod. 5. 50). In later Dionysiac
associations certain members bore the cult title βουκόλοι or βουκολικοί
and took part in that capacity in a mimetic dance or sacred drama:
lex Iobacchorum 121 ff.; χορεύσαντες βουκόλοι at Pergamum (*Ath. Mitt.*
xxiv [1899], 179); Lucian, *de saltat.* 79; cf. Dieterich, *Kl. Schriften*,
70 ff., Cumont, *A.J.A.* 1933, 247 f. These dances are probably, though
not certainly, a survival or revival of an old ritual feature, and may
well have had their αἴτιον in such stories as the herdsman tells here,
though the true meaning of the title was doubtless 'worshipper of the
bull-god' (cf. Ar. *Vesp.* 10 βουκολεῖς Σαβάζιον and Eur. fr. 203).]

657-9. ἐξ ὄρους: this could be inferred from the side (L. of audience)
on which the Messenger entered.   **σοι μενοῦμεν:** not 'I will wait for
you' (which would require σέ), but 'You will still have me there'
(dativus commodi) or 'You will find me waiting' (ethic dat.). [σῷ
(nom. pl. of σῶς) J. U. Powell, *C.R.* xxviii (1914), 48; but the sense
('unharmed', 'safe and sound') is not very appropriate.]

661-2. 'Where the white snow's glistening falls never loose their grip.'
If this means, as some suppose, that it never stops snowing on
Cithaeron, the exaggeration is monstrous; it is still considerable
if we take it to mean that the snow lies in places all the year round
(I found none when I climbed the mountain in April). We may have
here nothing more than a conventional poetic commonplace (Meurig-
Davies, *Rev. Ét. Gr.* lxi [1948], 366); but I suspect that Eur. insisted
on the snow because it was the right setting for a strange tale of
maenadism: on Parnassus, and probably on Cithaeron too, the
ὀρειβασία was a mid-winter rite. Like most southern peoples, the
Greeks felt (and still feel) snow to be a little uncanny: to early
poets the snowflakes were, like the lightning, κῆλα Διός, 'shafts of

God', a threatening visitation from the skies (*Il.* 12. 280, cf. Wilamowitz, *Die Ilias u. Homer*, 216). So Sophocles, describing the horror of Niobe's eternal vigil upon Sipylus, says χιὼν οὐδαμὰ λείπει (*Ant.* 830). βολαί, usually 'acts of throwing', can also mean 'things thrown', just as βαφαί can mean 'things dipped' (e.g. poisoned arrows, *Her.* 1190). The translation 'radiance' (L.S.⁹) is quite unjustified. For εὐᾱγεῖς, 'bright', cf. Parm. 10. 2 εὐαγέος ἠελίοιο and other passages quoted in L.S.⁹ The original spelling may have been εὐαυγεῖς, as in διαυγής, τηλαυγής, ἐξαυγής (πώλων . . . χιόνος ἐξαυγεστέρων, *Rhes.* 304).¹ [Verrall's notion that 662 is interpolated, the messenger having broken off his sentence at ἵν' οὔποτε, is surely incredible. And the line seems to have been known to Seneca, who was misled by it into citing the absence of snow on Cithaeron as a symptom of extreme drought, *Thyestes* 117 f.—ἀνεῖσαν χιόνος L. Dindorf, to avoid the tribrach composed of a single word coinciding with the foot. But this rhythm, which is rare in Aesch. and Soph. (except in the first foot), is admitted relatively often in the later plays of Eur. (Descroix, *Trim. iamb.* 159, 162). There are at least five other instances in the *Bacch.*: second foot, 18, 261, 1302; fourth, 731, 1147.]

663. 'And what weighty message do you bring?' lit. 'And you come contributing (or imposing) what seriousness of message?' Cf. *Hec.* 130 σπουδαὶ λόγων, 'earnest discussions'.

664–7. ποτνιάδας: a word of uncertain significance, perhaps 'wild women' or 'holy women'. Ποτνιάδες· αἱ βάκχαι· ἀντὶ τοῦ μαινάδες καὶ λυσσάδες Hesych. [At *Or.* 318 the Erinyes are called ποτνιάδες θεαί: there the scholiast explains it as μανιοποιοί, and connects it with the story of the mad mares of Glaucus, which was attached to Potniae in Boeotia. But is is difficult to separate ποτνιάδες in *Or.* 318 from πότνιαι, the title given to the Erinyes at Thebes and often in tragedy (*Sept.* 887, *Eum.* 951, *OC.* 84); and the possessed women are perhaps called ποτνιάδες here because their possession has conferred upon them the powers of πότνιαι.] αἱ . . . ἐξηκόντισαν: 'whose white limbs flashed away spear-swift in their madness.' For the metaphor cf. *IT.* 1369 f. κῶλα . . . ἠκοντίζετο. λευκός is the traditional epithet for women's flesh in Greek poetry; but its use here suggests the bare feet of the bacchants (called ἀπέδιλοι or ἀσάμβαλοι by Nonnus, and nearly always barefooted on vases)—cf. 863, *Cycl.* 72 βάκχαις σὺν λευκόποσιν, *Ion* 221 λευκῷ ποδί, 'barefoot'. On the supernatural swiftness of the maenads see 1090–3 n.; on the text of 667, 715–16 n.

669. λόγον στειλώμεθα: 'check my tongue', metaphor from shortening sail (cf. L.S.⁹ στέλλω iv. 2 and *Or.* 607 θρασύνῃ κοὐχ ὑποστέλλῃ λόγῳ). For the change of number cf. 616 f. Eur. seems to go farther in this

---

¹ Cf. now G. Björck, *Das Alpha Impurum*, 147.

than other poets: he even writes μαρτυρόμεσθα δρῶσα (*Her.* 858),
ἠγριώμεθα δοκοῦσα (*IT.* 349), διωκόμεσθα . . . κρατηθεῖσα (*Ion* 1250),
οὐ δικαίως, ἥν θάνω, θανούμεθα (*Tro.* 904).

671. τὸ βασιλικὸν λίαν: 'your all too royal temper', a cautious euphemism
for 'your irritable temper': θυμὸς δὲ μέγας ἐστὶ διοτρεφέων βασιλήων
(*Il.* 2. 196).

672–3. πάντως, in any case, 'whatever your story'.   **δικαίοις,** masc.,
governed by θυμοῦσθαι: the Herdsman is δίκαιος as not being
responsible for what he describes. [The partial coincidence with
fr. 287. I, τοῖς πράγμασιν γὰρ οὐχὶ θυμοῦσθαι χρεών, is not a reason
for rejecting the line, since Eur. often echoes his own earlier phrases;
the antithesis τοῖς δικαίοις∼τὸν ὑποθέντα τόνδε is a reason for retaining it.]

677–8. 'The pasturing herds of cattle were just climbing towards the
hill country, at the hour when the sun . . . .' The plural verb is
normal with neuter plural subjects which signify living agents,
e.g. *Cycl.* 206 f. βλαστήματα (lambs) . . . πρὸς μαστοῖς εἰσι. Some edd.
follow Musgrave in taking ὑπεξήκριζον (a ἅπ. λεγ.) as transitive and
first person singular, on the ground that the speaker must tell us
where he was himself when he saw the women; but 'ipsa boum
mentio satis ostendit bubulcum esse qui loquitur' (Elmsley), and all
the relevant evidence favours the sense 'climb', not 'drive up'.
[*Or.* 275 f. ἐξακρίζετ᾽ αἰθέρα πτεροῖς (scholion εἰς τὰ ἄκρα τοῦ αἰθέρος
πέτεσθε): Eustath. p. 1636. 47 ἀκρίζειν τὸ τὰ ἄκρα ἐπιπορεύεσθαι, ὃ καὶ
ἐξακρίζειν Εὐριπίδης φησίν: Aesch. *Cho.* 932 ἐπήκρισεν, 'reached the
summit' (metaph.): ὑπερακρίζειν, 'to climb over' (trans. Xen. *Eq.
Mag.* 6. 5, intrans. Strabo 15. 2. 10), or 'soar above' (Eur. *Supp.*
988). Hesych. ὑπεξήκριζον· †ὕβριζον† (ἥκριζον Heinsius) does not
help; nor do the meanings 'behead', 'walk on tip-toe', attributed
to ἀκρίζω by the lexicographers.]   **μόσχων** is used in a wider sense
than Eng. 'calves': it is clear from 735–45 that the μόσχοι *include*
δαμάλαι and ταῦροι, and they are called κεροφόροι βόες in 691. Cf.
IT. 163, where the μόσχοι are milch-cows, *El.* 813, where the μόσχος
is a bull, and the common poetic use of πῶλος for 'horse'. [The
position of the word has induced unconvincing attempts to construe
it with λέπας or even with ὑπεξήκριζον, or to emend it (βόσκων or
μοχθῶν Sandys). But the hyperbaton is no harsher than in 684,
where ἐλάτης belongs to φόβην.]   **λέπας,** not in the older sense
(Wilamowitz on *Her.* 121) of a naked cliff or rocky summit (which
would yield no grazing), but rather, as 751 and 1045 show, a collective
term for the broken country where forest, rock, and upland pasture
mix: cf. *Andr.* 295, where the herdsman Paris makes his home in
the Ἰδαῖον λέπας, and *Rhes.* 287.

680. θιάσους τρεῖς: in historical times there were three official θίασοι of
'maenads' at Thebes, as may be inferred from an inscription (Kern,

Inschr. Magnesia, 215 = 338 Parke–Wormell) which relates how on instructions from Delphi the Magnesians fetched from Thebes three maenads γενέης Εἰνοῦς ἄπο Καδμηείης to establish three θίασοι at Magnesia. This triple organization is attested also for Rhodes (*IG.* xii. 1. 937), and was probably universal; as at Thebes it is reflected in the story of the three mad princesses, its first leaders (cf. Theocr. 26. 2 τρεῖς θιάσως ἐς ὄρος τρεῖς ἄγαγον αὐταὶ ἐοῖσαι), so at Orchomenos Dionysus maddens the *three* daughters of Minyas, at Argos the *three* daughters of Proetus.

681–2. With δεύτερος, as with εἶτα and ἔπειτα, δέ is often omitted, even in prose (Denniston, *Particles*, 376): cf. Plato, *Legg.* 774 E πατρὸς μὲν πρῶτον, δευτέραν πάππου, τρίτην δὲ ἀδελφῶν. [τρίτη δ' Ἰνὼ χοροῦ (L P) may be corrected either to τρίτου δ' Ἰνὼ χοροῦ, which was probably the original reading of L, or to τρίτη δ' Ἰνὼ τρίτου (Hermann). The latter correction assumes χοροῦ to be an intrusive gloss; but the repetition χορῶν . . . χοροῦ has plenty of parallels (cf. 647 n.).]

683. σώμασιν: the so-called 'dative of relation' (apparently an extension of the locative use), in place of the normal accus. This dat. is common in Xenophon (e.g. *Mem.* 2. 1. 31 τοῖς σώμασιν ἀδύνατοι) and Hellenistic Greek, and appears occasionally in tragedy: Aesch. *Sept.* 895 f. διανταίαν λέγεις δόμοισι καὶ | σώμασιν πεπλαγμένους: Soph. *O.T.* 25 (πόλις) φθίνουσα κάλυξιν: Eur. *El.* 513 οἶν μελάγχιμον πόκῳ. In view of these parallels the text need not be doubted here. See Kühner–Gerth, i, pp. 317, 440.—With what follows contrast Chaeremon's lusciously elaborate picture of girls sleeping in the moonlight, fr. 14 (*Oxford Book of Gk. V.* 455): the austerity of Eur.'s description is significant of his attitude to his subject.

686–8. ὡς σὺ φής: 221 ff. The Herdsman was not present at that conversation, but as Aristarchus says of Homer, ὁ ᾔδει ὁ ποιητὴς τοῦτο τῷ προσώπῳ περιέθηκεν (schol. BT on *Il.* 16. 841).   θηρᾶν depends on φής: we might expect θηρῶσαι with ὡς σὺ φής parenthetic, but Eur. has to avoid an awkward accumulation of participles. For other and stranger cases of 'attraction' to a ὡς clause see Jebb on *Trach.* 1238.   λωτοῦ: on the 'intoxicating' character of flute-music see 126–9 n.   ᾐρημωμένας = εἰς ἐρημίαν πτωσσούσας (222) [but Wecklein's ᾐρημωμένην (with Κύπριν) improves the balance of the sentence and may well be right].

689–90. ὠλόλυξεν: see 24 n.   σταθεῖσα: 'standing up' (not 'standing', ἑστῶσα).

692–4. θαλερὸν . . . ὕπνον, only here: 'somnus qui est in ipso flore, i.e. altus sopor' (Hermann), or less probably 'somnus qui vires reficit' (Elmsley) like Lat. *alma quies*. For the latter (active) sense of θαλερός I can find no parallel, unless θαλερωτέρῳ πνεύματι is right at Aesch. *Sept.* 707 and means 'with a wholesomer wind'.   θαῦμ' ἰδεῖν εὐκοσμίας, 'a strange sight for its ordered calm': the members

of the θίασος are *en rapport* and move as one, like a flock of birds
(748). εὐκοσμίας, gen. of cause. The word and the ideal recur in later
Dionysiac cult: e.g. the Rules of the Iobacchi require εὐστάθειαν καὶ
εὐκοσμίαν (l. 16, cf. l. 64).   νέαι παλαιαὶ παρθένοι τε: in an enumeration it is against normal usage to attach a connective to the last item
only (for exceptions see Denniston, *Particles*, 501). But here παρθένοι
are not a third category co-ordinate with the other two : the sense
is rather 'young and old—and unmarried girls among them' (Bruhn).

695–8. Women tied up their hair under a μίτρα to sleep (*Hec.* 923 ff.).
ἀνεστείλαντο and κατεζώσαντο describe different actions. The former
seems to refer not to 'tucking up' the fawnskin under the girdle for
freedom of movement (Paley)—for on vases it falls little below the
waist—but to securing it on the shoulder (Sandys): cf. Accius,
Bacch. fr. 14 'tunc silvestrum exuvias laevo pictas lateri accommo-
dant'. The purpose of the snake-girdle, on the other hand, was
ritual rather than practical : cf. 101–4 n., and the ritual term βάκχος
or βάκχη ἀπὸ καταζώσεως (in the Great Bacchic Inscription of New
York, cf. Cumont, *A.J.A.* 1933, pp. 256 ff.).   λιχμῶσιν γένυν may
mean that the snakes licked the maenads' cheeks, as at 768, or
merely that they 'protruded their tongues as if licking their own
jaws' (Paley, comparing Hes. *Theog.* 826 and *Scut.* 235 where snakes
are said λιχμάζειν in this sense). Nonnus seems to have taken it
in the former way : he appears to be imitating this passage rather
than 768 when he describes the snake that coiled itself round
Cadmus' head καὶ γλῶσσα πέριξ λίχμαζεν ὑπήνην (44. 111). On the
other hand, the cheek-licking has more point at 768, and it may
be argued that the poet would not spoil his effect there by anticipat-
ing it here.

699–702. Maenads playing with the young of wild creatures appear in
vase-paintings (e.g. Phintias amphora, Beazley, *A.R.V.* p. 22. 2,
Pfuhl, fig. 381); but they do not suckle them, as they do here (and
in Nonnus, 14. 361 f., 45. 304 f.), save in a frieze at the Villa Item in
Pompeii, to which Prof. Merkelbach has called my attention. The
trait is hardly an invention of the poet's, for the act seems to have a
ritual meaning: the fawn or wolf-cub is an incarnation of the young
god, and in suckling it the human mother becomes a foster-mother
of Dion. (Διονύσου τιθήνη, Hom. *Il.* 6. 132, Soph. *OC.* 680).   ἐδίδοσαν,
'offered'.

702–3. ἐπὶ δ᾽ ἔθεντο: tmesis. On the μίλαξ see 108 n.; and on the ritual
significance of ivy and oak, 81 n., 109–10 n.

704–11. Dion. is a miraculous wine-maker (*H. Hymn.* 7. 35), and his
power is transmitted to those possessed by him when they wield
his magic rod. Since he is πάσης ὑγρᾶς φύσεως κύριος (Plut. *Is. et
Os.* 35), his rod can also, like Moses', draw water from the rock, and
its power extends likewise to the two other liquids which Nature

gives to man—milk and honey. [There was a spring at Cyparissiae which was called forth by Dion., θύρσῳ πλήξαντι ἐς τὴν γῆν (Paus. 4. 36. 7); and at several places there was an annual miracle by which Dion. was believed to transmute water into wine or to produce wine *ex nihilo* (Teos, Diod. 3. 66; Elis and Andros, Paus. 6. 26: cf. J. Vürtheim in *C.Q.* xiv [1920], 92 ff.). Of honey he was the first discoverer (Ov. *Fasti* 3. 736 ff.); milk he can produce from wood (Ant. Lib. 10). The tradition of Dion. as a miraculous milk-maker perhaps survives in the modern custom by which nursing mothers visit a cave on Pangaeum (where Dion. had his oracle, Hdt. 7. 111) in order to obtain an abundant flow of milk by touching a certain stone (P. Perdrizet, *Cultes et mythes du Pangée*, 38, n. 1). For the powers ascribed to the maenads cf. Plato, *Ion* 534 A αἱ βάκχαι ἀρύονται ἐκ τῶν ποταμῶν μέλι καὶ γάλα κατεχόμεναι, ἔμφρονες δὲ οὖσαι οὔ: Aeschines Socraticus fr. 11 Dittmar αἱ βάκχαι ἐπειδὰν ἔνθεοι γένωνται, ὅθεν οἱ ἄλλοι ἐκ τῶν φρεάτων οὐδὲ ὕδωρ δύνανται ὑδρεύεσθαι, ἐκεῖναι μέλι καὶ γάλα ἀρύονται: Hor. *Odes* 2. 19. 9 ff., Nonnus 45. 306 ff., &c. Similar miracles seem to have figured in Eur.'s *Hypsipyle* (see on 142–3) and in Soph.'s *Athamas* (fr. 5). See further Usener, 'Milch und Honig', *Rh. Mus.* N.F. lvii (1902), 177 ff.; C. Bonner, 'Dionysiac Magic', *Trans. Amer. Philol. Ass.* xli (1911), 175 ff.; and for the like miracles in a modern orgiastic cult, Brunel, *Aïssâoûa*, 119 f.]

710. ἐσμούς: not 'swarms' (an absurd metaphor) but 'springing jets': the word in this sense is connected not with ἕζομαι but (as Elmsley was the first modern to suggest) with ἵημι: cf. θεσμός (τίθημι). Similarly the New Comedy poet Epinicus calls honey ἐσμὸν μελίσσης γλυκύν, 'the bees' sweet sending' (fr. 1, Kock 3. 330). [Emendations have been proposed, but the text is confirmed by the echo in Philostratus, *vit. soph.* 1. 19 οἱ βακχεῖοι θύρσοι (ἐκδιδόασι) τὸ μέλι καὶ τοὺς ἐσμοὺς τοῦ γάλακτος.]

712. τόν, relative. Such forms, freely used by Aesch. and Soph. both in lyrics and (for metrical convenience) in dialogue, are in Eur. almost confined to the lyrics (Kühner–Gerth, i, p. 587 f.). The only other assured examples I know in Euripidean dialogue are *Andr.* 810 and *El.* 279: he probably felt the usage to be too remote from living speech.

715–16. 'To match reports in conclave concerning their strange uncanny actions.' [The text of 715 seems to me sound: λόγων ἔριν διδόναι is a typically Euripidean variation for λόγους διδόντες ἐρίζειν (cf. 618–21 n.). But the phrasing of 716 and 667 is suspiciously similar, and may originally have been identical: for *Chr. Pat.* (2212 f.) has ἥκω φράσαι σοι καὶ πόλει πολλὰ ξένα, | ὡς καινὰ πάντα θαυμάτων τ' ἐπάξια, which suggests that the author found θαυμάτων τ' ἐπάξια *in line 667*. If it stood there originally, we may suppose that (a) the line was quoted in the margin at 715, to define the contents of the κοινοὶ λόγοι, or perhaps deliberately introduced there for that purpose; then (b) at a later date θαυμάτων τ' ἐπάξια was altered in 667 to θαυμάτων τε κρείσσονα, to avoid recurrence of an identical line within the limits of a single speech.]

717. 'One who had tramped the town and had the knack of words' (Verrall).   τρίβων, 'rubbed', i.e. 'experienced' (cf. Lat. *callidus*), takes a gen. on the analogy of ἔμπειρος. It is one of the colloquial words introduced into tragedy by Eur. The poet has to explain why the herdsmen did not after all fall to prayer but instead (as tradition doubtless required) attacked the maenads. So he represents them as acting on the advice of an irreverent ἀγοραῖος ἀνήρ with an eye to the main chance (721 χάριν ἄνακτι θώμεθα), like the μάταιός τις at *IT*. 275. It is worth noticing that this is a type which Eur. elsewhere portrays with little sympathy: cf. especially *Or*. 902 ff., where the town-bred demagogue 'with no doors to his tongue' is contrasted unfavourably with the honest countryman 'who seldom went near town or market-place'.

719. θέλετε θηρασώμεθα, 'shall we hunt?': cf. Goodwin, *M. and T.*, § 287.

721. To 'oblige' some one is always χάριν θέσθαι, not θεῖναι, since the agent's interest is involved (he expects the favour to be returned): to 'confer a favour' gratuitously is χάριν δοῦναι. Hence the accepted correction θώμεθ' for θῶμεν here.

723–4. αὐτούς, first person, instead of the cumbrous ἡμᾶς αὐτούς: this is a fairly common usage even in classical prose, and is regular in Hellenistic Greek (Kühner–Gerth, i, pp. 571 ff.). The same tendency to make the third person reflexive serve for all persons is observable in other languages (Wackernagel, *Vorl. üb. Syntax*, ii. 94).   τὴν τεταγμένην ὥραν: 'at the appointed time (of day).' We might expect the dat., but in such phrases ὥρα, like καιρός, seems to be used in the accus. even where duration is not involved: cf. Aesch. *Eum*. 109 ἔθυον, ὥραν οὐδενὸς κοινὴν θεῶν, Hdt. 2. 2. 2 τὴν ὥρην ('at the due time') ἐπαγινέειν σφι αἶγας, Arist. *Ath. Pol*. 30. 6 τὸν μὴ ἰόντα εἰς τὸ βουλευτήριον τὴν ὥραν τὴν προρρηθεῖσαν. The two latter passages dispose of Verrall's idea (in his note on *Eum*. 109) that the words must mean 'in the appointed ritual'. So also ἀωρίαν 'at the wrong time', Ar. *Ach*. 23.

725. Ἴακχον: 'Lord of Cries' (if ancient and modern scholarship is right in connecting the name with the verb ἰαχεῖν): a local Eleusinian and Athenian title of Dion., here put rather inappropriately into the mouths of Theban worshippers. [Originally Iacchus may have been, as many scholars think, an independent local δαίμων, the presiding genius of the great Eleusinian procession, who lived for the rest of the year in the Ἰακχεῖον at Athens. But his eventual identification with Dion. in Athenian cult is shown in the ritual shout raised by the people at the Lenaea, Σεμελήι' Ἴακχε πλουτοδότα (schol. Ar. *Frogs* 482). The oldest extant authority for the identification is Sophocles, *Ant.* 1146 ff. and fr. 959 P. Νῦσαν ἦν ὁ βούκερως Ἴακχος . . . νέμει.]

726–7. 'And the whole mountain and its beasts were god-possessed as they were, and with their motion all things moved.' These strange and beautiful words startled ancient critics: πᾶν δὲ συνεβάκχευ' ὄρος is quoted in the *de sublimitate* as an example of imaginative boldness verging on extravagance, together with a line from Aesch.'s Lycurgus trilogy, ἐνθουσιᾷ δὴ δῶμα· βακχεύει στέγη, which the author finds still more παράδοξον. Hence Paley is surely wrong in supposing that συνεβάκχευε means merely 're-echoed'. The same thought that inanimate nature shares in the Dionysiac ecstasy seems to be implied in *IT.* 1242 ff. τὰν βακχεύουσαν Διονύσῳ Παρνάσιον κορυφάν: cf. also *Ion.* 1078 ff. and Soph. *Ant.* 1146, where the stars are represented as Dionysiac dancers; and for the behaviour of the beasts, Pindar fr. 61. 18 Bowra (70 b Snell) ὁ δὲ (sc. Διόνυσος) κηλεῖται χορευούσαισι κα[ὶ θη]ρῶν ἀγέλαις.

729. ὡς is logically superfluous, but emphasizes the fact that the seizure of Agaue never got beyond the stage of intention.

730. [ἐκρύπτομεν (L P) can perhaps stand, referring to the whole group of herdsmen (cf. 722). For the singular object cf. 744 ἐσφάλλοντο . . . δέμας. I do not know why Hermann says 'si activo usus esset, aoristum, nisi fallor, posuisset'.]

731. For the tribrach composed of a single word coinciding with the fourth foot cf. 1147. I suspect that in both places the exceptional rhythm is deliberately used for emotional effect. According to Descroix, it occurs in only seven other tragic trimeters, of which one at least is corrupt and another spurious.

732. ἀνδρῶν τῶνδ' ὕπο: in tragic senarii true prepositions rarely follow the noun they govern unless they come (1) at the end of a line or (2) in the middle of the governed phrase (e.g. *Tro.* 954 ναῦς ἐπ' Ἀργείων). The exceptions of which this is one, are listed and discussed by Denniston on *El.* 574. Cf. 1061.

734–47. On the significance of the σπαραγμός see Introd. pp. xvi ff. The rending of the cattle may have appeared also in the *Lucurgus* of Naevius, though fr. 19 'sine ferro pecua manibus ut ad mortem meant' was otherwise interpreted by Ribbeck (*Römische Tragödie*, 59).

737–8. τὴν μέν: not Agaue, but 'one of the madwomen': the picture is generalized, and the victims are named in order of *increasing* importance—πόρις (a young heifer), δαμάλαι (fully mature heifers), ταῦροι: cf. schol. Theocr. 1. 75 αἱ πόρτιες εὐτελέστεραι τῶν δαμάλεων. The humblest victim would hardly be assigned to the leader. ἔχουσαν . . . δίχα: can only, I think, mean 'holding apart'; but the sense required is surely 'wrenching asunder'. I would read, with Reiske, ἕλκουσαν . . . δίχα. Cf. Page, *Lit. Pap.* i, 10. 59 (from Eur. *Antiope*) ὁλκοῖς γε ταυρείοισι διαφορουμένη. [Not ἐν χεροῖν ἀκμαῖς (Nauck, &c.): one does not hold a cow in one's hands like a tea-cup. And not, I think, ἐν χεροῖν δίκῃ (Elmsley, &c.): the cow had committed no crime, and even if the phrase meant no more than ἔχουσαν ὑπο-χείριον it would still be, as Dalmeyda observes, rather too abstract an expression for a passage so gruesomely pictorial.]

743–5. 'Bulls that till then were arrogant, with anger mounting in their horns, stumbled to earth dragged by the multitudinous hands of girls.' **ἐς κέρας θυμούμενοι**, the source of Virgil's 'irasci in cornua' (*Georg.* 3. 232, *Aen.* 12. 104). Editors read into this simple phrase a reference to the beast glaring sidelong at his own horns (ἐς κέρας παρεμβλέπων, *Hel.* 1558) or staring at his adversary along the line of his horns. But the thought is rather that he concentrates his rage in his horns, as is clear from Ovid *Met.* 8. 882 'armenti modo dux vires in cornua sumo'. Cf. the archaic Eng. 'horn-wood' for 'fighting mad.'[1] **μυριάσι:** the 'multitudinous' hands suggest the terrible collective insanity of a mob (cf. 1109 μυρίαν χέρα, and the grim anonymous threat implied in πολλαὶ δὲ χεῖρες *Hec.* 1151); the effect is enhanced by the two resolutions, giving a swift, perhaps slightly hysterical rhythm.

746–7. **διεφοροῦντο:** best taken as passive (subject ταῦροι, ἐνδυτά 'retained accus.'). The change of subject then comes with the change of tense and topic at 748. **σαρκὸς ἐνδυτά:** probably not the hide, but 'the garment of flesh' (σαρκός genitive of material), like 111 ἐνδυτὰ νεβρίδων, *Her.* 1269 σαρκὸς περιβόλαια, Empedocles fr. 126 σαρκῶν χιτῶνι. **ξυνάψαι:** consecutive infinitive, 'faster than you could have closed': this is the normal construction after a comparative with ἤ (Goodwin, *M. and T.*, § 764), cf. e.g. *Hec.* 1107 κρεῖσσον' ἢ φέρειν κακά, and *infra*, 1285 πρόσθεν ἤ σε γνωρίσαι. [P has σύ, whence many edd. read σὺ ξυνάψαις with the Renaissance corrector *p*. But this receives only dubious support from *Hipp.* 1186 θᾶσσον ἢ λέγοι (λέγει V P) τις.] **βασιλείοις:** to palliate the homely familiarity of 'before you could wink', the Herdsman prudently inserts a deferential epithet (Denniston). [βασιλικοῖς Nauck, this being the usual form in tragic dialogue, as it is in Attic prose; cf., however, *Ba.* 60, *Med.* 960, *Hel.* 70, 144, 1526, *I.A.* 863 (which are overlooked in L.S.⁹)]

748–64. This raid on the Theban villages is probably, like much else in the Herdsman's narrative, traditional rather than invented by Eur. A fragment of Naevius' *Lucurgus* (see next note) suggests that

[1] Callimachus applied the phrase metaphorically to an angry poet, fr. 203. 52 Pfeiffer ἀοιδὸς ἐς κέρας τεθύμωται.

something of the kind figured in Naevius' (probable) model, the Lycurgeia of Aeschylus. Moreover, the description corresponds to the known behaviour of persons in abnormal states in many primitive societies (A. van Gennep, *Les Rites de passage*, 161 f., cf. 755-8 nn., and my *Greeks and the Irrational*, 275). And although such actions belong to a stage of social organization which fifth-century Greece had long outgrown, legend or ritual may well have preserved the memory of them; while in Macedonia Eur. may have encountered the actuality. An attenuated echo is perhaps to be recognized even to-day in the behaviour of the Viza mummers: 'in general', says Dawkins, 'anything lying about may be seized as a pledge to be redeemed, and the Koritzia (girls) especially carry off babies (cf. 754) with this object' (*J.H.S.* xxvi [1906], 197).

748-50. ὥστ' ὄρνιθες ἀρθεῖσαι δρόμῳ, 'like birds upborne by their own speed'. Naevius too compared the maenads to birds (*Luc.* fr. 7). πεδίων ὑποτάσεις, 'across the understretch of plain', accus. of space traversed (cf. 306-9 n.). Winnington-Ingram calls attention to the effective contrast between the maenads of the mountain, 'enemies of organised human society', and the lowlands, 'where men have laboured to subordinate nature, to grow corn and live in ordered settlements'. Naevius' maenads trampled the farmers' crops: 'quoque incedunt omnis arvas opterunt' (*Luc.* fr. 3). Erythrae is praised by the gourmet-poet Archestratus (*apud* Athen. 112 B) for the excellence of its bread.   ἐκβάλλουσι: so Hipp. *Nat. Puer.* 22 τὸν καρπὸν ἐκβάλλειν, 'to produce fruit'. [Brunck's Θηβαίοις is probable: the accus. sing. (P) may have been introduced by assimilation, and L's gen. pl. (for which I can find no good parallel) in an attempt to correct this.]

751-2. Ὑσιάς τ' Ἐρυθράς θ', governed by ἐπεσπεσοῦσαι (cf. *Her.* 34). These villages are situated among the northern foot-hills of the Cithaeron massif, where it runs down to the Asopus valley, and so are correctly described as 'standing in the hill-country (λέπας, cf. 677-8 n.) of Cithaeron, in its lower reaches (νέρθεν)'. The herdsmen would pass them in their flight towards Thebes.   ὥστε = ὥσπερ.

754. τέκνα should not be emended: the baby-stealing maenads reappear in Nonnus (45. 294 ff.), and cf. the behaviour of the Viza mummers cited above. They appear also on vases. The baby who sits astride a maenad's shoulders on a Bologna krater (Pfuhl, *Malerei*, Abb. 581) might be her own; but the maenad on a British Museum pyxis by the Meidias painter, E 775 (Beazley, *A.R.V.*, p. 833. 14; Curtius, *Pentheus*, fig. 15), who carries a child brutally slung by the leg over her shoulder, has surely stolen him. Perhaps she is going to eat him, as the daughters of Minyas in their madness ate the child Hippasos. The pyxis is closely contemporary with our play.

755-7. For the perfect sense of balance exhibited by persons in ecstatic states cf. Nathaniel Pearce's account of ecstatic dancers in Abyssinia: 'I have seen them in these fits dance with a bruly, or bottle of maize, upon their heads without spilling the liquor, or letting the bottle fall, although they have put themselves into the most extravagant postures.' If the text is sound, the 'bronze and iron' are not weapons—the maenads' only weapon is the thyrsus, 762—but domestic utensils (Wilamowitz, comparing Thuc. 3. 68. 3). In the Thucydides passage, however, the meaning is made obvious by the preceding word ἐπίπλα; here it is far from obvious, and it is at any rate a little odd that pots and pans should be specially named among the things which did not fall off the maenads' shoulders. I incline to agree with those who think that a line or more is lost after 756, and that the sentence beginning with ὁπόσα ended at πέδον. The Herdsman may perhaps have continued 'Nothing resisted their assault, not bolted doors, not bronze, not iron'. ὁπόσα ('all the things they carried') will then include the children—which would naturally be carried on the maenads' shoulders, and are so carried in Nonnus and on the B.M. pyxis—but will also include household goods (implied in πάντα διέφερον): what chiefly astonishes the Herdsman is that the latter did not fall off.[1] [This lacuna and the one at 652 may well be due, as C. Robert suggested (Hermes, xiii [1878], 137), to the same cause, viz. an accidental injury to a leaf of the archetype, if we assume that like P and L the archetype had two columns on each page of about 35 lines each (an assumption which agrees pretty well with Wilamowitz's calculation for the archetype of P in the Troades, Analecta Euripidea, 51): the interval between the lacunae will then be 3 columns (104 lines).[2] Some postulate another lacuna after 754; but the defectiveness of the antithesis, ἥρπαζον μὲν τέκνα, ὁπόσα δ᾽ ἐπ᾽ ὤμοις ἔθεσαν οὐκ ἔπιπτεν, may be due merely to the speed and compression of the narrative.]

757–8. Iamblichus, de myst. 3. 4, of religious ecstatics, πολλοὶ γὰρ καὶ πυρὸς προσφερομένου οὐ καίονται, οὐχ ἁπτομένου τοῦ πυρὸς αὐτῶν διὰ τὴν θείαν ἐπίπνοιαν. The same claim is made in modern times: e.g. painless fire-walking is practised today in Thrace by orgiastic dancers at the feast of Saint Constantine (Jeanmaire, Dionysos, 185, quoting C. A. Romaios, Cultes populaires de la Thrace, trad.

---

[1] A different solution of the puzzle has been offered by the late John Jackson, who suggests (Marginalia Scaenica, 17) that οὐ χαλκός, οὐ σίδηρος is the remains of a line which originally stood after 761, and that when it was misplaced the rest of the line was deleted and ἐς μέλαν πέδον introduced from 1065 to patch up the metre. The words would of course make excellent sense after 761, but I find the hypothesis too complicated to be very convincing.

[2] See now P. G. Mason, C.R. lxii (1948), 105 ff.

franç. 1949, 17 ff.); cf. also R. Benedict, *Patterns of Culture*, 176, T. K. Oesterreich, *Possession*, 264, 270 (Eng. trans.), Brunel, *Aïssâoûa*, 109, 158, and the feats attributed to Indian fire-walkers and to certain European 'mediums'. In our passage the fire could be supernatural in origin, like the lambent flames that played about Achilles' head in Homer (*Il.* 18. 205 ff.); but the context rather suggests that it is taken from the domestic hearths of the villagers.

758–60. οἱ δέ: the villagers.   φερόμενοι: 'being plundered'.   τὸ δεινὸν θέαμα: 'that dreadful sight' (which remains in my memory). Cf. *IT.* 320 οὗ δὴ τὸ δεινὸν παρακέλευσμ᾽ ἠκούσαμεν, and the many similar passages collected and discussed by Jebb on Soph. *Tr.* 476 (appendix). [Perhaps βάκχας ἔπι (Vitelli), to avoid second ὕπο.]

761–4. For the widespread belief that the possessed are invulnerable cf. Oesterreich, *Possession*, 353, Czaplicka, *Aboriginal Siberia*, 176. Persons in abnormal mental states are often in fact insensitive to pain (Binswanger, *Die Hysterie*, 756, cf. Iamb. *de myst.* 3. 4). That people were really afraid of maenads seems to be implied in the story of the fourth-century Macedonian king who used women dressed as maenads to frighten an invading army (Polyaenus, *Strat.* 4. 1, schol. Persius 1. 99). Cf. Aesch. *Sept.* 498 βακχᾷ πρὸς ἀλκὴν θυιὰς ὥς, φόβον βλέπων. But Alexandrine art and literature, not content with the indwelling magic of the simple thyrsus, usually provide their maenads with a θυρσόλογχος, a thyrsus with an iron spearhead (v. Papen, *Der Thyrsos*, 44 f.). [τᾶς μέν (P) may represent either τοῖς μέν or τὰς μέν. The latter gives an illogical but natural antithesis between the women as targets for missiles and the same women as assailants.[1]]

765–8. The Herdsman is allowed to round off his narrative by describing what he cannot well have seen. This is not unusual, and does not authorize us to regard him as a liar. To do that is to apply the standards of the modern detective story to a wholly different art form.   νίψαντο: the tragedians sometimes omit the syllabic augment (never or virtually never the temporal) in (*a*) lyrics (cf. 94, 100), (*b*) less often, narrative speeches, nearly always formal 'messenger' speeches, and nearly always at the beginning of a line. Usage (*a*) comes from the tradition of choral lyric; usage (*b*) is most naturally explained as an epicism.[2] It is interesting that the only certain in-

---

[1] I am now inclined to prefer it, since αἱμάσσειν, 'to make bloody', calls for an expressed object.

[2] I think this remains true despite L. Bergson, *Eranos*, li (1954), 121 ff., who argues that the only motive is metrical convenience. Although past tenses occur predominantly in messengers' speeches, I should nevertheless on his view expect a wider distribution of the usage.

stances of (*b*) in Eur. occur in the *Bacchae*, which contains four (767, 1066, 1084, 1134): he perhaps felt the suggestion of remoteness from common speech to be appropriate to these tales of the miraculous but not to more realistic narratives. Cf. Kühner–Blass, ii. 18 f., and Page on *Medea* 1141. **αἷμα**: not their own blood, as 761 shows, but that of the mangled cattle. **σταγόνα δ' ἐκ παρηΐδων**: probably used by proleptic attraction instead of *τὸν ἐν παρηΐσι σταγόνα* (cf. 49 n.): the presence of *χροός* makes it slightly awkward to take *ἐκ παρηΐδων* as dependent on *ἐξεφαίδρυνον*. The sense seems to be that while the maenads washed their hands (*νίζεσθαι* is used especially of hand-washing) the snakes were licking off (*ἐξεφαίδρυνον*, imperfect) the blood from their faces. [The only suspicious word in these lines is **αὐτάς**, which has little apparent point. Wilamowitz conjectured *κρήνας ἐφ' ἁγνάς*, but Bruhn's and Marchant's *κρήνας ἐπ'*, *αὐτός* has more chances of being right: the unusual position of *ἔπι* (for which cf. 732) would easily lead to corruption.]

769–74. The Herdsman ends, after the manner of messengers, by drawing the moral—which is that we should accept with reverent gratitude the god's normal gift of wine, lest we experience his stranger powers. This agrees with Teiresias' attitude (274–83). The last two lines, at which some critics have been needlessly shocked, reflect the persistent belief in wine as a magical source of vitality: according to Peripatetic theory wine contains *πνεῦμα*, the stuff of life, [Arist.] *Probl.* 953ᵇ25 ff.; or as Ovid more simply puts it, 'Venus in vinis, ignis in igne fuit' (*Ars. Am.* 1. 244). Cf. also the passages quoted on 402–16.

775–7. **ἐλευθέρους**, predicative (cf. 650): 'to make my speech free'. The Chorus-leader is by now, like the Herdsman (670), afraid of the King's temper, which has reached bursting-point; but she adventures her plea nevertheless. Such choral comments frequently mark the end of an important *ῥῆσις*: it is fantastic to attribute this one to a nameless citizen, as Norwood and Verrall do.

778–9. **ὥστε πῦρ ὑφάπτεται** 'blazes up like fire' (which is the type of τὸ δύσμαχον, Eur. fr. 429, Ar. *Lys.* 1014 f.). [*ἐφάπτεται* (P) may perhaps have the same sense: Theocritus uses it of a girl's cheek kindling (14. 23, with schol. *ἐφλέγετο*). It has also been explained as 'touches me to the quick' (Paley) or 'is reaching us' (Sandys); but we expect a verb which develops the simile.] **ψόγος ἐς Ἕλληνας**, 'a discredit in the eyes of the Greeks', like *IT*. 525 ὦ μῖσος εἰς Ἕλληνας, Thuc. 7. 56. 2 καλὸν σφίσιν ἐς τοὺς Ἕλληνας τὸ ἀγώνισμα φανεῖσθαι. Pentheus is full of racial pride (483).

780. The Electran Gate guarded the southern entrance to Thebes, where the road from Plataea and Cithaeron came in (Paus. 9. 8. 7), so is naturally chosen by Pentheus as the rallying-point for his forces.

781–6. This is, as Murray says, the typical 'Ercles' vein' of the tragic tyrant: cf. Thoas, *IT*. 1422 ff. Pentheus is unteachable: the palace miracle showed that bolts and bars availed nothing against Dion., yet he responded by locking the gates (653); the Herdsman's report has shown that weapons are equally unavailing, yet he calls out his army.   ἀσπιδηφόρους, i.e. hoplites (heavy infantry); πέλτας δσοι πάλλουσι, peltasts (light infantry).   οὐ γὰρ ἀλλά κτλ. = οὐ γὰρ (ἀνεκτά ἐστι) τάδε, ἀλλὰ ὑπερβάλλει (τὸ μέτρον), 'for this is indeed past bearing'. A colloquial ellipse (iambographi, Aristoph., Plato) used several times by Eur. (*Supp.* 570, *IT.* 1005, fr. 73), but otherwise foreign to tragedy: Denniston, *Particles*, 31.   πρὸς γυναικῶν: cf. Creon's bitterness at being worsted by a woman, *Ant.* 484 f., 525, 678 ff.

Scene 3 (c), the tempting of Pentheus. This is the crucial scene of the play. It begins with the psychological situation apparently unchanged, save that Pentheus is angrier than before. The patient god still recommends ἡσυχία (790, cf. 647); the man, blind with rage, threatens now not merely to arrest the bacchanals (231) but to massacre them (796). Yet by the end of the scene Pentheus is 'entering the net' (848). How is the change brought about? Not, I think, merely by the Stranger's persuasive tongue: I agree with Murray that from 811 onwards Pentheus appears to lose control over his own mind, though he fights against this (see on 810–12, 821–38). We should not try to rationalize this by following a superficial modern analogy and calling it 'hypnotism'. There is in fact no evidence that antiquity was acquainted with any hypnotic technique. [The incident described by Clearchus, *apud* Procl. *in Remp.* 2. 122. 22, has recently been called a 'séance d'hypnotisme', but I see no reason to suppose that the subject's sleep was other than natural. Apul. *Apol.* 42 and the Paris Magical Papyrus (*Pap. Gr. Mag.* 1. iv. 850 ff.) seem to refer not to hypnotism but to the artificial induction of 'mediumistic' trance.] What happens is rather the beginning of a psychic invasion, the entry of the god into his victim, who was also in the old belief his vehicle. Eur. is, however, too careful a psychologist to present an abrupt unmotived change of personality—a bare act of God like the conversion of the Eumenides in Aeschylus. In the maddening of Pentheus, as in the maddening of Heracles (cf. Wilamowitz, *Herakles*², p. 414), the poet shows us the supernatural attacking the victim's personality at its weakest point—working upon and through nature, not against it. The god wins because he has an ally in the enemy's camp: the persecutor is betrayed by what he would persecute—the Dionysiac longing in himself. From the first that longing has been skilfully excited by the Stranger (475); the barriers of self-control have been weakened by what happened in the stable; Pentheus' rage at the Herdsman's narrative shows the breaking-point to be near—it is his last desperate self-assertion. The Stranger's question at 811 releases the flood. Cf. Zielinski, *Neue Jahrbücher*, 1902, 649.

787. [πείσῃ (from πάσχω) was once suggested by Tyrrell, and has been proposed more recently by Cosattini (*Riv. di Fil.* xxxix [1911], 252). It looks neat as a retort to 686, yet can hardly be right, since it really destroys the force of the μέν . . . δέ antithesis. The author of the *Chr. Pat.* read πείθῃ (2277).]

791, εὐίων ὀρῶν, 'the hills of joy', hills that heard the cry εὐοῖ. Cf. the mountain in Messene which was called Εὔα, εὐοῖ Διονύσου πρῶτον ἐνταῦθα εἰπόντος, Paus. 4. 31. 4; and mount Euas near Sparta, Plb. 2. 65. [κινοῦντι P, but the dat. with ἀνέχομαι can hardly stand, here or at *Andr.* 980. Verrall's notion that it refers to Dion. (either transposing 791 to follow 789 or imagining the sentence to be interrupted by Pentheus) certainly will not do : εὐίων shows that κινεῖν has its usual implication of 'meddling'. The choice lies between κινοῦντα and κινεῖν τι: κινοῦν τι is too vague. Cf. *Hel.* 1045 f. οὐκ ἄν ⟨σ'⟩ ἀνάσχοιτο . . . μέλλοντα . . . σύγγονον κατακτενεῖν, which supports κινοῦντα.]

792–3. 'No preaching! You have broken gaol : then see you keep your freedom—or would you have me renew your punishment?' On the construction cf. 343–4 n.; for σώσῃ τόδε, Soph. *El.* 1256 f., where Electra says μόλις γὰρ ἔσχον νῦν ἐλεύθερον στόμα and Orestes replies ξύμφημι κἀγώ· τοιγαροῦν σώζου τόδε, 'guard your freedom' (rather than 'remember it', as some take σώσῃ τόδε here). ἀναστρέψω δίκην, lit. 'cause justice to turn back (and seize you again)' [Wecklein's χέρας is needless and improbable]. The rather marked sigmatism of these lines helps, I think, to suggest the King's rage : cf. *Med.* 476 (with Page's note), *Hipp.* 958 f., *Ion* 386, all expressive of anger. τὸ σῖγμα τὸ Εὐριπίδου, about which the comic poets teased him, is most often, as we should expect, purely accidental (O. J. Todd, *C.Q.* xxxvi [1942], 34 ff.); but this by no means excludes its occasional deliberate or instinctive use for emotional effect.

795. 'Kick against the goad, mortality striving against deity.' θεῷ is loosely governed by πρὸς κέντρα λακτίζοιμι (= μαχοίμην): so fr. 604 πρὸς κέντρα μὴ λάκτιζε τοῖς κρατοῦσί σου. For the proverb cf. also fr. iamb. adesp. 13 Diehl ἵππος ὄνῳ· πρὸς κέντρα μὴ λακτιζέτω and Pindar, *Pyth.* 2. 94, Aesch. *PV.* 323, *Ag.* 1624, Ter. *Phorm.* 776 'inscitiast, advorsum stimulum calces'. The author of *Acts* uses it (9. 5 and 26. 14) exactly as Eur. does, as a warning to the θεομάχος: he may in fact have borrowed it from the present passage (cf. 45 n., 443–8 n., and F. Smend, *Angelos*, i [1925], 41).

796–7. 'Sacrifice? Yes, of women's blood as they deserve; generously I shall unleash it in Cithaeron's glens.' (L.S. s.v. θῆλυς surprisingly mistranslates φόνον θῆλυν as 'murder by women'.) ὥσπερ ἄξιαι, sc. εἰσὶν ἀποθανεῖν αἱ γυναῖκες. [But I think we should read either ἄξιος (Wilamowitz, sc. ἐστὶν ὁ Διόνυσος) or, if this is thought too harsh, ἄξιον (Camper): the point must be that the female victims suit the womanish and woman-worshipped god.] For φόνον πολὺν ταράξας, cf. Aesch. Cho. 330 f. γόος ἀμφιλαφὴς ταραχθείς: ταράσσειν is 'to set in harassing motion' (Tucker).

798–9. 'To turn your shields of beaten bronze (i.e. take to flight) before the wands of bacchanal women.' The dat. is analogous to that used with ἐκστῆναι, ὑποχωρεῖν, &c., in the sense of making way for a person. [Nauck's ἐντρέπειν, 'put to shame', is not an improvement: this sense of ἐντρέπω appears only in late prose. βάκχας (Wecklein) would be a better correction if any were needed.—φευξεῖσθε P, perhaps rightly. Eur. uses this form of the future for metrical convenience (e.g. 659), but also, if the MSS. are to be trusted, without metrical necessity at Med. 604 (where both Murray and Page keep φευξοῦμαι) and according to M A B V at Hipp. 1093. Ar. similarly appears to use it with and without metrical necessity; Aesch. and Soph. not at all.]

800–1. ἀπόρῳ, predicative: 'I am at grips with this Stranger, and find no way with him.' συμπεπλέγμεθα, metaph. from wrestling: cf. Men. Epitrep. 60 (19) μετρίῳ γε συμπέπλεγμαι ῥήτορι, Aeschines 2. 153 συμπέπλεγμαι δ' ἐν τῇ πολιτείᾳ . . . ἀνθρώπῳ γόητι καὶ πονηρῷ. οὔτε πάσχων οὔτε δρῶν, i.e. in no circumstances: πάσχων refers to 788; and although the Stranger has not yet done anything, P. continues with the formal antithesis οὔτε δρῶν (instead of οὔτε ἐλεύθερος ὤν). On the influence of the Greek passion for antithesis see Wilamowitz on Her. 1106. Here, however, the audience may detect in the word δρῶν an unconscious admission that the initiative is passing to the Stranger (Winnington-Ingram).

802. ὦ τᾶν, 'Sir'. This expression (of uncertain derivation) is a polite and respectful form of address (πρόσρημα τιμητικῆς λέξεως Hesych.), not a condescending one as Bruhn asserts. It is used in speaking to parents (Ar. Nub. 1432, Vesp. 1161) or social superiors (servant to Iolaus, Heraclid. 688; Plato to Dionysius, Pl. Ep. 3. 319 E), as well as between equals who are not intimates. Frequently it calls attention to an admonition or a proposal as here (cf. Heraclid. 688, Cycl. 536, Soph. Phil. 1387, Ar. Eq. 1036). With 21 occurrences in Ar., none in Aesch., 3 in Soph. (1 satyric), 4 in Eur. (1 satyric), it looks like an Athenian colloquialism.[1]

803. δουλείαις, for δούλοις, like Lat. servitia for servi. Cf. Thuc. 5. 23. 3 ἢν ἡ δουλεία ἐπαναστῇ, and for the plural abstract Plato, Laws, 682 E τὸν συλλέξαντα τὰς τότε φυγάς (= τοὺς φυγάδας). That P. calls

---

[1] Cf. now G. Björck, Das Alpha Impurum, 275-7.

his subjects 'slaves' is significant of his character: he talks like Lycus in the *Heracles*, who calls the Chorus δοῦλοι τῆς ἐμῆς τυραννίδος (*Her.* 251).

804. I take this to be a genuine offer. Pentheus' earlier ὕβρις has been punished by his humiliation in the stable: if he will make terms now, man and god are quits. But he thinks it is a trick.

808. 'Certainly I made a pact—that much is true—(but I made it) with the god.' If ἔστι is retained, it must be so translated. But I rather doubt, despite Plato's use of ἔστι ταῦτα, whether τοῦτό γ' ἔστι could be used for τοῦτό γ' ἐστιν ἀληθές: and if it could, we should expect an adversative particle in front of τῷ θεῷ. I agree with the general view of modern edd. that we should accept Musgrave's ἴσθι, punctuating (with Elmsley) καὶ μὴν ξυνεθέμην τοῦτό γ', ἴσθι, τῷ θεῷ: 'Certainly I made *that* compact (viz. βακχεύσειν ἀεί), never doubt it, with the god.' The emphatic word is not τῷ θεῷ but τοῦτο. [Tyrwhitt's ἔς τι, 'for a certain purpose', has little point. P originally had καὶ μὴ, whence Hermann read κεἰ μὴ ξυνεθέμην, τοῦτό γ' ἔστι τῷ θεῷ, 'Even if I made no pact, *that* (viz. βακχεύειν) belongs of right to the god'. This is possible; but καὶ μήν looks genuine, in view of the frequency of καὶ μήν . . . γε in assent, often as here with repetition of one of the previous speaker's words: cf. Soph. *OT.* 345, 836, Eur. *Alc.* 713, &c., and Denniston, *Particles*, 353 ff. The copyist who misread ἴσθι as ἔστι doubtless had in mind the common use in late Greek of τοῦτ' ἔστι for 'i.e.'.]

810–12. Pentheus has broken off negotiations and turned to leave the stage when the Stranger recalls him with ἆ. This can hardly, like Eng. 'Ah'! signify resignation. It can be a gasp of astonishment (cf. 586, 596) or a groan of pain (*Rhes.* 799); but often it expresses urgent protest, 'Stop!': cf. *Her.* 1051 ἆ ἆ, διά μ' ὀλεῖτε, *Or.* 1598 ἆ ἆ, μηδαμῶς δράσῃς τάδε, *Hel.* 445 ἆ· μὴ προσείλει χεῖρα, Soph. *Phil.* 1300 ἆ, μηδαμῶς. This seems to be its force here (Tyrrell, cf. Verrall, *Bacchants*, 106). 'Stop! Would you like to see them, huddled there on the mountain-side?' 'Yes! I would give uncounted gold to see that.' It is the answer, if not of a maniac, at least of a man whose reactions are ceasing to be normal: the question has touched a hidden spring in Pentheus' mind, and his self-mastery vanishes.

813. Perhaps better punctuated, with Musgrave, τί δ'; εἰς ἔρωτα τοῦδε πέπτωκας μέγαν; The Stranger feigns a shocked surprise (Winnington-Ingram).

814. P. momentarily pulls himself together: 'I should be sorry to see them drunk.' As this is in itself no answer to the Stranger's question, we should probably read μέν for νιν: P. would have continued with a δέ clause—'Of course I should be sorry to see them drunk, but see them I must'—if the Stranger had not divined his thought and supplied the δέ clause himself. For the μέν clause left solitary as a result of interruption cf. *Her.* 555. [This is much better than writing 814 as a question (Hermann), which obscures and enfeebles the sense. λυπρῶς should not be altered: it is confirmed by ἅ σοι πικρά in the next line. If we punctuate 813 in Musgrave's way the difficulty is somewhat diminished, but not removed.]

816. [An epexegetic γε (cf. 796) is commonly used in tragedy with participial clauses which supplement the main statement (Denniston, *Particles*, 138), and δέ has been emended to γε here, as also at *Heraclid.* 794. But δέ is perhaps defensible if we give it an adversative sense, as introducing a *conditio sine qua non*: σάφ' ἴσθι· σιγῇ δ', ὑπ' ἐλάταις καθήμενος, 'Certainly I want to see them, but privily, crouched in the shadow of the firs.' For the modal dative thus added cf. *I.A.* 1456 f. ἄκων μ' ὑπὲρ γῆς Ἑλλάδος διώλεσεν.—δόλῳ δ', ἀγεννῶς Ἀτρέως τ' οὐκ ἀξίως. That P. abandons this condition a moment later (818) is entirely in keeping with his state of mind.]

820. τοῦ χρόνου δέ σοι φθονῶ: 'I grudge you the delay (the *intervening* time).' For this sense of χρόνος cf. Dem. *fals. leg.* 163 οὐδ' ἐποίησαν (ἐνεποίησαν Dobree) χρόνον οὐδένα. [P has δέ σ' οὐ, which cannot be defended as an elision or a crasis for σοι οὐ. Elmsley proposed δέ γ' οὐ, Dobree δ' οὖ σοι, Paley γάρ οὐ. If the negative is retained, Pentheus is saying merely 'I can spare you the time' (like *Hec.* 238 τοῦ χρόνου γὰρ οὐ φθονῶ); the words may be explained as 'a hasty attempt to deny the impatience the first half of the line betrays' (Winnington-Ingram). But it is perhaps likeliest on the whole that οὐ was introduced by a copyist who misunderstood τοῦ χρόνου.]

821–38. Pentheus' masculine pride (cf. 785 f.) is outraged by the proposal that he should dress up as a woman. Torn between dignity and lust, he accepts (824) and goes back on his acceptance (828). 'Then you have changed your mind and don't want to see the maenads?' (829). He hesitates, plays for time by asking questions, finally refuses (836). 'Then you will make bloodshed' (837). 'You are right: I must *reconnoitre* them first' (838). Yet a few minutes before he had fully intended to make bloodshed (796, 809). Now the lust to kill has vanished: it was only the substitute for a deeper, unacknowledged lust to pry into the women's doings, and it fades when he is able to rationalize the latter as a 'military reconnaissance'. Nowhere is Eur.'s knowledge of the human heart more subtly shown. [Failure to understand Pentheus' psychology has led Wecklein and others to propose unnecessary changes in the text. On the Stranger's motive, and the possible ritual significance of the change of dress, see 854–5 n.]

821–2. βυσσίνους πέπλους: 'a dress of eastern linen'. Though the πέπλος is properly a woollen garment fastened with a pin, the tragedians use πέπλοι as a general term for any kind of dress (Studniczka, *Beitr. z. Gesch. d. altgriech. Tracht*, 133 ff.). Here, as at Aesch. *Cho.*

30, it must be a long (833) linen χιτών: that βύσσος meant in the fifth century a kind of linen seems fairly certain from Hdt.'s statement (2. 86. 6) that it was the material of Egyptian mummy-wrappings. At the date of the *Bacchae* the long linen χιτών had gone out of fashion among Athenian males (Thuc. 1. 6. 3); the monuments of this period show it worn only by women and as a ceremonial dress by priests, musicians, or charioteers. Dresses of βύσσος were probably never worn save by women (Aesch. *Sept.* 1039, Theocr. 2. 73) and orientals (Anchises, Soph. fr. 373; Persian female mourners, Aesch. *Pers.* 125; male initiate in the mysteries of Isis, Apul. *Met.* 11. 24). Hence Pentheus's question. **ἐς γυναῖκας ἐξ ἀνδρὸς τελῶ**; 'am I to stop being a man and rank with women?' τελεῖν is (1) to pay taxes (τέλη), then (2) to be classified for taxation, then (3) to be classified (generally): cf. Soph. *O.T.* 222 εἰς ἀστοὺς τελῶ.

824. 'Well said again! What a clever fellow you have been all along (πάλαι)'! αὖ refers to 818, πάλαι perhaps to 655. [αὖ τόδ᾽· ὡς is Wecklein's convincing correction for αὐτὸ καί. αὐτό is the wrong pronoun, and the confusion of καί and ὡς is very common owing to the similarity of the shorthand symbols used to represent them in MSS.]

826. [The break between ἅ and σύ, the second and third syllables of a tribrach, would not have been allowed in older tragic practice. Hence ἁμέ Elmsley for ἅ σύ με, assuming that ἁμέ was read as ἅ με and σύ inserted to make up the foot. But cf. *I.T.* 728 πάρει|σιν· ἁ δ᾽ ἐ|πί and Soph. *Phil.* 1247 δίκαι|ον, ἅ γ᾽ ἐ|λαβες, both with a sense pause after the first syllable of the tribrach, as here. Late tragedy relaxed somewhat the earlier strictness in these matters (192 n., 475 n.).]

831-3. κόμην . . . ταναόν, i.e. a wig (φενάκη) or front of false hair (προκόμιον). It will not do to render 'I will loosen your hair into long curls' (ταναόν pred.): for (a) ἐπὶ σῷ κρατί would then have little point; (b) P.'s head must be close cropped if his jibe at 455 is to be effective. τὸ δεύτερον σχῆμα τοῦ κόσμου, 'the next feature of my costume.' πέπλοι ποδήρεις: cf. *Etym. Magn.* p. 191. 5 λέγονται βασσάραι χιτῶνες οὓς ἐφόρουν αἱ Θράκιαι βάκχαι... ἦσαν δὲ ποικίλοι καὶ ποδήρεις. Αἰσχύλος ἐν 'Ηδωνοῖς· ὅστις χιτῶνας βασσάρας τε Λυδίας ἔχει ποδήρεις (fr. 59); Sext. Emp. *Pyrrh. Hyp.* 3. 204 οὐδὲ ἀνθοβαφῆ καὶ ποδήρη τις ἄρρην ἐνταῦθα ⟨ἂν⟩ ἀμφιέσαιτο ἐσθῆτα.   μίτρα: usually a band or 'snood' passing round the head and across the temples. It was worn by women (*Etym. Magn.* μίτρα· λέγεται ὁ γυναικεῖος τῆς κεφαλῆς ἀνάδεσμος, cf. Ar. *Thesm.* 257, 941, Eur. *Hec.* 923), and also apparently by both sexes as part of the Dionysiac ritual dress. [Dion. himself is χρυσομίτρης (Soph. *O.T.* 209); a votaress speaks of her μιτροδέτου κόμης (*Anth. Pal.* 6. 165. 6); and both the god and his worshippers

sometimes wear the μίτρα in vase-paintings from the middle of the
fifth century onwards. This ritual use seems to be of eastern origin :
Alcman 1. 67 speaks of μίτρα Λυδία (? as a Dionysiac ornament,
Bowra, *Greek Lyric Poetry*, 46). We may perhaps interpret it as a
sign of dedication to the god's service (C. Picard, 'Dionysos Mitré-
phoros', *Mélanges Glotz*, ii. 709 ff.).]

836. [In the anecdote referred to in note on 314–18 Plato is made to
quote this line, followed in Suidas' version of the story (s.v. Ἀρίστιπ-
πος) by another—ἄρρην πεφυκὼς καὶ γένους ἐξ ἄρρενος. The words
ἄρρην πεφυκώς appear also in Sextus Empiricus' version (*Pyrrh.
Hyp.* 3. 204). The additional line has a Euripidean ring (cf. fr. 15
ἴδοιμι δ' αὐτῶν ἔκγον' ἄρσεν' ἀρσένων), and applies with special force
to Pentheus, whose father was not born of woman but sprung from
the dragon's teeth. Possibly, as Boeckh thought, it should be inserted here : if P. at this point breaks off the discussion and turns as
if to go, the breach of stichomythia would be in accordance with
Eur.'s practice elsewhere (842 n., 1269 n.). Schoene placed the line
after 852, but it is more natural in Pentheus' mouth than in the
Stranger's. It is hardly an anecdotist's invention, since the story
turns on capping quotations. But it may, I suppose, have been
taken from another play.]

837. 'But you will cause bloodshed if you join battle with the worshipping women.' Despite Housman (*apud* Tyrrell) and Campbell
(*Proc. Camb. Philol. Soc.* 1954, 13), I find nothing wrong with this
in point of sense (see above, 821–38 n.); but **αἷμα θήσεις** is rather
questionable Greek. [I know no clear and *exact* parallel. *Ion* 1260
τοῖς ἀποκτείνασί σε προστρόπαιον αἷμα θήσεις is, I think, different,
meaning 'You will make your blood a source of pollution to your
slayers'. At *Ion* 1225, ἔν τ' ἀνακτόροις φόνον τιθεῖσαν, the verb may
retain its local sense of 'putting'; at *Or.* 1641, θανάτους ἔθηκαν may
mean 'the gods *ordained* deaths'; while *I.A.* 1417 f. μάχας ἀνδρῶν
τιθεῖσα καὶ φόνους has been explained as a variation on the common
phrase ἀγῶνα τιθέναι. There are, however, other phrases in which
τιθέναι c. accus. undoubtedly means to 'make' or 'cause', e.g.
ὀρυμαγδὸν ἔθηκεν *Od.* 9. 235 ; στάσιν ἔθηκαν *Her.* 590 ; κραυγὴν ἔθηκας *Or.*
1510. αἱματώσῃ Kirchhoff (cf. 1135) ; αἷμα δεύσεις Wecklein (cf. Soph.
Aj. 376) ; αἷμα τίσεις W. A. Moore ; αἷμ' ἀφήσεις Colman, cf. *Heraclid.*
821–2 ; ἀλλ' εὐμαθὴς εἶ ('ibis') συμβαλὼν βάκχαις μάχην; Housman. The
last, though ingenious, can hardly be right, since ὀρθῶς (sc. ἔλεξας) is
no answer to it. If any correction is needed, I should be content to
propose αἷμα θήσῃ, 'you will lay upon yourself blood-guiltiness' :
cf. Soph. *OC.* 542 ἔθου φόνον, also Eur. *Supp.* 950 κατ' ἀλλήλων
φόνους τίθεσθε, *Or.* 833 ματροκτόνον αἷμα χειρὶ θέσθαι, Aesch. *Eum.*
226 πόνον πλείω (πλέον codd.) τίθου, 'lay more trouble on yourself' ;
and for the sense of αἷμα, Eur. *Supp.* 148 αἷμα . . . φεύγων, *Or.* 514

αἷμ' ἔχων. The change is very easy, as the later spelling would be θήσει and the next word begins with σ.[1]]

839. κακοῖς θηρᾶν κακά, to ask for trouble by inflicting it, 'to seek by wrath wrath's bitter recompense' (Murray). But the words are ambiguous: Pentheus can take them as meaning 'to hunt down one social evil (maenadism) at the cost of another (blood-guiltiness)'— cf. κακοῖς ἰᾶσθαι κακά, Soph. fr. 77 P., Aesch. fr. 349.

841. The strong break in the middle of the line seems to give weight to it and thus enhance its sinister effect. Cf. 922, 975, and Jebb on Soph. *Aj.* 855, also Denniston, *C.Q.* xxx (1936), 79.

842. An illogical but natural blend of πᾶν κρεῖσσον τοῦ τὰς βάκχας ἐγγελᾶν ἐμοί and πᾶν ἀγαπητὸν ὥστε ('provided that') τὰς βάκχας μὴ ἐγγελᾶν ἐμοί. With this line P. breaks off the discussion; with the next he turns towards the door: hence the asyndeton and the breach of stichomythia. [To avoid the latter, Hermann gave 843 to the Stranger and 844 to Pentheus. But it is P., not the Stranger, who has to take the decision; and 844, an expression of confident indifference, must be spoken by the Stranger. For breach of sticho-mythia where the speaker changes the subject or makes a gesture cf. *infra* 1269, *Her.* 1404, Soph. *Aj.* 541.]

843. ἐλθόντ', nom. dual. If the text is sound, the wavering construc-tion reflects P.'s wavering state of mind. He begins as if he meant to continue 'We will concert our arrangements together'; but he remembers his dignity and says instead 'I shall decide as may seem best'. The transition is felt to be possible because the 'I' is part of the 'we'. Cf. the combination of sing. ptcp. and plur. verb in Aesch. *Eum.* 141 ἀνίστω κἀπολακτίσασ' ὕπνον | ἰδώμεθα and Soph. *Phil.* 645 χωρῶμεν, ἔνδοθεν λαβὼν | ὅτου σε χρεία . . . ἔχει. [But ἐλθών γ' is technically an easy correction (Γ being frequently mistaken for Τ, and Ο confused with Ω) and may be right.[2]]

844. 'As you please: whatever you decide, I am at hand and ready.' ἔξεστι seems to be a formula of acquiescence rather than permission:

---

[1] Mr. Alan Ker points out to me that the transmitted text can also be interpreted as αἷμαθ' ἥσεις. Since ἱέναι is used of pouring liquids or shedding tears, this is perhaps not impossible Greek for 'you will shed blood' (Eur. often has αἵματα in this sense); but like αἷμα θήσεις it seems to lack any close parallel.

[2] Jackson (*Marg. Scaen.* 59), improving on Kirchhoff's proposal of a lacuna after 842, has now suggested that Euripides wrote something like

> Δι.   ἐλθόντ' ἐς οἴκους ⟨οἶα χρὴ στειλώμεθα⟩.
> Πε.   ⟨ἐπίσχες· αὐτὸς⟩ ἂν δοκῇ βουλεύσομαι.

This, though bold, has the attraction of simultaneously restoring stichomythia and normal syntax.

cf. *Hel.* 442, where it *must* have this sense, and Lat. 'licet' (Plaut. *Miles* 536). τό γ' ἐμόν, my course of action, my response to the situation. The words can be taken as an offer of collaboration, but they carry a veiled threat.

845–6. P. pretends to himself that his decision is postponed. But the Stranger knows that virtually it is already taken. στείχοιμ' ἄν, sc. ἐς οἴκους: 'I think I will go in.' He leaves the stage at 846.

847–8. ἐς βόλον: the βόλος (from βάλλω) was a casting-net for fish. For the metaphor cf. *Rhes.* 730 ἐς βόλον τις ἔρχεται, Eur. *Alexandros* fr. 43. 43 Snell (= Page, *Greek Lit. Pap.* 9. 37) εἰς βόλον γὰρ ἂν πέσοι, and Hdt. 1. 62. 4. βάκχας: the simple accus. of the goal of motion is often extended from places to groups of persons *as occupying places*. Cf. 1354 βαρβάρους ἀφίξομαι, Aesch. *PV.* 723 Ἀμαζόνων στρατὸν ἥξεις, Eur. *Her.* 409, *El.* 917, 1281. So here βάκχας represents 'Cithaeron', as οὗ shows. [The conjecture βάκχας (taken with δώσει δίκην) is thus needless. With βαίνω Eur. even uses this accus. of a single person, *Hipp.* 1371 ὀδύνα μ' ὀδύνα βαίνει, *Andr.* 287 ἔβαν δὲ Πριαμίδαν: cf. Ar. *Nub.* 30 τί χρέος ἔβα με; (a quotation from, or parody of, tragedy).—ἥξει κτλ. cannot as it stands be the opening line of the Stranger's speech, since he must turn to the Chorus *before* he speaks of P. in the third person. Murray's suggestion, ἥξεις . . . δώσεις (addressed *sotto voce* to P.'s back), would obviate the necessity of transposition. But the direct transition from 848 γυναῖκες . . . to 849 Διόνυσε . . . is a little abrupt. The same objection arises if 847 is deleted as an explanatory amplification added by someone on the model of *Her.* 740 ἦλθες χρόνῳ μὲν οὐ δίκην δώσεις θανών.]

849. σὸν ἔργον, an Attic colloqualism, frequent in Ar. and Eur., either (*a*) with dependent infinitive, 'it is yours to . . .' (so already Aesch. *PV.* 635); or (*b*) as a complete sentence, followed by a prayer or command, 'action rests with you'. οὐ γὰρ εἶ πρόσω, the same irony as in 500.

850–3. ἐλαφρὰν λύσσαν: a madness of inconstancy, 'a dizzy fantasy', rather than (Paley, Wilamowitz) 'a light attack of madness'. So Phocylides fr. 9 speaks of people who appear σαόφρονες but are really ἐλαφρόνοοι, and Philemon fr. 171 Kock calls the female sex ἐλαφρόν, 'inconstant'; cf. also Hesych. ἐλαφρία· μωρία. [οὐ μὴ θελήσῃ: this is the accepted reading, though P has θελήσει. But the old rule which limited οὐ μή with the future indic. to prohibitions cannot be sustained (see Ellendt, *Lex. Sophocleum* s.v. οὐ 7, Jebb on *OC.* 177, and Goodwin, *M. and T.*, Appendix II). And it is hardly logical to 'correct' the future here while letting it stand, as modern edd. do, at Soph. *El.* 1052, *Phil.* 611, *OC.* 177, Eur. *Phoen.* 1590, Ar. *Ran.* 508—all passages dating, like this one, from the last two decades of the fifth century.] ἔξω ἐλαύνων, an image from the race-course, more elaborately developed by Aesch., *Cho.* 1022, where Orestes, feeling himself lose control of his mind, says ὥσπερ ξὺν

ἵπποις ἡνιοστροφῶ δρόμου | ἐξωτέρω· φέρουσι γὰρ νικώμενον | φρένες
δύσαρκτοι: cf. also *PV*. 883.

854-5. The Stranger's insistence on dressing up P. as a woman has to
be motived, since the King was quite willing to go ἐμφανῶς (818).
But the motive assigned conflicts with the Stranger's promise at
841, and we do not learn that the King was in fact recognized and
mocked by the citizens. We may guess that the disguise was a
traditional feature of the story which Eur. had to accept and
account for (Murray). [*In origin* it is probably a reflection of ritual
(Bather, *J.H.S.* xiv (1894), 249 ff.). Putting on the dress of the
opposite sex is thought in many societies to be a strong magic,
and is practised with a variety of magical purposes (Frazer, *Golden
Bough*, IV. ii. 253 ff.; A. E. Crawley, *Dress, Drink and Drums*,
138 ff.). Its occurrence in Dionysiac ritual is attested by Lucian,
who says that the philosopher Demetrius μόνος τῶν ἄλλων γυναικεῖα
οὐκ ἐνεδύσατο ἐν τοῖς Διονυσίοις (*Cal*. 16); by Philostratus, *Im*. I. 2
συγχωρεῖ ὁ κῶμος . . . ἀνδρὶ θῆλυν ἐνδῦναι στολήν; and by Aristides,
41. 9 Keil, οὐ τοὺς ἄνδρας θηλύνειν μᾶλλον ἢ τὰς γυναῖκας εἰς ἀνδρῶν
τάξιν καθιστάναι Διονυσιακόν. The specific ritual reason for the disguising of Pentheus is perhaps that the victim of the womanish
god (453-9 n.) must wear the god's livery (as the calf sacrificed to
Dion. on Tenedos must wear the Dionysiac buskin, Aelian, *Nat.
Anim.* 12. 34). The victim, like the priest, is often invested with the
dress of the god, because (in Crawley's words) the sacred vestment
is 'a material link between his person and the supernatural'. This
would explain why Pentheus suffers a change of personality when
he puts on the holy dress, and why with the tearing off of the μίτρα
at 1115 his madness seems to vanish.]

856. ἐκ, 'after' (see L.S. s.v. II. 2). [The former ἀπειλαί are mentioned
as a contrast to the coming γέλως: hence Wecklein's transposition
of this line to follow immediately on 854.]

859-61. We expect the Stranger to say 'He shall learn what Dion. is'
(cf. 39 f.). Hence Elmsley and Hermann took **ὅς πέφυκεν** as equivalent
to τίς πέφυκεν or οἷος πέφυκεν (like Soph. *Aj*. 1259 μαθὼν ὅς εἶ φύσιν,
OT. 1068 μήποτε γνοίης ὅς εἶ). But the following words then come in
awkwardly, as an explanation of ὅς. [I incline to read ὡς πέφυκεν,
an easy change proposed long ago by Dobree (cf. W. Jaeger, *Hermes*,
lxiv [1929], 33).] **ἀνθρώποισι** must be taken with both superlatives.[1]
For its unusual position (which has led to unconvincing attempts at
emendation) Elmsley compared fr. 317 οὐ γὰρ ἡδονή, | γυναικὶ δ' (so
Elmsley for τ') ἐχθρὸν χρῆμα πρεσβύτης ἀνήρ, where γυναικί must be

----

[1] I cannot agree with Maguire and others that there is an intelligible
antithesis between ἐν τέλει, 'in his capacity as a god', and ἀνθρώποισι,
'in his relation to men'.

supplied with ἡδονή. Cf. also Soph. *El.* 929 ἡδὺς (sc. μητρί) οὐδὲ μητρὶ δυσχερής, and other passages quoted by Wilamowitz on *Her.* 237.[1] ἐν τέλει: meaning doubtful. (i) Hermann, &c., translate 'in the end'. But (a) this rendering receives only doubtful support from Soph. *OT.* 198 τέλει γάρ, εἴ τι νὺξ ἀφῇ, | τοῦτ' ἐπ' ἆμαρ ἔρχεται (where Hermann's own conjecture τελεῖν is easy and probable). The normal Greek for 'in the end' is τέλος or εἰς τέλος, though it is true that ἐν τελευτᾷ is so used by Pindar, *Ol.* 7. 26, *Pyth.* 1. 35. (b) It is not sense to say that Dion. 'is by nature (πέφυκεν) a god in the end': what he is by nature he is from the beginning. But to take ἐν τέλει with γνώσεται (as Hermann did) puts a quite impossible strain on the word-order. (ii) 'Omnino' (Elmsley), 'in fulness God' (Murray)— i.e. not a mere δαίμων or demigod. This likewise lacks any close parallel, though we may compare the adj. ἐντελής, 'complete', 'perfect', and Plato, *Epin.* 985 A θεὸν . . . τὸν τέλος ἔχοντα τῆς θείας μοίρας, 'a god who has full divine status'. (iii) Closely with δεινότατος, 'most terrible in the performance of his office' (Portus): cf. Aesch. *Ag.* 1202 μάντις μ' Ἀπόλλων τῷδ' ἐπέστησεν τέλει, &c. But Dionysus' *normal* office was not δεινόν, and we should expect τέλει to have the article. (iv) 'A god with a god's authority' (Brodeau): cf. οἱ ἐν τέλει, 'the authorities'. Perhaps likeliest, since τέλος is regularly used of divine authority: Hes. *Op. et Di.* 669 ἐν τοῖς γὰρ τέλος ἐστὶν ὁμῶς ἀγαθῶν τε κακῶν τε: Semon. Amorg. 1. 1 τέλος μὲν Ζεὺς ἔχει βαρύκτυπος | πάντων ὅσ' ἔστι: Eur. *Or.* 1545 τέλος ἔχει δαίμων βροτοῖς, τέλος ὅπᾳ θέλῃ and fr. dub. 1110 Ζεὺς ἐν θεοῖσι μάντις ἀψευδέστατος | καὶ τέλος αὐτὸς ἔχει. [Of the many emendations the simplest and best is ἐντελής (H. Hirzel). ἐν τέλει θεῶν, 'in the company of heaven' (Reiske, Headlam), is tempting but does not suit πέφυκεν very well; we expect ἠρίθμηται or the like.[2] I should be reluctant to delete 861 with Hirzel. Though P. is to learn only the terrible aspect of D., not the gentle, both are mentioned in order to set the theme for the song which follows. The man by his action has transformed the god's blessing into a curse.]

Stasimon 3 (862–911)

The Chorus express in passionate song the feelings evoked in

---

[1] Campbell objected (*C.Q.* xlix [1956], 60) that such ἀπὸ κοινοῦ constructions are not found where the two clauses concerned are antithetically opposed, as are δεινότατος and ἠπιώτατος. But cf. *Her.* 328–9 σὺ μὲν λέγ' ἡμᾶς οἷς πεπύργωσαι λόγοις, | ἐγὼ δὲ δράσω σ' ἀντὶ τῶν λόγων κακῶς, where Wilamowitz was surely right in taking κακῶς with both verbs.

[2] ἐν θεοῖς θεός (D. S. Robertson, *Proc. Camb. Philol. Soc.* 1945) avoids this objection, but has little transcriptional probability.

them by the new turn of events. Hope has been restored, and their first thought (862–76) is that they may one day know again the freedom and ecstasy of the παννυχίς. Their next, and equally natural, thought is that the tables are about to be turned on the aggressor: that will be καλόν and therefore φίλον (refrain, 877–81 = 897–901). The antistrophe, like the antistrophes of stasimon 1, 'universalizes' the situation, bringing it under the general law that 'God is not mocked' (882–90) and drawing a highly generalized moral —not that man must worship the personal god Dionysus, but that he must respect 'the rules' and 'the unknown daemonic' (890–6). To those who do so, the epode promises in words of liturgical gravity that inward happiness (εὐδαιμονία) which depends not on material prosperity (ὄλβος) but on the daily indwelling presence of a good daemon.

The song, one of the loveliest in Euripides, is entirely congruous with the Chorus's other utterances and with the dramatic situa-tion. The 'disharmony' which some modern critics find between the refrain, with its exaltation of revenge, and the quietism of the epode is rooted in the dual nature of Dion. as destroyer and libera-tor, master of the lightning and spirit of peace. The keynote of the whole is given in the words which immediately precede it—'a god most dangerous to man, yet most gentle to him'. There is no difficulty here. But if we go on to ask how far the poet himself sympathized, or expected his audience to sympathize, with the sentiments of the Chorus, we are on difficult and disputed ground. See below, on 877–81, 890–2, 910–11.

Metre. The dominant rhythm is throughout glyconic (see metrical note on stasimon 1); but there are a number of variations. Besides the standard forms ⏝⏝ –⏑⏑– ⏝(–) ('second glyconic') and ⏝⏝ ⏝⏝ –⏑⏑– ('third glyconic' or 'choriambic dimeter'), occasional use is made of abbreviated forms: 863 = 883, headless pherecratean or 'reizianum'; 869 = 889, 879, headless third glyconic; 873 = 893 (a third glyconic still further curtailed?). Extended forms also appear: 902, 904, 906, hypercatalectic glyconic or 'hipponacteum'; 876 = 896, 'enoplion'. Resolved syllables in the base, 864 = 884, &c.; in the choriambus, 865; resolved ending, 910. 875 = 895 is an iambic dimeter (glyconic systems often have interspersed iambics, cf. stasimon 1); 903 apparently trochaic dimeter. On text and metre of 877, 887, 905, see separate notes below. In several places the line-division is uncertain and disputed.

The rhythms of the epode, as Wilamowitz pointed out, seem to reflect traditional cult hymns: note especially the concluding lines, 3 pher.+glyc. +pher., the same arrangement as in the 'rhythmic refrain' which runs through the cult hymn in the *Heracles* (359–63, &c.), cf. also Aesch. *Supp.* 639–42, *Ag.* 381–4.

Scheme:

Strophe

	− − − ∪ ∪ − ∪ −	glyc.²
	− − ∪ ∪ − −	reiz.
	∪ ∪ ∪ − − − ∪ ∪ −	glyc.³
865 = 885	− − ⏕ ∪ ∪ − − −	glyc.²
	− − − ∪ ∪ − − −	glyc.²
	− ⏑̱ − ∪ ∪ − ⏑̱ −	glyc.²
	− ⏑̱ − ∪ ∪ − ∪ −	glyc.²
	· − − ⏑̱ − ∪ ∪ −	glyc.³
870 = 890	− − − ∪ ∪ − ∪ −	glyc.²
	− − − ∪ ∪ − ∪ −	glyc.²
	− − − ⏑̱ − ∪ ∪ −	glyc.³
	− − − ∪ ∪ − ∪ −	glyc.²
	− − − ∪ ∪ −	' Maecenas atavis'
	∪ ∪ ∪ ∪ ∪ ∪ − ∪ ∪ −	glyc.³
875 = 895	∪ − ∪ − ∪ − ∪ ∪ ∪	2 iamb.
	∪ − ∪ − ∪ ∪ − −	enoplion

Refrain

	∪ ∪ ∪ ∪ − ∪ ∪ − − −	glyc.² (corrupt?)
	∪ ∪ ∪ − ∪ ∪ − ∪ −	glyc.²
	· − − ∪ − ∪ ∪ −	glyc.³
880 = 900	− − − − − ∪ ∪ −	glyc.³
	∪ ∪ ∪ − ∪ ∪ − −	pher.²

Epode

	− − − ∪ ∪ − ∪ − −	hipp.
	∪ ∪ ∪ − ∪ ∪ ∪ ∪ ∪ ∪ ∪	2 tr.
	− − − ∪ ∪ − ∪ − −	hipp.
905	∪ ∪ ∪ ∪ ∪ − ∪ ∪ ∪ ∪ ∪ ∪	2 tr.
	− − − ∪ ∪ − ∪ − −	hipp.
	− ∪ − ∪ ∪ − ∪ −	glyc.²
	− ∪ − ∪ ∪ − −	pher.²
	∪ − − ∪ ∪ − −	pher.²
	∪ − − ∪ ∪ − −	pher.²
910	∪ ∪ ∪ − ∪ ∪ − ∪ ∪ ∪	glyc.²
	− − − ∪ ∪ − −	pher.²

862–5. 'Will the time come when barefoot I tread the night-long dances, in ecstasy flinging back my head in the clean dewy air?' A question mark should be introduced after ῥίπτουσα or after 872 κυνῶν: ἆρα must be interrogative, since the inferential ἄρα seems never to be placed first in tragedy (Denniston, *Particles,* 48). We

need not give it the force of ἆρ' οὐ: the Chorus hope, but do not
know, that the new turn of events will lead to the removal of the
ban on Bacchism.   παννυχίοις χοροῖς: cf. 485-6 n., and Plut. *de
curios.* 3, 517 A βακχεῖα καὶ χοροὺς καὶ παννυχίδας. On λευκὸν πόδα see
664-7 n.; on δέραν used where we say 'head', 241 n. (the throwing
back of the head exposes the throat to the air).   αἰθέρα suggests
the pure air of the mountain peaks (cf. 150, 1073, *Alc.* 594, *Med.* 830,
A. B. Cook, *Zeus,* i. 101, Wilamowitz, *Glaube d. Hellenen,* i. 138).—
The back-flung or wildly tossing head is a constant trait of bacchanals of either sex both in vase-paintings (Lawler, op. cit. 101,
reports 28 examples) and in literature: cf. 150, 185, 241, 930, Ar.
Lys. 1312 ταὶ δὲ κόμαι σείονθ' ᾇπερ Βακχᾶν, Pind. fr. 61. 10, Dionysius,
de avibus 1. 23, p. 112 Lehrs, (αἱ ἴυγγες) συνεχῶς τοὺς τραχήλους
κινοῦσιν, ὡς οἱ τῶν ἀνδρῶν ἀναδεχόμενοι καὶ θηλυδριῶν βακχεύειν ἐπὶ
τῆς τελετῆς τῆς Ῥέας εἰώθασιν, Ovid, *Met.* 3. 725 'ululavit Agave |
collaque iactavit movitque per aera crinem', Catull. 63. 23, Tac.
Ann. 11. 31, &c. This characteristic carriage of the head is also
associated with ecstatic states in modern times (I have quoted
some examples in *The Greeks and the Irrational,* 273f.) [Musgrave's
αἰθέρ' ἐς, to obtain syllabic correspondence, is unnecessary: for a
resolved choriambus in glyconics answering to an unresolved cf.
El. 435 = 445, 458 = 470, &c.]

866-70. 'Like a fawn at play in the green joy of a meadow when it has
escaped the frightening hunt, clear of the ring of watchers, leaping
the woven nets.' 'Green joy', a colour-word applied to an abstract
noun, is bold for a Greek poet, though not so bold as Marvell's
'Annihilating all that's made To a green thought in a green shade'.
χλ. λείμ. ἡδ. has perhaps the effect of a compound, 'green-meadow-
joy' (cf. Wilam. on *Her.* 468). For the function of the watchers cf.
the instruction to hunters, [Xen.] *Cyn.* 6. 12, συνιστάναι τὰς ἄρκυς καὶ
τὰ δίκτυα· μετὰ δὲ τοῦτο τὸν μὲν ἀρκυωρὸν εἶναι ἐν φυλακῇ. . . . [Dr. Maas
would keep P's θήραμ', here and at 1171. It is a late-Euripidean
word, otherwise rare. φοβεράν here may be due to preceding ἄν;
while at 1171 'θήραν is a corruption originating in one branch of the
transmission of Plut. *Crass.* 33' (cf. Lindskog's *app. crit.*).]

871-2. 'And the shouting huntsman braces the speed of his hounds.'
This introduces a new stage of the story, with the huntsman's
reactions on finding that the fawn has jumped clear; what follows
describes her final escape, and brings us back to the moment when
she ἐμπαίζει λείμακος ἡδοναῖς ('ring form', ἡδομένα echoing ἡδοναῖς).
[The narrative structure would be a little clearer if we read συντείνει
(Bruhn) and began the next line μόχθοις δ' (Matthiae). δρόμημα P,
but δράμημα seems to be the correct spelling, standing to ἔδραμον
as πέσημα to ἔπεσον: see Page on *Med.* 1180, where δραμήμασιν is
now confirmed by *P. Oxy.* 2337.]

873–6. 'With tenseness of effort, with gusts of swift racing, she gallops the water-meadow, rejoicing in the places empty of men and in the green life that springs under the shadowy hair of the forest.' The *Hymn to Demeter* had compared girls running eagerly on an errand to 'deer or calves galloping a meadow in the spring season' (174 f.); Anacreon had likened a maid's shyness to the timidity of a baby fawn astray in the forest (fr. 51, cf. Hor. *Odes* 1. 23); Bacchylides had likened a young girl making for the country on a holiday to a νεβρὸς ἀπενθής (12 [13]. 87); and the Chorus of Euripides' *Electra* had described themselves in a moment of joy as 'leaping sky-high in gaiety, like a fawn' (860). But though he is elaborating a traditional image, the poet has here enriched it with new tones: there is a hint of something very rare in Greek poetry, the romantic vision of nature not *sub specie humanitatis* but as a world apart from man, having a secret life of its own. This new feeling emerges elsewhere in the *Bacchae* (cf. esp. 726–7, 1084–5), and it is reasonable to associate it with the old poet's escape from the dusty thought-laden air of Athens to the untouched solitudes of northern Greece.

[The metaphorical use of ἀέλλαις need not be doubted, in view of *Hel.* 1498 ἄστρων ὑπ' ἀέλλαισιν, the adjs. ἀελλόπος, ἀελλοδρόμος applied to racehorses, and Homer's comparison of charging warriors to an ἀέλλα, *Il.* 11. 297, 13. 795. The story is slightly telescoped for brevity. I suppose μόχθοις to describe the painful effort of the fawn's initial dash for freedom, ὠκυδρόμοις ἀέλλαις the subsequent spurts which pass from painfulness to pleasure as she outpaces the hunt. Hermann's widely accepted suggestion ἀελλάς (nom.) provides μόχθοις with an epithet at the cost of eliminating this bridge between the μόχθοι and the ἡδονή. σκιαροκόμοιο for σκιαροκόμου is the neatest way of restoring correspondence with 896. This epic gen., which occurs about a dozen times in Euripidean lyrics (thrice in Aesch., once in Soph., fr. 142), was exposed to corruption by its rarity; it has been rightly restored also at *Rhes.* 909. Alternatively, we may insert ἐν (Aldine) or ὑπ' (Wilamowitz); but to my mind either preposition injures the poetry.]

877–81. 'What is wisdom?' The Chorus do not stay for an answer, but seek one indirectly by asking a second and easier question. 'Or what god-given right is more honourable in the sight of men than to keep the hand of mastery over the head of a foe? "Honour is precious": that is always true.' I apprehend that they reason thus. To punish an enemy is by general consent a καλὸν γέρας, a privilege to which one is honourably entitled; but men and gods are rightly jealous of their honour (ὅτι καλὸν φίλον): therefore we must approve the wisdom of Dion. in entrapping Pentheus. So by quoting two traditional maxims they argue themselves, not without a hint of uneasiness (for *qui s'excuse, s'accuse*), into the position which we shall find them attempting to sustain, against their natural feelings, in the latter part of the play. It is certainly not the poet's own position, as his revenge-plays sufficiently prove. A significantly different view of τὸ σοφόν and τὸ καλόν is offered by the Messenger, 1150-2. For ἐν βροτοῖς, 'in the judgement of men', 'before the tribunal of humanity', cf. *Hipp.* 1320 σὺ δ᾽ ἔν τ᾽ ἐκείνῳ κἄν ἐμοὶ φαίνῃ κακός, Soph. *OT.* 677 ἐν . . . τοῖσδ᾽ ἴσος ('just in their sight') with Jebb ad loc.—That we should do good to our friends, harm to our enemies, was an opinion accepted practically without question down to Eur.'s time, even by such as Solon (13. 5): see Adam on Plato, *Rep.* 331 E, Page on *Med.* 809-10. So Alcmene says in the *Heraclid.* (881) παρ᾽ ἡμῖν μὲν γὰρ οὐ σοφὸν τόδε, | ἐχθροὺς λαβόντα μὴ ἀποτείσασθαι δίκην, and the Old Servant in the *Ion* (1046) ὅταν δὲ πολεμίους δρᾶσαι κακῶς | θέλῃ τις, οὐδεὶς ἐμποδὼν κεῖται νόμος (and so Ion himself, 1328, 1334). κατέχειν seems to be merely a stronger ἔχειν (suggesting the firmness of the control), as in φυλακὰν κατέχουσα (*Tro.* 194). ὅ τι καλὸν φίλον was an old proverb (Plato, *Lysis* 216 C). Long ago at the marriage feast of Cadmus the Muses had sung ὅττι καλόν, φίλον ἐστί· τὸ δ᾽ οὐ καλὸν οὐ φίλον ἐστιν (Theogn. 15 ff., probably from Hesiod). To those who remembered that tradition (which seems to be recalled also at *Phoen.* 814, cf. 822) there would be a peculiar irony in this new application of the saying—to justify the murder of Cadmus' grandson (cf. Kranz, *Stasimon*, 235). τὸ καλόν was in fact an ambiguous and elusive notion (διολισθαίνει καὶ διαδύεται ἡμᾶς, Plato, l.c.). The proverb was explained in antiquity as applicable 'to those who pursue their own advantage' (schol. Plato, l.c. = Apostolius 16. 87); and it is evidently in this egoistic sense that the Chorus use it here.

[Divergent interpretations. (1) Several scholars understand τί τὸ σοφόν; in a contemptuous sense (cf. 203, 395)—'what is cleverness in comparison with revenge?' But I can see little point in this question; and such an interpretation is ruled out if I am right in regarding 1150-2 as an unconscious answer to the Chorus's questioning. (2) On the assumption that an exaltation of revenge is inappropriate here, it has been suggested that κατέχειν means 'to withhold', to have the whip hand and *not* use it. But (*a*) this is inconsistent with 991 ff.; (*b*) while κατέχειν χεῖρα might by itself mean 'restrain the hand', κατέχειν χεῖρα κρείσσω ὑπὲρ κορυφᾶς τῶν ἐχθρῶν can hardly mean anything but 'keep your hand superior'— the opposite of being ὑποχείριος (cf. Soph. *El.* 1090 ζώης μοι καθύπερθεν | χερὶ πλούτῳ τε τῶν ἐχθρῶν ὅσον | νῦν ὑπόχειρ ναίεις). (3) W. E. Blake (*Mnemosyne*, 1933, 361 ff.) would put a question mark after βροτοῖς and write ἢ χεῖρ᾽ . . . κατέχειν; as a third question: 'What is wisdom? or what is the more beautiful gift of the gods to men (i.e. more beautiful than wisdom)? is it keeping a strong

hand above your enemy's head (as Pentheus imagines)? (No: for)
"What is (really) beautiful is *permanently* precious" (and Pentheus'
triumph is not permanent).' This is ingenious. But it reads too
much into the last line, particularly into ἀεί, and it glaringly
contradicts 991 ff.—I agree with Blake on one point: the Greek for
'What right is more honourable than . . .?' is not τί γέρας τὸ κάλλιον
ἤ . . .; but τί γέρας κάλλιον ἤ . . .; (cf. e.g. *Or.* 832 τίς ἔλεος μείζων κατὰ
γᾶν | ἤ . . . θέσθαι; Pind. fr. 80 τί κάλλιον . . . ἤ . . . ἀεῖσαι;). The solu-
tion, however, is not, I think, to alter ἤ but to delete the article
before κάλλιον. As Paley saw, this improves the metre as well as the
Greek. From being a metrical oddity, seemingly a second glyconic
with proceleusmatic base (‿‿ ‿‿), the line then becomes a first
glyconic with the first syllable of the choriambus resolved, ‿‿ ‿ ‿ –
‿ – – – (or an ordinary iambic dimeter like 875, if we adopt the epic
and lyric prosody κάλλιον).]

882–7. For the traditional thought that divine justice comes late but
surely cf. Hom. *Il.* 4. 160 f., Solon 13. 25 ff., Eur. *Ion* 1615, frs. 223,
800, Soph. *OC.* 1536, &c.; for 883, Pindar, *Nem.* 10. 54 καὶ μὰν θεῶν
πιστὸν γένος.   τοὺς ἀγνωμοσύναν τιμῶντας, 'them that worship
the Ruthless Will' (Murray). The ἀγνώμων is the man who is
morally insensitive and without pity—the opposite of the συγ-
γνώμων who can put himself in another's place because he θνητὰ
φρονεῖ (cf. Soph. *Tr.* 473 θνητήν, φρονοῦσαν θνητὰ κοὐκ ἀγνώμονα).
The Chorus are thinking of Pentheus; the audience may think also
of such 'realists' as Cleon (cf. Thuc. 3. 40. 1), Callicles, Thrasymachus.
See 399–401 n., and Murray, *Eur. and his Age*, 194 ff.   σὺν μαινομένᾳ
δόξᾳ: for the preposition, where we might expect a simple dat., cf.
Aesch. *Supp.* 186 τεθηγμένος ὠμῇ ξὺν ὀργῇ, Soph. *OT.* 17 σὺν γήρᾳ
βαρεῖς. [τι (883) is inserted *metri gratia.* I see no reason to alter
αὔξοντας (cf. 209 αὔξεσθαι θέλει): τὰ θεῶν virtually = θεούς. Nor
need we doubt the correspondence of the 'impure' glyconic ending
δόξᾳ (887) to the 'pure' ending -δοναῖς (867): cf. *Hipp.* 741 = 751,
El. 144 = 162, 700 = 714 (Denniston, Metrical Appendix, p. 215),
Soph. *Phil.* 1128 = 1151.]

888–90. 'They have crafty ways to cover the unhastening stride of time
as they track the man without religion.' It seems easier to suppose
with Murray that κρυπτεύουσι is equivalent here to κρύπτουσι—cf.
the transitive use of θηρεύειν = θηρᾶν, of χορεύειν (21), &c.—than
to make πόδα an accus. of temporal extension as most commentators
do. Time is the long-distance runner (δολιχός, Plato, *Anth. Pal.*
9. 51) who always overtakes in the end. The notion of the deliberately stealthy approach of the gods to their victims is again traditional, though suggested here by the foregoing scene: cf. esp. Aesch.
Pers. 107 ff. and Eur. fr. 979 ἡ Δίκη . . . σῖγα καὶ βραδεῖ ποδὶ | στείχουσα
μάρψει τοὺς κακούς, ὅταν τύχῃ. Eur. had given time feet in the

Alexandros (fr. 42 καὶ χρόνου προῦβαινε πούς), and was, rather surprisingly, ridiculed for it in the *Frogs* (97 ff.) where it is called 'risky'.
It is true that the Greek imagination personified time less vividly
than the medieval; still, Aeschylus had made him cross a threshold
(*Cho.* 965), Simonides had given him teeth (fr. 176), and Sophocles
made him beget children (*OC.* 618).

890–2. τῶν νόμων : the πάτριοι παραδοχαί of 201. As in the earlier passage,
we may suspect a contemporary reference. In Eur.'s time the
validity of such traditional rules was challenged by men who set
'nature' (φύσις) in their place as a criterion of conduct : it was 'a
period which made the reason of the individual judge of all things
human and divine' (Nilsson, *Mélanges Fr. Cumont*, 365). Those who
regard Eur. as a purely destructive thinker overlook the many
passages where the ultimate validity of νόμος and the danger of
intellectual arrogance are dwelt upon by Choruses or by sympathetic
characters, e.g. *Hecuba* 799 ἀλλ' οἱ θεοὶ σθένουσι χὼ κείνων κρατῶν |
Νόμος (Hecuba) ; *Supp.* 216 ff. ἀλλ' ἡ φρόνησις τοῦ θεοῦ μεῖζον σθένειν |
ζητεῖ, τὸ γαῦρον δ' ἐν φρεσὶν κεκτημένοι | δοκοῦμεν εἶναι δαιμόνων
σοφώτεροι (Theseus) ; *Her.* 757 ff., 778 ff. νόμον παρέμενος, ἀνομίᾳ
χάριν διδοὺς | ἔθραυσεν ὄλ|βου κελαινὸν ἅρμα ; *IA.* 1089 ff. Cf. Stier,
'Nomos Basileus', *Philologus*, lxxxiii (1928), 251.

893–4. Cf. fr. trag. adesp. 350 οὐδεὶς κάματος εὐσεβεῖν θεούς.   ὅ τι ποτ'
ἄρα τὸ δαιμόνιον defines τόδε. The indeterminate formulation is an
expression of religious humility in face of the unknowable : cf. Aesch.
Ag. 160 Ζεύς, ὅστις ποτ' ἐστίν, Dem. *Meid.* 126 τὸ τῆς ὁσίας ὁτιδήποτ'
ἐστίν, τὸ σεμνὸν καὶ τὸ δαιμόνιον, Eur. *Hipp.* 191 ὅ τι τοῦ ζῆν φίλτερον
ἄλλο, perhaps *Tr.* 885 f. ὅστις ποτ' εἶ σύ, δυστόπαστος εἰδέναι, | Ζεύς,
εἴτ' ἀνάγκη φύσεος εἴτε νοῦς βροτῶν ('a law behind nature or a moral
insight in man'?). *Her.* 1263 and *Or.* 418 are different in tone, sceptical
and bitter.

895–6. These words admit of several grammatical constructions. Sandys,
taking the first τε as coupling τὸ νόμιμον πεφυκός τε with τὸ δαιμόνιον,
and the second as coupling φύσει πεφυκός with νόμιμον ἀεί, translated
'It costs but little to hold that *that* has (sovereign) power, whate'er
it be that is more than mortal, and in the long ages is upheld by
law and grounded in nature'. So also Mr. Lucas. But the Chorus
can scarcely take thus for granted the identity of two things
which Eur.'s contemporaries habitually contrasted, τὸ νόμιμον and
τὸ φύσει,[1] nor would they naturally equate either of these with τὸ
δαιμόνιον. It seems more likely that they *assert* the identity of τὸ

---

[1] Cf. F. Heinimann, *Nomos und Physis* (1945), 166 f., who, while
apparently accepting Sandys' view of the construction, rightly speaks
of 'the consciously paradoxical union of two predicates which are elsewhere sharply opposed'; and M. Gigante, *Dioniso* xviii (1955), 128 f.

νόμιμον and τὸ φύσει (cf. Bruhn, *Einl.* 23, where the construction is, I think, rightly explained though the implications of the passage are misunderstood). Translate 'And to consider what has been accepted through long ages (to be) an eternal truth and grounded in nature'. ἀεί has more force on this view: it is antithetic to the phrase ἐν χρόνῳ μακρῷ, instead of being a rather weak addition to it. If this is right, the Chorus anticipate in principle Plato's solution of the νόμος–φύσις antinomy, viz. that when the two terms are properly understood νόμος is seen to be founded upon φύσις (*Laws* 890 D δεῖ . . . νόμῳ αὐτῷ βοηθῆσαι καὶ τέχνῃ, ὡς ἐστὸν φύσει, ἢ φύσεως οὐχ ἧττον). Similarly the late-fifth-century writer known as Anonymus Iamblichi argues τόν τε νόμον καὶ τὸ δίκαιον ἐμβασιλεύειν τοῖς ἀνθρώποις καὶ οὐδαμῇ μεταστῆναι ἂν αὐτά· φύσει γὰρ ἰσχυρὰ ἐνδεδέσθαι ταῦτα (Diels, *Vors.* ii⁷, p. 402. 28 ff.).[1]

902–11. I am indebted to Prof. Fraenkel for light on the thought-structure of these deceptively simple lines. They have the form of a 'Priamel', i.e. a series of detached statements illustrating either by analogy or by contrast a rule of wisdom in which the passage culminates; the reader is left to make the connexion (cf. Dornseiff, *Pindars Stil*, 97 ff.). Here the connexion seems to be: 'There is the happiness of peril escaped, the happiness of hardship overcome, the pride of victory in the race for material success (ὄλβος καὶ δύναμις); there is besides (ἔτι) the pleasure of hope, which may or may not be fulfilled: but it is the happiness of the *here and now* that I call truly blessed.' All other εὐδαιμονία rests on the fading memory of yesterday's achievement or the insecure prospect of to-morrow's; what the Chorus long for is the *immediate* εὐδαιμονία of present experience which Dion. gives in his παννύχιοι χοροί, as they have told us in 72 ff.[2]

902–5. The language has a liturgical ring, vaguely recalling such religious formulas as ἔφυγον κακόν, εὗρον ἄμεινον (Sabazius mysteries, Dem. *de cor.* 259). [Cf. G. Thomson, *J.H.S.* lv (1935), 21 ff., and

---

[1] At *Ion* 643 νόμος and φύσις are represented as working in unison, but both terms have a more restricted sense than in our passage: νόμος is Apollo's rule, φύσις the inborn disposition of an individual.

[2] Since the above was written several critics have pointed out that lines 902–5 recall the theme of escape which was the subject of 866–76; ἔφυγε (903) and μόχθων (904) repeat φύγῃ (868) and μόχθοις (873). But in 866–76 the fawn symbolised the Chorus themselves. Hence the joy of escape cannot be placed on a level with the proverbially insecure satisfactions of ὄλβος, δύναμις and ἐλπίς; rather we must say with Diller (*Abh. Mainz*, 1955, 464 n. 3) that it *is* the happiness of the here and now; the closing makarismos reaffirms the opening one, but in a more generalized form.

M. Tierney, ibid. lvii (1937), 11 ff. I cannot agree with Tierney that the μόχθοι of the present passage 'are evidently the same as the πόνοι, πορεῖαι, πλάναι of the *Phaedo*'. The latter refer to post-mortem experiences of the soul, which are nowhere alluded to in the *Bacchae*.[1]]

905–6. For ἐτέρᾳ ἔτερος ἔτερον cf. Plato, *Gorg.* 448 c (quoting or parodying a pupil of Gorgias) μεταλαμβάνουσιν ἄλλοι ἄλλων ἄλλως. [Most edd. follow Elmsley in reading ἔτερα on metrical grounds. But ἔτερα 'in divers respects' seems to have less meaning in this sentence than ἐτέρᾳ 'by various methods'. And the long 'anceps' of ἐτέρᾳ is metrically possible.]

907–9. ἐν ὄλβῳ: we might expect ἐς ὄλβον, but the point is that all hope is, while it lasts, a kind of happiness, and some hopes '*remain* happy to the end', i.e. reach fulfilment.   ἀπέβησαν (gnomic aorist), 'withdraw', vanish. But the text is open to serious doubt. [In my first edition I defended ἀπέβησαν 'withdraw' as the opposite of ἦλθεν ἐλπίς 'my hope has arrived' (*Her.* 771), προσῆλθεν ἐλπίς 'my expectation has come true' (*Or.* 859, cf. *I A.* 785), ἐλπὶς προσήει (Aesch. *Ag.* 817), and as analogous to πέφευγεν ἐλπίς (*Heraclid.* 452), φροῦδαι ἐλπίδες (*Ion* 866). But the real difficulty, as Jackson pointed out (*Marg. Scaen.* 237), is that ἀποβαίνειν is regularly used in the contrary sense, of things 'coming true', e.g. Thuc. 4. 39. 3 καίπερ μανιώδης οὖσα ἡ ὑπόσχεσις ἀπέβη, Arist. *Div. Somn.* 463[b]10 πολλὰ τῶν ἐνυπνίων οὐκ ἀποβαίνει. He proposed, perhaps rightly, to give the word this sense here, and read ἀνόλβως for ἐν ὄλβῳ.]

910–11. τὸ κατ' ἦμαρ, adverbial, 'day by day' (cf. *Ion* 124). On the so-called hedonism of the *Bacchae* see 424–6 n. Those who are inclined to attribute it to the influence of old age or of Macedonia or of the poet's flight from the war may be reminded that some twenty years earlier his Hecuba ended her reflections on the vanity of wealth and power (*Hec.* 620 ff.) with an even humbler thought—κεῖνος ὀλβιώτατος, ὅτῳ κατ' ἦμαρ τυγχάνει μηδὲν κακόν. Cf. also Soph. fr. 536 ζώη τις ἀνθρώπων τὸ κατ' ἦμαρ ὅπως | ἥδιστα πορσύνων, Bacchyl. fr. 11 Snell, and the passages of Eur. quoted on 424–6.

Scene 4 (912–76)

Re-enter the Stranger from the castle, followed at 917 by Pentheus dressed as a maenad, wearing wig, μίτρα, and long linen χιτών, and carrying a thyrsus. Both antagonists are now transformed into something other than human (cf. F. Wassermann, *N. Jahrb.* v [1929],

---

[1] For religion as a 'haven' cf. the words of the priest in Apuleius, 'maximis actus procellis ad portum Quietis et aram Misericordiae tandem, Luci, venisti' (*Metam.* 11. 15), and other passages quoted by Campbell Bonner, 'Desired Haven', *Harv. Theol. Rev.* xxxiv (1941), 56 ff.

280). The Stranger reveals himself as more than man: he no longer
tempts, but commands; his tones are those which Athena uses in
the *Ajax* (71 ff.) when she summons the mad hero to be mocked.
And what follows him on to the stage is less than man: it is a
giggling, leering creature, more helpless than a child, nastier than
an idiot, yet a creature filled with the Dionysiac sense of power
(945–6 n.) and capable of perceiving the god in his true shape
(920–2 n.), because the god has entered into his victim. The scene
between these two is as gruesome as anything in literature, and its
gruesomeness is enhanced by a bizarre and terrible humour. The
situation of scene 2 is now reversed: the stage business with Pentheus' costume (925–44) is the counterpart of the stage business
with the Stranger's costume at 493–7; for the outrage then done to
his person the Stranger now takes a fantastic revenge on the pre-
text of playing the valet (θεραπεύειν 932).[1] Such a situation could
easily be exploited as pure farce: cf. the very funny scene in the
Thesmophoriazusae (213–68) where Mnesilochus is dressed up as a
woman. But here the effect of the farcical by-play is to intensify
the underlying horror which peeps out in lines like 922 and 934.
As Hermann said, the groundlings will laugh and are meant to
laugh; but for the sensitive spectator amusement is transmuted
into pity and terror.

912–14. σὲ τὸν . . .: 'the abrupt acc. calls the person's attention in a
rough and harsh way' (Jebb on Soph. *Ant.* 441, Creon to Antigone
σὲ δή, σὲ τὴν . . .). So Hermes to Prometheus, *PV*. 944 σὲ τὸν . . . τὸν
πυρὸς κλέπτην λέγω: Athena to Ajax, *Aj.* 71 οὗτος, σὲ τὸν . . . καλῶ:
Aegisthus to Electra, Soph. *El.* 1445 σέ τοι, σὲ κρίνω, ναὶ σέ, τὴν . . .
[Tyrrell wished to strike out 913, urging that it adds nothing to
the sense, spoils the symmetry (by giving the Stranger 6 lines to
Pentheus' 5), and may have been inserted by some one who objected
to leaving σέ without governing verb (for which cf. *Ant.* 441, *Hel.*
546, Ar. *Av.* 274). But when a speaker on the stage addresses an
invisible person off, the name is commonly supplied in this manner:
so Athena continues in the *Ajax* (73) Αἴαντα φωνῶ· στεῖχε δωμάτων
πάρος: cf. also *Phil.* 1261 σὺ δ', ὦ Ποίαντος παῖ, Φιλοκτήτην λέγω, |
ἔξελθε, Eur. *Heraclid.* 642 ὦ μῆτερ ἐσθλοῦ παιδός, Ἀλκμήνην λέγω, |
ἔξελθε. In the last passage, and at Aesch. *Ag.* 1035, the formula serves
to introduce a new character to the audience; it is needed no less here
to make clear the identity of the queer figure about to emerge.—For
σπεύδοντα ἀσπούδαστα cf. *IT.* 201 σπεύδει δ' ἀσπούδαστ' | ἐπὶ σοὶ δαίμων.
P's σπένδοντα is, *pace* Verrall, an example of a very common minuscule confusion: cf. 129 where both MSS. have ἐν ἄσμασι for εὐάσμασι.

---

[1] On such reversals of situation in other late Euripidean plays (*Ion,
Phoen., IA.*) see Diller, *Abh. Mainz* 1955, 470 f.

σπένδοντα ἀσπούδαστα 'would produce almost the effect of a bad pun' (Cyril Bailey, *CR*. xxv [1911], 144).]

915-16. γυναικὸς μαινάδος βάκχης: not mere pleonasm, but a climax of cumulative scorn: Pentheus is dressed as a woman, as a mad-woman, as a Dionysiac woman.   **τε:** correspensive.

917 is spoken as Pentheus enters.   **δέ,** 'well' (Denniston, *Particles*, 172).   **θυγατέρων ... μιᾷ:** this 'indefinite' use of εἶς with partitive gen. seems to occur chiefly (1) where something is predicated of one member of a group which by its nature can be true only of one, e.g. *Rhes*. 393 παῖ ... Μουσῶν μιᾶς (so also Hom. *Il.* 14. 275, Pind. *Nem.* 4. 65, Eur. *Ion* 2, *Hel.* 6); or (2) where, as here, a *definite* individual is classified as a member of a group, e.g. Soph. *El.* 1342 εἶς τῶν ἐν Ἅιδου μάνθαν' ἐνθάδ' ὢν ἀνήρ. [Elmsley and Tyrrell defended P's μορφῇ (cf. *Alc*. 1050 νέα γάρ, ὡς ἐσθῆτι καὶ κόσμῳ πρέπει). But it seems more likely that there has been a false assimilation than that Eur. wantonly juxtaposed two datives which look as if they agreed but do not.]

918-19. καὶ μήν: see 957-60 n.   **Θήβας καὶ πόλισμ' ἑπτάστομον,** like *Her.* 15 Ἀργεῖα τείχη καὶ Κυκλωπίαν πόλιν, καί linking two expressions which are virtually in apposition (Denniston, *Particles*, 291). From these lines some have leapt to the obvious inference that P. is merely drunk (Clem. Alex. *Protrept*. 12, p. 84. 2 Stählin, *Paed.* 2. 2, p. 170. 22, Verrall 108, Grube, *Drama of Eur.* 415). They are mis-taken: see next note. But 'if the result resembles that of intoxica-tion, is that strange when the power at work is that of the god of wine?' (Bailey, *CR*. xxv. 144). It is perhaps worth adding that 'seeing double' is in fact a not uncommon symptom in hysterical cases (Binswanger, *Die Hysterie*, 626). Cf. also Q. Smyrn. 12. 411 μαινομένῳ δ' ἤικτο, καὶ ἔδρακε διπλόα πάντα, of Laocoon.

920-2. 'I think you walk before me as a bull; I think your head is horned now. Were you perhaps (ποτε) an animal all the time? For certainly (οὖν) now you are changed to bull.' The dragging rhythm of the last line, due to the strong pause at the end of the third foot, suggests the King's slow bewildered utterance (cf. Jebb on Soph. *Phil*. 1369). Apparently he still sees the Stranger at his side in his wonted shape, but sees also another figure, the Stranger's exact double save for its horns, which becks him onward. This second figure is explained by his companion in the words ὁ θεὸς ὁμαρτεῖ. The vision is no drunken fancy, but a sinister epiphany of the god in his bestial incarnation, comparable with the visions of medieval satanists who saw their Master with the horns of a goat. The Chorus understand what it means, and recall it later (1159). Now at last—νῦν δέ in allusion to 502—P.'s eyes are unsealed to 'see what he should see', because now the bull-nature, the Dionysiac nature, has broken loose in his own breast. [ταῦρος ... ἡγεῖσθαι may

be intended to recall the associations of the god's cult title Καθηγεμών, if Cumont is right in suggesting that the title goes back
to the ancient conception of Dion. as the bull who leads the herd
(*A.J.A.* 1933, p. 238 n. 6).]

925-6. 'Well, how do I look? Have I not the very carriage of Ino or
my mother Agaue?' **δῆτα,** going on to the next point (Denniston,
Particles, 269). **γε,** not equivalent to 'utpote', but simply epexegetic, as often (Denniston, ibid. 138 f., *C.R.* xliii [1929], 59). [If γε
had causal force here we should expect μητρός γ' ἐμῆς οὔσης. And
P.'s presumable family resemblance to his mother is not the point:
he is pluming himself on his clever acting.]

927-9. οὐχ, sc. ἑστηκώς, which is easily supplied from ἐξέστηκε.—The
regularity of the distichomythia is broken here and at 934. Eur.
allows such breaches of symmetry especially towards the beginning
of a stichomythic passage (cf. Denniston on *El.* 651-2), perhaps in
order to soften the transition from natural dialogue to the artificial
stichomythic form. They seem to occur chiefly at places where the
actor may be expected to pause and make a gesture (A. Gross, *Die
Stichomythie,* 35): e.g. *Or.* 257 is evidently preceded by a pause in
which Orestes cowers away from the vision of the Erinyes. So here
927 may be followed by a pause in which the Stranger critically
inspects his victim's costume, and 934 by another in which he
rearranges the offending lock. Sometimes the pause is one of hesitation (1268-70 n.); sometimes it precedes a change of topic (842 n.).
[καθώρμισα, the original reading of P, is probably due to the scribe's
eye catching μεθώρμισα at the end of 931: the repetition of the
nautical metaphor would be flat.]

930-3. Cf. 862-5 n. Since 925 P. has evidently kept his head flung far
back in an exaggerated imitation of the typical maenad attitude:
hence **ὄρθου κάρα.**

934. 'There! You must play the dresser, since to you I am made over
now.' There is a sinister unconscious irony in P.'s choice of words:
to the audience **ἀνακείμεσθα** will suggest that the King is now in
some sense 'dedicated'.

935-6. 'And your girdle is slack, and the pleats of your dress hang
crooked below the ankle' (or 'at the ankle' if with Blass we alter
ὑπό to ἐπί). It was a ritual requirement that the linen χιτών of the
μύστης should be girt in such a manner as to hang in pleats: Pollux
7. 54 στολίδες δέ εἰσιν αἱ ἐξεπίτηδες ὑπὸ δεσμοῦ γινόμεναι κατὰ τὰ τέλη
τοῖς χιτῶσιν ἐπιπτυχαί. The loosening of P.'s girdle has disarranged
these pleats.

938. **τἀνθένδε,** 'on this side'. As he speaks, he looks over his shoulder
at the back of his left leg, a posture which involves bending the left
knee and raising the left heel: **παρὰ τένοντα** has thus pictorial pre-
cision, τένων being the tendon at the back of the foot which stands

out when the heel is raised. *Med.* 1166 τένοντ' ἐς ὀρθὸν ὄμμασι
σκοπουμένη describes the same typically feminine posture assumed
for the same purpose.

940. [The tribrach in the second foot is broken in the wrong place
(cf. 475 n.): hence Porson wished to write παράλογον, an adverb
which the MSS. present at *Or.* 391. But prep. and noun cohere so
closely that the break is not felt: cf. *I.A.* 1164 ἐπὶ τρι|σί, Theodectes
fr. 8. 5 (*T.G.F.* p. 804) διὰ φό|βον.]

943–4. ἐν δεξιᾷ: there was, apparently, no rule about this. Vase-paintings show the thyrsus carried in either hand, and so do literary
descriptions (right hand, Nonnus 14. 243; left, Callixenus *apud* Ath.
198 F).   **ἅμα δεξιῷ ποδί:** the thyrsus is to be lifted and brought
down (cf. 188 θύρσῳ κροτῶν γῆν) in time with the right foot. If it was
used like a walking-stick, this would be an unnatural movement,
'calculated to excite the pity or the amusement of the spectators'
(Sandys). But we do not know the movements employed in Dionysiac dancing or the part which the thyrsus played in them.   **μεθέστηκας φρενῶν:** 'the mind you had is gone.' P. will take the words as
meaning 'you have changed your mind', with reference to his refusal
to carry the thyrsus at 835–6. But they also hint that he is out of his
mind (ἀφεστάναι or ἐξεστάναι φρενῶν). 948 οἵας σε δεῖ has the same
ironic ambiguity.

945–6. Like the old men in Scene 1, P. feels himself filled with magical
strength; but with him this consciousness takes the form of megalo-
maniac delusions, like those of the mad Heracles (*Her.* 943 ff.) and
those which are in fact experienced by the insane. The god has
entered into him, but ἐπὶ κακῷ. The Stranger humours and soothes
him, and at 953 he obediently accepts the Stranger's suggestion.
[The phrase αὐτῆσιν ἐλάταις which a scholiast on the *Phoenissae*
quotes as occurring in the *Bacchae* most probably derives from an
inaccurate memory of this passage, blending αὐταῖσι βάκχαις with
ἐλάταισιν in 954.]

951–2. μὴ σύ γε, a friendly form of remonstrance, familiar and often
affectionate in tone (Jebb on *OC.* 1441); here it is tinged with
mockery. Cf. Athena's mocking words to the mad Ajax, μὴ δῆτα
τὸν δύστηνον ὧδέ γ' αἰκίσῃ (*Aj.* 111).—Pausanias 9. 3. 9 mentions a
νυμφῶν ἄντρον Κιθαιρωνίδων. But shrines of Pan and the Nymphs
were to be found everywhere in pastoral and forest country: cf.
Nilsson, *Greek Popular Religion,* 17 f.

954. [Murray's suggestion ἐλάταις δ' ἀμὸν ἐγκρύψω is designed to better
the rhythm. But lines in which the caesura follows an elision at
the end of the third foot are very common: Descroix has counted
173 instances in Eur.]

955–6. 'You shall find such hiding as a spy should find who would keep
secret watch on maenads.'   **ἥν . . . χρεών** has the same ambiguity

as 948 οἵας σε δεῖ and 964 οὓς ἐχρῆν. For the threatening effect of the threefold repetition cf. *I.A.* 1182, Clytemnestra to Agamemnon σὲ ... δεξόμεθα δέξιν ἥν σε δέξασθαι χρεών.

957–60. καὶ μήν (used here, and at 918, like 'I say' in colloquial English) calls attention to a new and delicious idea suggested by κατάσκοπον: 'Think of it! I fancy they are in the bushes now, like mating birds, hugged close in the grip of love.' 'Just so,' replies the Stranger drily: 'that explains your mission of vigilance.' Cf. 222–3 n.　ἦν σὺ μὴ ληφθῆς **πάρος**: presumably spoken 'aside'.

961–2. P. now courts the publicity which he shunned at 840.　**αὐτῶν,** sc. τῶν Θηβαίων, implied in Θηβαίας χθονός. [The transposition in the text (εἶμ' αὐτῶν P) is, I think, necessary: it produces a line with a normal type of caesura (cf. 954 n.) in place of one which is not merely caesuraless but falls into three distinct dipodies, a rhythm for which I can find no true parallel anywhere in Eur.—Nauck's πόλεως for χθονός is specious. But μέσος carries with it the notion 'public', so that διὰ μέσης χθονός implies 'by the public high road' in contrast with the ὁδοὶ ἔρημοι of 841.]

963–5. πόλεως τῆσδ' ὑπερκάμνεις: 'you bear the burden for this State'— which to P. means 'you toil on its behalf', but to the audience 'you suffer for its offences'. Perhaps a hint that P. is like the φαρμακός or scapegoat who carried the sins of the people and is put to death after being ritually mocked and pelted (cf. 1096–8 n.).　**μόνος ... μόνος:** for the emphatic repetition at the end of the line and sentence of the word which stands first cf. *Hipp.* 327 κάκ', ὦ τάλαινα, σοὶ τάδ', εἰ πεύσῃ, κακά, *Alc.* 722, *Rhes.* 579.　[**ἐχρῆν** should not be altered to σὲ χρή: the imperfect implies that what is coming to P. has been owed him for some time. On the form see 26 n.　**πομπὸς δ' εἶμι** (*ibo*), like Soph. *OC.* 70 ἆρ' ἄν τις ... πομπὸς ... μόλοι; Murray suppresses the δέ to avoid the awkwardness of the particle recurring three times in a line and a half with a different force each time. For **σωτήριος** Wecklein wrote θεωρίας on the ground that σωτήριος is not an equivocation but a plain lie. But it is true that P. *gets* there in safety. His return, says the Stranger, will be in other hands. A similar phrase is used at *Rhes.* 229, γενοῦ σωτήριος ἀνέρι πομπᾶς ἀγεμών.]

966–70. The Stranger makes ambiguous promises which Pentheus, excited beyond control by the prospect of his triumphant return, continually interrupts (cf. 188–9 n., and the similar use of ἀντιλαβή at the climax of the scene between Tecmessa and Ajax, Soph. *Aj.* 591 ff.).　**φερόμενος ἥξεις:** 'You shall ride home. . . .'[1] Pentheus, picturing himself in a chariot or litter at the head of a train of

---

[1] Claudian's 'laeti manibus portabere vulgi' (*in Rufinum* ii. 333) makes bitter use of the same ambiguity.

captives, protests coyly: 'You propose to pamper me.' (ἀβρότης
is the quality of an effeminate or over-fastidious person: so Agamem-
non meets his wife's flatteries with μὴ γυναικὸς ἐν τρόποις ἐμὲ | ἅβρυνε,
Ag. 918. For the litter as a mark of luxury cf. Athen. 12. 533 F
τρυφερῶς βιοῦντα περιφέρεσθαι ἐπὶ κλίνης.) Stranger: 'In your mother's
embrace.' P.: 'You are determined actually (καί) to spoil me.'
(τρυφᾶν is used of a petted child, e.g. *Ion* 1375 f. ἐν ἀγκάλαις | μητρὸς
τρυφῆσαι. Presumably P. takes the Stranger's words to mean, not
that his mother will carry him, but that she will share his litter.)
Stranger: 'To spoil you, yes—in my fashion' (τοιάσδε = such as
I have just promised, τρυφαί which will not be in fact τρυφεραί).
P.: 'I go to claim my due.' It is his last word, unconsciously significant, and the audience shudders.   ἀξίων μέν seems to mean
'what is at any rate deserved', the antithetic idea being left unexpressed, as at 1078 and often (Denniston, *Particles*, 380 f.).

971–2 are addressed to P.'s retreating back (P. could hardly take
δεινὰ πάθη to refer to the sufferings he will inflict on the maenads, as
Sandys supposes). οὐρανῷ στηρίζον: 'towering to heaven', an epic
phrase—*Il.* 4. 443 (Ἔρις) οὐρανῷ ἐστήριξε κάρη, cf. *Hipp.* 1207 κῦμ'
οὐρανῷ στηρίζον. The prophecy is literally fulfilled when P. mounts
the ἐλάτης οὐράνιον κλάδον (1064) which ἐς ὀρθὸν αἰθέρ' ἐστηρίζετο (1073).

973–6. Before leaving the stage the Stranger issues his orders to the
women far away on Cithaeron, and the audience knows that they
will hear and obey. The δέσις of the plot is now complete, the λύσις
about to begin. Mr. D. W. Lucas has called my attention to the
significance of the description of Pentheus here as τὸν νεανίαν. He
is in fact hardly more than a boy, as we may infer from 1185–7;
and that is the one plea which a Greek audience would accept in
extenuation of his conduct. The Greeks were very susceptible to
the pathos inherent in the rashness of inexperienced youth: cf. e.g.
Odyssey 7. 294 αἰεὶ γάρ τε νεώτεροι ἀφραδέουσιν, Eur. *Supp.* 580 γνώσῃ
σὺ πάσχων· νῦν δ' ἔτ' εἶ νεανίας, *IA.* 489 ἄφρων νέος τ' ἦ, fr. trag.
adesp. 538 τὸ νέον ἅπαν ὑψηλόν ἐστι καὶ θρασύ, and Aristotle's characterization of young men at *Rhet.* 2. 12, especially 1389b7 τὰ ἀδικήματα
ἀδικοῦσιν εἰς ὕβριν καὶ οὐ κακουργίαν. I think Mr. Lucas is right
in seeing here a first preparation for the shift of sympathy which the
next two scenes will bring about.   αἵ θ' ὁμόσποροι: short for ὑμεῖς
τε αἱ ὁμόσποροι, like Xen. *Cyr.* 3. 3. 20 ὦ Κῦρε καὶ οἱ ἄλλοι Πέρσαι.
[ἀγῶνα μέγαν: for the tribrach in the third foot followed (without
an elision) by a sense pause cf. *Cycl.* 577, *Hel.* 1241, *Or.* 1076. According to Denniston (*C.Q.* xxx, 79) this rhythm is peculiar to Eur.]
αὐτὸ σημανεῖ: 'the event will show', a Euripidean adaptation of the
colloquial proverb αὐτὸ δείξει (the answer given by the man who
was asked if the water were deep, Plato, *Theaet.* 200 E with schol.
ad loc.). So *Phoen.* 623 αὐτὸ σημανεῖ. [Sometimes τὸ ἔργον is added:

Andr. 265 τὸ δ' ἔργον αὐτὸ σημανεῖ τάχα, Soph. fr. 388 P., Ar. *Lys.* 375.
Sometimes again, in colloquial Greek, δείξει by itself has this force:
Ar. *Vesp.* 994, *Ran.* 1261, Plato, *Phlb.* 20 c.]

Stasimon 4 (977–1032)

A song of vengeance, consisting like stasimon 3 of one pair of
strophic stanzas, with refrain, plus an epode. In accordance with
an established convention, it covers an interval of many hours—
the time required for Pentheus' journey to Cithaeron, all the events
described in the next scene, and the Messenger's return to Thebes.
Developing the thought suggested by the Stranger's last words,
the Chorus in the strophe summon the demons of madness to enter
into the women on Cithaeron, as they have already entered into
Pentheus; then they describe in clairvoyant vision what shall happen, or is even now happening, somewhere in the mountains. 'What
conscious and unconscious prediction has given us as future, what the
Messenger's speech will give us as past, the Chorus lets us see in immediate visionary contemplation' (Wassermann). Eur. had used the
same device, though less powerfully, at *Med.* 976 ff. and *Hipp.* 769 ff.;
in the latter play it actually takes the place of a messenger's speech.
The antistrophe, like those of stasima 1 and 3, passes from the particular case of Pentheus to draw a generalized moral. The song
culminates in a prayer to Dion. to reveal himself, not this time, as at
553, in his human shape, but in his monstrous form as a destroyer.

Metre. With the approach of the climax of the action, the metre
of maximum excitement, the dochmiac, is introduced. The basic
form of μέτρον, at least in the type of dochmii here employed,
is ∪ − − ∪ −. Other forms are derived from this (*a*) by resolving
one or more of the long syllables, (*b*) by substituting an 'irrational'
long for one or both of the short syllables. The extreme forms
thus obtainable are exemplified in 986 = 1006, where the first
μέτρον consists of 5 longs, the second of 8 shorts. [The second
μέτρον of 998 is exceptional in that a substituted irrational long
is itself resolved, giving ∪ ∪ − − ∪ −. On this and on 983 = 1003,
see separate notes. Syllabic correspondence between στρ. and ἀντ.
is not invariably maintained: see scheme below. Synapheia is
broken by a *syllaba anceps* after 987, and correspondingly after 1007.]
The dochmii are varied, as often, by the introduction of occasional
iambic cola (including apparent cretics, · − ∪ −, and bacchiacs,
∪ − · −); once also by an iambelegus (iambic + dactylic phrase).

Scheme: Strophe

∪ ∪ ∪ − − − ∪ ∪ ∪ − ⏝ −   2 dochm.
∪ ∪ ∪ − ∪ − ⏝⏝ − − ∪ −   2 dochm.
      ∪ − − ∪ ∪ ∪   1 dochm.

980 = 1000	⏑⏑⏑–⏑– ⏑–––⏑–	2 dochm.
	–––⏑– ⏑–––⏑–	2 dochm.
	–––⏑– ⏝⏝⏑⏑⏑–	2 dochm.
	⏝ ⏝⏝ ⏑–⏑–	iambic tripody (corrupt?)
	⏑––⏑– ⏑––⏝–	2 dochm.
985 = 1005	⏑⏑⏑–⏑–	1 dochm.
	––––– ⏑⏑⏑⏑⏑⏑⏑	2 dochm.
	⏑⏑⏑–⏝– ⏑⏑⏑⏑⏑⏑	2 dochm.
	•–⏑– •–⏑–	2 iamb. (cretics)
	⏑––⏑– ⏑––⏑⏑⏑	2 dochm.
990 = 1010	⏑––⏑– ⏑––⏑–	2 dochm.

Refrain

	⏑– ⏑– ⏑⏑⏑ ⏑– ⏑– ⏑–	3 iamb.
	⏑–•– ⏑–•– ⏑–•–	3 iamb. (bacchii).
995 = 1015	⏑⏑⏑⏑⏑⏑⏑ ⏑⏑⏑–⏑–	2 dochm.
	⏑––⏑–	1 dochm.

Epode

	⏑–⏑–⏑ –⏑⏑–⏑⏑–	iambelegus
	⏑––⏑– ⏑–⏑–•–⏑–	1 dochm.+2 iamb.
1020	⏑––⏑– ⏑––––	2 dochm.
	⏑––⏑– –⏑⏑⏑⏑⏑–	2 dochm.
	⏑⏑⏑ ⏑⏑⏑ ⏑– ⏑–	2 iamb.
	⏑––⏑–	1 dochm.

977–8. Λύσσας κύνες: Lyssa, like Hecate, hunts with a pack of hell-hounds—cf. *Her.* 898, where she κυναγετεῖ τέκνων διωγμόν. An Attic fifth-century vase-painting (Pfuhl, fig. 515) shows her in the act of transforming Actaeon's hounds into such hell-hounds. In Aeschylus' Ξάντριαι she appeared in person (as she does in the *Heracles*), 'inspiring the maenads', fr. 169. [She is a figure akin to the Erinyes, who are, like her, daughters of Night (*Her.* 822, 834, Aesch. *Eum.* 321); they, too, cause madness; and they are imagined as a pack of hounds (Aesch. *Cho.* 1054, *Eum.* 246, &c.). Virgil's line, 'Eumenidum veluti demens videt agmina Pentheus' (*Aen.* 4. 469), implies either that in some version of the story the Erinyes took the place of Lyssa or that Virgil interpreted the Λύσσαι κύνες here as being the Erinyes. Cf. also Lucan 1. 574 ff. 'Thebanam qualis Agaven | impulit . . . Eumenis', and the Pompeian wall-painting, Pfuhl fig. 641.] **θίασον . . . ἔχουσι:** hold their congregation, 'are joined in worship', like 952 ἔχει συρίγματα.
981. λυσσώδη: Lyssa has already entered into P. (851). [With the manuscript word-order the attributive adj. λυσσώδη does not come

between article and noun as it should; and the line does not correspond metrically to 1001 which, if we accept the highly probable
correction τἀνίκατον, is a dochmiac dimeter. The transposition in
the text solves both difficulties.]

982–4. 'First of all (?) his mother will catch sight of him as he spies from
some sheer rock or (?) pinnacle.' The assertion of Elmsley, Sandys,
and L.S., that σκόλοπος here means 'tree', is not only unsupported
by authority but is hardly consistent with the evident root meaning
of the word, which is always applied to things having sharp points—
stakes for fencing or impaling (the only sense of σκόλοψ elsewhere
in classical poetry), thorns, pointed surgical instruments, the pointed
tip of a fishing-hook or of a date-palm (σκόλοπες αἱ τῶν φοινίκων
ἀκμαί Zonaras). Conceivably it was applied also to the pointed tip
of a fir-tree (date-palms do not grow on Greek mountains), or to
a rock-pinnacle (what climbers call a 'needle'); but it is surprising
that the ancient lexicographers, most of whom deal with the word,
should have preserved no notice of such a specific use if it occurred
in a work as famous as the *Bacchae*. Doubt about σκόλοπος is
enhanced by doubt about the metre. [983 could be read as a synco-
pated iambic dimeter, ·–∪∪∪ | ·–∪–. But if 1003 is sound, 983
must be taken as an iambic tripody –∪∪ ∪– ∪– with –∪∪ = ∪–,
an unusual though not unexampled irregularity of correspondence
(Denniston, 'Lyric Iambics', *Greek Poetry and Life*, 142). Many
metricians deny that iambic tripodies can occur at all (cf., however,
Denniston, ibid. 129 ff., who is inclined to admit them in rare
instances[1]): hence both lines are often emended to make dochmii.
ἢ σκόλοπος might be a corruption of εὔσκοπος (Nauck) or ἁ σκοπός
(Headlam, *J.Ph.* xxi [1893], 88). But we rather expect here some
vision, not necessarily exact, of the tree in which P. sat. Cf. Theocritus' echo of this passage, 26. 10 Πενθεὺς δ' ἀλιβάτω πέτρας ἄπο
πάντ' ἐθεώρει, | σχῖνον ἐς ἀρχαίαν καταδύς, ἐπιχώριον ἔρνος. If the true
rhythm of 1003 is ·– · – | ∪–∪–, something like ἢ κλωνός may have
stood here: cf. 1068 where the tree is called κλῶν' ὄρειον.—For the
rather pointless πρῶτα in 982 we should certainly write πρώτα
(Dindorf): cf. Ovid, *Met.* 3. 711 ff. 'prima videt . . . Penthea . . .
mater'.]

985–6. 'Who is he that is come to the mountain, is come to the mountain, tracking the Cadmean mountain-dancers?' For ἐς ὄρος ἐς ὄρος
cf. 116, 165: it seems to be a ritual repetition. [The transposition

---

[1] In addition to the instances quoted by Denniston, the MSS. offer
apparent iambic tripodies *among dochmiacs* at *Hipp.* 593, *Hec.* 1083,
Phoen. 114 and 183 (the two last emended in O.C.T.). A. M. Dale, *The
Lyric Metres of Greek Drama*, 113 f., treats some of these, and also the
present line, as variant forms of dochmius.

adopted by Murray produces syllabic correspondence with 1005–6. This is not, however, necessary; and if Καδμ. qualifies ὀρειδρόμων (fem.), Καδμειᾶν seems to be required (Maas, cf. 1160). I should be content to read τίς ὅδε Καδμείων | μαστὴρ ὀριδρόμων (Kirchhoff for ὀριοδρόμων), 'What man of the Cadmeans is this who comes . . . tracking the mountain-dancers?' The collocation of ὀριδρόμων and ὄρος is deliberate: the spy has penetrated to the fastnesses of the secret cult. The form ὀριδρόμος, which appears in a Pindar papyrus (fr. 41. 6 Bowra = 52 g. 6 Snell) and in the MSS. of Nonnus (5. 229, 25. 194), is confirmed by the analogy of ὀρίγονος Tim. Pers. 88 and ὀρίβακχος Opp. C. 1. 24. With either reading ὀρ(ε)ιδρόμων certainly depends on μαστήρ, not (as Wilamowitz and Lucas) on τίς: cf. Cornutus, ND. 30 ὀρείφοιτοι βάκχοι.]

987–90. τίς ἄρα κτλ.; 'what creature engendered him?' For the conventional suggestion that inhuman conduct implies inhuman origin cf. Il. 16. 34 γλαυκὴ δέ σε τίκτε θάλασσα, | πέτραι τ᾽ ἠλίβατοι, ὅτι τοι νόος ἐστὶν ἀπηνής: Catull. 64. 154 'quaenam te genuit sola sub rupe leaena?' and similarly Theocritus 3. 15 of Eros, βαρὺς θεός· ἦ ῥα λεαίνας | μαζὸν ἐθήλαζεν. But the Chorus see farther than they know: what they put into Agaue's mouth as a metaphorical *façon de parler* will in the true action be experienced by her as paranoiac delusion (1141). **Λιβυσσᾶν:** Hesiod situates the Gorgons in the far West (Theog. 274 f.), and the scholiast on Pindar, Pyth. 10. 72, tells us that some unnamed authorities placed them ἐπὶ τῶν περάτων τῆς Λιβύης. So too Hdt. makes Perseus return with the Gorgon's head ἐκ Λιβύης (2. 91. 6). [Hermann's transposition of ὅδε neatly puts the metre right in both 989 and 990: its insertion in 989 will be due to a reader who wished to make the construction clear by arranging the words in their prose order.]

991–6. 'Let Justice visible walk, let Justice sworded walk, stabbing home to the throat the godless, the lawless, the conscienceless one, earthborn of Echion's breed.' Cf. Aesch. Cho. 639 ff. τὸ δ᾽ ἄγχι πλευμόνων ξίφος | διανταίαν ὀξυπευκὲς οὐτᾷ | διαὶ Δίκας. Justice the swordbearer is seen on several of the South Italian vases which depict the punishments of the Underworld (Harrison, Themis, 520 ff.).—On Pentheus as γηγενής see 537–41 n. **φανερός:** used here only as feminine, cf. such adjs. in -ρος as βάρβαρος, ἥμερος, λάβρος. [Other adjs. exceptionally treated by Eur. as of two terminations, metri gratia, are δῆλος (Med. 1197), μέλεος (Hel. 335, &c.), ποθεινός (Hel. 623), δίκαιος (Heraclid. 901, IT. 1202), οἰκεῖος (Heraclid. 634). Some of these feminines in -ος may be old forms which disappeared from common speech through the influence of analogy but survived in poetic diction because of their metrical convenience (Wackernagel, Vorl. üb. Syntax, ii. 49 f.).] **τὸν ἄθεον ἄνομον ἄδικον:** almost exactly the same rhetorical effect was used in prose by Gorgias, Pal.

36 ἄθεον ἄδικον ἄνομον ἔργον. Cf. Aesch. *Cho*. 55 ἄμαχον ἀδάματον ἀπόλεμον, Soph. *Ant*. 876 ἄκλαυτος, ἄφιλος, ἀνυμέναιος.

997-1010. This passage is the hardest in the play, and full of textual uncertainties. Before discussing it in detail it may be useful to give a translation of the whole as it appears in the Oxford text, indicating by a query those places where I am inclined to doubt Murray's reading. 'Whosoever with conscienceless purpose and unlawful rage against thy worship, god of bacchanals, and against thy mother's worship sets forth with crazy craft and false daring, thinking to master by force that which cannot be mastered—for him death is a discipline (?) of his purposes, accepting no excuses (?) in things that are of the gods; and to act as befits mortality is a life secure from grief. I do not grudge the wise their wisdom; I rejoice to pursue it (?). Yet the other things are great and, manifest. O that life might flow (?) towards beauty, that day-long and through the night men might be pure and reverent, and casting away all customs that stray beyond the rule of justice, might respect the gods.'

997-1001. With Murray's punctuation this is a generic relative clause, the construction being θάνατος ἔφυ σωφρόνα γνωμᾶν (ἐκείνῳ) ὅς . . . στέλλεται. Most edd. put a stop after βίᾳ and attach the relative clause to what precedes it (cf. *El*. 156 and the examples cited by Denniston ad loc., p. 216): ὅς is then Pentheus. The choice depends on what we read in 1002.   περὶ . . . σᾶς is best taken with ἀδ. γνώμᾳ παρ. τ' ὀργᾷ (equivalent to ἀδικεῖ καὶ παρανομεῖ): if the words went with στέλλεται we should expect ἐπί (which Dobree conjectured). **ματρός**: Semele. On her place in Dionysiac cult, and the reason for it, see 6–12 n. Cf. *Phoen*. 1755 f. Σεμέλας | θίασον ἱερὸν ὄρεσιν ἀνεχόρευσα: Pind. fr. 63. 20 οἰχνεῖ τε Σεμέλαν ἑλικάμπυκα χοροί: Theocr. 26. 5 f. βωμὼς | τὼς τρεῖς τᾷ Σεμέλᾳ, τὼς ἐννέα τῷ Διονύσῳ: and the Fasti Myconenses (*SIG*[3] 1024, *circa* 200 B.C.), which prescribe an annual offering to her. [For the short syllable missing after περί, ⟨σά⟩ seems to be the right supplement in view of ματρός τε σᾶς, and in 1001 Wilamowitz's τἀνίκατον for τανανικατον is much the neatest correction.—In the second dochmius of 998 we should, I think, recognize the rare form ◡◡ – – ◡ – (Wilamowitz, *Gr. V.* 405) rather than emend or scan ὄργια as a disyllable (consonantalizing the ι). The same question arises in several other places: *Hipp*. 821 and 868 ἀβίωτος βίου (ἀβίοτος some MSS., but the form is foreign to classical Greek); *Her*. 878 μανίαισιν Λύσσας (μανιάσιν λύσσαις Dobree and Hermann); Soph. *Aj*. 358 ἁλίαν ὃς ἐπέβας (ἅλιον Hermann). I doubt whether all these are corrupt; and I should hesitate to explain them away by consonantalizing the ι, since apart from the word καρδία (κάρζα?) thrice in Aesch. I know no *certain* instance of this synizesis in tragedy (possible cases have been collected by Radermacher, *Sitzb. Akad. Wien*, clxx [1913], Abh. 9 and *Philologus*,

lxxxiv [1929], 257 ff.). On the other hand, apparent dochmii beginning ⌣⌣– occur e.g. at Soph. *OC.* 117 τίς ἄρ᾽ ἦν; ποῦ ναίει; and hesitation about admitting the form should be ended by the new fragments
of Sophocles' *Inachus* (Page, *Greek Lit. Pap.* i, No. 6) which present
a whole series of such dochmii—27 ff. μανία τάδε κλύειν | σὺ γὰρ οὖν,
Ζεῦ, λόγων | κακὸς εἰ πίστεως κτλ. (cf. R. Pfeiffer, *Sitzb. Bayer. Akad.,
Phil.-hist. Abt.*, 1938, Heft 2, p. 41 f.).]

1002–4. Text and sense uncertain. In Murray's text **γνωμᾶν** is gen. pl.,
σωφρόνα nom. sing. fem. The existence of a common noun σωφρόνη
(Dor. σωφρόνα) was elaborately argued by Housman, *C.R.* ii, 242 ff.
(cf. also Wilamowitz, *Pindaros*, 246 n. 2): it stands to σωφροσύνη as
δυσφρόνη to δυσφροσύνη, ἀφρόνη to ἀφροσύνη, εὐφρόνη (specialized in
the sense 'night') to εὐφροσύνη. Σωφρόνη is found as a proper name
('Prudence') in inscriptions and papyri, also Men. *Epitr.*, Terence,
Eunuchus, Aphthonius, *Progymn.* p. 32. 13 Spengel, &c. Meineke
wished to introduce σωφρόνη at Aesch. *Pers.* 829, Housman at
Ag. 181, Eur. *Hipp.* 1034, *Tro.* 1056; but its status as a tragic word
remains doubtful. [I think, however, that Murray's view of the
general sense is probably right: cf. Aristarchus tragicus fr. 3
(*T.G.F.* p. 728) ὦ θάνατε, σωφρόνισμα τῶν ἀγνωμόνων 'admonishment
of the ruthless' (Hense's collation establishes this as the true
reading); Choricius, p. 388. 16 Foerster-Richtsteig, θανάτου δὲ μείζων
οὐκ ἔστι σωφρονισμός. In view of these parallels, which have hitherto
escaped notice, I distrust emendations which eliminate θάνατος,
such as W. H. Thompson's γνώμα σώφρων, ἃ θνατοῖς (Heath) ἀπροφάσιστος ἐς τὰ θεῶν ἔφυ and Pohlenz's γνωμᾶν σωφρόνα κάματος
ἀπροφάσιστος περὶ τὰ θεῶν ἔφυ (to quote only the best). But Murray's
text will hardly do as it stands. (*a*) σωφρόνα cannot bear the sense
'castigatrix': the natural meaning of γνωμᾶν σωφρόνα θάνατος would
be 'sobriety of judgement spells death'. (*b*) ἀπροφάσιστος is not
found elsewhere in the sense 'indeprecabilis': it is always used of unquestioning obedience (cf. the synonyms in Pollux i. 43, λέγε δὲ περὶ
τοῦ μὴ βραδύνοντος ἕτοιμος, πρόχειρος, πρόθυμος, ἄοκνος, ταχύς, ὀξύς,
εὔτονος, ἐνεργός, ἀπροφάσιστος, and the numerous other passages
collected by Headlam, *J. Phil.* xxi, 95 ff.); and in the present context
its natural reference would be to that unquestioning obedience to
religious νόμος on which the Chorus repeatedly insist (387 ff., 428 ff.,
890 ff., &c.). To these objections may be added (*c*) the metrical
doubtfulness of the iambic tripody in 1003 (see on 982–4), and (*d*) the
inappropriateness of τε in 1004 (Murray's text seems to demand an
adversative). I suggest as the minimum alteration which will meet
all four difficulties

> γνωμᾶν σωφρόν⟨ισμ⟩α θάνατος· ἀπροφασί-
> στως ⟨δ᾽⟩ ἐς τὰ θεῶν ἔφυ
> βροτείως τ᾽ ἔχειν ἄλυπος βίος.

'for him death is a corrective of his purposes; but to accept without
question in things that are of the gods, as befits mortality, is griefless
life.' For γνωμᾶν σωφόνισμα cf. Thuc. 3. 65. 3 σωφρονισταὶ ὄντες τῆς
γνώμης: for the plural, Soph. *Aj.* 52. The position of ἔφυ, which
at first sight may seem wrong, is accounted for by the addition of
βροτείως (explanatory of ἀπροφασίστως): ἔχειν is attached to the
second adverb instead of the first. 983 = 1003 may now be scanned
as iambic dimeters · − · − ∪ − ∪ − (reading e.g. ἢ κλωνός in 983).
The second μέτρον of 1002 has the form ∪ ∪ ∪   ∪ ∪ − −, which like
the form beginning ∪ ∪ − (998) is unusual but not unexampled (cf.
Aesch. *Supp.* 350, *Sept.* 892, 893, Eur. *Med.* 1259, Wilamowitz,
Gr. V. 405). Those who find this rhythm unlikely may consider
reading γνωμᾶν ἀφρόνα θάνατος· ἀπροφασί|στως δ' . . . with a stop
after βίᾳ (for ἀφρόνα cf. *Alc.* 728 ἄφρονα); or γνωμᾶν σωφρόνισμα
θάνατος ἀπρόφατος | ἐς τὰ θεῶν ἔφυ· | βροτείως δ' . . ., 'death with-
out warning is a corrective of his judgements on things divine'.
The latter reading restores normal dochmiacs throughout, and as
Headlam pointed out ἀπρόφατος is more than once glossed ἀπροφάσιστος. On the other hand, the word appears only in Alexandrine
poets, and Pentheus' death was hardly 'without warning'.[1]]

1005–7. θηρεύουσα, sc. τὸ σοφόν.   ὤ, νάειν ... βίον: accus. and infin.
of prayer (Goodwin, *M. and T.*, § 785). But text and sense are highly
disputable. [Three questions are involved: (*a*) should we write
φθόνῳ (Aldine and many older edd.) or φθονῶ? (*b*) if the latter,
should we write θηρεύουσα τάδ' ἔτερα (Heath, &c.) or as Murray
θηρεύουσα· τὰ δ' ἔτερα? (*c*) what can we make of the corrupt words
τῶν ἀεί? A clue to the answer to (*a*) and (*b*) may, I think, be found
in 395 f., where similar language is used in a similar context of thought
(divine judgement on impiety). Since there τὸ σοφόν is clearly
equated with τὸ μὴ θνητὰ φρονεῖν, it is natural to suppose that it is
here contrasted with βροτείως ἔχειν. If so, the Chorus, whose constant
teaching is θνητὰ φρονεῖν, cannot say here that they rejoice to pursue
τὸ σοφόν. This points to the reading τὸ σοφὸν οὐ φθονῶ· χαίρω
θηρεύουσα τάδ' ἔτερα. . . . 'The wise can have their wisdom: my joy
is in pursuing these other aims. . . .' But we expect something
stronger than οὐ φθονῶ, especially in view of the asyndeton, and
Headlam may have been right in proposing οὐ ζηλῶ (*J. Phil.* xxvi
[1899], 235), on which οὐ φθονῶ might be a mistaken gloss: cf. schol.
Hec. 235 τὸ ζηλοῦν δύο δηλοῖ, τὸ φθονεῖν καὶ τὸ μακαρίζειν. The sense
required here is τὸ σοφὸν οὐ μακαρίζω. (Tyrrell's version of τὸ σοφὸν
οὐ φθόνῳ χαίρω θηρεύουσα, 'I care not to pursue rationalism in such

---

[1] On the manifold difficulties of lines 1002–10 see now A. Y. Campbell, *C.Q.* xlix (1956), 61 ff., who wished to solve them, *more suo*, by
re-writing the entire passage.

a manner as to offend the gods', cannot be got from the Greek: οὐ φθόνῳ could only = ἀφθόνως.)—In 1007 I find Murray's ὤ, νάειν (as also his earlier conjecture ἀέντων) more ingenious than convincing: the metaphor is violent and so far as I know unparalleled, and the construction improbable in the absence of an introductory voc. (Aesch. *Sept.* 253 θεοὶ πολῖται, μή με δουλείας τυχεῖν, Eur. *Supp.* 1 ff. Δήμητερ, . . . εὐδαιμονεῖν με, Ar. *Ach.* 247 ff. ὦ Διόνυσε, . . . ἐμέ . . . ἀγαγεῖν, &c.). The most widely accepted correction is φανέρ' ἄγοντ' ἀεί, and that some part of ἄγειν may have stood here is suggested by fr. 672 ὁ δ' εἰς τὸ σῶφρον ἐπ' ἀρετήν τ' ἄγων ἔρως | ζηλωτὸς ἀνθρώποισιν. But the hiatus after ἀεί is suspicious, and with μεγάλα φανερά we expect a causal participle ὄντα. I would read in preference φανερά τ' ὄντ' (Musgrave)· ἄ⟨γ⟩ει ⟨δ'⟩ ἐπὶ τὰ καλὰ βίον· ' My joy is in pursuing these other aims, being high and plainly set (for they lead man's life towards the good), day-long and through the night to be pure and reverent. . . .']

1008–10. With Murray's text these infinitives must be either consecutive or epexegetic of τὰ καλά. [With the reading proposed in the last note they are epexegetic of τάδε, as διαζῆν is of ταῦτα in 424–6.] ἦμαρ, 'by day', like Hes. *Op. et Di.* 176 οὐδέ ποτ' ἦμαρ | παύσονται καμάτου. ἐς νύκτα, 'on through the night', like Hom. *Od.* 4. 595 εἰς ἐνιαυτὸν . . . ἥμενος.—For the ideal here expressed cf. fr. 256, from the contemporary *Archelaos*, μακάριος ὅστις νοῦν ἔχων τιμᾷ θεόν, and *Andr.* 785 ff.

1017–19. The sense of the epode is clear, though metrical uncertainties render the text doubtful in some details. For the work of destruction the god is invoked (φάνηθι, cf. Soph. *Ant.* 1149, Aesch. *Pers.* 666 &c.) under his dangerous bestial shapes (Introd., p. xviii). So in *H. Hymn.* 7. 44 he manifests himself to his captors as a lion; so when he appeared to the unbelieving daughters of Minyas, ἐγένετο ταῦρος καὶ λέων καὶ πάρδαλις (Ant. Lib. 10); so in Nonnus (40. 40 ff.) his opponent sees him successively as leopard, lion, snake, &c. [Headlam's δράκων πυρίφλεγων θ' makes 1019 a dochmiac dimeter. As it stands, the line is dochmius (scanning πυρίφλέγων)+iambic dimeter,[1] which seems metrically defensible: cf. 1022.]

1020–3. γελῶντι προσώπῳ: 'now at last the meaning of that enigmatic smile with which the "gentle beast" surrendered to his captors (439) is made clear' (Winnington-Ingram). θανάσιμον is best taken with βρόχον. [In view of 1017–19 and of 436–9 Tyrrell's θὴρ θηραγρέτᾳ is attractive: the quarry shall hunt the hunter. θηραγρέτης is found at *Anth. Pal.* 6. 184, θηραγρευτής nowhere (ἀγρευτής Soph. *OC.* 1091).—In 1021 Murray's suggested transposition προσώπῳ

---

[1] Or bacchius plus paeon (πυρίφλέγων) plus dochmius (Dale, *Lyric Metres*, 105): cf. 1014, 1021.

γελῶντι gets rid of the questionable (545–6 n.) prosody γελωντῖ πρ-.
—In the next line P's πεσόντα is grammatically indefensible (for
Tyrrell's 'parallels' are not parallel); and P's ἐπὶ θανάσιμον impossible metrically, while ἐπί is also the wrong preposition—we
expect either ὑπό (cf. *Ion* 1270 ὑπὸ μητρυιὰν πεσεῖν) or possibly ἐς.
—Murray's colometry seems satisfactory : we need not rewrite the
passage to make dochmiacs throughout as Tyrrell and Headlam do.]

Scene 5 (1024–1152)

Pentheus' death is announced by his personal attendant (1046),
who had accompanied him to Cithaeron. The narrative is preceded
by a short passage of dialogue with the Chorus, which throws into
sharp relief the contrast between the narrator's and the Chorus's
reaction to the event. It is natural that the Chorus should feel only
joy that the Lord has delivered his people out of the hand of the
spoiler ; at the same time the Messenger's reproof at 1039–40 prepares
the ground for the change in the audience's sympathy which the
final scene will procure. The narrative itself is distinguished from
other Euripidean essays in the description of physical horror, such
as the Messenger-speech in the *Medea*, by the skill with which the
supernatural atmosphere is suggested, especially in the wonderful
lines 1084 ff. The episodes of the tree-climbing and the pelting, to
a modern taste slightly grotesque, are doubtless traditional, and
may be in origin a reflection of ritual (see 1058–75 n., 1096–8 n.).

1024–6. ἀν' Ἑλλάδα, 'in the sight of all Greece', like *Andr.* 449 ἀδίκως
εὐτυχεῖτ' ἀν' Ἑλλάδα. In 1026 Murray adopts Wilamowitz's idea
(*Hermes*, xxvi [1891], 199) that "Ὄφις was the dragon's proper name.
[I see no reason to embrace this rather odd and quite unsupported
hypothesis, which Wilamowitz seems to have abandoned later.
Nor need we try as some do to emend ὄφεος. Critics have overlooked
Hes. *Theog.* 322 ὄφιος, κρατεροῖο δράκοντος, ibid. 825 ὄφιος, δεινοῖο
δράκοντος, and Aristotle, *Hist. An.* 602ᵇ25 δράκοντος τοῦ ὄφεως.
Strictly speaking, though poetry does not always observe the distinction, ὄφις is the genus of which δράκων is a species (schol. *Or.*
479) ; and the two terms are conjoined as in ὄρνις . . . κύκνος (*infra*,
1365), ὄρνις . . . ἀλκυών (*IT.* 1089), ὄρνιθος . . . ἀηδοῦς (Soph. *Aj.* 629),
ὄρνιθος . . . πέρδικος (Soph. fr. 323), θηρός . . . λέοντος (*Her.* 465), συὸς
σιάλοιο (*Il.* 9. 208), βοῦς . . . ταῦρος (*Il.* 2. 480), &c. Usually the
general name is put first, but not invariably : cf. *Il.* 17. 389 ταύροιο
βοός, *Hel.* 19 κύκνου . . . ὄρνιθος, Ar. *Av.* 515 αἰετὸν ὄρνιν (Lobeck,
Pathologia Graeci Sermonis, ii. 364).]

1027–8. 'I am sad for you, slave though I am.' ἀλλ' ὅμως may end
a sentence, like 'but still' in colloquial English : cf. *El.* 753 ἤκουσα
κἀγώ, τηλόθεν μέν, ἀλλ' ὅμως, *Hec.* 843, *IA.* 904, Ar. *Ach.* 956. 1028
must have been added by someone who did not realize this and

failed to notice that he was not making sense (for τὰ [τῶν P] δεσποτῶν
can hardly = τὰ δεσποτῶν κακά). He borrowed the line from the
Medea (54) where it does make sense, since the sentence continues
κακῶς πίτνοντα, καὶ φρενῶν ἀνθάπτεται. [Such interpolations are late,
and should not be attributed to actors. Cf. *Or.* 1023, where the same
idiom gave rise (a) to a similar interpolation which appears in all
MSS. but is unknown to the scholiasts, (b) to an unmetrical (and
therefore late) emendation quoted in a scholion.]

1031. In questioning the Messenger the Chorus-leader used the ordinary
trimeter of spoken dialogue (1029); but on hearing of P.'s death she
becomes lyrical with joy (cf. the similar effect at *Phoen.* 1335–41). Her
remaining utterances, 1034–5, 1037–8 (probably), 1041–2, are dochmiac, and it is likely that 1031 should be restored as a dochmiac
dimeter by inserting σύ (Kirchhoff) or ὡς (O. Hense) before φαίνῃ.
With σύ, θεός should be scanned monosyll., as at *Her.* 347, *Or.* 399.
[A lyric iambic trimeter, such as Hermann wished to make, is
possible but less probable. I see no reason to doubt φαίνῃ: cf. 42
φανέντα θνητοῖς δαίμονα, a prophecy now fulfilled.]

1032–3. τοῖς ἐμοῖς ... δεσπόταις, 'one who was my master': the genera-
lizing plural has a slightly different force from the singular.

1034. ξένα: nom. sing. fem., as the metre shows. εὐάζειν is a μέλος βάρβαρον, since εὐοῖ is the cry of the new foreign cult.

1036. 'And do you count Thebes so poor in manhood ⟨that you shall
go unpunished⟩?' **ἀνάνδρους:** poor in men or poor in spirit or
both. That a complete couplet originally stood here seems fairly
certain; both symmetry and clarity demand it. Anyhow the Messenger cannot burst into song with a lyric line (iambic dimeter).

1037–8. κράτος ... ἐμόν, 'power over me', like Soph. *O.T.* 969 τὠμῷ πόθῳ
'longing for me', *OC.* 332 σῇ προμηθίᾳ 'forethought for you'. [1037
seems to be metrically faulty. Murray's διόγονος for the second
Διόνυσος is attractive (making a dochmiac dimeter), but the word
lacks authority; Διὸς γόνος (cf. 603) would be safer. Or we may
write with Hartung and Schroeder [ὁ Διόνυσος] ὁ Διόνυσος, οὐ | Θῆβαι,
dochmius + ? iambic μέτρον (· – · –).]

1039–40. This corresponds to civilized Greek sentiment. Cf. *Od.* 22.
412 οὐχ ὁσίη κταμένοισιν ἐπ' ἀνδράσιν εὐχετάασθαι, and the proverb
attributed to Pittacus (Stob. 3. 1. 172=Diels, *Vors.*⁷ 10 [73a]. 3)
ἀπραγοῦντα μὴ ὀνείδιζε· ἐπὶ γὰρ τούτοις νέμεσις θεῶν κάθηται. But the
Chorus-leader has still no word of pity.

1043–5. θεράπνας: a word of uncertain signification, used in a local
sense half a dozen times in Eur. but not elsewhere in classical poetry
(at *H. Hymn.* 3. 157 θεράπνη = θεράπαινα). Hesychius gives two
meanings, 'valleys' and 'farms', either of which would be appropriate
here and at *Her.* 370 Πηλιάδες θεράπναι. But a vaguer and wider
sense—something like 'settlement', 'dwellings'—seems to be required

at *Hec.* 482, *Tro.* 1070, *IA.* 1499, and at Orph. *Arg.* 1208; and so
Wilamowitz understood it here. [At *Tro.* 211 I take it, with the
scholiast, to be the Laconian place-name (cf. Isocr. 10. 63, Paus.
3. 19. 9); but there is little point in making it a place-name here,
though Strabo (9. 2. 24) mentions a village called Therapnae (like
Eng. 'Housesteads'?) in the neighbourhood of Thebes. E. Kretschmer, *Glotta*, xviii (1930), 73 f., connects the word with τέραμνον,
trabs, and explains θεράπων, θεράπαινα (θεράπνη) as originally 'house-
slave'.] λέπας ... εἰσεβάλλομεν: 'we began to strike into the hill-
country.' Cf. 677–8 n. and *Hipp.* 1198 ἔρημον χῶρον εἰσεβάλλομεν.

1049–50. 'Keeping silent every movement of foot or tongue.'   ἄπο
governs γλώσσης (not, as Tyrrell, tmesis with σῴζοντες). For the
variation in the choice of preposition cf. 118.

1051–2. 'There lay a glen, cliff-bound, refreshed with waters, close-
shadowing with pines.' With six words the Messenger makes a
picture (observe the double tribrach which mirrors the swift movement of the water). I apprehend that the 'grassy glade' where
Pentheus' party first established themselves is not identical with
this ἄγκος but is an open space in the forest traversed by the ἄγκος,
which is a deep-cut ravine with steep tree-clad sides. Pentheus'
tree grows at the edge of the ravine, since it commands a view of
the bottom and the maenads subsequently pelt him from the opposite
escarpment (1097). On its northern face 'the lower region of Cithaeron
consists partly of steep swelling banks, covered with green turf ...
or with dense masses of pine forest; partly of rocky dells, fringed
with brushwood or stunted oaks' (Mure, *Tour in Greece*, i. 264,
quoted by Sandys). [The anonymous line cited by the scholiast on
Hephaestion, ἠδ' (ἠδ'?) ἄγκος ὑψίκρημνον ὄρεσι περίδρομον, is *not*
a variant version of 1051 but comes from a satyr-play: it is cited
as a typical *satyric* trimeter. The same scholion is reproduced in
a Byzantine treatise on metre, *Anecdota Chisianà*; but there the
satyric line has been confused with *Ba.* 1051 which a reader had
probably cited for comparison, so that it appears as ἦν δ' ἄγκος
ὑψίκομον ὕδασι διάβροχον. This has no bearing on the text of the
Ba.]

1054–5. 'Some of them were restoring its crown of ivied locks to what
had been a wand of power.' The act described is not the wreathing
of the *stem* with ivy—stem-wreathed thyrsi appear first in Hellenistic art and Roman poetry (v. Papen, *Der Thyrsos*, 28)—but the
crowning of the νάρθηξ with the terminal bunch of ivy leaves which
transforms it into a thyrsus (cf. 176 n.). Hence **θύρσον ἐκλελοιπότα** =
a thyrsus which had ceased (to be a thyrsus). Cf. *Hel.* 1360 f. κισσοῦ
τε στεφθεῖσα χλόα | νάρθηκας εἰς ἱερούς, 'the ivy-bunch set as a crown
on the consecrated rods'; and for **κισσῷ κομήτην** (which is here proleptic), fr. 203 κομῶντα κισσῷ στῦλον εὐίου θεοῦ.

1056–7. 'Others were singing bacchic antiphonies, gay as fillies released from the patterned yoke.' For the comparison cf. 166–9 and *Or.* 45 πηδᾷ δρομαῖος, πῶλος ὡς ἀπὸ ζυγοῦ (s.v.l.).

1058–75. I doubt if the perching of P. on the tree was invented by Eur. 'to give Dionysus something to do' (Wilamowitz, *Textgesch. d. gr. Bukoliker*, 214). It looks more like a traditional element of the story for which the poet has found a neat motive in Pentheus' psychology. In origin it may well be a reflex of primitive ritual: 'the description suggests that the human victim was tied or hung to a pine-tree before being torn to pieces' (Frazer, *Golden Bough*, IV. ii. 98 n. 5). [Pausanias (2. 2. 6 f.) saw at Corinth two wooden statues, evidently ancient, which were named respectively Λύσιος and Βάκχειος and had their faces smeared with red paint. They were said to have been made from the tree on which Pentheus sat, in accordance with a Delphic oracle which ordered the Corinthians ἀνευρόντας τὸ δένδρον ἐκεῖνο ἴσα τῷ θεῷ σέβειν. This suggests that the tree is no less an agent and embodiment of Dion. than the Stranger who vanishes as soon as the tree comes into action (1076 f.).[1] Cf. 109–10 n.]

1058. 'This is not what P. came to see—and he does not see it' (Winnington-Ingram). We need not suppose him magically blinded.

1060. 'My sight cannot reach these counterfeit maenads.' P. had spoken earlier of their πλασταῖσι βακχείαισι (218) and had suggested that their maenadism was only a cover for immorality (224 f.). [ὅσσοις for ὅσοι (P) seems certain: ἐξικνοῦμαι by itself could hardly mean 'see', and ὅσσοιν, besides being uneuphonious, lacks support in tragic usage. If anything more were needed, I like J. Jackson's suggestion (*C.Q.* xxxv [1941], 49 = *Marg. Scaen.* 213), μανιάδων ὅσσοις νόσων, better than other guesses. But in view of P.'s earlier language I see no reason to doubt νόθων. For νόθος applied metaphorically to persons cf. Plato, *Rep.* 536 A χωλοῖς τε καὶ νόθοις χρώμενοι . . . φίλοις, Catull. 63. 27 'Attis . . . notha mulier'. μόθων (defined as φορτικὸν ὀρχήσεως εἶδος, schol. Ar. *Eq.* 697) is quite unsuited to this or any other tragic context. For the repetition of μαινάδων cf. 647 n.]

1061. ὄχθων δ' ἔπ': 'but on the banks (of the ravine)'. For the anastrophe in the middle of a line cf. 732 n. [If this is the sense—and the subsequent course of events suggests that it is (see 1051–2 n.)—we should probably accentuate ὀχθῶν (cf. L.S. s.v. ὄχθη). For ἀμβὰς (ἐμβὰς P) ἐς ἐλάτην cf. *Il.* 14. 287 εἰς ἐλάτην ἀναβάς, in a passage of which there

---

[1] We may perhaps compare another Dionysiac aetiology, the tale of Erigone, daughter of Icarius, who hanged herself on a tree and thus gave rise to an epidemic of similar suicides: this was told as the αἴτιον of the Attic 'swinging-festival', the Aiora (L. Deubner, *Attische Feste*, 187 f.).

are several apparent reminiscences in this speech (see 1070 n., 1073 n.).
The alternative restoration ὄχθον δ' ἐπεμβὰς ἢ 'λάτην (ὄχθον = 'hill')
is farther from the MS. and fits less well with the topographical
indications. (Elmsley's rule, 'ἐς apud tragicos nunquam in iambico
metro mediam pedis trisyllabi syllabam esse', is arbitrary: ∪ ἐς
ἐ|λάτην is no more objectionable than ∪ ἐν ἐ|κάστῳ (fr. 1018) or – ἐπ'
ἐ|λαχίστοις (*IA*. 541); and – ἐς ἐ|μέ seems to be right at *Or.* 394.)]
1063. τὸ θαῦμα: 'that miracle' (which so impressed me). Cf. 758–60 n.
[The article, being idiomatic, would easily be lost. τι (*p*) is merely
a Renaissance reader's conjecture.]
1064–5. γάρ: introductory, where English prefers an asyndeton.
οὐράνιον: sky-high, 'heaven-piercing'—a reminiscence of Hom. *Od.*
5. 239 ἐλάτη τ' ἦν οὐρανομήκης.   **κατῆγεν, ἦγεν, ἦγεν:** the threefold
repetition, unique in tragic dialogue, suggests the slow descent of
the tree-top. For the compound verb echoed by the simple cf. *Alc.*
400 ὑπάκουσον ἄκουσον, *Med.* 1252 κατίδετ' ἴδετε, *Hipp.* 1374, *Hec.*
168, *Or.* 181 (all lyrical). Ar. has πρόπαλαι πάλαι πάλαι, *Eq.* 1155.
Professor Fraenkel compares Schiller's description of the apotheo-
sis of Heracles in *Das Ideal und das Leben*:

> Froh des neuen ungewohnten Schwebens
> Fliesst er aufwärts, und des Erdenlebens
> Schweres Traumbild sinkt und sinkt und sinkt.

1066–7. 'And it was bent as a bow (is bent) or (as) a rounded wheel
drags its course when it is having its rim (?) marked out with peg and
line (?)' (**περιφοράν**, accus. retained after passive verb).   **ὥστε** 'as'
with finite verb is, like the dropped augment in κυκλοῦτο, an epicism,
and as such appropriate to a narrative passage: it occurs also
Aesch. fr. 39 (narrative), Soph. *Trach.* 112 (lyr.), 699 (narr.), fr.
474 P., *Rhes.* 972. Neither grammar nor the sense of the passage
as interpreted above requires us to alter **ἕλκει** (for ἕλκειν used of
a rotary movement cf. *Cycl.* 661 τόρνευ', ἕλκε addressed to one of
the men twisting round the stake in the Cyclops' eye). But since
περιφορά elsewhere means not 'rim' or 'circumference' (περιφέρεια)
but 'rotation' (Plato, *Laws* 893 C, is hardly a secure instance to the
contrary), we should perhaps read δρόμου (H. Stephanus)—'drags
the rotation of its course', i.e. 'its rotating course'. The meaning of the
second comparison has, however, been much disputed, and the translation given above is not offered with any confidence, though it represents the only sense I can extract from the text as it stands. The basic
question is whether **τόρνῳ** is here (*a*) the ancient equivalent of a pair of
compasses (as it certainly is in Eur. fr. 382) or (*b*) some ancient type
of lathe (as it certainly is in Aesch. fr. 57. 3 and in Plato, *Phlb.* 51 C).
Accepting (*a*), my translation follows Sandys in assuming that
the reference is to marking out the rim of a solid cartwheel, such as

may still be seen in parts of southern Europe. A disk is cut from a log, a hole is bored in its middle, and the disk is slipped over a peg fixed in the ground. To the top of the peg is attached a string with a piece of chalk at the other end. The string is held taut while the disk is revolved, so that the rim of the future wheel is marked out on it. [But if this is the comparison intended, it is a somewhat lame one, as several critics have observed: the sole point of similarity is the describing of an arc of a circle; we expect a more dynamic image to illustrate (as the bow does) the tension of the bent tree. Hence (b) the view that τόρνῳ here means a pole-lathe (as described by E. S. Robertson, *Hermathena*, iii, 387) is now widely accepted: see L. R. Palmer, *Eranos*, xliv (1946), 54 ff.; Kitto, *C.R.* lx (1946), 66; Campbell, *C.Q.* xlix (1956), 64 ff. In this primitive type of lathe 'the tension of the driving cord or strap is provided by a spring beam in the form of a bough or young tree' (Palmer). Robertson found something of the kind in use in India, although there the spring beam was 'a stout pole of some elastic wood, fixed into the wall so as to project at right angles'; and it is not impossible that similar lathes were used in ancient Greece, though their use is not attested. I should like to believe in this interpretation, but it will not fit the text as it stands, since (i) γράφειν is an unsuitable verb to describe the operation of a lathe, (ii) the tree is compared, not to the spring of a lathe, or even to the lathe as a whole, but to the wheel in process of manufacture. Palmer has met the former objection neatly by changing γραφόμενος to γλαφόμενος, 'being chiselled': γλάφειν is a by-form of γλύφειν (Hesych. γλάφει· γλύφει), and is used by Homer (*Od.* 4. 438, διαγλάψασα) and in the Hesiodic *Scutum* (431) in the related sense of 'scoop out' or 'scratch'. The second difficulty he would remove by altering ᾗ to ᾧ (or, with Verrall, ᾗ), thus reducing the two similes to one and making the sense 'It was bent like the τόξον whereby a rounded[1] wheel being chiselled on the lathe draws the rotation of its motion (δρόμου)'. This is less convincing. It eliminates the simple and apt comparison to a bow; and even if we assume that the spring of a lathe was called by carpenters the τόξον (of which there is no evidence), this technological use of the word seems inappropriate in tragedy. Campbell's more venturesome rewriting of the lines is open to the same objections. It may be thought better to acquiesce in view (a) despite its weaknesses.]

1068. ὥς = οὕτως, another epicism: so οἷα ... ὥς *El.* 151 ff. (lyr.), and

---

[1] κυρτός is simply 'convex', a purely ornamental epithet. Palmer translates it 'bulging', i.e. 'untrue', in need of rounding on the lathe. But cf. Arist. *Phys.* 222ᵇ3 ὁ κύκλος (ἔχει) ἐν τῷ αὐτῷ τὸ κυρτὸν καὶ τὸ κοῖλον, *Meteor.* 365ᵃ31 κυρτῆς καὶ σφαιροειδοῦς, and Campbell's discussion, loc. cit.

(probably) ὡς . . . ὡς Soph. *OC*. 1240 ff. (lyr.). Other tragic examples of demonstrative ὡς, except in the fossilized phrases ἀλλ' ὡς and οὐδ' ὡς, are open to question; but if ὡς is taken as temporal here (Tyrrell) the effect is intolerably flat. κλῶνα: 'stem'.

1070. [Bruhn read ὄχων with Hartman; but the line looks like a reminiscence of *Il*. 14. 289 ἔνθ' ἧστ' ὀζοισιν πεπυκασμένος εἰλατί-νοισιν.]

1073. 'Sheer to the sheer heaven it towered': like the Homeric ἐλάτη which δι' ἠέρος αἰθέρ' ἵκανεν (*Il*. 14. 288). The doubled epithet is a frequent trick of style in Greek and especially in tragedy—even in places where, as here, 'the repeated adjective serves for collective emphasis rather than for separate characterisation' (Jebb on Soph. *Tr*. 613). Cf. Soph. *El*. 742 ὀρθὸς ἐξ ὀρθῶν δίφρων ('himself and his car unspilt'), and the many examples collected by Denniston on Eur. *El*. 337.

1076–7. ὅσον γὰρ οὔπω δῆλος ἦν . . . καί: 'he was just becoming visible (only-just not-yet visible) . . . when . . .' Cf. Thuc. 6. 34. 9 ὅσον οὔπω πάρεισιν 'they are all but here'. The moment described is that at which the vibrations of the tree begin to subside, affording glimpses of its 'rider'.

1078–90. [This impressive passage is worth comparing with the almost contemporary lines in which the aged Sophocles described the supernatural summons to Oedipus, *OC*. 1621–9. The resemblances, individually trifling, are collectively rather striking:

Ba. 1078 φωνή τις ∼*OC*. 1623 φθέγμα . . . τινός
 1084 σίγησε δ' αἰθήρ κτλ. ∼*OC*. 1623 ἦν μὲν σιωπὴ
 1085 οὐκ ἂν ἤκουσας βοήν ∼*OC*. 1622 οὐδ' ἔτ' ὠρώρει βοή
 1087 ἔστησαν ὀρθαί ∼*OC*. 1624 ὀρθίας στῆσαι (τρίχας)
 1088 ὡς δ' ἐγνώρισαν | σαφῆ κελευσμὸν Βακχίου ∼*OC*. 1629 ὃ δ' ὡς
 ἐπῄσθετ' ἐκ θεοῦ καλούμενος

Some of these are adequately accounted for by the similarity of the situation; but not *OC*. 1624, which echoes the sound, not the sense, of *Ba*. 1087 and suggests unconscious reminiscence. If we accept the statement of the second Hypothesis that the *OC*. was first performed posthumously, which there is no reason to doubt, and ignore the bare possibility that a MS. of the *OC*. was sent to Eur. in Macedonia, it follows that if either poet echoed the other Soph. was the echoer. Soph., who died between July 406 and Feb. 405, may well have been at work on the last scene of the *OC*. in the spring or summer of 406, by which date we may suppose that copies of Eur.'s posthumous plays were circulating at Athens, even if they were not performed at the Great Dionysia of March 406.]

1078. ὡς μὲν εἰκάσαι, implying the unexpressed antithesis τὸ δ' ἀληθὲς οὐκ ἔχω εἰπεῖν: cf. 970 n. [Reiske's φωνήν (intern. accus. with ἀνεβόησεν) is pedantic and needless. Pap. Oxy. 2223, which preserves 1070–1136 in an incomplete condition (Introd. p. lvii), has φωνή.]

1081. [Pap. Oxy. has τ(ε)ιμωρεῖτ' ἐμοί here. There seems little to choose between the two readings.]

1082–3. 'And as the voice spoke these words, a light of awful fire was set betwixt heaven and earth.'   ἐστήριξε (which the author of the *Chr. Pat. may* have found in his copy of the *Bacchae*) implies a single flash, perhaps of lightning, which is called τὸ σεμνὸν πῦρ Διός, *Phoen.* 1175; ἐστήριζε (P), a continuous supernatural light (cf. *El.* 788, *Phoen.* 1177, where we have καὶ ταῦθ' ἅμ' ἠγόρευε καί . . . followed by an imperfect, expressing the simultaneity of two continuous actions). The verb is perhaps best taken as intrans., since to supply φωνή as the subject would be inappropriate and to supply Διόνυσος would make the Messenger assume more than he knows: cf. 972 and Plut. *Sulla* 6. 11 φλόγα λαμπρὰν στηρίξαι (intrans.) πρὸς τὸν οὐρανόν.—For Dion. as Master of the Lightning see 594–5 n. A supernatural light may accompany the epiphany of any god (*H. Hymn.* 2. 189, 3. 444, &c., cf. A. B. Cook, *Zeus*, ii, 114 ff.)[1]; but such manifestations seem to have been especially associated with the cult of Dion. [Cf. the αὐτόματον πῦρ which appeared at his sanctuary on Parnassus (schol. *Phoen.* 227), and the μέγα σέλας πυρός which was sometimes seen at his sanctuary in Crastonia in eastern Macedonia ([Aristot.] *mir.* 842ᵃ18 ff.). Eur. seems to have described a similar miraculous light in the Dionysiac ode in his *Hypsipyle* (fr. 31. 21 Hunt), where we have the fragmentary words φ]άος ἄσκοπον [ἀ]έρι.—Pap. Oxy. has σεμνόν, but *Phoen.* 1175, quoted above, tends to support P's σεμνοῦ (which appears also in the *Chr. Pat.*).]

1084–5 describe wonderfully the hush of nature at the moment when the pent-up forces of the supernatural break through: 'The high air went still (σίγησε aor.), and the woody glade held its leaves in stillness, and you could not have heard the cry of any beast.' The silence of the beasts here is the counterpart of their wild restlessness when the god is being summoned (727). Stillness is the traditional response of nature to a divine epiphany: cf. Ar. *Av.* 777 f. πτῆξε δὲ φῦλά τε ποικίλα θηρῶν, κύματά τ' ἔσβεσε νήνεμος αἴθρη, and the parody, *Thesm.* 42 ff.; Limenius 8 ff. (Powell, *Coll. Alex.* 149) ν]η-νέμους δ' ἔσχεν αἰθὴρ ἀε[λλῶν ταχυπετ]εῖς [δρό]μους κτλ.; Mesomedes, *Hymn.* 2. 1 ff. εὐφαμείτω πᾶς αἰθήρ κτλ. . . . μέλλει γὰρ πρὸς ἡμᾶς βαίνειν Φοῖβος. Prof. Fraenkel thinks that this type of description originally applied to the effects of Apollo's divine music (cf. Pind.

---

[1] In Heraclides Ponticus' account of the translation of Empedocles a mysterious voice is heard, as here, and then the watcher sees φῶς οὐράνιον καὶ λαμπάδων φέγγος, ἄλλο δὲ οὐδέν (fr. 83 Wehrli = Diog. L. 8. 67).

Pyth. i. 5 ff.), and was later transferred to the epiphany of Dionysus. [εὔλειμος (P) may be defended by the analogy of βαθύλειμος, but is a ἅπ. λεγ., whereas ὕλιμος (*Chr. Pat.*) is a word which Eur. is now known to have used elsewhere (fr. 495. 34), and one which suits φύλλα and νάπη: cf. *Andr.* 284 ὑλόκομον νάπος and *Hel.* 1303 ὑλάεντα νάπη. Moreover, Pap. Oxy. seems to have had ὕλιμος: there is a hole in it at this point, but Mr. Roberts judges the hole to be too small for εὔλειμος. For βοήν the papyrus has the more specific word βρόμον, which is likely to be right: it is used of stags belling (Alc. fr. 97) and horses neighing (Aesch. *Sept.* 476), and the adj. ἐρίβρομος of lions (Pind. *Ol.* 11. 21); βοήν would be a natural gloss. Cf. 151, where on ἐπιβρέμει L has the gloss ἐπιλέγει, ἠχεῖ: schol. *Phoen.* 113 βρέμων· ἠχῶν: Zonaras βρόμος· . . . ποιὰ φωνή.]

1087. διήνεγκαν κόρας: 'gazed about them', like *Or.* 1261 δόχμιά νυν κόρας διάφερ' ὀμμάτων. [But the papyrus has κ]άρα, which is supported by *Chr. Pat.* 673 καὶ διήνεγκαν κάραν (*v.ll.* κάρας, μάρας); the *Chr. Pat.* regularly makes κάρα feminine. κόρας looks like the result of a scribe's eye catching κόραι at the end of 1089.]

1090–3. The supernatural swiftness of the maenads is repeatedly stressed (165, 665, 748, *Hel.* 543). Cf. Pearce's account of a possessed dancer in Abyssinia who moved 'with such swiftness that the fastest runner could not come up with her' (*Life and Adventures of Nathaniel Pearce . . . 1810 to 1819*, i. 293). [This sentence as read in P is clearly faulty. ἔχουσαι cannot be construed with ὠκύτητα unless we alter ἥσσονες to ἥσσονα. But taken by itself it is meaningless: Tyrrell's rendering, 'holding their course', is not justified by fr. 779. 4 ἔχων δρόμον (where δρόμον makes all the difference), or by the non-tragic use of ἔχων with a present (not aor.) indic. to emphasize the continuous character of the action. Hartung's τρέχουσαι makes sense at the cost of some over-fullness of expression; but it is not safe to infer from the adaptation in the *Chr. Pat.* that the author found τρέχουσαι in his text of Eur. The papyrus cuts the knot by omitting both 1091 and 1092, which add nothing to the sense. I believe this to be right. 1091 was suspected by Paley and rejected by Wecklein and Dalmeyda. It may have been patched up from a note ἔχουσαι made by a reader unfamiliar with the 'accus. of respect' (which died out early), plus a recollection of 872 συντείνῃ δράμημα. 1092 (cf. 973–4) is an expansion of Κάδμου κόραι introduced, as often, πρὸς σαφήνειαν τῶν λεγομένων (schol. Soph. *Aj.* 841): see 182 n.]

1093. χειμάρρου νάπης: 'the torrent-flowing glade', i.e. the glade and the deep watercourse which intersected it.

1096–8. The pelting of Pentheus, which to a modern reader may seem below the dignity of tragedy, has not improbably a ritual origin (Bather), just as the tale of the stoning of Damia and Auxesia was invented to explain the Lithobolia at Trozen (Paus. 2. 32. 2). Cf.

perhaps the stoning of the φάρμακος at Athens (Harpocration s.v.).
[In view of this possibility, it is rash to reject 1098, as do most of the
recent continental critics, on the practical ground that fir-branches
would be ineffective missiles. Ballistics are one thing, ritual magic
another; and it may well be that the fir and (1103) oak branches,
like the thyrsi, were originally thought to be endowed with magical
virtue (cf. 109–10 n.). In any case the pelting *is* physically ineffective.
For the change of subject in 1098, which has been thought suspicious,
cf. 1124. The pap. has the line, and confirms Hermann's τ' for δ'.]
ἀντίπυργον: perhaps 'like a tower' (cf. ἀντίπαις), but more probably
'towering opposite', on the opposite escarpment of the ravine, where
missiles would not be obstructed by intervening trees; cf. the use of
ἀντιπυργοῦν at Aesch. *Eum.* 688.

1100. στόχον δύστηνον, 'cruel targeting' (Murray). στόχον for τ' ὄχον
(P) is now confirmed by the papyrus; it is accus. in apposition to the
sentence, and describes not the mark aimed at but the act of aiming.
[In my first edition I wrongly stated that for οὐκ the pap. has οὐχ,
which would agree with the statement of ancient grammarians that
ἀνύ(τ)ω was aspirated in Attic.]

1101–2. 'For beyond the reach of their fanaticism the poor wretch sat,
trapped past escaping.' Cf. Aesch. *Ag.* 1376 ὕψος κρεῖσσον ἐκπηδή-
ματος, of which the phrase here may be an unconscious echo. [The
pap. confirms the obvious corrections τλήμων and λελημμένος. It
agrees with P in reading καθῆ]στο, but usage favours the article:
cf. 1058, *Her.* 1013 εὗδει δ' ὁ τλήμων, *Or.* 1028 τέθνηχ' ὁ τλ., Soph.
El. 742 ὠρθοῦθ' ὁ τλ., 1477 πέπτωχ' ὁ τλ.]

1103. συγκεραυνοῦσαι, lit. 'shattering by a thunderbolt'; συν- has the
same force as in συντεθράνωται (633). The word is used elsewhere
of smashing a winecup (Cratinus fr. 187) and in the passive of a
person dazed by wine (Archilochus fr. 77), in both places with an
effect of comic exaggeration. Its use here seems intended to convey
the magical ease (cf. 194 n.) and swiftness of the act; the maenads,
like their master (594), command the magic of the lightning. That
they nevertheless fail in their attempts to hit Pentheus and to lever
up the tree-roots is inconsistent, but explicable on dramatic grounds:
the horror of the climax is intensified by its repeated postponement.
[The proposed emendation δρυΐνοις συντρια·νοῦσαι (or συγκραδαίνουσαι)
κλάδοις is not very convincing; and συγκεραυνοῦσαι (which the pap.
also had) looks much less like the chance product of a copyist's
blunder than like an element of the special Dionysiac vocabulary
on which Eur. draws repeatedly in this play. One is reminded of
the claim made today by orgiastic Arab sectaries that they can rend
objects without contact 'by the power radiating from their fingers'
(Brunel, *Aissâoûa*, 183).]

1104. ἀνεσπάρασσον: conative. [After this line the pap. has βακχαι τα Πενθεως.[....]πι.τω[. This appears to be the remains of a line omitted by P. But I cannot restore it with any confidence.[1]]

1106–10. φέρε ... λάβεσθε : φέρε, like ἄγε, ἰδέ and εἰπέ, has degenerated into an interjection, and is therefore used even in addressing a number of persons : cf. Ar. *Ach.* 541 ff. φέρε ... καθῆσθε, &c.   **πτόρθου:** 'the stem'.   τὸν ἀμβάτην θῆρα : Agaue sees Pentheus as a 'climbing beast', but the next words show that she sees him also as a human spy. What later becomes a fixed delusion (1141) begins as a fleeting fancy, perhaps no more than a metaphor. That is good psychology. The rationalism which would delete μηδ'—κρυφαίους (Paley, Merkelbach) seems to me imprudent.   **μυρίαν χέρα:** cf. 743–5 n.

1111–13. 'For rhetorical effect, the name of Pentheus is reserved to the end of the sentence, and the pause, at so early a point as the end of the first foot of the line, is admirably adapted to express the sudden fall' (Sandys). I see no sufficient ground for deleting 1113 with Nauck and others. [χαμαιριφής : this word is not found in classical Greek, though Dr. Maas quotes from Eustath. the gloss τὸ δὲ χαμαὶ ἐκπεσὸν χαμαιριφὲς λέγεται (1279. 45). χαμαιπετής (P) is ugly with πίπτει : cf., however, *Tro.* 506 ff., where χαμαιπετῆ is followed in the next line by πεσοῦσα. The pap. lacks the end of the line.   γάρ P and *Chr. Pat.* 1432 (explaining the οἰμώγματα) ; but the pap. has δ' ἄρ', which seems preferable : the Messenger knows Pentheus' state of mind only by inference from his behaviour.]

1114. ἱερέᾱ = ἱέρεια : Agaue becomes a 'priestess' because Pentheus is to be the victim of a ritual σπαραγμός. [ἱερεία P, ιερεια pap. But everywhere else in tragedy (*IT.* 34, 1399, *Or.* 261, Soph. fr. 456) the metre requires the penult. to be short, and we should almost certainly adopt the spelling ἱερέα, which is found in fifth-century inscriptions (Meisterhans, *Gramm. d. Att. Inschr.*[3], 40) and is transmitted in the Soph. passage. So probably here also. Herodian 2. 454 says that this word had ᾱ in Attic.]

1116. γνωρίσασα : the removal of the μίτρα—which was, as the vase-paintings show, a mere headband—would not in itself much assist recognition. Did it hold the wig (831–3 n.) in place, so that the latter would drop off when it was removed?

1117–21. Pentheus dies sane (cf. Nonnus 46. 189 τότε μὲν λίπε λύσσα) and repentant : along with the ritual μίτρα he has discarded the madness

---

[1] A. Y. Campbell's ⟨ἀθλίου⟩ πι⟨σ⟩τώ⟨ματα⟩ does not quite fit the traces : 'after Πενθέως a λ or a is probable ; before the πι, either σ or ε' (Roberts). The line may well have been interpolated πρὸς σαφήνειαν τῶν λεγομένων, as Merkelbach has argued (*Rh. Mus.* xcvii [1954], 374 f.) ; cf. 182 n., 1090–3 n.

which he acquired when he put it on. His repentance must be taken as sincere, and is fatal to the view which sees in him a blameless victim of religious fanaticism.   παρηίδος ψαύων, the traditional gesture of supplication. Cf. the parallel scene in the *Heracles*, 987 ff. Ἐγώ . . . εἰμί: 'It is I.'   ταῖς ἐμαῖς . . . παῖδα σόν: the antithesis is deliberate—the offence of an individual cannot justify the violation of the blood-tie. For the causal dative cf. *Andr.* 157 στυγοῦμαι δ' ἀνδρὶ φαρμάκοισι σοῖς. [In place of σέθεν the pap. had something beginning with ο, probably ὁ ⟨σός⟩ (C. H. ¦Roberts). Cf. *Rhes.* 90, where some MSS. have σέθεν, others τὸ σόν.]

1122–3. These are traditional (and genuine) symptoms of abnormal mental states: Hp. *morb. sacr.* 7 ἀφρὸς ἐκ τοῦ στόματος ἐκρέει . . . καὶ τὰ ὄμματα διαστρέφονται, of epileptics; Hp. *coac.* 476 ὄμμασι περι-βλέπουσαι, of states of ἐκστασις; *Aethiopis* fr. 3 Kinkel; Eur. *Med.* 1173 ff. with Page's note; *Her.* 932–4; *IT.* 308.

1124. ἐκ: regular in such phrases, because the god is conceived as the *source* of the mental state: cf. Xen. *Symp.* 1. 10 ἐκ θεῶν του κατε-χόμενοι.   ἔπειθε, sc. Pentheus.

1125–7. 'Seizing his left arm below the elbow (lit. "by the forearm") and setting her foot hard against the doomed man's ribs, she wrenched the shoulder out.'   ὠλένης, gen. of the part grasped (Kühner–Gerth, i. 348). χείρ 'arm', or rather, 'arm plus hand', is an occasional use from Homer downwards (L.S. s.v. I. 2, Wilamowitz on *Ion* 1337). —This moment is often represented in ancient works of art (cf. L. Curtius, *Pentheus*, 13 ff.; H. Philippart, *Iconographie des B.* 58 ff.). [ὠλέναις P, ωλεν[α]ισι pap. (i.e. ὠλέναισ', a rather artificial device for providing a caesura which was also suggested by Elmsley). This *inverts* the common usage of χείρ and ὠλένη, making the former mean 'arm' and the latter 'hand'. We might expect λαβοῦσα δ' ὠλένην ἀριστερὰν χερί (Minervini) or rather χεροῖν (Dunlop, *C.R.* li [1937], 57). But I am not satisfied that P's text is wrong. ὠλένη 'hand' occurs not only at *IT.* 966 (where Platnauer pronounces it 'impossible') but at *Her.* 1381 (where it has never been doubted). Wilamowitz calls it 'a specifically Euripidean κατάχρησις'. A probable further instance occurs in an anonymous tragic fragment (Page, *Gk. Lit. Papyri* i, no. 32. 7) ἐμῆς τόνδ' ὠλένης χερὸς λαβεῖν, where I think we must choose between reading ὠλέναις (Schadewaldt) and excising χερός as an intrusive gloss which has driven out e.g. πάρα at the end of the line (ὠλένη is regularly glossed by χείρ). In the present passage the inversion, as Rappold has pointed out, is not motiveless: it serves to avoid having χεροῖν as a line-ending twice within 4 lines.—The absence of caesura may be deliberate—a dragging line for the dragging movement. It is in any case an insufficient ground for drastic emendation, particularly in a play which shows Aeschylean influence. Cf. *Hec.* 1159 and fr. 495. 6, where the device of the elided long dative is applicable ; also *El.* 546, *Hel.* 86, *I A.* 630.—In 1126 the pap. has πλευροισιν, perhaps rightly.]

1128. A fresh sentence, as often, instead of a subordinate phrase parallel to ὑπὸ σθένους.—This is the last sinister manifestation of the Dionysiac effortlessness (194 n.).

1131–3. 'And every throat shouted together—he screaming with what breath was in him, but they were yelling triumph.' The sentence has the loose syntax of natural speech : ὁ μὲν στενάζων is in partitive apposition to πᾶσα βοή, like Aesch. *PV.* 200 ff. στάσις τ' ἐν ἀλλήλοισιν ὠροθύνετο, | οἱ μὲν θέλοντες . . . οἱ δὲ τοὔμπαλιν | σπεύδοντες, but in the δέ clause the expected participle is replaced for greater emphasis by a finite verb (cf. 225, 1128). So *Heraclid.* 39 ff. δυοῖν γερόντοιν δὲ στρατηγεῖται φυγή, | ἐγὼ μέν . . . καλχαίνων . . ., | ἢ δ' αὖ . . . | σῴζει. [The pap. confirms στενάζων, but does not help us to choose between ἐτύγχανεν πνέων and ἐτύγχαν' ἐμπνέων (Wecklein thought ὅσον impossible with the latter, but cf. *Alc.* 205, *Hipp.* 1246). For ὁμοῦ βοή the pap. offers λο·[: this may mean merely that the scribe repeated -λος τε πᾶς from the end of the previous line.]

1133–6. 'One carried an arm, another a foot still shod for hunting ; his ribs were stripped by rending nails, and every hand had blood on it as they tossed his flesh for their sport.' **ἴχνος :** properly footprint, then the foot which makes it : so fr. 530. 7 τὸ λαιὸν ἴχνος ἀνάρβυλοι ποδός, and Catullus 64. 162 'candida permulcens liquidis vestigia lymphis'. **πᾶσα** = ἑκάστη. **διεσφαίριζε :** lit. 'made it her handball'. Eur. does not shrink from the grotesque, which is, in Koestler's words, 'the reflection of the tragic in the distorting mirror of the trivial'. **γυμνοῦντο :** the augment is ordinarily omitted only at the beginning of a line (cf. 765–8 n., 1066, 1084). [Other apparent exceptions to this rule are (a) *Andr.* 1130, *Ion* 1205, Soph. *Trach.* 767, *Phil.* 371, Aesch. *Pers.* 313, of which the last may be spurious and the rest are easily emended ; (b) *Alc.* 839, Soph. *OC.* 1506, which are doubly suspect as not being narrative. All thes emay well be wrong ; but in the present passage Porson's γυμνοῦσι δέ | πλευρά does not carry conviction, still less other attempts at emendation. The pap. (which confirms the corrections in 1133 and 1136) has πλευραί, but the end of 1134 is missing.]

1137. χωρίς : 'scattered'.

1141. The carrying of the head transfixed on the point of the thyrsus is an additional touch of horror (cf. *Il.* 18. 176, Hdt. 9. 78 f.). This may be an innovation of Eur. In the pictorial tradition both before and after the date of the *Bacchae* it is carried by the hair. Farther on, at 1277, Agaue seems to have the head in her arms.

1147. 'The triumph-giver—in whose service she wins tears for triumph.' The last three words are added by the Messenger in bitter comment. ᾧ is the 'dative of advantage', like 66 Βρομίῳ. [No explanation of

P's ᾗ is quite satisfactory. (a) If ᾗ is Agaue (Barnes), νικηφορεῖ (a ἅπ. λεγ.) has to mean 'he gives as prize of victory'. Despite ξὺν δίκῃ νικηφόρῳ (*Phoen.* 781 and Aesch. *Cho.* 148), I doubt this sense for the verb: in this context it must surely have reference to the carrying of Pentheus' head, i.e. Agaue must be the subject. (b) If ᾗ is to refer to ἄγρας (Musgrave &c.), we have to reduce καλλίνικον to an adj. qualifying ξυνεργάτην (omitting comma at end of 1146). But the three epithets of Dion. are surely parallel and independent, representing respectively the chase, the kill, and the triumph. (c) To make ᾗ refer to νίκη understood from καλλίνικον (Tyrrell) is harsh and unlikely; and (d) if taken as an adv. (Marchant) it is hopelessly weak and unidiomatic. Heath's ᾗ is also unidiomatic, spoiling the balance of the sentence. There is more to be said for ᾗ (Kirchhoff, Madvig), introducing an ironical summing-up as at *Tro.* 383. But ᾧ is probably the right correction.]

1148-9. It is normal for a Messenger to leave the stage as soon as he has delivered his message (and in the present case indispensable, since all three actors will be needed in the next scene). The withdrawal is not as a rule specially motived, as it is here; cf., however, *IT.* 342, *IA.* 440.

1150-2. Like his predecessor (769 ff.) this Messenger draws a moral, and in doing so he answers the Chorus's question at 877, τί τὸ σοφόν; ἢ τί κάλλιον . . . ; What is at once κάλλιστον and σοφώτατον, dictate of honour and fruit of understanding, is σωφροσύνη and εὐσέβεια. It is the same traditional moral which Sophocles' Chorus drew from the fate of Creon—πολλῷ τὸ φρονεῖν εὐδαιμονίας | πρῶτον ὑπάρχει· χρὴ δὲ τά γ' ἐς θεοὺς | μηδὲν ἀσεπτεῖν (*Ant.* 1348).—For mental qualities as a κτῆμα cf. *Or.* 702 f., *IA.* 334, Soph. *Ant.* 683 f., 1050. [But σοφώτατον κτῆμα is perhaps a little odd, and I incline to prefer P's χρῆμα—'the wisest usage for those who use it'. The tragedians are fond of *figura etymologica*, and abstracts are often called χρῆμα, e.g. Mimnermus fr. 8 ἀληθείη . . . πάντων χρῆμα δικαιότατον: Andoc. 2. 1 δεινότατον ἁπάντων χρημάτων ἡγοῦμαι εἰ τῷ μὲν δοκεῖ ταῦτα τῷ δὲ μή.]

Stasimon 5 (1153-64)

As the action hurries to its climax there is time only for a brief song of triumph, a dozen lines without responsion. Similarly in the *Hipp.* and the *Ion* the last stasimon, sung at a moment of extreme crisis, is cut down to a single astrophic stanza; Aesch. at a like moment had replaced the stasimon by a dozen anapaests (*Ag.* 1331 ff.). The opening words suggest a joyful accompanying dance (ὑπόρχημα); but as the thoughts of the singers turn from Pentheus to Agaue horror, if not pity, creeps in. The last lines prepare the audience for what their eyes must now meet.

Metre. Similar to stasimon 4—dochmiacs interspersed with iambic and other cola. Synaphea is not observed.

Scheme:

	∪∪∪−−− ·−∪∪	dochm.+iamb.
	∪∪∪−−− ·−∪−	dochm.+iamb.
1155	−−∪−− −∪∪−∪∪−	iambelegus
	−− −∪∪− ∪−	glyc.²
	−−∪∪−∪−−	enoplion
	∪∪∪−−−	dochm.
	−−∪− −−∪− ∪−∪−	3 iamb.
1160	−−−·−−	dochm.
	−−∪− −−∪− ∪−∪∪	3 iamb.
	−∪∪−∪∪∪	dochm.
	∪∪∪−∪− ∪−−−−	2 dochm.
	∪∪∪−∪−	dochm.

1153–5. The verbs are parallel in sense, construction, and rhythm: 'Lift we our feet for the Lord Bacchus, Lift we our voice for the doom fallen On Pentheus the dragon's child.' [Wilamowitz's transposition in 1155 gives an iambelegus like 1018 and 1179–80 in place of an iambic trimeter with a highly improbable anapaest in the fourth 'foot'. For the word-order cf. *Heraclid.* 446 μητέρ' Ἀλκμήνην πατρός. A copyist has introduced the normal prose order.¹]

1157–8. 'And received the blessed wand of magic, which was death unfailing (?).' **νάρθηκα εὔθυρσον**, a fennel wand which has duly become a thyrsus (by the addition of the ritual ivy-bunch): see 113 n., 1054–5 n. **πιστὸν ῞Αιδαν**: probably corrupt. πιστός signifies 'worthy of trust or belief'; nowhere else does it mean 'certain', and the Homeric phrase σῶς αἰπὺς ὄλεθρος hardly justifies attributing that sense to it here. [I am fairly confident that the second word is Ἄιδα,² which under the influence of the neighbouring accusatives someone read as Ἄιδαν (cf. 475 n., and the similar confusions at *Hec.* 1105, *Her.* 736). πιστὸν Ἄιδα is, however, scarcely Greek for 'assurance of death': without an article the neut. sing. adj. cannot do duty as a noun. The most conservative correction is πίστιν Ἄιδα (Schroeder)³; but Wilamowitz's ὁπλισμὸν Ἄιδα, 'armature of death',

---

¹ The corruption is pre-Byzantine; for the new papyrus fragment from Antinoë (see Introd. p. lix) has πενθέως at the end of the line.

² This is now pleasingly confirmed by the new papyrus, which has πι..οναιδα (sic: *not*, apparently, αιδᾱ = Ἄιδαν). The preceding word seems to have been πιστὸν: Mr. Barns tells me that neither πίστιν nor (probably) ὁπλισμὸν will fit the traces.

³ Cf. Aesch. *Eum.* 670, where Murray's πίστις for πιστὸς would seem to be right.

is also attractive. Ἄιδα is often nearly equivalent to an adj. 'fatal' (Headlam on *Ag.* 1234): so δίκτυον Ἄιδου *Ag.* 1115, ξίφεσιν Ἄιδα *Or.* 1398, Ἄιδα κόσμον *Med.* 980. Of the conjectures which eliminate Hades altogether, Ingram's κισσοχαίταν is perhaps the most alluring (cf. 1054 θύρσον . . . κισσῷ κομήτην). But 857 κόσμον ὅνπερ εἰς Ἄιδου λαβὼν | ἄπεισι suggests the probability of a reference to Hades here. Verrall's interpretation of this passage, 'he took the pillbox, death in a drink', is one of the curiosities of scholarship. It is enough to say that νάρθηξ 'pillbox' is unknown to Greek poetry; that πιστός 'potable' is equally unknown save for one passage where the context excludes all ambiguity (Aesch. *PV.* 480); and that 'he took the bottle', i.e. its contents, is an English, not a Greek, locution.]

1161-2. 'A famous hymn of victory have you made—but the end is lamentation, the end is tears.' The reference is to 1145-7. **κλεινόν,** pred. **ἐξεπράξατε ἐς,** 'fulfilled into', i.e. 'transformed in its making to': their victory is also their punishment. The metrical hiatus between these two words indicates a pause (an English writer would put a dash) before the reversal of meaning. The καλλίνικος (ὕμνος) owed its name to the refrain τήνελλα καλλίνικε (Archilochus fr. 119, cf. Pind. *Ol.* 9. 1 ff. and schol., Ar. *Ach.* 1227 and schol.). [ἐξεπράξατο (P) can hardly be right in the absence of an expressed subject, nor is the middle elsewhere found in this sense.—For γόνον (P) I prefer Canter's γόον to Murray's στόνον (a word which does not occur in Eur.): cf. *Or.* 677 ἔς τε δάκρυα καὶ γόους, *IT.* 860 δάκρυα καὶ γόοι. γόος is technical for a dirge (Schadewaldt, *Monolog* 160²).]

1163-4. 'A pretty conquest—to plunge red hands (lit. "clothe a dripping hand") in the blood of one's child.' **στάζουσαν,** proleptic. [Reading uncertain. P has ἐν αἵματι στάζουσαν χέρα περιβαλεῖν τέκνου, which satisfies neither sense nor metre (we expect a concluding dochmius). Wilamowitz's conjecture, adopted in the text, does not convince me: the natural sense of χέρα περιβαλεῖν is not 'to clothe the hand' but 'to embrace', while χέρ' αἵματι στάζουσαν would naturally mean 'a hand dripping with blood' (αἵματι instrum. dat.). Wilamowitz's text might also be construed as meaning 'to embrace the blood-dripping arm of one's child' (cf. 1125). But to recall this detail of the σπαραγμός is inappropriate here, and tragic usage would require the addition of χερσί or the like. If περιβαλεῖν is sound, τέκνῳ seems to be needed—'to embrace one's child with blood-dripping hand'. The ἀγών, however, should be the actual kill rather than the subsequent parade. The neatest correction is that once suggested by Wecklein, ἐν αἵματι στάζουσαν | χέρα [περι]βαλεῖν τέκνου 'to lay red hands on the life of one's child'—an elaboration of the phrase found at *Med.* 1283, ἐν φίλοις χέρα βαλεῖν (προσβαλεῖν L P) τέκνοις. In each passage the simple verb was glossed (as often) by a compound; in each, P substitutes the gloss for the original text. For αἷμα 'life-blood' and so 'life' cf. Soph. fr. 799. 3 αἷμα συγγενὲς κτείνας, Aesch. *Sept.* 718 αὐτάδελφον αἷμα δρέψασθαι.]

Exodos (1165–end)

This falls into five sections: (*a*) the mad scene, Agaue and Chorus, 1165–1215 (the first part of this is lyrical, reflecting the excitement of Agaue's entrance); (*b*) the return of Cadmus with Pentheus' body, and the restoration of Agaue to sanity (ἀναγνώρισις), 1216–1300; (*c*) the lamentations for Pentheus (1301–29, latter part lost); (*d*) the *deus ex machina* (1330–67, beginning lost); (*e*) concluding anapaests (1368–92, mutilated). The whole is evidently designed to produce a revulsion of sympathy from the god who is so terribly avenged to the human victims of his vengeance (Introd., pp. xliv–xlvii, cf. nn. on 1184, 1197, 1249–50, 1296–8, 1302–29, 1348–9).

1165–7. The Chorus-leader interposes (ἀλλά) to break off the song and introduce the new character to the audience. **ἐν διαστρόφοις ὄσσοις :** in fifth-century poetry ἐν already begins to encroach on the simple dat. of accompanying circumstances, as on the simple instrumental (157–9 n.). A person is said not only to be 'in' the clothes he wears or 'in' a state of feeling, but to be 'in' anything which for the time being characterizes him, whether external (Eur. *Supp.* 593 καινὸς ἐν καινῷ δορί, &c.) or, as here, organic.

The *lyric dialogue* marks the climax of horror. It was accompanied by a formal dance, with *pas seul* for Agaue, as we may infer from the strophic structure and the distribution of parts between Agaue and Chorus, which was evidently identical in strophe and antistrophe though our MS. muddles it. The rhythms continue those of the preceding stasimon. [In 1173–5 = 1189–91 text and colometry are doubtful: see separate notes.]

Scheme:

	∪∪∪ – – – ∪∪∪ – – –	2 dochm.
	∪∪∪ – ∪ –	dochm.
1170 = 1186	∪∪∪∪∪∪ ∪∪∪∪∪∪	2 iamb. (tribrachs)
	∪∪∪ – – –	dochm.
	∪ – – ∪ – ∪ – – ∪ –	2 dochm.
	∪ – ∪ – ∪ – ∪ –	2 iamb.
	∪ – ∪ – ∪∪ – ∪∪ – ∪	iamb. + reizianum
1175 = 1191	– ∪ – ∪∪	hypodochmius
	∪∪∪ – ∪ –	dochm.
	∪ – ᐧ – ∪ – ᐧ –	2 iamb. (bacchii)
	∪∪∪ – ᐱ –	dochm.
	ᐱ – ∪ – ᐱ – ∪∪ – ∪∪ –	iambelegus

1180 = 1196   ∪–∪– –   –∪∪–∪∪–   iambelegus
              ∪– •– ∪– •–   2 iamb. (bacchii)
              ∪– •– ∪– •∪   2 iamb. (bacchii)
              ∪∪∪∪∪∪–   dochm.
              ∪∪∪–∪– ∪––∪–   2 dochm.

1168. τί μ' ὀροθύνεις, ὤ; 'Oh why do you urge me?' The words suggest
that despite their triumph-song the Chorus do not really welcome
the spectacle of Pentheus' head: they would prefer not to look at
it, but the madwoman insists. [ὀροθύνεις, or ἐρεθίζεις (cf. 148), seems
the best correction. Other proposals produce inferior sense with
more change. For postponement of ὤ cf. *Hipp.* 362.]

1169–71. ὀρέων, disyll.   ἕλικα, 'tendril' of ivy (or vine): the head with
its curling hair and beard (1185 ff.) takes the place of the ritual
bunch of ivy leaves on the tip of the thyrsus, and Agaue in her
delirium identifies the two. Cf. the story of Lycurgus, who in
Dionysiac madness believed his son to be a vine shoot and slashed
him down, [Apollod.] 3. 5. 1.   θήραν: best taken as 'hunting',
accus. in apposition to the sentence. [But θήραμ' has better
authority: see 866–70 n.] In the year 53 B.C. these lines were recited
'amid general applause' at the court of Parthia by an actor dressed
as Agaue who carried a real human head—the severed head of
Crassus, the Roman general (Plutarch, *Crassus* 33).

1173–5. Text mutilated, as antistr. shows; restoration is guesswork.
[P's νιν is more likely to represent ἷνιν, a favourite word in Euripidean lyrics, than the epic form λίν or λῖν, which does not appear in
tragedy: cf. Aesch. *Ag.* 717 λέοντος ἷνιν (λέοντα σίνιν codd.). Further
reconstruction depends on what view we take of the metrical
pattern. If we strike out θῆρα in 1190 (see below), we may perhaps
read here ἔμαρψα τόνδ' ἄνευ βρόχων, λέοντος ἶ|νιν ⟨ὀρέστερον⟩, ὡς
ὁρᾶν πάρα. Denniston suggests ⟨λεοντοφυῆ⟩ νέον ἷνιν = σοφῶς ἀνέπηλ'
ἐπὶ θῆρα, enhoplion, cutting out σοφός in 1190.]

1177. [τί Κιθαιρών; P. If τί is retained here we can get correspondence
by reading at 1193 ⟨τί δ'⟩ ἐπαινῶ; or better ⟨τί δ';⟩ ἐπαινῶ. But
we expect bacchiacs as in 1181–2: a pherecratean seems rather unlikely here (though cf. 1156 glyconic), an ionic dimeter impossible.
τί may have been intruded to show the interrogative intention.]

1178. [καταφονεύει would make the responsion syllabically exact. But
cf. 1172 = 1188.]

1179. πρῶτον ἐμὸν τὸ γέρας = ἐμοὶ πρώτῃ τοῦτο τὸ γέρας ἐδόθη. [πρῶτον
is the right correction, not πρώτα; (= πρώτῃ;): (a) a variation
between str. and antistr. in the distribution of parts between Agaue
and Chorus would throw out the movements of the dance, and in
1195 ματέρα surely belongs to Agaue; (b) epic shortening in hiatus
seems improbable where the hiatus coincides with a change of

singer (cf., however, *El.* 1331); (*c*) πρῶτον provides the motive for the
Chorus's next question, τίς ἄλλα;]

1180. [P gives **μάκαιρ' Ἀγαύη** to the Chorus: it is then an ironical comment like καλὸς ἀγών (1163), and Agaue replies 'That is what the
worshippers call me'. This is perhaps better: 1180 will repeat the
distribution, as it repeats the rhythm, of 1179. 1196 will be similarly
divided.]

1181–3. Ch.: 'Who else (struck him)?' Ag.: 'It was Cadmus . . .'
Ch.: 'Cadmus?' Ag.: 'Whose daughters laid hand on this creature—
but after me, oh after me! Yes, we have had lucky hunting.'   **τί
Κάδμου;** puzzled, like *Alc.* 807 τί ζῶσιν; 'Why do you say "live"?'
I A. 460 τί παρθένον; 'Why do I call her "maid"?'—It would seem that
as victor in a ritual competition Agaue enjoys some especial status
in the θίασος: she is the ἱερέα φόνου (1114)—hence, apparently, her
extraordinary exaltation (Bather, *J.H.S.* xiv, 255 f.). [Murray follows
Schöne and Wilamowitz (*Herakles*², 399 n. 1) in supposing that two
trimeters delivered by the Chorus-leader, answering to 1200–1, have
dropped out at the end of the strophe. The necessity seems very
doubtful: μέτεχέ νυν θοίνας follows naturally on εὐτυχής γ' ἅδ' ἄγρα,
and 1200–1 may be regarded as making the transition to the iambic
scene rather than as part of the lyrical dialogue.¹]

1184. The invitation to a feast—presumably with Pentheus' remains as
the principal dish—is too much for the nerves of the Chorus: their
attitude of forced approval breaks down. [τλάμων (P) would be
self-pity: τλᾶμον fits the situation better (cf. 1200 ὦ τάλαινα).²—We
may find here a hint of a tradition in which ὠμοφαγία as well as
σπαραγμός was practised on Pentheus. Cf. Oppian, *Cyn.* 4. 304,
where P. is *transformed* into a bull, the maenads into panthers who
rend and eat the bull; also the daughters of Minyas who tore and ate
the child of one of them (Plut. *Q. Gr.* 38), and the cannibal feast
prescribed by the god himself in a fragment of a late Dionysiac epic
(Page, *Literary Papyri* i, no. 134).]

1185–7. 'The bull is young: his cheek is just growing downy under his
crest of delicate hair.'   **γένυν . . . κατάκομον θάλλει,** lit. 'sprouts as to
his jaw (so that it is) hairy'.   **κόρυθα: κόρυς** does not occur elsewhere in this sense, but cf. κορυδός, the crested lark; κορύσσεσθαι,
of crested birds and crested waves; κορύπτειν, to butt with the top
of the head.—With the idea of a sacramental feast, Agaue's dream
has shifted a little: the head is a bull's head now, though bearded
like a young man's (cf. 1106–10 n.). As she speaks, she strokes it with
unconscious maternal affection. [L.S. still seems to take μόσχος to be

---

¹ If anything is lost, it was lost early: the new papyrus scrap, which
preserves parts of lines 1183–6, contains no more than is in P.
² And is now confirmed by the new papyrus.

a lion's whelp here, as did most scholars before Wilamowitz. But although a boy or girl could be called a μόσχος (*anglice* 'kid'), it does not follow that a young lion could—particularly without λέοντος, and in a play where μόσχος has been used more than once in its literal sense. (At *IT*. 163, which L.S. quotes, μόσχος is merely 'young cow'.) The tradition that P. was transformed into, or mistaken for, a bull appears elsewhere: Oppian (see 1184 n.); Val. Flaccus 3. 266; schol. Persius 1. 100 'Pentheum . . . quem mater . . . sub imagine vituli trucidavit'; Tzetzes, *Chiliades*, 6. 577 δόξας δὲ ταῦρος τῇ μητρὶ καὶ τῶν Βακχῶν ταῖς ἄλλαις (sc. ὁ Πενθεύς).]

1188. 'Yes, for its hair it looks like a beast of the wild.' Cf. Soph. *El.* 664 πρέπει γὰρ ὡς τύραννος. [P's text here is a good example of the Byzantine trick of filling out unrecognized dochmiacs to make iambic trimeters.]

1189–91. Sense clear, but exact text doubtful. ['Molestum est, rursus inculcari illud θῆρα', said Hermann, with justice. He read ἐπὶ θήρᾳ τοῦδε. But I incline to Wilamowitz's opinion that θῆρα (θήρα P) is a gloss on τόνδε. Its removal leaves a more convincing metrical pattern,

ὁ Βάκχιος κυναγέτας σοφὸς σοφῶς
ἀνέπηλ' ἐπὶ τόνδε μαινάδας,

iambic trimeter + anapaestic-iambic dimeter or Κυρηναϊκόν (cf. Denniston, 'Lyric Iambics', 135 ff.). If we retain θῆρα, 1190 has the unusual form ∪ – ∪ –   ∪ ∪ – ∪ – ∪, for which Denniston compares *Med.* 206, *Phoen.* 128.]

1192. Dionysus hunts the fawn or the wild goat (137 f.) at the τριετηρίς. He is also on occasion a hunter of men. [Despite Jeanmaire, *Dionysos*, 273, and others before him, I doubt if Eur. intends any reference to the name Zagreus, which the ancients derived from ζα- + ἀγρεύς (*Etym. M.* s.v.). Zagreus, originally, it would seem, a Cretan counterpart of Dionysus, was identified with him in Hellenistic times (Callimachus fr. 171, &c.). But it is not certain that this identification goes back to the fifth century (Eur. fr. 472 *may* imply it, but does not necessarily do so): cf. Nilsson, *Gesch. d. Griech. Rel.* i. 649 Anm. 3.]

1194. τάχα δὲ Καδμεῖοι . . . : Agaue would presumably have continued to the effect ἐπαινέσονταί με (cf. 1202 ff.), but the Chorus, curious to test the extent of her delusion, interject the name of Pentheus.

1197. Ch.: 'Strange spoil.' Ag.: 'And strangely taken.' The Chorus, who once warned us against περισσοὶ φῶτες (429), now find Agaue's deed περισσόν, though their god has willed it. But Agaue accepts the word as a compliment.

1198–9. μεγάλα καὶ φανερά: with unconscious irony Agaue echoes the words in which the Chorus described the splendours of Dionysiac irrationalism (1006). Denniston suggests that the phrase may be taken from ritual. **κατειργασμένα**, nom. sing. fem. mid.

1200. νυν: 'then', inferential (= εἴπερ μεγάλα καὶ φανερὰ κατείργασαι).

1203–7. θηρός, gen. of definition dependent on ἄγραν, but attracted into the relative clause, like Thuc. 2. 45. 1 παισὶ δ' αὖ ὅσοι τῶνδε πάρεστε.

ἀγκυλητοῖς ... στοχάσμασιν: 'with thonged javelins', missiles to whose middle a thong (ἀγκύλη) was attached, in a loop of which the thrower inserted his fingers (nicely shown in P. Jacobsthal, *Diskoi*, pl. II). Cf. Aesch. fr. 16 παλτὰ κἀγκυλητά, 'thongless and thonged javelins'. [But the form ἀγκυλωτοῖς (P and schol. *Hec.* 1156) is defensible on the analogy of λογχωτός, 'provided with a spearhead' (761), κοντωτός 'provided with a pole', &c. Cf. 19 n., and Ernst Fraenkel, *Gr. Denominativa*, 106 ff.] **Θεσσαλῶν**: Θεσσαλῶν γὰρ εὕρημα τὸ δόρυ, schol. *Hipp.* 221. Mr. Barrett compares Xen. *Hell.* 6. 1. 9 σχεδὸν δὲ πάντες οἱ ταύτῃ (sc. in Thessaly) ἀκοντισταί εἰσιν. **λευκοπήχεσι χειρῶν ἀκμαῖσιν**: 'with our hands' white blades'. χειρῶν ἀκμαί are probably hands, not fingers, as ποδοῖν ἀκμαί, Soph. *OT.* 1034, are feet, not toes. But the phrase suggests that the hands are sharp and deadly (cf. Aesch. *Pers.* 1060 πέπλον δ' ἔρεικε ... ἀκμῇ χερῶν). In λευκοπήχεσι the first part of the compound implies 'feminine', the second repeats the meaning of the noun as in λευκοτρίχων πλοκάμων (112). Cf. *Phoen.* 1351 λευκοπήχεις κτύπους χεροῖν.

1207–8. 'After that (**κᾆτα** = καὶ εἶτα), should huntsmen brag while they needlessly procure the armourers' engines?' What Agaue complains of is that huntsmen should *both* brag *and* hunt with weapons instead of the naked hand. [To read κᾆτ' ἀκοντίζειν (Sandys) would enfeeble the taunt.] For lion-killing without weapons see Paus. 6. 5. 5.

1209–10. αὐτῇ χειρί: to be taken with both verbs, as its position shows. **χωρίς** adv., as at 1137, strengthening διεφορήσαμεν. ['At θηρὸς post τόνδε languet' (Wilamowitz, *Analecta*, 67 n.1). Hence χωρὶς σιδήρου τ' Pierson; χωρίς τ' ἀθῆρος (= ἀθέρος) Ruhnken (but even if the form is defensible, ἀθήρ, 'point', is the wrong word); χωρίς τε δορίδος ('sacrificial knife') Wilamowitz, comparing *El.* 819, where Nauck conjectured δορίδ' ἀναρπάσας (but Δωρίδ' ἁρπάσας [MSS.] is confirmed by 836). These changes are unconvincing. Winnington-Ingram argues, perhaps over-subtly, that the poet has postponed θηρός so that the masc. pronoun may suggest Pentheus: 'τόνδε and θηρός represent the two discrepant parts of Agaue's consciousness.']

1213. [Cf. *Phoen.* 489 πηκτῶν κλιμάκων προσαμβάσεις, which confirms the conjecture πηκτῶν here.]

1214. τριγλύφοις: properly 'fluted beam-ends' (cf. L.S. s.v.). But the plural must be used here, and at *IT.* 113 εἴσω τριγλύφων, to describe the entire horizontal band composed of triglyphs proper alternating with metopes: it was to the *metopes* that βουκράνια, &c., were attached. The τρίγλυφοι would form part of the castle façade, which is still standing. Agaue proposes to follow the hunters' usage of nailing the head of the quarry to the housefront as a trophy. Cf. Posidonius fr. 116 Jac. (*F. Gr. H.* ii A. 304), where we learn that the Celts nail up on their houses the heads of their slain enemies ὥσπερ οἱ ἐν κυνηγίοις κεχειρωμένοι τὰ θηρία. The heads of sacrificial victims were sometimes similarly exhibited (Theophr. *Char.* 21 [7 Jebb]). Dedication of human skulls is attributed to the savage Taurians (*IT.* 74 f.), and to such legendary evil-doers as Antaeus, Evenus, Oeno-maus, and the Thracian Diomede (Pind. *Isth.* 4. 59 f. and schol., schol. BD *Il.* 9. 557, Pearson on Soph. fr. 473).[1]

1216–19. Πενθέως, defining gen. with βάρος. [Housman wished to take it with δόμων, putting comma after βάρος as in the Aldine, to avoid the slight awkwardness of φέροντες βάρος Πενθέως . . . οὗ σῶμα . . . φέρω. But Cadmus must make quite clear to the audience the identity of the veiled remains, and the anaphoric ἔπεσθε in 1217 should begin a new clause.] μοχθῶν, ptcp. Cadmus is an exhausted old man: the Dionysiac power that he experienced in the first scene has left him for ever. [Since the ζητήματα are now past, we expect an aor. ptcp. If μοχθῶν is right, it must imply μοχθήσας ζητήμασι καὶ μοχθῶν ἔτι. But we should perhaps read μόχθων, gen. pl. noun (Wecklein). The gen. of quality, equivalent to a qualitative adj., is rare in Greek; but cf. Aesch. *PV.* 900 ἀλατείαις πόνων 'laborious wanderings'.] τόδε, deictic: he points to the bier.

1220–1. πέδῳ apparently here 'spot', piece of ground.[2] δυσευρέτῳ, 'inscrutable' (bad for finding). [A prose writer would have at-tached the adj. to σῶμα, 'hard to find'. But that is no reason for writing δυσεύρετον (Reiske) or δυσευρέτως Hermann), or for rejecting the line (Nauck). The transference is not bolder than many others to be found in tragedy, and especially in the later work of Eur.]

1222. του depends on ἤκουσα, θυγατέρων on τολμήματα.—Observe the syncopation to which stage time is subject. Since the news of Pentheus' death reached the city Cadmus has had time to revisit Cithaeron, collect the remains, and return a second time to Thebes.

1224. Βακχῶν πάρα, with βεβώς. [Βακχῶν πέρι (P) is indefensible. Even if it stood near enough to ἤκουσα to be construed with it, ἤκουσα θυγατέρων τολμήματα περὶ Βακχῶν is mere nonsense.]

---

[1] For further evidence, and speculation about the original motive of the practice, see Nilsson, *Minoan-Mycenaean Religion*[2], 232 ff.; Meuli in *Phyllobolia für Peter Von der Mühll*, 233 ff.; Onians, *Origins of European Thought*, 96 ff.

[2] But Jackson (*Marg. Scaen.* 187, n. 1) may well have been right in suggesting πέδον, which would easily be corrupted by assimilation to the ending of the preceding word. For the partitive genitive cf. *Phoen.* 38 ἐς ταὐτὸν . . . ὁδοῦ.

1226. The normal order would be τὸν ὑπὸ Μαινάδων κατθανόντα παῖδα. But cf. *Supp.* 1036 τὸν μὲν θανόντα παῖδα Καδμείων δορί, and the many examples quoted by H. Schöne, *Hermes*, lx (1925), 158 ff.

1229. [The alteration of δρυμοῖς to δρυμούς appears arbitrary : for ἀμφί 'among' with local dat. cf. *Phoen.* 1516 (ὄρνις) ἀμφὶ κλάδοις ἐζομένα.]

1230–2. τὴν δ' . . . Ἀγαύην : 'but the other, Agaue', like *Hel.* 1024 f. ἱκετεύετε | τὴν μέν σ' ἐᾶσαι πατρίδα νοστῆσαι Κύπριν.   ὄψιν, 'a sight', accus. in apposition to the sentence.   [αὐτήν for αὐτῆς (P) is certain : cf. *Heraclid.* 929 f. Εὐρυσθέα . . . ἄγοντες . . . ἄελπτον ὄψιν, *Or.* 727 ff. εἰσορῶ . . . Πυλάδην . . . ἡδεῖαν ὄψιν. With αὐτῆς the sense could only be 'I see her face' (cf. Soph. *Phil.* 1411 f. αὐδὴν τὴν Ἡρακλέους | ἀκοῇ τε κλύειν λεύσσειν τ' ὄψιν) or 'I see a vision of her' (cf. *IT.* 150 ἰδόμαν ὄψιν ὀνείρων).]

1235–7. ἀπάσας εἶπον : 'I include them all.'   ἐς μεῖζον' ἥκω : 'I have risen to higher things' (different from εἰς τὸ μεῖζον ἦλθε, 'has grown greater', fr. 1025, or ἐπὶ μεῖζον ἔρχεται, 'increases', *Hec.* 380, Soph. *Phil.* 259). Cf. Plato, *Gorgias* 484 C ἂν ἐπὶ τὰ μείζω ἔλθῃ ἐάσας ἤδη φιλοσοφεῖν, *Menex.* 234 A ἐπὶ τὰ μείζω ἐπινοεῖς τρέπεσθαι. She feels herself to be like Pindar's Cyrene, who οὔθ' ἱστῶν παλιμβάμους ἐφίλησεν ὁδούς . . . ἀλλά . . . κεράϊζεν ἀγρίους θῆρας (*Pyth.* 9. 18).

1240. [In tragedy the final use of ὡς ἄν or ὅπως ἄν is normally restricted to clauses dependent on a main verb which expresses either a command (cf. 356, 510) or an intention on the part of the speaker (J. F. Dobson, *C.R.* xxiv [1910], 143 f.). Hence Hermann's ἀγκρεμασθῇ is probably right (though not for the reason he gave). ἀνακρεμάννυμι is, like ἀνατίθημι, a *vox propria* for dedication : cf. fr. 369. 4 f. πέλταν πρὸς Ἀθάνας | περικίοσιν ἀγκρεμάσας θαλάμοις.]

1241. [The notice about the occurrence of γαυριᾶν in the *Bacchae* (fr. 2 at end of text, p. 57) affords no real ground for reading ἐκγαυριῶν here. The word may well have occurred in the lost portion of the play.]

1245. ἐξειργασμένων, sc. ὑμῶν, gen. abs. The repetition of this word is not, I think, merely careless like the repetition of μαινάδων in 1060–2 : just as ὦ πένθος is a horrified rejection of μακάριος—addressed rather to himself than to Agaue—so φόνον ἐξειργ. is the old man's response to τοιάδ' ἐξειργ. [Middendorf condemned the line on the ground that it gives away the truth before Agaue is ready to receive it, and that she ignores it in her answer. But φόνος and its cognates can be used also of killing animals : cf. 1178.]

1246. καλόν, pred.   καταβαλοῦσα : 'having struck down' (or perhaps, 'having paid') : cf. *Or.* 1603 σφάγια πρὸ δορὸς καταβάλοις, Isocr. 2. 20 τοὺς ἱερεῖα πολλὰ καταβάλλοντας, Hesych. καταβολή· θυσία.

1248. The normal prose order would be πρῶτα μὲν σῶν. But cf. Soph. *Phil.* 919 σῶσαι κακοῦ μὲν πρῶτα τοῦδ', ἔπειτα δέ . . . . The omission of δέ is common with εἶτα and ἔπειτα, as with δεύτερος (681).

1249–50. ἐνδίκως μέν, ἀλλ' ἄγαν : cf. 1346. This is the voice of humanity ;

but we should remember that Sophocles, who did not design the *Ajax* as an attack on Athena, put a like criticism into the mouth of the Chorus-leader in that play, 951 ἄγαν δ' ὑπερβριθές γε τάχθος ἤνυσαν (sc. οἱ θεοί). **οἰκεῖος γεγώς**: Dion. has violated the family loyalty which is Cadmus' rule of life.

1251–2. ἐν τ' ὄμμασι σκυθρωπόν: Paley took ἐν ὄμμασι as 'in people's eyes'; but Murray's 'scowling in the eyes' is supported by *Or.* 1319 σκυθρωπούς ὀμμάτων ἔξω κόρας. For the use of ἐν cf. *Her.* 932 ἐν στροφαῖσιν ὀμμάτων ἐφθαρμένος.

1252–5. μητρὸς εἰκασθεὶς τρόποις: 'resembling his mother's ways'— 'compendiary comparison', like Soph. *OC.* 337 f. ἐκείνω τοῖς ἐν Αἰγύπτῳ νόμοις | φύσιν κατεικασθέντε.   **ἅμα:** best taken closely with ὀριγνῷτ', 'when he joined in hunting' (Elmsley). ἅμα σύν or ἅμα μετά, 'along with', is not uncommon (*Med.* 1143, *Ion* 717, Plato, *Criti.* 110 A); but ἅμα ἐν would be less natural. [Quite possibly one word or the other may be due to corruption. Murray suggested ἄγρᾳ for ἅμα, Jackson (*Marg. Scaen.* 67) ὁπότε for ὅτ' ἐν.]   **θηρῶν**, clearly noun, not (as Cruickshank) ptcp.   **ὀριγνῷτ'**, optative, the normal usage in indefinite relative clauses dependent on an antecedent optative (Goodwin, *M. and T.* § 177).

1256–7. σοῦστίν: this crasis of σοί or ἐμοί (μοι) with ἐστίν is attested by the MSS. at Aesch. *Cho.* 122, *Eum.* 913, Soph. *Aj.* 1225, and is accepted also at *Phil.* 812 (where MSS. have ἐμοί 'στι). [P, however, has σοί .τ' ἐστιν. This may mean that something is lost; but the supplement printed by Musurus in the *editio princeps* is presumably mere conjecture.]

1257–8. τίς ... ἄν ... καλέσειεν; virtually = καλείτω τις. This is a common idiom, e.g. *Hel.* 435 ὤή· τίς ἂν πυλωρὸς ἐκ δόμων μόλοι;   **τὴν εὐδαίμονα:** the word is carefully placed. Its unconscious irony becomes the more devastating if the hearer recalls all that the Chorus sang concerning the Dionysiac εὐδαιμονία, 72 ff., 426, 910 f.

1262. 'Fortunate I will not call you; but in your dream you will escape misfortune.'   **δόξετε**, because εὐτυχία is an objective condition ('good fortune'), not a state of mind ('happiness'). For the thought cf. fr. 205 τὸ μὴ εἰδέναι γὰρ ἡδονὴν ἔχει τινὰ | νοσοῦντα, κέρδος δ' ἐν κακοῖς ἀγνωσία, and Soph. *Aj.* 552 ff. Tyrrell is strangely wrong in saying that **οὐχί** must be taken with δόξετε as otherwise 'grammar would demand μή': οὐ is normal with infin. after δοκεῖν, e.g. *Andr.* 77 δοκῶ γὰρ οὐκ ἂν ὧδέ σ' ἂν πράσσειν κακῶς, Plato, *Rep.* 329 B δοκοῦσιν ... οὐ τὸ αἴτιον αἰτιᾶσθαι, &c.

1264–7. Cadmus begins his treatment by getting Agaue to concentrate on something in the external world. She does so (ἰδού, like *voilà*, calls attention to the performance of the act requested, cf. *Cycl.* 211 f.). He then *suggests* to her that its appearance has changed, and she thereupon feels as if a mist were lifting from her eyes. So Heracles says on recovering his sanity (*Her.* 1089) δέδορχ' ἅπερ με δεῖ, | αἰθέρα τε καὶ γῆν τόξα θ' Ἡλίου τάδε. This may be founded on actual observation: one of Binswanger's subjects described his recovery from an attack by saying that 'a veil was removed from his eyes' (*Die Hysterie,* 729).   διειπετέστερος : 'more translucent'. So *Etym. M.*, which quotes this passage as evidence for the sense διαυγής. And at *Rhes.* 43 διειπετῆ δὲ ναῶν πυρσοῖς σταθμά no other sense is possible. [Homer applies the word to rivers, and its original meaning was probably 'sky-fallen', i.e. 'rainfed'; but Zenodotus maintained that it meant διαυγής in Homer (schol. *Il.* 17. 263). The latter explanation was doubtless already current at Athens in Eur.'s day.]

1268–70. Cadmus next suggests that Agaue's inward excitement is fading. She tries to reject the suggestion ('I don't understand what you mean'). Yet it works, and her next words admit it: 'But my head is somehow . . . clearing: something has changed in my mind.' 'She speaks very slowly and simply: we shudder as we watch her beginning a new life' (Wilamowitz). The decisive moment is marked, as at *Alc.* 1119, by a breach of stichomythia: after 1269 we may suppose a pause of hesitation, during which Cadmus waits in expectant silence. Cf. *El.* 965, which is similarly followed by a pause while Electra gazes at the approaching figure, and *IT.* 811, where Orestes pauses to think of a test.

1272. 'Yes, for indeed I have forgotten what we said to each other just now.' Eur. knows that sudden alterations of personality are often accompanied by amnesia (cf. *Her.* 1094 ff., *Or.* 215 f.), and brilliantly exploits the dramatic possibilities of the situation. Agaue is like a subject coming out of deep hypnosis, or a Siberian shaman when he has finished shamanizing (Czaplicka, *Aboriginal Siberia,* 231, 240). —On ὡς . . . γε, a favourite combination with Eur., see Denniston, *Particles,* 143.

1273–84. Cadmus skilfully leads up to the ἀναγνώρισις, appealing to older memories that have not been repressed. She remembers her husband? Her son? Then at 1277 he shoots the crucial question at her. With averted eyes she answers 'A lion's—*or so they told me in the hunt*'. Gently but relentlessly he forces her from this last refuge: 'Come, you must look properly: it is only a moment's effort.' Then she knows; but she will not or cannot speak the name until he drags it from her (cf. Phaedra's inability to pronounce the name of Hippolytus, *Hipp.* 351). The whole dialogue is magnificently imagined. It is interesting that Goethe, who considered the *Bacchae* 'Euripides' finest play' (*Gespräche,* ed. Biedermann, iv. 435), chose lines 1244–98 to render into German verse as a specimen (*Werke,* Weimar edition, vol. 41. ii, pp. 237 ff.).

1274. ὡς λέγουσι must qualify Σπαρτῷ: cf. *Med.* 684 παῖς, ὡς λέγουσι, Πέλοπος εὐσεβέστατος where ὡς λέγουσι, despite its position, qualifies

εὐσεβέστατος. The words sound like an acknowledgement that the
Sown Men, who grew from the dragon's teeth, belong to legend, not
to the real world of human suffering in which this part of the action
moves. Cf. the non-committal language used elsewhere in Eur.
about miraculous births, *Her.* 826 φασιν, *Hel.* 17 ἔστιν λόγος τις.
[Bruhn's idea, that Agaue is teasing her father for asking questions
to which he knows the answer, involves a misconception of the whole
tone of the passage.]

1277. δῆτα : 'Well, then'—indicating that Cadmus has reached what he
was leading up to.

1280. ἔα : cf. 644 n.　　φέρομαι differs from φέρω in that it implies a
reflex effect of the action upon the agent: Agaue carries the head
as her prize—and as her pollution (cf. fr. 1 at end of text, p. 57, ἴδιον
ἔλαβον ἐς χέρας μύσος). To alter to φέρομεν would destroy a significant
if untranslatable nuance; and, as Hermann said, 'pluralis a tanto
animi motu, praesertim in interrogatione, alienus videtur'.

1281. ἄθρησον : 'look closely'. Cf. Suid. ἀθρεῖν· τὸ ἐπισκοπεῖν καὶ μετ'
ἐπιτάσεως ὁρᾶν : Soph. *OC.* 252 οὐ γὰρ ἴδοις ἂν ἀθρῶν 'For you will not
see him however closely you look'. [The alteration of **αὐτό** to αὖθις is
thus needless.]

1285. 'Mourned (by me) long before you recognized him.' Until now,
Cadmus has had to bear his sorrow alone. [In his translation Murray
adopted ᾑμαγμένον, 'blood-drenched', which is at first sight more
vigorous; but is it not in reality a mere affirmation of the obvious?]
σέ, emphatic. We need not assume (with Descroix, *Trimètre*, 20) that
it remains short, contrary to usage, before γν-. For the fifth foot
beginning with a long monosyllable see 246–7 n.

1286. [Since Byzantine word-division has no authority, P's ἦλθες can
equally represent an original ἦλθες or ἦλθ' ἐς. Without an accompanying vocative (as in 1308) the former is hardly possible. But ἦλθ' ἐς
should not be hastily rejected as 'unmetrical' : the admission of this
type of ending is characteristic of Eur.'s later work (246–7 n.). In
earlier plays his phrase was χεῖρας εἰς ἐμάς (*Alc.* 1020, *Heraclid.*
976).]

1287. ἐν οὐ καιρῷ : 'at the wrong moment', stronger and more vivid than
οὐκ ἐν καιρῷ, 'not at the right moment'. As Wackernagel points out
(*Vorl. üb. Syntax*, ii. 264), the expression was made natural by the
existence of the phrase οὐ καιρός (ἐστι), Aesch. *PV.* 523, Soph. *El.* 22,
although in that phrase the οὐ, strictly speaking, negatives the
sentence, not as here the noun. Cf. 455 n., and *Or.* 579 ἐν οὐ καλῷ
μὲν ἐμνήσθην θεῶν.

1288. τὸ μέλλον, accus. governed κατὰ σύνεσιν by καρδία πήδημ' ἔχει =
καρδία πηδᾷ = φοβοῦμαι. This is common in tragedy where a transitive verb, especially one denoting emotion, is replaced by a peri-
phrasis: *Or.* 860 τὸ μέλλον ἐξετηκόμην γόοις (= ἐγόων), Aesch. *Sept.*

290 μέριμναι ζωπυροῦσι τάρβος (= ποιοῦσι με ταρβεῖν) τὸν . . . λεών, Supp. 566 θυμὸν πάλλοντ' (= ἐφοβοῦντο) ὄψιν ἀήθη, &c. So Ar. Nub. 1391 τὰς καρδίας πηδᾶν ὅ τι λέξει, and so even in prose, Dem. 4. 45 τεθνᾶσι τῷ δέει τοὺς τοιούτους ἀποστόλους, 19. 81.

1291. See 337–40 n. διέλαχον: 'parted among them', a grim euphemism for 'tore to pieces'.

1293. ἐκερτόμει . . . μολών: 'he was trying to insult, having gone (there)', i.e. 'he went there to insult'. θεόν, monosyll. here and in 1297.

1296–8. Agaue recognizes with horror the agency of Dion., as Hippolytus the agency of Aphrodite, Hipp. 1403 τρεῖς ὄντας ἡμᾶς ὤλεσ', ᾔσθημαι, Κύπρις. But Dion. had the same justification as Aphrodite: 'you denied his godhead' (ἡγεῖσθε, impf.). To that Agaue makes no response—she turns instead to ask for her son's body.

1300. 'Is limb laid decently to limb?' καλῶς shows that this must be the sense, not (as Wecklein, &c.) 'Did you find the body intact?' She has not been told since her recovery that P. was the victim of a σπαραγμός; but from the evidence in her hand, and her knowledge of the cult, she may well guess it.—The answer to her question is lost. It was probably in the negative: Apsines' words (see note at end of text) suggest that the *compositio membrorum* was performed on the stage by Agaue herself. That the question *was* answered seems to me certain. If the poet had intended that Cadmus should keep silence while Agaue lifted the veil of the bier and saw for herself, he would, I think, have indicated this in the text; and in any case the abruptness of the transition to 1301 points clearly to some textual disturbance. Its character and extent we do not know. [Three lines would seem to be the minimum required for a natural transition from 1300 to 1301. Carl Robert (*Hermes*, xxxiv [1899], 645 ff.), arguing that 1300 must lead up to the *compositio membrorum*, held that the missing lamentation of Agaue over Pentheus' body (see 1329 n.) must have occurred at this point, and that 1301, which he understood as an indignant rhetorical question, was the last line of her ῥῆσις. But 1301 seems to belong more naturally to an earlier stage, at which Agaue is still trying to get the facts clear. Moreover, 1329 looks as if it were intended to motive some request; and what would this be, if not a request to pay a last farewell to her son's body (which in ordinary circumstances the murderess would not be allowed to touch)? Wilamowitz attributed the disturbance in the present passage not to an omission but to a displacement: he thought that 1301 originally followed 1297, and supposed 1298–1300 to have stood originally somewhere in the 'great lacuna' after 1329. This is not impossible. But does not Cadmus' apostrophe to the dead man (1308 ff.) come with greater effect after the bier has been brought forward and its contents made known?]

1302–29. The dramatic function of this speech is to move the sympathy of the audience not only for Cadmus himself but in some measure also for Pentheus, by exhibiting, belatedly, the more attractive side of the young man's nature. It is true that even here P. is presented as a man of violence; he was 'a terror to the city' (1310), and was anxious for an opportunity to punish people (1322)—that fits perfectly with what we have seen of him in action. But at least he was fond of his old grandfather.

1302. ἐγένεθ᾽: 'proved himself' (not 'became'): cf. 270–1 n.

1305–7. ὅστις, as so often, = *quippe qui*, introducing the ground for the statement that Cadmus is ruined. **ἄτεκνος ἀρσένων παίδων**, like *Andr.* 714 ἄπαιδας . . . τέκνων, *Phoen.* 324 ἄπεπλος φαρέων λευκῶν: cf. 112 n.—Elsewhere (*Phoen.* 7) Eur. follows Hesiod (*Theog.* 978) and Hdt. (5. 59) in giving Cadmus a son Polydorus, who was evidently invented as a genealogical link between the oldest figures of Theban saga and the later Labdacid kings. But here the complete sweeping away of the guilty Cadmean house is assumed, so the shadowy Polydorus is ignored. Cf. Wilamowitz, *Glaube d. Hell.* i. 408; Robert, *Oidipus*, ii. 26. **ἔρνος . . . κατθανόνθ᾽**: a normal sense construction (Kühner–Gerth, i. 53 f.), cf. *Od.* 6. 157 λευσσόντων τοιόνδε θάλος χορὸν εἰσοιχνεῦσαν, *Tro.* 740 ὦ περισσὰ τιμηθεὶς τέκνον, Thuc. 4. 15. 1 τὰ τέλη καταβάντας ἐς τὸ στρατόπεδον βουλεύειν, &c.

1308. ᾧ δῶμ᾽ ἀνέβλεφ᾽: 'by whom (instrum.) the house had recovered sight'. The heir of a family is often thought of as its *eye*: Aesch. *Pers.* 169 ὄμμα γὰρ δόμων νομίζω δεσπότου παρουσίαν: *Cho.* 934, Orestes is called ὀφθαλμὸν οἴκων: Eur. *Andr.* 406 εἷς παῖς ὅδ᾽ ἦν μοι λοιπὸς ὀφθαλμὸς βίου. So in the *Ion* when the lost heir is found, the house of Erechtheus οὐκέτι νύκτα δέρκεται, | ἀελίου δ᾽ ἀναβλέπει λαμπάσιν, 'recovers sight in the rays of dawn' (1467). ἀνιδεῖν is similarly used, Aesch. *Cho.* 808. In view of these parallels we must abandon the traditional rendering 'to whom the house looked up'; ἀναβλέπω never elsewhere means 'look up to' in the sense 'respect'. [ἀνέβλεπεν (P) is usually and no doubt rightly altered to ἀνέβλεφ᾽ because in tragedy βλ normally lengthens a preceding syllable in the same word. This seems to be invariably the case with compounds of βλέπω. Exceptions are ἀμφίβληστρα Eur. fr. 697, ἔβλαστ- fr. 429 and six times in Soph., ἔβλαψε fr. adesp. 455, βύβλου ἀναβλέπ᾽ Aesch. *Supp.* 761.] **συνεῖχες**: στῦλοι γὰρ οἴκων παῖδές εἰσιν ἄρσενες (*IT.* 57).

1312. ἐλάμβανες, sc. εἴ τις ὑβρίζοι: the reference is to 'the actual results of a former experience' (Paley). [It is hardly safe to reject P's ἐλάμβανεν. Although δίκην λαβεῖν commonly means 'to exact justice', it is used of suffering justice not only by Hdt. (1. 115. 3) but in a fourth-century Attic inscription, Dittenb. *Syll.*³ i. 165. 37 Μανίτα . . . τὴν δίκην λαβόντος ἐν χειρῶν νόμῳ 'M. having been lynched'. Cf. τὴν ἀξίην λαβεῖν 'to get one's deserts', Hdt. 7. 39. 2; and τὴν δίκην ἔχειν, *infra* 1327, Xen. *Anab.* 2. 5. 41, &c.]

1313–15. ἐκβεβλήσομαι: fut. perf. 'I shall be an exile'—more pathetic than ἐκβληθήσομαι. **τὸ Θηβαίων γένος:** Cadmus made the surviving Σπαρτοί citizens of his new town (Pherecydes fr. 22 Jacoby), and from them the Theban nobility traced their descent (*Phoen.* 942, Aesch. *Sept.* 474, Paus. 8. 11. 8).—For Cadmus as a type of the insecurity of mortal ὄλβος cf. Pind. *Pyth.* 3. 86 ff. That he already foresees his banishment may strike the modern reader as odd. Murray finds in it 'probably another mark of the unrevised state of the play'. But in the Greek way of thinking a pollution so abominable could hardly be expiated save by the expulsion of the whole guilty family. And some reference to the likelihood of this may have disappeared in the lacuna after 1300.

1317. ἀριθμήσῃ, fut. pass. in meaning, though middle in form.

1319 recalls 254, where Pentheus addresses Cadmus as ἐμῆς μητρὸς πάτερ.

1326. ἡγείσθω θεούς = νομιζέτω θεούς, 'let him believe in gods'. Cf. *Supp.* 731 f. νῦν τήνδ' ἄελπτον ἡμέραν ἰδοῦσ' ἐγὼ | θεοὺς νομίζω, fr. 913 τίς τάδε λεύσσων θεὸν οὐχὶ νοεῖ; Cadmus' faith has a new accent here: what once seemed to him possible matter for a καλὸν ψεῦδος (334) has proved its reality by laying his whole world in ruins.

1327–8. σὸς . . . παῖς παιδός: not σοῦ, since παῖς παιδός is treated as a single expression = 'grandson'. So οὑμός . . . παῖς παιδός, *Andr.* 584. Cf. Wilamowitz on *Her.* 468 πεδία τἀμὰ γῆς.—These lines with their double μέν and δέ reveal the wavering sympathies of the Chorus, torn between gratified revenge and human pity.

1329. There is a gap here of at least 50 lines, perhaps caused by the accidental loss of a leaf or a half-leaf (2 columns) from one of P's ancestors. The injury does not go far back, since the full text was known not only to Apsines (3rd cent. A.D.) but, as Porson was the first to perceive, to the author of the *Christus Patiens*, which is now assigned to the twelfth century (Introd., p. lv f.). From Apsines' description of Agaue's ῥῆσις, the account of Dion.'s speech at the end of the first ὑπόθεσις, and the adaptations in the *Chr. Pat.*, now supplemented by a couple of mutilated papyrus fragments, we can form a general picture of the contents of the lacuna [for the evidence, see Murray's note at the end of the text, and my appendix]. Agaue, flung in a moment from ecstasy to despair (1329, *Chr. Pat.* 1011), and conscious of being a polluted creature (schol. Ar. *Plut.* 907), begs permission to lay out the body for burial—'a scanty consolation to the dead', *Chr. Pat.* 1449—and to bid it a last farewell. Cadmus consents, warning her of its condition (pap. fr. 2a 3, cf. *Chr. Pat.* 1471). Over the body she 'accuses herself and moves the audience to pity', embracing each limb in turn and lamenting over it (Aps., cf. *Chr. Pat.* 1257, 1311 ff., 1466 ff.). Dion. now appears above the castle, on the θεολογεῖον, and first addresses all present (*Hyp.* I), speaking of the Theban people who denied his divine origin and rejected his gift (*Chr. Pat.* 1360–2, 1665 f.) and of the outrages for which Pentheus has paid with his life (ibid. 1663 f., 300). He then predicts the future of the survivors, each in turn (*Hyp.* I). The Cadmeans will one day be expelled from their city (*Chr. Pat.* 1668–9, where βαρβάροις may replace πολεμίοις, cf. Hdt. 5. 61. 1): they have themselves to blame for it (*Chr. Pat.* 1715). Agaue and her sisters must at once leave Thebes for ever, 'for it is against religion that murderers should remain' (ibid. 1674 ff., cf. pap. fr. 2b 6). Finally the god turns to Cadmus (*Chr. Pat.* 1690), the description of whose fate survives apparently almost complete.—Such prophecies are common form on the Euripidean stage: of Eur.'s extant tragedies all except *Alc.*, *Tro.*, and *I A.* end with a forecast, usually in the shape either of an utterance by a god or of a reported oracle, which links the stage action with the future as the narrative prologue links it with the past (cf. Grube, *Drama of Eur.* 77 ff.).

1330–9. [This bizarre prediction has puzzled mythologists no less than it startles the common reader. The story bears traces of having been put together at a relatively late date out of heterogeneous older elements. None of these (apart from the marriage to Harmonia) appears in extant literature before the fifth century; but it is possible to make some guess at their original character. (1) The transformation into snakes may well be rooted in early Theban belief. If Harmonia was once, as seems likely, the house-goddess and divine consort of the early kings who built the Mycenaean palace on the Cadmeia, the snake-shape was proper to her from the beginning (cf. Nilsson, *Minoan-Mycenaean Religion*², 310 ff.). And it was natural that Cadmus, like Erechtheus and other heroes, should be imagined as living on in his house in the shape of an οἴκουρος ὄφις (Gruppe, *Gr. Myth.* i. 86). This fits ill, however, with the banishment—and with the rest of the story. Was Cadmus already a snake when he drove the ox-wagon (cf. 1358)? and is he still one in Elysium? (2) The exile of Cadmus and Harmonia (1354) may reflect the overthrow of the Mycenaean kingship (cf. Hdt. 5. 61 ἐξανιστέαται Καδμεῖοι ὑπ' Ἀργείων καὶ τράπονται ἐς τοὺς Ἐγχελέας) and the decline of the cults associated with it; the local goddess is supplanted by Aphrodite and becomes in mythology the daughter of her supplanter (Hes. *Theog.* 933 ff., cf. Wilamowitz, *Pindaros*, 38). (3) Cadmus is to become the chief of a barbarian horde, presumably identical with the Ἐγχελεῖς of Hdt. 5. 61 and 9. 43. Hecataeus (fr. 73 Jacoby) located these Ἐγχελεῖς in northern Epirus; later writers put them farther north, in Albania or Montenegro, and so, it would seem, did Euripides—for the ox-wagon of 1333 must have been brought into the story to account for the name of the town Βουθόη, mod. Budua, on the coast of Montenegro, which Cadmus was said to have founded (*Et.*

Magn. Βουθόη· πόλις 'Ιλλυρίδος· εἴρηται ὅτι Κάδμος ἐπὶ βοῶν ζεύγους ἐκ Θηβῶν ταχέως εἰς 'Ιλλυρικοὺς παραγενόμενος ἔκτισε πόλιν). And there is evidence in later times of an actual cult of Cadmus and Harmonia on these coasts, where their tomb or 'stones' or ἱερόν was shown in various places (Eratosthenes ap. Steph. Byz. s.v. Δυρράχιον, Ap. Rhod. 4. 516, Dion. *Perieg.* 390 ff., ps.-Scylax 24). How this came about is unknown. It has been suggested that Greek colonists on the Dalmatian coast, finding traces of earlier Phoenician settlements, attributed them to Cadmus 'the Phoenician'; but we have at present no good evidence of the existence of Phoenician settlements there (Beaumont, *J.H.S.* lvi [1936], 163 f.). Wilamowitz thought that a local snake-god was identified by the Greeks with Cadmus (*Pindaros* 37, cf. Beaumont, l.c. 196). (4) Cadmus is to lead his barbarians against Hellas (1356, 1359), but when they sack Delphi disaster will overtake them. This is presented as a θέσφατον (1355) or χρησμὸς Διός (1333). And we know that in fact such an oracle was current at the time of the Persian Wars: according to Hdt. (9. 42 f.), Mardonius applied it to the Persians but its true application was to 'the Illyrians and the host of the Encheleis'; while Pherecydes (fr. 41 e Jacoby) seems to have connected it with the expedition of the Phlegyes against Thebes, which he placed *before* the time of Cadmus. The primary element here is evidently a warning put out by Delphi for its own protection (Latte in P.-W. s.v. Kadmos). Of an actual Illyrian invasion we know nothing. (5) Finally, Cadmus and Harmonia are to be translated bodily to Elysium—a privilege which Cadmus, like Menelaus and Peleus, owes to his wife's family connexions (1338 σὲ δ' Ἄρης . . . ῥύσεται). This is the only part of the prophecy which Pindar knows (or, as a good Theban, chooses to mention), *Ol.* 2. 78. It must originally have been alternative, not additional, to the snake story.]

1332. Ἄρεος, sc. θυγατέρα οὖσαν. ἔσχες: 'took (not 'had') to wife.' Ἁρμονίαν: the proper name in apposition to the antecedent is attracted into the relative clause, as often: cf. *Hec.* 771 πρὸς ἀνδρ' ὃς ἄρχει τῆσδε Πολυμήστωρ χθονός, Kühner–Gerth, ii. 419.

1338. [τε ῥύσεται: for the vowel remaining short before initial ῥυσ- (as Porson's law here requires) cf. Aesch. *Eum.* 232 τε ῥύσομαι, Soph. *OT.* 72 τήνδε ῥυσαίμην. Dr. Paul Maas suggests writing ἐρυσ- in all three places (*Gött. Nachr.* 1934, i. 1. 58); but ἐρύομαι is otherwise unknown to tragedy, and see 59 n.]

1339. σὸν καθιδρύσει βίον: 'shall translate you living', cf. *Alc.* 362 ἐς φῶς σὸν καταστῆσαι βίον 'bring you back alive to the daylight'.

1341–3. 'If you had had the sense to be wise, when you would not, you would now be happy' (εὐδαιμονεῖτε impf.). [P's εὐδαιμονοῖτ' ἄν, though defended by Wilamowitz and others, is probably an instance of the frequent confusion between Ε and Ο. The combination of a past indic. in the protasis with optative plus ἄν in the apodosis is indeed not uncommon (Goodwin, *M. and T.* § 503). But (*a*) in this combination the protasis almost always (except in Homer) expresses an *open* condition, e.g. Soph. *El.* 797 f. πολλῶν ἂν ἥκοις, ὦ ξέν', ἄξιος τυχεῖν, | εἰ τήνδ' ἔπαυσας ('if you have really stopped her'); whereas the condition here is clearly unfulfilled. (*b*) The sense required by the context is not, I think, 'you could, or might, be happy',[1] but 'you would be happy'—as enjoying that especial εὐδαιμονία which Dionysus has in his gift (73, 902 ff.). The optative would fatally weaken the rhetorical contrast.]

1344–51. All modern edd. except Murray and Lucas transfer 1344, 1346, 1348 to Agaue, thus making her the interlocutor throughout the stichomythia: 'non enim aequum est, ut Cadmus, in quem nulla impietatis suspicio cadit, culpam hoc modo agnoscat, veniamque precetur' (Elmsley). But the change does not really remove the difficulty: for the condemnation implied in 1342, οὐκ ἠθέλετε (σω-φρονεῖν), must include Cadmus, the last person individually addressed; and he is presumably included also in the 'you' of 1345, 1347, as he certainly is in the 'you' of 1351. It is possible that the god has seen through the equivocal motives of Cadmus' earlier conformism (334 n.), and has said so in the missing part of his speech; but the underlying implication is perhaps rather that when great natural forces are outraged we can expect no nice adjustment of the punishment to the magnitude of the individual offence (cf. Grube, *Drama of Eur.* 419). At any rate, Cadmus *is* condemned with the rest of his house. And it is entirely in character that the old man whose rule of life is the solidarity of the family should accept the consequences of that solidarity and make himself the spokes-man of the family group instead of pleading his individual case. His reaction to the god's award is the same as his reaction to the murder of Pentheus (1249 f.): he finds it just—but merciless (1346).

1345. ᾔδεμεν, ᾔδετε, ᾔδεσαν and ᾖσμεν, ᾖστε, ᾖσαν are both good Attic ; ᾔδειμεν, ᾔδειτε are probably, ᾔδεισαν certainly, Hellenistic (Kühner–Blass, ii. 65, 242). [That ᾔδετε, not εἴδετε, is the true reading here is confirmed by the fuller text of the *Etym. M.* published by Reitzen-stein (from Oros περὶ ὀρθογραφίας), which cites Menander for the form ᾔδεμεν and the present passage for the form ᾔδετε. Cf. also

[1] A. O. Hulton, *C.Q.* lii (1958), 141, claims that the optative is oc-casionally used with present reference even in Attic Greek, and cites this passage as an example. But even if his claim is justified, objection (*a*) remains: neither Isocr. 12. 149 nor Xen. *Mem.* 3. 5. 8 is a safe parallel, since in both places MSS. are divided between optative and indicative, as they are also at Dem. 18. 206.

Bekker's 'Antiatticist' (quoted in the *apparatus criticus*) and *Chr. Pat.* 2560 ὄψ' ἐμάθομεν, ὅτ' ἐχρῆν οὐκ εἰδότες.]

1348–9. Cadmus pleads with Dion., as the old servant in the *Hippolytus* with Aphrodite, *Hipp.* 120 σοφωτέρους γὰρ χρὴ βροτῶν εἶναι θεούς. And both plead in vain: for such gods as these the human 'ought' has no meaning. We need not conclude that the poet denies their title to worship: to do so is to confuse the Greek with the Christian conception of deity. 'Because Dion. as god represents a universal law, the operation of this law is not to be measured with the measure of human good and evil' (Wassermann, cf. Introd., pp. xliv f.). This may be the underlying sense of 1349, which has been stigmatized by Bruhn, Robert, and others as a weak evasion—and is one, so long as we think of gods as personal agents having moral responsibility for their acts. Other Euripidean *dei* fall back in the same manner upon 'Destiny' or 'the Father's will', *Hipp.* 1331 ff., *Andr.* 1269, *El.* 1247 f., 1301, *Hel.* 1660 f., 1669, to justify their own actions (or failure to act) and the fate of the human characters. 'The appeal to Zeus is an appeal to ultimate mystery, to a world structure in which the forces Dion. represents are an inescapable element. With that there is no quarrelling, and Agaue recognizes that this word is final' (Winnington-Ingram).

1350. δέδοκται . . . φυγαί: the so-called σχῆμα Πινδαρικόν or Βοιώτιον— an inappropriate term which is used to cover several different types of irregularity, some of them quite natural, others much less so and very possibly due to textual corruption (cf. R. S. Haydon, *A.J.P.* xi. 182 ff.). In the present instance we may say that φυγαί is added in explanatory apposition to the impersonal subject of δέδοκται: 'It is settled—exile.' [Kühner-Gerth (i. 68 f.) calls φυγαί an exclamation, denying that σχῆμα Πινδαρικόν genuinely occurs in Attic writers save with ἔστι, ἦν, γίγνεται, used quasi-impersonally and nearly always standing first in the clause (cf. the regular ἔστιν οὕς, *il est des hommes qui . . .*). But our sentence is not very different in principle from this standard type. Bolder and more surprising are *Phoen.* 349 ἐσιγάθη σᾶς ἔσοδοι (M V) νύμφας (where ἔσοδοι, like φυγαί here, is singular in meaning); Aesch. *Pers.* 49 στεῦται (M¹ and schol.) δ' ἱεροῦ Τμώλου πελάται (where στεῦται, like δέδοκται here, has no available plural form); fr. trag. adesp. 191 ἦλθεν δὲ λαοί, 'there came folk', quoted by Herodian as a solecism. A different explanation applies to examples like *Hel.* 1358 ff. μέγα τοι δύναται . . . στολίδες κισσοῦ τε . . . χλόα . . . ῥόμβου τε . . . ἔνοσις κτλ., where a collection of subjects are mentally unified (cf. Meisterhans, *Gramm. d. att. Inschr.* § 83); in this type the verb need not come first (Plato, *Symp.* 188 B, *Legg.* 925 E, &c.).]

1352. It is not clear whether the god vanishes at this point or is simply ignored by the two human beings as they turn to each other for comfort. See on 1377–8.

1355-6. 'And there is besides (ἔτι) for me the oracle, that I must lead....' [The text is sound: θέσφατον has the article because it refers back to χρησμός (1333); the adaptation in the *Chr. Pat.* is dictated by the difference of context and by the author's avoidance of trisyllabic feet.]

1358. [Cf. *Med.* 1343 Σκύλλης ἔχουσαν ἀγριωτέραν φύσιν. ⟨σχῆμ'⟩ is technically the neater supplement (a copyist's eye might jump from CX to EX), and is supported by *Ion* 992 μορφῆς σχῆμ' ἔχουσαν ἀγρίας, but involves accepting Dobree's ἀγρίας for ἀγρίαν.]

1360-2. Cadmus finds in his eventual translation to Elysium only a culminating cruelty. That is psychologically right: the god's mortal victims have nothing left for comfort but their mortality—τὸ γὰρ θανεῖν | κακῶν μέγιστον φάρμακον νομίζεται, *Heraclid.* 595—and the tired old man sees himself robbed even of that. **καταιβάτην:** L.S. translates here 'to which one descends'; but there is no difficulty in giving the word either its normal sense, 'downward-plunging', or the active sense 'downward-carrying' (as in Sosiphanes fr. 1, *T.G.F.* p. 819). The Acheron was believed to run for part of its course on the surface of the earth, for part through the underworld (Plato, *Phd.* 112 E f.). That Lycophron took it so appears from the phrase Ἀχερουσία τρίβος | καταιβάτις (*Alex.* 90 f.), which he applies not to the underworld but to Taenarum, where there was an entrance to Hades; cf. also Ap. Rhod. 2. 353 εἰς Ἀίδαο καταιβάτις ἐστὶ κέλευθος.

1365. 'As the young swan shelters the old, grown hoary and helpless.' The swan is a type of filial piety (*El.* 151 ff.).   **κηφῆνα:** properly a drone-bee, then any creature too weak or old to look after itself (κηφήν . . . λέγεται καὶ ἄνθρωπος ὁ μηδὲν δρᾶν δυνάμενος, Suid.). **πολιόχρων** applies both to the white plumage of the mature swan (πολιὸς ὄρνις *Her.* 110) and to Cadmus' white hair (cf. 258): the two ideas are similarly combined at *Her.* 692, κύκνος ὡς γέρων ἀοιδὸς πολιᾶν ἐκ γενύων κελαδήσω, while Ar. *Vesp.* 1064 makes the comparison explicit, κύκνου . . . πολιώτεραι δὴ αἵδ' ἐπανθοῦσιν τρίχες. [The parallel with *Her.* 692 confirms the soundness of this reading, which also improves the balance of the clause and makes clear the sense of κηφῆνα. πολιόχρως (P) would be a pointless ornamental epithet. πολιόχροα Heath, Nauck: but this is metrically clumsy, and cf. λιπαρόχρων, Theocr. 2. 102. There is nothing to be said for changing κύκνος (and/or ὄρνις) to the accus.; the proposal was based on a mistaken notion that κηφήν must be adjectival here. For ὄρνις . . . κύκνος cf. *Hel.* 19 κύκνου . . . ὄρνιθος, and 1024-6 n.]

1366. γάρ: she clings to him *because* she feels herself suddenly alone in the world.

1368. [One of the many places in Eur. where our MSS. offer πατρῷος with shortened penult. See Jebb on Soph. *Phil.* 724, Page on *Med.* 431.]

1369. ἐπὶ δυστυχίᾳ : 'in misery'. In such phrases ἐπί introduces an attendant condition (L.S. s.v., B.I. 1. i): *IT.* 1490 ἐπ' εὐτυχίᾳ, Soph. *OC.* 1554 f. κἀπ' εὐπραξίᾳ | μέμνησθέ μου.

1371. The sentence is incomplete and its meaning unknown (there is no real parallel for the ellipse of οἶκον postulated by editors before Hermann). Aristaeus, originally a god of hunters and herdsmen (Wilamowitz, *Glaube der Hell.* i. 248 ff.), in Virgil a shepherd bee-keeper (*Geo.* 4. 317 ff.), was brought into the Theban Dionysiac cycle as husband of Autonoe (Hes. *Theog.* 977) and father of Actaeon (*supra* 1227); according to Pausanias (10. 17. 3), he left Thebes after the latter's death. Cadmus may have advised his daughter to join A. in some foreign land, or to go for the moment to A.'s house in Thebes where her sisters awaited her (cf. 1381–2). I cannot believe with Bruhn that he sent her back to Cithaeron to collect Ino and Autonoe; 1381–2 do not require us to assume this stupid and unkind procedure, and 1383–5 seem to exclude it. The return of the sisters from the mountain may have been announced by Dion. in the missing part of his ῥῆσις. [If Hermann was right in thinking that 1368–73 were originally symmetrical with 1374–80, only one line is lost here. Others suppose a bigger lacuna, containing further lamentations by Cadmus, traces of which Brambs thought he could detect in the *Christus Patiens* (942, 944, 1078–11). The evidence is insufficient for any decision.]

1372–92. These lines were attributed to an interpolator by Nauck, Robert (*Hermes*, xxxiv [1899], 648), and at one time Wilamowitz (*Analecta Eur.* 51, but cf. *Her.* i.¹ 211, n. 179). Certainly 1372–80 are weak and repetitive, and in the form in which the MS. transmits them are full of metrical faults and oddities suggestive of the doggerel 'anapaests' at the end of the *IA.*, while 1388–92 occur as a tail-piece to other Euripidean plays. On the other hand, (*a*) the moving lines 1383–7 seem much too good for an *ex hypothesi* late and ignorant interpolator; (*b*) passages of weak and repetitive pathos occur elsewhere in Eur. (cf. e.g. the parallel scene in the *Electra*, 1308–41); (*c*) the metrical peculiarities of 1373–5 may be explained by their threnodic character (see below), while the remaining metrical defects yield very easily to treatment and seem sufficiently accounted for by a copyist's haste to finish; (*d*) if the interpolator's motive was to fill the gap after 1371, we should expect him to have completed the unfinished sentence. I am inclined to accept the whole passage as genuine.¹

---

¹ Professor Merkelbach has suggested to me that lines 1372–8 may have been composed by some one as an *alternative* to the genuine ending from line 1352 onwards, for some occasion when it was desired to shorten the Exodos. In this shortened version 1377–8 would have been

1373. [In 'strict' as distinct from 'melic' or 'threnodic' anapaests Eur. (unlike Aesch.) adheres pretty rigidly to the rule which requires a caesura between the two metra of a full dimeter. Of the other lines quoted as exceptions by Page on *Med.* 1099, fr. 114. 2 is not one, being a 'paroemiac' (catalectic dimeter); fr. 897. 4 is easily emended; *IA.* 592 is perhaps excused by a proper name; while *Hipp.* 1374 occurs in a passage where there seems to be a transition from strict to threnodic anapaests (Wilamowitz, ad loc.). The last explanation possibly applies also to the present line: see next note.]

1374-5. αἰκείαν: 'outrage', 'brutality'—a bitter word, and significant of Agaue's state of mind. [These anapaests are either threnodic or corrupt: in strict anapaests a purely spondaic *paroemiac* is almost unknown (? Aesch. *Supp.* 976), and two successive paroemiacs impossible. Assuming γάρ to be, as often, intrusive, we could write, e.g., ⟨δεινὸς⟩ δεινῶς τήνδ' αἰκείαν, and perhaps insert ⟨πάτερ⟩ (Hermann) before εἰς. But in view of 1373 it is, I think, safest to let the text stand. There is a partial parallel in the *Ion*, 859 ff., where threnodic anapaests, ὦ ψυχά, πῶς σιγάσω; | πῶς δὲ σκοτίας ἀναφήνω κτλ., are followed by strict ones (862–80) and then by more threnodics. For a paroemiac ending with a prepositive (εἰς) cf. Aesch. *Pers.* 935 πρόσφθογγόν σοι νόστου τάν. If the present lines are threnodic the Doric spelling τάνδ' is justified, but not otherwise (cf. Jebb on *Ant.* 110 ff., App.).]

1377-8. If the text is right, the god is heard here once more (possibly as a voice 'off'?), still implacable, still complaining of his injured honour. [Hermann and others write ἔπασχεν (a technically easy correction) and give the lines to Cadmus, urging (*a*) that Dion. has said his say and should vanish at 1351 instead of remaining a silent spectator for 27 lines, (*b*) that with this change we get a symmetrical distribution between speakers (1368–73 = 1374–80). 1351 certainly sounds like the god's last word (cf. Soph. *Phil.* 1449–51); and the present lines are not out of character for Cadmus (cf. 1296–7). It may be urged on the other side that this is not (at least to a modern taste) the right moment for Cadmus to insist on his daughter's guilt, and that there is no instance of a *deus* vanishing before the end of the scene except in the *Hippolytus*, where Artemis' withdrawal is specially motived (1437 ff.). But the balance of probability is, I think, in favour of Hermann.]

1380. τόδε: sc. τὸ χαίρειν. A similar bitter play on the literal meaning of the word and its conventional use occurs *Hec.* 426 f.

the last lines of the play, and would have been spoken by Cadmus (see below). This is a tenable hypothesis, but not in my view a necessary one.

1381. ὦ πομποί: not 'guides' (for she needs none) but 'friends' who will see her off (προπέμπειν). Hippolytus makes a like request to his friends when he is going into exile (*Hipp.* 1099 προπέμψατε χθονός). These πομποί must be Theban women, not the alien Chorus.

1384. ⟨ἔμ' ἴδοι⟩ may have fallen out through the eye passing from *MIΔ* to *MIA*. The optative is right, for 'the clause with ὅπου is an integral part of the wish' (Paley), whereas ἀνάκειται below refers to something existent. Cf. *Hipp.* 732 ff.

1386. 'Where no dedicated thyrsus can remind' (Winnington-Ingram). θύρσου, gen. of definition. For such dedications cf. *Anth. Pal.* 6. 158 θύρσα Λυαίῳ, 165, 172; 13. 24. [I should prefer, with Wilamowitz, μηδ' ὅθι, 'nor yet where': this clause is not strictly parallel to the other two.]

1387. μέλοιεν, sc. Κιθαιρὼν καὶ ὁ θύρσος. She would forget the ὀρειβασία and all that is associated with it.

1388–92. A modern producer would bring down the curtain on 1387, but a Greek dramatist had to get his Chorus out of the orchestra. Soph. and Eur. regularly end their tragedies with a brief anapaestic clausula delivered by the Chorus as they march out (*OT.*, *Ion*, *Tro.* are the only exceptions, and even there the Chorus have the last word). Commonly this tail-piece either motives the exit or draws an obvious moral; in *IT.*, *Phoen.*, *Or.*, the Chorus break the dramatic illusion with a prayer for victory, identical in all three plays. The present lines are used also in *Alc.*, *Andr.*, *Hel.*, and with a slight variation in *Med.* They are in fact appropriate to any play having a marked περιπέτεια (cf. schol. *Andr.* 1284 ταῦτα εἴωθεν ὁ ποιητὴς λέγειν διὰ τὰ ἐν τοῖς δράμασιν ἐκ παραδόξου συμβαίνοντα). Verrall discovered in them a sly dig at improbable myths, while a more recent writer (J. Mewaldt, *Wien. Stud.* liv [1936], 13) calls them Eur.'s personal sign-manual, the expression of his tragic resignation. But a survey of all the clausulae in Soph. and Eur. suggests that this is not the place to look for deep significance. Possibly, as Hermann conjectured, the words were liable to be drowned by the clatter of the departing spectators, and therefore mattered little. If so, Aeschylus' audience had better manners: the last words of the *Eumenides* were written to be heard.

APPENDIX

Additional fragments attributable to the Bacchae

I

I print below the papyrus fragments referred to in the Introduction, p. lviii, as read by Mr. Roberts. The supplements, which are my own, are for the most part offered only *exempli gratia*.

P. Ant. 24 fr. 2a (Verso)

[Κα.]   ] ε σ θ α λ [
              ] ρ ο σ ε [
        Πενθέως κατ]ηλοκ[ι]σμέν[' αἱμόφυρτά τε
        μέλη κομί]ζων, ἴσθι, κη[δείοις πόνοις.
  5   ὁ ταῦτ' ὁπω]πὼς ἐκδιδαχ[θήτω βροτῶν·
        Διόνυσον] ὁ Ζεύς ἐστιν ὁ [σπείρας θεόν.
              ]τεκαιτισητ[
              . . . . . . σ . .

3]ηλωκ·σμεν[pap., added between the lines by another hand: τὰ δ' αἱμόφυρτα καὶ κατηνλοκισμένα (al. κατηνλακισμένα) Chr. Pat. 1471.
4 μέλη Chr. Pat. 1472. But Roberts now thinks]κων likeliest and suggests τάδ' ἄρθρ' ἐνεγ]κών.

fr. 2b (Recto)

[Δι.]   λο]ισθια[
        οὗ δ' ὠλέναισ]ι τὸν δυ[σάθλιον νέκυν
        ἔχεις, Ἀγαύ]η, σαῖς ἐβούλ[ετ' ἀντέχειν
        μανίαις ὁ Πενθε]ύς· τοὺς δ' ἀ[
  5   τη]ν γε δυσσέβε[ιαν
              ]ν εἴργει νόστιμ[ον βλέπειν φάος
              ] . . . [ ]φ[

6 Cf. Aesch. Pers. 261.

fr. 3a (Verso)

              . . . .
              ]φηδ[
              ]οντι . [
              ]νσοιτ[
              ]ιαι[
              . . . . . .

fr. 3b (Recto)

The grounds for attributing fragments 2*a* and 2*b* to the *Bacchae* are (i) the fact that they were found with fragments containing extant lines of the *Bacchae* (P. Ant. 24 frs. 1*a*, 1*b*), and are written in the same hand with similar materials; (ii) the high probability that ηλωϙ·ϲμεν in fr. 2*a* 3 represents the rare word (κατ)ηλοκισμένα (cf. *Supp.* 826), and that if so this line is the source of *Chr. Pat.* 1471, which has long been recognized as a borrowing from the *Bacchae*. Consideration (i) applies also to frs. 3*a* and 3*b*; but they are too minute and too badly blurred for anything to be said of them with confidence.

The relationship of frs. 1*a* and 1*b* shows that the codex had 37 lines to a page: hence 29 lines (37 minus 8) must be missing between the end of 2*a* and the beginning of 2*b*. The passage 1301–29 is clearly too long to be inserted in this gap, if we allow for the necessary transitions. Therefore 2*a* and 2*b* must either both precede 1301 or both follow 1329. On the former assumption, 2*a* might be part of Cadmus' reply to Agaue's question at 1300, while 2*b* 6 might be interpreted as a reference on Agaue's part to the probability of exile, leading up to Cadmus' ἐκβεβλήσομαι in 1313. If this is right, we must also accept Robert's view that Agaue's great speech and the *compositio membrorum* preceded 1301. For 2*a* almost certainly led up to the *compositio*; moreover, the lacuna in which these fragments occurred was at least 50 lines long, and if we place it before 1301 it is difficult to imagine its contents unless it included Agaue's big speech. But the balance of probability seems to me to be against Robert's view (see 1300 n.). I should therefore prefer to situate Agaue's speech, and with it the two fragments, in the lacuna after 1329. 2*a* 3–4 will then form part of Cadmus' reply to the request introduced by 1329. 2*a* 5 and 6, if I have divined their sense rightly, will be either a concluding couplet spoken by Cadmus (cf. 1325–6) or a comment by the Chorus-leader. 2*b* will be Dionysus announcing her banishment to Agaue.

II

The following beginnings of lines, on a detached fragment of papyrus, were found with the Oxyrhynchus fragment (P. Oxy. 2223) containing *Ba.* 1070–1136, and are in the same hand. Since no group of lines with these beginnings seems to occur in any extant tragedy, they *may* come from the lost portion of the *Bacchae*.

ατη
ορε
ελ
οφ

III

Most of the lines in the *Christus Patiens* which can plausibly be assigned to the lost portion of the *Bacchae*, and several which cannot, were listed by Kirchhoff, *Philol.* viii (1853), 78 ff. Subsequent critics seem to have relied on K.'s investigation; they have rightly thinned out his collection, but have added little to it. The quarry is perhaps not quite exhausted. In addition to the lines printed by Murray at the end of the play, the following may with some probability be attributed to the *Bacchae*:

Chr. Pat. 1011 καὶ δυστάλαιναν τὴν πάλαι (μακαρίαν)

This could follow immediately on *Ba.* 1329. The last word presumably replaces some adjective unsuited to the Virgin Mary, such as γαυρουμένην. δυστάλας is one of Eur.'s pet words.

Chr. Pat. 1449 βαιὸν παρηγόρημα τοῖς τεθνηκόσι

This line, whose tragic origin is unmistakable, may well have been spoken by Agaue with reference to the *compositio membrorum*.

Chr. Pat. 1360–2 οὐκ εὐπρεπεῖς ἔθεντο (πολλοί μοι) λόγους,
ψευδῶς τεκεῖν βάζοντες ἔκ τινος βροτῶν.
κοὐκ ἤρκεσέν (-σάν codd.) μοι ταῦθ' ὑβρισθῆναι μόνον

I suspect that πολλοί μοι replaces Καδμεῖοι and that these lines are adapted from Dion.'s ῥῆσις, which would naturally begin with a state-ment of his wrongs. Cf. 26 ff. and 1297.

Chr. Pat. 300 (μάθῃς γὰρ) εὑρὼν τὴν κατ' ἀξίαν τίσιν

Perhaps spoken by Dion. of Pentheus.

Chr. Pat. 1756 δεῖ γάρ σε τὴν φονῶσαν ἐκλιπεῖν πόλιν

Perhaps spoken by Dion. to Agaue: the people will demand her blood if she remains.

INDEXES

I. ENGLISH

II. GREEK